La Conquistadora

La Conquistadora

The Virgin Mary at War and Peace in the Old and New Worlds

AMY G. REMENSNYDER

OXFORD
UNIVERSITY PRESS

OXFORD
UNIVERSITY PRESS

Oxford University Press is a department of the University of Oxford.
It furthers the University's objective of excellence in research, scholarship,
and education by publishing worldwide.

Oxford   New York

Auckland   Cape Town   Dar es Salaam   Hong Kong   Karachi
Kuala Lumpur   Madrid   Melbourne   Mexico City   Nairobi
New Delhi   Shanghai   Taipei   Toronto

With offices in

Argentina   Austria   Brazil   Chile   Czech Republic   France   Greece
Guatemala   Hungary   Italy   Japan   Poland   Portugal   Singapore
South Korea   Switzerland   Thailand   Turkey   Ukraine   Vietnam

Oxford is a registered trademark of Oxford University Press
in the UK and certain other countries.

Published in the United States of America by
Oxford University Press
198 Madison Avenue, New York, NY 10016

Some material in Chapters Three and Six has appeared in Amy G. Remensnyder, "Christian Captives, Muslim
Maidens and Mary," *Speculum* 82 (2007): 642–677. It is re-used here with the permission of The Medieval
Academy of America.

Library of Congress Cataloging-in-Publication Data
Remensnyder, Amy G. (Amy Goodrich), 1960–
La Conquistadora : the Virgin Mary at War and Peace in the Old and the New Worlds/
Amy G. Remensnyder.
pages cm
Includes bibliographical references and index.
ISBN 978–0–19–989298–3 (alk. paper)—ISBN 978–0–19–989300–3 (alk. paper)
1. Mary, Blessed Virgin, Saint.   I. Title.
BT603.R45 2014
232.91—dc23
2013027151

1 3 5 7 9 8 6 4 2
Printed in the United States of America
on acid-free paper

CONTENTS

ACKNOWLEDGMENTS

My quest to understand La Conquistadora led me far afield from medieval France, the focus of my earlier work. My ensuing odyssey across first the Pyrenees and then the Atlantic would not have been possible without the intellectual and personal generosity of many individuals and institutions who offered support along the way.

During my research and writing, I relied heavily on the skill of librarians on both sides of the Atlantic. For their collective patience and knowledge, I thank the staffs at the Biblioteca Nacional de España (Madrid), the Fray Angélico Chávez History Library (Santa Fe, NM), the John Carter Brown Library (Providence, RI), and Brown University's John Hay and Rockefeller libraries. I am especially grateful to Karen Bouchard of Brown's Rockefeller Library and to Tomas Jaehn of the Fray Angélico Chávez History Library, who, it is important to say, is *not* the librarian referred to in this book's introduction.

Generous fellowships from a range of organizations allowed me spend years in those libraries while also introducing me to new scholarly communities. A fellowship at the Institute for Advanced Study in Princeton helped lay the foundations for the book. The opportunity to participate there in the late and much regretted Sabine MacCormack's lively Mellon seminar on the colonial Andes opened new doors. I am deeply grateful to Professor MacCormack for the warm interest that she took in my project from its beginnings through to its final stages. Further phases of research and writing were supported by a John Simon Guggenheim Memorial Foundation Fellowship as well as an ACLS/SSRC/ NEH International and Area Studies Fellowship and sabbatical leave from Brown University. A remarkable year at the Ruhr-Universität's Käte Hamburger Kolleg (KHK) was crucial for the book's completion. I thank Nicolas Jaspert not just for the generous invitation that led to my KHK fellowship, but above all for his unflagging hospitality and the rich intellectual community he so masterfully fosters. Exchange of ideas and work with him and with Jenny Oesterle

was invaluable. Discussions with international fellows at the KHK, especially
Abhishek S. Amar, Georgios Halkias, and Jason Neelis, widened my horizons.
Thanks are owed also to Volkhard Krech and Marion Steinicke, whose wise lead-
ership and oversight of the KHK make it so vibrant.

Many other people shaped this book in important ways. Some were the
undergraduates and doctoral candidates at Brown University with whom I have
thought about medieval Iberia over the years. They have pushed me to define
my ideas more clearly, as have the student-prisoners at the Rhode Island Adult
Correctional Institute, whose discussions of medieval Muslims, Jews, and
Christians gave me new perspective on the problems of living together. Rachel
Gostenhofer helped with the tricky business of image acquisition and permission. Jason Dyck kindly shared his scan of Cisneros's difficult-to-find *Historia*.

Many colleagues and friends, including the faculty and staff of Brown's
History Department, provided vital intellectual direction and community.
Louise Burkhart's generous invitation to participate in her panel at a meeting of
the American Society for Ethnohistory in Mexico City encouraged me to believe
that medievalists really could offer something to the study of the colonial New
World. Her own work remains a touchstone and constant source of inspiration.
Sharon Farmer's incisive comments as I was conceptualizing key aspects of the
book saved me from my worst instincts. Ever since my undergraduate days, she
has helped me become a more subtle thinker. Karen Graubart and Kenneth
Mills generously shared their keen insights about colonial New World societies.
Discussions with Simon Barton and John Tolan deepened my understanding of
high medieval Iberia.

Professors Barton, Graubart, and Tolan belong to that select group of
supremely generous people who read and commented on drafts of some of this
book's chapters. Among them are also Douglas R. Cope, Linford Fisher, and
Karl Jacoby, who read the New World chapters in particular. Philippe Buc and
Moshe Sluhovksy heroically read a draft of the entire manuscript when it was
much longer than it is now, while Deborah Cohen even more heroically read
multiple drafts of the whole book and spent many summer afternoons helping me think through challenging points. Particular thanks are owed to these
last three readers. The comments of all these people made this a better book, as
did the two readers' reports from Oxford University Press. At the Press, Susan
Ferber's interest in this project ever since she first heard about it spurred me on.
I am grateful for her astute editing.

I also thank Jeff Cook, Lisa Fink, Janelle Greenberg, Shana Klinger, Evelyn
Lincoln, Ellen Reeves, Margaret Rezendes, and Ed Shea for their friendship and
constant support. Laura Mason has helped me to remember what really matters.
Though my father, John Remensnyder, did not live to see the book completed,

he was always enthusiastic about it, as were my mother, Mary Remensnyder, and my siblings, Margaret and Stuart Remensnyder. My gratitude to them is lifelong.

Finally, this book would not exist without two people. Margaret Malamud was there in Chimayó in 1992 when I first encountered La Conquistadora. Her own bold change of historical fields encouraged me to believe I could do the same. She read this book in all its iterations and helped me realize its vision, while always providing warm hospitality during my New Mexico research trips. My life partner Linda Heuman, journalist and master wordsmith, taught me that writing is an adventure. Leading me to take risks in writing and in life, she has shaped every page of this book. Her patience in living with the Virgin Mary for so many years is saintly.

Introduction

New Mexico, 1992

I first encountered La Conquistadora in the tranquil backyard of New Mexico's most famous pilgrimage shrine, Chimayó. It was a hot August day. Sunlight filtered through the trees, leaving filigree shade on the church's rough adobe walls. Inside, pilgrims dressed in everything from dark formal suits to tight short dresses shot through with sparkle—some leaning on crutches or seated in wheelchairs, some teetering on high heels—waited their turn to enter the church's cramped back room. There they knelt down on the earthen floor and scraped up dirt famed for its curative powers. The room's antechamber was filled with dozens of candles, so many that their flames fed the heat. No wonder that a sign cautioned: "One candle per family. The others take home."

I was not a pilgrim but a tourist. Ill at ease being a spectator to devotion, watching people in these intimate moments as they offered fear in exchange for hope, I went outside. There, on a shady stone wall behind the sanctuary, I found La Conquistadora. She was one among a number of saints whose images were set into the stone: Saint James, Saint Francis, the Virgin of Guadalupe. Their shrines dwarfed the small colored ceramic tile depicting her as a dainty Madonna clad in white and blue (Figure 0.1). Yet she clearly had her imposing side—her name was "La Conquistadora," proclaimed the blue lettering beneath the image. Disquieted, I lingered in front of the tile. Conjuring all the aggressive violence of warfare, "the Conqueress" hardly seemed a suitable title for the Virgin Mary, crowned with her halo of tenderness.

As a medievalist, I had been taught that Mary embodied boundless maternal love; though the powerful queen of heaven, she was always ready to intervene on behalf of human sinners to soften her son's judgment.[1] The modern world often fosters this view of her. Popular magazines such as *Newsweek* and *Life* run lavishly illustrated articles about "the Story of Mary" and her age-old readiness to intercede for human beings.[2] Every year, images of the compassionate Madonna adorn Christmas stamps, while countless tourists and the occasional devotee

Figure 0.1 La Conquistadora tile. El Santuario de Chimayó, New Mexico. Author photo.

contemplate the portraits of the maternal Mary housed in museums across the globe.[3] Modern feminist spiritual seekers find inspiration in her as a loving mother whose joys and tribulations echo their own, while intellectuals such as Octavio Paz declare her "the consolation of the poor, the shield of the weak, the shelter of the oppressed."[4] The newest edition of the official catechism of the Catholic Church—issued in 1997 on the feast day of the Virgin's assumption into heaven and with the imprimatur of John Paul II, a pope known for his passionate Marian devotion—presents Jesus' mother as an inexhaustible fount of mercy.[5] Whether feminist theologians find in Mary's maternity a way to rethink power relations in an effort to "humanize" the church, or a patriarchal, oppressively impossible ideal of femininity, they agree that she symbolizes perfect motherhood.[6]

Mary's reputation as a kind mother with a capacious heart does not leave much room for the belligerence implied in a title like "La Conquistadora." In the 1990s, Mexican American women told researchers that aggression of any sort was one of the characteristics they would least expect to find in the Virgin, while the affectionate warmth of a nurturing parent was one of the traits they most associated with her.[7] How then could the iconic loving mother, "the sign of hope and mercy. . . for so many centuries," as one writer has called Mary, possibly merit the title of "La Conquistadora"?[8]

There wasn't anything military about the Madonna on the tile in Chimayó, apart from her name. She did not wave a bloody sword or wear armor. Yet her title was plainly written below the fringe of her dress. La Conquistadora cut through my sunny summer day, bringing with her the shadows of the violent men who had shared her name: Cortés, Pizarro, Coronado. Disturbing anywhere, these specters of conquest seemed particularly alien to Chimayó, a shrine where, as pilgrims note in letters stuck into the frames of the saints' pictures crowding the sanctuary's walls, they have found peace of spirit, if not of body.

Some thirty miles south of Chimayó, La Conquistadora holds court over a much larger audience. Enshrined in Archbishop Lamy's famous cathedral at Santa Fe, New Mexico, and cared for by a loving confraternity founded sometime before 1684 is the late sixteenth- or seventeenth-century statue of Mary depicted on the tile (Figure 0.2).[9] Saint Francis may be the patron of Santa Fe's cathedral, but La Conquistadora is its devotional heart. People sit on the benches in front of the statue, murmuring prayers to the Virgin. A bent woman in black tends the thicket of candles left by supplicants. La Conquistadora has so many outfits provided by the confraternity that a woman who grew up in Santa Fe recalls how, as a child, she used to walk through the cathedral every day just to see what the statue was wearing.[10]

By 1686, La Conquistadora could appear in any one of five dresses, three skirts, six hoods, six mantles, and seven chemises, all made from rich materials. The confraternity inventory from that year records "a dress of white lamé with its gold galoon and small red fringe, lined with blue; a dress of flowered tapestry with scallops of silver and gold lined with red linen"—and more.[11] The leading men and women of Santa Fe's colonial society clearly cared about keeping their Virgin well clad. In 1698, the governor of New Mexico, Don Diego de Vargas, bestowed on the statue "a blue figured–silk dress and white mantle," a gift that publicly demonstrated not only his Marian devotion but also his considerable social status.[12]

At the cathedral in Santa Fe, I bought a pamphlet about the statue entitled *La Conquistadora, Our Lady of Conquering Love.* Her shrine in Chimayó hadn't inspired me to think of the ancient proverb inscribed on Chaucer's prioress's brooch: "Love conquers all."[13] Yet perhaps La Conquistadora wasn't associated

Figure 0.2 Statue of La Conquistadora. Cathedral of Santa Fe, New Mexico. Photo courtesy of Maureen Jameson.

with Spanish military conquest after all but instead with divine love. Then I opened the brochure.

It read like a Spanish chronicle of the seventeenth century, eulogizing the Spanish who conquered and settled New Mexico as heroic and "isolated pioneers" whose victories over the Indians had the aura of divinely ordained triumphs.[14] According to this pious narrative of colonial bravery, La Conquistadora had been brought to Santa Fe in 1625, in the "days of [the] founding fathers... the conquistadores" and accompanied their descendants into exile to El Paso in 1680 after the Pueblo Indians carried out one of the most successful rebellions ever against Spanish colonial rule. In 1693, related the pamphlet, the displaced

settlers came north again, determined "to reconquer Santa Fe beneath the protection of La Conquistadora.... But the Spaniards had to fight hard for Santa Fe;
from their encampment northwest of the town walls the people gathered around
their Queen and prayed the soldiers to final victory." Leading the colonists in this
enterprise was not only La Conquistadora, but also Don Diego de Vargas, who
five years later expanded the statue's wardrobe.

In its celebration of how "La Conquistadora has been venerated and feted ... as
a long-enduring symbol of a people's unfailing love for the Mother of God," the
pamphlet clearly referred to the Spaniards, not the Pueblos. As for the "conquering love" promised on the cover, there was no affection in the narrative, except
of this "people" for their Virgin, and the conquering was all of the military kind.

A year later, I went to the history library at Santa Fe's Palace of the Governors.
When the librarian asked me to sign in, I wrote my name and research subject: "the Virgin Mary as a symbol of military conquest and conversion—special
interest in La Conquistadora." He smiled and said gently: "But you know, she was
never associated with anything military. She's Our Lady of Conquering Love."
Already I had begun to suspect the situation was more complicated than that.

*　*　*

Not everyone in northern New Mexico was willing to interpret La Conquistadora's title benignly, particularly some members of the Pueblo Indian communities whose ancestors had been violently subdued when the Spanish bore the
statue triumphantly into Santa Fe centuries ago. "One thing that's been bothering the tribes is that name," Joe Savilla, a Pueblo Indian who codirects the Native
Ministries of the Archdiocese of Santa Fe, told a reporter from an Albuquerque
newspaper in July 1992.[15] During that summer, in the heightened atmosphere
of soul-searching and celebration that accompanied the five-hundredth anniversary of Columbus's voyage, Pueblo resentment of La Conquistadora's title
simmered over into open protest.

The ensuing controversy rocked Santa Fe. At stake were deeply divergent
interpretations of New Mexico's colonial past of Spanish conquest and Native
American subjugation, all embodied by the cathedral's elegantly dressed
Madonna. On one side were the Pueblos who declared her title to be an offensive commemoration of Spanish victory over their ancestors. On the other were
some Hispano residents of the city who hewed to the cathedral pamphlet's
version of history.[16] Angered by the Pueblo protests, they retorted that La
Conquistadora's name had nothing to do with military conquest, but referred
only to Mary's winning of souls for Christianity.[17]

Whose vision of New Mexico's colonial past rang truer: the Pueblos' or the
Hispanos'? Had the Spanish colonizers flaunted their military and cultural conquests in the shape of the statue? Or had Mary been instead a figure of compassionate love, inviting Indians to convert to Christianity?

Both parties in the Santa Fe controversy had hit upon the truth: the Virgin Mary figured in the Spanish colonization of New Mexico as an embodiment of military conquest *and* of religious conversion. The Spanish colonizers assigned these starring roles to Mary not just in New Mexico but almost everywhere in their far-flung American empire. In fact, Mary as conqueror and as evangelist made the Atlantic crossing to the New World with Spanish conquerors and missionaries. During centuries of contact, cohabitation, and confrontation with the members of the other religious cultures who inhabited the Iberian Peninsula—Muslims and Jews—Spanish Christians had developed an understanding of the Virgin as an icon of the conquest and conversion of non-Christians.

The significance of this Marian history for pre-modern Spanish Christians as well as those peoples whom they dominated militarily and culturally is the subject of this book. Spanning the Atlantic Ocean to bring together the histories of Spain, Mexico, and the United States, this book covers seven centuries and connects medieval and early modern understandings of Mary to explore a legacy that continues to fuel ethnic and religious politics today. Defying chronological and geographical boundaries that historians often treat as sacrosanct, it shows how the medieval Mary persisted into much later centuries and offers an expansive view of the Middle Ages.[18]

Parts One and Two take place in the medieval Christian kingdoms of Castile-León and the Crown of Aragon, with the occasional foray into Muslim territory—al-Andalus, as Islamic Iberia was known to its inhabitants.[19] These sections of the book begin with the eleventh century—which marked the first major successful efforts by Christians to retake territory that the Muslims had held since arriving in the Iberian Peninsula in 711—and continue into the high and late Middle Ages, when Castile and Aragon gradually took control of most of the peninsula and some Christians began to dream of converting Muslims and Jews to Christianity.

Part Three explores the early modern Spanish worlds of the sixteenth and seventeenth centuries. In the momentous year of 1492, the last Muslim foothold in the Iberian Peninsula—the culturally luminous if politically fractious kingdom of Granada—fell to the Christians; the Jews of Castile and Aragon were presented by the Spanish Crown with the agonizing option of abandoning either their Spanish homes or their ancestral faith; and Columbus made his voyage across the Atlantic Ocean, opening the Americas to Spanish colonization. Soon, all subjects of the Spanish empire were Christian, at least in name. The forced conversion of Spain's Muslims followed close on the heels of the baptism of those Jews who had not fled Castile and Aragon in 1492, and many natives of the New World gathered in crowds for Franciscan friars to fling holy water over their heads in efficient if theologically dubious ceremonies of mass baptism. Part Three especially focuses on Mexico and its daughter colony to the north, New Mexico.

The book ends in the late seventeenth century, when the Spanish conquests in the Americas were complete and the remaining descendants of the Spanish Muslims—the Moriscos—suffered forcible expulsion from the peninsula their ancestors had once ruled. After this period, Mary hardly vanished from the Spanish vocabulary of conquest and conversion.[20] But between the eleventh and the seventeenth centuries, Spanish Christian expansion had made conquest and conversion inescapable realities—even matters of life and death—for many women and men in the Iberian Peninsula and the Americas. Christians, Muslims, Jews, and the indigenous peoples of the Americas had to negotiate their ways through the complex cultural and religious situations that inevitably accompanied these twinned colonizing enterprises. As individuals and as groups, and as colonizers and the colonized, they had to devise ways to forge their identities in situations of enormous diversity.

Living side by side in medieval Castile and Aragon were Christians of all sorts, as well as Jews and Mudejars—Muslims subject to Christian rule. Just beyond the porous frontiers of these kingdoms lay the Islamic realm of al-Andalus, a polity as often admired by Christians as it was targeted by their polemical and military attacks. In the sixteenth and seventeenth centuries, the human landscape of Castile and Aragon remained diverse. Although all inhabitants technically were Christian, the Muslim and Jewish converts often retained elements of their former cultures. Some even clandestinely practiced the religion of their ancestors. Meanwhile, across the Atlantic, a particularly radical form of cross-cultural encounter occurred as Tainos, Nahuas, Mayans, Andeans, and myriad other natives of the New World were caught in the rip tides generated by successive waves of Spanish colonizers—the violent and abrupt meeting of peoples who, unlike the Muslims, Jews, and Christians of the Iberian Peninsula, knew nothing of each other, at least at first.

Mary was drawn into these cross-cultural and cross-faith encounters—whether peaceful or hostile—for the Christians, Muslims, and Jews of medieval Iberia, followed by the Spanish colonizers and the indigenous peoples of the New World, often turned to her to articulate their identities. Much of this book explores how lines of demarcation between Christians and non-Christians were drawn through Mary. These could be the metaphoric lines of fixed identities created by doctrinal differences and religious polemic, or the physical ones of war. In either case, Christians and non-Christians ended up on opposite sides of Mary and of each other. While Mary could symbolize military confrontation and religious borders, as this book shows, she could also embody borderlands, where seemingly stark distinctions dissolved and the actual malleability of identities became apparent. Though Christian knights who warred against Muslims made her a patron of their conquests, they recognized that she belonged as much to Islam as to Christianity, a fact that created situations of complexity for members of both faiths. Mary could even open the way for non-Christians to make the border crossing to Christianity. Accordingly, this book considers Christian stories depicting her as a particularly effective agent in the conversion of Jews, Muslims, and native peoples of the Americas. It also explores how, in situations of Christian domination, converts might use her as a figure of power through which to narrate their experiences and express identities blending old and new, as did some New World peoples, who appropriated from their Spanish colonizers the idea of Mary as Conquistadora.

This, however, is not to suggest that in the pre-modern Spanish world, Mary played only these roles. Attempting to capture all the meanings she had for her devotees inevitably risks becoming encyclopedic, as numerous studies of her are—she possesses so many faces.[21] The anonymous author of a twelfth-century Latin text from Catalonia lovingly listed sixty-eight different terms for her, each corresponding to a different trait of her personality. "Goddess, virgin…rod, flower, cloud, queen, empress, lady, peaceful one, handmaiden, earth, garden, spring…" began his lengthy catalogue.[22] Though average Christians perhaps were not familiar with all sixty-eight of Mary's metaphoric identities, they would have experienced her as many things: mother, queen, intercessor, virgin, miracle worker, apocalyptic messenger, the second Eve, handmaiden of God, the heavenly bride.[23]

Mary's traits have waxed and waned according to the spiritual and emotional needs of the era and of the individual men and women who have loved her. From her abundance of qualities, Christians have been able to choose those most likely to bear the desired fruit if cultivated with devotion. This is perhaps part of the attraction she has exercised over the centuries. There is not just one Mary, but many. In modern Madrid alone, some fifty Madonnas, each bearing her own name, command the reverence of the city's Catholic inhabitants.[24]

Some members of the Marian pantheon embody specific characteristics or important moments of her life: Our Lady of the Sorrows, or Our Lady of the Immaculate Conception, Our Lady of the Annunciation, even La Conquistadora.[25] Many other Virgins take their names from the places where they are venerated: Our Lady of Guadalupe, Our Lady of Lourdes, Our Lady of Montserrat, Our Lady of Czestochowa, Our Lady of Rocamadour. So too do the less renowned Madonnas bearing the names of the countless humble Marian shrines scattered across Europe and Latin America. Firmly rooted in the landscape, these Virgins nonetheless can multiply, transplanted to new locations by enthusiastic pilgrims and enterprising churchmen. By the twelfth century, for example, devotees could venerate Our Lady of Rocamadour not only in her southern French home but also at the numerous churches named for her in the Christian kingdoms of the Iberian Peninsula.[26]

Our Lady of Guadalupe is particularly well traveled. Many of the Spanish adventurers who subjugated the New World—including Hernán Cortés and Francisco Pizarro—came from the region of western Castile where her original shrine still attracts pilgrims. Once on the other side of the ocean, the conquistadors remembered this Madonna from home warmly. Sometime in the mid-sixteenth century, the Spanish established a shrine to her amidst the rubble of Tenochtitlan, the capital of the Meso-American empire that Cortés and his men had destroyed.[27] The Mexican Guadalupe now far outshines her Old World sister. More than sixteen million pilgrims arrive annually in Mexico City to pray before the miraculous image of this dark Virgin.[28]

Other than its dusky tint, the Mexican image of Guadalupe bears little resemblance to the Castilian Madonna for whom it is named. One is a painting in soft colors on a rough piece of cloth, the other a diminutive statue carved of cedar wood. The Mexican Guadalupe stands alone on a sliver of moon, while her Old World counterpart sits on a throne, the infant Christ perched on her lap. Wonders—but different ones—accompanied the discovery of each image. Each is a likeness of the Virgin of Guadalupe, but to what degree are they the same Madonna? How much have they been shaped by the force of devotion to fit their particular settings?

The answers to these questions vary with historical circumstances as well as individual devotees' perspectives. But in the pre-modern world, efforts to ensure uniformity as the cult of a particular Virgin spread were bound to fail. So a friar named Diego de Ocaña from the Castilian monastery of Guadalupe learned when, in the very last years of the sixteenth century, he set out for the viceroyalties of Peru and New Spain to collect alms for his community.[29] In many places Ocaña visited in Peru, he saw paintings and statues of the Virgin whom he so loved. To his dismay, he discovered that the material and spiritual fruits of devotion to these New World images of Guadalupe were not being ferried across the Atlantic to his home monastery. The local people considered these Madonnas their own, not representatives of one located thousands of miles away. Ocaña energetically attempted to manage Guadalupe's New World cult. Blessed with artistic talents, he painted new portraits of her and left them on the altars of Peruvian churches as insistent reminders of *his* Virgin, the one in Castile.[30] Although news of the miracles performed by these Guadalupes filtered back to Spain, Ocaña's artistic endeavors offered people living in Peru yet more Madonnas to make their own.[31]

The story of the New World Guadalupes is testimony to the needs of Mary's devotees to bring the transcendental, universal Virgin of doctrine and legend down into the human realm, making her personal, local, and tangible.[32] Baser human desires, too, can express themselves through this multiplication of

Madonnas. The communities that control her shrines often directly compete with each other for the fame and profit brought by the pilgrim trade.[33]

If there was a strong sense in the pre-modern world that each Madonna was different from her sisters, there was also the knowledge that, ultimately, all of them were one and the same figure. Christopher Columbus, a man deeply devoted to Mary, seems to have known this well, at least according to the sixteenth-century redactor of his diaries.[34] As the explorer sailed for home after his first New World voyage, he ran headlong into a storm so fierce it threatened to sink his ship.[35] Like countless other medieval sailors, Columbus and his men hoped Mary's mercy would save them. They turned at first to Our Lady of Guadalupe, whose church Columbus had probably visited as a pilgrim in 1486.[36] Using the ship's store of dried chickpeas, they drew lots to choose one of them to make a thanksgiving journey to her shrine if she helped them come ashore safely. Chance singled out Columbus himself. Yet the storm did not abate. The men drew lots again. This time they appealed to Our Lady of Loreto. The sailor who found in his hand the marked chickpea pledged a pilgrimage to her shrine in Italy. Still the winds remained menacing. A third round of lots—to decide who would go as a pilgrim to the church of Santa Clara of Moguer, a saint also known to rescue mariners in need—did not help.

In desperation, Columbus and the ship's crew abandoned all thoughts of particular Madonnas and simply invoked the universal Mary. They made a collective vow that, if they survived the storm, at their first landfall they would hasten in a solemn procession wearing only their shirts—a mark of humility often adopted by late medieval pilgrims—to the nearest church of Our Lady. Mary seems to have been satisfied by their promise. The seas gradually subsided, allowing Columbus's ship to reach the haven of the Azores, where the sailors made their pilgrimage to a chapel dedicated to her.

Some of the Virgins important to conquest and conversion in the pre-modern Spanish world had titles to prove it—Our Lady of Battles, or La Conquistadora. But a Madonna did not need to bear such an explicit name for Christians to believe she had power in these realms. Our Lady of Remedies, Our Lady of Guadalupe, Our Lady of Tentudia, Our Lady of the Immaculate Conception— these are just a few of the Madonnas to figure in narratives of conquest and conversion. Almost any Virgin had the potential to take on traits of conqueror or missionary, including the universal Mary, who needed no name beyond "Our Lady." Following the lead of the medieval and early modern writers, when they mention a particular Madonna, I give that Virgin her title and attributes. But when, as is often the case, the authors simply call her "Mary" or "Our Lady" or "the Virgin," so do I.

Whether writing of the universal Mary or a particular Madonna, medieval and early modern Christian authors often used the language of marvel. Miracles, visions, and apparitions were indeed arenas in which pre-modern Christians hoped to meet Mary. Pronouncing on the reality of encounters between people and the transcendent lies well beyond the province of the historian. Yet as I write about the politics, cultural ideals, and social situations that could be expressed in stories about Marian marvels, I am acutely aware of another layer of meaning. These tales relate the startling, wondrous encounter of humans with the sacred, which is what mattered to so many people listening to them.[37]

But not to everyone. Although Jews, Muslims, and the pre-Columbian peoples of the New World had their own traditions of the miraculous, some of them heard in Mary's marvels not the awesome poetry of the divine, but the coercive rhetoric of Christian colonization. They could experience these tales as heavy-handed, oppressive propaganda. Some Jews in late medieval Castile, for example, sang songs that would have angered the sailors of Columbus's crew; these ballads lampooned Christian stories about the Madonna's ability to calm the seas.[38] A twelfth-century Andalusi Muslim who scornfully debunked the most famous Marian miracle associated with the Castilian city where he spent two long years in captivity was probably not the only follower of Islam who found Christian tales about the Virgin's wonders hard to swallow.[39] Their perspectives too figure in this book.

This exploration of the passions that Mary aroused centuries ago is written in the hopes that modern Christians, as well as people of other faiths or of no faith, might better understand historical circumstances in which people of diverse cultures and religions lived in proximity. It asks how the language of the sacred could both underscore potential differences between people and help to smooth out those very differences. While the answers of men and women of the past bear the stamp of their times and places, there is much to be learned from their successes and their failures, for these same questions starkly face our own world.

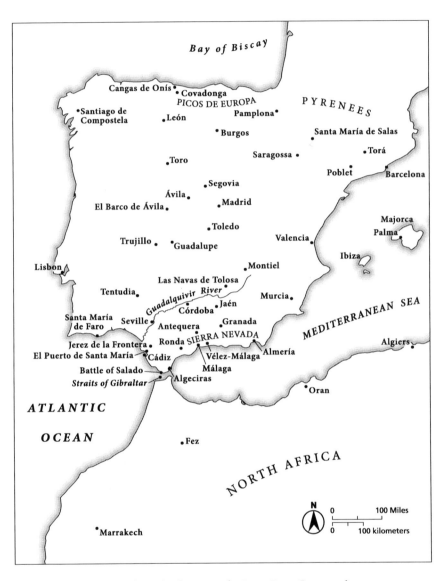

Bay of Biscay

Cangas de Onís • Covadonga
PICOS DE EUROPA
PYRENEES

• Santiago de
Compostela
• León
Pamplona •

Santa María de Salas

• Burgos

Saragossa •
• Torá

• Toro
Poblet •
• Barcelona

• Segovia
Madrid •

Ávila •

El Barco de Ávila •
• Toledo

Majorca
Palma •

Trujillo •
• Guadalupe
Valencia •

Ibiza

• Montiel

Lisbon
Las Navas de Tolosa

Tentudia •
Guadalquivir River
Murcia •

Jaén •
MEDITERRANEAN SEA

Córdoba •
Santa María
de Faro
Seville •
Antequera
Granada •

Ronda SIERRA NEVADA
Algiers •

Jerez de la Frontera •
Almería

El Puerto de Santa María
• Cádiz
Vélez-Málaga

Battle of Salado
Málaga

Straits of Gibraltar
Algeciras
Oran •

ATLANTIC

OCEAN
• Fez

NORTH AFRICA

N
0   100 Miles

0   100 kilometers

• Marrakech

Iberia and North Africa. Map by Pease Press Cartography.

PART ONE

THE VIRGIN AND THE RECONQUEST

Introduction

"Our Lady is powerful in battles....[S]he is the hope of...knights who fight.... [W]ithout her aid, knights cannot win."[1] So wrote a Catalan Christian named Ramón Llull in the rapturous book of Marian praise he composed around 1290. Llull was a religious contemplative, a tireless missionary, and a prolific author. He often spoke in allegory, but not here. He did not mean that Mary helped souls struggling in the battles between virtue and sin, or between Christ and the devil, although he knew she could do so. Nor did Llull want merely to express his desire that Christian knights, often undisciplined and frighteningly violent, might become paragons of chivalry and virtue, fighting for God, the Church, and justice.[2] Instead, he meant that Mary had a place in actual battles, the kind in which warriors slashed and thrust with weapons of steel and wood.

With these phrases, Llull captured the hope that many Christian men of war, medieval and modern, have placed in Mary.[3] He also situated her at the heart of a central arena of human experience in the high Middle Ages. The violence of warfare too often broke into the daily life of medieval people. William the Conqueror's invasion of England in 1066, stitched in graphic detail on the Bayeux Tapestry, the conflicts that pitted popes, German emperors, and Italian city-states against each other, and the Hundred Years' War between England and France were among the great clashes that roiled this period of European history. Vicious territorial contests between local lords and their gangs of knights also plagued the landscape—medieval combat was as often carried out by raiders as it was by royal armies.[4] No wonder some saints specialized in miracles that rescued the unarmed members of society from the ravages of men with weapons.[5] Mary often had to shield pilgrims journeying to her shrines, protecting them from bandit knights who saw unarmed travelers as easy prey. Any knight who did succeed in robbing or harming her devotees had to fear that he might be struck with sudden illness, the punishment she often meted out to miscreants in miracle stories.[6]

Ramón Llull had seen enough war that it was to him as much a regular part of life as the other fortunes and misfortunes over which he assured his readers that Mary had dominion: health and sickness, wealth and poverty, perils on land and at sea, the deprivations suffered by widows and orphans.[7] He did not assign geographical limits to her battlefield powers, believing them as universal as her other talents. The Iberian Peninsula was indeed not the first place in western Europe where Mary inspired hope in men of war. As early as the ninth century, Christians living in southern Italy told stories of how in 663 she had appeared on the walls of a Lombard city under siege and helped its inhabitants to victory.[8] This tale probably owed something to a Latin translation of a famous Byzantine hymn in Mary's honor whose prologue celebrated her defense of the imperial city of Constantinople centuries earlier.[9]

When the Italian story was written down, Mary had not yet entered the arena of warfare in the Iberian Peninsula, for conditions were not ripe. She had still to gain the prominent place in the affections of the Christians living there that she would enjoy by Ramón Llull's day. All across early medieval Europe, martyr saints eclipsed Mary as Christians' devotional choice, except in areas like southern Italy that were heavily influenced by the Byzantine Empire, where she already reigned in Christians' hearts. Only around the year 1000 would the first tentative shoots of the deep love for Mary that would later flower everywhere in high medieval Europe begin to grow. Nurtured by monks and nuns and clerics and friars as well as by lay men and women, this burgeoning devotion would lead to the "marianization" of high medieval European Christianity.[10]

Mary's arrival on the battlefield in medieval Iberia belongs to the story of her rising fortunes in Europe. Gradually, the shifting currents of politics and power in the land bordered by the Pyrenees, the Mediterranean, and the Atlantic would draw her into warfare there. Though she would also exercise her military talents elsewhere in Europe, this is a particularly Iberian story.[11] Just as a Virgin venerated at one shrine was both the same as and different from one enthroned in another church, so the martial Mary of medieval Iberia had her own distinctive character, shaped by local conditions.[12] As the hope of knights, she in fact had her work cut out for her in the high medieval Christian kingdoms of the Iberian Peninsula such as Castile-León and Ramón Llull's home in the Crown of Aragon.

These kingdoms have been called "societies organized for war."[13] To be sure, goldsmiths, rabbis, bakers, nuns, priests, fishwives, peasants, and countless other sorts of people lived in Castile and Aragon, not just men who identified themselves primarily as warriors. For many if not most of these men and women, combat was often a distant rumor or something they heard about in epic poems or chivalric romances. Knights and soldiers themselves often put down their weapons, for medieval hostilities were rarely continuous. Yet between the late eleventh and the late fifteenth centuries, warfare and its ethos impressed themselves on life in Castile and Aragon perhaps more profoundly than elsewhere in western Europe, because these kingdoms shared borders with a succession of Muslim polities.

Peace often prevailed between Muslim and Christian lands, fostering neighborly exchanges across the frontier.[14] Yet the ever-present possibility of raids, skirmishes, or battles cast the shadow of danger over the shifting boundary zones. The potential for military conflict between Christian and Muslim polities had been a fact of life in the Iberian Peninsula ever since 711, when a large force of Muslims, mostly composed of North Africans recently converted to Islam, crossed the Straits of Gibraltar and defeated the reigning power, the Christian Visigoths. Over the next decade, Muslims established themselves as the peninsula's new rulers, concentrating their energies on controlling the fertile plains of the south. Many Hispano-Visigoths accommodated themselves to life under the new regime, but others fled, finding refuge in the much less desirable mountainous regions in the north and east of the peninsula. There Christians established the small kingdoms and principalities, like Asturias and Pamplona, that would later develop into León, Castile, Portugal, Navarre, and Aragon, while in the south, the Muslims created the expansive realm they called al-Andalus.[15]

Mary's role in warfare against Muslims became sharply defined only a few decades before Ramón Llull composed the *Libre de Sancta Maria*. But the martial Mary whom he celebrated did not spring fully formed into the world of thirteenth-century Iberia, an Athena born in armor. Instead, she gestated in the same womb where, not coincidentally, Castile and Aragon would become something like "societies organized for war"—the centuries-old history of war and peace that bound the kingdoms of the Iberian Peninsula, Muslim and Christian, together into an unstable political constellation.

War, Peace, and Reconquest

For four hundred years, most of what is now called Spain belonged to the Islamic world. From 711 until the eleventh century, al-Andalus, under the rulership of the Umayyads, men descended from Islam's first caliphal dynasty, dominated the physical and political geography of the Iberian Peninsula. Muslim authors were wont to compare al-Andalus to the lush gardens of paradise promised the faithful by the Qur'an. With its scientific and philosophical learning, technological accomplishments, and cultural sophistication, this early medieval polity far outshone its Christian rivals in western Europe. Rumors of its treasures of erudition and tales of the magnificence of its cities and towns—of Seville, Toledo, and especially Córdoba, its capital—reached Christians living well beyond its borders. Inspired by such reports, a tenth-century German nun who had never been south of the Pyrenees confidently proclaimed Cordoba the "ornament of the world."[16] A visitor to al-Andalus's capital could stroll through paved and well-lit streets, cross the River Guadalquivir on graceful arched bridges, and peer into the elegant courtyards of aristocrats' mansions. Everywhere was the sound of water splashing in fountains, nourished by a great aqueduct, which also ensured that the city's numerous gardens remained green.[17]

Though afflicted by serious internal political turbulence, Umayyad al-Andalus commanded the respect of its much smaller Christian neighbors. Many rulers of these kingdoms eagerly struck alliances with the reigning caliph or amir, while some Christians even took military service with the Umayyads. Around the turn of the millennium, enough Christian mercenaries from Catalonia were in al-Andalus's pay that the gold dinars they received as wages became the currency of choice in Christian Barcelona.[18] Other dinars circulating in this Catalonian city in the early eleventh century were instead plunder seized during raids by Christian men who fought against al-Andalus's armies. The frequent political unrest troubling the Muslim polity offered enticing military opportunities for Christian rulers. In the ninth and tenth centuries, the Christian kingdoms eroded the northern and eastern edges of al-Andalus, gradually advancing as far south as the Duero River and as far west as the upper reaches of the Ebro River.[19] Yet in the early Middle Ages, the majority of the Iberian Peninsula remained under the control of al-Andalus.

Everything began to change after al-Andalus's long-standing ethnic tensions and political antagonisms ignited into full-on civil war in the first decade of the eleventh century. By the 1030s, the caliphate had shattered into a multitude of fragile statelets known as the *taifa* kingdoms, each centered on a city.[20] The political fragmentation of al-Andalus precipitated a new balance of power. Although the territory under Islamic rule would retain all its sophisticated urbanity, the geography of Muslim Iberia would gradually shrink while the Christian kingdoms expanded. This shift brought subtle changes in the Christian kingdoms' stance toward the Muslim polities with whom they shared borders. New ideas re-arranged old attitudes into fresh patterns that would eventually foster Llull's declaration that Christian knights could not win without Mary's aid.

Enterprising eleventh-century Christian monarchs and adventurers were quick to perceive the possibilities of self-enrichment offered by the birth of the *taifa* kingdoms. In return for hefty payments in gold, men like Alfonso VI, ruler of Castile-León, or his sometime vassal Rodrigo Díaz de Vivar, better known as the Cid, hero of the famous thirteenth-century epic poem, offered their military services to one *taifa* kingdom in its struggles against another, or in its battles against other Christians.[21] Equally often, these Christian strongmen extorted astronomical sums from *taifa* rulers in exchange for peace. Buying protection did not always work, however, especially when men as hungry for land and power as Alfonso VI and the Cid were involved. Alfonso conquered the *taifa* kingdom of Toledo in 1085, while the Cid mastered Valencia in 1094. Fearing the same fate, the rulers of other *taifa* kingdoms appealed for military aid to a vigorous new Muslim dynasty in North Africa, the Almoravids. Once across the Straits of Gibraltar, the Almoravids quickly turned against their hosts and established themselves as the reigning Muslim power in the Iberian Peninsula. By the mid-twelfth century, they were displaced by a rival North African group, the Almohads, who established a trans-Mediterranean caliphate headquartered in Marrakech and Seville.[22]

Despite fierce infighting, the Almoravids and then the Almohads regained some of the territory that had been lost to León, Castile, and the nascent kingdom of Aragon. But Christians themselves conquered land that had been under Muslim control. Mapping the conquests and reconquests, whether Christian or Muslim, of the twelfth century is a dizzying task. Raids and skirmishes were more or less constant along the fluid frontier between the Christian kingdoms and their Muslim neighbors, the broad swath of land along the Tagus and Ebro rivers.[23] No wonder that the Christian settlers who moved to this and other frontier areas founded civic militias and built massive walls encircling their towns; the crenellated granite and brick fortifications crafted by twelfth-century stone masons around Ávila were one and a half miles long, some forty feet high and ten feet thick.[24] Less tangible expressions of Christian expansionist energies appeared in the form of ideas that would invite Mary onto the battlefield.

As Christian knights and soldiers of Castile and Aragon took up arms to defend their communities or to launch raids against the Muslims, they could think with pious satisfaction about how just their actions were; God wanted them to retake the land that their Christian ancestors, the Visigoths, had held until they lost it to the unbelieving Muslims. They were participating not just in conquest, but in a holy reconquest, legitimated by God and the past. This marriage of holy war and holy history, which became particularly pronounced in high medieval Castile, trampled the truth. It flattened the confused realities and mixed loyalties of the Iberian Peninsula, hiding the fact that Muslims might fight for Christians (and vice versa) behind a mirage of monolithic and implacable religious conflict. And it ignored the fact that due to generations of intermarriage and conversion in both directions, the Muslims of high medieval Iberia probably had as much right as the Christians did to claim the Visigoths as their forebears. With its false front of inexorable and incessant warfare, it also masked the many years of peace and truce between Muslim and Christian polities. But ideologies are almost always rooted in a useful worldview, rather than in historical veracity. It was clearly advantageous for the chroniclers, monarchs, prelates, and warriors of the medieval Christian kingdoms to have available a set of ideas that could justify aggressive territorial warfare against Muslim polities.

Exactly when this notion of what modern historians call the reconquest coalesced is much debated, in part because the term itself—a post-medieval coinage—suggests a kind of ideological consistency and constancy not found in the medieval sources.[25] It is evident, however, that the potential for Christians to frame combat against al-Andalus with the inflammatory rhetoric of battle against the infidel increased once knights from the lands north of the Pyrenees began to be inspired by the ideals of crusade, and an army of French and German warriors calling themselves pilgrims wrested Jerusalem from its Fatimid over-lords in 1099. In the twelfth century, the pope even declared Iberia as worthy a theater for crusade as the Levant.[26] By then, writers in the Christian Iberian kingdoms sometimes ornamented their panegyrics to conquest with flourishes drawn from the vocabulary of territorial recovery and restoration, a lexicon that later authors would use more frequently.

These ideas, however, neither possessed an iron grip on the hearts and minds of the men who fought under their banner nor dictated how they thought and behaved all the time. Christian and Muslim rulers continued to esteem each other as diplomatic partners and military allies, and Christian admiration for the refined beauties wrought by the artists and artisans of al-Andalus persisted. So highly did Christians prize Muslim craftsmanship that they often deemed the famed silks woven in Andalusi workshops worthy shrouds for their bish-ops, kings, queens, princes, princesses, and even the wonder-working relics of saints.[27] In some Castilian and Aragonese churches, saints' relics wrapped in such silk were housed in intricately carved ivory boxes and finely molded silver caskets that had been made in al-Andalus but taken by Christians as trophies.[28] While many high medieval Castilian and Aragonese men of war strove to win such battle spoils, others fought for pay in the armies of the Muslim rulers of the Iberian Peninsula and North Africa, just as Muslim mercenaries wielded weap-ons for Christian rulers.[29] Religious difference thus hardly split Christian and Muslim Iberia into two implacably antagonistic armed camps. Nonetheless, the emergent ideas of reconquest offered Christian knights and soldiers the heady possibility of believing—when convenient—that their wars against al-Andalus were willed by God and by history.

Holy enterprises call for holy patrons. According to the chronicles recounting the crusades in the eastern Mediterranean, the dragon-slayer archangel Michael and popular Byzantine warrior saints such as George, Mercurius, and Demetrius often galloped astride heavenly white horses in the midst of the Christian armies.[30] These saints' evolution into the holy defenders of Christian knights had its counterpart in medieval Iberia. There, relics could repose in Andalusi silks, but some saints began to join Christian knights and soldiers in waging war against al-Andalus itself.

Early Stories

Amidst the blood, sweat, and fear of combat, warriors have often experienced the sudden, intense epiphany of divine or saintly aid. Authors from the ancient and medieval Western world—pagan, Jewish, and Christian—recounted many such wondrous moments, lingering especially over the dread these apparitions instilled in the enemy.[31] These stories were not merely literary devices intended to impress the reader with the superior power of one's gods and the failure of the enemies' protectors. They also expressed a worldview shared by writers and warriors, all of whom could gladly believe that supporting their cause were invincible holy forces. As the tides of power slowly turned against al-Andalus in the eleventh and twelfth centuries, Christians began to declare their belief that Mary was among those heavenly forces helping them win.

In this early period, only a handful of texts mention Mary on the battlefield. Spare and sparse as they are, these early stories nonetheless hint that as the concepts of crusade and reconquest were crystallizing, the foundations were being laid for her entrance into these charged arenas. Some eleventh- and twelfth-century writers suggest little more than that Christian warriors would do well to pray for Mary's aid against al-Andalus. A laconic document of 1045 from the kingdom of Navarre-Pamplona, for example, depicted the tenth-century ruler Sancho Garcès I petitioning Mary in her church at Irache before successfully investing a castle held by "Saracens," which he then gave to her.[32] The scribe who penned this charter refrained from characterizing Sancho's Muslim enemies in overtly religious terms—"Saracen" was an old ethnic term that predated the emergence of Islam.[33] An early twelfth-century monk from the Catalonian monastery of Nájera who included similar anecdotes in his chronicle was more inclined to underline divine support of Christian warfare against Muslims, but he was no more forthcoming about Mary's exact role in victory. According to this author, two tenth-century Christian rulers—Ordoño II of León and one of the many men named Garcés who sat on the throne of Pamplona—had built churches for her in the wake of triumphs over al-Andalus.[34]

While these writers were cobbling together their reticent accounts, some of their contemporaries fashioned more dramatic stories in which Mary rehearsed some of the battlefield roles in which she would later star. "How the Virgin Mary triumphed over...the infidel nation...supported with the power of the most holy archangel Michael and the help of the holder of the keys to the highest palace"—it was with these ringing words that an early eleventh-century monk opened his account of a battle fought in the shadow of the castle of Torà.[35] It was probably in 1003 that four great counts of Catalonia—Bernat Tallaferro of Besalú, Guifré II of Cerdanya, Ermengol of Urgell, and Ramón Borrell of Barcelona—gathered with their knights at this fortress in the hills near Ermengol's seat of power.[36] These men had put aside their considerable differences to unite against the troops of al-Andalus.

According to the monk's narrative, the Andalusis promised to be as successful during this expedition into Catalonia as they had been some twenty years earlier when they plundered the wealthy port city of Barcelona. At Torà, their forces, swollen with Christian mercenaries, far outnumbered the comital armies—or so the panicked Christian lookout shouted as he caught sight of the enemy. The counts' followers, wrote the monk, began to retreat. Then, as medieval war leaders often did to bolster their men's courage, Bernat Tallaferro cried out that divine favor was on their side.[37] Why, he harangued his troops, had they forgotten the many times that Mary, Saint Michael, and Saint Peter had already led them to victory? Mary would triumph over five thousand of the enemy, Michael trample another five thousand, and Peter destroy the same number. The Christians regrouped. Beseeching Mary, Peter, and Michael, they prevailed over the Andalusis.

This victory apparently pleased the Virgin (she was "happier than usual," commented the monk), although it made her late for an assembly of saints at the Archangel Michael's famous Italian mountainside shrine, Monte Gargano. Apologizing for her tardiness, Mary explained to the holy congress that she had been detained by a delegation of Christians begging for her military aid. This, at any rate, is what Andrew, the writer from the French monastery of Saint-Benoît-sur-Loire who so colorfully narrated the events at Torà, told his readers. He slipped this story of saintly warfare into a book he composed in the 1040s celebrating the miraculous powers of his abbey's holy patron, Benedict.[38]

With his highly educated pen, Andrew embellished this tale of Mary and the celestial contingent at Torà, but he did not invent it. He would have had little reason to do so, for the saint whose reputation really mattered to him was not Mary but the holy monk whose name his monastery bore. Andrew must have heard the story when he made the arduous journey from northern France to Catalonia in order to collect evidence that Benedict performed miracles even in this southwestern fringe of Christian Europe.[39] Among the stories of saintly power with which local people filled his ears must have been the account of Torá, a battle still fresh in their minds as a Christian triumph so remarkable that it made sense only as a result of saintly intervention.

It is impossible to know if at Torá the Christian warriors actually invoked Mary and her male saintly companions. As news of the victory spread, her name may simply have crept into the tale, as dramatic details have a way of doing when stories travel from person to person. Andrew's informants may not have vaunted Mary's martial leadership by placing her as squarely in the limelight as he did, or even have used the stark language of Christian and infidel with which he sharpened his narrative. After all, Andrew was from France, where the language of crusade became popular long before it did in the Iberian Peninsula.

Yet already in the early twelfth century, when a monk from the kingdom of León looked back over the centuries to an event of mythic importance for nascent notions of reconquest—the first Christian victory over Muslims in the Iberian Peninsula—he was willing to grant Mary an important part in it. As he composed his narrative, this monk believed that he was commemorating the crucial Christian triumph that gave birth to Asturias, the kingdom that would become León and eventually give rise to Castile. In his story, Mary lent her halo to this twinned foundational moment that stamped the political conscious-ness of many Christian Spaniards well into the twentieth century: the battle of Covadonga.[40] This engagement probably took place around 718 or 722 in the difficult if spectacular mountainous terrain of the Picos de Europa. The rest is legend, for the earliest extant Christian reports of Covadonga date some two hundred years after the purported events, appearing in Asturian royal chronicles in the first or second decade of the tenth century.

The monk from twelfth-century León was familiar with his tenth-century predecessors' narratives of Christian heroism, which read as follows.[41] A decade or so after Muslim armies first arrived in the Iberian Peninsula, a Visigothic noble named Pelagius gathered his handful of fighters deep in the mountains. Ever since 711, he had stoutly resisted the invaders, even drawing his sword against prominent Christians who collaborated with these new overlords. As Pelagius and his men sought the protection of a cave in Mount Aseuva's rock face at the place that would be called Covadonga, they were confronting a Muslim army numbering in the hundreds of thousands. With God's help, they miraculously defeated this vast host. The jubilant Pelagius then established his seat of power at nearby Cangas de Onís, bequeathing the title of "king" to his descendants.

The story of Covadonga had surely pleased Alfonso III of Asturias-León if he was still alive when his chroniclers included it their fulsome celebrations of his military campaigns against al-Andalus. They crafted Pelagius into a flat-tering reflection of their royal patron; the legendary Visigothic hero triumphs with divine aid against the Muslim invaders, just as Alfonso III—occupying the throne Pelagius had established—battles Muslims to repossess land that right-fully belonged to Christians. To heighten the sense that Covadonga was a divinely willed victory, Alfonso III's writers styled the Muslims after Old Testament foes of Israel. They further consecrated the battle by describing the rocky refuge from which Pelagius makes his stand as "Saint Mary's cave."[42] Although Pelagius fights from this place sacred to the Virgin and rocks hurled by the Muslims miracu-lously rebound from her cave onto the enemies' heads, there is no hint that Mary herself had a hand in the victory.

When the legend of Covadonga was resurrected in the early twelfth century, Mary was enthroned at its center. In his chronicle, the anonymous Leonese monk transformed the little band of Christian warriors into her devotees.[43] Carefully reworking the Asturian chroniclers' version of Pelagius's speech on the eve of battle, this twelfth-century monk made it into a manifesto for holy war and created an opening for the Virgin. Pelagius still angrily defies Oppa, the traitorous archbishop of Toledo who has colluded with the Muslims and is urging the hero to back down from battle. But now the hero is a proto-crusader. Declaring his confidence in Christ and scorn for the "multitude of pagans" whose war tents are massed before the "blessed cave," Pelagius accuses Oppa of having delivered the Visigothic kingdom to Satan and confidently predicts that "the Gothic people" will triumph "through the intercession of Our Lord's mother, she who is the mother of mercies." During the long days and nights in the cave on Mount Aseuva, he and his men beseech the Virgin for her aid, something they had not done in the tenth-century texts. It was with this decidedly Marian twist that the story of the first victory of Spanish Christians over Muslim foes would most often be repeated in later centuries.[44] Covadonga itself would eventually become a flourishing Marian shrine, attracting crowds of pilgrims who braved the mountain paths in order to offer their respects to the Virgin of the battle; according to the twelfth-century Leonese monk, already in his day the cave resounded with people's prayers to her.[45]

In retouching the legend of Covadonga, this monk revealed exactly how some people in the early twelfth century thought Mary could help men of war to victory. Her powers of merciful intercession were the key to her new importance in the story of Covadonga. The fearful knowledge that God would punish his sinful followers with the bitter taste of military defeat was as old as the Hebrew scriptures. Any saint, by virtue of being enthroned in heaven close to Christ, could potentially win the heavenly king's pardon before a battle for those penitent warriors who prayed hard enough. But by the time the anonymous Leonese monk composed his version of Pelagius's deeds, Mary was earning a reputation as the most efficacious saintly intercessor.

Mediation at Christ's celestial court, the softening of the heavenly ruler's justice through his mother's tender pleas—this is what twelfth-century Christian women and men often hoped for from Mary. They beseeched her to persuade God to forgive their sins and to smooth their path through life's difficulties. This longing for her intercession arose from the newly vibrant Marian devotion apparent everywhere in late eleventh- and twelfth-century Christian Europe. Shaped increasingly in text and image as an approachable human figure, Mary acquired a new intimacy with her devotees to balance the awe elicited by more formidable regal representations of her. Hence prayers imploring her to have mercy on sinful humanity flowed from the pens of monks and clerics.[46]

By the mid-twelfth century, Christian men of war could rely on Mary's ability to win forgiveness for her devotees, according to the anonymous cleric who chronicled the reign of Alfonso VII of Castile-León. Like Andrew of Fleury, this author wrote about her role in military conflicts between Muslim and Christian forces that happened during his own lifetime. He was particularly eloquent about an engagement on the plains around Montiel, where the Christian militias of Toledo, Ávila, and Segovia trounced the Almoravids in 1143. In winning this important victory, wrote the chronicler, they relied not only on their own strength but on Mary's mediation. "Oh great Virgin of virgins, intercede for us with your son Our Lord, Jesus Christ. And if you will free us, from all the things which you have given or will give to us [as booty in battle] we will faithfully give tithes to your church in Toledo," intoned the Christian forces while arming themselves spiritually for the clash with the Almoravids.[47]

This prayer drew from the same deepening wellspring of belief in Mary's powers of intercession that spilled into the twelfth-century retelling of Covadonga. But these militia men did not rely on Mary alone for spiritual aid on the battlefield. Alfonso VII's chronicler described how their fervent prayers at Montiel and other engagements paired her name with that of the apostle James, also known as Santiago. In the future, many other battles against non-Christians would bring the Virgin and the apostle together. James would become Mary's rival and then her most frequent saintly comrade at arms not only in medieval Iberia, but also on the other side of the Atlantic.

Medieval Christians like the militia men who fought at Montiel, believed that James, fired by the evangelical zeal that had perhaps caused Jesus to name him a "son of thunder" (Mark 3.17), had traveled from Judea to the Iberian Peninsula and labored to convert its inhabitants. Returning to Jerusalem, James met martyrdom at the hands of Herod's henchmen. But even decapitation could not sever his connection to Spain. Cradled in a rudderless boat, James's headless body miraculously made its way back to the land he had tried to evangelize. For some nine hundred years, his relics lay hidden until their wondrous revelation at the place that would be called Compostela. Medieval people interpreted this name to mean "the field of stars," believing it commemorated the celestial signs that had allegedly guided a hermit to discover James's resting place. In the ninth century, the first in a series of ever more capacious churches was built at Compostela to honor Spain's evangelist.[48]

By the twelfth century, throngs of pilgrims from all over Europe prayed to James in Compostela's magnificent Romanesque cathedral, hoping for cures, forgiveness of sins, and aid with trials of daily life.[49] Tucked into the *Liber Sancti Jacobi*, the twelfth-century book celebrating the apostle's most famous miracles, was a story indicating that he was developing some other talents that would make him as smart a devotional choice as Mary for the militia men massed at

Montiel. This tale, which would become a part of Santiago's biography, was already well-known when the shrine keepers at Compostela were compiling the *Liber Sancti Jacobi*. It also reached the ears of the Leonese monk who was busy revising the story of Covadonga. Their versions of this anecdote about James differ in some detail, but the gist is the same.

Set in a much less distant past than Covadonga but nonetheless enjoying the gilded glow of history, this story told how a Greek pilgrim who arrived in Compostela in 1064 was appalled to overhear some local people calling Santiago a "good knight." The pilgrim believed that a humble apostle like James would never have engaged in the bloody practices of knights or even ridden a horse. A terrifying vision proved him wrong. James appeared and upbraided the Greek for doubting that an apostle could be a "most powerful knight." He then produced a white horse, leapt on its back and galloped around the church, thundering that he would help King Ferdinand I of Castile-León take the city of Coimbra from the Muslims.[50] The pilgrim was convinced. As James had foretold, a few days later, Ferdinand conquered Coimbra with his aid.[51]

By the mid-twelfth century, men who called on Santiago in battle believed that this haloed knight had supported Christians in their wars against al-Andalus for generations. Legend told them that during the ninth-century battle of Clavijo, James's appearance on a shining white steed had spurred Christian forces to a great victory over the Umayyads and thus freed the rulers of Asturias from the humiliating obligation of supplying one hundred virgins a year to the harem at Córdoba.[52] Both battle and tribute payment were figments of twelfth-century Christian imagination, but Clavijo still became a respectable chapter in reconquest history.

James the knight might have Clavijo, the legendary battle that ended the political and sexual submission of the first post-Visigothic Christian kingdom to al-Andalus—but Mary the intercessor had Covadonga, the Christian triumph that lay at the kingdom's very roots and thus had made all other victories over the Muslims possible. Clothed with charisma in the evolving Christian vision of past wars against al-Andalus, Mary and James could join forces during battles of the present, as the prayers uttered by the militias of Ávila, Toledo, and Segovia at Montiel suggest. Yet some people, including the prelates who presided over James's burgeoning cult, considered the Virgin and the apostle instead as contenders for one prize.

The bishops of Compostela had great ambitions. During the twelfth century, they sought nothing less than to steal the title of head of the Spanish church from the archbishops of Toledo, the old Visigothic capital that Alfonso VI had returned to the Christian fold in 1085.[53] In their bid for primacy, the bishops of Compostela heavily promoted James and styled him as a rival to Toledo's saintly patron, who happened to be Mary. Stung in their considerable pride, the archbishops of Toledo countered with vituperative polemics underlining the superiority of the mother of God, a blood relative of Christ, over a mere apostle, and, like the prelates of Compostela, they tried to insinuate their own patron saint into the particular affections of the monarchs of Castile-León.[54] The militia men at Montiel were not bothered by the heated game of high ecclesiastical politics being played out through Mary and James. According to Alfonso VII's chronicler, they invoked both saints in the same breath as holy allies who might help Christians in armed clashes with Muslims.

Shortly after their triumph at Montiel, these militia companies jubilantly processed into Toledo and wound through the steep streets toward the city's cathedral, which bore Mary's name. Some of these men shepherded groups of chained Muslim captives, some brandished spears spiked with the heads of defeated Almoravid leaders, while others led captured horses and camels laden with less gruesome trophies of silver, gold, armor, and shields.[55] They had come to Toledo to fulfill their battlefield vow to offer Mary a portion of the booty if her intercession helped them to win. As these Christian fighters entered the city's cathedral for the ceremony of thanksgiving, they knew they were stepping into a building that was itself both a monumental victory offering to her and testimony to the Christian triumph that several decades earlier had made the *taifa* kingdom of Toledo a Castilian possession. It was equally powerful evidence of a final important aspect to Mary's involvement in the early years of reconquest.

Christian men of war wanted not just to win their battles against al-Andalus but also to transform the Muslim territory they conquered into Christian land. They took practical measures, such as appropriating the choicest houses and properties for themselves while leaving less desirable real estate to those Muslims who chose to remain. Christian rulers offered enticing terms to their subjects who were willing to move to the newly acquired regions. But settlement and immigration alone could not accomplish the difficult task of Christianizing territory that had borne Islam's imprint for centuries. Mary was the saint perhaps best suited for helping Christians achieve this conversion of the landscape. She already commanded this field of operations in the era when men like Alfonso VI of Castile-León and the Cid were busy supporting and terrorizing the *taifa* kingdoms, a fact written into the fabric of Toledo's cathedral.

Alfonso VI presided over the cathedral's dedication to Mary just a year after he had taken Toledo in 1085 from its Muslim ruler and his former ally, al-Qadir.[56] This building had actually graced Toledo for many years, for it was the city's main mosque (*'jami*). Only in the thirteenth century would the Islamic complex with its spacious courtyard, fountains, and columned prayer hall be knocked down and replaced by the undeniably Christian forms of the ornate Gothic cathedral that still stands.[57]

Dislodged in 1086 from the building where they had gathered every Friday for prayer, Toledo's Muslim residents had been stripped of one of the most important architectural ornaments of their community. Now within the walls where they had prayed, ceremonies they considered wrong at best and idolatrous at worst would unfold, a thought that would have been hard to bear, even if Muslims did not consider mosques sacred in the same way that Christian did churches.[58] This bitter reminder of their humiliating subjugation to Christian rule had the added flavor of betrayal if what some later writers assert is true: that according to the conditions of surrender, Alfonso VI had allowed Toledo's Islamic community to retain its 'jami.[59] Whether or not the ruler of Castile was breaking a promise when he called his bishops together in 1086 to perform the ritual of turning the mosque into Mary's church, for the Muslims, the loss of the building was yet another painful stage in the Christian conquest of their city.

Toledo's Muslims thus joined the multitudes of vanquished peoples who have watched as their religious buildings are seized by conquerors and given over to the victors' gods. This spiritual dispossession was intended to rub salt in the wounds of defeat, for Alfonso VI and his prelates presented their appropriation of the mosque in Mary's name as the ritual complement to the military victory that had ushered Toledo back into Christendom a year earlier. According to a document purporting to bear Alfonso's signature and dated 1086, the cathedral's consecration ceremony celebrated the city's restoration to Christian rule and to the Church after centuries of Muslim domination.[60]

In the early years of Christian military expansion, other triumphant Christian warriors often chose Mary as the saintly protector for mosques converted into churches. The Cid, for example, marked his triumph over the *taifa* of Valencia in 1098 by dedicating this prosperous Mediterranean city's 'jami to Mary, and Alfonso VII of Castile-León appears to have done the same at Coria in 1142.[61] It was perhaps natural for victorious Christians to incorporate former mosques into the church by giving them to Mary. Ever since the early days of Christianity, writers and artists had played with her likeness to the allegorical figure of the Church, *Ecclesia*.[62] As spiritual mothers and Christ's virginal spouses, both held out the promise of redemption to humankind. Mary's identity with *Ecclesia* even compensated for the fact that these new places of Christian worship often looked almost exactly as they had when Muslims prayed there; for reasons including cost and convenience, Christian kings and knights were reluctant to undertake major architectural modifications of the 'jamis they claimed for their own religion.[63] Instead, they relied on ritual strategies to cleanse the buildings of Islam's polluting touch. Here, too, Mary could offer particularly powerful aid.

In mosques, Muslims adored "the heinous idols of demons and of the most impure Muhammad," wrote a Christian scribe in 1097 as he recorded the consecration of Huesca's *'jami* to Mary, her son, Saint Peter, and John the Baptist a year after Peter I of Aragon won this important fortress city from the *taifa* kingdom of Saragossa.[64] Muslims did not pray before images of Muhammad, never mind of "demons," but one would never know this from Christian descriptions of mosques converted into churches.[65] To remove the stain of supposed Islamic idolatry from mosques, priests and bishops performed the ritual gestures with which they consecrated any church, sprinkling the building's walls and altar with holy water, drawing crosses on the floor and threshold, and waving thuribles to send forth clouds of incense.[66] They would also stand at the building's entrance and intone the name of the new church's saintly patron.

Every time Christian prelates pronounced Mary the guardian of a converted mosque, they exorcised perhaps as many unclean demons of Islam as they did with their crosses and incense, for her name conjured perfect Christian purity.[67] Mary was, as a twelfth-century author from Catalonia rhapsodized, "immaculate," "inviolate," "without any stain of corruption," "chaste in mind and body with no blemish or wrinkle," "the pure woman" who cleansed her devotees from the stain of sin.[68] Once houses of filth, converted mosques dedicated to the purest saint were purged of their Islamic past and joined the ranks of Christian churches.

The Christianization of the main mosques of important towns and cities wrested from al-Andalus would become almost standard procedure over the next centuries, as would the dedication of these new churches to Mary.[69] This pattern, set during the Christian victories of the eleventh and twelfth centuries, never lost the edge it had even in those early years: the dedication of mosques to Mary, spotless icon of Christian purity and living embodiment of the Church, framed the conflict between Muslims and Christians in religious and not just political terms. This edge would sharpen by the thirteenth century as Christians from Aragon and Castile increasingly availed themselves of the language of holy war against the infidel.

This more pronounced attitude of crusade would profoundly affect how men of war experienced their saintly patrons. Santiago, for example, soon took up weapons to complement the warhorse he had acquired in the twelfth century—Castilian knights and chroniclers began to tell of how the heavenly rider appeared in the midst of Christian armies, arrayed in full military gear and swinging his sword.[70] Other male saints, too, began to ride to the rescue of Castilian knights fighting Muslim foes: Isidore, an erudite bishop of Visigothic Seville; Aemilianus, an ascetic hermit of the sixth century; and Pelagius, an equally reclusive monk.[71] This saintly troop, often headed by James, however, was not as popular among knights and soldiers in the Crown of Aragon. Aragonese men of war preferred Saint George, a military saint imported from the Byzantine East via the crusaders, to any of these saints associated with their rival, Castile.[72]

If knights' affections for these male saintly patrons divided along the lines of political allegiance, the same was not true of their feelings toward Mary. High medieval Christian knights and soldiers from both Castile and Aragon freely called on her as they went to war against Muslims. Although Mary did not mount a warhorse and ride by the knights' side, she became as much their defender and champion as James himself. In the process, she would become the "hope" not just of ordinary knights but also of the men who sat on the thrones of Castile and Aragon. Perhaps as much as the members of new religious orders like the Cistercians and Franciscans, these monarchs belonged to the vanguard of European Marian devotion.

1

Marian Monarchs and the Virgin's Realm

In July 1212, the lands between Toledo and Córdoba lay simmering in the heat as two great armies prepared to face each other in the hills and plains that fall away from the flanks of the Sierra Morena just south of the Despeñaperros Pass. Attacking from the north was a Christian coalition that included Alfonso VIII of Castile, Peter II of Aragon, and Sancho VII of Navarre, as well as some contingents from León. Some one hundred and fifty French knights rode with them. A few months earlier, this host had assembled at Toledo, filling the old Visigothic capital with noise and keeping its famed sword makers busy. In late June the force had pulled out of the city, heading south on a campaign that promised not just glory and booty but also spiritual benefits. Much to the satisfaction of the expedition's leaders—especially Alfonso VIII and the indefatigable and erudite archbishop of Toledo, Rodrigo Jiménez de Rada—Pope Innocent III had officially baptized the enterprise with the waters of holy war.[1]

These men advanced toward the enemy to fight one of the most important pitched battles of the reconquest, the first to bear the name of "crusade" so openly. They wore the sign of Christ's passion on their clothes—but wielded their weapons under his mother's aegis. During this engagement, which helped to irrevocably tip the balance of power in the Iberian Peninsula in favor of the Christian kingdoms, Mary visibly loaned her halo to the warfare against Muslims for the first time.

Massed on the rough terrain below the Despeñaperros Pass were the forces commanded by the Almohad caliph, Muhammad al-Nasir li-dini llah. That day, al-Nasir probably did not have at his disposal troops numbering over half a million, as his chroniclers claimed.[2] He was nonetheless a formidable enemy, who had already used his military talents to extend his power in al-Andalus and North Africa and to win important victories against Castile. Now he wanted to add another triumph to his tally. Fear that al-Nasir might achieve his aim had prompted some of the Christian kings of the Iberian Peninsula to interrupt their incessant wars with each other and make common cause against him.

According to panicky Christian rumor, al-Nasir had vowed to lead his troops over the Pyrenees and march across Europe until he reached Rome. Reports of his supposed boast sowed fear among Christians well beyond the Iberian Peninsula and even made their way to Innocent III. Hence in May 1212, the pope ordered the citizens of Rome to throng the city's streets and pray for the success of the crusader army then gathering in Toledo. By July, Innocent and other Christians across western Europe waited eagerly for news of the campaign. The surrender of several important Muslim castles to the crusaders had already raised hopes that the host would prevail over al-Nasir and halt the seemingly inexorable advance of the Almohads into Christian Europe.

When battle was joined on July 16, not far south of the Sierra Morena at Las Navas de Tolosa, al-Nasir could survey operations from the hill at the rear of the Muslim lines where his majestic red war tent was pitched. He wore a black cape that had belonged to his great-grandfather, the first member of his family to bear the title of caliph.[3] The white war standard used by the Almohad rulers flew overhead.[4] Streaming in the wind on the other side of the field was Alfonso VIII's own battle banner, which told the crusaders that they fought in the name of the king of Castile—and in honor of the Virgin Mary.[5]

In a letter to Innocent III written shortly after the engagement, Alfonso described his banner as bearing "an image of the blessed Virgin and her son placed above our emblems."[6] Though the king gave no other details, the figures of Mary and Jesus above the crenellated towers of the Castilian royal coat of arms were probably embroidered in bright thread onto a solid colored background, as a very warlike Saint Isidore is on an extant banner from high medieval León.[7] Perhaps the Virgin held her son in her lap, as she does in a late thirteenth-century Castilian illumination depicting a Marian war standard.[8] In any case, she apparently dominated Alfonso's banner, for when Rodrigo, the archbishop of Toledo who accompanied the Castilian troops at Las Navas, described the object, he omitted any mention of Jesus.[9]

This Marian banner was in good company. By the eleventh century, banners decorated with saints' figures served as more than colorful drapery for church walls and altars. Ritually blessed by priests, they went to war alongside Christian knights and soldiers, declaring to friend and foe alike the saints' approval of the bloody proceedings.[10] Mary's appearance on a battle standard that bore the royal arms of Castile placed her at the heart of the hostilities that scorching July day in 1212. Banners, plainly visible with their bold colors and shapes even in the confusion of combat, were used to signal men scattered across a battlefield. Woven into their fabric was also a more symbolic value as a statement of the army's courage, persistence, and unity. This was especially true of royal banners. Accordingly, the *alférez*, the bearer of the king's standard, was usually chosen from among men of very high rank.[11] In battle, he rode close to the monarch. If the *alférez* fled with the banner, the rest of the army would not be far behind. Muslim warriors such as those fighting under al-Nasir's direction in July 1212 felt just as strongly about their own war standards.[12] In high medieval Iberia, both Muslim and Christian armies vigorously defended their respective banners, while making equally strenuous attempts to seize their opponents'. Each side prized standards captured from the enemy, proudly hanging them in public places as great victory displays.[13]

On July 16, 1212, Alfonso VIII's Marian banner spectacularly fulfilled its function as a Christian rallying point. Both the king and the archbishop believed that this cloth image of Mary had decisively turned the tide of battle in the right direction, at a moment when all seemed lost.[14] Al-Nasir's forces had the upper hand at Las Navas until Alfonso VIII, Peter II, and Sancho VII resolved to make a united charge. Accompanying the monarchs' contingents were presumably the royal standards of Aragon and Navarre as well as that of Castile. But in their reports of the battle, Alfonso VIII and Rodrigo singled out the Marian banner of their own kingdom. Flanking this standard as the monarchs plunged into the Almohad lines, wrote both king and archbishop, was the sign of Mary's son, a processional cross.

According to Alfonso, the Almohad troops pelted the banner and cross hurtling toward them with arrows and rocks. This "dishonoring of Christ's cross and of his mother's image" enraged the Castilian king, as he wrote in his letter to the pope. Ready to die "for the Christian faith," Alfonso charged with such force that the Almohad ranks parted before him.[15] Rodrigo simply said that the Almohads turned tail and fled at the sight of the Castilian standard.[16] Those who did not retreat before the Marian banner, added the archbishop, were so terror-struck that they let themselves be slaughtered by the Christians. No wonder Alfonso richly rewarded his *alférez* after the battle.[17]

Jubilant Christians would commemorate the triumph won that day in the shelter of the Marian war standard as shattering Almohad power in the Iberian Peninsula, though the reality was considerably more complex.[18] As they repeated the story of the battle over the next few decades, the Marian standard gained an ever larger part in reversing the Christian army's fortunes. By the late thirteenth century, some royal chroniclers in the kingdom of Castile proudly wrote that the "miraculous arrival" of the "image of Saint Mary the virgin mother of God" had saved the day for the Christians.[19] It is perhaps not surprising to find the banner so soon embroidered with the gold thread of miracle; in Rodrigo's account of Las Navas, it already seemed to have an aggressive power of its own, capable of terrorizing the enemy. With their choice of words, the late thirteenth-century chroniclers went one step further than the archbishop, conjuring up the possibility that this was no mere battle standard, but instead a wonder-working Marian image.

In later centuries, legends proliferated about Las Navas that openly insisted the banner had wielded the power of miracle on the battlefield.[20] Sometimes in these stories, the processional cross given such weight by Alfonso VIII and Rodrigo took its place at the Marian standard's side.[21] A beloved martial talisman of Christian kings for centuries, the symbol of the crowned Christ and his eternal triumph over death would have its own complex history as an emblem of reconquest.[22] The cross, however, did not always appear in Las Navas's legendary afterlife, while the Marian banner remained an almost constant feature. Its enduring presence paid fitting homage to the battle in the shadow of the Sierra Morena, which was after all the first time Mary's role as a patron of reconquest came into sharp focus.

Las Navas not only inaugurated a swath of Christian victories that within thirty years would trim Muslim Iberia to one small kingdom, but also heralded a period of several centuries during which the Christian men of war who whittled away al-Andalus's territory and the writers who chronicled their deeds openly celebrated Mary's involvement in this enterprise. The Castilian royal standard used at Las Navas in fact articulated something that would deeply mark her future. This banner's stitches bound Jesus' mother together with the sort of Christian men who by the early thirteenth century increasingly led the campaigns against al-Andalus, monarchs like Alfonso VIII. Sharing the colored field of cloth, the Marian image and the royal arms announced an alliance that would only strengthen as successive rulers of both Castile and Aragon invoked the Virgin in their wars against Muslims.

The bond between Mary as a patron of the reconquest and the Christian kings as its commanders was already tight by the time news of the victory at Las Navas traveled across the Pyrenees. By the 1240s, a monastic chronicler in northern France named Alberic of Trois-Fontaines knew enough about the battle that in his brief account of it, he made the Marian standard the centerpiece. But the story that really interested him was a fanciful narrative of how the Virgin personally had provided the war banner to Alfonso VIII.[23] Alberic explained that she had entrusted the banner to a sacristan serving at her church of Rocamadour, a famous pilgrimage shrine located hundreds of miles away from Las Navas among the limestone cliffs of southwestern France. Handing the carefully folded cloth to this man, Mary instructed him that it was for the king of Castile, who was about to fight the "Saracens." It should not be unfurled until the day of the battle, she said, and then only in the Christians' hour of greatest need.

According to Alberic, this standard, which eventually made its way to Alfonso, bore a likeness of Our Lady of Rocamadour with the royal arms of Castile at her feet. This French Madonna ranked high in the affections of many men and women living in the Christian kingdoms of high medieval Iberia.[24] But there is no evidence suggesting that anyone in the Castilian contingent at Las Navas—least of all Alfonso VIII himself—believed that Our Lady of Rocamadour was emblazoned on the royal banner. Alfonso had once given some land to her monastery, but it was a poor gift in comparison to the wealth he lavished on his favorite Marian churches, both of which lay in Castile.[25] Whether Alberic of Trois-Fontaines was the first to give the banner a French twist is not clear. Perhaps Our Lady of Rocamadour's name had already slipped into the war stories that the French knights who fought at Las Navas told on their return home from southern Spain—in France, she was renowned for gracing men of war with her miraculous favors.[26] Yet even this tale that tried to credit a Madonna from the other side of the Pyrenees with the victory at Las Navas preserved the tie between Mary and the king sewn into the fabric of the actual banner.

In his letter to the pope, Alfonso VIII felt no need to explain why his battle standard sported a Marian image. Rodrigo Jiménez de Rada was more forthcoming, declaring in his description of the banner that "the blessed Virgin Mary ... has always been the protector and patron of the province of Toledo and of all Spain."[27] This was a rather self-serving statement, given the archbishop's political interests. In his relentless efforts to assert Toledo's primacy in the face of continuing competition from the bishops of Compostela, Rodrigo promoted every possible association between the rulers of Castile and Toledo's holy patron.[28] His readiness to interpret the Madonna of the royal standard in relationship to his own see suggests that he might have urged the king to take her as the emblem for the campaign in which Toledo had so much at stake—Rodrigo hoped that his energetic promotion of the crusade of 1212 might incline the pope to take his side in the dispute with Compostela.[29]

After Rodrigo's death in 1247, Toledo's machinations to establish a privileged relationship between Mary and the Castilian monarchy continued, as a late thirteenth-century manuscript indicates. It contains a fairly standard version of the ritual used to crown an emperor—with a few telling changes of wording. Typically, a newly minted monarch was proclaimed the defender of the "Roman church" and its patron saint, Peter. The Toledo manuscript instead anointed the ruler as the champion of "the church of Toledo" and of Mary. It also stipulated that when the prelate officiating at the ceremony girded the king with the blessed sword representing the military side of monarchy, he was to call the ruler not "Saint Peter's knight" as was usual, but instead "blessed Mary's knight."[30]

It is unlikely that any thirteenth- or fourteenth-century archbishop of Toledo ever stood in his cathedral and pronounced the sonorous words that would have dubbed a king of Castile "Mary's knight." Few Castilian monarchs of this period chose to be formally crowned, and those who did probably did not follow the ritual prescribed by the Toledo manuscript.[31] The rulers were not always inclined to indulge the ambitions of the archbishops who sought to restore Toledo to its Visigothic glory as the royal city. Alfonso VIII himself shifted his realm's center of gravity away from Rodrigo's see to the city of Burgos.[32] In doing so, however, he hardly distanced himself from Mary. As Alfonso would have known, the city he favored belonged as much to her domain as did Toledo.

Mary was the saintly protector of Burgos's cathedral, in the king's day a Romanesque building dating from the late eleventh century whose heavy arches rose on a site granted by one of his predecessors on the throne of Castile, Alfonso VI.[33] Whenever Alfonso VIII rode by the cathedral, he could have been reminded of a heroic knight who, according to legend, had delivered his fate into the Virgin's keeping right there. The *Cantar del Mio Cid*, the popular epic poem that by 1207 had transformed the opportunist and adventurer Rodrigo del Díaz into an exemplar of virtuous Christian chivalry, used this building as the setting for a finely wrought Marian scene. In the *Cantar*, as the Cid leaves Burgos to ride into exile, he wheels his horse around to face the cathedral, crosses himself, and promises Mary that if she watches over him "night and day," he will make her rich gifts and order a thousand masses said in her church.[34] Later in the epic, he sends to the Virgin of Burgos a boot filled with gold and silver won in battle against the *taifa* king of Valencia.[35]

At Burgos, Alfonso VIII made lavish offerings of his own to Mary. In 1187, the king and his wife Eleanor formally established a monastery for Cistercian nuns called Las Huelgas on the outskirts of the city.[36] Its church, like all those belonging to this successful new monastic order (which Alfonso helped to implant in Castile), was dedicated to Mary.[37] Known in Latin as Sancta Maria Regalis (Saint Mary the Royal), the abbey more than lived up to its name. As the king doubtless intended, it became for a time the royal monastery, home in the thirteenth and fourteenth centuries to many Castilian princesses who took the veil. In 1204, Alfonso announced his intention to be buried there, entrusting himself for eternity to Mary's care.[38] His tomb still stands in the abbey's church, alongside those of his wife and several of their children, many of them laid to rest in Andalusi silk shrouds.[39]

This king who founded a monastery whose very name proclaimed a connection between Mary and monarchy probably did not require the archbishop of Toledo's urging to take up a war banner graced with her image some twenty-five years later at Las Navas de Tolosa, though he may have been influenced by the Cistercians monastics he favored. Like Alfonso's establishment of Las Huelgas, the standard that led the Castilian troops to battle in 1212 announced Mary's significance in the politics of royal self-fashioning. Paired with the processional cross that the king mentioned in his letter to the pope, the banner adorned with his coat of arms and the figure of the Virgin expressed how Alfonso VIII wished to be understood by his contemporaries and by posterity: as a Christian king who fought to defend *Christianitas*, Christianity writ large.[40] High medieval Christians often coupled Mary and the cross to evoke the central truths of their faith: the Incarnation and the Passion. In paintings and sculptures that told the tale of the Crucifixion to the faithful, she stood sorrowing beside the instrument of her son's death.[41] As a thirteenth-century Franciscan associated with the court of Castile explained, together Mary and the cross offered the sweet promise of redemption to humankind mired in the desperation of sin.[42] A ruler who rode to war against Muslims behind this holy pair proclaimed himself the champion of Christianity.

Yet Alfonso's banner itself twinned Mary with the royal arms—and thus brought her close to the core of kingship, as the rulers of Castile and Aragon and their advisors increasingly understood it: martial prowess. Military leadership was one of the more important foundations of royal power everywhere in Christian Europe. Those medieval kings who did not prove themselves capable warriors could expect to face especially grave challenges to their rule. In Castile and Aragon, this aspect of monarchy was particularly developed, shaping rulers' sense of themselves so profoundly that until the early fourteenth century, they saw little need for the religious rites with which their peers in France, England, and Germany consecrated royal authority.[43]

The kings of Castile and Aragon preferred to display their power with ceremonies flaunting their nature as warriors. In particular, they emphasized the prerogatives they believed graced them by virtue of the royal office that Alfonso VIII fulfilled under Mary's banner at Las Navas: leadership of warfare against Muslim polities. As indefatigable defenders of the faith, such monarchs occupied the pinnacle of Christian kingship, at least according to some flattery penned by Alvarus Pelagius, a fourteenth-century bishop. In a mirror for princes addressed to one of Alfonso's successors on the throne of Castile, Alvarus wrote: "Other kings live trapped in houses and swimming in luxury—you inhabit war tents and the castles of Christ, content with austere food. They sleep and drowse—you spend your nights sleepless, so that your mother the Church may be expanded and live quietly . . . other kings praise God with their voices—you risk your body for him."[44] Therefore, the bishop concluded, the kingdom of Castile was simply better than all others.

If Alfonso VIII's war banner added a Marian tinge to his self-image as champion of Christendom, this hue deepened in the careers of many later kings of Castile and Aragon as they carried out the most royal of tasks and waged war against Muslims. In intertwining the Virgin with their personae as Christian warriors, these monarchs may have been encouraged by members of new religious orders like the Franciscans and the Dominicans, who promoted Marian devotion as eagerly as the Cistercians funded by Alfonso VIII; friars often served as courtiers and royal advisers.[45] Yet rulers had their own reasons for drawing her into the Christian conquest of al-Andalus, not least of which was the royal diadem that she often wore.

Mary was a "queen without equal," as a poem composed under the direction of Alfonso VIII's great-grandson put it in the late thirteenth century.[46] Despite the biblical portrayal of Jesus' mother as a woman of humble origins, medieval Christians believed that the blood of King David flowed in her veins.[47] Mary's triumph over death—when she was assumed, body and soul, into heaven—made her a queen in her own right. She received her celestial crown from angels or from her son the King of Heaven, a scene carved onto church façades and painted onto the stained glass windowpanes of cathedrals all across Europe.[48] Crowned and enthroned in due majesty, statues of the Queen of Heaven adorned the altars of Marian shrines and received pilgrims' prayers.[49]

Many kings of Castile and Aragon would burnish their rulership with the heavenly brilliance of Mary's crown without having recourse to the ritual trappings of sacral monarchy so popular among their French, English, and German counterparts. Sanctifying their majesty through hers, these monarchs made the Queen of Heaven as important to their self-understanding as her royal son was.[50] They also often found in her an apt embodiment of their kingdoms, particularly of the Christian land whose reach they sought to extend at al-Andalus's expense, though the ways that they and their contemporaries made her stand for their territorial claims against Islam would change over the centuries. The career of a king who for a decade or so was Alfonso VIII's son-in-law—James I of Aragon—suggests why Mary had such potential in the realm of martial monarchy.

A King's Marian Deeds

In July 1276, James I of Aragon summoned his son to Alzira, a town just south of Valencia. The king was heavy with a sudden sickness from which he suspected he would not recover. At sixty-eight, he no longer possessed the vigor that had made him one of the more successful rulers of his day—a man who had vastly expanded his kingdom's territory through military conquests and made Aragon a trading powerhouse in the Mediterranean—but age had not curbed his arrogance or extinguished his notorious passion for women.[51] Severely ill and in great pain, he realized it was time to turn away from earthly concerns and fortify himself for the next world. As the king did so, he committed himself to the care of a saint whom he had loved all his life, Mary.

At Alzira, James formally abdicated in favor of his son and exchanged the rich garb of royalty for the simple white robes of a Cistercian monk. He did so, he said, "in honor of God and his blessed mother, who have given us much honor and help in this world, and for the remission of our sins."[52] Then, sick as he was, James set out on the long journey north toward the place where he wanted to be buried: Saint Mary of Poblet, a wealthy monastery in the mountains outside Tarragona that was home to a community of monks who wore the same habit he had just put on. In a testament drawn up some thirty years earlier, James had recorded his wish that his remains rest in a plain tomb "before Saint Mary's altar" in Poblet's abbey church.[53] The body of one of his predecessors, Alfonso II the Chaste, already lay in state in this graceful if austere Romanesque building.[54]

When James renounced his kingdom in 1276, he gave instructions that if death should overtake him on the road north, his body should temporarily be interred at another church dedicated to Mary until it could be moved to Poblet.[55] Yet the ailing king hoped to survive the voyage to the monastery in the mountains, for he longed to spend his last days alive in service to her there. "I had it in my heart to go to Poblet and to serve the Mother of God in that place of Poblet. I had already left Alzira and was in Valencia, when my sickness increased and it was not God's pleasure that I complete the voyage I wanted to make"—James dictated these lines as he lay dying at Valencia.[56] They were the final touches in his account of how he turned to the Virgin as life ebbed from his body.

Medieval Christians often looked to Mary in the hour of their death, seeking her mercy as the terrifying moment neared when her son would judge their sins and virtues.[57] At the end of his life, James thus joined his more ordinary fellows in finding refuge in her, but he was, until the last, conscious of himself as a king. He died as he believed he had lived: as a ruler devoted to God and Mary. With his description of his fervent wish to finish his time on earth as the Madonna's monastic servant, he provided a fittingly regal conclusion to the *Llibre dels feits*, the memoirs in which he carefully crafted his self-portrait as a monarch.

While high medieval Christian kings rarely composed autobiographies, Muslim rulers often did. Whether or not this Islamic tradition influenced James, he used the *Llibre* to justify his decisions as a monarch, much as his Muslim counterparts often did in their memoirs. Like them, he wrote to show what he had "achieved with the help of God" during his reign, as he explained in his pious preface. James may also have intended his memoirs to fulfill the same purpose as those testaments outlining the principles of good rulership that some of his Christian peers left their heirs. He ended the *Llibre*'s preface with the hope that his life would serve as an "example" and encourage "other men of the world" to put their faith in God.[58]

If any later rulers of Aragon looked to the *Llibre* for guidance, they would have learned that one of their main tasks was to wage war against Muslims, a royal duty that, James wrote, he bequeathed to his son, along with the throne itself.[59] They would have understood as well that as the leaders of such warfare, they should devote themselves not just to God, but also to Mary, the saint whom

James wove into the narrative of his last days. James's devotion to her is such a strong leitmotiv in his descriptions of the campaigns with which he claimed huge slices of al-Andalus for Aragon that the *Llibre* often reads as an account of a king's Marian military exploits.[60] This remarkable text allows us to hear for the first time a Christian king of the Iberian Peninsula putting into words his belief that Mary watched over his wars with Muslims and explaining how his love for her profoundly influenced his own self-image as a crusading king.

James cultivated cordial and politically useful relations with some of his Muslim counterparts. He was nonetheless the son of a king who had joined Alfonso VIII in triumphing over al-Nasir at Las Navas, only to fall a year later on another crusading battlefield. Orphaned at age five, James spent his formative years in the castle-monastery of Monzón under the tutelage of the Templars, men even more inspired than his father by the ideals of holy war. By age twenty, he was ready to embark on his first major expedition against a Muslim polity. His target was the archipelago beloved of modern sun-seekers, the Balearics, then under the wavering control of the Almohads and, James knew, key to Aragon's commercial expansion in the Mediterranean. In September 1229, the young king set sail with some one hundred and fifty ships to lay siege to Majorca, the largest and most important of these islands. It would be the first of his Marian campaigns.

In the *Llibre*, James described how his forces would never have reached their target without Mary's aid. He recalled how soon after his fleet sighted Majorca's mountainous outline silhouetted against the sea, strong winds began to roil the waves. All the ships took in their sails. On the royal galley, the king beseeched Christ and Mary for aid. Perhaps his prayer was not quite as elegant as he remembered it in the *Llibre*: "Mother of God, you who are the bridge and passageway of sinners, I beg you, in the name of the seven joys and seven sorrows that you had from your son, to remember me and ask your son to save me from this suffering and danger."[61] But his invocation of her had the desired effect, and the fleet made it to Majorca. Mary, the "star of the sea," was the mistress of the waves.

For the king, Mary was not just the merciful intercessor of his traditional shipboard prayer. She was also the mother of triumph, as James showed repeatedly in his account of the battle for Majorca, a campaign largely fought not on the turquoise waters surrounding the island but on its plains and craggy hillsides. In the *Llibre*, James remembered how right before his first big engagement on Majorca, he listened to the bishop of Barcelona preach a sermon proclaiming Mary as much a patron of the expedition as God. To steel the young king and his men for combat, the bishop first reminded them that they were fighting a holy war, promising them the paradise of martyrdom if they were slain by the Muslims. Then, wrote James, the prelate exhorted the knights never to forget that God and Mary would always be with them in battle. "God and his mother...will give us victory," thundered the bishop.[62] Whether or not the bishop actually uttered these pithy words, there is no mistaking the king's conviction that he and his knights had won their first fight on Majorca under Mary's aegis. He believed the same of the triumph that finally made the island his. During this battle in December 1229, the king and his men loudly invoked Mary, giving voice to what the royal banner at Las Navas had silently suggested.

James remembered how, on December 31, the end to his troops' wearying siege of Majorca's main city seemed near. His scouts reported that the town's streets were littered with Muslim corpses and the watch on its walls slack—the perfect moment for an attack. At dawn, the king and his host attended Mass. Then as light filled the camp, James turned to his men and commanded them to take up their arms. To his shock, none of them, not even the knights, moved. In the *Llibre*, James contrasted his army's cravenness with his own inspirational courage as a crusading stalwart, ever confident in Mary's aid. When his men refused to budge, he "turned to the Mother of God," pleading with her to intercede with her son so the knights' cowardice would blot neither their own honor nor his. Three more times James ordered his knights to pick up their weapons. Eventually they obeyed, if reluctantly. As they surged forward, the king wrote in the *Llibre*, suddenly "the whole host all at once began to shout 'Saint Mary! Saint Mary!'" As he remembered it, this rallying call echoing his own prayer rang out at least thirty times, growing louder and louder—a passionate, vocal eruption of Marian devotion.[63]

Later that day, some fifty of James's knights yelled out "Saint Mary!" again as they charged against the king of Majorca, who rode a white horse.[64] The defeated Muslims, wrote James, would report that on December 31, they had seen another white rider, though on the Christians' side. The king identified this knight as Saint George, thus introducing the holy soldier into Aragonese accounts of Muslim-Christian warfare.[65] If the fall of Majorca was the first time that George would appear in such combat, it also seems to be the first time that Mary's name was used as a battle call by a Christian army in the Iberian Peninsula, apparently at the instigation of a king who loved her. James wrote in his memoirs of other important conflicts with the Muslims during which his forces yelled her name.[66]

Like war standards, battle cries played an important part in maintaining an army's morale.[67] Shouting Mary's name, James and his men told themselves and their enemies that they were her warriors. In the *Llibre*, the king even recalled having said as much to Mary herself. During his battlefield prayer, he told her that the Christian host "serve[s] me in your name and the name of your son."[68] If military service to the king was military service to Mary and Jesus, James's army belonged as much to this heavenly pair as it did to the earthly king.

James made sure to give Mary her due share of the territory won from the Muslims. He wrote that after vanquishing Majorca, he "built" a church dedicated to "our Lady Saint Mary" in the island's main town.[69] Elsewhere in his memoir, he boasted that "in all the large towns which God has granted that we take from the Saracens, we have built a church of Our Lady, Saint Mary."[70] Styling himself the active creator of a Marian Christian geography from formerly Muslim land, the king suggested an overlap between the expansion of the Virgin's earthly realm and his own.

James's description of exactly how he studded the landscape of royal conquest with buildings bearing Mary's name is, however, misleading. It was perhaps only in the seaside city that was the greatest prize of his crusading wars—Valencia— that he "built" a Marian church as we would understand that verb. In September 1238, Valencia fell to the king's forces, marking the end of the prolonged series of campaigns with which James claimed the extensive and rich lands of this Muslim kingdom for Aragon. By the late 1240s, at the king's orders, the ground was laid for work to commence there on a Gothic cathedral dedicated to the Virgin.[71] The city's late medieval bishops would pay fitting homage to James's Marian devotion when they depicted their see as originating in a warrior-king's generosity toward the Virgin. In the miniature heading an early fifteenth-century manuscript listing the cathedral's possessions, an armor-clad ruler girt with a sword and sporting the gold and maroon bars of the Aragonese royal arms kneels before the enthroned Madonna, an azure cape gathered softly about her. Flanking the king is a bishop of Valencia, who also humbles himself before Mary's majesty.[72]

Unlike the cathedral from which Valencia's prelates watched over their Mediterranean city, there was little that was obviously Christian about the lines of the church James claimed to have "built" for Mary on Majorca. Until at least the early fourteenth century, Majorca's cathedral of Our Lady looked very much like the mosque its original architects had intended it to be.[73] In the wake of the island's conquest, James had ordered his prelates to consecrate the main town's ʿjami to her. Almost forty years later, he would preside over the same ceremony in another conquered Muslim city, Murcia, which lay south of Valencia. Although the king would watch as this community's mosque was splashed with chrism and baptized in Mary's name, he would use the same language as at Majorca, writing that in Murcia, he had "built" (haviem edificada) a "church of Our Lady."[74] His insistent use of this verb suggested that the consecration of former Muslim prayer halls to Mary was such a potent rite of Christianization that it effectively destroyed these structures' Islamic foundations, rendering actual architectural changes almost superfluous.

In his account of Murcia's conquest, James expressed his belief that the Muslim lands he conquered became Mary's domain. Given this city's wealth, power, and strategic location, James naturally eyed it as a possible quarry after his victory over Valencia. In 1243, however, Murcia's Muslim lord accepted Castilian suzerainty, in return for which this man was allowed to retain de facto control over a city that for all intents and purposes remained very much part of the Islamic world. Then, in the 1260s, the inhabitants of Murcia joined their fellow Muslims across Castile in a violent rebellion against Christian rule. It was not the ruler of that Christian kingdom, Alfonso X, who subdued the city in 1266, but his father-in-law, James I.[75]

In the *Llibre*, James described how he rescued Murcia for Christianity both with Mary's help and for her. If his memoirs are to be believed, he had long dreamed of taking the city in her name: "I never passed through the region of Murcia without praying to [Mary] that I would be able to put there the name of the glorious Virgin Mary."[76] James remembered uttering such pleas to her during the actual battle for the city, even reminding her at one critical juncture of his desire to make her "venerated and believed in" at Murcia.[77] She granted his wish, he wrote, "and through petitioning her dear son, made me accomplish my will."[78]

Immediately after his triumph, the king hastened to realize his hopes of making Murcia into Mary's city: "because this was the greatest and most honored city of all of Andalusia (with the exception of Seville), I wished to honor the name of the mother of God so that she would be honored here forever."[79] Hence he offered one of the city's most important buildings to her: its ʿjami. Ignoring the enraged protests by Murcia's leaders, who brandished their 1243 agreement with Castile guaranteeing them continued use of all their mosques, James made Mary's new church the focus of a public ceremony announcing that this formerly Muslim city was now irrevocably part of Christendom. A signal to the Muslim community of the dramatic changes that were to come, this was also a ritual of thanksgiving, proclaiming that royal victory, Christian victory, and the Virgin's victory were one and the same.

In the *Llibre,* James recalled how he summoned all the church dignitaries he could find, including the bishops of Barcelona and Cartagena. The king ordered that each be dressed in robes of samite and gold. This crowd of clerics accompanied James as he left his military camp outside Murcia and ritually entered the city. Swaying in time with the steps of the procession as it moved through a city still full of Muslim residents were the emblems of all that the king had fought for: an image of Mary and several crosses. Slowly the king and his companions approached Murcia's main mosque, or, as James preferred to call it, the "church of Our Lady...that we built." Once inside the building, James fell to his knees before the newly constructed altar, which, as he had ordered, was decorated with sumptuous cloths from his own collection. Overwhelmed with joy that God had granted his desire "to put here the name of the glorious Virgin," the king wept as though he would never stop. The sound of hymns, followed by the solemn words of the Mass, filled the mosque-church.[80]

In reading the *Llibre*'s description of this procession, one cannot help but be struck by the sincerity of the king's gestures of gratitude to God and Mary.

Yet this ceremony also provided an opportunity for powerful political theater, as James and his contemporaries doubtless knew. The whole procession was orchestrated as a statement that Murcia had two new rulers: the king of Aragon and the Queen of Heaven. Under the sign of the cross, these earthly and celestial monarchs wended their way through the streets, tracing out their ownership of the city in front of a largely Muslim audience. Together, they then took possession of the mosque-church.

Just how strongly the king believed that Murcia had become Mary's city is evident in his apparent reluctance to transfer control of his prize to Alfonso X of Castile's proxies—men whom James feared would let Murcia slip from their fingers and return to Muslim dominion. James contemplated this prospect unhappily, considering it a threat to Mary's own safety. In the *Llibre*, he wrote poignantly of his anxiety that by yielding the city "where I had erected an altar of Our Lady Saint Mary" to such unworthy guardians, he would be deserting the Virgin and leaving her to face an uncertain fate all "alone." "For nothing in the world would I abandon her in such a position and time," he declared, again verbally conflating the Virgin with the city he had conquered in her name.[81]

In the end, James did deliver Mary and Murcia to his son-in-law, Alfonso X. In doing so, he was actually entrusting the Virgin and her newly acquired city to a man who, if anything, loved her even more passionately than he did and thought of her as even more important to the duties incumbent on a reconquest king. But the ways in which James intertwined the Virgin with some of his most important martial achievements as a Christian ruler pale in comparison with his son-in-law's Marian language of monarchy. In the admiring portrait that Alfonso X created of his father—Ferdinand III of Castile, a king who won victories over al-Andalus as important as those of James—and then in his own self-image, something emerges that might be called "Marian monarchy." While Alfonso's vision of Mary's relationship to the royal house of Castile shared some traits with James's understanding of her patronage of his own military enterprises, it also represented a significant evolution in her history as a patron of Christian wars against al-Andalus and as an embodiment of newly Christianized landscapes. These later developments occurred primarily in Castile, not because James I's successors lacked either Marian piety or crusading zeal, but because the events of 1266 altered Aragon's situation vis-à-vis al-Andalus.[82]

With the definitive transfer of Murcia to Castile, Aragon's border with al-Andalus vanished and Castile's expanded. Hence when, in 1269, James I set off on his last campaign against the Muslims under the banner of holy war, his target lay on the other side of the Mediterranean in the Levant. (When his fleet ran into bad weather, the king prayed to Mary to save his ships, thus ending his crusading career under her protection as he had begun it.)[83] Over the next few centuries, the energy of the reconquest would be largely centered in Castile, the Christian kingdom that shared a border with what remained of al-Andalus, which was not much after the conquests by James I and his peer, Ferdinand III of Castile, the man whom Alfonso X would make into a Marian hero.

Like Son, Like Father

"Señor, I leave you all the land here, which the Moors won from King Roderic [the last Visigothic king]. It is now in your dominion. And if you manage to keep it in the condition in which I gave it to you, you are as good a king as I. If you win more for yourself, you are better than me. And if you diminish it, you are not as good as me."[84] Thus a late thirteenth-century Castilian royal chronicle rendered Ferdinand III's dying words to his son and heir, Alfonso X. Ferdinand may never have uttered such a deathbed speech proclaiming himself the warrior king who had recovered the old Visigothic lands from the Muslims. But Alfonso X certainly inherited a warrior's legacy—and a heavy Oedipal burden—from his father, which he would sublimate in intense devotion to Mary.[85]

It would have been hard for anyone to live up to Ferdinand's military achievements. A savvy and accomplished military man, he pushed the Muslims ever farther south toward the Mediterranean. In 1236, he took the old Umayyad capital of Córdoba, riding with his knights over the Guadalquivir River on the elegant bridge leading into the city that had once been the showplace of the caliphate. The Almohads, their power crumbling on both sides of the Mediterranean, were in no position to halt Ferdinand's advances. By the late 1240s, he was the master of most of the Guadalquivir valley, a fertile swath of land stretching from Jaén in the west to the gates of Seville itself in the east. Ferdinand then set his sights on Seville, the seat of Almohad power in al-Andalus, which succumbed to his siege engines in November 1248.[86]

By the time Ferdinand lay dying four years later, he could pride himself on having reduced al-Andalus to a rump state. Almost all that was left of Muslim Iberia after his conquests and those of James I of Aragon was a diminutive polity ruled by a new dynasty, the Nasrid kingdom of Granada. Swelling Granada's population were Muslim refugees from the areas conquered by Castile and Aragon who could not bring themselves to live under Christian rule. Leaving behind centuries of memories, they wrenched themselves from their homes and relocated in the one area of the Iberian Peninsula still under Muslim control by the 1250s. The kingdom of Granada, bounded by the Mediterranean and protected by the snow-peaked bulwark of the Sierra Nevada, occupied a modest strip of land on the southeastern coast of the Iberian Peninsula.

If the Nasrids' realm was squeezed by mountains and the sea, the inflated self-image of its sultans had lesser limits. The Alhambra, the palace-city they built for themselves on the hill above their capital city, flaunted their claims to be great rulers, almost the equals of the Umayyad caliphs. What remains of the Alhambra today—a labyrinth of graceful courtyards and ornate chambers whose walls are covered with cascades of delicate carved tracery—suggests majesty, wealth, and power. But while the Umayyads had adorned their palaces with imported marble, the Nasrids used the far cheaper stucco, an apt index of their actual power.[87] This dynasty's founder ensured his political survival first by helping Ferdinand III conquer Seville and then by offering his kingdom's vassalage to Castile. Granada would never quite cast off this status of ritual and political subjection to its hulking Christian neighbor, though it would try, often through the force of arms.

Ferdinand III, the first king of Castile to command Granada's homage, would be endlessly eulogized for his military feats. By the seventeenth century, he had even fought his way to official sainthood, the only medieval Castilian ruler ever to be canonized.[88] This commemorative process began during his lifetime, when he was praised as a king who waged war as much for Christianity as for his own gain, to borrow words from a Castilian abbot who celebrated Ferdinand's victory at Seville in lengthy, tedious verse.[89] After Ferdinand's death in 1252, his reputation would only grow. His son and heir, Alfonso X, especially tended Ferdinand's memory, crafting such a compelling portrait that it would determine how future generations of Castilians saw this reconquest hero.[90] Slowly but surely, Alfonso's filial piety transformed Ferdinand into a man who had wielded his sword for the Virgin and had ruled Castile as a Marian monarch.

If the formal language of official documents produced by the Castilian royal chancery can be trusted, Ferdinand in fact seems to have shared the devotion to Mary so characteristic of high medieval Christian piety. In a donation he made in 1237 to a monastery near Burgos, the king declared: "we have [the glorious Virgin, Saint Mary] as our lady and advocate in all our deeds."[91] Ferdinand might even have believed that his wars against al-Andalus were among the royal deeds she tended. In his grant of privileges and laws to the newly Christian city of Seville in 1251, he thanked Mary, "whose servant we are," for her heavenly intercession, which, he said, had helped him achieve his victory there three years earlier. Yet in the same document, Ferdinand expressed gratitude for exactly the same thing to Saint James, "whose standard bearer we are and whose banner we carry and who always helped us to conquer"—a phrase that almost hides the Virgin in the holy knight's shadow.[92]

This is quite a contrast with how Alfonso X remembered his father's greatest victory over al-Andalus in his own privileges for Seville. Banishing Santiago as Ferdinand's special battle patron, Alfonso tellingly featured a father-and-son pair of Marian knights as the city's conquerors: "My father, the noble and much honored King Ferdinand won and founded [the cathedral of Seville]. I did it with him. We won [Seville] from the Moors and we populated it with Christians in the service of God and the glorious Virgin Mary."[93] These phrases, repeated like a litany by royal scribes, expressed Alfonso's pride in having fought at his father's side during the long hard siege of Seville—a prince and a king, as Alfonso remembered it, inspired to feats of arms against the Muslims by their shared love for the Virgin.

James's demotion in favor of Mary in these documents reflected Alfonso's own preferences.[94] In making Ferdinand her passionate devotee, Alfonso may in fact have been projecting his own love for her onto his father. Even when measured against the fervent Marian piety of many of his contemporaries, Alfonso's veneration of her can only be termed flamboyant. He built churches for the Virgin, commissioned beautifully dressed statues and richly decorated containers for her relics, acquired fine ivory carvings depicting scenes from her life, had masses said in her honor for the spiritual welfare of his family, and ordered hundreds of poems composed in celebration of her miracles.[95] Commanding his Christian subjects to show her relics the greatest respect, this king wrote Mary right into the law of his land.[96] His love for her, influenced perhaps by a prominent Franciscan at his court, only grew more extravagant in the course of his reign.[97] Alfonso certainly deserved the title he bears in numerous royal documents as Mary's faithful "servant."[98]

As the wording of Alfonso's privileges for Seville indicates, it was a title he believed his father merited as well. Suggestive as these documents are of Alfonso's desire to present his father to posterity as the Virgin's knight, they do not begin to match the deeply Marian picture the king traced of Ferdinand in his lyrical homage to the Virgin, the *Cantigas de Santa María*. Written in Galician, the elegant language of courtly love poetry in Castile and Portugal, this extraordinary collection of some four hundred poem-songs in honor of her miracles was produced with Alfonso's patronage and close supervision. The *Cantigas* married the king's love of Mary with his passion for poetry. He set the poets who crowded his court to work on these lyrics and spent a princely sum on the project. Two of the four extant manuscripts of the *Cantigas* are exquisite luxury objects. Made from the finest quality parchment, the folios of these king-sized codices boast sumptuous full-page series of illuminations for each poem. Painted at regular intervals into the blue, red, and gold borders framing each set of miniatures are the castle tower and lion rampant of Castile-León's royal coat of arms. Alfonso had instructed his artists to create manuscripts fit for a king—and for the Queen of Heaven.

So committed was Alfonso to this Marian project that he apparently wrote some, if not many, of its poems.[99] The opening *cantigas* even present the king as the collection's author. One of the accompanying miniatures shows Alfonso at work.[100] At the center of the scene, he sits in majesty, holding an open book and dictating to a crowd of scribes gathered at his feet. In the wings, musicians hold stringed instruments and practice their parts.

Whenever singers and musicians sounded out the melodies of the *Cantigas*, they gave voice to what Alfonso believed was the close relationship between Mary and the royal house of Castile. Whether this king composed many or only a handful of songs for the *Cantigas*, the collection articulates his understanding of himself and his world.[101] In this poetic counterpart to James of Aragon's *Llibre dels feits*, Alfonso is very present, sometimes speaking in the royal "we" or even the more intimate "I." Some of the *cantigas* celebrate wondrous favors that the Virgin had showered upon him and his close relatives, proof that "Saint Mary does many miracles for kings whenever it pleases her," as the refrain of one song puts it.[102] Expressions of Alfonso's hopes, fears, and memories, the family stories included in the *Cantigas* also reveal how deeply Marian his conception of monarchy was. The king's much admired father, Ferdinand III, stands tall in these poems as an exemplar of such rulership.

According to Alfonso and his poets, Ferdinand had enjoyed Mary's miraculous attentions ever since childhood. One *cantiga* relates how as a young boy, he was stricken with such severe illness that everyone despaired of his life except his mother, who insisted on taking him to a Virgin watching over a church in the province of Burgos.[103] There the queen pled with Mary for her son's life. Through the Virgin's grace, Ferdinand survived to become king. This was, however, an office he commanded only at her pleasure for, according to the *Cantigas*, he owed her not just his life, but also his throne.

"From [Mary] and her beautiful son I held my kingdom. And I am loyally hers because I was made a knight in her church in the royal monastery of Burgos," declares Ferdinand in one poem.[104] In 1219, the twenty-year-old Ferdinand had in fact solemnly laid down his sword for its ritual blessing on the altar of Las Huelgas, the abbey church founded by his grandfather. There, amidst the tombs of his royal ancestors, he had undergone the rite of passage so important for Castile's warrior kings, kneeling while he was dubbed a knight.[105] When Ferdinand lifted his sword from Mary's altar, a new knight ready to defend the realm over which he had been made king only two years earlier, perhaps he felt the rush of gratitude toward Mary that the *Cantigas* so lyrically describe. In any case, his son and heir believed that Ferdinand's stature as both king and knight had depended on her.

In the *Cantigas*, Ferdinand as the ideal Castilian warrior king naturally fights against Muslims in the name of the Virgin and her son. His spectacular military feats against al-Andalus become so many devotional offerings to his holy patrons. As one poem declares: "the good king Ferdinand . . . always loved God and His mother and was on their side and for them he conquered most of Andalusia from the Moors."[106] Whenever he conquered a Muslim town, asserts another *cantiga*, he celebrated by "put[ting] an image [of the Virgin] above the entrance to the mosque."[107]

Ferdinand III actually did mark some of his most important triumphs over al-Andalus by transforming mosques into homes for images of Mary. Under his direction, the ʿjamis of Córdoba, Jaén, and Seville all became cathedrals bearing her name.[108] It was the king's appropriation of Córdoba's great mosque for Mary that won him the most accolades from many Christian writers. With its canopy of red and white horseshoe arches casting lacework shadows among a forest of columns, and its blue and gold mosaics evoking the sun-lit pleasures of Islamic paradise, this Umayyad building was indeed, in the words of one of Ferdinand's grandsons, the "greatest and most perfect and most noble mosque that the Moors had in Spain"—and thus a fitting offering to the Virgin.[109] Ferdinand's son and heir, however, assiduously cultivated instead the memory of his father's expansion of her ecclesiastical empire in Seville.

Alfonso described how "in honor and praise of the Virgin, Saint Mary, mother of Our Lord Jesus Christ," Ferdinand had transformed Seville's Almohad mosque into a church that ranked among "the most noble in the world."[110] This building embodied the caliphal pretensions of the Almohad rulers, showcasing their desire to be the "leaders of the faithful" on both sides of the Mediterranean. Constructed in the late twelfth century to display their might and to ornament their Andalusian capital, the mosque boasted a soaring minaret embellished with rhythmic patterns worked in tawny brick, making it a near twin to the ʿjami in the Almohads' Moroccan seat of power, Marrakech. The Christian conquerors hung church bells in this imposing tower when they claimed Seville's mosque and its princely meanings for Mary and themselves. And when Alfonso X decided, late in his reign, to create an elaborate tomb complex for his parents, he housed it in this mosque-cathedral, the building that spoke so eloquently of his father's greatest victory over al-Andalus and of this warrior-king's generosity toward Mary. In the memorial chapel Alfonso designed, he tried to ensure that the two would be entwined forever.

Alfonso commissioned a sumptuous set of statuary for the chapel and ordered it arrayed in an arresting tableau.[111] Crowned effigies of Ferdinand and his queen, Beatrice, rested on silver encrusted thrones. In front of them was an altar bearing a statue of the Queen of Heaven, her own golden crown heavy with precious stones and her richly dressed royal son ensconced on her lap.[112] Near the images of Ferdinand and Beatrice lay their tombs, covered in silver and ornamented with the arms of Castile. Alfonso thus cast his parents as the Virgin's eternal devotees and staged a scene of earthly monarchy mirroring heavenly majesty.

In one hand, Ferdinand's effigy brandished a naked, glittering sword. It is still guarded as a precious treasure in the cathedral of Seville today, something that would have pleased Alfonso X. He attached much importance to this detail of the statue, intending it as an unambiguous emblem of his father's quintessential achievements as a Marian king. As a *cantiga* that provides the earliest extant description of the tomb complex explains, "Ferdinand holds in his hand his sword with which he had given a mortal blow to Muhammed."[113] In the accompanying illumination, the sword dominates the scene, its broad blade almost as long as Ferdinand's statue is tall (Figure 1.1). With Ferdinand's effigy seated respectfully in front of Mary, the chapel's design announced in whose honor the king had struck his blows against Islam.

Whether or not Ferdinand would have recognized himself in this gilded warrior rendering eternal reverence to the Queen of Heaven, Alfonso X could observe in the statue a satisfying family resemblance between himself and his father, suggesting that he had indeed lived up to his weighty paternal legacy. In his verbal and visual portraits of Ferdinand, Alfonso fashioned a flattering prince's mirror in which to gaze at his own reflection, and he established a distinguished and legitimating lineage for his own practice of Marian monarchy.

Expanding Mary's Kingdom

Mary's sanctifying halo spread wide over Alfonso X's self-image as a ruler.[114] Late in his reign when he faced serious criticism, even opposition and rebellion, he must have hoped that its sheen would blind his challengers, among them his own son.[115] A king who received his office from Mary as Alfonso believed he had surely had the right to his crown. "I have praised and praise and will praise Mary...because she made me the lord of this good land," sings the poet-king in the *Cantigas*.[116] One *cantiga* even proposes her as the foundation of all rulership: "Kings and emperors should give great praises to Mary because through her they are the lords of everyone."[117] Alfonso seems to have believed that Castile was as much her kingdom as it was his.

Like Ferdinand, Alfonso always "was on the Queen of Heaven's side against Muslims," declares a poem in the *Cantigas de Santa María*, prudently ignoring the alliances with Granada or with Moroccan dynasties that sometimes put the king on a rather different side.[118] Introducing the king as the author both of the Marian lauds that follow and of a long string of victories against al-Andalus, the first song in the collection artfully juxtaposes his military accomplishments with his ardor for the Virgin.[119] The list of the lands that he had "won from the Moors" did not equal the tally of Ferdinand's conquests, but it was impressive enough. The *cantiga* mentioned the Algarve (a Mediterranean region Alfonso would cede to Portugal) and the western Andalusian towns of Jérez de la Frontera, Medina Sidonia, Vejer de la Frontera, and Niebla (all of which he would keep for Castile).

Figure 1.1 Miracle accompanying the construction of Ferdinand III's tomb in Seville's royal chapel. *Cantigas de Santa María*. Florence, Biblioteca Nazionale Centrale, MS Banco Rari 20, folio 12r. Reproduced with the permission of the Ministerio per i beni e le attività culturali della Repubblica Italiana, Biblioteca Nazionale Centrale di Firenze.

Alfonso's grant of privileges to this latter town in 1263 bluntly described his military service to Mary: Niebla was "the first [city] we won after we began to reign…we expelled the Moors and populated it with Christians in the service of God and Saint Mary and all the saints."[120]

The privilege that Alfonso issued two years later for another of the towns itemized in the *Cantigas'* catalogue of his Marian conquests rendered him even more the Virgin's warrior than he thought his father had been. "It wasn't by our merits, but through the great goodness of the Holy Savior and through the entreaties and merits of Saint Mary and through the help she gave us with her blessed son that we took this our city Jerez Sidonia from the Muslims," says the king in this grant of 1265 to the birthplace of sherry.[121] Alfonso believed that both he and Ferdinand fought on Mary's "side." But he did not describe his father as sharing the conviction that the Virgin herself was the source of royal victories against al-Andalus.

The poet-king of the *Cantigas* went so far as to intimate that he owed all his military successes to the saint who stood at the foundation of his reign. Mary "aided me on every military expedition when I called out to her," rhapsodizes Alfonso in one poem.[122] In another, she provides the cash-strapped king with the miraculous infusion of funds he needs to continue his wars against Granada. Repeated ten times over, this *cantiga's* refrain left no doubt about Alfonso's confidence in the handsome rewards awaiting the Christian men who served her with their swords: "Saint Mary well shares her favors and her treasures with those who serve Her and Her son well against the Moors."[123]

Alfonso was not the first Christian ruler in the Iberian Peninsula to attribute his crusading victories to Mary, as James I's *Llibre dels fets* indicates. But the Aragonese king had rarely made such programmatic statements about her patronage of royal wars against al-Andalus. Alfonso was, in fact, the first monarch to institutionalize a Marian vision of reconquest. In 1272, he founded a military order called Santa María de España (Saint Mary of Spain), whose knights, according to a document of 1273, were to fight in her name "against the nefarious Saracens, against perfidy and for the faith."[124] Seated in majesty on the new order's seal was the Virgin holding her son. The outline of an eight-pointed star embraced mother and child, styling Mary as the "star of the sea" and symbol of the order's duty to protect Castile's seacoasts against Muslims.

Through his foundation of this Marian order, the king hoped to counterbalance the other military orders in his kingdom.[125] Frustrated by his inability to rein in these powerful and wealthy organizations, Alfonso made sure that his Marian knights were subject to his direct control. Santa María de España was a royal order or even, as Alfonso probably saw it, an imperial one. He thirsted after the title of emperor of Germany, to which he laid claim through his mother, Beatrice of Swabia, a German princess.[126] In his energetic if fruitless attempts to style himself a suitable candidate for this office, Alfonso often imitated German impe-rial fashions. His Marian order was likely modeled on the rather more famous and successful one patronized by German rulers, the Teutonic Knights.[127]

If the establishment of Santa Maria de España expressed Mary's importance to Alfonso's vision of the kind of ruler he wanted to be—imperial and sover-eign—it also suggested her presence in his image of his kingdom as he dreamed it should be. The members of Alfonso's military order bore the charge of extend-ing Christian territory in her name. According to a document of 1273, they were to defend and enlarge the frontiers of Castile and Christendom "for the faith and for the *patria* against the barbarian nations."[128] In the Latin word *patria,* Alfonso and his subjects would have heard all the physical and juridical resonances then possessed by its Castilian equivalent, *la tierra,* a term evoking plains and moun-tains and rivers, the soil on which one lived and walked, the expanse of earth one loved. For a king like Alfonso, the word conjured up the actual contours of his kingdom.[129] In high medieval Castilian thought, *patria* was increasingly twinned with *fides* ("the faith"), as it was in Santa María de España's mission statement, becoming one grand cause for which a man should be willing to fight and to die.[130] As Alfonso's law code put it: "one has to love the land (*tierra*) and enlarge it and die for it if necessary."[131]

The name Alfonso gave to his military order—not "Saint Mary of Castile," as one might expect, but the far more grandiose "Saint Mary of Spain"—reveals his Marian conception of the *tierra* on whose behalf his knights were to wield their swords. If James I had conflated Mary with the city of Murcia, Alfonso appar-ently saw in her all of Spain as he believed it should be—a Christian land.[132] She was well suited to embody the king's ample territorial aspirations. In cultures where earthly power and authority are as heavily identified with men as they were in high medieval Iberia, allegorical representations of collective political identity usually take shape as women.[133] As a virgin, Mary offered a particu-larly potent image of the polity as monarchs like Alfonso wished it to be: whole and intact, or, to use the Latin word so often applied to Mary herself, *integer.*[134] Medieval writers seeking metaphors for the health of Christian society found them in her body as well as her son's.[135] Like Christ, she suffered injury when society itself was lacerated. Perhaps Alfonso X was familiar with a story told in a Leonese chronicle composed in the 1230s at his grandmother's behest: right before a "horrible...war" broke out between two Christian kings in the Iberian Peninsula, a statue of the Madonna began to bleed, foretelling the rending of the political fabric to follow.[136] It is no accident then that as medieval Christian writ-ers increasingly emphasized the *patria* as a military cause, Mary's role as a battle patron became more pronounced.

The Virgin's potential to stand for the integrity of Christian Spain must have been appealing to Alfonso X, a ruler who, at the same time that he strove to expand his kingdom, faced the colossal task of welding its rather disparate regions into a governable whole. Mary often figured in the measures he took to incorporate the newly acquired Andalusian territories into his *tierra*, a responsibility he believed belonged to his duties as a reconquest king.[137] Undertaking in her name the work of what he called "populating" these lands, but which might more properly be termed their colonization, Alfonso made them hers as much as they were his.[138] He also suggested that the Queen of Heaven participated in the royal task of transforming former Muslim land into Christian *tierra* as energetically as she had patronized his efforts to win it.

The king undertook his most Marian colonization project in al-Qanatir, a port that looked out onto the Atlantic from the Gulf of Cádiz. By 1260, Alfonso had mastered this Muslim town. He immediately took advantage of its strategic location by making it the launching pad for an abortive naval attack on Morocco's Atlantic coast. Al-Qanatir remained important in the king's tactical calculations as he sought to realize his ambitions of a crusade to North Africa, a project he hoped would bolster his claims to empire and restore Christian Spain to its old Visigothic fullness, which he believed had extended across the Mediterranean. This town also figured prominently in his plans to erode the remaining pockets of Muslim power in southwestern Andalusia through intensive Christian settlement as well as military action. In the late 1260s, Alfonso's efforts to populate al-Qanatir with Christians began in earnest.[139]

By then, the king called al-Qanatir "Saint Mary's Port" (El Puerto de Santa María), a name that unmistakably announced the town's integration into Christian Spain and thus into the Virgin's domain. In the very first clause of the text of 1281 laying out the terms for the port's Christian future, he stipulated that the community should always be called after Mary.[140] A lengthy poem in the *Cantigas* that recounts El Puerto's christening declares that from the start, al-Qanatir's Christianization had been as much her project as Alfonso's. This *cantiga* relates how, in the wake of the king's first North African campaign, Mary commands that the port be called after her and Alfonso makes sure she eventually gets her wish.[141] It is a desire that she expresses in terms of a bitter rivalry between herself and the founder of Islam: Mary wants her name and that of her son to be exalted, while Muhammad's is to be denigrated. She also claims the honor of conqueror and colonizer of al-Qanatir. The poem's title reads: "How Saint Mary took a place for herself in the kingdom of Seville and made them call it Saint Mary of the Port."

In the twenty or so other poems in the *Cantigas* chronicling El Puerto's development, Mary continues her involvement in the royal work of colonization.[142] The king did his best to lure Christian settlers to her young colony, but it was not easy, especially after an army sent from North Africa by a new Moroccan dynasty, the Marinids, sacked and burned El Puerto in the late 1270s. Alfonso was undaunted, for he knew he could rely on the support of the saint "whom we believe is our lady and advocate and helper in all our deeds," as he wrote in his privilege of 1281 for El Puerto.[143] Interweaving stories of Mary's miracles in the town with accounts of the king's efforts to woo Christians there, the El Puerto *cantigas* attest to Alfonso's confidence that she watched carefully over his settlement project. In some of these poems, Mary protects the town's new inhabitants; in others, she oversees the construction of its church that would bear her name.

As the Virgin supervised the progress of her church, she even aided Alfonso to accomplish his final royal task at El Puerto: the construction of fortifications to defend his realm.[144] The king conceived of Mary's port as both a Christian gateway to the Atlantic and a fortress shielding his Andalusian possessions that spread eastward toward the city where Ferdinand was entombed. As Alfonso put it in his privilege for El Puerto, he intended to "make a noble city in the service and praise of God and Holy Mary his mother…as a guard and defense for the kingdom of the noble city of Seville."[145] Whenever the king looked at the imposing walls of the church of Our Lady standing almost at the edge of El Puerto's waterfront, he was reminded that the celestial queen had lent her own hand to this royal labor. "The Queen of Heaven, Saint Mary of the Port, very quickly made a church on the sea coast where she could be much venerated. It was to guard the Christians from the Moors and be a fortress to wage war against the Moors of Spain and the Africans," wrote the poets of the *Cantigas*.[146] At Alfonso's orders, masons raised this church on the site of a partly ruined mosque. Adapting what remained of the Islamic building into the new structure, they realized in stone the military ambitions for El Puerto nurtured by both Alfonso and Mary. This church was part of a castle complex, girded with crenellated walls and topped with four heavy towers. Fittingly, in 1272, Alfonso designated this set of fortifications as the headquarters for his newly created order of Marian knights.[147]

In transforming al-Qanatir's crumbling harbor-front mosque into Mary's castle-church, Alfonso used her as a symbol of Christianization, like so many rulers before him. He was also mining a rich vein of Marian metaphor where he could find the materials to solder the already strong bond between the Virgin, lands conquered from the Muslims, and his *tierra*. If Mary's perfect virginity suggested wholeness to medieval thinkers, it also inspired them to reach for the vocabulary of impenetrable enclosure. To find the right imagery for her inviolability, erudite clerics and monks had only to lift their eyes from the parchment and glance at the heavily fortified landscape surrounding them. The Virgin was a walled city, King David's tower from the Song of Songs, and a "castle entered only at God the Father's pleasure," to borrow the words of a Franciscan friar closely associated with Alfonso X's court.[148] The illuminators of the *Cantigas* played with this conceit when they painted the images to accompany a poem in which a statue of Mary placed on the battlements of a Christian castle under

Figure 1.2 A statue of Mary placed in the battlements protects a Christian castle under Muslim attack. *Cantigas de Santa María*. Biblioteca Monasterio del Escorial, Codice Rico, MS. T.I.1, folio 247r. Madrid, Spain. The Bridgeman Art Library.

attack by Muslims successfully wards off the enemies (Figure 1.2).[149] Alfonso's artists tucked the image of the Madonna into a turret so neatly that it blends into the fortifications. One of the captions reads: "How Saint Mary defended the castle well like a very good castellan."

In the stones and mortar of El Puerto's fortress-church, Mary's meaning as citadel took shape, as it had in German castle chapels of Our Lady and Byzantine churches bearing her name built into city ramparts or along urban boundaries.[150] This building was thus the perfect sentinel to stand guard over the passage of ships in and out of the newly Christianized port town named for her. Literally and metaphorically, El Puerto's former mosque became a castle defending Mary's town—and the kingdom she shared with Alfonso—from the Muslims. Maybe the king thought of her as similarly fortifying the mosque-churches that he dedicated to her elsewhere.

Enshrined as the patron of these new churches located along the ever-shifting frontier of military engagement, Mary guarded the perimeter of her Christian *tierra*, just as she would watch over Alfonso's remains for all eternity. In his testament of 1284, the king suggested two possible burial sites for his body.[151] Not coincidentally, both were churches dedicated to her and reminders of Alfonso's successes on the battlefield against the Muslims. One was the cathedral of Seville, the converted mosque where his parents' bodies were enshrined with such Marian magnificence. The other was the monastery of Santa María la Real, located in Murcia, the city which, as the king says in his testament, "was the first place that God willed we should take in his service." The church honored with his remains, Alfonso stipulated, was also to receive the exquisite illuminated manuscripts of the *Cantigas*, tangible evidence of his lifelong devotion to Mary. In the end, the king's body joined his parents' in Seville.[152] And so in death, Alfonso became part of the Marian reconquest geography of Castile that he had done so much to create in life.

This king, who had so diligently fashioned himself and his revered father as crusading monarchs expanding the Virgin's *tierra* with their swords, died leaving one set of questions about his relationship to Mary unanswered. Nowhere in the abundance of texts and images of which Alfonso was the patron is there one that described exactly how the king invoked her on the battlefield, as James I's *Llibre dels fets* did. Did Alfonso pray to Mary before he faced Muslim foes and make her victory offerings afterward? Did he shout out "Saint Mary" when he faced Muslims on the battlefield, as his Aragonese father-in-law had done? Was Alfonso's royal war standard decorated with an image of the Madonna like the one carried by his great-grandfather at Las Navas?

The answers to all these questions are probably yes. But it is hard to know, since the most detailed account of Alfonso's activities as a warrior—the *Crónica de Alfonso X*—dates from the early fourteenth century.[153] Hardly a saint appears in its pages, and none in its battle narratives. Yet the very king of Castile who ordered the *Crónica de Alfonso X*'s composition would himself loudly invoke Mary during the combat that led to a major Christian victory in 1340. The battle of Salado provides a final measure of the changes that had occurred since 1212 in the Virgin's role as a patron of Christian rulers' campaigns against al-Andalus.

The Battle of Salado

The priests of the parish church of Barco de Ávila could not boast that they belonged to one of the great ecclesiastical communities of Castile so prominent in royal affections. They nonetheless did their part to send crusading kings into battle armed with saintly aid. A fourteenth-century manuscript made for the clerics serving this church in the diocese of Ávila contains prayers to be intoned on behalf of a ruler named Alfonso when he set out for war against the Muslims. The prayer recited on weekdays invoked Santiago as the ruler's battle patron, while on Saturdays—Mary's day—it was the Madonna, "queen and virgin," whom the priests beseeched to defend the monarch.[154]

Together, these saints would help the only fourteenth-century Castilian ruler named Alfonso to win a victory over the Muslims so stunning that it would take its place next to Las Navas de Tolosa in reconquest mythology. Fought in October 1340 on the hilly terrain surrounding the Salado River within eyeshot of Tarifa's Atlantic coast, this battle was the greatest Christian triumph and the most resounding Muslim defeat in fourteenth-century Iberia.[155] Although it did not result in the kind of sweeping territorial gains made by James I and Ferdinand III a hundred years earlier, the victory at Salado so neatly hamstrung Nasrid Granada that for nearly a century afterward, the project of the reconquest would lose its urgency. Salado, as one historian has said, represents the culmination of a period of Castilian expansion that began with Las Navas de Tolosa.[156] Jubilant Christians would write of the victory that crowned this expansionist era in even more Marian terms than they did the triumph that had opened it.

As Muslim and Christian forces gathered in 1340 for battle on either side of the Salado, they knew that whoever won was likely to become master of that nearby narrow but vital strip of water, the Straits of Gibraltar. Some months earlier, the combined forces of Yusuf I of Granada and Abu al-Hasan ʿAli, the Marinid emir of Morocco, had inflicted a crushing defeat on the Castilian fleet at Algeciras, a much contested port city near the Straits. Now, in October, Alfonso XI of Castile, the great-grandson of the poet-king of the *Cantigas,* allied himself with the Portuguese and struck back in the hills around the Salado.

At Salado, as at Las Navas, a king of Castile and his knights turned to Mary as they sought victory over the Muslims. Yet if in 1212 her battlefield presence had been subtle, confined to her image on Alfonso VIII's war banner, in 1340 she was explicitly woven into the fabric of the engagement, an integral part of the experiences of the ruler and his men—at least according to the *Poema de Alfonso XI,* a vivid epic composed during the king's lifetime to celebrate his crusading valor and one of the most detailed contemporaneous Christian account of the victory.[157] The men and women listening to the *Poema's* rhythmic verses heard of a heroic ruler who rode to war believing that Mary was a particularly efficacious battle patron who had already helped him win military successes against Granada.[158] Before Alfonso arrayed his men in the arid hills near Tarifa, relates the epic, he placed himself in her care again. He chose to hold his war council at Seville in the mosque-cathedral where the tomb of his Marian besotted great-grandfather, Alfonso X, lay near the warrior-effigy of Ferdinand III brandishing its sword before the Queen of Heaven. There Alfonso XI rallied his nobles for the hard struggle that lay ahead.[159]

At the blessing of his arms just hours before the fight on the Salado began, Alfonso officially gained Mary's sanction. This ceremony took place in the king's field tent, as the sun rose and the ranks of Castilian and Portuguese knights assembled. First Alfonso received absolution, readying himself for possible death. Then he lay prostrate in prayer and listened to the archbishop of Seville intone the Mass of the Holy Cross. After this invocation of the triumphant Christ, the prelate placed Alfonso's weapons on an altar, probably a portable one made to be carried on military campaigns, and chanted verses in honor of Mary. Alfonso took his sword back girded with the Virgin's blessing for the deeds he was about to do.[160]

In the *Poema*, Mary's power, as much as her son's, thus clothed the king when he rose from prayer and called to his men to mount their horses and follow him. As they advanced, all of them—"noblemen and foot soldiers" alike—prayed to her. In voices hoarse perhaps with anticipation, this Christian host sang the *Salve Regina*, a famous hymn invoking the Queen of Heaven.[161] Then they engaged the enemy. During this battle that began with such a dramatic display of Marian piety, the *Poema* relates, Alfonso's men punctuated the swing of their weapons by shouting the Virgin's name, a rallying call as powerful as the cries of "Santiago!" that also filled the air.[162] When they quailed before a particularly fierce assault by the Muslims, it was Alfonso's firm reminder of Mary's potent backing that gave them the courage to resist: "Saint Mary, advocate of Christians, does not want the African Moors to boast this day," shouted the king.[163] According to the epic, after their triumph the Christian troops joyously praised "God and the Virgin Mary."[164]

Epics often exaggerate. Yet whether or not the *Poema* accurately represented Alfonso's battlefield piety, it eloquently captured the changes that had occurred over the course of the more than century-long association between Mary, Christian warrior-kings, and wars against al-Andalus. So, too, did the wartime liturgy of Barco de Ávila. From its silent beginnings on Alfonso VIII's war banner at Las Navas de Tolosa, the connection between the Virgin and royal victory over the Muslims had grown ever stronger. By the mid-fourteenth century, Mary was known as a royal battle patron equal to Santiago himself. Priests in local churches could pray for the king to ride to war flanked by both Spain's apostle and the Virgin, while a poet singing of a Castilian monarch's prowess could use Marian touches to elevate his hero. Kings who fought for Mary's sake, kings who shouted out her name in the heat of battle, kings who triumphantly claimed Muslim cities and mosques for her—these are the sort of rulers one often encounters in the chronicles and poetry of thirteenth- and fourteenth-century Castile and Aragon.

A pilgrim who entered the royal chapel of Seville's cathedral in the mid-fourteenth century would have seen evidence of the shifts that had occurred in the many decades since Las Navas de Tolosa. Large candles and silver lamps burned night and day in the chapel.[165] The light flickering over the gilded surfaces of the monarchs' effigies gathered before Mary illuminated a court of rulers paying homage to the Queen of Heaven. As the sword that Ferdinand III held in his hands would have reminded viewers, she had presided over the monarchs' wars as she now guarded their bodies. The location of the royal tombs revealed the changes in the relationship between rulers and Mary since Alfonso VIII's reign. The Castilian king who had defeated al-Nasir in 1212 also chose to place his tomb under her guard, but the royal sarcophagi of Las Huelgas lay within the walls of a monastery built in the north, safely far away from the frontier. The tomb complex at Seville was instead part of the frontier, just like the patron saint of the mosque-cathedral herself. The shifting map of royal burials signaled that Mary's reign extended from the heart of Castile to its southernmost reaches and even reached toward Granada itself.

After Alfonso XI's death in 1350 during the siege of Gibraltar, his mortal remains lay for some decades beside those of Alfonso X, Ferdinand III, and Beatrice in the cathedral of Seville before being moved to their final resting place in Mary's other great frontier mosque-cathedral, the *mezquita* of Córdoba. Alfonso XI had founded at least one such cathedral of Our Lady; in 1344, he took the port city of Algeciras and had its main mosque dedicated to Mary.[166] Yet during his lifetime, this ruler most visibly expressed his devotion to her at a different sort of church whose contours indicated that by the mid-fourteenth century, the Marian geography of the reconquest had begun to expand in a new way, as would the alliance between monarchs and the Madonna.

2

Heroes and History

A few months after his triumph at the Salado River, Alfonso XI of Castile made a pilgrimage to the young church of Santa María de Guadalupe, located deep in the rugged hill country west of Toledo. A few years earlier, he had granted royal land to this shrine so that its ramshackle chapel could be expanded into a building big enough to hold the crowds of pilgrims who increasingly sought Mary's miraculous favor there.[1] In December 1340, the king took the church at Guadalupe under his protection and endowed it with property and legal privileges. This new round of donations was Alfonso's thanksgiving offering to the Virgin for his success on the steep banks of the Salado, although the king did not exactly say so in the document that recorded his generosity: "When we had just vanquished the powerful Abu al-Hasan, king of Morocco... and the king of Granada in the battle we fought with them near Tarifa... then we came to this place [Guadalupe] because of the great devotion we had toward it."[2]

This reticent if proud expression of royal affection for a Marian shrine would not have been out of place in a text signed by the king's great-grandfather, Alfonso X. It betrays no hint that Alfonso XI's affection for Guadalupe actually helped open a new dimension in the relationship between the rulers of Castile and the Virgin as patron of their wars against Granada. An account of Salado written some thirty years after the king made his gifts to Guadalupe suggested what was to come. A new Marian history of reconquest was being written onto the landscape, a prestigious past that could be summoned on behalf of monarchs of the present as it already was in the 1370s, when the chronicle describing Alfonso XI's reign received a thorough official revision.

Under the supervision of the Castilian royal chancery, writers reshaped the original chronicle and introduced additional material.[3] Among the passages they touched up was the description of the famous victory of 1340. In this retelling of Salado, Guadalupe figures so prominently that Alfonso readies himself for battle by making a pilgrimage to the shrine and "commend[ing] himself" to Mary's care there. Immediately after his triumph, Alfonso's first thought is to return to Guadalupe and thank its Virgin for her military aid. But the shrine is a long hard ride north from the battle site, and victory celebrations are awaiting him in Seville. So the king contents himself with a visit to a nearby place of Marian pilgrimage, the waterfront church-mosque of El Puerto de Santa María established by his great-grandfather. Later, he makes his way to Guadalupe to deliver handsome gifts to its Madonna in gratitude for what the chronicle calls "the marvelous victory that God, because of His Mother's request, had given him against the kings ... of Morocco and Granada."[4]

This new story of Salado explicitly made the Virgin of Guadalupe into the royal battle patron at which Alfonso's own privilege of 1340 had hinted. The chronicle's authors, however, slipped something far more interesting about the relationship between the king and this Madonna into the laconic last lines of their account. Alfonso, they said, "ordered that it be written in his chronicle how Our Lady appeared in that place to a cowherd and how her holy image was found buried there and how that holy church of Guadalupe was founded there."[5] At Guadalupe, a Marian geography of Christian Spain gilded by miracle and grounded in history had been revealed. With these simple phrases, the men who revised Alfonso XI's chronicle became among the first writers to record a story destined for a great future. This foundation legend would help make Guadalupe one of the most popular Marian pilgrimage places of Castile, even of western Europe. By the early fifteenth century, droves of Christian men and women, kings and queens among them, traveled winding and often treacherous roads to pray before a stern-faced cedar wood statue of the Virgin, which, they were told, had been unearthed right on the spot where a large Gothic church now stood.[6]

In this church and its Madonna, the balance between Muslim past and Christian present came to rest in an equilibrium that was not exactly the same as at the other shrine where Alfonso XI supposedly had given thanks to the Virgin for her battlefield aid, El Puerto de Santa María. The difference might not have been immediately apparent to a medieval pilgrim who traveled first to one and then to the other of these places. Built of ochre red and flinty grey stone, Guadalupe's church is practically as imposing a Marian fortress as El Puerto's; its architects used Gothic arches to support austere square towers that would not have been out of place on a castle (Figure 2.1). Although Guadalupe's church borrowed from the vocabulary of military architecture almost as heavily as El Puerto's did, the two were built on radically different foundations. Constructed over the remains of a mosque, the church of El Puerto appropriated Islam's terrain for Christianity, as did the army of Mary's other church-mosques established by triumphant Castilian and Aragonese rulers. Guadalupe's church instead stood on intrinsically Christian ground, its walls rising from the soil where a statue of the Madonna was reputed to have lain hidden during the long centuries of Muslim rule.

Figure 2.1 Monastery church of Santa María de Guadalupe, Spain. Ken Walsh. The Bridgeman Art Library.

Still hazy in the brief version of Guadalupe's foundation legend mentioned by Alfonso XI's chronicle, this historical vision snapped into focus in a story fostered by the Jeronymite friars who in 1389 became the royally appointed guardians of this increasingly famous Virgin and her shrine. Although art historians now date Guadalupe's Marian image to the twelfth century, medieval pilgrims believed that the Madonna before whom they knelt had actually arrived on Spanish soil at the height of Visigothic power.[7] The visitors who crowd into Guadalupe's church today and crane their necks to contemplate the statue (Figure 2.2) enthroned at the summit of a towering altarpiece are themselves received by the modern shrine keepers with a tale that is more or less the one that the Jeronymites had committed to parchment by the early fifteenth century. The story as they told it then was as follows.[8]

In the sixth century, Pope Gregory the Great sent this image of Mary from Rome to the bishop of Seville. It was a generous gift, for the statue was already a proven and powerful wonder-worker. The bishops of Seville cherished the image and kept it in their city until the Muslims invaded Spain in 711. Faithful Christians ensured that the precious statue did not fall into the hands of the

Figure 2.2 Statue of the Virgin of Guadalupe. Monasterio Real, Guadalupe, Spain. The Bridgeman Art Library.

conquerors. They took it and abandoned Seville, heading north away from the Muslim armies. Their flight brought them to the hills around the River Guadalupe. There they buried the statue, along with a piece of parchment detailing its illustrious lineage.

The early fifteenth-century telling of Guadalupe's legend dispensed of the ensuing centuries of Muslim domination with a few brief sentences, telescoping time to erase the hundreds of years during which the region around the future shrine had lain squarely within al-Andalus's borders. Medieval pilgrims to Guadalupe learned little of those long years from the eighth to the thirteenth centuries, when Muslim lords had trod the ground over the Madonna's hiding place. Instead, they heard much about the heady days when "it pleased God to strengthen the hearts of Christians so that they began to recover the lands they had lost," as the early fifteenth-century version of Guadalupe's foundation story put it. Not until this era when Christians "took much land...possessed by the Moors" did Mary decide to manifest her presence at Guadalupe.

In a series of visions, Mary appeared to a cowherd, a humble Christian man, right on the spot where the Visigothic refugees had concealed the statue. Revealing the secret that waited in the earth, she told the man that she wanted the local clergy to excavate the image and build a church to house her statue on the site of its centuries-long sojourn underground. It took a few more miracles to persuade the cowherd's community that he really bore a message from Mary, but soon the image was disinterred and enshrined in a chapel constructed of dry stone, green wood, and cork. According to the legend, pilgrims from all over Spain began to flock to the chapel, drawn by rumors of the statue's miraculous powers.

Over the course of the fifteenth century, new details appeared in the story cultivated by the Jeronymite friars who enjoyed the spacious precincts of the monastic buildings attached to Guadalupe's church. The discovery of the statue was related at greater length to give the shrine more prominence. The image itself acquired increasingly ancient origins, until it was presented as no less than a work of Saint Luke, the apostle whom medieval people believed had been the first artist to capture Mary's likeness. Guadalupe could thus boast of an apostolic connection rivaling Santiago's.[9] The statue's new pedigree also enhanced its power as a symbol of the fundamental continuity between Spain's Visigothic past and its Christian present.[10] Lying hidden in the earth for all the centuries of Muslim rule, this Madonna was concrete proof of the land's essential and eternal Christianity.

Guadalupe was not the only place where Mary appeared to an animal herder and revealed her role as the guardian and guarantee of Spain's natural Christianity. Transcribed into a late fifteenth-century manuscript is the record of the visionary experiences of a young shepherd boy from Santa Gadea, a village north of Burgos.[11] In 1399, he repeatedly beheld Mary in the shape of a woman dressed in white and shining with such bright light that he had to shade his eyes. She sat atop a hawthorn, a type of tree often associated with the Madonna in the High Middle Ages.[12] Around its grey trunk gathered a company of people also clad in white. As was increasingly the case in Marian apparitions, the Virgin had a message for the seer that she wished him to convey to his community.[13] It was a tale of heroes and history beginning with 711.

Mary told the boy how "at the time of the destruction of Spain...there was a church here that bore my name." A group of local Christians had tried to shelter themselves within its walls from the "great troublesomeness of the...infidels," but had been captured "by force of arms." Staunchly refusing to convert to

Islam, they "were all beheaded" as "glorious martyrs." So freely had their blood flowed for the faith that the "whole church and the cemetery and the surrounding area" had been "bathed" in it. Now Mary wanted to resurrect the memory of these heroes whose sacrifice had indelibly stained the soil with the color of Christianity. She ordered that a monastery be built on the site of their death and her apparition, that place where the Christian past and present met in a seamless whole, hardly scarred by the Muslim interlude. In this sequence of apparitions, the Virgin both revealed the land's enduring Christianity and embodied it in the form of her tree, the hawthorn, with its roots plunged in the earth drenched with the Visigothic martyrs' blood.

These stories from Santa Gadea and Guadalupe date from an era when tales of Marian apparitions leading to the establishment of new shrines enjoyed great popularity in the Christian kingdoms of the Iberian Peninsula.[14] They also bear the marks of the renewed fascination with the Visigothic past often apparent in fifteenth-century Castilian representations of Spain's history. Recently ennobled families eager to mask their arriviste origins with the dignity of the deep past and poets and propagandists looking to enhance rulers' reputations found it useful to invoke the Gothic era as the foundation for the present political order. So strong was the appeal of this slice of history to Castile's fifteenth-century literati that they created a "neo-Gothic" portrait of their own world, asserting that the Visigothic past continued in the person of contemporary rulers and aristocrats.[15]

In late fifteenth- and sixteenth-century Castile, churches and monasteries seeking to enhance the reputation of their own Marian images often plagiarized the story of Guadalupe's miraculous discovery. Such legends proliferated, transforming many statues of the Virgin enthroned on church altars into repositories of a Christian continuum that had persisted through time and space in defiance of the Muslims. Some of these stories would even work their magic on church-mosques, recounting how Christian conquerors had found an old statue of the Virgin hidden in the building's fabric, a sign that Islamic prayer halls themselves asserted Spain's essential Christianity. It is perhaps no accident that beginning in the late fourteenth century, some church-mosques were pulled down and replaced with recognizably Christian cathedrals.[16] To be sure, there were practical considerations. Earthquake damage, for example, had rendered Seville's mosque-cathedral a dangerous place in which to pray. Yet the new Gothic buildings visibly erased the Islamic contours of cityscapes in the same era when Marian legends like Guadalupe's began to construct a fundamentally Christian landscape for Castile.

These tales often placed the moment of the Madonna's revelation so close in time to Christian military victory that it participates in the triumph. By the early fifteenth century, the friars at Guadalupe told the story of their Madonna's discovery as part of the movement of the reconquest itself. Flanked by accounts of Christian conquests, the statue's unearthing becomes the centerpiece in the unfolding drama of Spain's return to its true Christian nature, with the kings of Castile starring as heroes.[17] These monarchs' triumphs over Muslims prepare the way for the discovery of the Marian image, an event that also receives a royal spin. Guadalupe's legend carefully locates the miracle in the flow of royal history: "In the time when this King Don Alfonso reigned in Spain, Our Lady the Virgin Mary appeared to a cowherd in the mountains of Guadalupe." It also proudly proclaims that at this king's command, the text on the Visigothic parchment buried with the Madonna was "transcribed into his royal chronicles."[18] Here, history as conceived by the Jeronymite friars who tended Guadalupe's cult intersected with the view of the past cultivated at court by the 1370s, for the tale of the statue's revelation actually did become part of the official record of Alfonso's reign.

The overlap between Guadalupe's history, royal history, and reconquest history culminates at Salado, where the king invokes as his patron none other than the Madonna whose statue has just been revealed. The friars enthusiastically embellished the story, recasting the royal chronicle's simple account of Alfonso's pre-battle prayer and post-battle pilgrimage of thanksgiving in order to feature Our Lady of Guadalupe as the source of his most important triumph over the Muslims. Pilgrims to the shrine would learn that the king had called on this Madonna in the heat of combat at Salado—and "she gave him victory over those enemies of our faith."[19] The friars usually concluded the tale by detailing how the king celebrated his victory with lavish offerings to Guadalupe's shrine. It was a pious act of royal generosity that the Jeronymites were happy to see Alfonso XI's successors on the throne of Castile imitating. The late fourteenth- and fifteenth-century monarchs of Castile held the shrine high in their affections, enriching it with a steady stream of largesse and gracing it with their own presence. Often, members of the royal family came and stayed at Guadalupe for days, even months at a time. In the sunshine of royal favor, the shrine grew wealthy, powerful, and influential. "To be prior of Guadalupe is better than being count or duke," ran a sixteenth-century proverb.[20]

The rulers of Castile had practical reasons to elevate Guadalupe to such prominence. By promoting the shrine, Alfonso XI hoped that the lure of the Virgin, combined with the business opportunities generated by pilgrimage, would bring settlers to this under-populated and inhospitable part of his kingdom.[21] Guadalupe was also a logical place for monarchs to break their journey as they traveled between northern Castile and the important Andalusian cities in the southwest of their realm, such as Córdoba and Seville.[22] Equally advantageous was Guadalupe's location in the imaginative geography of Christian conquest. By focusing their piety on this shrine, the rulers signaled the importance of the historical vision embodied by its Madonna and her shrine. In the second half of the thirteenth century, the mosque-cathedral of Seville—testimony to the

Virgin's power to Christianize Muslim lands conquered by Castilian kings—had challenged Las Huelgas's role as the church embodying royal affection for Mary. Now Seville had a rival in the form of Guadalupe, a shrine that proposed her as proof that when kings took territory from the Muslims, they were restoring the land to its true Christian nature.

In venerating Our Lady of Guadalupe, late medieval Castilian rulers were worshipping at the shrine of the Visigothic past, which they believed they were resurrecting in the present. As these monarchs fought the actual battles that eventually led to the demise of the kingdom of Granada, they would seek to realize the vision of Marian history embedded in the landscape. To be sure, they would still Christianize conquered territory by dedicating mosques to the Virgin, for her new role in the imaginative project of creating an eternally Christian Iberia complemented rather than replaced the part she had played at El Puerto and elsewhere. In this era, rulers would also develop new aspects of Marian monarchy. As they did so, they often believed that they were imitating their illustrious predecessors. By the beginning of the fifteenth century, the Marian past had impressed itself as heavily on the contours of Iberia's human history as on its geography. Looking back to earlier Christian eras, rulers of the fifteenth century found heroic models in men who had won the great victories that had set Christian Iberia on the road to recovery—and who had done so under the Virgin's shield.

Ferdinand III's Avatar

Mary's crusaders of the past had often worn crowns, learned the readers of Fernán Pérez de Guzmán's lengthy poem celebrating the illustrious deeds of the great men of Castile. An important player in the bloody politics of the first half of the fifteenth century and a knight who had drawn his sword against Granada, Pérez de Guzmán was also an aristocrat with a taste for history who shared with his learned Castilian contemporaries the conviction that the foundations of the current Christian polity lay in the Visigothic past. With his writings, he hoped to foster a renewal of Spain's former splendor and to encourage ethical behavior in the leading men of the realm, including its rulers.[23]

Among the exemplars Pérez de Guzmán held out to his audience were Alfonso VIII, who "had . . . at Las Navas de Tolosa a most heroic victory with the glorious cross and the Virgin Mary," and Alfonso XI who at Salado had fought "a glorious battle, famous throughout the world . . . against Abulhacen, king of Fez and Tlemcen. He pray[ed] to the very precious Virgin for the Spanish people, [and] the Christian nation, thanks be to God, was victorious."[24] With these last lines, Pérez de Guzmán evoked Mary not just as the battle patron of crusading kings

but also as the keeper of the Spanish people, a "nation" as inevitably and fundamentally Christian as Guadalupe's legend proposed the land of Spain itself was.

Mary naturally made an appearance when this poet turned his pen to the
ruler who, more than any other past king, embodied Christian military virtue
and commanded the imagination of late medieval Castilians, Ferdinand III.
The men who made up Castile's ruling class in the fifteenth century were the
enthusiastic heirs of Alfonso X's cult of admiration for his father. The conqueror
of Seville belonged to a select trinity of knights from the past who epitomized
Christian chivalry as Pérez de Guzmán's peers believed it should be lived in the
present.[25] In his verse portrait of Ferdinand III, the poet celebrated the king's
crusading victories and devotion to the saint watching over his wars. Ferdinand,
wrote Pérez de Guzman, had "won Andalusia, calling for his glory on the Lord,
whose servant he was, [and] with the intercession of Mary, with whom he was
in love."[26]

In conjuring Ferdinand III as the sort of Marian military monarch whom
Alfonso X had memorialized, Pérez de Guzman was summoning his fellows to
imitate the king's deeds and devotion. He found few members of the contemporary royal house of Castile who measured up to his ideal of rulership. The
man who came the closest—and whom the poet supported during Castile's civil
strife—would himself explicitly invoke Ferdinand III's ghost.[27] He would also
make devotion to Mary central to both his considerable political aspirations
and his wars against Granada. This man even bore the same name as the monarch whom Pérez de Guzmán celebrated as her lover. Known as Ferdinand of
Antequera, he was the second son of Juan I and brother to the man who inherited the Castilian throne in 1390, Enrique III "el Doliente" ("the Sick"). A formidable warrior as well as a deeply ethical man, the *infante* Ferdinand would take
his nickname from the Muslim city that was his greatest conquest, while Enrique
was remembered for the severe illnesses that sent him to the grave sixteen years
after he became king.[28]

As the fifteenth century opened, Ferdinand was the second most powerful
man in Castile, beholden only to his ailing brother. Fabulously wealthy, he commanded armies of vassals and bore a long string of titles that made him lord over
huge stretches of Castile. All he lacked was the crown itself. But Enrique had yet
to father a son, and his health was rapidly degenerating. In first few years of the
new century, Ferdinand consciously cultivated an image of himself as a paragon of Christian knighthood and thus as eminently throne-worthy. As he sought
to enhance his public persona, he combined two marks of royalty into one by
founding a chivalric order dedicated to the saint who was so important in Pérez
de Guzmán's vision of heroic crusading rulers of the past.[29]

Ferdinand's inauguration of the Order of the Jar and Griffin at the church of
Santa María de la Antigua in his city of Medina del Campo on August 15, 1403

(the feast of Mary's Assumption into heaven) was the first time in Castile that a chivalric order would be founded by anyone other than the reigning king.[30] Unlike military orders such as the Templars or the Knights of Santiago, the members of these organizations did not live together as religious communities following a monastic rule. Instead, high-ranking aristocrats met at prescribed times for ceremonies designed to display their status, honor, and chivalric virtue. The founding of chivalric orders was practically a tradition in Ferdinand's family, at least for the men who sat on the throne. His father Juan I had established several, and his great-grandfather, Alfonso XI, had been the first European monarch ever to do so. Alfonso XI's Order of the Band created quite a stir among his crowned contemporaries. Soon it became the vogue for Christian kings to create such orders. Eager to promote themselves as exemplars of the chivalric values so central to the male aristocratic ethos, rulers recognized the considerable advantages of binding the magnates of their realms together in a society whose chief was usually the sovereign himself. Accordingly, loyalty to the order's leader was much stressed in these organizations' statutes, and monarchs bestowed memberships upon men who served them faithfully. There is every indication that Ferdinand assigned his own Marian chivalric order such duty in the politics of fidelity.[31]

The *infante*'s establishment of the Jar and Griffin was perhaps a sign that the founding of such orders was no longer a jealously guarded royal prerogative in Castile. It could equally indicate his aspirations to equal his forebears who had occupied the throne. In any case, in Ferdinand's creation of the Order of the Jar and Griffin, personal piety coincided with political expedience, as they had in the origins of Alfonso X's short-lived Marian military order, Santa María de España. Ferdinand was especially dedicated to Mary, as he announced in the preface to the statutes for the Jar and the Griffin, and he intended the whole order to share his veneration of her.[32]

As one sign of their allegiance to Mary, members were always to wear the ornamented neck chain bearing the Order's insignia. Its weight would have been a constant reminder of the service they owed her. The metal links of this collar were cast in the shape of jars filled with blossoming lilies, Mary's flowers. From the heavy chain hung a griffin-pendant, with wings outstretched and talons flexed. Lauded in the Order's statutes as the "most powerful of all animals," the griffin was perhaps intended to evoke the might of Mary's son, for medieval theologians often pointed to this creature's hybrid identity when discussing Christ's own mixed nature as god and man.[33] Wrought into this collar were the intertwined qualities of Marian devotion and Christian prowess that Ferdinand hoped the members of his Order would display.

Fortified by the griffin's strength and their love of God and the Virgin, the knights of the Jar and Griffin, declared the Order's statutes, would naturally perform deeds of great valor.[34] Ferdinand intended that they achieve these chivalric feats by fighting for God and Mary against one set of foes in particular. The Order's statutes exhorted its members to defend "churches, widows, orphans and all the servants of God against the attack of pagans"—shorthand in fifteenth-century Castile for the Muslims.[35] Ferdinand himself would undertake this Marian military mission in 1407 when he set out on the first of his campaigns against Granada.

As the *infante* rode south toward Seville in 1407, it is likely that he obeyed his Order's statutes by wearing the collar of the Jar and Griffin. The glint of its metal on his chest would have ceremoniously announced that he battled Muslims in Mary's name. Some of Ferdinand's contemporaries, in any case, believed that forged into this neck chain was the *infante*'s identity as her crusader. As renowned Castilian poet Alfonso Alvarez Villasandino lyrically put it, "Day and night [Ferdinand] is devoted to the blessed Virgin. And it is through the collar, the bright emblem which he has in honor of Saint Mary, that he vanquishes and conquers the great land of the Moors."[36] Even if Ferdinand did not sport this collar during his campaign of 1407, he was accompanied by at least one "bright emblem" proclaiming him the Virgin's knight. It was an even more brilliant ornament than the Order's neck chain, for it bore the sheen of history and the halo of that saintly Marian hero from the past, Ferdinand III.

By 1407, the *infante* evidently believed that he had a right to claim as weighty a heritage as Ferdinand III's Marian mantle. He was as close to occupying the Castilian throne as he would come. In 1406 Enrique III had finally succumbed to his ailments, having lived just long enough to see the first birthday of his son and heir. In his will, the dying king designated as the regents of Castile his wife, Catalina of Lancaster, and his brother, Ferdinand. It was an unhappy condominium that degenerated into open strife within a few months of Enrique's death. When, in 1407, Ferdinand summoned the Crown's vassals and his own for war against Granada, he was hoping this display of martial leadership would help to consolidate his position against Catalina.[37] He was also fulfilling his responsibilities as co-regent by protecting the realm from attacks by Granada, the likes of which had not been seen for years.

During the decades since Alfonso XI's triumphs against Granada's Nasrid rulers and their North African allies, Castile had devoted little energy to war with its Muslim neighbor. Though raids continued on the late medieval frontier, as did piracy along the Mediterranean coast, official truces between Castile and Granada had become the rule rather the exception.[38] Then, in 1401, the Nasrids opened hostilities with Castile and struck again in 1405. In the year of Enrique's death, they launched an offensive that took little territory but many Castilian lives. The Cortes, Castile's version of the parliamentary institutions emerging across western Europe, began raising funds for a counterattack.[39] Riding at the head of the Christian troops would be the regent of Castile so devoted to Mary.

Ferdinand would fight with the Virgin's blessing and a martial talisman of that famous Marian monarch from the past whose name he bore. Both were bestowed on him at an elaborate ceremony in Seville on September 7, 1407. A few weeks earlier, the regent had ordered his vassals and mercenaries to muster in this city. On the evening of September 6, he prepared himself spiritually for the ritual to unfold the next day. He spent the night under the Virgin's protection in a church located near one of Seville's main gates, a sanctuary selected, as a Castilian court chronicler later explained, "because of his great devotion to the image of Saint Mary of Iniesta" housed there.[40] Why Ferdinand felt such affection for this Madonna the chronicler did not say, but perhaps rumor already had begun to gild her with the Guadalupe-like history that by the sixteenth century would make her famous; a Visigothic Madonna concealed from the Muslims in 711 and later miraculously revealed to true believers would have been a good patron for a Christian prince about to do battle with Granada.[41]

Ferdinand passed the long night hours praying and sleeping before Our Lady of Iniesta. As September 7 dawned, he heard Mass at her altar and then left her care to enter the realm of a Virgin who definitely would connect him to the glories of the Christian past, the Madonna enthroned in the royal chapel of Seville's cathedral. Waiting for the regent in Mary's mosque-cathedral were all its canons and clerics, dressed in their finest ceremonial garb. In a long line, they processed with the *infante* down the nave to the main altar, whose steps were covered by a cloth woven of gold and silk threads. Ferdinand paid homage to a cross there and then made his way to the royal chapel—crowded with Seville's civic officials and a host of noblemen—for the ceremony's main act. As they all watched, the regent prayed before the statue of the Queen of Heaven who reigned over the tombs and bejeweled effigies of Ferdinand III, Beatrice of Swabia, and Alfonso X.[42]

The regent had come to the cathedral not only to beseech Mary for victory in the hushed presence of his ancestors, but also to acquire a relic of the past from one of her eternal royal devotees, the sword brandished by the statue of Ferdinand III. The dean of the cathedral gently loosened the blade from the effigy's grip and laid it in the statue's arms. Then the regent leaned forward to take the weapon. As he closed his hand around its hilt, he believed he was seizing the very blade with which his saintly namesake had wrested Seville from the Almohads in 1248, wrote the fifteenth-century royal chronicler who described the ceremony.[43] True, Alfonso X, who had commissioned Ferdinand's III's effigy, had written of this weapon as a symbol of his father's triumphs over Muslims rather than as the warrior king's actual blade. But already in the fourteenth century, pilgrims to Seville pressed into the royal chapel so they could kiss the sword, believing that it had been powerful enough to defeat the Muslims and therefore possessed the force to vanquish their own maladies.[44]

The sword that the regent of Castile held in his hand that day was thus sheathed with all the strength of a holy relic. As the Count of Las Marchas, one of the nobles present at the ceremony, explained to Ferdinand: "Lord, it seems that this sword is power (*virtud*). Therefore you should carry it around the church and then ride through the city with it."[45] The *infante* followed this astute public relations advice. Everyone who beheld him in the streets of Seville, the blade firmly in his grasp, would know that this new Ferdinand commanded the weapon's *virtud*.

The sword would accompany the regent on his campaign against Granada, consecrating his actions with the halo of history. The entire ritual in the cathedral had in fact been choreographed to suggest continuity between his wars against Granada and those prosecuted centuries ago by the weapon's original owner. On the eve of the ceremony, he had slept before an image of Mary, just as the other Ferdinand slept for all eternity entombed in front of another Virgin. The next day, as the regent took hold of Ferdinand III's sword in the Madonna's presence, he made himself into an avatar of the Marian hero represented by his ancestor's effigy.

A few months later, the regent returned the sword to Seville's cathedral in a ceremony as impressive as the one in September.[46] As he knelt before the Madonna in the royal chapel, he gave thanks that God had helped him bring this precious relic back safe and sound from the campaign. But the sword had not really worked its magic. The regent's only major success had been the capture of Zahara de la Sierra, a Muslim town perched on a rocky hump of land in the Sierra de Grazalema. There, the triumphant Ferdinand had presided over the ritual transformation of the community's mosque into a church dedicated to Mary.[47] Even though the tally of victories was not what the regent had hoped for, his ambitions to establish a special relationship with his illustrious ancestor persisted. Back in Seville, he prayed before the Madonna in the royal chapel, placed the sword into the hand of Ferdinand III's effigy, and then kissed the image's fingers and its feet. The crowd of spectators would have immediately understood the meaning of his gestures. In high medieval Castile, vassals touched their lips to the hands and feet of their lord as a sign of submission and loyalty.[48]

It was as Ferdinand III's vassal and ritual heir—and as Mary's loyal devotee— that the regent rode again to war with Granada several years later. During this campaign, he would earn his nickname by taking Antequera. It would be a spectacular victory for Castile and a major loss for the Nasrids, because this town lying some fifty kilometers north of Málaga guarded the crossroads of the main ways traversing Andalusia. As the regent prepared to lay siege to Antequera in April 1410, Ferdinand III's sword was brought from its Sevillean home to the

Christian battle camp.[49] During the long months before the city's fall, the sword remained with the *infante*, as did other holy talismans, including a cross, a banner of Saint Isidore, and one bearing Santiago's image.[50]

Some of Ferdinand's subjects did their best to obtain Mary's favor for his bold venture. At one point in 1410, the streets of Jérez de la Frontera, a town far west of Antequera, were full of Christians uttering solemn prayers on the regent's behalf. Perhaps led by friars from Jérez's convent of Our Lady of Mercy, they beseeched God and "the Holy Virgin Mary with the whole court of heaven to grant conquest and victory against the Moors, enemies of the holy catholic faith" to the *infante*.[51] As the Castilian forces gradually tightened the noose around Antequera, Ferdinand was indeed confident that he went to battle fortified by Mary's aid, as he wrote in a letter of May 1410 describing his confrontation with an army led by the brothers of Nasrid sultan. These princes had ridden from Granada in the hopes of breaking the Castilian siege lines, but Ferdinand fended them off. It was to God and Mary that he owed this victory that was crucial to his eventual triumph at Antequera, wrote the regent. Ferdinand was, after all, the Virgin's "knight" and she was his "advocate", commented the fifteenth-century chronicler who preserved the letter.[52] According to one of his contemporaries, the regent had even promised her that if he took Antequera, he would have "all the silver he acquired on the frontier" melted down and offered to her in the form of a lamp bearing the town's likeness.[53]

Immediately after his victory, the regent hastened to fulfill his vow, commissioning a heavy silver lamp in the shape of the defeated city and giving it to Mary at the cathedral of Toledo.[54] Installed in front of her altar, this ex-voto commemorated the past and predicted the future, for the battle of Antequera would earn its place in the pantheon of great Marian victories. Within a decade or so of the city's submission, the Castilian poet Villasandino composed verse celebrating how during the siege the Virgin had "ordered" Santiago and Saint John to accompany the regent on his forays and to ensure that he won (here Mary acts a general, outranking the male saints whom she commands as if they were her troops).[55] By the sixteenth century, Castilians who listened to one of the many ballads that figured "Moors" mourning the city's fall would have had their spirits lifted by the exultant concluding lines: "And so was Antequera taken / In honor of Saint Mary."[56]

The events of 1412 proved that once Ferdinand de Antequera acquired a royal crown, he would more than live up to the Marian reputation of the ruler whose sword-relic had cast its blessing on his campaigns against Granada. In that year, he was crowned king in a ceremony that proclaimed him a ruler obviously in love with the Virgin. It was not, however, the throne of Castile the *infante* gained, but that of Aragon, a kingdom to which he laid claim through his mother. The electors of Aragon had chosen Ferdinand out a field of contenders, many of whom had good reason to believe the crown should be theirs. Not all of Ferdinand's rivals were willing to renounce their claims immediately. His formal accession to the Aragonese throne in August 1412 thus took the form of a ritual extravaganza choreographed to show that none other than the Queen of Heaven had approved the electors' decision. It has even been suggested that Ferdinand intended the whole display to prove that Mary had bestowed the crown on him, the message of a painting made a few years later.[57] The festivities that took place in the graceful halls of Saragossa's old Muslim palace styled Ferdinand as perhaps even more a Marian monarch than Alfonso X of Castile. If the poet-king of the *Cantigas* had sung of how he owed his kingdom to the Virgin, Ferdinand repeatedly invoked her in the very spectacles that proclaimed him king.

Several days of ceremonies, feasting, and pageants of the sort popular in late medieval Christian Europe accompanied the coronation. The fifteenth-century chronicler who detailed these festivities wrote that Ferdinand wore white to display himself to his guests as a "devoted knight of Saint Mary."[58] The new king announced his love for her with a lavish tableau vivant portraying her coronation as Queen of Heaven.[59] Shrewdly furthering Ferdinand's political agenda, this spectacle suggested that the celestial ceremony it depicted was both sanction and model for the more earthly one taking place before the audience of Aragonese grandees. Ferdinand's coronation could not be contested, implied the tableau, for it mirrored Mary's own.

From a theatrical piece acted out during one of the banquets, Ferdinand's guests learned even more about Mary's importance to his understanding of monarchy. This pageant proclaimed that at the heart of his kingship would be the values symbolized by the collar of the Order of the Jar and Griffin: valorous combat against Muslims in Mary's name.[60] As the second course was served, "celestial music" sounded and an angel came forth from an ingeniously contrived cloud and presented Ferdinand with a jar full of lilies from heaven. This angel announced itself as "the messenger of the resplendent Virgin who sent [the king] this jar which he should always carry with him on his conquests," a speech implying that Mary had chosen Ferdinand to vanquish the Muslims. Next came an elaborate staged battle. An eagle, a griffin, "Moors," and a young man bearing the Aragonese royal insignia contested for a Marian prize, a castle decorated with a jar of lilies. The victor was, of course, the youth, intended to represent Ferdinand.

With Ferdinand's accession to the throne of Aragon, the Jar and Griffin attained the dignity of a royal institution, just like the chivalric orders that had been founded by his brother, father, and great-grandfather. Its emblem even became a royal crest bequeathed to his successors on the throne of Aragon.[61] Until the end of the fifteenth century, the collar with its jars of lilies and griffin pendant proclaimed the link between the monarch, the Virgin, and the chivalric fight against Granada. The Order was still in existence when the second man named Ferdinand to rule Aragon took the throne in 1479, a monarch for whom the Marian fight against "the pagans" of the Jar and Griffin's raison d'être was very much a current reality.[62] Together he and his wife—Isabel I, the sovereign of Castile—would lead the military campaigns that ended the almost eight hundred–year period during which Christian and Muslim polities had shared the Iberian Peninsula.

The Catholic Monarchs

Among the many treasures owned by the Prado Museum in Madrid is a wood panel painting dating from the early 1490s, known as *The Virgin of the Catholic Monarchs* (Figure 2.3).[63] The brush strokes of an anonymous artist produced this image some years before the pope dubbed Isabel and Ferdinand with the honorific of "los Reyes Católicos." Yet from the panel gaze portraits of these rulers reflecting the reputation they already enjoyed as Christian paragons. In the last decade of the fifteenth century, the painting belonged to a Dominican convent in Ávila so high in royal favor that the monarchs' personal coat of arms and the royal shields of Castile and Aragon were sculpted over and over onto its walls. The king and queen may have commissioned this image of Mary or may have been involved in deciding its composition.[64] Whoever paid the artist's fees oversaw the production of a politically charged vision of the Madonna suggesting that Ferdinand and Isabel's agenda as rulers expressed the Virgin's will.

The painting's center is a gentle-faced, red-robed Mary. Seated on an ornate throne on a dais, she cradles the infant Jesus in her arms. Flanking the platform's broad steps stand two haloed saints. In the foreground Isabel and Ferdinand kneel at prie-dieux, one to either side of the tiled path leading to the Virgin. Several of their children, as well as some pious Dominicans, appear in the wings, but the monarchs and the Madonna to whom they pray dominate the painting. Not only are Ferdinand and Isabel physically closer to Mary, but the artist also made them the same size as Jesus' mother, while reserving for the royal offspring and the friars the traditional hierarchy of scale that required ordinary humans to appear smaller than saints. The rulers' piously folded hands almost reach the bottom edge of Mary's mantle, practically joining their terrestrial sphere of action to her celestial one. Further blurring the boundaries between these two realms, the painting hints that Ferdinand and Isabel are actually in Mary's presence. It is no coincidence that the stalk of lilies one saint holds out toward the Virgin rises from his hand directly above Isabel's own head, making the queen participate in Mary's purity.[65] Exceeding the usual parameters for portraits of Marian devotion, this painting boldly proposed that a certain unity reigned among the king,

Figure 2.3 The Virgin of the Catholic Monarchs, ca. 1490. Prado Museum, Madrid, Spain. The Bridgeman Art Library.

the queen, and the saint whom they venerated. The viewer was invited to see the monarchs' Christianizing endeavors as being Mary's projects as much as the rulers' own.

The queen was doubtless pleased with this painting. Isabel was a learned woman of strong will, uncompromising piety, and pronounced austerity.[66] She loved many saints, but Mary was chief among them. Not only did the queen own a copy of Alfonso X's *Cantigas de Santa María,* but she also surrounded herself with tapestries and paintings depicting Marian scenes.[67] The man whom Isabel married in 1469 enjoyed good living and was more moderate in his Christianity. Yet Ferdinand shared his wife's Marian devotion, as he would demonstrate during the crusade against Granada. It was a war first urged by Isabel, of which

Ferdinand soon became an enthusiastic proponent; despite the differences in their personalities, these ambitious, energetic, and competent sovereigns often successfully combined the resources of their respective kingdoms to great effect.

During their Granadan campaigns, Ferdinand and Isabel would actualize the Marian monarchy suggested by the Prado's painting. But before the king and queen were able to contemplate crusade against Muslims, they first had to defeat their Christian enemies. The Virgin would help the royal couple to do so—and so would her prestigious past. From the tumultuous beginnings of their reigns, Ferdinand and Isabel consciously played with the power of reconquest history and Mary's connection to it. By the late fifteenth century, this history that Ferdinand of Antequera had drawn on to consecrate his own campaigns against al-Andalus had evidently become potent enough to be marshaled in the service of a monarch fighting to assert her right to the throne.

When Isabel had herself crowned as the sovereign of Castile in 1474, many considered her a usurper. They believed their rightful ruler was her niece, Juana, daughter of the last reigning king of Castile, Enrique IV, and fiancée to the king of Portugal. But Juana had her own legitimacy issues. By the time Enrique died in 1474, it was widely rumored that she was not really his offspring and therefore had no claim on his crown, gossip eagerly fostered by the supporters of the late king's half-sister, Isabel. Five years of civil strife ensued, with Castile's prominent aristocrats split into factions. Alfonso V of Portugal championed his betrothed, while Ferdinand of Aragon battled on behalf of the woman whom he had married in 1469.[68]

As Isabel and her husband strove to realize her sovereignty by force of arms and propaganda, they mustered many vocabularies of legitimacy. Sometimes they went so far as to frame their war against Juana as divinely willed, even holy, by mobilizing the ritual and rhetoric that previous Castilian monarchs had used during campaigns against Granada.[69] It was a repertoire that included Mary wearing her ever more capacious cloak as patron of Spanish royal crusaders, past and present. Through public alliances with Madonnas of distinguished reconquest pasts, Isabel would style herself the legitimate successor to a long line of Castilian rulers and consecrate her bid for the throne with the authority of history.

Just how much practice Ferdinand and Isabel gained during the contest over the crown for holy war against more traditional opponents is evident from the Marian tone of the celebrations they staged in honor of an important military victory over Juana's defenders, the battle of Toro, fought in March 1476. In a letter composed shortly after this engagement, Ferdinand declared that during the fighting, he had placed his trust in "the mercy of Our Lord and his blessed mother and in the help of the apostle Santiago."[70] His confidence in the holy trinity that had so often led Spanish crusaders to triumph paid off. A Castilian chronicler reported that after Toro, Ferdinand had rejoiced and "giv[en] thanks to Our Lord and his mother, who had guided his hands in the fight and his fingers in the battle."[71] Isabel and her husband accordingly ordered public thanksgiving processions in nearby Zamora in praise of God and Mary "for the victory it pleased them to give me in this battle," as Ferdinand wrote.[72] If God and his mother had seconded Ferdinand at Toro, the justice of Isabel's cause was proven.

The royal couple staged their ceremonial entry into Toledo in February 1477 to give the same Marian message. Keenly aware of the political efficacy of public ritual, Ferdinand and Isabel came to the old Visigothic capital both to win its allegiance and to display themselves before its citizens as the victors of Toro.[73] They paraded through the city streets to the cathedral of Our Lady. Awaiting them in the building's Gothic portal was a tableau vivant intended to cast the aura of the holy over their presence in Toledo.[74] On either side of the cathedral's door stood ordered ranks of "angels," while above them was installed a richly dressed young woman wearing a golden crown "in the likeness of the blessed mother of God, Our Lady," as the Bachiller Palma, a chronicler writing in 1479, remembered the scene. When Isabel and Ferdinand passed through the portal and entered the cathedral "to give thanks to Our Lord and his blessed mother," they visibly received the Queen of Heaven's blessing on their reign, a celestial endorsement underscored by the music of the angel-actors. As the royal couple processed under the feet of the Virgin-come-to-life, the heavenly ensemble sang, "Yours is the power, o Lord, yours is the kingdom," an antiphon that in some parts of western Europe belonged to the liturgy of holy war.[75]

In his description of this scene of political legitimization through liturgical pageantry, the Bachiller Palma intimated that Ferdinand and Isabel had come to Toledo in order to venerate a Virgin who could connect them to the Visigothic era. Castilian court writers would stress the Gothic theme in their portraits of the Catholic Monarchs, even creating a pedigree for Isabel that led straight back to the Christian kings who had ruled Spain before 711.[76] Palma made sure to point out that the cathedral where Isabel and Ferdinand came to pray after Toro was built on the site where Mary had famously graced Ildefonsus, a Visigothic archbishop and author of an important treatise about her virginity, with her miraculous favor. By the thirteenth century, Christians all across western Europe knew how hundreds of years ago, the Virgin had appeared in Toledo and given the city's saintly prelate a priestly garment from paradise.[77] As Palma put it, she had "descended in person in the time of blessed Saint Ildefonsus" right where Isabel and Ferdinand offered their prayers to her.[78]

According to the same chronicler, the Marian Visigothic connection had been at work during the battle of Toro itself; Saint Ildefonsus had acted as Mary's "good chaplain" by helping Ferdinand trounce Juana's supporters.[79] Thus the status of Isabel's fight for the throne as a crusade continuing those waged by earlier Castilian rulers was reinforced. As the would-be queen was well aware, four decades earlier, a king about to depart on campaign against Granada had come to Toledo's cathedral to acquire the favor of the Madonna who had been so generous to Ildefonsus. This royal warrior, who spent the night in prayer with his arms before the Marian image marking the spot where the Visigothic bishop had received the Virgin's gift, was none other than Isabel's father, Juan II.[80] As the queen uttered her prayers of thanksgiving in Toledo, she doubtless intended to evoke the memory of Juan's pre-battle vigil and thus to armor her quest to occupy his throne with yet another legitimizing layer of Marian history.[81]

As Isabel traveled around Castile to receive the submission of town after town, she made sure to institute a liturgical celebration of Toro at the shrine of Guadalupe, whose Madonna even more powerfully embodied the continuum between the Visigothic past, the royal present, and victories over God's enemies. The Jeronymite friars who tended the famous image of Mary had not all supported Isabel, and the community had even benefited from the largesse of her enemy, Alfonso V of Portugal. It was important to the queen to secure the allegiance of this influential and quintessentially royal monastery and to gain the sanction of its Virgin.

Isabel got what she wanted when she visited Guadalupe in 1477. During her stay, the friars offered prayers of thanksgiving to their Virgin for the triumph at Toro. As they pronounced these words that declared their Madonna to be Isabel's patron, they would have realized that they were also admitting the queen's right to the throne, for Mary could only be on the side of justice. Isabel asked to be received as the Jeronymites' spiritual affiliate. Then she openly hitched her royal destiny to the Virgin by providing revenues to support annual liturgical services at Guadalupe that would honor the Madonna and commemorate Toro. Over the next few years, Isabel would return often to the shrine, turning the monastery and her devotion to its Virgin into a platform for her cause.[82]

A further stop on the queen's 1477 tour of her intended realm brought her to Seville, another place where Mary proffered the legitimating power of reconquest history. In July, Isabel entered the city in a ceremony at least as elaborate as the one at Toledo. It would have been logical for her to visit the city's cathedral and give thanks for the victory at Toro before the crowned Marian statue watching over the tombs of Ferdinand III, Beatrice, and Alfonso X and thus to lay immediate claim to the collective charisma of these monarchs, celestial and earthly. In any case, one of the first things Isabel did during her prolonged stay in Seville was to establish a new liturgical feast in honor of Toro. Every March on the battle's anniversary, the queen decreed, Sevilleans were to listen to a sermon praising Saints James and Michael for their military aid and then offer prayers to God and the Virgin, asking them to bless the royal family.[83]

The beautifully illuminated document recording this feast's foundation left no doubt that Mary was as intimately connected to the ritual celebration of Isabel's victory as she was to the memory of the monarchs buried in Seville's cathedral. Inside the broad curves of its heavily decorated initial letter, the Queen of Heaven sits on a golden throne wearing a heavy crown and a royal blue cloak.[84] In her arms is her son, clad in almost nothing but a halo. He extends his fingers in a gesture of blessing toward a kneeling woman dressed in gold—Isabel. The queen's hands are raised in prayer and her head is bare. Her crown rests at the Virgin's feet, its gold fleur-de-lys only slightly less impressive than those adorning the Madonna's own diadem. This illumination proclaims that Mary and her son are the true guardians of Isabel's crown and the authors of the triumph that had helped the queen secure it.

The similarity between the headpieces belonging to the two queens even suggests that Isabel is in some ways Mary's likeness on earth and thus an indisputably legitimate sovereign.[85] It was an audacious idea, almost flirting with blasphemy, which marked much other Isabelline propaganda. The men who crafted the queen's image during the succession struggle energetically promoted the notion that she was a new Virgin Mary, who had come into the world to rescue Castile from the moral decay into which it had fallen under its previous ruler, Enrique IV, a king whom the queen's party slurred as an effeminate sodomite. Elevating Isabel as Mary also promised to mitigate the anxieties provoked by the paradox of sovereign power being invested in a woman.[86]

After 1479, the queen's propagandists could put their Marian rhetoric to other uses. In that year, Isabel and Ferdinand emerged victorious in the succession crisis when Alfonso V of Portugal agreed to renounce both his betrothal to Juana and his support of her struggle to gain her father's crown. Stripped of most of her titles under the agreement's terms, Juana would spend the rest of her life in a Portuguese nunnery. Free to consolidate their power and pour their energies into new enterprises, Ferdinand and Isabel armed an expedition in 1480 to relieve the Mediterranean island of Rhodes, then under siege by the Ottoman Turks.[87] Two years later, they turned their eyes toward Granada.

In the decades since Ferdinand of Antequera's victories, Castile's rulers had sought truce more often than war with their Muslim neighbor, although skirmishes along the frontier had continued.[88] Then, in the 1460s and 1470s, Castilian aristocrats captured important cities from the Nasrids. But bold offensives mounted by Granada caused Castile to lose territory too. In 1481–1482, Muslim forces recaptured Zahara de la Sierra, the Andalusian stronghold that Ferdinand de Antequera had won for Castile decades earlier. This defeat goaded Ferdinand and Isabel into taking up arms against Granada. In 1482, they petitioned the pope to declare their war against the Nasrid kingdom a crusade. A decade of campaigns followed, during which Castilian forces laid siege to

Granada's cities and towns, ratcheting up the earlier practice of draining the enemy kingdom's lifeblood by burning its fields and chopping down groves of carefully tended olive and mulberry trees. Ferdinand and Isabel also divided in order to conquer, pursuing strategic and sometimes secret alliances with disaffected members of Granada's deeply factionalized ruling house. One by one, the Muslim kingdom's major cities surrendered or were taken by the Christian besiegers.[89]

As the Catholic Monarchs engineered Granada's military destruction, they often looked to the future, as did many of their subjects. Theirs was an era of rampant prophecy and wild apocalyptic expectation, nurtured by the intense fears aroused across western Christendom by the fall of Constantinople to the Ottoman Turks in 1453. The thought of this quintessentially imperial Christian city, a treasure house of holy relics second only to Jerusalem, in Muslim hands was deeply disturbing. The loss of Constantinople was also a wake-up call, for it brought the Turks alarmingly close to the frontiers of western Europe. To many Christians, it seemed that an apocalyptic struggle between their faith and Islam was at hand. Some people hoped for a new crusade, one that might even be led by the emperor of last days, foretold for centuries by Christian prophecy, the world ruler who would take Jerusalem in anticipation of Christ's second coming, or as an Aragonese version put it, the king who would crush Islam as easily as a bat eats mosquitoes.

Court writers in Aragon and Castile declared that this long-awaited ruler had come to life in the person of Ferdinand II, who enthusiastically donned the cloak of apocalyptic emperor.[90] Nobles and lesser folk eager to flatter the king proclaimed that this lofty destiny had been predicted by the utterances of saints.[91] According to one Aragonese man, the Virgin herself had foretold that Ferdinand would conquer the Holy Land.[92] Mary invoked the same apocalyptic project when she appeared in a vision to one of Castile's most powerful nobles, Rodrigo Ponce de León, Marquis of Cádiz. Predicting victory for Rodrigo in an upcoming battle, the Virgin announced that his triumph would be the "knife-edge and beginning of the whole destruction of the kingdom of Granada and of all Moors in the world."[93]

If Mary had a part in these visions of the future that Ferdinand and Isabel intended to realize through their Granadan wars, she also was present as they sought the sanction of the past. During the years that the Catholic Monarchs fought to make Granada their own, they pressed into service the Marian history of reconquest that they had so carefully cultivated in the 1470s. In 1482, as Ferdinand and Isabel returned north from their first major Granadan expedition, they stopped in the hills of Extremadura to pray before the Virgin of Guadalupe, whose legendary history emphatically demonstrated the justice of their desire to make all of Spain Christian territory. The wealth that her monastery had

accumulated through pilgrims' offerings and the Jeronymites' astute management of their revenues would even help finance the royal crusade against the
Nasrids.[94]

In the first half of the sixteenth century, a friar of Guadalupe wrote that during
their Granadan wars, "Don Ferdinand and Doña Isabel, because of their devotion to Our Lady, came many times to this her house and entrusted themselves
to her in all their enterprises and thus they enjoyed her favor in all the things they
did."[95] This was a fairly accurate characterization of the shrine's place in the crusading monarchs' affections. As one late fifteenth-century visitor to Guadalupe
reported, Isabel was wont to say that at the monastery, she felt she "was in her
paradise." She even had her own oratory high above the church choir, which
doubtless afforded her a privileged view of the famous Madonna.[96]

The monarchs returned to Guadalupe in 1486 and again in 1489 on their way
southward for the campaigning season. By then, they could inspect the progress on an imposing royal residence attached to the monastery, a construction
project begun at their command in 1487. Isabel must have been pleased when
she and Ferdinand could finally stay in their elegant new quarters at Guadalupe.
Testimony that the Catholic Monarchs' love for this monastery and its Virgin
rivaled Alfonso XI's own, Isabel and Ferdinand's visits to Guadalupe and their
establishment of a residence there showed that as crusaders against the Nasrids,
they remained in firm command of the Visigothic Marian connection they had
established in the 1470s.[97]

During their Granadan campaigning years, the monarchs would also repeatedly stop in Seville. There they would imitate Ferdinand of Antequera and summon the legacy of Ferdinand III, who reigned over the vision of reconquest
history cherished in their realm. Already in 1477, Isabel had witnessed the
elaborate ceremonies with which Seville annually celebrated its centuries-old
reincorporation into Christendom through the saintly king's sword.[98] After the
Catholic Monarchs secured Castile and began their own war against al-Andalus,
they often came to Seville to share in the civic rites extolling the virtues of a crusader king from the past; 1484, 1490, 1499, and 1501 saw them in the city for
these festivities. The city's archbishop even tried to recruit Ferdinand II to the
cause of canonizing Seville's conqueror, pointing to all that the ruler of the present owed to the monarch of the past: his name, his lineage, and the very *tierra*
he ruled.[99]

The archbishop's sermon probably fell on receptive ears. Isabel and Ferdinand
were convinced they were Ferdinand III's heirs, as they flamboyantly demonstrated in 1484. A Polish visitor to Seville recorded how during the pageantry of
the feast days honoring Ferdinand III's triumph, he saw the Catholic Monarchs
solemnly ride through the city's streets, preceded by a man carrying a sword that
was "short, badly made, dirty, black and old."[100] It was this unprepossessing blade,

the Pole learned, that had severed Seville from its Islamic past so many centuries ago. Like Ferdinand of Antequera, Ferdinand and Isabel must have hoped the relic would lend its power to their own expeditions against the Muslims and cast its saintly owner's ever larger halo over their endeavors.

The Catholic Monarchs doubtless realized that the famed sword brought with it Mary's blessing on their wars. By the end of the fifteenth century, Ferdinand III's reputation as the Virgin's devotee had attained nearly epic proportions, as evinced by an elaborate Marian military fable circulating in Seville that became inseparable from the saintly king's heroic biography. Hieronymus Münzer, a sharp-eyed German physician who composed a detailed account of his travels through Aragon and Castile, heard this story when he toured Seville's cathedral in 1494. In the royal chapel, he lingered before the tombs of Ferdinand III, Beatrice, and Alfonso X, no longer arrayed in the setting conceived by Alfonso X, but not yet moved into the nearly completed Gothic building that would replace the city's old mosque-cathedral.[101] While Münzer admired the statues of the three monarchs and the crowned Virgin, the cathedral guardians, or perhaps some local who served as his guide, told him about the Madonna's role in Ferdinand III's rescue of Seville from centuries of Muslim domination.[102]

Ferdinand III, Münzer was told, had been passionately devoted to Mary and believed "firmly" that she would help him take Seville from the Muslims. And so the king had a wooden statue made of her, with Jesus sitting on its lap. The Muslim city also had an image of the Virgin, an old one "in their mosque which they had taken from Christians." This Madonna in the mosque stood for Seville's true nature as a Christian city, defying the centuries of Muslim rule, just like the Marian statue unearthed at Guadalupe. Münzer does not say if it was the mosque's image of Mary or Ferdinand's own that figured in heaven-sent instructions the king received one night. In a dream, the ruler was admonished to focus his devotion on "this image" of the Madonna and that he would shortly take Seville. The king obeyed and a few days later captured the city. From then on, Ferdinand's devotion to Mary knew no bounds, as did his conviction that her image could bring him victory. He declared the wooden Madonna his battle talisman and always brought her along on his expeditions against the Muslims, even carrying her right onto the field in a litter of gold and silver. This statue of Mary so beloved by Ferdinand III was, Münzer learned, none other than the image that sat resplendent before the royal tombs—a thirteenth-century Madonna who probably already bore the richly allusive title of "the Virgin of the Kings."[103] Although the German did not mention this name, he remarked on the statue's jointed limbs, one of Our Lady of the Kings' striking features.[104] He also commented on the Madonna's heavy crown made from "purest gold, with emeralds, pearls and other jewels," a description that matches the diadem that the regally titled Virgin wore until it was stolen from her in 1873.[105]

Münzer's account is among the earliest extant renderings of the Marian legend that would become an indelible part of Ferdinand III's identity as a saintly warrior. But it is not the only one. The Catholic Monarchs might have known the story of how the Madonna had helped their ancestor vanquish his unbelieving foes as it was told by another Castilian writing in the 1490s. Lauding "the very saintly king Ferdinand" as a chivalric hero who was "very devoted to Our Lady," this author described how, on the eve of Seville's surrender, Mary had appeared to the monarch and handed him the keys to the city.[106] However the story was told, it proclaimed that the greatest triumph of the iconic reconquest king was indisputably the Virgin's victory, a message reinforced in later centuries by some of Spain's most accomplished Baroque painters.[107]

As the Catholic Monarchs paraded through Seville's streets behind Ferdinand III's sword in 1484, they laid claim to this venerable alliance between Mary and heroic crusading rulers. Some of their subjects were keen to see it as a partnership that persisted in the present, including Pedro Marcuello, a civic official of the Aragonese town of Calatorau and a member of the lower nobility, who composed some overblown verse in honor of Ferdinand and Isabel and their wars against al-Andalus. As he put it in an apostrophe to the rulers: "Make war [against Granada] and prosecute the feud with great fervor, because the Virgin without blemish will be part of your armed company and she will always favor you!"[108] Marcuello reiterated this sentiment so often that it reads as a refrain in his verse; the rulers, the poet repeatedly told the Virgin, "make this war to serve you."[109] The centerpiece of his poetic work was a seventeen-folio long version of the Ave Maria, a prayer known to most high medieval Christian.[110] Marcuello turned its sonorous praises of Mary into a litany of war chanted on behalf of Ferdinand and Isabel. Then, after performing the same martial alchemy on that famous Marian hymn, the Salve Regina, the poet closed his verse with words from the Virgin herself. Speaking to Isabel and Ferdinand, she predicts that they will conquer the Holy Land and make all of its mosques into churches.[111]

If the king and queen ever leafed through the sumptuous presentation copy of Marcuello's oeuvre sent to them in 1502, they probably admired the manuscript's full-page illuminations. Many depicted the saint whom Marcuello's poetry presented as the patron of their crusade, while others flattered Ferdinand and Isabel with their own royal countenances.[112] One of the painted folios brought both sorts of majesty together. In it, Isabel, wearing a crown on her red-blonde hair, is enthroned under a green pavilion.[113] Gold letters border the canopy's top edge, forming a litany of sacred names: "Mary, Jesus, Mary, Jesus . . . " If this legend identifies the heavenly rulers who watch over the queen, a frieze behind the royal tent suggests that Isabel was a new Virgin Mary, an idea still popular among royal propagandists during the years of the Granadan campaigns. Inscribed along its length are the opening words to the Ave Maria.[114] This conceit of Isabel as

Madonna, which Marcuello also applied to his celebration of the energetic involvement of both women in the Granadan campaigns, helped him heighten the messianic quality of the Catholic Monarchs' martial mission.[115]

Sometime during the Granadan wars, a painter working at the behest of the community of nuns of Las Huelgas produced an image showing how, as the champion of Christianity, the queen literally wore Mary's mantle. Sometimes called the *Mater Omnium*, this painting depicts a very regal Madonna, complete with crown and majestic gold and blue robe (Figure 2.4). Sovereign and serene, she may indeed be the "mother of all," but here she singles out a select coterie

Figure 2.4 Mater Omnium. Las Huelgas de Burgos, Spain. Art Resource, NY.

that includes Ferdinand and Isabel. This Virgin extends her cape to enfold on the one side the kneeling royal family and, on the other, a group of nuns clad in the black and white robes of Las Huelgas' residents. In the world beyond Mary's embrace, two black demons race across the landscape. One hurls arrows at the faithful gathered beneath the cloak of protection, but the Virgin, who already grasps in each hand a bundle of shafts with their tips facing downward, will doubtless catch them. With this gesture, the Queen of Heaven reproduces the heraldic device of the earthly queen, for Isabel's emblem was a sheaf of arrows tied together facing down. Here Mary mirrors Isabel such that the queen of Castile's terrestrial campaigns against the enemies of Christianity fuse with the Virgin's celestial battles against the forces of evil.[116] Late medieval viewers of the *Mater Omnium* probably got the point. Pedro Marcuello expressed an opinion shared by many of his Christian contemporaries when he said that the arrows of the queen's heraldic device were aimed right at the kingdom of Granada.[117]

Given Mary's place in the royal ideology of the Granadan crusade, it is not surprising that the king and queen felt her presence when they took the field. The centuries since Las Navas de Tolosa had taught Christian monarchs to expect her military aid against al-Andalus. When Isabel and Ferdinand sent the pope a letter in 1485 celebrating their recent capture of Ronda and Marbella, they assured him that, "with the aid of God and the glorious Virgin his mother," they intended to "continue their conquest until they had gained the whole kingdom" of Granada.[118] Court writers repeatedly described how during the campaigns, Ferdinand and his high-ranking knights expressed their confidence that God, Mary, and Santiago would grant them victory.[119] War banners bearing Mary's image, at least once twinned with the royal arms of Castile, reminded the monarchs' forces of her patronage.[120] Sometimes these banners even reigned over conquered Muslim communities. A Christian chronicler reported that when in April 1487 Isabel and Ferdinand rode up the steep streets of Vélez-Málaga to take possession of this hilltop town, "[a] banner of Our Lady and [a] standard of Santiago" were at their side. Trumpets blew as the cloth images of the saints were raised over Vélez's castle and the royal guidon installed below them.[121]

Following in their ancestors' footsteps, Ferdinand and Isabel thanked the saints who brought them victory. After the triumphs of 1485, the king went to Córdoba, knelt below the elegant red and white horseshoe arches of the city's old Marian cathedral-mosque, and offered his grateful prayers to God, the Virgin, and Santiago.[122] Ferdinand, often accompanied by Isabel, also staged more dramatic ceremonies of thanksgiving in cathedrals that had only recently come to bear the Madonna's name. At the monarchs' orders, bishops consecrated the *jamis* of Alhama (1482), Álora (1484), Ronda (1485), Loja (1486), Vélez-Málaga (1487), and Málaga (1487), converting them all into Mary's cathedrals in a tidal wave of ritual that kept pace with the advance of the frontier.[123]

In making mosques into Mary's churches, Ferdinand and Isabel were following well-established royal custom. Yet the king and queen surpassed even those great monarchs of reconquest history, Ferdinand III and James I, in the quantity of architectural offerings to her. This escalation in the Virgin's role in the Christianization of Islam's territory was partly a function of the war's swift progress as the monarchs' troops neared the Nasrids' capital city. These new Marian cathedrals also appear to have been key to the strategy that Isabel and Ferdinand adopted in order to heighten the effect of their *entradas* into defeated Granadan towns. By centering the ceremonies on buildings that had just been transferred from Muhammad's jurisdiction to Mary's, they could hammer home the message of Christian dominion, as reports of the thanksgiving celebrations with which the monarchs concluded their siege of Málaga in 1487 suggest.

The months during which the Christian forces had encircled this immensely wealthy Mediterranean port city had been traumatic for both sides. The siege lasted much longer than Ferdinand and Isabel expected, costing them time, money, and men. Málaga's lord, confident that his city's extensive fortifications would defeat the attackers, had rejected the humiliating terms proposed by the Catholic Monarchs at the start of the siege. Málaga's inhabitants paid the price. Many starved to death, while slavery awaited those who survived to see the Christians march into the city in August.

Isabel and Ferdinand were determined to celebrate their dearly won victory in the building whose fate unequivocally embodied Málaga's change of fortunes, its *'jami*. Founded by an Umayyad ruler in the ninth century, this building became Mary's cathedral at the orders of Málaga's new lords. A Castilian chronicler wrote that Ferdinand and Isabel even deliberately delayed their *entrada* into the conquered city to give their prelates time to consecrate the mosque to the Virgin; the king and queen, he said, wanted to be able "to go there first to pray."[124] This author added that the monarchs were also waiting for the heaps of corpses rotting in the summer heat to be removed and the stink of death to be chased from Málaga's streets. After the city was made pure, the bishops performed the ritual that cleansed the mosque from the pollution of Islam and rendered it Mary's church. Only then did Isabel and Ferdinand, accompanied by their retinues and various dignitaries, enter Málaga. Another Christian chronicler described how as the monarchs rode into the city, its remaining inhabitants were trudging in the opposite direction, herded into captivity by the victors. This spectacle of human misery hardly dampened the victory celebrations. Upon setting foot in Málaga, Isabel, her daughter, and their entourages fell to their knees and offered thanks to God, Mary, and Santiago, while bishops solemnly intoned the *Te Deum* and Christian banners waved from the citadel.[125] The king and queen paraded through the city toward the new cathedral of Our Lady, where they heard Mass.[126]

Ferdinand chose to end his elaborate *entradas* into some other defeated Muslim cities at their equally new church-mosques of Our Lady.[127] Such buildings remained the stage for royal rites of possession well after the king's departure. Castilian chroniclers detailed how Isabel provided the necessary liturgical furnishings—bells, chalices, crosses, books, holy images—for Mary's cathedral-mosques in Alhama, Loja, Ronda, and Vélez-Málaga.[128] With these gifts, Isabel displayed the pious generosity befitting a Christian ruler, while at the same time marking these buildings as monuments to the monarchs' victories. The queen also adroitly cast herself as a Christianizer who was the equal of her husband. Ferdinand might have had the more active part in the military victories over the Nasrids, but Isabel ensured that Granada's religious landscape became identifiably Christian. The queen even fashioned some of the liturgical items (doubtless vestments or altar cloths, as embroidery was a pastime of queens and noblewomen) for Alhama's mosque-cathedral of Our Lady with "her own hands," wrote one chronicler. Isabel graced it with this honor, he said, because it "was the first church she founded in the first place won during this conquest."[129]

In the last and most important place that the Catholic Monarchs took during their crusade—the city of Granada—Mary would acquire more than one such church. By 1491, Ferdinand and Isabel were closing in on the Nasrid capital. In April, they laid siege to the city. They oversaw military operations from a fortified town they erected on the plains just to the west of Granada. Named Santa Fe ("Holy Faith") and designed to accommodate not only the monarchs and the war tents of their army but also houses for future settlers, it announced to Granada's inhabitants that the Christians were there to stay.[130] From Santa Fe's towers, Isabel and Ferdinand had a clear view of the ochre walls of the Alhambra, the palace-city that would soon be theirs.

As the winter of 1491–1492 approached and Granada's residents—even the rich ones, wrote one Muslim chronicler—increasingly suffered the ravages of hunger, the last Nasrid sultan came to terms with the besiegers.[131] On January 2, 1492, Isabel and Ferdinand made their formal entrance into the city. According to a Christian eyewitness, the monarchs' banners, along with ones bearing the cross and images of Santiago, were hoisted high in one of the Alhambra's towers. From the same turret, a Christian herald shouted out across the city words that proclaimed Mary part of the celestial triumvirate who had led the rulers to victory: "Santiago, Santiago, Santiago, Castile, Castile, Castile, Granada, Granada, Granada, for those very exalted and powerful lords Don Ferdinand and Doña Isabel, king and queen of Spain, who have won from the infidel Moors this city of Granada and all its realm, with the aid of God and of the glorious Virgin, his mother, and of the blessed apostle Santiago, and with the aid of the most holy pope."[132]

Mary had helped the Catholic Monarchs become Granada's masters and bring to an end the 781-year history of al-Andalus. She herself became the mistress of what had been the Nasrids' personal mosque in the Alhambra. Admiring the fabled beauty of the palace's chambers and courtyards, Ferdinand and Isabel declared it one of their official residences and had the royal mosque baptized in Mary's name. When Hieronymus Münzer visited this new church in 1494, he marveled at it, describing it as "proud and noble" and "most beautiful."[133] In the Nasrids' day, lamps seven and a half feet long had hung from the mosque's ceiling. Sheltering faceted prisms under metal shades as delicate as lacework, they cast rainbows of light onto the ornate mosaics adorning the walls. Mary's magnificent church in the Alhambra would serve as the seat of Granada's archbishop until 1502, when it lost the title of cathedral to a mosque-church of Our Lady located in the city sprawling beneath the palace's massive walls.[134]

As Ferdinand and Isabel put the final touches on the Marian churchscape they created from so many mosques of the Nasrids' former kingdom, they did not forget those places further to the north where, they believed, the Madonna had for centuries preserved Spain's essential Christianity. On the same day that Granada officially became part of Castile, the queen composed a letter to the prior of Guadalupe. According to a late sixteenth-century member of the community, Isabel wrote both to announce the good news that all of Spain now belonged to Christendom and to request that the prior offer praises to the Madonna enshrined in his church "in recognition of how the victory and glorious triumph over the kingdom [of Granada] came from her generous hand." The text of the letter itself was more ambiguous, seemingly referring to God as the author of Granada's fall. Yet the queen's missive arrived at Guadalupe accompanied by a sizable portion of the plunder seized from the Nasrids, just the sort of trophies with which Christian warriors often rewarded their saintly patrons. Isabel's victory offering to the Virgin included weapons of exquisite manufacture, probably some of the renowned swords forged in Granada's smithies, their hilts and scabbards encrusted with elaborate metalwork worthy of the ornament on the Alhambra's walls. Displayed among Guadalupe's other treasures until at least the late sixteenth century, the battle spoils reminded pilgrims of the monarchs' esteem for Our Lady of Guadalupe and commemorated her role in Granada's demise.[135] In June 1492, Isabel and Ferdinand came to the shrine to express their gratitude in person to the Madonna whose history had predicted the inevitability and justice of the conquest they had achieved six months earlier.[136] There they prayed before the statue of Mary that had anchored their wars against Granada in the mythic continuum of an eternal Christian Spain, stretching back beyond Salado to the days of the Visigothic kings.

After Granada's defeat, the connection between the Virgin of Guadalupe and Castile's crusading rulers seemed timeless to some of Isabel and Ferdinand's contemporaries. When Münzer visited the shrine in 1495, he toured its sacristy and admired the opulent liturgical furnishings neatly organized in boxes and chests: vestments and altar cloths of gold brocade, along with crosses, candelabra, and chalices, most made from gold or silver and some decorated with precious stones. As the German contemplated this show of wealth that led him to conclude "not the least of the treasures of the kings of Castile is this monastery," his eyes were drawn to a "great cross... of purest gold which the king of Castile gave to the blessed Virgin [in gratitude] for a certain victory."[137] Münzer did not specify which Castilian ruler or which victory, perhaps because he did not know or perhaps because it did not matter. Collapsed into this golden cross were all the moments of the Virgin of Guadalupe's battlefield aid to the long line of monarchs who had been so generous to her monastery.

Mary's patronage of the monarchs who led the reconquest may have seemed eternal, but it was not. Its long history had a beginning—probably in July 1212, when Alfonso VIII's Marian war banner had presided over a Christian crusading coalition's defeat of the Almohad caliph at Las Navas de Tolosa, the first time a ruler so visibly declared faith in the Virgin's military aid in an explicitly crusading context. During the centuries between that Christian victory and Isabel and Ferdinand's triumphant entry into Granada in January 1492, many Castilian rulers and at least two kings of Aragon had practiced their own versions of Marian monarchy. They drew the Virgin into their understanding of themselves as the royal captains of the reconquest and into their strategies to proclaim even the most freshly conquered corners of their realms as Christian. Appointed the saintly guardian of many mosques made into churches, Mary helped rulers fulfill their task of Christianizing Muslim territory, a responsibility she bore beginning with Alfonso VI's conquest of Toledo in 1085. By the mid-fourteenth century, as she started to feature in stories insisting on the immutable Christian nature of Castile's very soil, a Marian vision of history joined with that of the realm's present to predict a firmly Christian future for the lands ruled by her crowned devotees.

It was doubtless easier for an earthly queen to see herself in the Queen of Heaven than it was for a king to find his likeness in the Madonna—both Isabel and Mary were women enjoying exalted status, if in rather different ways. Yet male monarchs too admired their reflections in Mary's haloed majesty. As these men exercised their royal duty and waged war against al-Andalus with the Virgin's patronage, they had an advantage that Isabel's sex denied to her. They were, after all, as much knights as they were monarchs, and Mary especially loved the men of chivalry, whatever their rank, who fought Muslims in her name.

3

In a Man's World

In 1488, Rodrigo Ponce de León, the marquis of Cádiz and the middle-aged but still vigorous scion of a noble family that controlled much of southern Andalusia, clattered into Guadalupe with a train of fifty pack animals. Each of them was probably loaded with plunder from a recent string of successful campaigns against the Nasrids during which this proud aristocrat had seconded the Catholic Monarchs. Grey had perhaps begun to tinge the marquis' red hair, but he was as vigorous in battle as ever.[1] He came to the shrine of Guadalupe as a victorious crusader eager to fulfill a vow to Mary.[2] Rodrigo was a deeply religious man. Though short-tempered and possessing little tolerance for some of the more tedious pastimes enjoyed by his social peers, the marquis impressed his contemporaries with his ability to kneel patiently during the Mass he insisted on hearing every day.[3] Yet as he bent his knees before the Virgin of Guadalupe and made rich offerings to her, he might have admitted to himself that some politics mingled with his pilgrim's piety.

For years the marquis had contributed his military talents, his wealth, and his men to Ferdinand and Isabel's wars against Granada. But during the succession crisis of the 1470s, he had been on the wrong side. By the time he arrived in Guadalupe, he had done much to repair his relations with the Catholic Monarchs. In 1486, Rodrigo had even publicized his loyalty to the crown by circulating a letter among his fellow Castilian magnates that called on them to recognize Ferdinand as the emperor of prophecy who would "destroy all the Moors."[4] Now two years later, the marquis openly professed his devotion to the Madonna who ranked so high in Isabel and Ferdinand's affections.

Politically expedient as Rodrigo's pilgrimage to Guadalupe was, it was also a sincere expression of one of his fundamental character traits. The marquis "was very devoted to Our Lady Saint Mary," the chronicler Andrés Bernáldez wrote.[5] The Catholic Monarchs themselves recognized his love for the Virgin.[6] Rodrigo's life story reveals that Mary belonged as squarely to the ethos of the knights who fought against Granada as she did to the royal ideology of reconquest.

The deeply flattering biography of the marquis composed shortly after his death in 1492 etched a portrait of him as "the man of our time most devoted to the Virgin Mary" and as a knight driven by the sole ambition to "inflict as much harm as possible on the Moors" in the "service of God and of His blessed mother the Virgin Mary and of the royal crown."[7] The anonymous author set the tone with his description of the marquis' lineage. Glossing over Rodrigo's birth as an illegitimate child, the biographer made him into the spiritual heir of generations of Spanish Christian heroes who had "defended and exalted the holy catholic faith against the Moors and infidel, enemies of the faith of Jesus Christ."[8] Included in this brotherhood of Christian bravery that stretched back to the Visigoths were two men whom the biographer vaunted as sharing Rodrigo's love for the Virgin.[9] One of these Marian paladins of the past was the great leading man of royal reconquest history, Ferdinand III of Castile. The other was a knight and a noble like Rodrigo: Don Pelayo Correa, a thirteenth-century master of the military Order of Santiago, who enjoyed a posthumous reputation as the epitome of chivalry.[10] If, by the fifteenth century, Christian kings could look back over the long centuries of the reconquest to find among their predecessors Marian heroes upon which to model themselves, so too could knights.

To style Don Pelayo Correa "a devotee of Our Lady the Virgin Mary," the marquis of Cádiz's biographer ornamented his portrait of Rodrigo's spiritual ancestor-at-arms with an anecdote about a legendary frontier skirmish.[11] Late one day, Don Pelayo and his men clashed with Muslim forces on the crest of a hill. The master of Santiago soon realized that night would fall before he could finish off the enemy. He rode out of the scrum, dismounted, knelt, and implored Mary to "stop the day" and speed him to victory. Heeding his prayers, she halted the sun. This miracle story vaulted Don Pelayo into the ranks of those heroes whom God had graced with the same battlefield favor: the biblical Joshua, leader of the Israelites (Joshua 10:12–13), and the Frankish emperor Charlemagne in his epic incarnation in the *Song of Roland*.[12] It also substituted the Madonna for God as controller of the skies and patron of righteous warriors and demonstrated that knights could star in the Marian vision of reconquest history.

The marquis of Cádiz, wrote his biographer, proved worthy of this Marian heroic heritage. The writer reveals little of Rodrigo's childhood, save that he always humbly obeyed his father and that beginning at age nine, he virtuously honored all of the Virgin's feast days by fasting.[13] A few years later, it became evident just how close the marquis was to the saint in whose name he would launch so many campaigns against Granada. As Rodrigo grew into an adolescent itching to show off his knightly prowess, he made Mary his confidante. In his late teens, he began to pray "secretly" twice daily before an image of her, begging her to grant his wish to "participate in some battle against the unbelieving Moors."[14]

One day, as Rodrigo repeated his pious petition, he was rewarded by a vision of Mary. Addressing Rodrigo affectionately as "good knight, my devotee," she told him that his faith and constancy had impressed her. She and Christ had therefore decided that he would always be the "victor" whenever he fought against Muslims.

Neither this vision of Mary, nor an equally hawkish one that the biographer says Rodrigo later experienced, figures in other Christian chronicles of the Granadan wars. Perhaps this episode in the marquis' life was invented by a biographer bold enough to pilfer from the apparition genre in order to enhance his chivalric subject. In late medieval Castile and Aragon, visions of Mary usually blessed either animal herders or men and women following the religious life, not high-ranking knights.[15] But it is entirely possible that the story originated with Rodrigo himself. This Marian vision reflects what must have been a dream common among young knights: to know that they had been specially chosen to perform deeds of valor.

Rodrigo's military career was almost as successful as the Virgin had predicted. During the decades when he reaped victory after victory over Granada, he never lost the Marian fervor of his adolescence. According to his biographer, on his expeditions against the Nasrids, Rodrigo often called on the Madonna and God for help. Such invocations, whether private prayers or battlefield speeches, resound throughout the biography, as do the marquis' fervent expressions of gratitude to the same celestial duo for his triumphs.[16] Yet if God's name was often on his lips, the marquis was Mary's man. It was to the Virgin that Rodrigo made his victory offerings, it was in her honor that he and his wife commissioned masses to celebrate his triumphs, it was to her shrines that he went as a pilgrim after battle, and it was she who sent Saints James, George, and Eustace to his rescue in one particularly fierce skirmish with Granada.[17] When the marquis came to another turning point in his life after some twenty years of campaigning, Mary appeared once again to offer her guidance.

In 1482, Rodrigo organized his forces for an assault on the Granadan town of Alhama. This audacious opening salvo in Ferdinand and Isabel's crusade against their Muslim neighbors could easily have backfired. Because Alhama lay deep inside the Nasrid kingdom, the attackers would be exposed as they advanced toward their target. Some fifty kilometers southeast of Granada, this town surrounded by ravines and river gorges protected the principal road connecting Málaga and the Nasrid caspital. With its natural defenses and manmade fortifications, Alhama could have held out for a long time against Rodrigo, if its residents had known of his plans. But he unleashed his offensive on an unsuspecting population. The lightly guarded town quickly fell to his men. Almost immediately, however, the besiegers became the besieged, as Granadan troops arrived to recapture Alhama.

After gruesome deaths on both sides, the Christians won a pyrrhic victory. Yet Rodrigo's biographer clothed the whole campaign in glory by describing how Mary had urged the attack on Alhama. Before embarking on this risky operation, wrote the author, the marquis did not know whether to trust his scouts' reports about the town's vulnerability. So, late one night, Rodrigo took counsel with his best military advisor. In the room where he was accustomed to perform his devotions before an image of Mary, he knelt, raised his hands in prayer and beseeched her to reveal the "truth." She appeared, assured him that he would conquer Alhama, and instructed him to turn its mosque into her church. Predicting that this Christian triumph would trigger Granada's downfall, the Virgin announced: "Know that you will prevail with a great victory and that in the thick of battle I will be with you."[18]

Mary's rousing words eloquently capture her importance to Rodrigo's self-image as a Christian knight. Uttered only ten years before the Nasrid capital would fall to Ferdinand and Isabel, they also articulated the belief that a man of war did not have to be a king to count on the Virgin for help against Muslim foes. Knights' and soldiers' trust in Mary was evident as early as 1143, when the Christian militias of Toledo, Ávila, and Segovia prayed to her as they gathered to fight the Almoravids on the plains of Montiel. During the hundreds of years separating this brief battlefield invocation of the Virgin from the shrewd war counsel she dispensed to the marquis of Cádiz, she had become an ever more active presence in the wartime experiences of kings and of the less exalted Christian men of war who campaigned against Muslims. Mary's patronage of the reconquest was institutionalized not just by royally founded military and chivalric military orders dedicated to her, but also by similar organizations established in her name by knights or men who aspired to be like them.[19]

This prized intimacy between Mary and Christian men of war—whatever their rank—suggests that in Castile and Aragon, she was becoming as central to the definition of Christian manhood as she was to Christian monarchy, for on the battlefield, men fought not only to defeat their enemies but also to prove themselves as men.

Military Manhood

"The honor of the feminine sex lies in the mother of Christ," declared Saint Augustine.[20] Yet according to an early fifteenth-century Castilian author and man of war named Gutierre Díaz de Games, also residing in Mary was the honor of men who considered themselves the epitome of manliness—knights. God, wrote Gutierre Díaz, had three orders of knights. A holy battle chief (*caudillo*) captained each divinely ordained rank of chivalry. First came the army of angels commanded by the archangel Michael. Next were the martyrs, led in their spiritual battles by the victorious Christ, conqueror of death. Last, but not least, followed the company of "good kings of the land" and "good knights" who wielded their arms to protect the Church, the faith, their king, and his realm. Heading this troop was Mary, attended by a host of angels and saints. As the *caudillo* of this earthly "knighthood of good defenders," she presided over the virtuous campaigns that Gutierre Díaz believed would win men like him a place in heaven.[21]

Appointing Mary to this elevated military grade helped Gutierre Díaz stake out his position in the debate about the nature of knighthood that raged so fiercely in his day.[22] If God's mother directed chivalric feats of arms, then such deeds surely lent as much luster to knighthood as did the book learning so highly prized by some of Gutierre Díaz's contemporaries. More important, by making the Virgin into the *caudillo* of earthly paladins, Gutierre Díaz expressed his belief that *all* men of chivalry, regardless of rank, fought under her command.

A generation later, Ferran Mexía, a Castilian who shared Gutierre Díaz's mastery of sword and pen, repeated this Marian sentiment in a treatise dedicated to Ferdinand II of Aragon and published in 1492. Men readying themselves for the ritual that would make them into knights, wrote Mexía, should spend the eve of the ceremony praying in a church dedicated to Saint James, Saint George, or the Virgin.[23] Mexía obliquely underlined Mary's prominence among these saintly patrons of knighthood when he mentioned that the Cid, the great reconquest hero and popular model of chivalric virtue, had been dubbed in a church of Our Lady.[24] Perhaps some aspiring knights who followed Mexía's advice even chose to perform their vigils in one of the churches in fifteenth-century Castile and Aragon named for a Madonna most sympathetic to men like them, Our Lady the Warrior's Guide.[25]

Gutierre Díaz and Mexía were not the only high medieval authors to weave Mary into their visions of chivalry. Already in the late thirteenth century, the poems of the *Cantigas de Santa María* emphasized Mary's affection for Christian knights. In Alfonso X's miracle collection, the Virgin saves men of war from dishonor or death at their enemies' hand, sorts out their love lives, and enforces their Christian virtue.[26] All across Europe, those aristocrats who embraced the martial virtues of knighthood tended to be Mary's fervent devotees, proclaiming her their special protector.[27] In the looking glass of her nobility, they could gaze at a magnified reflection of the elite status that they themselves enjoyed.[28] Yet the values that knights often strove to embody were as bound up with manliness as they were with nobility. Mary's stature in knightly culture suggests that in her, men of war somehow found confirmation not just of their social rank, but of their manhood itself.

The Castilian and Aragonese kings, knights, and soldiers who fought Muslims in Mary's name would have joined their peers elsewhere in Christian Europe in declaring that they proved their manliness through combat and feats of arms.[29] One of Gutierre Díaz's near contemporaries, the battle-hardened and exquisitely literate marquis of Santillana named Iñigo López de Mendoza, put it well. In a poem chastising knights of his day for preferring talk to action, Iñigo wrote: "It is not in words nor in threats uttered without fierce countenance that noble souls show themselves to be great, strong and virile, brave, bold...let one's acts be not at all base, but virtuous and knightly and let us leave behind feminine weapons, hateful to all warriors."[30]

As Iñigo's words suggest, warfare was a crucible for the forging of ideas about masculinity and femininity.[31] A knight who acted valiantly on the battlefield affirmed his manliness, but lost it if he displayed cowardice: fearful knights are "like women," declared a thirteenth-century Castilian epic.[32] If the prized virtues of courage, battle prowess, and endurance in the face of hardship made one manly, the actual activities of warfare—the right to bear arms, the organized and legitimate shedding of enemy blood—were considered male prerogatives.[33] Although in some medieval frontier societies, the intense militarization of daily life included opening combat roles to women, this was not true in Christian Iberia.[34] Women could not be knights, nor could they belong to the municipal militias of frontier towns or claim a share of spoils from raids into Muslim territory.[35]

To be sure, in emergencies, women would do battle rather than suffer rape or death. Queens and aristocratic women sometimes exercised their powers as lords by sending their vassals into war or even leading troops onto the field, as did Isabel I of Castile during the wars of succession and the campaigns for Granada. Warfare nonetheless remained a matter of manhood. Such women, writers explained, were exceptions proving the rule: shedding feminine fear and vulnerability, they donned virile courage to act like men on the battlefield.[36] So Isabel's chroniclers praised her manly bravery, constructing a portrait of a queen who exhorted her knights with "words more like those of a bold man than of a fearful woman."[37] Ambivalence deeply strains their portrait of Isabel on the battlefield, as it often did descriptions of women who boldly strode into the man's world of warfare.[38] Laudable as such women were for their courage, they threatened the proper order of the sexes. The decidedly Marian twist that writers sometimes gave their accounts of Isabel's role in Granadan campaigns was one rhetorical solution they devised to deal with the ideological challenge posed by a queen who participated in warfare far more actively than women were supposed to: if Isabel was like Mary, who could be present on the battlefield, then the queen had every right to be there too.[39]

Much less culturally problematic was the stance toward war attributed to one of Isabel's predecessors as queen of Castile, Berenguela, wife of Alfonso VII. A mid-twelfth century Castilian chronicle relates how Alfonso once left the city of Toledo in her capable hands when he was off campaigning.[40] The Almoravids took advantage of his absence to besiege the city. Despite the "great crowd" of knights, soldiers, and archers at her disposal, the queen did not engage these Muslims in combat. Instead, she sent a message to the Almoravid leader, asking if he really wished to fight against a woman, an enterprise that, she pointed out, would bring him no honor. Looking up at Toledo's alcazar, he saw Berenguela sitting enthroned among the battlements and surrounded by her female attendants. The Almoravids retreated from this city held by women, "ashamed and humiliated," having won neither "victory nor honor." Summoning the shame that a warrior should feel in fighting women, the queen brandished a weapon as sharp as those of the men under her command.

This face-off between Berenguela and the Almoravids may belong to the domain of legend, but it reveals the deeply engrained belief that a man who raised his sword against a woman jeopardized his honor and his manliness. In medieval Iberia, this belief even cut across religious lines to unite the cultures of Muslim and Christian men of war.[41] Sometimes Christian writers praised the manly valor displayed by Muslim warriors, a favor that Muslim authors could return.[42] Genuine as such expressions of respect could be, they also magnified the victories of one's own forces. Yet both Christian and Muslim chroniclers could vilify the other side by depicting the enemies' ranks as filled with women.[43] Serving the same purpose was Christian rhetoric that stripped Muslim warriors of manliness; the triumph of virile Christian knights over such effeminate foes was as natural as the domination of women by men, and the subordination of Islam by Christianity.[44] Christian authors could even paint Muslim men as effete lovers of other men, whose deviant sexuality sapped their manhood.[45] To further underline the virile strength of Christianity, Christian writers imagined Muslim cities and towns as seductive women eagerly awaiting conquest.[46]

In medieval Castile and Aragon, military manhood was thus doubly prized, signaling the elite stature of a warrior and the natural superiority of Christians over their Muslim foes. As men like Rodrigo Ponce de León strove to embody this ideal on the battlefield, they could turn for inspiration to the holy host of male saintly patrons of warfare. From their youth, aspiring knights learned to emulate these saintly paragons of military manhood. "Take as your example the knight Santiago," the future count of Buelna, Pero Niño, was instructed at age ten. "Every single one of his limbs was cut from him, from his fingers to his toes, one by one, every joint sliced through. But they never could make him deny Jesus Christ. Before this [too] he was strong, like a good knight. That's good triumphant chivalry, that's the way to win the haloed crown which God has promised victors."[47] From this graphic description of steadfast courage, Pero Niño might have learned that virtuous knighthood could be as profound a confession of Christian faith as martyrdom and bring as great a reward. Santiago perfectly modeled such virile Christian chivalry.

Pero Niño's lesson about Santiago as knightly exemplar was recorded by the count's own loyal lieutenant and biographer, Gutierre Díaz de Games. Yet Gutierre Díaz had anointed Mary—and not Santiago—as the *caudillo* of the order of "good defenders" on earth. Like her saintly male peers, as the Virgin commanded her troops, she helped them see themselves as virile Christian men of war. For all her rank in heaven, however, Mary was a woman and so had to resort to different strategies. The men who fought in her name experienced her not as a mirror image of their better selves, but as merciful mother, lady love, and virgin warrior—or even all three at once. Whichever face she turned toward her devotees in the man's world of warfare, they gazed upon a woman who reinforced their manhood and reminded them of their mission to fight Muslims.

Mother of Mercy

"Let us trust in the glorious Virgin, mother [of Christ], that we will be safe and free through her intercession, and that she will help us because she is the mother of mercy."[48] So a late thirteenth-century Castilian chronicler imagined the Visigothic hero Pelagius rallying his handful of men before the legendary battle of Covadonga, where Christians believed they had won their first victory against al-Andalus's forces. By the time this chronicler wrote, legend had gilded Pelagius's every action with the sheen reserved for mythic heroes. Yet this battlefield prayer to Mary as mother of mercy could have been uttered by any of the less fabled Christian men of war who turned to her in high medieval Iberia. These men knew her as a mother whose love never failed her devotees, a belief shared by Christians all across Europe.[49]

Mary often displayed her maternal affection for men of war by exercising her influence as God's mother.[50] Pleading their case with her son, she could persuade him to grant them victory over Muslims. If confidence in Mary's powers as the most efficient intercessor between humans and God tinged the earliest depictions of Christian men invoking her on the battlefield in medieval Iberia, it colored the later Aragonese and Castilian chronicles of war more deeply.[51] At the battle of Salado in 1341, Christian troops even rode to war against their Muslim enemies intoning the *Salve Regina*, a hymn that poignantly voices the longing for Mary's intercession at the court of heaven: "Hail to the Queen of mercy . . . to you we cry out, the exiled children of Eve. To you we sigh, groaning and weeping in this vale of tears. Oh our advocate, turn your merciful eyes toward us."[52]

Military victory actually required Mary's intercession, according to Ferdinand of Antequera. The statutes of his Order of the Jar and Griffin declared that although "full victory lies" in God's "hands," he dispensed such triumph "at the prayers of [his] mother, the most glorious Virgin."[53] Don Pero Niño, whose life Gutierre Díaz de Games chronicled, echoed this sentiment in an epitaph he designed for himself in 1435. He wished his tombstone to read: "Here lies Don Pero Niño, count of Buelna, who through the mercy of God, with the holy Virgin Mary his mother interceding, was always victorious and never defeated, on sea and on land."[54]

Men of war believed that Mary would naturally do everything in her power to help them, for she was the spiritual mother of *all* Christians. As the thirteenth-century Castilian priest Gonzalo de Berceo sighed in his book of Marian praise: "Men and women, we all look to you as mother.... We shall be as your children. Sinners and just people alike, we hope for your mercy."[55] Miracle stories proved the truth of his words, celebrating how Mary embraced even the most wayward of her spiritual children with her boundless mercy and compassion. The Virgin, as Gutierre Díaz wrote, always "help[s] people in grief and distress at the time of their great need."[56]

So when off the coast of North Africa, Pero Niño attacked a Muslim warship and accidentally ended up alone on its prow to face the entire crew, he drew his sword and entrusted himself to the loving mother who never abandoned her devotees. Just as the Muslims were about to fall upon him, he called out Mary's name and made a vow to her.[57] It is easy to imagine the comfort that Pero Niño found in the thought of this heavenly mother watching over him during his struggle on the Muslim galley. When death in battle stalks men as closely as it did the count that day, they often take refuge in fantasies of all-powerful maternal figures.[58] During the reconquest, other Christian men caught in dire combat situations consigned themselves to Mary's care.[59] Confidence in this omnipotent mother's protection helped them to confront their fears and to keep fighting, even when all seemed lost. Immediately after calling on the Virgin, Pero Niño leapt on the Muslims as "boldly as a lion on its prey" according to Gutierre Díaz, and held them off until reinforcements arrived.

Pero Niño triumphed that day. But if he had been defeated and suffered the fate common to Christians and Muslims taken by the enemy in battle—captivity—he might have relied on the mother of mercy to rescue him from his new plight. The shifting configurations of alliances and rivalries among Christian kingdoms, Muslim Granada, and various North African polities all sowed rich crops of captives, as did civil strife within kingdoms. While high-ranking captives might await ransom in comfort befitting their status, most often the human spoils of war were shackled, crowded into prisons, forced to labor, or even sold into slavery.[60] If they were Christians, they might pray for the balm of Mary's mercy to ease their misery.

Christians all across Europe knew that the Virgin's maternal love shattered chains and defied prison walls, bringing solace and freedom to captives. Miracle after miracle demonstrated her compassionate presence in this traumatic arena of wartime experience.[61] By at least the thirteenth century, Castilian and Aragonese knights and soldiers were familiar with her renowned powers of liberation, for the poets who worked on Alfonso X's *Cantigas de Santa María* were able to collect many stories of how "Saint Mary's hands, which directly touched Jesus Christ, can very well free captives from prison."[62] One such poem showing her merciful hands in action featured a squire from Quintanilla de Osoña, a Marian devotee who was taken prisoner while campaigning against the Muslims. Brutally beaten by his captors, he wept piteously and implored the saint he so loved for his freedom. His faith was rewarded when Mary suddenly illuminated his dark prison with her radiance and unlocked his fetters.[63]

The saintly heroine of this *cantiga* was one of Alfonso X's favorites, the Virgin of Villa Sirga.[64] Many other Madonnas in high medieval Iberia enjoyed reputations as specialists in the art of freeing captives.[65] Yet by the late fifteenth century, Our Lady of Guadalupe far outperformed her sisters. The fifteenth- and sixteenth-century compilations of her miracles include tale after tale of how she liberated Christians from their Muslim captors in Granada and on the more distant shores of North Africa.[66] When Rodrigo Ponce de León visited her shrine in 1486, he would have noticed the heaps of shackles that grateful former captives had left as ex-voto offerings. A few years later, Hieronymus Münzer was impressed by the sight of the "innumerable iron fetters" brought to Guadalupe by "captives freed from the Saracens through the intercession of the blessed Virgin."[67] The thicket of chains adorning the shrine even made it into the pages of a novel written by Miguel de Cervantes, a man scarred by the trauma of five years of captivity in Algiers.[68]

"The most merciful Virgin... can leave no one without comfort," explained a late sixteenth-century friar from Guadalupe, as he recounted how she had freed a Christian captive from a "cruel Moor."[69] Cervantes agreed, for he knew from personal experience that captives placed their hopes in Mary as the mother of mercy. At the end of one of his plays set in Muslim North Africa, Christian captives cry out in a sad chorus to "our intercessor, [Christ's] mother who is our mother," begging her to "use mercy" and "free [us] from the hands of these Moors."[70] Here Cervantes applied his literary genius to an idea inherited from the Middle Ages. As liberator of captives, Mary is "the compassionate mother of God" and is "always able to help those in need," wrote Alfonso X's poets in the *Cantigas*.[71] The *cantiga* about the squire from Quintanilla de Osoña even concludes with this former captive arriving at Mary's church in Villa Sirga and brandishing his shattered chains as he shouts: "The Virgin did this, she who helps people in misery."[72]

More than any other saint, Mary possessed the qualities that a Christian captive would desire in a heavenly guardian: a mother's boundless compassion and infinite mercy, along with unrivaled influence in heaven. Although she was not the only wonder-worker in whom captives might place their hopes for freedom, many other saints' reputations as liberators eventually withered, while hers continued to flourish.[73] Mary, in fact, dislodged another saint to become the patron of the Mercedarian friars, a Spanish religious order dedicated to the redemption of captives.

This order owed its existence to Pere Nolasc, a Catalan layman troubled by the plight of Christians captured by Muslims. During the 1230s, Pere began to raise funds to ransom captives, efforts that soon won him and his companions the status of a new religious order. At first, his followers took as their saintly patron Eulalia, a female martyr who had presided over Barcelona's cathedral for centuries. But by the 1240s, Mary seconded Eulalia in the task of assisting the members of this order as they traveled to Granada and North Africa to purchase Christian captives' liberty. Soon, Our Lady of Mercy began to eclipse the Barcelonan saint in the friars' self-image. In painting and sculpture all across high medieval Europe, this increasingly popular Madonna tenderly gathered her devotees beneath her capacious cloak as if returning them to the shelter of the womb.[74] By the fourteenth century, the friars had taken her name, styling themselves the "Order of Saint Mary of Mercy of the Redemption of Captives."[75] They may have done so in part because of a pleasing word play: the Catalan word for "ransom"—mercè—also meant "mercy." Just as important, Our Lady of Mercy's maternal affection stood for the compassionate charity at the heart of the order's mission.

Whether rescuing Christian men of war from the dungeons of Granada and North Africa, protecting them from Muslim enemies on the battlefield, or pleading with her son to gain victory for them, the maternal Mary eschewed the fierceness that mother goddesses and human mothers can summon on behalf of their children.[76] Choosing tenderness instead, she modeled motherhood as infinite love. Thus the mother of God was disarmed of any potential to threaten the masculine pride of the military men in her care.[77]

Drafting Mary's loving maternity into the service of the reconquest even enhanced the masculine solidarity that Christian men of war were to feel for each other and therefore the enmity they were to feel for the Muslims.[78] As the mother of mercy's spiritual sons, Christian warriors became a band of brothers. Outside this kin group lay the enemy. With her trademark cloak, the Madonna of Mercy erected a boundary between her family and its foes. When the fifteenth-century Castilian poet Fernan Pérez de Guzman wrote "may the sweet Virgin Mary cover you with her mantle," he knew that her cloak could not cover everyone.[79] Revealing who was not huddled beneath her cape was often the point of stories and images featuring Our Lady of Mercy, as in Las Huelgas's Isabelline portrait of her (Figure 2.4).[80]

Among those left out in the cold were the Muslims against whom Christian kings and knights fought, according to a poem from the *Cantigas de Santa María*. This *cantiga* recounts a legend that originated centuries earlier in Constantinople. It celebrates how Mary foiled a Muslim siege of the imperial city (probably the blockade of 717–718). Draping her cloak over Constantinople, she fended off the Muslims' weapons and forced the sultan's surrender. In the illumination, Alfonso X's artists painted her cape descending right onto the city walls, its soft folds a stronger bulwark between the Christians and the Muslims than the stone fortifications themselves (Figure 3.1).[81]

The maternal mercy with which Mary embraced captives drew just as firm a line between Christians and Muslims. It is no accident that among the Madonnas most renowned for bursting the bonds of Christian captives was that icon of reconquest history, Our Lady of Guadalupe. Her powers to free Christian men and women from their Muslim captors, wrote one of her sixteenth-century devotees, proved that Christianity was the "true and holy faith."[82] Such miracles could even predict the inevitability of Christian military victory, according to a letter quoted in a fifteenth-century Castilian chronicle.[83]

Written in the spring of 1409, the letter brought welcome news to Prince Ferdinand as he mustered his forces for a campaign against the kingdom of Granada. Mary, the saint who watched over his Order of the Jar and Griffin, had just performed a great wonder in Antequera, one of the Nasrid towns he was eyeing as a possible target. The letter related how the Virgin had visited two Christian boys held hostage in Antequera. Urging them to put aside their fears, she promised them they would safely escape their Muslim dungeon. A few days later, the boys slipped out through a sewer. But once beyond the city walls, they lost their bearings and wandered hopelessly for several days. Hungry and scared, they were about to give up and return to captivity when Mary appeared and led them to a nearby Christian town.

The regent must have been pleased by this heavenly sign. If Mary had delivered the boys from Antequera to Christian territory, she would surely help him deliver Antequera itself to Christendom. The chronicler who preserved this letter underscored the convergence between her merciful aid to the young hostages and her "compassion for Christians" as their "advocate" in wars against the Muslims. Both the miracle at Antequera and Mary's loving intercession on behalf of Christian warriors crossing swords with Muslims, he wrote, showed how the "mother of consolation" supported Christians in "their work of war against the infidel."[84]

Mary's spiritual sons returned her affections. Yet their love for her could exceed the bounds of filial devotion, as suggested by some poems composed by Pero López de Ayala, a former lieutenant of the royal Order of the Band. After being captured in battle in 1385, Pero López wrote verse prayers imploring the

Figure 3.1 With her cape, Mary protects Constantinople from a Muslim army. *Cantigas de Santa María.* Biblioteca Monasterio del Escorial, Codice Rico, MS. T.I.1, folio 43r. Madrid, Spain. The Bridgeman Art Library.

Madonna –"the cloak and cape of sinners"—to have mercy upon him and free him from prison.[85] "I love to serve you now and every day," he declared, "my heart does not wish to quit your service, for all my happiness lies in praising you."[86] Addressing one of his delicate laments to Toledo's "White Virgin," an exquisitely beautiful marble statue, he recalled her "noble countenance" which he longed to "adore" in person.[87]

These lyrics are more worthy of a knight celebrating the charms of his lady than of a son speaking to his mother. Indeed, though medieval men of war may have channeled oedipal longings into their devotion to Mary, they knew her not just as their mother, but also as their lady—and a woman as desirable as those beauties for whom the heroes of romance broke lances.[88] The chivalric literature popular in high medieval Europe taught knights how to treat such an exalted lady. Although few real men of war ever became as courtly as characters like Lancelot and Tristan who quested for glory in their lady's name, some did cast themselves as heroes in a spiritual romance featuring Mary in place of Guinevere and Isolde. Preening for Our Lady, singing her praises, and suffering the pangs of lovesickness, Christian men of war took up arms as her knights and rode into battle against Muslims wearing her colors.

Lady Love

Knights needed a lady love in order to accomplish the feats of arms that made them men, or so the culture of chivalry schooled its students. Without the strength inspired by the thought of their ladies, wrote Alfonso X in his law code, knights lacked the courage necessary for warfare.[89] The statutes of the Order of the Jar and Griffin suggested that love of Mary might be this spur to manly prowess: members "should be strong and firm in their love of God and the Virgin Mary, and...in all works of knighthood."[90] Alfonso X's poets in fact counseled knights seeking worthy objects of their ardor to choose Mary: "He who wishes to love a beautiful and good lady, let him love [Mary] and he will not err."[91] "Rose of beauty and of form," the Virgin was, they explained, the "lady of ladies"—and the loveliest of all.[92]

No ordinary woman could rival Mary's attractions. "The beauties of Our Lady surpass all other beauties," declared Catalan mystic and missionary Ramón Llull a few years after Alfonso's poets dispensed their love advice.[93] Llull and other religious writers emphasized the spiritual benefits of contemplating her beauty, for they believed that in her countenance, humans glimpsed the splendor of the divine.[94] The ubiquitous statues and paintings of Mary adorning church altars might have aroused some less pious thoughts, for they often lent earthly curves to her heavenly charms. Toledo's "White Virgin," whose smooth features inspired some of Pero de Ayala's prison poetry, had many equally lovely sisters. Among them was Alfonso X's favorite Madonna in the cathedral of Seville, a statue "so beautiful and so well fashioned that the heart of whoever saw it rejoiced," as the king's poets put it.[95] Striving to capture Mary's comeliness in stone, ivory, wood, and paint, high medieval artists and artisans produced images so seductive that Llull worried they might cause Christians to praise the Virgin for her "bodily beauties" alone.[96]

Llull should also have worried about the depiction of Mary in the love lyrics of the troubadours, verse that became increasingly popular among the European elite. Deeply influenced by the elegant poetry recited in the palaces and night gardens of al-Andalus, troubadour lyric sung in sensual words of knights' yearning for their ladies. Its aristocratic authors often created scenarios of impossible love, with a young knight longing for a married woman of much higher stature. By the thirteenth century, the lush language and sonorous forms of this poetry played with the rapturous imagery of love that ecclesiastical writers themselves increasingly used for Mary. Troubadours began to celebrate the passionate desire that men might feel for the Virgin, the most unattainable—and most alluring— lady of all.[97] She became Notre Dame, the Madonna, and Our Lady. Male poets applied to this celestial object of their affections the same literary conceits they used for the earthly women whose charms excited their pens.

If the poetry that men of war enjoyed in their leisure moments and the images that they prayed before in churches revealed to them Our Lady's incomparable attractions, miracle stories instructed them to "give to the devil all other loves" for her, as the *Cantigas de Santa María* bluntly put it.[98] A tale popular in Christian Europe illustrated the wisdom of casting aside ordinary ladies in Mary's favor. As Alfonso X's poets tell the story, a valiant knight seeks to court a lady by winning tournament after tournament. Unmoved by his prowess, she spurns him. In his despair, the knight consults an abbot, who advises him to pray to Mary every day for a year. At the end of that time, Mary cures the knight's lovesickness by offering to become his *amiga* (beloved) if he will renounce the haughty lady. Naturally, he decides to pledge his love to her, declaring "you are the most beautiful thing my eyes have ever seen." After he prays to his ravishing new lady for yet another year, death joins him to her forever.[99]

By 1200, Christians even regaled each other with miracle tales about men of war who betrothed themselves to Mary; lovestruck at the sight of a gorgeous statue of Our Lady, a knight slips a ring on its finger, effectively taking the Madonna as his wife. In previous centuries, Venus featured in stories of men who married statues, but the Virgin had become the new goddess of love.[100] Unlike Venus, she required absolute fidelity, as the *Cantigas de Santa María* admonished its audience. In one poem, a young squire who has offered his ring to a statue of the Madonna yields to the devil's prompting and marries another woman. On their wedding night, a jealous and angry Mary prevents the couple from consummating their relationship. After she upbraids the squire for his faithlessness, he flees to a lonely hermitage where he loyally serves her for the rest of his life.[101]

These miracle stories all imply that the secular life is inferior to the religious: carnal pleasures cannot compare with the raptures of chastity. Mary had other miraculous means of setting her knightly devotees on the path of celibacy.[102] But most of the actual men of war who followed the *Cantigas'* advice and took her as their lady had no intention of imitating their counterparts in the miracle stories and rejecting other loves. True, they might have agreed that in serving the most beautiful of all *amigas*, they pledged themselves to a love that offered more than an ordinary woman ever could. Not only could knights hope for Mary's miraculous favors, but they expected from her pleasure far more intense than any ever felt in the arms of an earthly woman; the joys of salvation awaited the Virgin's lovers at the moment of consummation—death. Yet they served Mary according to their own values, not those of the celibate monks and clerics who so often recorded her miracles. The Madonna's knightly lovers offered her their swords, their praise, and their loyalty to the religion named for her son.

A poem from the *Cantigas* even suggests that the story of the man married to the Madonna could be tailored to suit the culture of knighthood. In this reworking of the tale, the man who commands that his ring be placed onto the finger of a Marian statue is no less a knight than Ferdinand III. But Ferdinand's battlefield days are well behind him, for the miracle occurs after his death. Its setting is the magnificent burial complex that Alfonso X was preparing for his parents in Seville's mosque-cathedral. In the *cantiga*, Ferdinand appears in a dream to one of the master metalsmiths working on the tombs and orders that a bejeweled gold ring intended for his effigy adorn Mary's hand instead (Figure 1.1).[103] The king also stipulates that his own statue should be shaped to kneel in front of her statue, his hands proffering her the ring. Upon awakening, the smith rushes to the cathedral and discovers that the ring has miraculously slid off Ferdinand's finger. The poem does not say whether the jewel was transferred to the Madonna's hand as per Ferdinand's commands. But a fourteenth-century visitor to Seville's cathedral admired a ring glittering on the Marian statue's finger.[104] Gold and set with a large ruby, it exactly fit the *cantiga*'s description.

In this poem, Ferdinand's gesture does not marry him to Mary. Yet medieval men and women listening to the tale would naturally be reminded of the knights who famously bestowed rings upon the statues of their celestial lady love. The humble posture that Ferdinand dictates for his own effigy evoked the realm of courtly love, where knights kneel before their *amigas* in homage to love itself. Knights also bent their knees to their lords. But in the Middle Ages, there was no divorce between the languages of love and of lordship. Ferdinand wants to be on his knees before Mary to show that he "was loyally hers," a lover's declaration as much as a vassal's. The *cantiga's* opening lines explicitly place the king among Mary's knightly lovers, while elsewhere the poem lauds him for having served her as lovers did their ladies: Ferdinand praised her and dedicated his feats of arms against al-Andalus to her.

Here the royal patron of the *Cantigas* fondly cast his father in his own image. The first poem in the collection presents Alfonso X as a man who serves his heavenly lady Mary with song and sword. Alfonso, it declares, is a royal warrior who has wrested from al-Andalus a whole string of towns. He is also a poet "who made this book...for the honor and praise of the Virgin. . . . [H]e composed songs. . . that are pleasant to sing."[105] As Alfonso himself writes in the second poem of the collection: "I want from now on to be [Mary's] troubadour and I ask her to take me as her troubadour and accept my singing...and I intend from now on not to sing for any other lady."[106] As the king exuberantly celebrates his passion for her, he often composes his love songs in the vocabulary that troubadours used for more mundane love affairs: Mary is Alfonso's *dona* (lady) and he is her *entendedor* (lover).[107]

Well into the sixteenth century, Christian men of war from the Iberian Peninsula wrote love poetry to the Virgin.[108] Like Alfonso X, some of these poets also styled themselves as Our Lady's champions on the battlefield, as did Iñigo López de Mendoza, the fifteenth-century marquis of Santillana, who reprimanded knights for preferring conversation to combat. No one could have levied this reproach at Iñigo, who campaigned against Granada and wielded a sword during the civil wars that wracked Castile during his lifetime. As adept with words as with weapons, he composed some of his most lyrical verse in Mary's honor, including a rapturous cascade of imagery inspired by the Virgin of Guadalupe.[109] Iñigo, however, turned his hand to religious poetry only as an aging man readying his soul for death.[110] In his younger years, he devoted his literary energies to distinctly profane subjects, including love affairs with women whose names his poems did not disclose.[111] The motto borne by his war banners was as coyly suggestive of a mysterious lady love: "God and you."

Only as Iñigo lay dying did he reveal the identity of the woman whom he had loved and for whom he had fought all those years. It was neither his wife nor any of the other women who had been attracted to this handsome man.[112] The *Vos* fluttering from his banners, Iñigo confessed to the priest administering the last rites, had always referred to the Madonna. He had even chosen this motto "in order to have Our Lady continuously present in my mind." Face to face with death, Iñigo relied on his heavenly lady to save him from the torments of hell.[113]

Offering their love service to Mary, knights played the manly roles of faithful suitor and valiant champion. They also announced their Christian virility, for warriors often make themselves men by defending the women they cherish.[114]

"Fight for your wives!" medieval lords might shout to their troops, mustering the army of emotions commanded by battlefield evocations of women beloved by warriors.[115] Wartime rhetoric and propaganda, as well as the stress of combat itself, often encourage soldiers to imagine the women they love—whether wife, mother, or lover—as pure and innocent icons of the values for which they fight.[116] For a Christian knight of medieval Iberia, what woman could more perfectly represent the purity, innocence, and moral order he was supposed to defend than Mary, embodiment of the Church, the monarchy, and the land?

Ramón Llull implied that Mary stood for the integrity of Christianity when he urged knights to take her as their lady love and to champion her against the Muslims. He worked this message into the *Blaquerna*, a spiritual romance-cum-chivalric adventure story he composed in 1238.[117] The title character of this piece sets out on a quest for the religious life. At one point in his odyssey, Blaquerna, now a pious abbot, passes through a forest, where he encounters a knight resting under a tree. This knight, who "seeks adventure for love of his lady," is singing a melody complaining of the troubadours who have not lauded her above all other women. Blaquerna asks him whether if a lady were to be found who was "better and more noble and more beautiful," the knight would renounce his own love in her favor. The knight concedes that he would, but doubts that any such woman exists. When Blaquerna insists that he knows one, the knight bristles. Wielding words rather than weapons, the two men joust for their ladies. The knight vaunts his lady's beauty and virtues, which have inspired such passion in him that he has vanquished many of his peers on the battlefield. When Blaquerna reveals that the lady whom he himself loves is "Our Lady Saint Mary," the knight admits defeat. Recognizing that his own lady could never protect him from hell fire or lead him to celestial glory, he joins his chivalric peers from the miracle stories in pledging love and service to Mary alone.

"Through arms I wish to honor the lady whom God honored above all other women," the Madonna's new knight says. He sets off to fulfill his chivalric Marian duty by spending "all the days of [his] life in battles and wars against those who do her dishonor." "I shall," he declares, "go to fight in the land of the Saracens against a knight who is not Our Lady's servant and . . . vanquish him so that he will never defeat another." In battle against Muslim foes, the knight eventually offers Mary the ultimate proof of his love, dying as "Our Lady's martyr."

By dispatching this knight to combat Muslims, Ramon Llull deftly transforms the idea of Mary as lady love into an argument for crusade. Constructed from complex layers of allegory and metaphor, the whole episode also reads as propaganda for holy wars conducted on the Madonna's behalf with weapons of the spirit rather than the flesh. Yet Llull knew how to write words that might appeal to men who wielded real steel, for he had served as a knight at the royal court of Majorca. His fictional knight, in love with Mary and fighting in her name against the Muslims, is not so far removed from the self-image of actual men of war like Alfonso X.

Our Lady's Christian champions could believe that they owed her military service against the Muslims because they were her vassals as well as her lovers. The *Cantigas de Santa María* and other thirteenth-century Castilian compilations of Mary's miracles told them so, invoking the bond of fidelity often projected onto the relationship between saints and devotees.[118] And if knights were Our Lady's vassals, she was not just their *amiga,* but also their *caudillo* (war chief), as Gutierre Díaz reminded his readers. After all, she possessed the courage, strength, and military prowess needed to lead men to victory. Mary was herself a warrior.

Virgin Warrior

Sometime late in the thirteenth century, a band of Castilian *almogávares*— Christian men of arms who lived tough lives in frontier areas, haunting the wilderness and launching frequent raids into Granadan territory—grew frustrated at their repeated lack of military success. Realizing that their sins lay at the root of their defeats, they decided to enlist the Virgin's help. They gathered as pilgrims at a nearby Marian shrine, a chapel in the former mosque of the old Muslim fortress in Jérez de la Frontera. There, they passed the night in prayer and promised Mary the richest cut of the booty if she ensured that their next foray across the frontier was profitable. According to the poem in the *Cantigas de Santa María* that relates this tale, she accepted the *almogávares'* proposition. After she "made them defeat a very large pack of Moors," their prize loot, a length of purple and gold cloth, lent its shimmer to her altar in Jérez. Mary even granted her permanent military favor to these Christian raiders: "henceforth [that company] made no expedition on which they did not win a lot, because the crowned Virgin arranged that each time they set out, they made a good journey."[119]

In this *cantiga,* Mary does not supplicate her son on behalf of the penitent *almogávares* but instead grants military favors herself.[120] After all, she was Our Lady of Victory, as the Duke of Medinaceli knew when, in 1506, he founded a church dedicated to this Madonna in an Andalusian town not far from Jérez, El Puerto de Santa María.[121] The Virgin deserved this title, for she not only dispensed victory but could also win it herself. To show her in action on the battlefield, many writers recruited the same distinctly military vocabulary that Díaz de Games used when he named her the *caudillo* of Christian kings and knights.

In one *cantiga,* for example, Alfonso X's poets celebrated how the Virgin "destroyed" a band of Muslims trying to sack a nameless Christian city.[122] In the accompanying illumination, a statue of Mary floats above the Muslim men of war who lie flat on their faces, quivering in terror.[123] Not coincidentally, the *Cantigas'* royal patron used the verb *destruyr* later in the collection to express the military fate he intended to inflict on the "infidel Moors."[124] Another *cantiga* written in Alfonso X's voice deployed an even more martial verb to predict that Mary would triumphantly accomplish the reconquest's mission: "she will conquer Spain and Morocco, and Ceuta and Asila." The miracle recounted by this poem itself proved her prowess as conqueror. When a North African Marinid amir colluded with Muslims living under Christian rule in Murcia, Mary "defeated" his plans and "drove" the Islamic community from the city. "She conquered there," concluded the *cantiga* baldly.[125]

A late thirteenth-century Castilian chronicle limned an equally martial portrait of Mary when explaining why Alfonso VIII had fought under a banner decorated with her likeness during the crusading triumph of Las Navas de Tolosa: because she was a "victor and patron" who always exercised her powers on behalf of Christian Spain.[126] The Virgin of Guadalupe earned similar praise from Iñigo López de Mendoza, the marquis of Santillana who had emblazoned his love for Mary on his own war standard. In his poetry, he lauded her as "invincible and victorious over our persecutors" and even termed her the "weapons of Christianity."[127]

By the late fifteenth century, Mary's military talents had become legendary. Visitors to Seville's cathedral who lingered in front of the Virgin of the Kings learned from locals that this Madonna enthroned above the tombs of Alfonso X and his parents had combat experience: she had always accompanied Ferdinand III onto the battlefield. In fact, their guides might tell them, it was "with the blessed Virgin's power" that the saintly warrior king had won his campaigns against al-Andalus.[128] With such stories in circulation, it is no wonder that a late sixteenth-century friar from Guadalupe styled Mary a whirlwind of military energy when commemorating how she had aided Alfonso XI against his Muslim foes during the battle of Salado hundreds of years earlier. The "sovereign princess...helped in the war. She weakened the enemy, she conquered them, she subjected and vanquished and killed and despoiled them."[129] Just a few years later, another Christian author recorded a miracle demonstrating that Mary fought as fiercely in the present. In 1610, he wrote, she brandished a sword during a bloody clash on the battlefield with the descendants of Spain's Muslims. Wielding her weapon with "unheard of valor and strength," she "defeated" and "routed" the enemy, forcing them to abandon the Iberian Peninsula.[130] This story spectacularly vindicated Alfonso X's conviction that the Virgin was a conqueror who would herself drive the "Moors" from the lands he longed to claim for Christianity.

Centuries of Christian commentary on the Bible may have encouraged these portrayals of Mary as a woman who donned the mantle of crusading warrior and thus defied the strictures on her sex.[131] It was not the meager information about the mother of God provided by the canonical Gospels that suggested her military potential, but instead some passages of the Old Testament that Christians had read for centuries as predicting her role in salvation history. Clerics, monks, and nuns seeking to unravel the meaning of scripture interpreted the "strong woman" of Proverbs 31.10 as the Virgin.[132] From the Song of Songs' lushly erotic lyrics imagining the passionate play between a bride and her betrothed, erudite high medieval Christians borrowed militant as well as sensual metaphors for Mary.

Like the Song's bride, Mary was "beautiful and gentle" yet "as terrible as an army drawn up for battle" (Song of Songs 6:3), and her neck was a proud tower from which hung a thousand shields and weapons (Song of Songs 4:4).[133] The comparison between the Virgin and a host arrayed for war particularly inspired men seeking the right words to describe her greatest victory; this quotation from the Song of Songs appeared among the sonorous phrases of the liturgy for the church feast celebrating Mary's triumph over death when she was assumed bodily into heaven.[134] The marquis of Santillana wove these words with their unmistakable ring of battle into one of his poems praising the Virgin.[135]

In the very first book of the Latin Bible, medieval Christians found the name of the enemy against whom Mary would marshal her valor: the serpent, mankind's ancient foe, author of Adam and Eve's Fall, and source of perpetual temptation. By the high Middle Ages, clerics and poets alike read the words of Genesis 3:15 as prophesying the Virgin's powers over the snake and its descendants.[136] "She will crush your head," declares God when informing the serpent of the enmity that would henceforth exist between its kind and "the woman." Identified with this triumphant "woman," Mary began her battle with the snake at the start of all things. This war would continue until the end of time, as a story in the last book of the Christian Bible revealed to the Virgin's devotees. One of the violent contests that roils the pages of the Book of Apocalypse pits a pregnant woman "clothed with the sun and with the moon beneath her feet and on her head a crown of twelve stars" against a red dragon sporting ten horns on seven heads (Apocalypse 12:1–3). When this woman bears a "man child who would rule all the nations with an iron rod," the raging beast tries to devour him (Apocalypse 12:5). By the twelfth century, Christian authors and artists increasingly turned this apocalyptic event into Marian allegory, adorning the mother of God in the woman's luminous raiment.[137]

Facing off against dragon and snake—embodiments of the devil and his minions—Mary entered into a contest with evil itself. As a twelfth-century author from Catalonia put it, Mary "governs hell, because she crushed the head of the ancient serpent, that is, the king of hell."[138] In many miracle stories, she wrestles with the devil, often bringing him to his knees. Christians thus knew her as a triumphant warrior in the combat between good and evil, the spiritual struggle that played out within the soul of every Christian as well as on the vast stage of the cosmos.

The distance between allegory written and allegory realized was not always so great in the pre-modern world, where political events were often read through the screen of scriptural paradigms. The wars waged by Christian knights and soldiers against Muslims might have inspired writers to think of the martial Mary of biblical commentary, for they knew that unbelievers marched in the devil's armies. It was against such adversaries that Mary girded herself, declared the twelfth-century Catalonian author who lauded her powers over hell: "the blessed Virgin is a tower of fortitude armed with all sorts of weapons against heretics, Jews, and all infidel."[139]

Even those descriptions of Mary's belligerence on the actual battlefield penned by highly educated writers, however, rarely alluded explicitly to the scriptural passages that lent her such military mastery. Perhaps more fundamental in opening the way for her as warrior was one of her traits known to all Christians, whether literate or illiterate: her virginity. Evocations of Mary as the Song of Songs' army, arrayed for battle, and the strong tower bristling with weapons often mingled with praises of her perfect purity, for virginity and valor were close intimates.[140]

Medieval Christian authors summoned their best military metaphors to celebrate the spectacular spiritual strength displayed by virgin saints in the struggle against evil.[141] Mary's own powers to best the devil sprang from her virginity, asserted many writers.[142] As the fifteenth-century Valencian poet-physician Jaume Roig elegantly put it, the Virgin "is the strong wall / of defense against the attack / of the enemy, since her chastity / drives him back. / She conquers him / with purity. Against sin, / she is a fighter."[143] Sexual purity, medieval Christians believed, fueled prowess and clad the saintly men and women who embraced it with armor impenetrable by the forces of evil. The inviolate bodies of female virgins particularly inspired such imagery, and Mary herself could be likened to an invulnerable battle shield. "All places that have Saint Mary as their shield can be well defended," insists the refrain of a poem from the *Cantigas de Santa María*.[144] "Virgin who alone is worthy of this name, place the shield of salvation, the renowned sign of your strength against the enemies' weapons," intoned the priests of an early fourteenth-century Castilian parish church as they implored Mary to aid a king setting off for war.[145]

Holy virginity possessed such military potential that it could even exempt maidens from the taboo against women on the battlefield and forge them into warriors who fought physical foes. It is no accident that the few female warrior saints venerated by medieval Christians were virgins, just like the warrior goddesses of classical antiquity, Athena and Diana. Among them was Saint Thecla, who valiantly seconded Byzantine armies in their wars by the fifth century. A devoted companion of Saint Paul during her life, after her death this virgin saint performed many military miracles, often glorying "victorious" over the enemy, as one fifth-century writer said.[146] Further west in Christendom, high medieval pilgrims traveled to shrines housing relics from a legendary army of maidens, Saint Ursula and her holy host of eleven thousand virgins. The Christians who prayed before Ursula's remains in the city of Cologne venerated her as a devout princess of the distant past who had trained her battalions of eleven thousand maidens in warships, preparing to defend her virginity and her faith with a sword against the assaults of the pagan prince to whom she was betrothed. In the tenth-century text recounting the slaughter of Ursula and her saintly army in battle with the Huns, men wonder at these female warriors readying themselves for death, each girded with the "sword-belt of virginity."[147]

Virginity allowed some women of the medieval present to join these maidens from sacred history in waging warfare. The remarkable fifteenth-century French peasant girl now known as Joan of Arc who took up arms to save her king and her country during the Hundred Years' War was in her day more often called "the Maiden," at least by her supporters. Her sexual innocence guaranteed her mission's divinely ordained nature and served as the license for her to wield a weapon. It also rendered Joan an example held out to Isabel of Castile, who almost as energetically turned the battlefield into her domain. Though this monarch was no maiden, some of her propagandists shaped her as a virgin warrior and intimated that this pure woman would save Castile, just as Joan had rescued France.[148] With this rhetoric of virginal belligerence, the queen's courtiers also reinforced the identification of Isabel with Mary herself.

Mary and other virginal women could step into the man's world of warfare because in renouncing sex, they had triumphed over their feminine nature. Since late antiquity, Christian authors had lauded saintly female virgins as "manly" women, high praise in an era when manhood was associated with reason and the spirit, and womanhood with the flesh and its sinful desires.[149] Female virgins exchanged the carnal life for the spiritual one, eschewing the roles of wife and mother that defined women as women. Straddling the boundary between manliness and womanliness, female virgins in many cultures have access to realms normally reserved for men, including warfare and hunting.[150] Virginity, medieval Christian authors declared, armed female saints with the masculine virtues of strength and courage.[151]

Mary's own perfect purity itself communicated manly fortitude to her whole gender. "After a virgin [Christ] came forth from a virgin [Mary] ... the fragile sex has become virile, the fragile sex is made strong. Therefore, in the sex in which formerly was the weakness of sinning is now the joy of conquering," intoned priests reciting the Mozarabic liturgy, the church rite of early medieval Iberia.[152]

These solemn words endowed Mary with the same manly courage she displayed as a warrior on the battlefield.

As virgin and warrior, this famous paragon of womanhood not only elevated her own sex, but also modeled the valor that Christian men of war expected from themselves. To these men, Mary thus held out a rather different mirror from the one she offered her male devotees dedicated to life in cloister and cathedral. Monks strove to imitate her humility, while priests saw the magnificence of their office reflected in her majesty and believed that their performance of Mass echoed the miracle of her motherhood: just as Christ had taken on flesh in Mary's womb, so the host became body in the priest's hands.[153] These traits, however, belonged to Mary's feminine side, unlike her strength and courage as virgin warrior.[154] The Christian men of war who fought in her name in medieval Iberia identified with her manly martial virtues, as the poem from the *Cantigas de Santa María* that named her a conqueror suggested.

This *cantiga* provides a particularly intimate view of Alfonso X's sense of self.[155] The king proclaims himself not only the poem's narrator, but also its protagonist and eyewitness to the miracle it celebrates. In predicting that Mary will "conquer Spain and Morocco, and Ceuta and Asila" as she has already "conquered" at Murcia, this *cantiga* identifies her as the patron of Alfonso's cherished projects, the Christian conquest of Spain and Morocco. She is the explicit subject of the verb "to conquer," but the implicit one is surely the ruler who nourished these dreams. The *cantiga* collapses the two subjects—Alfonso and Mary, male and female—into one conquering figure.

Mirroring the prowess that men of war sought to display, Mary's potent purity could blaze the way for them to identify with her. Some miracle stories urged her warrior devotees to believe that she made them invincible by loaning them her virginal inviolability. This is the message of a poem from the *Cantigas* that borrows a miracle tale from an early thirteenth-century Latin text featuring knights who take up pilgrim staffs to pay their respects to the Virgin at Notre Dame of Chartres, where they kneel before the revered relic of her tunic.[156] In the *cantiga*, the knightly pilgrims touch pieces of cloth to the reliquary containing Mary's garment and then have their own war shirts stitched from the lengths of fabric. This Marian armor affords far more protection than does chain-mail, the *cantiga* declares, and even saves a knight from a deadly assault. Although his squires watch with horror as lances bristle from his body, due to his special shirt he survives without a scratch. The original Latin version of the story indulges in some erudite word play to explain that the knights' shirts are rendered inviolable (*intemerabiles*) through contact with the inviolate (*intemerata*) Virgin's tunic. Thus clad with impenetrability, warriors' bodies remain unwounded and "whole" (*integer*), a word more often used to describe Mary's virginal nature.[157]

This miracle tale does not suggest that donning the shirts made the knights themselves into virgins. Yet medieval Christian men of war were often exhorted to embrace chastity, at least temporarily. Their counterparts in other times and places have received similar counsel, for many cultures understand sexual desire and armed aggression as twinned energies.[158] Medieval Christian warriors were urged to drive away the demons of desire and save their forces for the battle-field: a chaste man made himself pure and might gain divine favor in war. Sexual restraint led to military victory, declared the Portuguese bishop Alvarus Pelagius in a manual of instruction for princes composed in Alfonso XI of Castile's honor. Alvarus delivered this stern lesson as an anecdote about knights belonging to a military order stationed along the frontier with Granada. Though few in num-ber, these men always triumphed over their Muslim foes because "they girded their loins with chastity." But one day the knights ceded to lust and slept with some local women. From that moment onward, "they were always defeated and killed by the Muslims."[159]

Purity—or, to use the term favored by high medieval Castilian authors, *limp-ieza*—was thus as much a warrior's virtue as it was Mary's.[160] Knightly purity required nobility of character and purpose, chastity of soul as well as body. In his law code, Alfonso X urged knights to be "pure" in their habits and their dress.[161] Gutierre Díaz de Games, Count Pero Niño's biographer, praised Charlemagne, the Cid, and Ferdinand III of Castile as paragons of purity. These model knights, he wrote, "saved their souls by fighting with great faith against the Moors and for truth, and by living pure lives."[162] By the late fifteenth century, Castilian treatises portrayed purity as a prized moral and genealogical trait elevating those people who possessed it—aristocrats—above those who did not—commoners.[163]

The source and sign of knights' virtue and exalted class, purity joined some very high-ranking men of war in fifteenth-century Castile right to the Virgin herself. The court poet Alfonso Alvarez de Villasandino, for example, boldly appropriated the vocabulary of purity to suggest an almost blasphemous paral-lel between Mary and Ferdinand of Antequera. In some lyrics celebrating this Castilian prince's capture of the Granadan town that gave him his nickname, Villasandino lauded Ferdinand as "handsome without any blemish."[164] This was quite a claim. Borrowed from the Song of Songs (4:7), the phrase "without blemish" traditionally appeared in praises of the Virgin and her perfect purity, not in panegyrics to princes and their victories over Muslims.[165] As erudite as he was playful, Villasandino surely intended his audience to hear the Marian echoes in his verses flattering Ferdinand.[166]

Ferdinand of Antequera would likely have been pleased to think that he rode to battle against the Muslims fortified with Marian purity. After all, the prince dubbed the Order of the Jar and Griffin in the name of the Virgin's maidenhood; the "jar" was understood as a vase holding white lilies, flowers whose heavenly color and clear scent reminded medieval Christians of Mary's radiant purity.[167] The curving petals of these virginal blossoms adorned the heavy neck chain worn by the Order's members. And, during Ferdinand's coronation as king of Aragon one tableau featured a "very large jar of Saint Mary" filled with lilies of burnished silver and accompanied by six "maidens" singing sweet songs.[168] Matching the flowers' Marian hue was Ferdinand's white ceremonial dress, a color he donned as a sign, wrote a fifteenth-century chronicler, that "from then on, [he] would maintain chastity, which virtue it is rumored that he always maintained as Saint Mary's devoted knight."[169]

A few decades later, another of Mary's most devoted knights, Rodrigo Ponce de León, would earn praise and military favors from the Virgin for possessing purity reflecting her own. The marquis' biographer underscored at some length the "virtue" and "excellen[ce]" of purity as a knightly quality and delineated its connection to his subject's favorite saint. Chastity and virginity, he continued, "are the honor and purity of Jesus Christ and Our Lady" and, when found in the individual Christian, reflect the soul's beauty and endow the body with "clarity and grace." Purity was also, he wrote, a source of spiritual prowess: "blessed" are those people "pure and strong in will and deed," for they "battl[e] against the wicked enemy who always tries … to deliver us to perdition."[170]

According to the biographer, Rodrigo's deeds of arms proved that the men of war who shared this Marian virtue of purity would triumph in physical battles as well as spiritual struggles. Because Rodrigo was "pure" in his body and in his will to fight Muslims, God and Mary were "with him" when he waged war against Granada.[171] The biographer's insistence (probably contrary to fact) that the marquis had been born on the feast day of the Madonna's own conception also encouraged readers to view Rodrigo's purity through a Marian glass.[172] This increasingly popular liturgical celebration, which arrived in Castile late in the fourteenth century, elevated the Virgin as the only human being besides her son to have been conceived without the stain of original sin, thus remaining immaculate in body and soul.[173] Although the Immaculate Conception would not become church dogma until the nineteenth century, by Rodrigo's day many Castilians had become passionate partisans of the controversial idea.[174] Prominent among them were Queen Isabel and a host of aristocrats, including the marquis himself.[175]

According to his biographer, Rodrigo was determined to promote the cult of Mary's perfect purity. Every year he poured funds into the celebrations of her immaculate conception that were staged in all of "his cities, towns and villages," ordering particularly lavish solemnities wherever he himself happened to be residing.[176] After winning a series of campaigns against Granada, the marquis commissioned a sumptuous thanksgiving offering to the Madonna of the Immaculate Conception: ten masses "of the Conception of Our Lady" to be performed by a crowd of richly dressed clerics to the sound of organ music.[177]

Rodrigo was right to see this Madonna as a formidable ally in his clashes with Muslim foes. A few years after his death in 1492, Spanish artists began to experiment with ways to draw out the militant edge to her potent purity. They claimed for her the imagery of Genesis 3 and Apocalypse 12, which dramatized Mary's age-old war against the devil and his henchmen: crowned with stars, Our Lady of the Immaculate Conception crushes a serpent beneath her feet.[178] It was perhaps natural that this most pure Madonna would inspire the loyalties of a man as dedicated to crusade against Granada as the marquis of Cádiz. For centuries, Christian writers had accented the opposition between their faith and Islam with the same charged language of purity with which they lauded both Mary and the men who battled al-Andalus in her name. So in one of his treatises, Juan Manuel, a Castilian prince as active in the domain of letters as in the politics and wars of the fourteenth century, first extolled the Virgin's purity and then praised Christianity for the same quality.[179] Purity, he declared, made Christianity a better faith than Islam.

Juan Manuel did not specify what kind of purity his religion possessed and Islam lacked, but other authors revealed that it was just the sort exemplified by Mary. Reserving the virtue of chastity for themselves, Christians charged Muslims with the corresponding vice of lust and slurred Islam as a religion of carnal lechery.[180] As the bishop Alvarus Pelagius sermonized in his prince's mirror: "the Saracen sect is completely flesh; the law of Christ is spiritual."[181] Accordingly, a stock Muslim character of high medieval Christian romance and epic was the Virgin's exact opposite: a seductive infidel maiden who vamps her way into the bed of a Christian man.[182]

If it was the literary destiny of these Muslim temptresses to become the booty of Christian warriors and thus to serve as metaphors for the Christian conquest of al-Andalus, the perfect purity of the saintly woman for whom so many Christian knights fought suggested the inevitability of this victory. The alluring Muslim women of Christian fantasy aroused immoderate fleshly desire. But the Virgin inspired in her devotees a chaste love that, according to the fifteenth-century Castilian poet Pérez de Guzman, extinguished the "carnal fire of lust."[183] Mary's purity proclaimed that just as the spirit reigned over the flesh, and chastity over desire, so Christians would triumph over Muslims.

Such ideas would have appealed to men of war eager to find signs that victory would be theirs. But it was not only swaggering soldiers who could appreciate this Marian vision of the right order between Christianity and Islam. Many Christians living in Aragon and Castile who did not participate in skirmishes, raids, and expeditions against al-Andalus found themselves face to face daily with Muslims. Religious difference confronted them too in the shape of Jews. In medieval Iberia, Mary offered Christians, Muslims, and Jews many ways to negotiate relations with each other, away from the clash of weapons.

PART TWO

SPIRITUAL POLITICS

Introduction

"Ah Saint Mary, because your mercy does not fail those who ask for it, protect us, we who are yours, from falling into the power of these unbelievers who will not for anything believe that you are the mother of God."[1] Thus one of Alfonso X's poets who worked on the *Cantigas de Santa María* imagined Christians, besieged by Muslims in the Holy Land, imploring the Virgin for aid. With these simple words, the thirteenth-century writer transformed the conflict between Christians and Muslims from a mere military encounter into an inexorable clash of religious identities defined around her. Repeated elsewhere in the *Cantigas*, the potent phrase "we who are yours" erects Mary as the boundary between Islam and Christianity.[2]

This is the rhetoric of warfare, which often draws battle lines between self and enemy sharper than those that prevail in actual combat. Yet one has only to open the thick registers of notarial records, leaf through proud town chronicles, or glance at law codes to realize that in high medieval Aragon and Castile, the small stuff of daily life offered situations as opportune for the articulation of religious difference as holy war did. Those Christian men and women carving out new lives in the towns that sprang up along the frontier in the wake of Christian conquests knew the Muslims of Granada not just as armed raiders but also as neighbors.[3] A Castilian village could lie so close to a Granadan one that today the same exit off the highway serves both. As between all neighbors, good relations or bad might prevail. But even during moments of open hostility, Muslim and Christian villages often were linked across the frontier by the ties of trade, if only in the form of smuggling and contraband. During the long years of truces with Granada, such commerce was usually conducted openly with the stamp of royal and papal approval.[4] Hence the famed gold and purple silks of Granada made their way into the hands of those Christians rich enough to pay for such luxuries. In exchange, Castile offered the staples so often in short supply in the tiny Muslim kingdom whose mountainous landscape could not produce enough food for the population.

Muslims and Christians also dickered and struck deals, some on a grand scale, in the busy seaports under Castilian and Aragonese rule. The island of Majorca, after its conquest by James I, saw brisk trade between its Christian colonizers and Muslim merchants from nearby Morocco.[5] So too did El Puerto de Santa María, the formerly Muslim port near Cádiz that Alfonso X claimed for Christianity and the Virgin. In his foundation charter for Mary's port, the king encouraged Muslim and Christian merchants to bring their business there. He also extended the invitation to Jews, who actively participated in much of this Mediterranean commerce.[6]

Most of the Muslim traders who strode through these ports in their long flowing robes came from Granada or one of the Islamic states lining the shores of North Africa. Some of the Jewish merchants also had traveled from far away. Among the Jews who conducted their business in Palma de Majorca were men from Morocco, while others were Majorcans, residing on the island among its Christian lords.[7] All across Aragon and Castile lived Jews and Muslims who had as much right to claim these kingdoms as their homes as did the Christians with whom they rubbed elbows in streets and marketplaces. From the thirteenth to the early sixteenth centuries, the Castilian town of Ávila, for example, sheltered behind its massive walls not just Christians, but Jews and Muslims as well.[8] So vital to Ávila were its Muslims and Jews that by 1300, they ran the majority of shops serving the town's four thousand residents.[9]

The Muslim presence in Castilian and Aragonese towns and villages resulted directly from the Christian conquests of Islamic territory. Monarchs and other lords did their best to attract Christian settlers to the lands they had taken from al-Andalus. But also inhabiting many areas newly under Christian control were vanquished Muslims, who either could not bear to leave the villages and towns where their ancestors had lived for centuries or could not afford the expense of relocating to Muslim-held territory. Known as Mudejars, these Muslims could be the object of scorn and cause of discomfort among their co-religionists elsewhere. Their lives raised awkward questions about where the *dar al-Islam* (the "house of Islam") ended and the *dar al-harb* (the "house of war") began. In the eyes of some Muslim jurists, no less than the boundaries of the *umma*, the community of believers, were at stake. Many jurists issued fatwas urging Muslims to emigrate rather than remain willingly in areas subjugated to the powers of non-believers. Others instead argued that the infidel might be moved to conversion by the example of pious Muslims in their midst.[10] Whatever the jurists' opinions, by the late thirteenth century most high-ranking Muslim nobles had abandoned the territories of al-Andalus that had been conquered by Christian rulers. Some moved to Granada, while others chose exile in North Africa. Left behind under Christian rule were the middling and more humble classes, along with a handful of aristocrats. Although some Mudejars were skilled artisans who made a good living from their trades as bricklayers, potters, tile makers, carpenters, or smiths, most worked the land as peasants or tenant farmers. Others had the misfortune to labor as slaves in Christian or Jewish households.[11]

If Mudejars represented a relatively new element in the medieval Castilian and Aragonese populations, Jews did not.[12] Thriving Jewish communities had existed in the Iberian Peninsula ever since at least the fourth century. Between 711 and the late eleventh century, most resided in al-Andalus, where they enjoyed what some historians have termed a Golden Age, an era of outstanding cultural achievement and relative prosperity that ended with the arrival of first the Almoravids and then the Almohads. Fleeing the religious persecution that these Berber dynasties unleashed contrary to the Quranic prescriptions of toleration for the "peoples of the Book" observed by most previous rulers of al-Andalus, many Andalusian Jews sought refuge in the Christian kingdoms of the north. In Castile and Aragon, they joined communities of Jews who had lived for centuries among Christians. These communities expanded in the course of the thirteenth and early fourteenth centuries when their co-religionists expelled from Christian kingdoms north of the Pyrenees found a new home in the Iberian Peninsula. There they prospered, at least for a time. So culturally vibrant did the Jewish communities of Castile and Aragon become that one historian has declared that in the thirteenth century, Christian Iberia was the "centre and heart of European Jewry."[13]

In contrast to Mudejars, who tended to live in the countryside, most Jews resided in towns and villages. Many gained modest livelihoods as artisans, working in professions that they shared with Mudejars and Christians. But on the whole, Jews commanded more wealth than did Mudejars. The gold buttons painted on the dress of a dignified Jewish matron seated at a sumptuously laid Passover table in a fourteenth-century Haggadah from Catalonia were not wishful thinking. At medieval Jewish sites in Castile and Aragon, archaeologists have unearthed such buttons, along with silver necklaces, silver plates and saucers, and gold rings heavy with jewels.[14] Some Castilian and Aragonese Jews rose to great prominence due to their skills as financiers or physicians. They enjoyed royal favor and high positions at court, sometimes suffering disastrous, even fatal, falls from grace.

Fittingly, medieval Castilian kings such as Alfonso X proclaimed themselves the "ruler of the three religions."[15] Aragonese rulers also made this notion part of their royal ideology.[16] Population figures, notoriously difficult to calculate as they are for the pre-modern era, support these royal pretensions. It has been estimated that in the high Middle Ages, as many as six or seven hundred thousand of the approximately six million inhabitants of Aragon and Castile were Mudejars, while Jews made up perhaps two to three percent of the total population.[17] Outside the Iberian Peninsula, the only other western European Christian

kingdoms characterized by anywhere near such religious diversity were Hungary
and Sicily. In some places in the Crown of Aragon, notably the region of Valencia,
Mudejars even outnumbered Christians for much of the high Middle Ages.

A Mudejar who lived in the Valencian countryside toiling on the land of a
Christian lord might encounter only other Muslims in his or her daily round
of activities and even speak only Arabic. But such insulation from contact with
Christians was impossible for many Mudejars, as for most Jews in Castile and
Aragon. Scattered across these kingdoms, they spent their lives as religious and
numerical minorities among an overwhelmingly Christian population. To be
sure, many towns and villages had their *morería* and their *judería*, the Muslim
and Jewish quarters, where residences and shops clustered around synagogues
or mosques. The sense of cohesion that such neighborhoods could provide was
reinforced by Christian laws recognizing Jews and Mudejars as self-governing
communities.

Yet many Jews and Muslims chose to live not in these quarters, and defied
royal and municipal legislation by residing in predominantly Christian parts of
the city or town. Nor did the *juderias* and *morerías* create impermeable barriers
between their residents and people of other faiths. In medieval Barcelona, for
example, Christians came into the Jewish quarter (*call*) to sell fish or transact
other business. Some Christians even had to walk through the *call* on their way to
church, for Barcelona's Gothic cathedral casts its shadow over the neighborhood
where the Jews lived for so long. A Christian passing through the *call* might have
seen not only Jews, but also their Mudejar slaves and servants.[18] Well-off Catalan
Christians also enjoyed the services of Muslim servants in their own homes.[19]

The Christians, Jews, and Mudejars of Castile and Aragon in fact had all sorts
of dealings with each other. A Jew renting a room in the house of a Muslim,
a Mudejar steward managing the estates of a Christian monastery, Muslims
and Jews laboring as tenants on lands belonging to Christian military orders,
Christians and Mudejar shoemakers belonging to the same guild, ailing
Christians turning to Jewish or Mudejar doctors or midwives, Jewish painters
exercising their talents in the pay of a cathedral chapter—these and countless
other transactions bound members of the three faiths together. Such relations
were not confined to the realm of business. Christian women could invite Jewish
or Mudejar friends to accompany them to church, while their menfolk drank
and diced together in the local taverns. There were Jews who joined Mudejar
gangs to terrorize the countryside and Christian bandits who cleaned out the
pockets of Jewish, Muslim, and Christian travelers alike. Jewish men fell in love
with Mudejar slave girls, and Christian men were consumed with passion for
their Jewish mistresses.[20]

Many of these forms of cross-faith interactions were perfectly legal. Others
were socially condemned and some even prohibited by ecclesiastical, royal, or

municipal legislation. Nonetheless, examples of each abound, along with evidence that cultural borrowing among Muslims, Christians, and Jews was more the rule than the exception. Christian nobles might sport Muslim garb; it was more practical than Christian clothing, wrote Ramon Llull.[21] In the fifteenth century, Muslim dress was all the rage at the Castilian court: Enrique IV surprised some German visitors by receiving them while seated on cushions strewn about the floor and wearing clothes that would not have been out of place on his Granadan counterpart.[22] Enrique's political enemies found in his Islamophilic habits a convenient target for their spite. Yet Alfonso X had not been criticized when he openly expressed admiration for the intellectual achievements of al-Andalus by commissioning extensive translations of Muslim scientific works. For the challenging task of capturing these texts' complexities in Castilian, Alfonso employed erudite Jews who were fluent in the language of science as well as in Castilian and Arabic.[23]

Cultural entanglement even molded the townscapes of Castile and Aragon. The Jewish communities of Toledo and Córdoba, for example, chose Islamic architectural styles for their synagogues.[24] Rows of horseshoe arches and walls adorned with cascades of stucco work as delicate as lace greeted the faithful who came to worship in these synagogues. As numerous churches across Castile and Aragon demonstrated, Christians were just as eager to appropriate the magnificent architectural vocabulary of al-Andalus.[25] Just a few streets away from Toledo's synagogues stands the thirteenth-century church of Santiago del Arrabal, whose minaret-like bell tower is just one of the building's many deliberate Islamic echoes.

Mudejar artisans knew best how to shape a horseshoe arch or lay out the intricate patterns of wood to make the honeycomb ceilings that adorned the domes of Christian churches as well as the halls of the Alhambra, for these were their own familiar techniques and materials, even if used in the pay of Jews or Christians. According to one of the *Cantigas*, Alfonso X even hired a Muslim master architect, Ali, to oversee the transformation of El Puerto de Santa María's decaying mosque into the fortified church dedicated to the town's saintly namesake.[26] Although the king intended Mary's church as a bastion guarding this frontier port against Muslim invaders, it was a Muslim mason who, with the Virgin's help, made sure that the building's fortress-thick walls and powerful towers boasted the finest dressed stone.[27] The church bore the marks of his hand just as clearly as the *Cantigas* betrayed Christian fascination with the high culture of al-Andalus; Alfonso and his poets often chose to sing Mary's praises using a verse form derived from Arabic poetics, the *zajal*.[28] The *Cantigas*, the building history of Mary's church at El Puerto, and the Jewish and Muslim merchants who crowded this town's streets are all eloquent testimony that Castile and Aragon were kingdoms characterized by the coexistence of the three faiths.

Such coexistence, or *convivencia*, as it has often been called, did not, how-ever, erase the fact that Jews and Mudejars were religious minorities living under Christian rule.[29] Local and royal law codes from Castile and Aragon recognized and reinforced a hierarchy of faiths, restricting public expressions of Judaism and Islam and placing certain legal burdens on Jews and Mudejars from which Christians were exempt.[30] These laws guaranteed a certain amount of security to Jews and Mudejars. They were the "king's people," ultimately subject to the mon-arch's jurisdiction alone and thus enjoying his special protection. But this did not prevent Christians from acting as majorities are all too wont to do and violently reminding Jews and Mudejars of their minority status. Interfaith violence was an ever present possibility in Castile and Aragon, erupting in lynchings, riots, and attacks on *morerías* or *juderías*, as well as in other acts of aggression: the stoning of synagogues; the horrific punishments inflicted on Jewish or Mudejar men accused of having slept with a Christian woman; restrictions on the height of synagogues and mosques to ensure that they would not challenge Christian urban skylines; angry complaints about the noise of the *muezzin*'s call to prayer; or efforts to force Jews and Mudejars to wear distinctive clothing flagging their status as non-Christians.[31] The period up to the early fourteenth century was less scarred by episodes of mass Christian physical hostility against Jews and Mudejars than subsequent years would be. But then as later, awareness of reli-gious difference often provided the excuse, if not always the underlying reason, for interfaith violence.[32]

Christian, Muslim, and Jew—these were fundamental identities in the Christian kingdoms of medieval Iberia. Religion was not the only way that people understood themselves, nor was it always paramount in their minds, but it shaped the boundaries of their lives in countless ways. Even in Christian texts recording worldly transactions like property sales, Jews and Muslims were almost invariably named as such.[33] So important was religious affiliation that it determined one's legal identity. Jews, Christians, and Muslims were each gov-erned by their own law. Every local Mudejar or Jewish community had its own officials responsible for administering that law and managing its finances.[34] Even if individual Jews or Mudejars on occasion found it to their advantage to take their legal business to a Christian court, Jewish and Mudejar communities jeal-ously guarded these rights of self-governance.[35]

Depending on circumstance, time period, social situation, even personality, different people drew the lines separating themselves from members of the other faiths in different places.[36] Fluid and multiple as religiously defined boundar-ies could be, they nonetheless existed, a bulwark perhaps against the fact that centuries of living together in close proximity had flattened many of the social and cultural differences among the Muslims, Christians, and Jews of medieval Iberia.[37] Day-to-day interactions with neighbors, stories passed down in families, erudite writings of religious polemicists, and high-level political maneuverings all provided opportunities for the articulation of religious identity.

Whichever way people chose to express religious difference, they often used Mary to do so.[38] The Marian declaration of identity uttered by the besieged Christians of the *Cantigas*—"we who are yours"—only begins to hint at her extensive role in the spiritual politics of medieval Iberia. As the symbol of the Church and the virgin whose bodily integrity represented that of Christianity itself, she perhaps naturally offered Christians a vocabulary of inclusion and exclusion. So, at moments when Christians felt the boundaries of their community threatened, they might particularly stress her physical purity. It is no accident that Castilian aristocrats became passionately devoted to the Virgin of the Immaculate Conception in the fifteenth century, when debates began to rage over whether Jewish converts to Christianity could be successfully integrated into the Christian communal body, and purity was forged into a sword defending the faith from Jewish and Muslim taint.[39] Embodying purity defined by lineage and reproduction, this Madonna was the holy counterpart of the notorious, if largely ineffective, "purity of blood" statutes devised to exclude men or women of Muslim or Jewish ancestry from membership in some Christian institutions in late fifteenth-century Castile.[40]

Nor was it Christians alone who exploited Mary's potential as the powerful enforcer of difference between themselves and the members of other monotheistic faiths with whom they lived side by side. Jews and Muslims, well aware of her centrality to Christian identity, could respond in kind. Compare the phrase from the *Cantigas*—"we who are yours"—with an accusation first levied against Christians in the Qur'an(Suras 5:77, 5:116) and repeated throughout the centuries by Muslim polemicists in their anti-Christian tracts.[41] In the words of ʿAbdallah al-Taryuman, a fourteenth-century Christian from Majorca who converted to Islam and then, from his new home in Tunis, wrote a fiery treatise attacking his old religion: "Some [Christians] say that the three [members of the Trinity] are God—may he be praised—Jesus, and Mary."[42] This incendiary charge acknowledged the special bond between Christians and Mary, but only in order to proclaim Islam's superiority: if Christians are polytheistic Jesus- and Mary-worshippers, Muslims are righteous and uncompromising monotheists.

Then listen to a ballad sung first among Castilian Jews of the late fifteenth century and later by their descendants scattered across eastern Europe after the expulsion of 1492.[43] The song's words could vary, but the substance was always the same. A storm threatens to sink a ship. The captain, a Christian, prays fervently to Mary for her aid, promising her offerings of gold. But his invocation of Mary as "idol, my idol" presages an evil end. In contrast to the countless Christian stories in which the Virgin saves sailors, the Mariolatrous captain of this tale is swept overboard. The pious crew members, who direct their prayers to God alone, survive. Jews who sung and listened to this ballad would have learned the same lesson as Muslims could from the Quranic passage: idolaters who elevated a mere woman to the level of God, Christians belonged to an inferior religion. The only true recipients of God's favor were real monotheists.

There is then as much to learn about Jewish and Muslim religious identities from an examination of Mary in medieval Iberia as there is about the Christian sense of self. Understanding how Christians, Muslims, and Jews found in her a way to articulate religious difference requires drawing on evidence from beyond the borders of Castile and Aragon as well as from within. The documentation for the religious life of Mudejars is slim enough that exploring the Muslim perspective on Mary means venturing into the succession of Islamic polities that occupied parts of the Iberian Peninsula for centuries. She in fact figured in many dialogues between these polities and their Christian neighbors. To fully grasp her role in spiritual politics among Christians, Muslims, and Jews, it is even necessary at times to leave the Iberian Peninsula and consider the general currents of Christian, Jewish, and Islamic exegesis, polemic, and legend that swirled around her.

The men and women who lived in the Iberian Peninsula participated in these wider trends, each according to his or her situation. The difference in perspective among peasants, princes, and polemicists could be just as great as the distinctions separating Jews, Christians, and Muslims. A Mudejar housewife did not necessarily share the concerns of an erudite commentator on the Qu'ran any more than a wealthy Christian merchant from Barcelona shared those of a poor Christian peasant living next door to Mudejar farmers. To lump together these very different lives into monolithic categories of Muslim, Christian, and Jew runs the risk of accepting what some writers from all three faiths intended their audiences to believe: that Mary created one immutable religious boundary. Careful attention to social distinctions reveals that the religious lines of demarcation drawn through her were as varied as the people who created them.

If Mary had certain qualities that naturally suited her to divide Christians, Muslims, and Jews, she had others that have led some modern writers to characterize her as "a bridge builder" between the three monotheistic faiths.[44] Medieval Christians themselves could understand her as the patron of the more peaceful aspects of *convivencia*. Alfonso X believed that Mary benevolently watched over his efforts to attract Jewish and Muslim merchants to El Puerto de Santa María. After all, he knew she had once punished a group of Christian pirates for abducting Muslim merchants making their way to this town that lay under her protection. As the poem in the *Cantigas* that relates this miracle concludes, Mary "does not want any harm to befall…people coming to her home by sea or by land. Although the Moors sometimes wage war on her, she never closes the door of salvation to them."[45] An even more expansive vision of Mary as universal mother, spreading her cloak of infinite mercy across religious frontiers, appears in another *cantiga*'s declaration that she could "pardon Christian, Jew, and Moor if they have their intentions strongly turned toward God."[46]

A Jewish woman and the mother of a man viewed by Muslims as a prophet and by Christians as the son of God, Mary indeed straddles the borderlines between Judaism, Christianity, and Islam. In medieval Iberia, recognition of this fact could create situations of considerable complexity, especially for Muslims and Christians. Yet medieval rhetoric rarely shaped Mary as a truly ecumenical figure. Even the lines from the *Cantigas* present her within an unmistakably Christian worldview of penance and salvation. Instead of finding in Mary the "bridge-builder" hopefully celebrated by some people in the modern world, medieval authors from all three faiths—but especially Christianity—preferred to mask the potential for religious overlap that she offered. In these wars of words, Christians brandished Mary as a sign of their faith's triumphant superiority, much as they did on the battlefield.

4

Mary's Enemies, Mary's Friends

One night in 1502, a Christian man named Andres of Jaén stood guard in a watchtower overlooking the Mediterranean coast near the port of Almería.[1] He had every reason to be alert as his eyes swept the sea. Almería had been a Christian city since 1489, the year its Granadan lord had handed it over to the Castilians. Yet even after a decade of belonging to Castile, it remained a frontier town. Although Granada had fallen to Isabel and Ferdinand in 1492, the early sixteenth-century residents of Almería still feared Muslim attack. The narrow strip of the Mediterranean was all that separated the city from the Muslim polities of North Africa. The sea that licked Almería's shores could bring Muslim traders and merchants, but it also could carry the ships of Muslim corsairs, the famed Barbary pirates, as rapacious as their Christian counterparts who also prowled the Mediterranean.

As Andres watched for "Moors" that night, he suddenly saw a light shining from the waves breaking on the shore. At its heart sat a beautiful image of Mary, miraculously undamaged by the foaming salt water. According to the story that Andres would tell later, he wanted to rush off and announce the wondrous news to everyone. The reason he did not do so says much about Mary's importance in the complex politics of how Christians thought about Muslims. Andres did not dare leave his sacred find alone on the seashore even for a moment, lest "some Moor come along and take [it] in order to mock it."[2] With these simple yet eloquent words, he drew Mary into his vulnerable frontier world, envisioning her as prey to the same dangers stalking the townspeople of Almería.

The rest of this tale of the Madonna from the sea reveals how on the charged field of Muslim-Christian relations, the ubiquitous Marian images of Castile and Aragon served as lightning rods. Andres decided to take the Madonna to his guard tower for safekeeping. But he was unable to lift the holy flotsam from the waves. In desperation, he resorted to prayer. Admitting to the Virgin that he was a sinner unworthy of touching a representation of her, he urged her to let him do so nonetheless "because of the danger from the Moors." The possibility that Muslims might desecrate her image must have alarmed Mary, for the second time Andres tried to move it, he was able to do so. Until a more suitable home was found, the image stayed in the tower where he had put it.

Finding a permanent home for this Madonna posed quite a problem. The clergy of Almería's cathedral and the friars of the city's Dominican convent practically came to blows over the right to become her guardians, engaging in such unseemly wrangling that the case had to be adjudicated by the archbishop of Granada. This Marian gift from the sea was the ideal steward for a newly Christian frontier city deeply wary of Muslim enemies. The Virgin, the "star of the sea" whose image had been borne to Almería on the same waves that sometimes brought more violent visitors, could help protect the city against its foes. Thus in 1520, the confraternity of soldiers who watched this coastline took this Madonna as their patron saint.[3]

The discovery of the image drew a veil of miracle over Almería, divinely confirming the city's Christian identity. As this Marian wonder shrouded the Muslim past, it defied the Muslims who threatened the community in the present. Part of the miracle was that the image had washed up on the Christian side of the Mediterranean and not on the shores of Muslim North Africa that were so dangerously close. To quote the documentation that the Dominicans sent along to the archbishop of Granada to support their claims: "by chance, the sea could have cast the image on the land of the Moors over there, and Our Lord wanted it to fall into the hands of Christians."[4] God's favor lay with the Christians, not the Muslims.

If the story of the image's arrival expressed the hopes of Almería's Christian inhabitants, it also betrayed their fears. The expectation that Muslim ships could swoop down to raid the coast at any moment is palpable in Andres's tale. So too is the trepidation over what these Muslims would do to the image of Mary. Any Christian who heard this story could only conclude that Muslims posed at least as much of a threat to the Virgin herself as they did to Almería, a disturbing thought, but not a new one. For hundreds of years, Christians had harbored the fears that haunted Andres. This anxiety rippled through a story well-known to the crowds of pilgrims who came to the church of Guadalupe in the fifteenth century and laid their cares at the feet of this shrine's diminutive Madonna: the tale of how after Tariq's army crossed the Straits of Gibraltar in 711, pious Christians spirited away this statue to protect it from the Iberian Peninsula's new masters.[5] Even older miracle stories warned graphically of the gruesome fates supposedly awaiting images of Mary that fell into the hands of the followers of Islam. Muslims could hack at Marian paintings with axes, set fire to statues of the Madonna, or hurl them into the sea, according to the late thirteenth-century poets and painters who worked for Alfonso X on the *Cantigas de Santa María*.[6]

The most extreme of these fantasies of violence created by Alfonso's artistic team was so lurid that it recalled the endless torments inflicted on Christian martyrs by their pagan executioners. Andres of Jaén might even have known the story, for the action—the invasion of Castile by the Marinids of North Africa in 1277–1278—took place close to the town whose name he bore. The poem sadly details the havoc that this Berber army wreaks as it cut a wide swath through the Andalusian countryside.[7] In a church near Jaén, the Muslims seize a statue of the Virgin and fall on it with their swords. But when one of them chops out part of Mary's arm and then suddenly loses the use of his own, they all shout in alarm. Dropping their weapons, they retreat to a safe distance and stone the statue. The rocks fall harmlessly. Undeterred, the Muslims build a bonfire and leave the statue to roast for two days. When it emerges from the flames unscathed, they tie a boulder around the image's neck and toss it into a pond. The statue bobs to the surface, and the Muslims finally give up. With such stories as part of his cultural heritage, Andres was right to fear for the image he found on Almería's shores.

Whether such fears were grounded in reality is another matter. There is little evidence other than these miracle tales to suggest that medieval Muslims made images of Mary into targets of their wrath.[8] Yet these Christian stories do capture a truth of sorts about Islam: to avoid idolatry, Muslims were not supposed to use images as devotional objects. Muslim miniaturists might adorn the pages of manuscripts with delicate renderings of courtly love stories and legendary heroes, while frescoes of human figures paraded across the walls of some Muslim palaces. But stern prohibitions on figural representation in the realm of the sacred limited mosque decoration to stylized calligraphy and floral ornament.[9] Erudite Muslim authors railed against the dangers of venerating images, especially when they turned their pens to anti-Christian polemic—the profusion of paintings and statues in churches offered an easy target.[10] Christians riposted by fervently defending devotional images.[11]

The high drama of Almería's legend and the tales from the *Cantigas* transformed this heated polemical exchange over images into an impassioned narrative about Mary and Muslims. In these stories, the Virgin's painted, carved, or sculpted body became the battlefield for war between Islam and Christianity. Like the "Moors" of Andres of Jaén's imagination, the Muslims of these miracle tales were Mary's enemies. As one of Andres of Jaén's contemporaries, the Aragonese official and would-be-poet Pedro Marcuello, put it in his verse celebrating Ferdinand and Isabel's Granadan crusades, Muslims were "blind people who with blind error wage war against the Mother and Maiden and her Son."[12]

Marcuello's blunt words and the stories of image desecration suggest just how similar in Christian imagination Muslims could be to Mary's other fierce foes, the Jews. Jews too were reputed to express their scorn for Mary and all she represented by viciously desecrating images of her. The famous story of a Jew who pitches an icon of her into his stinking privy featured in pungent detail in many Marian miracle collections, including the *Cantigas de Santa María*.[13] The tale came to life in 1302, when three Jewish merchants of Barcelona were charged with insulting and spitting on a image of Mary.[14] The accusation of blind refusal to see Christian truth that Marcuello flings at the Muslims brings them into this dubious company, for Christians usually made this charge against the original children of Israel.[15] In high medieval Christian sculpture and painting, Jews clasp their hands tightly over their eyes while Synagoga, the allegorical figure of the Jewish community, slumps defeated with her eyes blindfolded. Marcuello's blind Muslims recall the blind Jews, the error of one in waging war against Mary as grave as the error of the other.

In a poem composed by the thirteenth-century Riojan priest Gonzalo de Berceo, Mary herself suggests the likeness between Muslims and Jews. Berceo's Virgin is the sorrowful mother keening for her son at the foot of the cross, the grieving Mary of that great liturgical lamentation, the *Stabat Mater*. As she pours forth her anguish, she accuses "Moors" (*moros*) of colluding with the Jews in her son's torment. At the behest of Jews, she says, "Moors" arrested Jesus, cruelly bound him, and loaded the cross onto his back. In the same poem, "Moors" mockingly deny Mary's plea to die in her son's place.[16] For Berceo, as for many of his Christian contemporaries, *moros* meant either the pagans of old or the followers of Muhammad.[17] Although the poet doubtless intended the word here as a reference to the Roman soldiers who had participated in the Passion, for his readers it also would have conjured up the Muslims of the Iberian Peninsula. Some images produced by Berceo's near contemporaries indeed suggested Muslim participation in Christ's death.[18] This priest's reverie hints at what some Christians believed to be a timeless truth: enemies of Christ and enemies of Mary, the Jews and the Muslims had to be in cahoots.[19]

If Christian writers blurred the lines between Mary's Muslim and Jewish antagonists, they did not always erase the differences completely. They often ranked the Virgin's adversaries to suggest that in the war against her, Jews made up the relentless vanguard, not Muslims. Mary "hates" the "Jews, her enemies...more than [she does] the Moors," declared one *cantiga*."[20] Accordingly, in the *Cantigas*, Jewish perpetrators of evil against her images suffer the most. Immediately after the Jew throws the icon of Mary into his latrine, he dies and is dragged off by the devil to an excruciating and endless sojourn in hell.[21] Although the Muslims of another poem who rampage through a Christian town trying to destroy images of Mary are punished by such keen pain that they think they will die, they do not.[22] Nor do the Muslims who attempt to harm images of her in other *cantigas*.

The more closely one reads these *cantigas*, the more ambiguous their portrayal of the relationship between Mary and the followers of Islam becomes. In two of these miracle stories, the same Muslims who attack Marian images are eventually forced to admit some measure of respect for them and thus for the Virgin

herself. Those Marinid soldiers who subject a statue of her to torments worthy of
the martyrs eventually recognize that the image possesses great "power."[23] To rid
themselves of the troubling object, they give it to Muhammad II, ruler of Granada.
As befits a man allied at that moment with Castile, Muhammad treats the image
well and hastens to send it to Alfonso X.[24] Another *cantiga* borrowed a story from
twelfth-century Christian chroniclers to describe a less politically motivated display of Muslim respect for an image of Mary following on the heels of its desecration. The Muslims of the coastal city of Faro cast a stone statue of the Virgin into
the sea, only to retrieve it later when they realize that in Mary's absence, their supply of fish has dried up.[25] According to such Christian tales, Muslims, unlike Jews,
were capable of capitulating to and even admitting Mary's power.

If Muslims were Mary's enemies, as Andres of Jaén and Pedro Marcuello
believed, they were not then quite as bad as the Jews. The clear-cut oppositions
between Muslim and Christian drawn through the Virgin on the battlefield
dissolved beyond the arena of war. A deep ambivalence often complicated the
Christian portrayal of Muslims as Mary's enemies, while rarely tingeing depictions of Jews. The gulf between Jewish views of the woman called Miriam in
Hebrew and Muslim attitudes toward the woman known in Arabic as Maryam
told Christians which palette to choose when painting Mary's relations with the
other monotheistic faiths.

Gaude Maria Virgo

By the ninth century, clerics and monastics across western Christendom raised
their voices three times a year to proclaim the Virgin's power to crush all heretics
and opponents of the faith. They concluded by singling out the Jews as her special foes. During the services for three Marian feast days (the Annunciation, the
Purification, and the Assumption), the officiants intoned these lines:

> Rejoice, Mary the Virgin (*Gaude Maria Virgo*)!
> You alone destroyed all heresies,
> You who believed the words of the Archangel Gabriel
> When as a virgin you gave birth to one who is both God and man
> And after the birth you remained an inviolate virgin...[26]

This liturgical celebration closed by pointing to Judaism as first among all the
wrong beliefs that Mary was destined to slay: "Let the miserable Jew blush with
shame / Who says that Christ was born from Joseph's seed."[27]

These vituperative phrases savored in the mouths of clerics and monastics
each year set up implacable conflict between Jews and Christians, with the Virgin

as the flashpoint. Although not all laypeople in attendance at these services were able to understand the Latin phrases, the Marian miracle stories that clustered around this liturgical text taught them its vehemently anti-Jewish meaning.[28] The best-known of these tales makes singing the *Gaude Maria Virgo*, as the liturgical piece was called, into a belligerent act of Christian faith in the Madonna and a declaration of war to which Jews are quick to respond. Accordingly, the poem in the *Cantigas de Santa María* recounting this Marian wonder opens by praising "the Holy Virgin Mary, with whom the Jews have great war."[29] As the rest of the *cantiga* reveals, if the Jews wage war on Mary, she and her devotees in turn wield the *Gaude* to battle the Jews.

The story centers on the fate of a Christian boy who possessed a sweet singing voice. As Alfonso X's poets relate, this child's exquisite rendition of the *Gaude* particularly moved his Christian listeners, but angered Jews. This is no wonder, for the *cantiga* pointedly characterizes the *Gaude* as "say[ing] bad things about the Jew, who fights against this." Another version of the *cantiga* even more baldly reduces the Marian liturgical text to its anti-Jewish elements, underscoring the boy's delight in singing "a song to Saint Mary that says: 'Gaude Maria Virgo, woe to the Jew who argued stubbornly against you!' "[30]

The contest between Mary and the Jews of which the child sings takes flesh one day when he performs before a group of Jews and Christians gambling together. Enraged by the stinging words of the *Gaude*, one of the Jews lures the boy to his house. There he kills the child and conceals the body in a hastily dug grave in his cellar. Distraught when her son fails to come home, the boy's mother implores Mary for aid. Her prayers are answered when the child's voice resounds from the Jew's house, singing the offending words of the *Gaude* more beautifully than ever before. A crowd of Christians rescues the resurrected boy. They learn from him that after his death at the Jew's hand, he lay "sleep[ing]" when Mary appeared and commanded he sing for her. His report prompts the *cantiga*'s ugly end: the Christians massacre "all the Jews," reserving for the child's murderer a particularly painful death by fire (Figure 4.1).

The *Gaude Maria Virgo* and its attendant anti-Jewish miracle tales were right in suggesting that Mary often sparked angry dialogues between Christians and Jews. Through her, Jews and Christians built some of the high barricades intended to keep their faiths apart. As a Jewish woman and the mother of a man whom Christians believed was the Messiah but whom Jews considered at best an erring human being, Mary offered the members of these two faiths so dangerously close to each other an opportunity to articulate their irreconcilable difference.[31] Much of this boundary building took place on the contentious field of religious polemic, where clashes between Jewish and Christian leaders became more frequent during the High Middle Ages. Learned Jews and Christians alike composed treatises defending their respective faith while attacking the

Figure 4.1 Mary resurrects a Christian boy killed by a Jew for singing the *Gaude Maria Virgo*. *Cantigas de Santa María*. Biblioteca Monasterio del Escorial, *Codice Rico*, MS. T.I.1, folio 13v. Patrimonio Nacional.

other. They often intended such texts to strengthen the beliefs of their own co-religionists rather than to persuade the other side of its error, as their choice of languages indicated (Jews usually wrote in Hebrew, Christians in Latin or the vernacular). Yet at staged public debates—where Christians were always declared the winners—Christian and Jewish thinkers actually had a chance to break lances with each other.[32]

One of the most hotly contested issues in high medieval Jewish-Christian polemic was whether Jesus was the Messiah and enjoyed divine paternity. As Christians strove to affirm his right to such exalted status and Jews sought to demote him, both sides inevitably drew his mother into the debate. In constructing their case that Jesus was not God's son but a mere human being, rabbis and Jewish thinkers often targeted Mary by doing exactly what the *Gaude* accused them of—they denied her sexual innocence. Mary must have slept with a man to produce Jesus, they argued, for how could a virgin possibly give birth? Nor, they declared, did Mary merit the title of "mother of God." Erudite Jews recoiled from the idea that God could have dwelt in a woman's womb for nine months; the squalor of humble female flesh and the majesty of ineffable divinity could never meet in this way.[33] They were unimpressed when Christians summoned passages from the Hebrew Bible as prophetic evidence of Mary's virginal motherhood. Chief among these texts was Isaiah 7:14, cited by the evangelist Matthew as proof that Jewish scripture predicted Jesus' miraculous conception (Matthew 1:23). Jews charged their Christian opponents with being poor linguists who misconstrued Isaiah's reference to the *almah* who would be the Messiah's mother by reading the Hebrew word as "virgin," when it simply meant "young woman." Needless to say, high medieval Christian polemicists stuck to their own translation of this Biblical verse.[34]

To be sure, some high medieval Jews appropriated the rich Marian imagery with which they were surrounded. Ashkenazi writers and artists in northern and eastern Europe could portray rabbis and teachers of the Torah as loving maternal figures who sat Madonna-like on a throne, holding in their lap the child whom they were instructing.[35] Further south, Jewish mystics in twelfth-century Provence wrote lyrically about the Shekhinah, a feminine manifestation of the divine, as God's sister, daughter, spouse, and the mother of his sons. Their descriptions of a female figure mediating between God and humanity may well have been influenced by the Christian devotion to Mary, so visible in the high medieval European world in which they lived.[36]

Although Jews could play with the potential inherent in the notion of a tender maternal figure, they did not think positively about Mary herself. As indicated by some folktales elaborated by Jews over many generations in reaction to Christian denigration of their faith, it was not just learned men who had little good to say about her. Known as the *Toledot Yeshu* (*Life of Jesus*), these stories circulated for centuries orally before being written down sometime before the year 1000.[37] They fleshed out the sketchy details in the Talmud about some shadowy figures that might or might not be Mary and Jesus, transforming these cryptic references into a full-blown anti-Nativity tale.[38]

The ordinary Jewish men and women who repeated tales from the *Toledot Yeshu* knew that Mary was no virgin, or even a virtuous wife, but rather an unclean adulterer. They agreed with their Christian neighbors that she had been betrothed to a good Jewish man. But while Christians celebrated how the angel Gabriel came to Mary to announce Christ's birth, Jews listening to the *Toledot Yeshu* stories learned that she had received a far less reputable visitor: a man who was not her fiancé yet had sex with her anyway. According to many versions of the story, he was not even a Jew, but a Roman soldier. The fruit of this adulterous liaison was Jesus, whose birth was further stained by Mary's ritual impurity; she had been menstruating when she conceived him. Jesus then grows up to live a degenerate life consonant with his shameful origins. The details could vary according to the storyteller's inspiration, yet the message remained the same. As a Jewish woman who had doubly contravened Jewish law, Mary could hardly be the mother of the Messiah. An adulterous polluted woman who bore a bastard son, she embodied the falsity of Christianity.

These stories slurring Mary and her son had reached Jews in the Iberian Peninsula by at least the early years of the twelfth century. Jews say that Christ "was a magician born from a harlot," declared Petrus Alfonsi in his *Dialogi*, a Christian polemic against Judaism.[39] This Aragonese man was in a privileged position to relay Judaism's perspective on Jesus and Mary since he had been born in that faith and converted to Christianity only as an adult in 1106.[40] Perhaps he had been raised on tales from the *Toledot Yeshu* and had enjoyed them in the years before his baptism. But from the vantage point of his new religion, he could only see these stories as weapons in a millennial war waged by Jews against Christianity. In pronouncing such calumnies against Mary and Jesus, wrote Alfonsi, Jews repeat the Crucifixion and "kill Christ the son of God."[41]

Christian thinkers discovered more evidence of Jewish danger to Mary when in the twelfth century they started to pay attention to the Talmud.[42] They learned Hebrew and combed this compilation of rabbinic opinions for ammunition to turn against the Jews, seizing on its ambiguous references to a man and a woman who seemed to be Jesus and Mary. Despite rabbis' efforts to the contrary, many influential Christian leaders became convinced that this collection of Jewish texts maligned Mary and her son. After a public debate in 1240 at Paris between Jewish leaders and a representative of Christianity predictably failed to exonerate the Talmud, wagonloads of copies of it were burned at the order of an ecclesiastical court. Chief among the Parisian charges against the Talmud was its alleged defamation of the Virgin.[43]

James I of Aragon apparently shared this fear that the Talmud slandered Mary and her child. In 1263 and again in 1264, he commanded that the Jews of his kingdom expunge from their books and writings all "blasphemies against our Lord Jesus Christ and his mother, the blessed Mary, glorious Virgin."[44] This ruler's efforts to safeguard from Jewish derision the saint who had so often helped him in battle hardly allayed Christian anxieties. "Oh queen, the Jews dishonor you...and call you a corrupt woman and the mother of the son of another man," complained Ramón Llull to Mary some thirty years after James's decrees.[45] During a debate at Tortosa in 1413–1414 that pitted a set of powerful Christian clerics against a group of rabbis, Christianity's champions launched another frontal attack on the Talmud. They listed among this text's many offenses "the abominable and foul things" it said "about our Savior...and his most blessed and glorious mother Mary." After the Christian triumph at Tortosa, the pope forbade Jews to possess or read any books (including the *Toledot Yeshu*) insulting Jesus, Mary, or the saints and even prohibited Jewish bookbinders from exercising their craft on any Christian texts containing the name of the Virgin or her son.[46]

Based on fantasy as much as reality, the Christian conviction that Jews disparaged Jesus' mother spread its poison widely. The aggressive anti-Jewish paranoia apparent in Christian readings of the Talmud seeped into high medieval Marian miracle stories, eucharistic theology, and other Christian texts, as well as being enacted in church drama and urban theater. Christian readers and audiences learned how Jews threatened the Virgin and her son and thus merited terrible punishment, even gruesome death. In the *Cantigas de Santa María*, Jews who have crossed the Madonna die twisted in the agonies of bonfires or crushed under falling buildings.[47] Marian devotion became such a common vehicle for the emergent anti-Semitism of the Christian high Middle Ages that one historian has labeled the era a time of "militant anti-Jewish Marianism."[48] In this period when some Christian thinkers feared that the sacred and social body of Christendom was under attack by Jews and polluted by their presence, the woman whose powerful purity was celebrated in the *Gaude Maria Virgo* was naturally called in to police the boundaries.

Maryam

If Mary stood between high medieval Jews and Christians like a mountain range—immovable and forbidding passage—between Muslims and Christians she was instead a fault line, an unstable suture joining two religious continents. The sacred book of Islam itself suggests why. "O Mary, indeed God has favored you and made you immaculate, and chosen you from all the women of the world

(Sura 3:42)."[49] Thus the angels hail Mary in the Qu'ran, their words distinctly echoing those Gabriel famously utters in the Gospel of Luke (1:28) as he greets the future mother of God. According to the Qu'ran, Mary, or Maryam as she is known in Arabic, fully deserves this angelic praise. She is one of the great figures of virtue that Islam inherited from its monotheistic predecessors. The poetry of Islamic revelation spreads her fragmentary story over several *suras*, including one entitled *Maryam*, the only *sura* to be titled after a woman.[50]

From conception, Mary is the model of obedience to and service to God—of *islam*. While she is still in the womb, her mother, wife of Imram, dedicates her to God. Upon her birth, her parents give her into the keeping of Zachariah, a pious man. She is miraculously nourished with food from God and grows up. Lots are cast to see who will "take care" of her, though it is never mentioned who wins. Angels, according to one *sura*, and a divinely sent "spirit," according to another, bring her the startling news that she will bear a special son, "a sign for men and a blessing" (Sura 19:21) from God—a prophet. "How can I have a son," she protests, "when no man has touched me, nor am I sinful?" In response, she receives a lesson in submission to God's will: "That is how God creates what He wills" (Sura 3:47). After Mary conceives through God "breath[ing] a new life" into her (Suras 21:91, 66:12), she withdraws to a "distant place" (Sura 19:22). There, alone in the shade of a date palm, she gives birth.[51] When she cries out in the anguish of labor, a voice comforts her, telling her to drink from a stream that has miraculously appeared and to eat the fruit of the tree under which she has taken shelter. One more trial awaits her. Mary presents the child to "her people," who accuse her of fornication. A mere newborn yet already an eloquent prophet, Jesus answers their charges and clears his mother's name.

This is the Qu'ran's spare portrait of Mary: a woman chosen by God and touched by miracle from a young age, the virginal mother of a prophet, a model of devotion "who believed the words of her Lord and his Books and was among the obedient" (Sura 66:12). If it seems reminiscent of the Mary of Christian scripture, that is no accident. From her inception, the Muslim Mary grew in tandem with her older Christian sister. The Quranic portrayal of her owes much to the canonical gospels, but even more to the so-called apocryphal gospels. Widely circulated and much beloved by Christians, although formally condemned by early church councils, texts such as the *Protoevangelium of James* and the *Gospel of Pseudo-Matthew* provided all the details about Mary lacking in Matthew, Mark, Luke, and John, including her conception, her childhood, and the selection of her husband/guardian.[52] Drawing from this rich fund of information, the Qu'ran's vision of Jesus' mother refracts the Mary that medieval Christians knew from the apocrypha.[53]

Muhammad probably had not read the Christian apocrypha himself; he may not even have been literate in the modern sense of the word.[54] But he could have heard these stories about Mary repeated by Christians who lived in the great oasis towns of the Arabian Peninsula, or by traders who crossed the desert to bring news and wares to Mecca's marketplaces. Muhammad could even have been raised on such tales, for his own wet nurse was an Ethiopian Christian. At a busy trade fair not far south of Mecca he had listened to at least one sermon delivered by Quss ibn Sa'ida, a silver-tongued Christian bishop who sometimes preached from the back of a camel. Perhaps this orator renowned for his stately Arabic drew on the stories about Mary as he strove to convince his pagan audience of Christianity's benefits.[55]

As Muhammad shaped the revelations that God had sent him about a new form of monotheism into the verses that would become the Qu'ran, he wrestled with what he knew of Christianity and Judaism. In his efforts to work out the relationship between Islam and its monotheistic predecessors, he might have visited the "oratories of Mary" located near his home town or have exchanged ideas with a Christian man named Pachomius, who put Jesus' mother's imprint on Mecca's sacred shrine, the Ka'aba.[56] Pachomius was a Coptic Christian who, after being shipwrecked on the coast of Arabia in the early seventh century, made his way to the desert town. There he lent his skills as an artisan to the project of transforming the Ka'aba from a rude open-air structure into a building more worthy of housing the sacred black stone venerated by Meccans and pilgrims alike.[57] Pachomius left the traces of his own faith in the paintings of Abraham, Jesus, and Mary with which he decorated the inside of the refurbished shrine.[58]

The respect accorded Mary in the formative years of Islam is evident in the fate of Pachomius's artwork. On Muhammad's triumphant return to Mecca after the long sojourn in Madina, he resolved to purge the Ka'aba of pagan idolatry. According to one of the Prophet's early biographers, Ibn Ishaq, Muhammad ordered the destruction of all the shrine's idols and the erasure of the pictures on its walls. Muhammad exempted only the portraits of Mary and her son, "on both of whom be peace!" exclaims Ibn Ishaq. This eighth-century writer goes on to relate a tradition that just as crisply claims Mary for Islam and the Arabs. A woman who came to Mecca on pilgrimage took one glance at the painting of Mary and declared, "You are surely an Arab woman!"[59]

Despite the acceptance of Mary and her son in early Islam, the idea that Muhammad would have spared images of them made some Muslims uncomfortable. When Ibn Hisham abridged and edited Ibn Ishaq's text in the ninth century to produce the authoritative biography of Muhammad, he altered this passage to read that Muhammad had *all* the images in the Ka'aba removed.[60] Ibn Hisham's changes did not, however, suggest a demotion of Mary herself. If anything, she became a more developed and pronounced personage in Islam as the authors of the so-called "legends of the prophets" and other texts filled in the many details of her life left blank by the Qu'ran. In dialogue with the ever evolving Christian apocrypha, Islamic texts began, for example, to mention Joseph and to describe the Flight to Egypt.[61]

The most miraculous and puzzling aspects of Mary's life received intense scrutiny. How, wondered Muslim writers, had she actually conceived her son? The compilers of the *hadith*, authoritative texts recording the sayings and deeds of Muhammad and his companions, gradually devised an ingenious solution to this problem that also worried Christians: Jesus had been borne into Mary's womb on the angel Gabriel's breath. Did Mary menstruate? If so, was her purity defiled? As early medieval commentators on the Qu'ran sought to understand the questions posed by the scriptural portrait of Mary, they helped to articulate a place for her within Islam.[62]

Pondering the exalted status ascribed to Mary by their sacred book, some Muslim theologians wondered if she was perhaps a prophet—a *nabiya*, a person upon whom God conferred revelations but not the mission to speak about them that burned in a *rasul* like Muhammad. Enthusiastic as some writers were about this idea, many concluded that Mary instead enjoyed the role of a saintly friend of God. So much was at stake in this debate that the discussion was not always polite. The conflict over Mary and prophecy raged particularly fiercely in early eleventh-century Córdoba, rousing such acrimony among the city's learned men that al-Andalus's ruler believed that it threatened the peace. He squelched the feud by banishing some protagonists from each camp.[63]

As these men left Córdoba behind and headed into exile, some still hotly defended Mary's right to the title of *nabiya*, while others continued to believe she did not deserve it. Those theologians who were reluctant to concede this honor to her openly expressed their doubts that any representative of the female sex could achieve prophethood. Yet even they were willing to agree that among women, Mary stood out as a paragon of virtue and purity. After all, the Qu'ran itself declared that she was "chosen…from all the women of the world" (Sura 3:42) and an "example" to be followed (Sura 66:12), language that elevated her above the other exemplary female figures of early Islam: Khadija, Muhammad's first wife; 'Aisha, his youngest and supposedly favorite wife; and Fatima, his daughter.[64] By the tenth century, Islamic writers who were slowly sculpting these members of the Prophet's household into epitomes of feminine virtue looked to Mary as their model and worked to bring out their subjects' likeness to her. Virginity per se held little interest for these authors, who belonged to a culture in which lifelong abstinence from sex was not a spiritual ideal for women. But Mary's perfect chastity could easily be appropriated for these other idealized figures, as could her piety, her loving maternity, her honesty, and her constant obedience to God.[65]

How strongly Mary's role as exemplar in the scriptural and theological traditions of medieval Islam translated into the world of living devotion is another question. She certainly did not elicit the pious ardor aroused by Fatima, whose name today is attached to the stylized hand amulets ubiquitous to the Middle East that are believed to ward off bad luck and the evil eye.[66] Yet even though Mary could not rival Muhammad's daughter, she had an honorable place in the larger landscape of Islamic belief and practice.

Sufis seeking to capture their mystical ecstasies in poetry evoked Mary as a living metaphor of the soul's desire for God and honored her as a guardian of divine wisdom.[67] In some parts of the Islamic world, two of the Quranic verses narrating her story were used more literally to frame the rituals of devotion that brought Muslims together for worship. When they pray in mosques, Muslims face the *mihrab*, the wall niche indicating the direction of Mecca. Usually the most richly decorated part of a mosque, the *mihrab* often is ornamented with Quranic inscriptions. Among the verses commonly used are two with Marian associations, Suras 3:37 and 3:39. Both mention the chamber—*mihrab* in Arabic—where the young Mary lived, and one describes the priest Zachariah paying his devotions to God there. Though chosen for the word echo and their portrait of prayer rather than their Marian connotations, these Quranic verses nonetheless belong to the story of a prophet's virginal mother.[68]

Many of the *mihrab* inscriptions invoking these Marian *suras* come from the Ottoman Empire. Further west in the Mediterranean, Islam's devotional geography was marked more explicitly by affection for Mary. By the twelfth century, Muslim women and men from as far away as al-Andalus made pilgrimages to see the places where she and Jesus had stopped during the Flight to Egypt, including the date tree that leaned over to offer its fruits to the exhausted mother and the spring from which she had drunk.[69] These travelers could collect keepsakes from their journey to the lands where the mother of a prophet had lingered. In 1494 an elderly Muslim resident of the city of Granada proudly showed a German visitor a set of prayer beads made of date pits from one of the trees that had generously fed Mary.[70]

The items Muslims brought home from these Marian pilgrimage sites were more than just souvenirs. Reverently kissing the date-pit-beads, the old man in Granada explained that they could help "pregnant women."[71] Surely the circlet was believed to ensure a safe birth or to ease labor pains, for its beads came from the fruit that had comforted Mary in her anguish.[72] According to a fourteenth-century German author, Muslim women attributed similar powers to roses that grew along the roads where she had walked.[73] In al-Andalus, people attending births thus often raised their voices in prayer not just to God, but also to Mary, asking her to watch over the mother and bring a male child.[74]

Some Muslims living in Córdoba at the height of the city's splendor felt that Mary extended her beneficence to their whole community. In a niche over one of the capital's main entrance gates stood a statue of a woman. It was perhaps an old Roman image of a goddess, but some medieval Islamic writers reflecting on the glories of al-Andalus confidently asserted that it was an image of Mary. One even went so far as to call her the patron of Córdoba.[75] It is hard to know if the comments of these learned men reflected the opinion of the crowds who passed under the statue every day on their way in and out of the busy city. But Córdoba's statue was famous enough that in the ninth century, the founders of Pechina, a town deliberately modeled on al-Andalus's capital, made sure to ornament one of its gates with a similar image, or so said a late medieval Muslim geographer.[76]

One eleventh-century man who surely had walked beneath the statue at Córdoba many times was Abu Muhammad 'Ali ibn Hazm, a member of a prominent family and a prolific author. He was silent on the subject of the statue, but not about Mary. Ibn Hazm displayed his mastery of the erudition prized among al-Andalus's upper classes by writing over four hundred works. In one of them, he methodically laid out the arguments in support of Mary's prophethood.[77] He also mentioned her in his book on the rather more profane theme of love. In one of the poems ornamenting this famous account of the joys and sorrows awaiting lovers, Ibn Hazm quoted from the Qu'ran's description of her.[78]

By the twelfth century, Andalusi court poets permitted themselves to sigh with desire and longing for Mary, inviting her into the pleasure palaces they erected in verse for their masters. They did so by inventively reworking a popular erotic poem that originated in Bagdad at the court of Harun al-Rashid, the great 'Abbasid ruler fancifully depicted in *The Thousand and One Nights*.[79] Linked by the tenth century to a suggestive story in Shahrazad's narrative about three women quarreling over one pleasure-giving object, the original poem described a man in love with three women at once. Several centuries later, the poets of Granada gave these verses from Baghdad a decidedly more elevated tone by identifying the three women in question as Fatima, 'Aisha, and Mary. Lines written by 'Ali ibn al-Jayyab, court poet and vizier to a fourteenth-century Nasrid ruler, eloquently represent the Granadan tradition:

Ah, I love three women, all virtuous of conduct!
'Aisha, who enjoyed great glory and whom God saved from calumny;
And ahead of her, Fatima, she of high lineage;
But in first place, the most pure of the three, [Mary].[80]

The Nasrid sultan probably enjoyed these verses, as he did Ibn al-Jayyab's other compositions, some of them traced in stucco on the walls of the Alhambra's sumptuous apartments. As popular in its more pious phrasing as the bawdy earlier version had been, the poem also attracted quite an audience in the dense jumble of streets that lay below the precincts of Granada's famous palace complex.

In the late fifteenth century, some Granadans blessed with three daughters even were inspired to name them after the poem's three damsels.[81]

By the late fifteenth century, this poem circulated so widely that crossed into Christian territory. Castilian court poets appropriated its conceits, as did the singers of ballads who moved in less fashionable circles. Somewhere in the process of translation from Arabic into Castilian, the poem's descriptions of Islamic virtue disappeared in favor of an emphasis on the more physical attractions of the "three Moorish girls," as Fatima, 'Aisha, and Mary were called in the Christian songbooks.[82] Hence, when the Christians occupying Granada in 1499 and 1500 encountered trios of Muslim sisters bearing these names, they immediately recognized the literary allusion.[83]

Not all of the women known as Mary who lived in Granada when Castile took possession of the city had sisters called Fatima and 'Aisha. The name Mary by itself enjoyed much popularity among Granadans. According to Hieronymus Münzer, the reason for this naming pattern was simple: "the Saracens venerate the Virgin Mary very much."[84] Was the same also true of those Muslims who spent their lives under Christian rule? Did the Mudejars of high medieval Castile and Aragon perceive Mary differently from their co-religionaries across the frontier? These questions are frustratingly difficult to answer. Most of the extant texts written by Mudejars themselves rather than by Christians about Mudejars do not open the kind of broad window onto the religious life of these Muslims that would be helpful. It is clear, however, that despite the grave difficulties posed by their political subjugation to unbelievers, most Mudejars wanted be good Muslims and strove to abide by the legal and ritual precepts of Islam.[85] The few scattered references to Mary that appear in some late fifteenth- or early sixteenth-century Mudejar texts suggest as much. Quoting the Qu'ran's description of Mary and her son, and recounting the legendary events of her life, these Mudejar authors did not deviate from mainstream Islam.[86]

These writers were learned men who had some access to Islamic scholarship. How and whether Mary was present in the devotional lives of the less literate men and women who made up the bulk of the Mudejar population remains an open question. Yet any Mudejar, literate or illiterate, male or female, who thought about Mary must have been keenly aware of her importance to their Christian neighbors. She was, after all, the mother of the man on the omnipresent cross. Nor could Mudejars fail to see the churches of Our Lady that densely blanketed the Christian landscape by the thirteenth century, many of which occupied the sites of their former mosques. In some towns, a church of the Virgin stood right in the Muslim quarter, as in late fifteenth-century Ciudad Rodrigo.[87] Even those Muslims who lived in al-Andalus had to admit that she did not belong to Islam alone. Yusuf I's court poet Ibn al-Jayyab may have called Mary "the purest of the three" women who had stolen his heart, but he also recognized her as "the lady of the enemies," wistful words that concluded his famous poem about the trio.[88]

"The lady of the enemies"—Ibn al-Jayyab's elegant phrase lays bare a world of spiritual and religious complications clustered around Mary. How were the Muslims of Granada to follow the Qu'ran's injunctions and honor her if their enemies, the Christians of Castile and Aragon, loved her as their "lady"? What did they think when they heard Christian knights call out her name in battle or when they saw her image fluttering on Christian war banners?[89] For Mudejars, living among Christians and subject to their rule, such questions must have been even more acute. The Christian lords on whose lands they labored, the Christians for whom they built churches and houses, and the Christians who required their services in countless other ways all claimed Mary as advocate and intercessor.

The answers to these questions lie in the dialogues about Mary—whether imaginary or real, physical or intellectual, hostile or friendly—in which the Muslims of the Iberian Peninsula engaged with their Christian neighbors both across the frontier and down the street. The Christian side of these conversations also needs attention, for the followers of Christ themselves had to negotiate the Virgin's ambiguity as a figure who stood astride the boundary between their faith and Islam.

5

Lady of the Enemies

Whether the average Castilian or Aragonese Christian peasant realized that the sacred scripture of her Mudejar neighbors praised Mary, more learned members of the faith certainly did. Alfonso X of Castile and his court poets provide the most lyrical evidence. "In the Qu'ran I have read that Saint Mary was...a virgin," sings one Muslim sultan in the *Cantigas de Santa María*.[1] Other poems in the collection evoke the Qu'ran's elevation of Mary above all women and its praise of her miraculous virginal conception of Jesus.[2] Alfonso's poets once even allow a Muslim character to call Jesus's mother by her Arabic name: Maryam, or *Mariame* in its Galician corruption.[3] Like a boulder in a river, this garbled Arabic word rudely interrupts the flow of "María"s in the *Cantigas*. In the way that only a name can, it stands as testimony to the strength of Islam's claim on Alfonso's beloved *amiga*.

Few of Alfonso X's immediate descendants rivaled his erudition. But some of them knew that Muslims believed in Mary's virginity and Jesus' conception through God's breath. Alfonso X's son, Sancho IV, as well as the learned king's nephew, Juan Manuel, both said as much in books they wrote.[4] So, too, did men who dedicated themselves not to affairs of swords and crowns, but instead to wars of words: Christian polemicists. In Aragon and Castile, as elsewhere in Christian Europe, such writers by the thirteenth century readily admitted that Muslims, in Ramón Llull's succinct formulation, "honor Mary by calling her holy and virgin and Jesus Christ's mother through the Holy Spirit."[5]

So aware were Christian polemicists of the Qu'ran's positive vision of Mary that they mustered it as a weapon in their fight against Judaism: if even Islam's scripture proved Christianity's claims about the virgin birth, how could Jews stubbornly cling to their disbelief in Mary? The thirteenth-century Catalan Dominican friar Ramón Martí, as at home in Arabic as in Hebrew, marshaled quotations from the Qu'ran in his monumental *Dagger of the Faith* when Pugio Fidei railed against Jews for not recognizing Mary as virgin mother.[6] Several centuries later, the Castilian friar Alonso de Espina did the same in his vitriolic polemic against all "enemies" of Christianity, *Fortalitium Fidei* (1461). As Espina

147

so bluntly put it: "To the greater confounding of the Jews, the scriptures of the Saracens declare the sanctity of the Virgin Mary."[7]

One Christian text circulating in late thirteenth-century Castile went much further. The unknown author of the *Libro de las tres creencias* championed Christianity as the best of the three religions.[8] Judging by the text's discussion of Mary, Islam came second with Judaism a distant third. Aiming directly at the Jews, the *Libro*'s author quotes (although inaccurately) the Qu'ran's praise of Mary. Using as his foundation this triumphant proof hewn from Islamic scripture of Jewish error and Christian truth, the writer proceeds to construct a Marian hierarchy that places Islam above Judaism. He declares that "Muslims, in contrast to Jews, enjoy worldly glory and temporal power because they honor" Mary, a neat explanation of why Muslims had a polity on the Iberian Peninsula but Jews did not.[9]

Muslims would have agreed. After all, their own holy book told them that one of the many reasons they were better than Jews was precisely because they respected Mary. The Jews "denied and spoke dreadful calumnies of Mary." Reminiscent as this accusation is of Christian anti-Jewish rhetoric, it actually comes from the Qu'ran (Sura 4:156). It appears in a passage that seeks to establish the superiority of Islam over the original Abrahamic religion by severely rebuking the Jews for their offenses against God. If the Jews disparaged Mary and thus incurred God's wrath, Muslims, this *sura* implies, would not commit the same error. These words that, just like all the others in the Qu'ran, would be memorized by countless medieval Muslims made Mary into a firm boundary between Islam and Judaism. Medieval Muslim polemicists themselves pointed self-righteous fingers at the Jewish legends slurring Jesus' mother.[10]

The Christians and Muslims of high medieval Iberia then both thought that their belief in the special status of Jesus' mother elevated them above their Jewish neighbors. Some Christians also recognized that Muslims' respect for Mary distinguished Islam from Judaism. What did it mean to Christians and Muslims to share this figure so resoundingly rejected by the members of the other Abrahamic religion? How did they deal with the unsettling potential for proximity offered by the "lady of the enemies," as the Granadan poet Ibn al-Jayyab dubbed Mary? Though the answers to these questions depend on whom we ask and when, this much is evident. At times, Mary, a figure belonging to both Christianity and Islam, offered the possibility of practical ecumenicism. She created a space where Muslims and Christians could ignore religious difference for a whole host of reasons—political, economic, even spiritual. In other situations, she became yet another sharply drawn line between the worlds of Muslims and Christians, a medium through which some members of these faiths could express their implacable difference and thus their inevitable bloody conflict.

Sharing Mary

In the eleventh century, the ancient port city of Ossonoba acquired a new name: "Saint Mary." For an era in which European Christian devotion to the Virgin began to flourish, this change would hardly be worth noting—except this urban community did not lie within the frontiers of Christendom. The city jutted into the Mediterranean from the southern tip of the Algarve, a swathe of coastline whose white sand beaches and groves of fig and orange trees belonged to Muslim masters. Ossonoba had been part of al-Andalus ever since the eighth century and would not come under Christian control until some two hundred years after its name change. During the intervening centuries, its residents knew their home as Shantamariyya, eventually tacking on the name of one of their rulers, Ibn Harun. Beyond the frontiers of al-Andalus, Romance speakers reshaped the Arabic words, dubbing the city Santa María de Faro.[11]

Behind Ossonoba's startling transformation into Mary's city lay some complicated urban politics. Like many towns and cities in early medieval al-Andalus, Shantamariyya housed within its walls not just Muslims but also Christians, descendants of those Visigoths and Hispano-Romans who had not fled Tariq's army in 711 but stayed on under Muslim rule. These men and women enjoyed the religious protections that Islamic law granted to Christians and Jews, who, as monotheists, were allowed to maintain their own devotional beliefs and practices, albeit within prescribed limits. Many Christians in al-Andalus would eventually convert to Islam, although they had no legal obligation to do so.[12] Perhaps the ever-increasing numbers of new Muslims influenced Ossonaba's name change; converts might have been comforted to know that Mary, a woman whom their old religion had taught them to love, could continue to watch over them in their new faith. Her appeal as a crossover figure to people who had left Christianity for Islam was a factor in city politics elsewhere in al-Andalus. The learned Muslims in early eleventh-century Córdoba who so vehemently insisted on Mary's right to the title of prophet may have been trying to reassure new members of their faith that she commanded almost as exalted a place in Islam as she did in Christianity.[13]

Not all of Ossonoba's Christians, however, had renounced the religion of their parents by the time their city adopted Mary's name. Between the ninth and the eleventh centuries, this Christian community was vibrant, well-organized, and influential. These men and women funneled some of their apparently considerable resources into a church dedicated to the Virgin. Often filled with pious visitors from well beyond Ossonaba's walls, it welcomed a steady stream of Christian pilgrims, many offering Mary thanks for having been liberated from captivity through her graces.[14] The Muslim authorities permitted and perhaps even encouraged this traffic, since pilgrims generated income. To remind everyone that this was nonetheless a Muslim city, a mosque was built right next to Mary's church.[15]

Some Muslims obviously knew the Virgin's church well and considered it an ornament of their city. Anyone who entered the church and gazed at the massive white columns lining its nave—each wider than a grown man's arm span, boasted an eleventh-century Muslim author—would have been impressed by this showy display of wealth by the city's Christians.[16] Matching the church's magnificence was the apparent political influence commanded by the Christian community in the late ninth and early tenth centuries. In those years, the leading Muslim family of Ossonoba, the Banu Becre, shook off the unsteady hand of the Umayyad rulers of al-Andalus. Even after the great tenth-century caliph 'Abd al-Rahman III subdued the majority of his rebellious subjects, the Banu Becre maintained an unusual degree of autonomy. Their success in establishing Ossonoba's independence resulted in no small part from the allegiance and support of the city's Christians.[17]

Shantamariyya—the new name that began to appear in the eleventh century for Ossonoba—eloquently captured the Christians' importance to the city's political and economic life, and its sense of self. A woman who commanded the respect of both Muslims and Christians, Mary was the ideal symbol for this civic community bound together by a web of alliances between members of the two faiths. According to Christian miracle stories circulating by the twelfth century, a statue of her may even have topped the city's walls, looking far out over the sea slapping against the stone fortifications.[18] The artists of the *Cantigas de Santa María* painted the scene with their usual attention to detail, setting an imperious Madonna into a tower flanked by a city gate, its horseshoe arch visual shorthand for the land of Islam. Grey waves curl and foam beneath the walls.[19]

A statue of Mary would have been an unusual emblem for a Muslim city, but not an impossible one in an era when some learned Muslims identified the image over one of Córdoba's gates as the Virgin. Muslim authors, however, did not breathe a word about Shantamariyya's statue, though they often praised the city's famous Marian church.[20] Perhaps the image did not actually exist anywhere but in the overly active imagination of Christian hagiographers, or perhaps the statue did cap Shantamariyya's walls, but Muslims were reluctant to admit it in writing. They might not have wanted to commemorate a feature of the city that so blatantly contravened Islamic prohibitions against religious imagery. It is even possible that some Muslims expressed their displeasure with the statue's prominent location and tried to have the image removed, as medieval Christians beyond the frontiers of al-Andalus evidently believed. According to a tale recounted by twelfth-century Christian chroniclers and taken up by Alfonso X and his poets in the *Cantigas*, some of Shantamariyya's Muslims threw the statue of Mary into the sea, only to repent when the schools of fish on which the city depended had vanished. They retrieved the image and replaced it in its lofty perch, thus restoring its status as civic symbol.[21] This miracle story may be the product of Christian fantasy, or it may reflect something that really happened to disturb Muslim-Christian relations in Mary's city by the sea. Whether or not a statue of the Virgin ever decorated the town's sturdy walls, the name Shantamariyya bore testimony to a long history of interfaith solidarity.

Perhaps similar relations between Muslims and Christians prevailed in Shantamariyat ibn Razin (now known as Santa María de Albarracín), another town in al-Andalus named for Mary.[22] Yet a Muslim city did not have to experience a Marian christening for its Muslim and Christian residents to form a united front under her aegis, or so a poem in the *Cantigas de Santa María* relates. The story is set in thirteenth-century Marrakech, a Moroccan city whose political fortunes greatly mattered to Alfonso X. He dreamed of conquests on the southern side of the Mediterranean and was acutely aware that the tumultuous politics of North Africa often had repercussions in the Iberian Peninsula. Marrakech, the capital city founded by the Almoravids and further embellished by their successors, the Almohads, was usually at the center of the storm.

In the 1260s, Almohad Marrakech twice suffered assault from a new Berber dynasty, the Marinids. Among the residents who feared for their property and their lives when the city lay under siege were Christians, most of them mercenaries serving the Almohad caliph with their swords.[23] They were a significant enough community that they perhaps had their own church, maybe even one dedicated to Mary.[24] According to the *Cantigas,* they at least owned a banner of the Virgin and some processional crosses, concrete emblems of Christian identity in a city dominated by the soaring red brick minaret of the Almohad mosque. When Marrakech trembled under Marinid attack, the Christians apparently were willing to loan these precious objects to the Almohad army in hopes of their city's miraculous deliverance.

An evocative poem in the *Cantigas* commemorates these events.[25] It relates how under the leadership of Abu Yusuf Ya'qub, Marinid forces encircled Marrakech, imprisoning its residents behind the city's walls. The desperate Almohad caliph, probably 'Umar al-Murtada, holds a war council, where his advisors exhort him to make a sally accompanied by a handful of his best fighters and the "banner of the Holy Virgin Mary." Where he should get this banner they do not say, though they assure him that victory will be his when the standard unfurls before his enemies' startled eyes. For good measure, the caliph's council advises him also to ask the Christians to make a procession from their church carrying their crosses. The Marinids flee in disarray before the Marian banner and the crosses, and the city is saved.

It is possible that the caliph's advisors did counsel him to ride to war behind this Christian banner bearing the image of a woman lauded by the Qu'ran, as the *cantiga* insists. Another scenario, however, seems more plausible: during this crisis, the Christian mercenaries living in Marrakech turned to the battle icons from their own faith that just fifty years earlier had presided over the great victory of Las Navas de Tolosa. The *cantiga*'s illumination even suggests that Christian men of war, not their Muslim fellows-in-arms, carried the banner and crosses into the fight with the Marinids.[26] Alfonso X's artists meticulously painted knights with typically Christian war gear massed right under these Christian emblems (Figure 5.1). Close to the banner and crosses but not quite under them comes a company of bearded turbaned knights obviously meant as the Almohads. It is an arresting scene of Christians and Muslims united by Mary on the battlefield instead of separated by her. Ironically, the two panels depicting the banner shared by this interfaith army are the only representations of a Marian war standard in all of the *Cantigas de Santa María*. In the artists' rendering, it is a large red square of cloth decorated with Mary seated in stiff majesty, Jesus on her lap.

Alfonso X's poets did not entirely agree with their painterly colleagues' tale of Muslim-Christian military cooperation. They countered the illuminators' version of events with lyrics that created a story of Mary's intervention in an episode of Islamic history. They set the scene with the poem's title, omitting not just Marrakech's Christian mercenaries, but the crosses too in order to give the Virgin sole credit for the miraculous victory: "How Abu Yusuf was put to flight in Morocco by Saint Mary's banner." In the subsequent verses, no Christians appear to carry the Marian banner into combat, though they do hold the crosses, a tacit admission that, unlike Mary, such symbols belonged exclusively to Christianity. According to the poem, Muslims suggest that the caliph adopt the banner as his war standard, only Muslims fight on the battlefield, and Mary presides over a victory of good Muslims against bad Muslims. As the *cantiga* declares in its last lines, this is a story about Mary and Muslims: "So Saint Mary helped her friends, even though they were of another faith, to smash their enemies."

As so often in the *Cantigas*, Mary's sentiments mirror Alfonso X's own. The king had every reason to dislike the Marinids, for the vigorous state they were building threatened Castile as the largely decrepit Almohads did not. Yet the poem papers over such politics to craft a narrative of mutual affection between Muslims and Mary, insisting in its refrain that "the Virgin helps those who love her most, even though they are of another faith and unbelievers." Similar things are said of Muslims elsewhere in the *Cantigas*, but never of the followers of that other unbelieving faith, Judaism.[27] All the while recognizing the otherness of Islam, Alfonso's poets were as ready to share Mary with Muslims as the Christians of Marrakech apparently were to loan their Marian banner to the Almohad caliph's troops.

These instances of the Virgin's potential to play a bridging role in city politics had as their stage the medieval Muslim polities of al-Andalus and the Mahgreb,

Figure 5.1 A war banner decorated with an image of Mary miraculously protects Almohad Marrakech from attack by the Marinids. *Cantigas de Santa María*. Biblioteca Monasterio del Escorial, Codice Rico, MS. T.I.1, folio 240r. Patrimonio Nacional.

places that belonged to the *dar al-Islam*, the "house of Islam," where the follow-ers of Muhammad reigned supreme over all other faiths. There, Muslims could be sure that granting the Christian version of Mary occasional entrance to the civic arena would not threaten the proper hierarchy of religions. Yet her ability to serve as the medium for positive exchanges between Christian and Muslim neighbors did not depend on this particular political configuration. In the kingdoms of Castile and Aragon, where Christian monarchs ruled over those Muslims known as Mudejars, Mary also had this capacity.

The Christian and Mudejar ironsmiths of fourteenth-century Teruel, an Aragonese town near Santa María de Albarracín, seem to have thought so. The statutes of the confraternity to which these men belonged suggest the kind of practical Marian ecumenicism that prevailed in a place like Shantamariyya ibn Harun or besieged Marrakech. Watching over Teruel's smiths was Saint Eloy, the Merovingian metal- and miracle-worker after whom the confraternity was named and whom Christian smiths across Europe considered their patron. But every week the town's Christian and Muslim smiths pooled their resources to offer a candle to Mary. It is true that once the family of a Muslim smith violently refused to pay up for that week's candle, but it is unclear whether this incident revealed anything more than tight finances. Over a century later, the Mudejar and Christian smiths of the Castilian town of Segovia joined a confraternity of Saint Eloy, founded in 1484 in "honor and reverence and praise of the blessed Saint Mary…and all the male and female saints of the celestial court." But in Segovia, the Mudejar smiths did not have to contribute to the confraternity's candle expenses.[28]

These Christian and Muslim artisans were driven by mutual economic inter-est to band together in confraternities. Their decision to honor Mary institution-ally may have been dictated as much by common sense as by the fact that she was one of the most popular saints in high medieval Christian Europe. If the smiths realized that both Muslims and Christians could respect her without transgress-ing the precepts of their respective religions, she would have been a logical choice as a devotional focus for their cross-faith confraternities. Equally prag-matic considerations motivated the instances of sharing Mary in Shantamariyya ibn Harun and Marrakech. Yet Muslims and Christians of medieval Iberia could also conceive of sharing Mary in a purely devotional context, motivated by faith rather than by politics, economics, or fear.

If Alfonso X and his literary entourage are to be believed, some thirteenth-century Christian and Muslim mercenaries operating in the eastern Sierra Morena were united in unexpected ways by their mutual love for Mary. In the years leading up to and immediately following Ferdinand III's conquest of Seville, this region of rolling hills not far from that city was a wild border-land, officially part of the kingdom of Castile-León but subject to raids from

Figure 5.2 Church of Tentudia. Author photo.

al-Andalus and populated with restive Mudejars and newly arrived Christian settlers. According to the *Cantigas de Santa María*, one oasis of interfaith peace in
the eastern reaches of these hills was the tiny church of Santa María de Tentudia
(Figure 5.2). Founded sometime in the early thirteenth century, Tentudia
belonged first to the Templars and then to the Order of Santiago.[29] A frontier
church whose masters were Christian men dedicated to fighting the infidel
would seem an unlikely place for Muslims and Christians to come together in
rituals of devotion to Mary, but that is what the *Cantigas* recount.

One poem describes how a band of Muslim raiders pitch camp right next to
the church.[30] They then enter the sacred precincts of Mary's shrine. The *Cantigas'*
Christian audience probably knew what to expect—a shocking scene of loot-
ing with Muslims falling upon the church treasure of rich liturgical vessels and
robes, gleaming statues and candlesticks, as they do in other poems. The poet
instead surprises with a peaceful portrait of Muslims revering Mary. One by one,
these men approach the altar and lay upon it offerings of gold and silver coins "in
honor of the holy Virgin." Then they pray. Such love for Jesus' mother is enjoined
upon Muslims by their own religious traditions, explains the poet. "Although the
Moors do not hold our faith," Muhammad "wrote in the Qu'ran" praise of Mary
that "the Moors well believe without fail."

This poet betrayed no sense that his story could be interpreted as a narrative
of the infidel desecrating a building sacred to Christians. Instead, his evocation of
the Marian beliefs and offerings of these Muslim raiders is as respectful as other

cantigas' descriptions of Christians rendering thanks to statues of the Madonna. So comfortable was the poet with the presence of Muslims in Tentudia's church that it did not seem wondrous to him. The miracle he celebrated was instead Mary's punishment of a greedy Muslim soldier. This man, who slips back into the church at Tentudia and swipes his companions' offerings from the altar, is immediately struck with blindness and paralysis, just like those Christians who commit similar offenses in the *Cantigas*. Only a renewed display of devotion to Mary by his fellow Muslims saves him. They pat him down, discover the purloined coins, and return the offerings to "the Lady worthy of praise." The Virgin in turn restores the malefactor's health—a great miracle that, writes the poet, Christians learned of from the Muslims themselves.

If, in the poetic world of the *Cantigas*, love for Mary could bring Muslim men of war into this frontier church and make them tell tales of her miracles, it could also create peace between them and their Christian adversaries. In the days when Seville still belonged to al-Andalus, relates one *cantiga*, a hard-riding band of Muslim knights set out from the city and pushed deep into the Sierra Morena, searching for Christian prey. At nightfall, they camp beside the church of Tentudia, just a stone's throw away from the men of a Christian company. But even though these heavily armed Christians and Muslims water their horses at the same fountain, they never so much as notice each other and sleep the night away "in peace." Only as the sun rises do they all realize what has happened. Astonished at this "miracle" caused by Mary's "power," the Muslims and Christians petition each other for truce and depart from Tentudia without bloodshed. The shared devotion of these Muslims and Christians to the Virgin of Tentudia, the "crowned Queen, whom they all obeyed that night," makes both miracle and truce possible. As the poem's refrain insists: "Saint Mary causes agreement between those who know how to revere her, even if they do not love each other."[31]

This scene of harmony set at Tentudia justifies some of Alfonso X's policies late in his reign, such as occasional truces with Granada and military cooperation with Muslim allies.[32] It also reflects the patron of the *Cantigas*'s political ideology as "ruler of the three faiths": his desire to command obedience from the non-Christians in his realm as well as the Christians, just as Mary does in both Tentudia poems. Although Alfonso's political agenda was well served by these *cantigas*, they may well have been accurate in their assertion that at this Christian shrine, Muslims honored Mary and even made offerings to her.

After all, Muslim geographers from al-Andalus could include in their worldview famed Marian churches located as far away as southern France.[33] The learned thirteenth-century French encyclopedist, Vincent of Beauvais, even praised Spain's Muslims (*Sarraceni occidentales*) for sending "gifts" to the cathedral of Our Lady at Le Puy. Vincent says that these pious Muslims hoped that their offerings would inspire this Virgin to "protect them and their fields from lightning bolts and storms."[34] This report from France may have been booster-ism intended to show the universal reach of Le Puy's Madonna, but Christians traveling the pilgrimage route linking this shrine to Compostela may have told tales of her power that impressed not only their co-religionaries in Castile and Aragon (the *Cantigas de Santa María* include five stories about her), but also Mudejars living there.[35]

From at least the late twelfth century onward, Muslims mingled with Christians in some Marian churches elsewhere in the Mediterranean. Crowning a rocky outcropping north of Damascus stands the most famous of these shrines, Saidnaya, still bustling with pilgrims, most of them Christian, but many Muslim.[36] In the high Middle Ages, too, Muslims and Christians, some of the latter crusaders, jostled for room in this church, especially on the feast days of Mary's Assumption and Nativity.[37] There the Muslims prayed and "offered their ceremonies with the greatest devotion," noted Burchard of Strasbourg in the late twelfth century.[38] As the German ambassador to Salah al-Din, the great Kurdish sultan who had retaken Jerusalem from its crusader kings, Burchard would have had the opportunity to visit Saidnaya and see for himself what went on at the shrine. He also had learned enough about Islam to report favorably on the Muslim belief in Mary's virginity and special motherhood.[39] By the thirteenth century, even Christians who had never been to the Holy Land knew about the miraculous benefits that Our Lady of Saidnaya conferred on Muslims who believed in her. Perhaps it was crusaders returning home who brought to Europe the uplifting if fanciful tale of how a blind sultan of Damascus recovered his sight through her good graces.[40]

By the time this legend circulated in French and Latin, Muslim authors began to mention the presence of members of their faith at Saidnaya.[41] Muslims went to the church, they wrote, for the same reason as Christians. All pilgrims to Saidnaya, whatever their faith, hoped to acquire a vial or even just a drop of the sweet wonder-working oil oozing from the church's icon of Mary. Such healing oil more typically trickled from saints' bodies than from paintings. But accord-ing to ever more elaborate Christian miracle stories about Saidnaya's renowned image, this icon was not so different from a bodily relic, for its paint and wood had become true flesh.[42] This living image of Mary was the shrine's devotional heart. Although "none dared touch [it], all were allowed to see it," wrote Burchard of Strasbourg.[43]

At Saidnaya, Muslims thus joined Christians in venerating a Marian image, just the kind of object that Andres of Jaén, the lookout posted near Almería in 1502, feared the followers of Islam would desecrate. If the *Cantigas* are right and Muslims came to Tentudia's frontier church to make offerings to Mary in the thirteenth century, they probably laid their gold and silver coins before a statue of her. By then, Christian Europe was crowded with images of the Madonna, many of them miracle workers.[44] Even churches far more humble than the sturdy stone building in Tentudia usually could muster the resources to purchase or commission a statue or painting of her. Images of Mary probably also decorated the altars of other Christian shrines in the medieval Mediterranean, where Muslims could be found paying their respects to Jesus' mother.[45]

The potential for cross-faith rituals of Marian devotion—even ones that openly defied Islamic strictures on venerating images—in these churches was conditioned by the specific historical circumstances of Muslims and Christians living in close proximity. It is also testimony to the possibilities for interfaith devotion that figures shared by two religions can offer. The continuous contact and exchange between Muslims and Christians characteristic of places like the Granada-Castile frontier could even occasionally produce saints who were no more constrained by territorial boundaries than the people living there. Such was the case with Saint Ginés de la Jara, whose relics were housed in a church on the Mediterranean coast near Murcia. In the fifteenth century, Muslims from Granada and North Africa often crossed the frontier to visit this shrine, which perhaps occupied the site of a former Muslim holy place. While Christian pilgrims to this rural church believed that the saint was the pious brother of the epic hero Roland, Muslims may have thought of him as a paladin of their own faith, even Muhammad's blood relative.[46]

The emergence of a saint like San Ginés resulted from the slow processes of legend building, religious acculturation, and even, as one historian has said, religious "confusion among the semi-literate" in the borderlands.[47] No such developments were necessary for Muslims to know they should honor Mary, for the Qu'ran taught them to do so. But the sacred book of Islam hardly urged its audience to venerate her in Christian religious buildings. The apparent ease with which some Muslims did so is a sign of the fluidity of religious cultures in medieval Iberia so dramatically embodied by Saint Ginés, as well as evidence of the more worldly side to the co-existence of the three faiths. In medieval Aragon and Castile, Jews, Muslims, and Christians visited each other's places of worship for all sorts of mundane reasons, whether to accompany friends, to work, or even just to satisfy their curiosity about what went on there—visits that Christian authorities did not condone but could not always control.[48] For some Muslims, it was not a big step to enter a church to honor Mary, a woman praised in their own scripture.

Is it reasonable then to imagine a peaceful Mediterranean Marian ecumenicism for which Christian churches were the setting, a kind of counterweight to Mary's involvement in reconquest? Events at Tortosa in 1498 caution otherwise. In that year, King Ferdinand II of Aragon issued an angry decree denouncing the Christian officials of this city for allowing Mudejars from Valencia, Catalonia, and

Aragon to celebrate Muslim festivals in the church of Santa María de la Rápita. Though the church stood kilometers south of Tortosa in the marshy expanses of the Ebro River delta, it fell within the city's jurisdiction.[49] The thought of Muslims ululating and performing the rituals of the "infernal Muhammadan sect" in this space dedicated to Christ's "inviolate mother" made the king shudder. So too did the knowledge that Muslims lit candles in the church (whether in honor of Mary, the document does not say, although as the church's patron, she would have been the logical recipient of such offerings). The harsh punishments that Ferdinand threatened for any civic or religious officials caught permitting these practices in the future—heavy fines, even execution—betrayed the depth of his outrage, as did his pronouncement that any Muslim who dared to enter the church risked enslavement or death. The king ordered that his decree be well publicized. To reclaim the church for Christianity, Ferdinand commanded that images of Christ and Mary be painted over the window in the part of the church where the Muslims had gathered. Only then would "all impurity be purged and abolished," he declared.[50]

What Ferdinand considered to be repugnant sacrilege and heinous offense against God and Mary, Tortosa's civic officials must have believed was a benign gesture of neighborly sharing. The divergence between their viewpoint and the king's signaled more than the distance between the practicalities of local *convivencia* and the lofty exigencies of royal policy. After all, centuries earlier, Alfonso X of Castile had expressed no disgust at the idea of Muslims praying in the church of Tentudia. The contrast between the *Cantigas'* stories of Muslims and Christians sharing Mary and Ferdinand's response to the situation at Santa María de la Rápita reveals distinct limits to the potential Mary offered for cross-faith devotion.

Geography begins to explain the gulf between these two rulers' reactions to what seem like similar circumstances. Built among forested hills only recently conquered by Christian forces, the church of Tentudia lay along the uncertain frontier of Alfonso X's realm, whereas by Ferdinand II's day, the Ebro Delta, home to Santa María de la Rápita, had belonged to Aragon for almost four hundred years.[51] Since the area surrounding Santa María de la Rápita was a favorite hunting preserve of Aragonese rulers, the church had received many royal visitors over the centuries.[52] It was probably easier for a king to countenance Muslims performing rituals of devotion in Christian churches in the borderlands of his realm than it was for a monarch to contemplate such mixed forms of worship in a place that he very much considered his own.

Changes in royal attitudes toward contact between Muslims and Christians surely played a part as well. Although during Alfonso X's lifetime, the Cortes of Castile decreed that Mudejars should not dress like Christians or live in houses next to them, such measures were rarely enforced.[53] In the sections of his law code that dealt with the Muslims, Alfonso did not even mention such statutes.[54] Thirteenth-century Aragon too saw little effort to implement the provisions aimed at segregating Mudejars (and Jews) from the Christian populace that were announced with the papal stamp of approval at the Fourth Lateran Council in 1215. If in the thirteenth century, the kings of Castile and Aragon did not energetically support such laws, the same was no longer true two hundred years later. Ferdinand II of Aragon was an enthusiastic proponent of maintaining strict boundaries between his Christian and Muslim subjects and harbored what has been called a "[fear] that Christians would be morally contaminated by extensive social interactions with Muslims."[55] No wonder he was so shocked by what he discovered at Santa María de la Rápita in 1498.

The biggest difference between the situations described in the *Cantigas* and the events at Tortosa, however, lay in what the Muslims were actually doing in these churches, or at least in what the Christian texts said they were doing. At Santa María de la Rápita, Mudejars prostrated and ululated like Muslims everywhere. Even if they offered candles to Mary as Tortosa's Christians did, their reason for gathering in the church on Islamic holy days was to perform the rituals affirming their identity as Muslims. They had apparently been doing so for several centuries. A document issued in 1304 by one of Ferdinand's predecessors on the throne of Aragon confirms how well-established and intentionally Islamic the gatherings of Muslims at Santa María de la Rápita were.

Muslims had the custom of making "pilgrimage" and of "congregat[ing]" at the "tower named Rápita," said James II of Aragon in 1304. It was entirely natural for them to do so, since this "tower" was actually an eleventh-century Muslim fortress, complete with mosque. It is unclear whether by the time that James II's document was drawn up, the fortress's mosque still belonged to the Muslim community or had already been transformed into Mary's church. Nor is it known if any traces of the original building survived into Ferdinand II's day. This much, however, is certain: in the early fourteenth century, Muslims visited this tower for devotional purposes that would have pleased the men of their faith who had built it. James II forbade this practice and gave the building to a community of nuns recently installed on the site.[56] Yet almost two hundred years later, Ferdinand II found Mudejars congregating in the same place and for the same purpose.

Alfonso X would have been disturbed had he heard that Muslims in his kingdom were turning Mary's churches into virtual mosques. After all, this king had no more complimentary things to say about Muhammad and his revelations than did Ferdinand II. The *Siete Partidas* deride Islam, while the *Cantigas de Santa María* label it a "sect of the demon" founded by a "false, vain...dog," as Mary herself uncharitably declares in one poem.[57] In the *Cantigas*, no Muslim was imagined as using a Marian church as a setting for Islamic devotional practices.

Instead, Alfonso's poets firmly cast Muslim devotion to Mary into the mold of Christian veneration of the Virgin and thus celebrated something rather different from the activities at Santa María de la Rápita.

In the *Cantigas*, the followers of Islam express their love for Mary with gestures taken straight from the Christian devotional repertoire. Muslims lay offerings on the altar of her church at Tentudia and respect the shrine as a place of peaceful sanctuary; in Marrakech they ride into battle with a banner bearing her image; and at Santa María de Faro, they install an image of her on the city walls. The other Christian authors who seemed to be comfortable with the notion of Muslims venerating Mary in Christian churches—including Vincent of Beauvais, Burchard of Strasbourg, and the anonymous writer who first recorded the tale of the Muslim sultan cured at Saidnaya—also depicted Muslims participating in Christian rituals of Marian devotion.[58] Whether or not they were documenting real events, they were spiritual imperialists, subtly shaping their material to give the message that Muslims could enjoy Mary's favor, but only by acting like Christians. Thus Christian writers admitted that the Virgin was a point of commonality between their religion and Islam, yet adroitly kept her for Christianity.

By performing even more spectacular rhetorical sleights of hand, Christian authors could transform even apparently innocuous stories about sharing Mary into brazen narratives of Christianity victorious. In one poem in the *Cantigas*, the poet deftly organizes his tale to convince his audience that a Muslim venerating Mary in a church was not evidence of Muslim-Christian rapprochement, but instead proof of Muslim military defeat. This was a neat trick, since the Muslim in question was none other than Baybars, the formidable Mamluk sultan who, as the members of Alfonso X's court surely knew, was executing a series of brilliant military campaigns that would lead to the final ignominious collapse of crusader power in the Levant.[59]

This *cantiga* built its Marian fantasy around one of Baybars's few reversals, his failure to take the Syrian port of Tartus from its crusader lords in 1270–1271. Naturally, the poet had a miraculous explanation: when Baybars lays siege to Tartus, the city's Christians beg Mary to protect them.[60] She responds by summoning an army of celestial soldiers. Informed by his lieutenant that this host of white-clad warriors took their orders from "the Virgin, mother of Iça," the sultan responds with a confession of Marian faith. Exclaiming that he has read in the Qu'ran that she was a virgin, he declares that he will not wage war against her. He then commands that the drums roll to signal his troops to withdraw. Before his final retreat, Baybars makes rich offerings to Mary in the city itself. The accompanying illumination shows him humbling himself before a statue of her in the same church where earlier the Christians had entreated her aid (Figure 5.3).

Whoever first told this story probably imagined as the setting for this final scene Tartus's crusader cathedral of Our Lady. Whether or not Alfonso X's poets

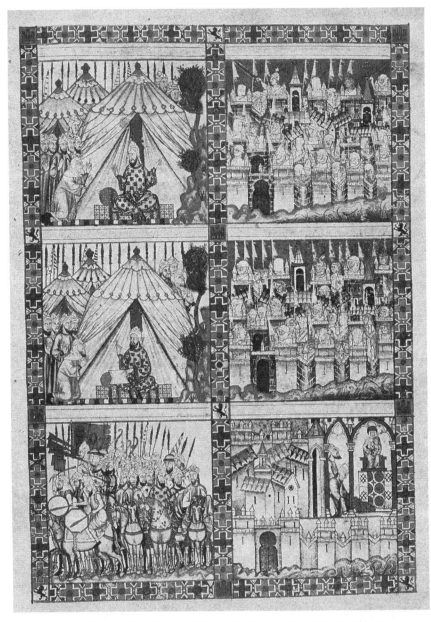

Figure 5.3 Miracle of Baybars' defeat at Tartus. *Cantigas de Santa María*. Biblioteca Monasterio del Escorial, Codice Rico, MS. T.I.1, folio 222r. Madrid, Spain. The Bridgeman Art Library.

and painters knew it, in the thirteenth century, men and women of the sultan's faith actually did pray among the massive pillars and heavy arches of this building, for it was one of Mary's churches that drew both Christian and Muslim pilgrims.[61] Soon after 1290, when another Mamluk sultan finished what Baybars had started and conquered Tartus, the city's new masters converted the cathedral into a mosque.[62] But they were not the first to remove this church from the peaceful pastures of Marian ecumenicism and thrust it into the tense arena of Muslim-Christian antagonism. Alfonso X's artists and poets had already done so, if more metaphorically, in their *cantiga* about Tartus. As their Baybars bows before Mary in her church, thwarted in his military enterprise not just by her heavenly army but also by his belief in her, he teaches the *Cantigas'* audience that the source of his defeat is internal to Islam. It is even enshrined in Islam's sacred book, which lies open in front of the sultan in the illumination.

The Castilian men and women who heard of this Marian miracle set in the Levant would have had little difficulty understanding its relevance to their own crusading world. If Muslim respect for Jesus' mother could cause Muslim defeat, the Christian narrative of reconquest remained intact, untroubled by Mary's role in Islam. Christian kings and knights were propelled to victory by their Marian faith, but Muslims instead were vanquished by it. Subtly—and at times not so subtly—Alfonso X and his poets thus made moments of sharing Mary part of the military contest between Islam and Christianity.

When the Granadan poet and vizier Ibn al-Jayyab composed his own version of the famous verses about the three women who captured one heart, he was more accurate than he could have suspected in describing the third damsel as Mary, "the lady of the enemies." Although in practice, Muslims and Christians could share devotion to this woman, Christian rhetoric never truly figured her as common ground between the two faiths. Earlier stories such as those in the *Cantigas* came the closest to doing so, yet even these tales failed to imagine Muslims doing anything other than conforming to Christian patterns of Marian devotion.[63]

A fifteenth-century king like Ferdinand II would never have given his approval to stories like those that so pleased Alfonso. As the official rhetoric promoting segregation intensified in Aragon and Castile, and as Christian polemic against Islam became more aggressive, there was much less room to recognize the points of overlap between the two faiths.[64] This was the era when Christian legends began to erase the Islamic past by making statues of Mary into the guardians of Spain's eternal Christianity, and men such as Pedro Marcuello sought to curry favor at court by writing verse for Ferdinand and Isabel that excoriated Muslims as the Virgin's enemies. Yet Marcuello and his fellows did not invent this kind of aggressive Marian rhetoric, though they certainly sharpened its edge. As fifteenth-century polemicists and poets brandished the Madonna in their war against Islam, they drew on a time-tested arsenal of weapons.

Fighting over Mary

One of the duties incumbent on King Peter the Ceremonious of Aragon in 1347 was to answer a "humble supplication... and petition" from Mudejars living under his rule in the kingdom of Valencia. These Muslims wanted the right to punish according to their own law any member of their community, male or female, who "spoke evil of or attacked God, the blessed Virgin Mary, or the [Christian] saints."[65] The king granted his Mudejars' request. But whatever efforts they made at self-policing did not prevent one of Peter's fifteenth-century successors from fearing that Muslims might "blasphem[e]" against God and Mary. Alfonso V decreed that any Mudejar of his realm caught uttering such insults would suffer the full weight of the law.[66]

These royal documents suggest that Mudejars in the villages of medieval Aragon could give vent to their frustrations by disparaging the holy figures cherished by their Christian lords and neighbors. Both the Mudejar leaders and the king of Aragon believed that such verbal assaults spelled danger for their respective communities. The monarch strove to protect his religion, while the Mudejars hoped to prevent violence by disciplining their own people. But just what kind of calumnies did these Mudejar leaders worry that their fellow Muslims might hurl against the woman lauded by the Qu'ran as a prophet's pious virginal mother? Perhaps they were concerned about curses taking the name of this icon of Christianity in vain, a sin of which Christian men and women could be guilty, too. In the high Middle Ages, even the kings of such very Christian countries as France had to work hard to impose moral order on their realms by curbing their subjects' affection for swearing in the name of the holy. More likely the anxiety captured in these Aragonese royal decrees resulted from an awkward truth about Mary: Jesus' mother as she was celebrated in Islam did not share all the traits possessed by the Virgin of Christian tradition. Hence words that Muslims might regard as simply telling the truth about Mary would be heard by Christians as unpardonable insults, uttered by people who therefore had to be her enemies.

As an anonymous Christian from Toledo who wrote a vicious tract against Islam and Muhammad sometime between 1085 and 1132 declared, the Qu'ran's Mary simply is not "one of us."[67] This apparently did not trouble the Christian custodians of Marian churches like Tentudia or Saidnaya, where Muslims came seeking favor from Jesus' mother and offering coins and wax as good as those brought by Christians. Nor did the finer points of Islamic and Christian theology matter much to Muslim pilgrims who could gaze at Christian paintings and statues of Mary and see in them Maryam as they knew and loved her. But when Muslims and Christians clashed, whether in written polemic or casual conversation, over the urgent question of which faith possessed the truth, the distinctions between Mary and Maryam could matter very much indeed. Seeking to proclaim their own religion the sole guardian of God's full revelation, Muslims and Christians each used Jesus' mother to prove the falsity of the other faith and to articulate their differences.

Even simple matters such as Mary's genealogy provoked disagreement between Muslims and Christians. Christian polemicists mocked the Qu'ran for describing her as the "sister of Aaron" (Sura 19:28) and gleefully pointed to this passage as a sign of Muhammad's mendacious ignorance. According to the Book of Exodus, Aaron and his more famous brother Moses did have a sister named Mary (Miriam), but Christian writers pointed out that this woman who had lived many centuries before Jesus' birth could not possibly have been his mother. They scoffed when Muslim apologists defended themselves by reading this passage metaphorically. Christian polemicists remained convinced that "Muhammad lied...saying that Mary, the sister of Moses and Aaron was the mother of Our Lord Jesus Christ, [since] there were nearly a thousand five hundred fifty years between these two women," as the writer from twelfth-century Toledo declared.[68] Erudite Christians disputed other details of the Qu'ran's portrait of Mary, deriding, for example, the notion that she gave birth under a date tree.[69] These quarrels, however, were no more than effete intellectual jousts compared to the ferocious battles over more fundamental divergences. As both sides in these acrimonious exchanges realized, nothing less was at stake than the central truths of Christianity embodied by Mary.

Christians and Muslims skirmished over Mary's body, arguing about how long Jesus' mother had kept herself free from the stain of sex. Any Muslim familiar with the Qu'ran could agree with Christians that Jesus' mother conceived and gave birth as a virgin, but Islam's scripture was mute about her subsequent sexual career. The same was not true for the Christian Bible, at least after respected fathers of the Church such as Jerome explained away the Gospels' references to Jesus's brothers.[70] This dubious linguistic hocus pocus allowed the men who laid the foundations of Christian doctrine to argue that Mary had remained a spotless virgin for her whole life, a belief they bequeathed to medieval Christians. Since no lesser siblings ever sullied the womb where Christ had dwelled, Mary's eternally chaste body offered irrefutable proof of her only son's absolute difference from the children born of all other women.

Some Christian writers interpreted the Qu'ran's silence on Mary's perpetual virginity to mean that Islam shared this belief with Christianity. Burchard of Strasbourg, the poets of the *Cantigas de Santa Maria*, and Alfonso X's nephew Juan Manuel all made this assumption, but events recounted by the late medieval Castilian chronicler Andrés Bernáldez proved just how wrong they were.[71] With evident satisfaction, Bernáldez reported on the service a Christian named Juan de Vera rendered to Mary during a stint in 1482 as royal ambassador to the Nasrid court at Granada.[72] Lingering in the shaded patios of the

Alhambra, Juan overheard some Muslims discussing "matters of faith." One of them provocatively mentioned that Mary did not remain a virgin after Jesus' birth. Enraged, Juan accused the man of lying, drew his sword, and attacked. This undiplomatic deed was apparently much appreciated by Juan's lord, King Ferdinand II of Aragon, who soon was busy in Tortosa stamping out a different form of Muslim sacrilege against Mary.

Some forty years later, Ignatius Loyola, the founder of the Jesuits, proudly championed Mary's sexual honor in a similar situation. He was walking through the craggy hills northwest of Barcelona on pilgrimage to the famous shrine of the Madonna of Montserrat when he began to chat with a fellow traveler, a Mudejar man. As Loyola's sixteenth-century biographer wrote, "one thing led to another" until soon the travelers arrived at the touchy subject of religion, in particular "the virginity and purity of the most glorious Virgin." The Mudejar praised Mary's virginity "before and during" Christ's birth, but flatly denied the notion of her perpetual chastity. Only divine intervention stopped Loyola from stabbing the man to death to avenge this insult to Mary's honor.[73]

In their willingness to draw their swords on behalf of their celestial lady's perpetual virginity, Juan de Vera and Loyola proclaimed themselves Christians in the face of Muslims who misunderstood Mary's nature and thus the truth that was Christianity. Their contests with these Muslims were as eloquent expressions of religious difference as the bitterest polemical exchange. Juan's altercation in the Alhambra even suggests that Mary's perfect purity could be a matter of international politics. His Muslim antagonist was no mere palace servant but a member of the Banu Sarraj family, a kin group so powerful in Granadan politics that a Nasrid sultan once tried to eliminate its leading men in a bloody purge.[74]

This man of the Banu Sarraj would have fired even more rage in de Vera had he chosen to utter words resoundingly rejecting Mary's identity as God's mother, another of the traits Christians most cherished in her that Muslims denied. The Virgin had enjoyed this lofty status in Christendom ever since the bishops assembled at the raucous council of Ephesus (431) and the less contentious one of Chalcedon (451) had proclaimed her *Theotokos*—"Mother of God." Mary's family relationship to divinity made Christian men and women confident in her powers of intercession, for God could not refuse to listen to his mother's pleas. Muslims, however, found the idea that God had a mother entirely offensive.

In the *Cantigas de Santa María*, Christians cry out to Mary that Muslims are "unbelievers, who absolutely refuse to believe that you are the Mother of God."[75] Even Islam's acceptance of Mary's virginity could not compensate for this insult that rattled Christianity's very foundations. As Ramón Llull wrote late in the thirteenth century: "Saracens honor [Our Lady] when they call her holy and virgin and mother of Jesus Christ through the Holy Spirit, but they dishonor her when they deny and refuse to believe that she is the mother of God."[76] For Llull,

Muslims' refusal to grant Mary this honor made them just like her other enemies, the Jews. In his book of Marian praise, he complained bitterly to her that
"the Jews and Saracens... do not believe that you could be the Mother of God."[77]

On this point, the Jewish and Muslim positions coincided: no woman could
be the mother of God. The line between the human and the divine could not be
breached in that way. It was sacrilege, unpardonable offense against God's majesty, to imagine that he had a mother or a son. Would God, limitless and eternal,
have consented to enclosing himself in a woman's gurgling belly?[78] Rejecting this
shocking scenario with the same disgust as their Jewish counterparts, erudite
Muslim polemicists deftly dethroned Jesus himself. He was not God. Nor was
he, as Christians claimed, God's son. How could God, unique and wholly one,
possibly have a child? Did God cut off some little part of himself to create Jesus?
So a fourteenth-century Muslim polemicist mockingly wondered as he underscored the irrationality and implausibility of the doctrine of the Incarnation, the
belief on which the entire edifice of Christianity rested.[79] The Jesus of Islam was
fully human, the guarantee of which was none other than his mother. "Son of
Maryam" is the title he most often enjoys in Islam's holy book.

Learned Muslims knew that other equally heinous offenses against God
lurked in Christians' insistence on Mary's status as God's mother. This claim
threatened to inflate Mary to the level of a quasi-divine figure, even a rival to
God. The Qu'ran accuses Jesus of having exhorted humankind to "worship
me and my mother as two deities apart from God" (Sura 5:116). In a heartfelt
profession of obedience to God, Jesus denies these charges (Sura 5:117–118).
But his words were not enough to dispel some Muslim writers' suspicion that
Christians did indeed practice Mariolatry, a hunch that ripened into conviction
when they contemplated another heady title that Christians bestowed on Jesus'
mother, "Queen of Heaven."[80]

Those Muslims who lived among Christians and observed what went on in
churches realized that their neighbors did not actually pray to Mary as a god. In
the late fifteenth century, a Mudejar author who invoked Sura 5:116–118 to warn
his audience against the many errors of Christianity altered these verses to better reflect Mary's standing in the surrounding society. For the Qu'ran's "deities,"
this man substituted the words "advocates and lords."[81] The passage nonetheless
packed the punch of the original, with Mary's position as Christians' intercessor
and celestial advocate replacing her pretensions to divinity as the sacrilegious
encroachment on God's territory.

This telling adjustment to the Quranic vocabulary appears in a treatise composed by a learned Mudejar who wanted to remind less knowledgeable members of his faith about the fundamentals of Islam.[82] Although he did not reveal
his name, it is likely that he was the consummately erudite Yça Gedelli, a man
who by 1450 was the religious leader (*faqih*, pl. *fuqaha*) of the Mudejar *aljama*

in Segovia and commanded the respect of Christians and Muslims alike.[83] Like his fellow *fuqaha* elsewhere in Castile and Aragon, Yça worked hard to keep Islam alive in his community.[84] For Mudejars isolated in a sea of Christians, this was never an easy task. But perhaps it was particularly challenging in late fifteenth-century Segovia, where not only did Christian and Muslim black-smiths belong to the same confraternity, but the Christian authorities forced the city's Mudejars to gather every Wednesday on the plaza abutting the church of San Miguel and listen to Christian sermons.[85]

Whether or not Yça succeeded in persuading his fellow Mudejars that it was sacrilegious to appeal to Mary's intercession like their Christian neighbors did, just a few years later, in the seaside church of Santa María de la Rápita, hun-dreds of miles east of Segovia, Mudejars would be lighting candles—a decid-edly Christian ritual form of petitioning saintly intercessors. At their Wednesday assemblies in the shadow of San Miguel, the men and women of Yça's own flock themselves had doubtless heard Christian preachers urging them to look upon the Virgin and her son exactly as their *faqih* had instructed them not to: as "lords and advocates."

Yça's rather accurate characterization of Christians' understanding of Mary and Jesus probably would not have offended any member of that faith. The original wording of Sura 5:116–118 was another matter altogether. Predictably enough, Christian polemicists who read these verses in Islam's sacred book were outraged to find themselves accused of being polytheistic Mary-worshippers. Lies, all lies, like so much else in the Qu'ran, wrote one; Christians certainly knew Mary was no "goddess," but "they most firmly believed she was God's mother," he said.[86]

Defense of Mary's right to the exalted title of "Mother of God" spurred Christian polemicists to impressive verbal exertions. They exorcised the ugly details of pregnancy conjured up by Muslim authors with the holy water of her perpetual virginity. Her pure body, untouched by even the slightest trace of worldly filth, offered a fit receptacle for God's grace, for God's son, and for God himself, Christian writers insisted. Nor did God's limitless majesty suffer injury from the narrowness of the womb: only Christ's humanity was held within by Mary's belly, while his divine "infinity" remained wholly "uncircumscribed." In a maneuver beloved by religious polemicists of all stripes, Christian authors even marshaled evidence for their points from the very faith they attacked. They tri-umphantly flourished the Qu'ran's own assertions of Mary's unblemished vir-ginity as eloquent confirmation that she was a worthy vessel for divinity.[87]

Clever Christian writers could even twist Islam's sacred scripture so that it seemed to prove the logical necessity of the very doctrine Muslims found so abhorrent, a tactic of which two princes in Alfonso X's family availed them-selves.[88] One was the learned king's rebellious son and eventual successor to the crown of Castile, Sancho IV. A man who gained the throne after leading a revolt against his father, a monarch excommunicated by the pope for much of his reign, and a ruler who continuously had to fight off other claimants to the crown, Sancho was keenly aware of how fragile his purchase on power was. Hence in the 1290s, he provided for the future by composing a book of instruction for his six-year old son and heir, Ferdinand IV. Among the information Sancho thought important to pass on to the future ruler of a kingdom often at war with Granada was a knowledge of Islam, at least of the points on which it coincided and diverged with Christianity. "It is written in the Qu'ran . . . that Jesus Christ came into Saint Mary from God's breath . . . which means that Jesus Christ was born from Mary by the grace of the Holy Spirit"—this is the rather Christianized rendering of the Quranic story of Mary's motherhood in Sancho's book. To make sure his son would grasp the doctrinal significance of this statement, the king underlined how it proved that "Christ is the true son of God."[89]

Sancho's cousin Juan Manuel put it more bluntly. He declared that if according to the Qu'ran "Jesus Christ wasn't engendered by a human father, but by the spirit of God" and if the same text asserted that Mary conceived and gave birth as a virgin, then logically her child could be none other than the son of God. "[Christian] priests can [thus] easily vanquish (*vençer*) the Moors with their own religion, because [Muslims] believe that Jesus Christ was conceived in the womb of Saint Mary," he concluded.[90]

It is no coincidence that as this prince turned the sword of Islam's own sacred book against those people who would deny Mary her prized title as mother of God, he chose a verb with obvious military overtones: *vençer.* Sancho IV also used this word as he hammered the doctrine of the Incarnation into a weapon for his son to brandish in battle against "Moors."[91] Religious polemicists on both sides eagerly wielded the language of war in their treatises. The very genre in which they wrote reflected the course of military conquest; only when armed forays by Christian knights and rulers began to threaten al-Andalus's political dominance did the Muslims of the Iberian Peninsula join their fellows elsewhere in the Islamic world by developing polemics against Christianity.[92] In medieval Iberia, Muslim and Christian authors alike often used their attacks against the other faith as a platform from which to prophesy military victory or to urge grandiose projects of holy war on rulers.[93]

The bitter contest over the Virgin's right to the title of mother of God evoked vivid fantasies of martial ardor among her Christian champions, including Ramón Llull, who in his *Blaquerna* imagined a Christian knight throwing over his own lady for Mary and venturing into the "land of the Saracens" to seek combat with knights who are not "servant[s]" of Our Lady."[94] In Llull's story, an abbot blesses this Marian quest, even bestowing upon it a title drawn from Luke 1:42 and repeated in the Ave Maria, the prayer murmured by high medieval Christians

to the click of rosary beads: "Blessed art thou among women." Guided by God's
sure hand, the knight, or "servant of *Benedicta tu*" as Llull often calls him, arrives
in Muslim territory. He seeks out its king and announces his intention to cross
swords with any man who would deny Mary the honor of being called "mother
of God and man."

Llull's firm grasp of the finer points of Islamic doctrine is evident in the
Muslim ruler's answer. Combat, says the king, surely is not necessary, since
Muslims believe that Mary is a saintly woman, a virgin, and the mother of a
prophet, although not the mother of God. But the knight knows just as well
as Christian polemicists the danger of the Muslim position: "he responded to
the king that the best honor that Our Lady had was to be the mother of God."
Shouting his Marian motto, he fights one Muslim to the death and is about to
dispatch another when the man admits defeat, professes that Mary is the mother
of God, and declares allegiance to the "rule and order of *Benedicta tu*." Seething
with rage, the Muslim ruler orders the arrest and execution of both men. Llull
deems them "martyrs for Our Lady." Perhaps it would be better to see these
Marian knights as sacrificial offerings on the altar of an idea that, as many heresy
trials of the thirteenth century show, some Christians found as difficult to accept
as Muslims did.

The combat over Mary's motherhood that Llull describes is fictitious, contained by his spiritual romance, and set in a nameless, timeless, featureless Muslim
land. Yet during the actual battles that resulted in the erosion of Muslim power
in the Iberian Peninsula, Christian knights sometimes wielded their weapons to
safeguard the Virgin's status as God's mother. So a twelfth-century English priest
recalled in his proud record of the deeds of his crusading compatriots who had
paused on their way to the Levant long enough to help King Alfonso Enríquez
of Portugal win Lisbon for Christianity in 1147. This priest remembered how
the Muslims defending the port had jeered at the besiegers for venerating Jesus
as the son of God when he was really no more than the offspring of a "poor
woman."[95] Immediately after capturing Lisbon, the crusaders ordered the emaci-
ated Muslim survivors to drag themselves to the city's main mosque and publicly
retract their insults against Mary's maternity. Kissing a cross, they confessed in a
pathetic chorus that Mary was indeed the "blessed mother of God."[96]

Lisbon's Muslims pronounced these words in a building that used to be theirs,
but which the triumphant crusaders had just baptized with the splashing of holy
water and chrism, proclaiming it a church in honor of Mary and her son.[97] Several
centuries later, other mosques consecrated as Mary's cathedrals became a different sort of monumental setting for statements of Christian victory in the contest
over her right to the title of mother of God. In the final years of the campaign for
Granada, as Muslim city after Muslim city fell to Ferdinand and Isabel's military
captains, the jubilant victors often made mosques into churches by dedicating

them to a figure straight from the pages of Muslim-Christian polemic, Our Lady of the Incarnation.

After his victory at Alhama in 1482, Rodrigo Ponce de León, the marquis of Cádiz, ordered that the city's Friday mosque would henceforth bear Our Lady of the Incarnation's name, or so his biographer claims.[98] According to a chronicler working in the service of the Catholic Monarchs, Isabel and Ferdinand personally chose this Madonna as the patron of Alhama's new church.[99] The king and queen went on to dub the mosque-churches of Álora (1484), Ronda (1485), Loja (1486), Vélez-Málaga (1487), and Málaga (1487) in her honor.[100] By 1492, Almería boasted a similar monument to Christian victory. Described by the German physician Münzer as a "most beautiful building," adorned with "over eighty columns" and lit "with more than one hundred lamps," Almería's cathedral-mosque of Our Lady of the Incarnation was obliterated by an earthquake in 1522.[101] But for thirty years, the title of its saintly patron had offered eloquent testimony to the hostility between Muslims and the mother of God incarnate.

The Christian chroniclers who reported on the campaign for Granada did not spell out the weighty meaning of placing former mosques under the protection of the Virgin of the Incarnation. But surely the Christian prelates and princes who proclaimed her the patron of these cathedral-mosques were aware that they thereby extended the sweep of Christian military victory to the realm of theology. Enthroned among the pillars of former Muslim prayer halls, Our Lady of the Incarnation reigned over the twinned triumphs of Christian doctrine and Christian knights against her Muslim enemies.

On this Virgin's feast day in 1523, the Archbishop of Granada solemnly laid the cornerstone for the Renaissance cathedral that would slowly rise in the heart of the capital city of the former Nasrid kingdom. Our Lady of the Incarnation's new cathedral was a crucial building block in the grand project of Christianizing Granada.[102] Its ornate classicizing forms would carve through the Islamic cityscape, imposing the designs of Granada's new masters on the skyline. Triumphal arches adorned its principal façades, setting the stage for the riot of carved, painted, and sculpted statements of Christian victory that lay within. In keeping with the theme were images of the cathedral's patron saint. Plans drawn up in the late sixteenth century specifying that reliefs depicting the Incarnation and other episodes from Mary's life should crown the cathedral's main entryways were fulfilled some decades later.[103]

This building crowded up against the city's equally capacious former main mosque. Its minaret stood as a defiant reminder of Granada's Muslim past until 1588 when its stones were cannibalized for use in the new cathedral. When the rest of this mosque, slowly crumbling into ruin, was finally destroyed in 1704, any architectural threat it posed to the new cathedral had long ago been neutralized by its conscription onto the Christian side in the debate over Jesus' mother. Appropriated in Mary's name as a parish church in 1501, by 1502 the former mosque became Granada's cathedral, an honor it relinquished when the new Renaissance building was ready.[104]

This mosque-church was dedicated to Our Lady of O, also known as Our Lady of the Expectation.[105] Often depicted in late pregnancy, this Madonna offered a less flamboyant proclamation of the doctrinal differences dividing Islam and Christianity than her sister who would reign over the new purpose-built cathedral, Our Lady of the Incarnation. Yet many sixteenth-century Granadans who walked by Santa María de la O believed that the mosque-church enjoying the expectant Virgin's protection itself bore deep scars from the battle over her right to the title of mother of God. Tales circulating in the city drew this building into the contest between Muslims and Christians over Mary's maternity. Representing the culmination of this centuries-old conflict, these stories suggest that the view of Muslims as the Virgin's implacable adversaries had finally rhetorically triumphed over the possibilities of sharing her.

These legends originated in rumors that began to spread soon after Granada's fall to the Christians. They focused on the exploits of one of Ferdinand and Isabel's knights, Hernan Pérez de Pulgar, who reputedly slipped into Granada under the cover of darkness one night when the city was still ruled by the Nasrids. Once inside the walls, he made his way to the main mosque and, according to his epitaph of 1531, snubbed the city's Muslim lords by "tak[ing] possession" of the building. These words were inscribed on the Christian hero's tomb, which would lie in the mosque-church itself; reports of Pulgar's intrepid deed reached the highest circles, inciting Charles V to allot him a burial place in Santa María de la O.[106]

By the later sixteenth century, imagination had filled in the details of Pulgar's adventure. Everyone knew that he had announced Christianity's claim to Granada's mosque by defiantly nailing to its door a piece of parchment on which was written the Ave Maria, the prayer whose closing line succinctly summed up the Marian doctrine Muslims so abhorred. "Holy Mary, Mother of God, pray for us sinners"—every time Christians intoned these words that had been added to the Ave Maria in the late fifteenth century, they affirmed their belief that the Virgin had given birth to the son of God. No wonder this prayer appeared in a tale about a knight seeking to goad Muslims.

Before long, this story about Pulgar blended with another one in which the Ave Maria starred in the conquest of Granada. Early modern Spaniards knew many versions of this tale, but the gist remained the same. Tarfe, brother to the last Muslim king of Granada, rides out from the city to prove his valor against Ferdinand and Isabel's forces. When he reaches the Christian lines, he wheels his horse around. Fluttering from its tail is a parchment bearing the words of the

Ave Maria (in many renderings of the tale, it is the document Pulgar had tacked onto the mosque). To rescue the Ave Maria from its ignominy and to avenge the Virgin's honor, a young knight named Garcilaso de la Vega challenges Tarfe to single combat. This Christian man returns triumphant from the field, chanting Mary's praises and bearing as trophies the Muslim's bloody head and the Ave Maria parchment.

By the late sixteenth century, Spaniards from all walks of life listened to balladeers sing of the duel of the Ave Maria.[107] This story of Marian triumph also featured in popular plays. Even the celebrated Golden Age author Félix Lope de Vega devoted his considerable talents to extolling the Marian heroism of Pulgar and Garcilaso. His two plays on the subject borrowed their material from the ballads and their structure from the *Moros y Cristianos* (Moors and Christians) mock battles that were important civic rituals in sixteenth-century Spain.[108] By the seventeenth century, Granada chose a play based on Lope's work as the centerpiece for its annual festivities commemorating Ferdinand and Isabel's ceremonial entrance into the city. For centuries, every January 2, actors would don costumes to perform the ritual exchange of Marian insults, the elaborate battle scenes, the burlesque interludes, and lovers' trysts required by the script of the *Triunfo del Ave Maria*—"The Triumph of the Ave Maria."[109] Cities across Andalusia and Valencia staged their own performances of the *Triunfo* well into the twentieth century.[110]

The meaning that this play held for its Granadan audiences changed over the centuries. But watching the unfolding drama—Pulgar driving his nail into the mosque door, the Muslims tearing off the parchment insulting their faith, Tarfe taunting the Christians with his horse's hindquarters, and Garcilaso vanquishing the Moor—the citizens of Granada could always learn that their city's former Muslim lords had been remorseless enemies of the Ave Maria and its words about God's mother. The play did not, however, hint at the complexities and ambiguities intrinsic to the ways that medieval Muslims and Christians had thought and written about Mary as a figure whom they shared as well as fought over.

In the thirteenth century, Alfonso X and his poets had sung of a Muslim sultan paying homage to Mary, and Ramón Llull had willingly imagined a king of the same faith lauding her in an effort to curb the bloodthirsty enthusiasm of one of her Christian devotees. But Tarfe, the Muslim prince invented by sixteenth-century Christian legend as the villain of the *Ave María* cycle, does not even know who she is and, in one of Lope de Vega's plays, only learns of her existence from a Christian convert to Islam. This renegade informs the prince that the Christians rely on "a powerful princess whom they say is the holy mother of the god they adore."[111] The other theatrical and poetic versions of the *Ave María* figured Mary as equally alien to Islam. These early modern Marian legends thus denied what so many medieval Christians had been willing to admit: that Jesus' mother belonged almost as much to Muslims as she did to Christians. In one mid-sixteenth-century ballad from another cycle, a Muslim ruler of Granada is even seized by a violent rage at the mere mention of the Virgin.[112]

This literary erasure of Mary's status as a shared religious figure owed much to the political configuration of Muslim-Christian relations in the sixteenth century.[113] Yet these early modern plays and poems were also the natural offspring of changing Christian attitudes in late medieval Castile and Aragon. By the time Andrés of Jaén stood guard by the sea in 1502, Mary's ambiguity as a woman celebrated by both the Bible and the Qu'ran had acquired far more potential to disturb Christian ideology than it had possessed in earlier centuries. As the old laws requiring the segregation of Mudejars from Christians were increasingly enforced in fifteenth-century Castile and Aragon, Mary's ability to be at home in both *morería* and Christian quarter had to be masked, lest it make a mockery of the boundary between neighborhoods. After the fall of Constantinople to the Ottoman Turks in 1453 projected the struggle between Islam and Christianity onto the apocalyptic stage and Ferdinand II and Isabel eagerly embraced the divisive rhetoric of crusade, Christian leaders and propagandists had little motivation to imagine their military enemies venerating Christ's mother. Rather, they did their best to contain and control Mary's ability to cross the lines between the two faiths, as Ferdinand did quite literally in his decrees forbidding Mudejars to gather at Santa María de la Rápita.

In the fifteenth and early sixteenth centuries, erudite Christians thus no longer permitted themselves fantasies of Islam's closeness to Christianity by asserting that Muslims believed in Mary's perpetual virginity. Instead, they celebrated Christian knights like Juan de Vera who dueled with Muslims denying this doctrine. Although followers of Islam and Christianity continued to mix at many Mediterranean Marian shrines, the respectful—if ideologically loaded—portraits of Muslims praying to the Virgin in churches painted by texts like the *Cantigas de Santa María* increasingly vanished from the fifteenth-century Aragonese and Castilian literary scene. Christian authors instead teased out the subtle message of these earlier stories and then pushed it to its logical extreme. If in Alfonso X's poems, Muslims visit churches to pay their devotions to Jesus' mother like Christians do, in fifteenth-century miracle stories, the followers of Islam enter such buildings in order to become Christians. Driven by their love for Mary, they renounce Islam and embrace the religion named for her son. The Christians of Castile and Aragon had believed for centuries that Mary could win the ultimate victory over her Muslim—and Jewish—enemies by summoning them to the baptismal font.

6

Mother of Conversion

Sometime in the mid-thirteenth century, a man in search of miracles came to Segovia. Rodrigo de Cerrato was a Dominican friar busy compiling a book of the lives and wonders of the saints.[1] Just before his visit, this Castilian town had been blessed with a spectacular demonstration of Mary's powers in a particularly fraught arena of spiritual politics on the Iberian Peninsula: conversion. The tales the friar heard at Segovia of how the Virgin had saved a Jewish woman's life and brought her into the Christian fold must have pleased him, belonging as he did to a religious order famed for its missionary aspirations.[2] But one did not have to sport the black and white robes of a Dominican to be awed by these happenings. The miracle was apparently the talk of Segovia. "I heard reports of this miracle...and I saw many people bearing witness to it," wrote Rodrigo.[3] By the 1270s, word of this Jewish woman's change of faith had even reached the royal court of Castile. Alfonso X and his poets, ever alert for evidence of Mary's powers, fashioned a *cantiga* from what they knew of the wondrous events at Segovia.[4]

Like all miracle tales, both the *cantiga* and Rodrigo's account were creative stories shaped to suit the tastes and needs of author and audience. Yet the friar's language suggests the possibility that, like many other miracle tales, this story crystallized around the experiences of a real person. Rodrigo claimed not only to have interviewed people at Segovia, but also to have glimpsed the convert. From what he learned, he pieced together the story of how, in Mary's name, this woman abandoned her ancestral faith for Christianity.[5] In his tale, the sheen of Mary's miracle gilds the messy realities of conversion—the constellation of forces that might have compelled a Jewish woman to cast off the bonds of faith, family, and community in order to embrace Christianity.

According to Rodrigo, the events that led to this Marian wonder began prosaically enough. The woman in question was a member of Segovia's Jewish community, which in the thirteenth century numbered perhaps some fifty households.[6] Though the *Cantigas* describe her as guilty of an unspecified crime, Rodrigo says that a Christian unjustly accused her of an adulterous liaison with a Christian knight—a serious charge. Adultery between a Jewish woman and a Christian man both violated the sanctity of marriage and flouted the prohibitions of sex across religious lines issued by Jewish and Christian authorities alike.[7] Execution often awaited those convicted of this cross-faith crime, as it did this woman. She was to die by being pushed off a steep rocky ledge on the town's outskirts.

Rodrigo wrote that a Christian court handed down this sentence. He could be right; the punishment decreed for this woman resembled the form of execution prescribed in a nearby town's law code for Muslim and Jewish men who slept with Christian women.[8] But Alfonso X and his poets implied that Jews judged her; in Castile, Jewish communities indeed had the right to try members of their own faith in certain capital cases.[9] In any case, as this woman stood at the edge of the bluff, she was stripped of all her clothes except for the thin shift that Jewish law prescribed for modesty's sake to females facing execution.[10]

Officials tied her hands behind her back. Then they pushed. Rodrigo wrote that jagged rocks reached out greedily from the cliff, ready to lacerate the victim before she even reached the ground. Yet the woman landed gently, completely unhurt. The word "miracle" must have been murmured by at least some people in the "multitude" of Jews, Christians, and Mudejars who, says Rodrigo, had gathered in anticipation of the "spectacle" of her death—judicial punishments in the Middle Ages were often staged as a grisly form of public entertainment and instruction.[11] By the time the Dominican arrived in Segovia, the potent language of marvel was certainly in use and Mary was considered responsible for the woman's remarkable escape from death.

As the Jew plummeted toward the ground, she "continually invoked blessed Mary, saying, 'Saint Mary, help me, because you know I'm innocent of this sin,'" to quote Rodrigo's evocative re-creation of the events.[12] A white dove appeared from nowhere and fluttered down to the ground with her, its presence calming her fears, details that the friar claimed the woman herself related. The wonder of the moment when the Jew landed unharmed was more effectively captured by the painterly art of Alfonso X's miniaturists than by the Dominican's spare prose. In the *Cantigas'* illumination, the woman stands at the foot of the cliff and raises her hands in gratitude to her protector, the Virgin, who leans deeply into the picture space from heaven (Figure 6.1). The would-be executioners gesture in astonishment. From Mary's outstretched fingers, blessing rains down on her new devotee.

The account Rodrigo heard of what happened next confirmed for him the presence of miracle: the Jewish woman requested baptism. The Christian name she insisted on taking announced the Virgin's role as the author of her salvation, physical and spiritual. She wanted, wrote Rodrigo, to emerge from the baptismal waters as Mary, although by the time that the friar came to Segovia, she was known as Marisaltos. As he parsed it, "Mary because she was freed through her invocation of blessed Mary" and *saltus* ("jump") because rather than falling to her death from a height, "she jumped onto the ground as if from a low rise."

Figure 6.1 Miracle of Marisaltos. *Cantigas de Santa María*. Biblioteca Monasterio del Escorial, Codice Rico, MS. T.I.1, folio 154r. Patrimonio Nacional.

How exactly had Mary become so associated with whatever happened that day at the foot of the cliff that this convert—if she was indeed a real person and not a product of Christian imagination—felt compelled to take her name? Despite the hostility to Jesus' mother so deeply engrained in Jewish culture, it is possible that this woman called on her for help as Rodrigo and the poets of the *Cantigas* insisted. Out of sheer desperation, she might well have invoked any source of heavenly aid she could think of, including ones that she knew Christians appealed to. Even if she did not utter Mary's name during her fall, she would have had good reason to do so afterward when facing the crowd that had expected her death and could still demand it. Conversion to Christianity offered a way out. She had probably already been condemned by her own religious community and expelled from it. Perhaps Christians would offer her shelter if she accepted their faith. Those Jews and Mudejars of high medieval Castile and Aragon who, like Marisaltos, ran into serious legal or personal trouble with their co-religionaries often tried to escape their problems through baptism.[13] If the decision to convert came from within, the woman must have cast about for some way to explain her sudden desire to embrace Christianity. The language of Marian miracle would have offered convenient cover. But she would only have reached for this vocabulary—so alien to the faith she had been raised in—if she thought it had a chance of winning over the Christians in the crowd.[14] It did.

By the thirteenth century, any Christian familiar with Mary's miracles had ample reason to expect her merciful hand in a tale of conversion. Stories that bore the weight of centuries told of Jews, Muslims, and even pagans who came to Christianity through her graces. So famed were Mary's powers to defeat the stubbornness of unbelievers and bring them to the truth that Segovia's Christians themselves very well could have introduced her name into the story of the events at the cliff, whether in the shock of the moment as they stared at the woman safe and sound in front of them, or days later as the tale grew more fantastic in the retelling.

How and why Mary became associated with the miracle of conversion in the high Middle Ages is the subject of this chapter, as is the relationship between Marian marvels and the more mundane forces that could induce a Muslim or Jew of high medieval Castile and Aragon to embrace Christianity. The day-to-day proximity among Christians, Jews, and Muslims made the exchange of one set of religious beliefs for another as much of an ever present possibility there as it was in the Christian Levant, where members of the three faiths also coexisted.[15] In Castile and Aragon, the broad avenue leading from the minority religions to Christianity was naturally the most trodden walkway of conversion, but other paths existed. Some Jews traded the Torah for the Qu'ran, while some Mudejars did the opposite.[16] Some Christians even embraced Islam, although very few chose to become Jews.[17] It was one thing to convert to the religion espoused by proud Granadans and powerful North African rulers, and another to voluntarily join the ranks of a people who knew only subjugation in medieval Europe. Almost no one, however, embarked lightly on the journey from one faith to another; until 1391, relatively few people set out down this road at all. As Marisaltos's story so vividly demonstrates, those men and women in Castile and Aragon who turned away from their ancestors' religion had to have compelling reasons. Conversion tore the social fabric cut from the cloth of religious identity, often rending the ties of family and community that were of a piece with one's faith. Converts risked losing everything, from their friends and their spouses to their property and even their lives.[18]

Those Muslims and Jews who voluntarily made the difficult passage to Christianity perhaps found that the vocabulary of Marian miracle smoothed the way. But for Jews and Mudejars who remained true to their faiths, the stories of Marian conversion must have seemed like oppressive Christian propaganda. In private, Segovia's Jews perhaps scoffed at the tale of the Virgin's rescue of the woman who once belonged among them, but it was a story that no Christian, Muslim, or Jew in the city would be allowed to forget.

Marisaltos's miraculous change of faith was commemorated publicly for hundreds of years. By the fifteenth century, frescoes depicting how the Virgin had saved this woman, body and soul, ornamented Segovia's cathedral of Our Lady.[19] As visitors admired these paintings, they might be told stories about the power of prophecy that Marisaltos enjoyed after her conversion—a saintly gift of clear vision appropriate for a woman who through baptism had shed the willful blindness to the Christian truth that shuttered Jewish eyes.[20] Pilgrims could even pay their respects to her bodily remains, which reposed in a tomb near the frescos, a commemorative arrangement described in a text dating from 1523.[21] Three decades later, Marisaltos's bones were transferred to a purpose-built niche in the city's new cathedral.[22] On the wall above her final resting place, a sixteenth-century painting with an accompanying inscription still recounts the miracle that earned this woman her name.[23]

By the time this convert's body was enshrined in the new cathedral, a chapel consecrated the spot at the foot of the cliff where she had been spared from death.[24] Rebuilt in the seventeenth century, this church became home to a statue of Marisaltos' savior and namesake. To celebrate the building's completion, Segovia staged costly festivities lasting ten days. Processions featured *tableaux vivants* sponsored by the city's guilds, including one depicting Mary's genealogy and another the miracle that led to the Jewish woman's baptism.[25] A few decades later, Segovians gathered in the shadow of the fateful cliff to watch Marisaltos's story come to life in performances of a play commissioned by municipal leaders.[26] Today, the chapel's Marian statue is Segovia's patron saint.

The miraculous imprint of the Virgin's evangelical hand thus lingered on Segovia's civic landscape for centuries after Marisaltos's baptism. All these monuments to the woman who was born a Jew but died a Christian reveal that the Christian belief in Mary's wondrous ability to win souls could quite literally shape the world in which the men and women of high medieval Castile and Aragon lived. Understanding how the Virgin's power to expand the Christian flock became so real requires exploring why Christians thought she offered a compelling language with which to make sense of conversion.

"Through Her the Whole Human Race Is Born into the Faith of Christ"

Some decades before baptismal water would trickle down Marisaltos's forehead, a monk from Catalonia suggested that Mary naturally opened the way from unbelief to Christianity. His task was to assemble and explain the many epithets that Christians used to honor her qualities. In grand rhythmic phrases intended to be read aloud on Saturdays, Mary's special day of the week, he set down the words that would have been familiar to his twelfth-century audience. Queen, rose, lily, moon, dew, star, river, empress, Christ-bearer and more—the list of the Virgin's "sacred names," as the monk called them, was long and poetic. It evoked power, nature's beauty, and Mary's closeness to Christ. It also conjured up places of passage. Mary was, wrote the monk, a "bridge," a "road," a "path," an "open door," a "ladder."[27] He would doubtless have been disturbed to learn that the pagans of antiquity had praised their own mother goddesses as such mistresses of transition. Gates, entrances, and portals abound in the iconography of those divine beings in whom the qualities of motherhood are distilled, symbolizing the womb as doorway into the world.[28]

The Catalonian monk would have been much more comfortable knowing that his fellow Christians in the East used such imagery for Mary. As the residents of late medieval Constantinople strode through the city's doors and portals, they could glance up at images of the Virgin adorning the archways' curve. Christians there even called her the "Gate of the Word."[29] This title expressed both Mary's similarity to every other mother and her absolute difference. Since the son of God himself had chosen her as his gateway, she occupied a very privileged place in the Christian geography of the in-between. No other mother—or saint—could stand as she did squarely on the threshold between the old religious dispensation and the new one created by her child.

Anyone sorting through the metaphors so carefully catalogued by the twelfth-century Catalan monk would realize that Mary was the mother of conversion. She could give birth to new Christians, the miracle of their spiritual regeneration mirroring Christ's physical birth from her body. So the monk declared as he contemplated one of the most melodious of her "sacred names": aurora (dawn).[30] Because in Christian imagination Jesus was the sun casting light on the world, his mother naturally personified that pregnant moment when day is born from night. As aurora, Mary illuminated the path leading out of the spiritual shadowlands into her son's radiant realm. In the monk's words: "God's mercy placed [her] just like dawn between night and day…between death and life, between sin and its remission, between the old law and the new" so that she could bring sinners from the darkness of the old to the light of the new.[31] "The mother of God," he continued, "was a well of living waters, because just as waters flow into a well from all directions, so the peoples who were to be saved, namely from paganism and Judaism, rose by baptism to faith in her."[32] In his exegesis of another of Mary's titles, the monk proposed such an expansive vision of her evangelical motherhood that all of humanity was baptized in her womb: "because through her the whole human race is born into the faith of Christ, the mother of God is called generation."[33]

As the monk sat in his scriptorium and searched for the right words with which to glorify Mary, he probably consulted learned commentaries on the Bible for guidance. Had the works of distinguished Cistercian abbot Bernard of Clairvaux, or renowned theologian Thomas Aquinas, already been available, he would have found in them further reason to associate her with conversion. While the monk grounded his proof in Mary's maternal body, these authors focused on words she had spoken. In the Gospel of Luke, John the Baptist's mother, Elizabeth, greets Mary as the mother of God and Jesus leaps in the womb, a joyous scene known as the Visitation that was a favorite of medieval artists. Mary responds by chanting God's praises. Her sonorous phrases passed into the Christian liturgy as the *Magnificat*, a hymn of thanksgiving.

Christian thinkers meditated on the words of the *Magnificat*, seeking their hidden meaning. What to make, for example, of Mary's bold assertion that "all generations will call me blessed"? As Bernard of Clairvaux and Thomas Aquinas pondered the significance of this utterance, they elaborated an interpretation that would be repeated by other high medieval theologians: the Virgin was predicting that unbelievers would recognize her powers, cede to the truth she embodied, and convert to Christianity.[34]

Medieval Christians knew it had not taken long before these powers announced in the *Magnificat* became reality. From the beginning, false gods had trembled before Mary. When she and Joseph fled into Egypt to save Jesus from Herod's hired swords, they came to a town where 365 idols received daily worship in a temple. Finding nowhere else to take shelter, Mary brought her family to the shrine. The moment she entered holding Jesus, the army of idols toppled over and shattered on the ground. Immediately, the town's lord threw himself down before Mary and her child, "adored" Jesus, and proclaimed the infant the master of his own deities. He urged his friends and followers to join him in the worship of this divinity who had so easily conquered his idols. Prostrating before Mary and her son in recognition of the truth they embodied, these Egyptians were converts to a religion that had just been born.[35]

This stark story about the spontaneous suicide of paganism in the presence of the Madonna and child does not appear in any of the four canonical gospels. Yet it purports to come from the hand of one of the familiar evangelists—the apostle Matthew. The tale belongs to a sixth- or seventh-century Latin text known to modern scholars as the Gospel of Pseudo-Matthew, a title indicating its classification among the apocrypha, writings never formally approved by the church. But in the Middle Ages, most Christians, whether peasants in the fields or learned clerics, considered the stories it told of Mary and Jesus to be as true as anything in the canonical gospels. The fall of the idols thus belonged to the Virgin's story as her medieval devotees knew it. This primal episode of conversion was told and retold by clerics and monks, as well as by artisans and artists.[36]

Some medieval Christians even believed that Mary's miraculous motherhood caused false gods to disintegrate, a role that was foreordained for her in Jewish prophecy, wrote Peter Comestor in the twelfth century. Comestor was the author of the *Historia Scholastica*, an enormously influential and rather colorful commentary on the Bible. Within a few years of its composition, copies of the *Historia* lay open on masters' lecterns in universities across western Europe. Clerics-in-training were taught the curious stories contained in its pages, including one about a prophecy attributed to Jeremiah. According to the *Historia*, this Old Testament prophet revealed to the pagan Egyptians that "when a virgin gave birth," their idols would be destroyed. Anticipating the future, the Egyptian priests fashioned a statue of a virgin and a boy-child, and worshipped it.[37]

Some thirteenth-century authors transposed this prophecy to ancient Rome, an equally authoritative layer of the pagan past. Gil de Zamora, a prominent Franciscan friar who served as tutor for one of Alfonso X of Castile's sons, wrote that when Mary bore Christ, "right then a golden statue fell over—the one that Romulus had placed in the Romulian palace, saying 'this will not fall until a virgin gives birth.' "[38] This passage comes from one of the friar's more secular compositions, a tract praising the old Roman city of Numantina. In Gil de Zamora's pious poetry in Mary's honor, Roman idols also tumble when she becomes a mother. But in these verses, no prophecy prepares the way. The Franciscan simply writes that when Mary gave birth, "the temple of Peace [at Rome] was overthrown and the idols fell."[39]

All these stories about the fall of the idols, Egyptian and Roman, told how unbelief inevitably gave way before the virgin birth. These scenes could occasion meditations on Christ's powers. Yet Gil de Zamora's poetry leaves no doubt that the fall of the idols was a triumphant moment as much for Mary as for her son. Not only did the friar intend his verses as liturgical pieces praising Jesus' mother, but he included them in his *Liber Mariae*. Organized neatly into subdivisions, the *Liber* lays out the Virgin's genealogy, narrates her life, her death, and her miracles, and provides words to be sung in her praise.[40]

If pagan idols tumbled before Mary, so too did the false beliefs of Christianity's monotheistic rivals. She was an ideal symbol for the intoxicating hopes nurtured by some Christian preachers beginning in the late twelfth century: the belief that Muslims and Jews teetered on the edge of the baptismal font. The evangelical interpretation of the *Magnificat* proposed by writers like Bernard of Clairvaux and Thomas Aquinas was just one of the ways in which Mary was drafted into the service of the new aspiration to Christianize Muslims and Jews.

Until the thirteenth century, Christians had shown markedly little interest in any sort of mission to the Muslims in the Iberian Peninsula or elsewhere.[41] Jews had not been the target of Christian evangelical fervor for centuries, except for a few hideous interludes like the forced conversions during the waning years of Visigothic rule. Across western Europe, princes and prelates followed Saint Augustine's dictum: Jews, although stained with guilt for the crime of Christ's death, were allowed a place in Christian society because they offered living testimony both to the Passion and the Old Testament's truth. No active measures were to be taken for their conversion, an event that Christian apocalyptic texts predicted would occur en masse at the Second Coming.[42]

As the apostolic awakening of twelfth-century Christianity matured into what one historian has called the thirteenth-century "dream of conversion," new ideas began to compete with traditional modes of thought about the place of unbelievers in Christian society.[43] A more aggressive attitude toward Islam and Judaism emerged, along with a desire expressed by some churchmen to make Muslims and Jews into Christians. This evangelical passion burned the brightest in men who, like Gil de Zamora and Rodrigo de Cerrato, belonged to new religious orders—the Franciscans and Dominicans. Saint Francis himself preached the Gospel not just to the men and women of Italy's urban landscape but to the birds that flocked in its fields. He also tried to ignite the love of Christ in the sultan of Egypt, a spectacularly unsuccessful effort that would nonetheless be commemorated in Christian art and literature for centuries.[44]

Some Franciscans and Dominicans tried to realize their vision of bringing all people to Christianity.[45] In the thirteenth century, they founded schools to train their preachers in the necessary languages. Soon, friars readying themselves for missions could study Arabic or Hebrew at Játiva, Murcia, Barcelona, Valencia, on the island of Majorca, or even in Tunis itself.[46] A handful exercised their newly acquired linguistic skills on the Muslims of North Africa and al-Andalus, or at least on those few who would listen to them in Islamic lands where disparaging

Muhammad was punishable by death. Other friars prudently focused their evangelical energies on Mudejars and especially Jews living under Christian rule in Aragon and Castile.

One prong of the missionary strategy was to prod Jews and Muslims into admitting the irrationality of their own religions while at the same time proving to them—and to any doubting Christians in the audience—Christianity's superiority. Staged debates, carefully managed so that the Christian side had no chance of losing, offered the public forum for such religious combat. Although occasionally Muslims and Christians thrust and parried in these verbal duels, the dangerous dance of words typically pitted Judaism against Christianity, as in the famous disputations at Barcelona in 1263 and Tortosa in 1413–1414.[47] Such large-scale formal debates, however, happened infrequently. A more common evangelical tactic was preaching, the occupation that Francis and Dominic prescribed for their followers in imitation of Christ and the apostles. In thirteenth- and fourteenth-century Aragon, friars and other preachers received royal licenses to deliver missionizing sermons to Jews and Mudejars, and some put this privilege into practice.[48]

The work of evangelization was hard. But Ramón Llull believed that Christians would be inspired to undertake this labor if they considered how badly Muslims and Jews treated Mary in not believing all that was true about her. Llull, who shared the Franciscans' missionary fervor whether or not he was formally affiliated with the order, argued that devotion to the Virgin and her son should move all Christians to dedicate themselves to the enterprise he so cherished.[49] Men and women who really loved her, he wrote, would not be able bear the dishonor that Jews and Muslims did to her daily. Instead, they would strive to bring unbelievers to the baptismal font so that she would no longer suffer disrespect.[50]

Some of Llull's contemporaries thought of Mary not as the muse of mission but rather as a fellow evangelist. Many Muslims, declared Jacques de Vitry, "have asserted [that] they have been warned in their dreams by Jesus Christ or by the blessed Virgin or by some saint that they should cross over from the Muhammadan error to the grace of Christ."[51] The thirteenth-century author of these words wore the bishop's miter of the crusader city of Acre and blazed with a missionary fervor rare among his peers in the episcopate, hoping to convert the Muslims surrounding him in the Levant. Had Jacques directed his energies toward Castile and Aragon, he would have found there evidence confirming his conviction that it was Mary who especially seconded Christ in the miracle of conversion. A writer surveying the landscape of wonders in these medieval kingdoms probably would not have been tempted to make even the kind of perfunctory reference that Jacques did to the evangelical powers of other saints.

The conversion of Muslims and Jews was not a common theme in the books of miracles kept at the shrines guarding the relics of most holy men and women in high medieval Castile and Aragon. Not even the apostle James, who bore a title declaring his status as a master evangelist, enjoyed a reputation for such wonders. The pilgrims who made their way to his shrine at Compostela believed that they were visiting the tomb of the man who had led Spain from pagan darkness to the light of the Christian truth centuries ago, as the clerics who tended this apostle's cult told them. But his promoters did not include a scrap of evidence in the twelfth-century book of his posthumous miracles to suggest that his apostolic powers of persuasion continued into the present. James cured pilgrims of dire illnesses, saved them from tempests at sea, held open prison doors so captives might flee, but never in this collection did he induce a Jew or a Muslim to embrace Christianity.[52]

This compilation of James's miracles predates the great surge of missionary hopes in the thirteenth century, but the thick book celebrating the wonders performed in that evangelical century by a saint who had ample posthumous dealings with the Muslims—Saint Dominic of Silos—barely registers contemporaneous missionary aspirations. Venerated at a northern Castilian monastery, in the thirteenth century this saintly abbot was best known for his posthumous sternness with Muslims. Story after story collected by the eager note takers at Silos proved how he could free Christian captives from Muslim masters.[53] Not once, however, did they record a tale of Dominic liberating a Muslim from the spiritual prison of Islam. He was no anomaly among local Spanish saints of the era. Isidore, for example, a humble farmer saint whose relics were venerated in Madrid, then no capital city but merely a backwater village, certainly had no posthumous knack for conversion. The late thirteenth-century collection of his miracles mentions only a failed conversion, describing how he punished a Mudejar who reneged on a vow of baptism.[54]

This contrasted sharply with the vast Marian project on which Alfonso X and his poets embarked during just the same years. Though this monarch did little to encourage actual missionary activity in his kingdom (Jews and Mudejars were useful to the Crown just as they were), he lauded his favorite saint for doing such pious work with select individuals. In the *Cantigas de Santa María*, Marisaltos rubs shoulders with an array of people whose conversion to Christianity is, like hers, the fruit of Mary's miracles. The learned king and his literary team celebrated Marian-inspired conversions in twelve poems.[55] A Christian hearing the songs of this collection would even be tempted to believe that when the Virgin directed her attention to Jews and Muslims, she often did so not to harm them, but to escort them down the path of truth.[56] The refrains to each of these twelve *cantigas* announced which of her many miraculous powers she had exercised in order to bring a given unbeliever to Christianity. Some of these tales about conversion praised the motherly comfort that Mary extended to people in distress, while others extolled her talents as a physician or lauded the power inherent in

images of her. Yet as Alfonso X's illuminators limned these stories in paint and
gold leaf, they deftly captured these miracles' family resemblance. The pictorial
narrative for each culminates with the formulaic scene of baptism that served as
shorthand for a change of faith. In the last (or sometimes the next-to-last) panel
of these paintings, the convert sits naked in a baptismal font, the holy water of
spiritual rebirth cascading over his or her head and shoulders. Usually from one
edge of the picture frame, a crowd of people looks on, each time bearing public
witness to Mary's miraculous ability to acquire souls for Christianity.

Alfonso X and his collaborators plucked at least six of the *Cantigas'* tales of
conversion from the Marian miracle collections that had begun to grow in western Europe a century or so earlier.[57] Some of these six stories had roots sunk
deep in the soil of the early Middle Ages, while others were more recent. Some
even had germinated in Byzantium, taking hold in Latin sources only after having flourished for centuries in the cosmopolitan eastern Christian world.[58] Each
of these tales of conversion adapted by the learned king had already been given
narrative shape by other assiduous Marian hagiographers of the high Middle
Ages, including the French monk Gautier de Coinci and the erudite encyclopedist Vincent of Beauvais. As they were passed from author to author, the
details that originally placed the miracle in a precise moment, a local context,
were rubbed away.[59] When place names remained, it was only as so many bright
pins on a far-flung map of Marian miracle. Bourges, Constantinople, England,
the Levant—the Virgin could touch the hearts of unbelievers everywhere in the
Christian world. Even more expansive in their claims were those miracles that
floated free of any mooring to town or city or kingdom, as if Mary's evangelical
talents knew no geographical limit. These stories of conversion borrowed from
the standard Marian repertoire even transcended time itself. Almost without
exception, they unfold in a deliberately featureless past that through its lack of
definition is no different from the present. The timelessness of these tales suggested that Mary's power to dispel unbelief was an eternally present possibility.

Four *cantigas*, however, showed her powers to sway the hearts and minds of
unbelievers at work in the world of thirteenth-century Castile, where Muslims
and Jews lived side by side with Christians, and Christian rulers claimed sovereignty over not just one but three faiths. The *Cantigas* present these poems as
tales told by the king's contemporaries about their own experiences. This is a
plausible enough provenance for stories that brought the Marian miracle of conversion down to earth, turning it from timeless potential into immediate reality
and anchoring it firmly in history.

In the fourteen and fifteenth centuries, Christians in Castile continued to
believe that Mary could bring the Jews and Muslims who were their neighbors
to baptism. One Castilian Madonna, Our Lady of Guadalupe, was particularly
reputed for her evangelical ability in the later Middle Ages and exercised this

talent well into the sixteenth century. So enduring was the Virgin's fame in this domain that it inspired two brilliant writers of the Spanish Golden Age, Miguel de Cervantes and Lope de Vega, to create literary portraits of Muslim Marian converts. These memorable characters speak with all the eloquence of their Renaissance makers, but follow a route to the baptismal font that had been blazed centuries earlier by the medieval miracle tales.[60]

It takes careful observation to chart how Mary's miracles of conversion changed over time, for their evolution was subtle rather than dramatic; hagiography was a genre deeply constrained by tradition. Some of the shifts in emphasis and tone reflected the changing conditions under which Muslims and Jews came to embrace Christianity, others the developments in ways that Christians in Castile and Aragon thought about conversion. Yet all of these stories made Mary's conversion of Jews and Muslims into part of God's plan for the triumph of Christianity over Islam and Judaism in high medieval Iberia.

The Miracle of Conversion and the Triumph of Baptism

Mary's miracles imposed the crisp lines of divine will onto conversion, a spiritual landscape clouded by the ambivalence and taboos that always shadowed the places where religious borders were openly crossed.[61] In its very essence, conversion was subversive, involving a series of decisions or actions that led an individual or a group to betray one faith for another.[62] The dangerous passage it necessitated aroused both individual and collective anxiety.[63] Hence Jewish, Muslim, and Christian leaders did not view apostasy with a kind eye. The law of each community heaped heavy penalties on any member who abandoned the faith (though naturally, the rulers of Castile and Aragon repeatedly decreed that any Jew or Muslim who wished to become a Christian should be able to do so freely).[64] These severe legal constraints attempted to contain anxiety about conversion, but miracle could alleviate it.

To those men and women like Marisaltos who changed faiths voluntarily, miracle could serve to justify their radical religious choice. Dreams and visions often figured prominently in the autobiographical narratives of high medieval converts, these signs from God sometimes working in tandem with reason to move the author ineluctably toward his or her new faith.[65] In these texts, converts could be speaking to themselves as much as to an external audience, salving any uneasiness about their decision with the balm of confession.[66] They also could be attempting to proclaim the authenticity of their conversion to the community they had just joined. For Jews and Muslims who became Christians in high medieval Castile and Aragon, this could be a hard task. Miracle eased the way, offering a strong antidote to the suspicion that converts to Christianity often stirred up in the members of their new faith.[67] In both kingdoms, monarchs tried to protect the newly baptized from scorn and hostility, spelling out punishments for Christians caught mocking or abusing converts.[68] Christians were warned against calling converts from Islam *tornadizo*, a insulting term meaning "renegade" or "turncoat."[69] After all, if these men and women had been willing to abandon their religion for Christianity, might they not also be willing to shed Christianity for their old faith?[70] The fear that converts might apostatize was compounded by worry that their conversion to Christianity might have been neither sincere nor complete.[71] In Christian imagination, the convert often was a hybrid monstrous creature, no longer overtly a Jew or a Muslim, but not fully Christian.[72]

Miracle stories cut through these anxieties about where in the person of the convert the Jew or Muslim ended and the Christian began. Wonders prompting or accompanying baptism proved that there had been a real change of faith, one that could be trusted because God surely could not err.[73] If miracle drew a line between the convert and his or her former faith, placing the convert clearly on the Christian side, it also reassured Christians that the resistance of Jews and Muslims to the truth of Christianity could be defeated. Hence Mary's miracles of conversion could be drafted into the service of religious polemic, as Marisaltos's story was in the mid-fifteenth century by the Franciscan Alonso de Espina, author of a particularly vicious diatribe against Judaism and Islam.[74] Echoing the high medieval theologians who read the *Magnificat* as the Madonna's proclamation of the inevitable victory of Christianity over all other faiths, these conversion tales suggest that from a Christian perspective, baptism, whether accomplished by the Virgin or by men in preachers' robes, was a form of spiritual conquest.[75] Even those tales that may have begun as actual converts' accounts of their own experience took on the coloring of this triumphalist ideology when incorporated into Marian hagiography.[76]

The many wondrous ways that the Virgin brings Jews and Muslims into the Church serve as weapons brandished in this war of faiths. Like high medieval preachers who tailored their sermons to suit the social status of their listeners, Mary was sensitive to the differences in her audience.[77] She adjusted her methods to fit Muslims and Jews, as well as men, women, and children. Sometimes her miracles of conversion inflicted gaping wounds on Islam and Judaism, while at other moments she sliced more subtly. Mary as evangelizer could also wear her cloak of compassion. But always in these narratives, baptism and the triumph of Christian doctrine converge, just as missionaries like Llull hoped they would.

In the world of Mary's marvels, the overwhelming power of the Christian truths embodied by the Virgin and rejected by Islam and Judaism could bring Jewish and Muslim men to the baptismal font. Conversion is just such a vehicle for the affirmation of Marian doctrine in a miracle story of Byzantine origins included in the *Cantigas de Santa María*.[78] It might have been forged in the crucible of the iconoclastic debate, the bitter struggle over the validity of worshipping images that inflamed Byzantium in the eighth and ninth centuries.[79] In those troubled years, the tale would have offered comfort to iconodules ("lovers of images") because it provided graphic proof of devotional images' power. Later hagiographers also made the protagonist's progress to baptism into the story of a Muslim who comes to believe in the Christian version of Mary.

In the *Cantigas'* lyrical version of this much-told miracle, a Muslim acquires a beautiful image of the Virgin. He treats it with respect, wrapping it in gold cloth, and safeguarding it in his home. He visits the statue often, standing in front of it and puzzling over the challenge Mary poses to his faith. The twelfth- and thirteenth-century French authors who composed their own versions of this tale confidently asserted that it was the idea of the virgin birth that particularly troubled this man.[80] But Alfonso X and his poets were more informed about Islam than were their counterparts north of the Pyrenees.[81] Their Muslim wastes no time hesitating over a trait of Jesus' mother that is praised by the Qu'ran but instead agonizes over the Incarnation, a doctrine that, as the learned king and his collaborators were well aware, Islam really denied.

In words that could have been taken directly from Muslim polemics against Christianity, this man wonders how God, "who is so great," would possibly have abased himself by enclosing himself in flesh. Yet the Muslim is willing to be persuaded of this difficult truth. He declares that if God will only give him proof of the Incarnation, he will convert to Christianity. No sooner have the words left his mouth than the breasts of his cherished image of Mary turn into "living flesh" from which milk pours forth. The Muslim hastens to keep his promise, even bringing his followers with him to the baptismal font in collective witness to the twinned triumph of Marian miracle and Christian truth over Islamic error.

If Alfonso X and his collaborators trimmed this old miracle story to make it fit the polemical conflict between Islam and Christianity over the Virgin as it was fought in their world, other Marian tales culminating in conversion sprang right from the heated discussions that Muslims and Christians in high medieval Iberia really had about Jesus' mother. A late medieval miracle story from Guadalupe, for example, made the conversion of a Muslim man into testimony to Mary's right to the title "Mother of God."[82] According to this tale, sometime before 1489, a company of Christian soldiers was captured by a squadron of Muslims in the countryside near one of Granada's last strongholds. The group's captain was enslaved and endured the added humiliation of laboring under a master who liked to ridicule the notion that Mary was God's mother. Angered by these insults to his faith, the Christian entreated the Virgin of Guadalupe to bring "this miserable infidel to his senses" and began to recite the Ave Maria.

When he reached the phrase "mother of God," the words were so "powerful," wrote Guadalupe's hagiographer, that "the Moor's very hard heart turned into the softest wax." Capitulating to this "great force," the Muslim embraced his captive's faith and began to deride "the miserable Qu'ran, invention of the demon."

According to the hagiographer, the "great force" that defeats this "obstinate" Muslim and brings him to the Christian truth is not just the Ave Maria but also the "most powerful arm of Our Lady." It is a sweet form of coercion, but coercion nonetheless. In other conversion miracles, Mary intervenes even more brusquely, instructing Muslim men to embrace Christianity and brooking no resistance, no matter how hard they fight against her. Three times in the course of the fifteenth and sixteenth centuries Our Lady of Guadalupe appeared in dreams or visions to Muslim men and summarily ordered them to convert.[83] She succeeded in defeating even the most recalcitrant of them—a man who tried to strike her with his scimitar.

The hagiographers' characterizations of Islam in these stories make it clear why Mary had to be so imperious to bring Muslim men to baptism. Enslaved to "the miserable superstition of Muhammad," they were "tenacious" members of a "sect and a madness," whose holy book was "an invention of the devil."[84] To liberate these men from willing servitude to the devil, Mary could not afford to be gentle. Accordingly, the author of a fourteenth-century text from Aragon depicted Mary as a celestial field captain who once "commanded" a Muslim prince in North Africa to "come out of the diabolical captivity" of Islam and to convert to the "true catholic faith."[85]

Sometimes, as the missionary Mary forcefully overcomes Muslim men in these starkly framed religious wars between good and evil, she confronts the devil himself, as in a tale from the Cantigas set in a town near Toledo. The target of her evangelical zeal is a Muslim slave, whose Christian owner tries to convert him but to no avail. As punishment, his master locks him up in a dank chamber. There, the Muslim's resistance to Christianity crumbles before forces far more potent than his owner's admonishments. First a demon attacks him, sensing easy prey and a soul ripe for the plucking. After fighting back desperately for two nights, he is visited by Mary. In the accompanying illumination, the darkness that filled the prison during the demon's assaults bursts into golden light when she appears. The slave falls to his knees and holds out his hands in supplication, while the ugly spirit of Muslim evil flees through a hole in the roof.[86] The only way to escape the "bonfire of hell," Mary instructs him, is to renounce the devil and that "false, vain, very crazy and villainous dog Muhammad." Her stern sermon brings the slave to his senses. Ridiculing Muslims for uselessly "holding out their hands toward Mecca," he admits his error, converts, and becomes Mary's fervent devotee.[87]

This tale introduced the Virgin's authoritarian evangelical presence into a social setting where conversions from Islam to Christianity often occurred in high medieval Aragon and Castile: Christian households served by Muslim slaves. Though some enslaved Muslims were browbeaten by their Christian masters into accepting the Gospel, others converted voluntarily.[88] Those requesting baptism often did so in full awareness of a principle enunciated in canon law: Christ's followers were not to exist in a state of bondage. Through the Christian holy waters, numerous slaves passed to freedom, so many that in the thirteenth century Christian slave owners protested, worried that their wealth of human chattel would dissolve in the baptismal font. In response, civic and church officials diluted the promise of liberty that conversion continued to offer in principle.[89]

The poem from the *Cantigas* may be translating into Marian miracle the experience of a real Muslim slave who broke down in the face of relentless pressure from his Christian owner and renounced his faith. Yet the final frame of the *cantiga*'s accompanying illumination suggests the physical and spiritual freedoms this slave could have acquired through conversion. In this painting, the newly baptized man kneels before a statue of Mary, offering a candle to the author of his salvation. He is completely alone in the church, with no master in sight. This tender devotional scene balances the preceding panels that highlight Mary's awesome powers to force Muslim men to abjure the diabolical beliefs of Islam.

The evangelical Virgin could compel Jewish men, too, to admit the infernal nature of their faith and exchange it for Christianity, as she does in a poem in the *Cantigas*.[90] One of the stock Marian miracles, this tale was of recent vintage, dating perhaps from the twelfth century. In fact, all the stories in which conversion becomes a command performance carried out at the Virgin's behest come from the high Middle Ages. While some miracles of conversion inherited from earlier centuries bore the heavy impress of force, in these older tales Mary was no missionary. She wielded her wondrous powers not to bring a Jew or Muslim to Christianity, but to thwart unbelievers and reveal the impotence of their evil designs against Christians. Conversion was an aftereffect, the glow that lingered as the fireworks of the miracle itself faded.

One *cantiga* of Byzantine origins, for example, culminates in a Muslim sultan's baptism, but focuses on the miracle of his preceding military humiliation by Mary (she foiled his siege of Constantinople).[91] Alfonso X and his collaborators also applied their literary talents to an even more famous and equally venerable story from the eastern Christian empire in which conversion is similarly the offshoot of a barbed Marian miracle, but not its point.[92] In this tale, a Christian in Constantinople borrows money from a Jew. The two men decide that Mary and her son will stand as surety for the loan, an agreement they formalize in the presence of a statue of the holy pair. When the payment falls due, the Christian is far away from Constantinople. Relying on God's help, he counts out the money, locks it in a chest, and tosses the box into the sea. The chest washes up on the shore and the Jew's servant finds it and delivers it to his master. On the Christian's return to Constantinople, the Jew pretends not to have received payment and accuses him of defaulting on the loan. Summoning the Jew before the statue of the Madonna and child that had witnessed the agreement, the Christian calls on Mary to prove that he has already paid his debt. She clears the Christian's name, then reveals the Jew's trickery, and declares the perfidy of his people. Overcome with horror, the Jew admits his guilt and converts to Christianity.

Only in the stories originating in the high Middle Ages does baptism become more than a grace note to Mary's dealings with Jews and Muslims, and only then is she inspired with a missionary zeal equaling that of men like Ramón Llull. The high medieval evangelical awakening thus left its traces in Mary's miracles. As friars and other preachers started to sermonize Jews and Mudejars, lauding the glories of Christianity awaiting the convert, the Virgin began to wrestle with the demons of Islam and Judaism with the aim of conquering them through baptism.

Transposed into the idiom of Marian wonder, the dream that Muslims and Jews could be made into Christians gained a plausibility that it often lacked in reality. Only rarely did Jews and Muslims voluntarily heed Christian calls to conversion.[93] They often argued with missionaries, prompting James I of Aragon to command the Jews and Mudejars of his realm to listen silently to the mendicants' sermons.[94] But Jews and Muslims hardly ever dared talk back to Mary when she ordered them to the baptismal font. Even the most obstreperous eventually capitulated and obeyed her commands to convert, as did their less bold fellows. Mary's missionary successes both captured the optimism that initially inspired some thirteenth-century preachers and offset their disappointment as they realized how ill-founded their hopes had been. The same ebb and flow of missionary tides surged through her changing miraculous methods in the high Middle Ages. In that evangelical era, Mary become as active and forceful a proselytizer as the preachers who exhorted restive audiences of Jews and Muslims to cast off their ancestral error and embrace the Christian truth. The history of evangelization in high medieval Castile and Aragon is in fact one of escalating, if sporadic, pressure and coercion, whether spiritual, emotional, or physical.

Until 1492, no ruler of Castile or Aragon would adopt an official policy imposing conversion on either of the religious minorities that enjoyed the status of being "the king's people." "Not by force or by coercion" should Christians try to convert Jews and Muslims, wrote Alfonso X in words echoed over the centuries by later monarchs of Castile and Aragon. Jesus, Alfonso explained, did not wish people to serve him out of "fear" or force but welcomed those who followed him of their own free will. So, said Alfonso, Christians could "work to convert" Muslims and Jews using "good examples," the "sayings of the holy scriptures," "sweet words," and "appropriate preaching."[95] Church law itself prescribed nonviolent methods of conversion. As the famous canonist Gratian declared decades before Alfonso X's birth, "blandishment" was the preferred form of evangelization.[96]

The "blandishment" and "sweet words" prescribed by ecclesiastical and royal ideology sounded quite a bit harsher to Jewish and Muslim ears. Though most Mudejars and Jews had no desire to listen to preachers' calls for conversion, they sometimes had little choice. James I was the first in a long line of Aragonese rulers, who, despite their considerable ambivalence toward conversion efforts, articulated the mendicants' right to compel Jews and Mudejars to attend missionizing sermons, which were often preached in synagogues and mosques.[97] Medieval kings might not have believed that commanding Jews and Mudejars to listen to Christian proselytizing in the presence of Torah niche and *mihrab* constituted force, but missionaries' sermons could ignite anti-Jewish or anti-Mudejar rioting, as James I was acutely aware. Hence he forbade Christian laypeople from accompanying these preachers as they went about their duties.[98] Even when the friars' words were gentle, touting the rewards of Christianity rather than laying out the eternal punishments that awaited unbelievers, they were vehicles for spiritual aggression.

The Christian champions in this battle against unbelief grew more violent as it became evident that Jews and Mudejars were not converting of their own accord. Missionaries like Llull who began their careers firmly committed to peaceful, positive methods of evangelization ended their lives believing in the necessity of compulsion or even the sword.[99] By the late thirteenth century, the language of crusade had entered the missionaries' vocabulary.[100] In fact, only at those moments when the taint of coercion that always clung to these evangelizing efforts ripened into actual violence did the ranks of Christians swell with new converts. Driving these waves of men and women to the baptismal waters was exactly the "force" that Alfonso X and so many other monarchs of Castile and Aragon had outlawed in the arena of conversion—the weapons of knife, sword, and rock, or the simple menace of the mob. These forced conversions could be the poisoned fruit of Christian riots targeting Jews and Mudejars, when the crowd offered its quarries the choice between death or baptism.[101] Jews and Mudejars could also face this agonizing decision during moments of less extreme tension with their Christian neighbors.

Until 1391, episodes of interfaith violence severe enough to cause clusters of conversion were rare.[102] But that June, crowds of Christians took to the streets of Seville, inflamed by a local preacher's violently anti-Semitic rhetoric. They sacked the Jewish quarter and murdered those Jews who refused baptism, a fever of destruction that rapidly spread across Castile, then Aragon, and even the island of Majorca. Monarchs, the Jews' traditional protectors, tried to stop the slaughter, as did some town councilmen, but to little avail. Over the summer, thousands of Jews were killed and thousands of others forcibly baptized.[103]

Although not all Christians countenanced such violence or even believed that Jews and Muslims had to be converted, coerced mass baptisms, especially of Jews, continued into the fifteenth century.[104]

This dark potential for violence lurked in the missionaries' sermons, it exploded into riots, and it stained Mary's miracles of conversion. Yet Christians did not believe that Mary indiscriminately bullied potential converts. Almost all the protagonists of the miracles in which she used evangelical tactics edged with force were adult male Jews or Muslims. These targets required the heaviest weapons in her arsenal. In Christian imagination, the iconic Jew and the iconic Muslim, the figures embodying the unpardonable error of each religion, were adult men. High medieval Christian illuminators such as the artists who worked for Alfonso X on the *Cantigas de Santa María* often gave adult male Jews grotesque features signaling their association with the devil, but spared women and children from such vicious visual stereotyping. Nor did Christian polemicists ever create a Jewish or Muslim woman as the fictive opponent with whom they sparred. Instead they always imagined victory over Muslim and Jewish men, for, Christians thought, these unbelievers clung most firmly to infidel ways.[105]

In the Marian stories of conversion, it is men whom the Virgin must persuade to leave behind their ancestral religion for Christianity, men whom she commands to come forth from the diabolical prison of Islam or Judaism, men whose ferocious animosity toward Christianity and Christians she tames, and men who demand proof of the truth of Christianity and its doctrines.[106] The language of religious conflict is used openly in these tales, and Mary's spiritual victory is plain to see. Only rarely did hagiographers write of Jewish and Muslim men whom she converted with a miraculous display of maternal tenderness.[107]

When hagiographers described how Mary brought women and children to Christianity, however, they almost always moved to a much gentler rhetorical register. The leitmotiv in these tales is her universal compassion, and mercy is her method. These miracle stories about female and child converts teach that Mary extends her "clemency and generosity" not only to "her faithful followers" but also to people "who are beyond her range of acquaintance, in order to convert them to the good that they do not [yet] enjoy," to quote the reassuring words with which a late medieval hagiographer from Guadalupe prefaced his account of an adolescent Jew's conversion.[108]

These tales, however, were not entirely innocent celebrations of the evangelical side of Mary's maternal mercy. They too narrated the triumph of baptism, although blurring its sharp outlines with the camouflage of her compassion. In these miracles, women and children hardly need to be persuaded to convert. Instead, so lightly do they hold the religion into which they were born that they happily shrug it off. Their willing progress to the baptismal font suggests that Islam and Judaism are feeble faiths, incapable of commanding lasting allegiance, easily undermined and betrayed from within. Muslim and Jewish men are exposed as impotent creatures unable to prevent the spiritual defections of their women and children.[109]

This double edge to Mary's activity as the loving mother of conversion runs through one of the most popular of all her miracles, a story that came from the Byzantine Empire.[110] As Alfonso X and his poets tell the tale, a little Jewish boy accompanies his Christian friends to church. In the presence of a statue of Mary enthroned in majesty, he innocently receives the bread and wine of communion. It even seems to him that the Virgin distributes the sacrament. When the Jewish boy goes home, his father discovers what he has done, flies into a rage, and shoves him into a hot oven. His mother rushes into the street, shouting in alarm. Aroused by her cries, Christians crowd into the house and fling open the oven door, only to find that the child has survived his ordeal without so much as a singed finger. As he explains to everyone, Mary shielded him from the flames. In gratitude to her, the boy and his mother convert to Christianity. Meanwhile, the angry Christian mob tosses the father into the stove, where he burns to death.[111]

The contrasting fates of the boy and his father epitomize the different roles allotted in Mary's miracles to Jewish children and Jewish men. While Jewish men aggressively embodied the enmity between their religion and Christianity, Jewish children were easy to shape and form, as impressionable as children in general were in medieval imagination.[112] A mere visit to church, a pleasant vision of Mary, and a moment under her cape of love were enough to detach this boy from his father's faith. In fact, even before his baptism, he is well on his way to Christianity, attending church, receiving communion, and gazing with delight at apparitions of Mary.[113]

The susceptibility of children to conversion was expressed rather literally in a late fifteenth-century miracle story from Guadalupe.[114] In this tale, the missionary Mary extended her compassion to a Jewish youth with the explicit goal of bringing him to baptism. She appeared to him one night and "plac[ed] her hand on his breast." The touch of her fingers left traces visible long afterward, a gentle brand that made the boy hers—and a Christian—before he even knew it.[115] She then instructed him to "leave the bad life" of Jews and "convert to the holy faith of Christians," but her tone was tempered with a kindness she rarely showed his elders. After she promised the youth that only good would come of his conversion, he needed no further encouragement. He not only rushed to baptism, but also took up arms for his new faith; the hagiographer detailed how this convert fought alongside the members of a Christian military order during the siege of the Granadan city of Loja (probably the ill-fated Castilian expedition of 1482). Badly wounded there by a Muslim archer, this eager convert recovered his health through a renewed display of Mary's mercy.

This story dates from the era when Jews were an increasingly small and often embattled minority in Castile. It is perhaps the tale of a calculated choice made by a real adolescent boy who hoped for a brighter future.[116] For all that the Jews and Muslims of medieval Castile and Aragon stood to lose by becoming Christians, they also could gain much. Well into the fifteenth century, converts could be catapulted to positions of social and political eminence that they could never have reached without the sanction of baptism.[117] Converted Jews could exchange the mantle of rabbi for that of archbishop, even papal nuncio and royal chancellor, as did Solomon Halevi of Burgos, better known as Pablo de Santa María, his Christian name that ingeniously managed to evoke both his new god's mother and one of the most famous Christian converts of all times.[118] Through baptism, the Jewish adolescent of Guadalupe's miracle story gained full access to the military, a profession that could not easily be undertaken by members of his original faith.[119] Upward mobility, however, was of little interest to the hagiographer. For him, this was the story of a youth whose flesh was twice marked with the impress of Mary's mercy as she worked to save him, both body and soul.

If in medieval Christian imagination children were impressionable, women were often seen as changeable, easily influenced, spiritually fragile, and thus more prone to conversion than men.[120] Real Jewish and Mudejar women rarely conformed to this Christian stereotype, typically resisting baptism much more strenuously than did their menfolk.[121] Yet in the world of Mary's miracles, all that was necessary to tip them toward the Church was the delicate touch of her compassion. Just as Jewish boys are graced with tokens of her love before their baptism, women are blessed with signs of her wondrous favor marking them as budding Christians. Children are the passive recipients of these miracles but women actively solicit them, as if inviting Mary to conquer Islam and Judaism. So determined are these women to become Christians that they argue with any of their co-religionists who try to stand in their way.[122]

Just how eagerly in Christian imagination Jewish and Muslim women betrayed their own faith by succumbing to Mary's mercy is evident in a story from the *Cantigas de Santa María* that may have originated in the Iberian Peninsula in the tenth or eleventh century.[123] A Jewish woman struggles to give birth to a child who will not come. Alfonso X and his poets give an explanation for her torment that does not appear in other versions of the story: she is being punished for not "believ[ing] anything about Saint Mary that was true and proven." The Virgin, nonetheless, is ready to help her. A heavenly light breaks through the woman's anguish and a voice instructs her to call on Mary. When she does, her labor eases, and the baby is born. After the obligatory days of purification, the woman takes all her children to a church. There, the members of this fatherless family shed their Judaism (as the *cantiga* puts it, the women was not "waiting for the Messiah" any more) and receive baptism.

This woman has to be prodded to turn to Mary's mercy, but then calls on her without hesitation. Perhaps, as one historian has recently suggested, such stories reveal that Jewish women giving birth occasionally copied their Christian neighbors and entreated Mary when the pain of labor seared through their bodies—Jews were well aware of the reputation she possessed in Christian circles of offering succor at such moments.[124] In any case, this woman's readiness to act like her Christian counterparts conveyed a confident message to the *cantiga*'s audience: some Jewish women were embryonic Christians, willing to give birth to the faith in Mary that already lay within them.

In other conversion miracles, Jewish and Muslim women are even more enthusiastic Christians-in-waiting. As in the stories circulating in thirteenth-century Segovia about Marisaltos, they need no heavenly cues to prompt their appeals to Mary's mercy. A *cantiga* that probably originated at Salas, a popular Marian pilgrimage shrine in Aragon, tells of a Mudejar mother from nearby Borja who practically joined the Christian faith before she arrived at the baptismal font.[125] This moving poem begins by evoking this woman's overwhelming grief after the premature death of her beloved young son. Distraught, she decided to "trust in the Virgin." Her heartache was the impetus, and her Christian neighbors the inspiration—she "saw how Christian women went to Saint Mary at Salas and heard of the miracles [the Virgin] did there." This woman prepared for pilgrimage like any good Christian described in the *Cantigas*, "commend[ing]" her child to Mary and buying an ex-voto offering to take to Salas. At the shrine, her behavior was equally Christian; she spent the night in prayer before a statue of the Madonna, joining her fellow pilgrims in vigils. Each of her actions was a further step down the path of conversion, a spiritual journey this Mudejar completed voluntarily. She herself proposed baptism, telling Mary she would renounce Islam in exchange for her child's resurrection. The Virgin came through on her end of the bargain, and so did the woman.

Behind this miracle story may well lie the suffering and vulnerability of a real person, as in the case of Marisaltos. True, it is difficult to reconcile a miracle of resurrection with the awful finality of death. But in another *cantiga*, Mary revives a "dead" girl, Alfonso X's own sister Berenguela, who actually survived for many years after a severe childhood illness robbed her of the signs of life.[126] Perhaps a modern parent would diagnose coma where medieval people saw death. In any case, a Mudejar mother in despair quite plausibly could have grasped at any possible source of hope. If, like many Mudejars of Aragon, she lived not in a *morería* but side by side with Christians, she would in fact have had ample opportunity to observe their religious practices, just as the *cantiga* claims. She probably spoke Romance, the Aragonese lingua franca, and so could easily have discussed remedies for sick children with her Christian neighbors and heard them praise Mary's miracles.[127] If this woman actually did go to Salas, she would hardly have been the only medieval Muslim to pray to Jesus' mother in a church.

Christians, in any case, tailored this woman's story to their own design, just as they did other Marian tales in which the veil of miracle softened the sharp bones of actual situations provoking conversion. Her baptism joins with those of other female converts in predicting the inevitability of Islam and Judaism's defeat even more forcefully than did the submission of Jewish and Muslim men to the Virgin's commands. These women's willing and natural affection for Mary—symbol of the Church—suggests that Islam and Judaism harbor a hidden longing for evangelical love that vindicates Christian missionary aspirations.

In the world of Christian hagiography, Muslim women can even openly yearn for the Virgin and the baptismal font, unlike their Jewish sisters. The Marian literature of high medieval Iberia proposes no Jewish counterpart to Fatima, a wealthy young Muslim maiden of late fifteenth-century Tangiers featuring in a miracle story from Guadalupe, a woman with such "an acute and intimate desire" for Mary and Christianity that she decides to commit suicide when her plans to convert are thwarted. Only a reassuring vision of Our Lady of Guadalupe prevents Fatima from leaping to her death. To "reach the desired good" of baptism and closeness to Mary, she eventually abandons her North African home, crosses the Mediterranean, and comes to Guadalupe. She spends the rest of her life there serving Mary, her ardor for her new faith earning her the nickname of "the good Christian."[128]

Fatima's pre-baptismal passion for the Madonna, which was shared by a Muslim maiden from a late fifteenth-century French miracle story, perhaps served as the hagiographer's tacit admission that Christianity and Islam crossed ways at the shrine of Marian devotion.[129] Yet like so many Christian authors, this writer twisted Mary's role in Islam to serve decidedly un-ecumenical ends: the love Fatima feels for Jesus' mother inexorably propels her onto a spiritual path leading to baptism. Suggesting likenesses between this woman and the object of her spiritual desire, the hagiographer further reinforced this message. While still living as a Muslim, Fatima is virginal and merciful, just like Mary. Her ability to mirror Jesus' mother makes Mary's place in Islam visible. But the clearest reflection in the glass of Fatima's virtues is the Christian Madonna—a prefiguration of this Muslim woman's inevitable future as "the good Christian."

Hagiographers could even write the destiny of Marian conversion directly onto the bodies of Muslim women by literally forming them in the Virgin's image, as a haunting poem from the *Cantigas de Santa María* describes. This *cantiga* brings forth from the baptismal font a torrent of Christian triumphs. It relates how in the early thirteenth century, the Castilian magnates Alfonso Téllez de Meneses and Gonzalo Yáñez besieged a Muslim castle somewhere on the frontier.[130] When their men set fire to the fortress's tower, the Muslims ran out onto the battlements where all died, except for a woman who sat on the edge of the tower clutching her son in her arms. When the Christian attackers saw her, they drew in their breaths with wonder. As the poem says: "this image seemed to them like the way that the Virgin Mary is depicted holding and embracing her son." Alfonso X's artists did their best to bring out the likeness of the Muslim woman and child to the image of the Virgin and child (Figure 6.2). The Muslim pair are perched in the battlements in exactly the same way that, in an earlier *cantiga*, a statue of the Madonna and child nestles in the tower arch of a Christian frontier castle under Muslim attack (Figure 1.2).

Weakened by fire, the tower was about to collapse. So, the *cantiga* says, the Christians implored Mary to save these Muslims. Miraculously, when the tower fell, the Muslim woman and her child landed without injury. The poem concludes with their baptism. The illuminations underline the Marian quality of this female convert even more explicitly than do the poem's words. In one frame, a Christian points with one hand at a statue of Madonna and child, and gestures with the other to the Muslim woman, explaining the miracle to her and calling the viewer's attention to the resemblance of the two mothers. In the final frame, under the impassive gaze of the Marian statue, the Muslims, still in mother-and-child mode, sit in the baptismal font.

In this story, the likeness between the woman's maternal body and Mary's own both saves and betrays her. A living Marian icon, this Muslim has no choice but to abandon Islam for the religion of the Virgin's son and surrender to the faith of the castle's conquerors, her baptism consecrating their victory. Perhaps this was how the sweat-stained warriors who fought to take the castle made sense of the events of that day, for the tale probably originated with them. When this *cantiga*'s poetic veneer is stripped away, the unmistakable lines of a war story emerge. Alfonso X might even have heard this anecdote from one of the noblemen who led the attack, Alfonso Téllez de Meneses, a regular at Ferdinand III's court who had fought alongside Alfonso's own knights at the siege of Seville.[131] Wherever this tale came from, it was a narrative that staged Mary's miracle of conversion against the bloody backdrop of actual war between Christians and Muslims.

Other Marian tales more literally militarized the triumph of baptism, sometimes promoting it to the front lines of Christian-Muslim combat. Jacques de Vitry, the crusading bishop of Acre, was convinced that the Virgin wielded her evangelical sword to thin the ranks of Muslim hosts. In a letter of 1216–1217, he mentioned Muslims who converted because Mary warned them that otherwise they would be vanquished by Christian armies and "die a miserable death."[132] Few Marian stories from high medieval Castile and Aragon coupled battle and baptism this aggressively. Yet if the evangelical ideology of men like Jacques de Vitry could coincide with crusade, some Christians in the Iberian Peninsula

Figure 6.2 A Muslim mother and her child are miraculously saved from death in a
castle set on fire by Christian attackers. *Cantigas de Santa María*. Biblioteca Nazionale
Centrale di Firenze. Florence, Biblioteca Nazionale Centrale, MS Banco Rari 20, folio 6r.
Reproduced with the permission of the Ministerio per i beni e le attività culturali della
Repubblica Italiana.

believed that Mary's missionary domain encompassed the field of holy war. In the *Cantigas*, for example, Alfonso X and his poets sharpened a timeless, place-less miracle of conversion inherited from earlier writers by locating it in the cru-sader world of the Levant.[133] They also discarded the featureless Muslim of the earlier versions in favor of a fierce Moorish warrior who delights in "ravag[ing]" and "rob[bing]" Christians. Baptism precipitated by a Marian miracle subdues this man who could not be tamed by the force of arms, and presumably places his sword at Christianity's service.

Christians who had survived one of the most traumatic theaters of war with Muslims—captivity—could even tell stories transforming Marian conver-sions into an extension of their battlefield experiences. In some of these tales, gathered from former captives making thanksgiving pilgrimages to shrines like Guadalupe, the Virgin commands Muslim men who hold Christian prisoners of war to convert.[134] Muslim women too can feature in these captivity narratives; Fatima of Tangiers, longing for Mary and for baptism, reaches her end by con-spiring with Christian captives languishing in her father's dungeon. Whether featuring Muslim men or Muslim maidens, these stories depicted conversion as the source of spiritual liberation for the followers of Islam and physical emanci-pation for Christians shut up in Muslim slave houses; after Mary releases these Muslims from the prison of Islam, they turn their energies to freeing Christian captives from much more tangible fetters. Together, the converts and former captives then flee Islamic territory and journey to Christendom, where they has-ten to Guadalupe.

Some of these Marian stories of captivity and conversion date from the late fifteenth century, others from a century later. During the Golden Age of Spanish literature, these Marian miracles even made their way into Miguel de Cervantes' *Don Quijote*. At the inn where much of the novel's action transpires, Cervantes' hero encounters Zoraida, a Muslim maiden–turned-Christian whose life story echoes that of Fatima, the convert from Tangiers: she is a virginal, merciful, North African Muslim woman brought to Christianity by her passionate love for the Virgin. By the time Don Quijote meets her, she even insists on being called Mary.[135] Accompanying Zoraida is a Christian man whom she helped to escape from her father's prison in Algiers. In one of Cervantes' lesser-known plays, an almost identical Muslim Marian convert named Zahara flees from North Africa with her father's Christian captives.[136]

In borrowing these motifs from Guadalupe's miracles, Cervantes was giving literary expression to his own long years in a slave house in Algiers and seeking to make sense of his ordeal.[137] Less lettered captives did the same through the stories assiduously collected by the shrine keepers at Guadalupe in the fifteenth and sixteenth centuries. These Marian tales had an enduring power to help men and women transmute the trauma of their time in chains, subject to the whims of Muslim masters, into cathartic narratives of suffering and redemption.[138] The abjection of captivity becomes a progress toward Christianity triumphant, as the captives return to Christendom with Muslims whom Mary has primed to defect from Islam. These stories created a world in which she vanquished Islam on its home territory and won spiritual victories, reversing the military defeats that led to the capture of Christians in the first place.

Yet if anyone was likely to convert in the late medieval and early modern slave houses and prisons of Granada and North Africa, it was Christian captives themselves, not their Muslim captors.[139] Sometimes it was pressure from their masters that caused Christian captives to utter the words of the *shahadah*, the profession of faith in God and his prophet Muhammad that if twice repeated brought one into the *umma*, the community of Muslims. Other captives, despairing of ever returning to Christendom, willingly sought the freedom that came with conversion to Islam. So many Christians captured by Muslims chose the path of conversion that in Castile and Aragon, captivity gained notoriety as a peril to the Christian soul.[140] Mary herself sometimes had to intervene to shore up captives' wavering allegiance to Christianity.[141]

The Marian miracle stories that culminated in the baptism of Muslims turned the realities of captivity and conversion inside out. These were narratives of hope, personal and political. Countering the fears aroused by the fate of those thousands of medieval and early modern men and women captured by Muslims on the battlefield, in border raids, or pirate attacks, these stories reassured Christians that the Virgin had the power to transform their jailers into their allies, their liberators, and their companions in the faith—and thus to redraw the political map in favor of Christianity.

Marian conversion miracles had such weight that they could even figure in actual political maneuverings between Muslims and Christians, as an enigmatic set of letters from the Barcelona archives dated 1325 and addressed to Pope John XXII suggests.[142] These documents focus on a man described as "Bobacre," the Muslim "lord of the city of Africa," better known as Abu Bakr, an early fourteenth-century governor of the Tunisian port town of Mahdia.[143] In a letter purportedly written by the Muslim lord himself, Abu Bakr relates how one night as he lay sleeping, a beautiful woman appeared, announced herself to be Mary, and commanded him to convert to Christianity. Not only did Abu Bakr bow to her wishes, but he also decided that his friends and followers should renounce Islam along with him—a mass conversion of high-ranking Muslims that would create a veritable army of new Christians. He even requested that the pope appoint a Christian king as the ruler of Mahdia. With this important site in Christian hands, declared Abu Bakr, "Christians will gain a great advantage and great damage will be inflicted on the Saracens."[144]

The letters describing Abu Bakr's conversion pose many interpretive challenges, not the least of which is determining exactly where to locate these documents between fiction and fact. These letters may be relating a spiritual experience Abu Bakr really had, for dreams often figured in autobiographical narratives of conversion. But his use of the language of Marian miracle could just as easily represent a canny effort to gain Christian military support against Muslim rivals by dangling the enticing bait of baptism before a potential ally, a game that Maghrebi strongmen and rulers before him had played with Christians.[145] It is also possible that Abu Bakr's conversion and all its anticipated political and military benefits owed something to the active imagination of the Christian men who signed their names to two of the letters: Dominicus Sancii and Alfonsus Petri. They were Mahdia's *alcayts*, leaders of the Aragonese mercenaries employed by the city's Muslim ruler.[146] As such, they were also the unofficial representatives of the king of Aragon and well aware of how nicely his territorial ambitions in the Maghreb would be served by the submission of Mahdia to Christianity.[147] Whether Abu Bakr's Marian conversion was a Christian literary fabrication, his own invention, or a genuine spiritual experience, the letters render it an act as pregnant with military and political consequences as it was with religious meaning. On both the secular and spiritual stages, Mary plays a leading role. She is the mother of Abu Bakr's baptism and all the triumphs for Christianity to which it gives birth.

Two and a half centuries later, Mary was still winning political victories for Christian Spain through her conversions of Muslim men, according to the story that a Moroccan named Brahen, son of the *qadi* of Fez, told in 1598 to Guadalupe's shrine keepers about his Marian-inspired journey from Islam to Christianity.[148] By the time Brahen came to the hills of Extremadura to kneel in thanksgiving before the diminutive statue of the Virgin who had, says the hagiographer, "brought him to the light of the Gospel when least he expected it," many Christians had heard his tale and were willing to vouch for its truth. The list of illustrious witnesses began in Fez with the Spanish ambassador, continued in Portugal where the archbishop of Lisbon baptized Brahen "with great pomp and majesty," and culminated at Philip II's court in Madrid, where the sovereign himself received the convert.

It is no wonder that these great men of Spanish politics took such keen interest in Brahen, celebrating his baptism with extravagant and "infinite thanks to God and his most holy mother, the Virgin of Guadalupe," in the words of the hagiographer. The defection of a high-ranking Moroccan would have been welcome news in the 1590s. In those years, Philip II was no friend to the man who sat on Morocco's throne, Ahmad al-Mansur, an ally of Spain's formidable enemies, the Ottomans and Elizabeth I of England. In his efforts to contain al-Mansur, Philip extended his protection to the aristocratic leader of the opposition to the Moroccan ruler.[149] Though the hagiographer from Guadalupe does not reveal

Brahen's political allegiances, it is not hard to imagine why Philip would have been willing to harbor yet another influential refugee from al-Mansur's Morocco, especially one who had decided to renounce Islam. It was a political miracle consecrated by the intervention of the mother of God herself.

It is not clear who first thought to frame Brahen's conversion with the language of Marian miracle. Was it Brahen himself, perhaps influenced by the Christian captives his father held prisoner in the slave houses of Fez? Or was it one of the many Christians whom he met during his long journey from Morocco to Madrid? It is plain, however, why Philip II and his court found the language of Marian miracle a convincing explanation for Brahen's decision to leave his faith and his home. For centuries, Christians had understood Mary as an open door through which all could pass to escape the prison of wrong belief and enter Christianity. The medieval miracle stories depicting the wondrous shattering of unbelief in her presence, as Jews and Muslims submit to her and Judaism and Islam lie broken before Christianity, were deeply imprinted on the early modern Spanish consciousness. The tale of Brahen's conversion is in fact almost a treasury of the familiar motifs from the medieval stories. In it figure a threatening vision from the Virgin as she commands this Muslim man to convert, his violent resistance to her orders, a struggle with the devil, the liberation of Christian captives, and the inevitable outcome of Brahen's complete capitulation to Mary's will.

Brahen was baptized in a political world very different from that of high medieval Iberia. Yet like Cervantes' literary creations, the narrative of this man's experience eloquently attests to the continuing vitality of the medieval Marian evangelical marvel as Spain moved into its imperial period. Early modern men and women even inherited from the Middle Ages the belief that the Virgin's victories on the spiritual battleground of conversion could be intertwined with triumphs gained on the fields where men and states crossed swords. By the time Brahen made his way to Guadalupe, the shrine keepers there pointed proudly to evidence that their Madonna's powers of conversion reached all the way to the new worlds that the Spanish had conquered on the other side of the Atlantic. Tucked into Guadalupe's miracle books is an account of an enigmatic Caribbean "princess," sister to the "king of Santo Domingo." She came as a pilgrim to Guadalupe in 1542 to thank Mary for having saved her life and her soul.[150] The Virgin had calmed the waters when the boat bearing this woman from her island home to Spain had been on the verge of foundering in a storm, a miracle that convinced the "princess" to seek permanent refuge in the god of the Spanish. When her ship made landfall in the Cape Verde islands, she requested and received baptism in gratitude for Mary's mercy.

This newly minted Christian was not the first native of the New World to tread the broad steps of Guadalupe's church. That dubious honor belonged instead to two Taino men whom Christopher Columbus brought back from his second voyage to the Caribbean. In July 1496, various dignitaries gathered at Guadalupe to watch as Columbus's two Indian "servants" were solemnly baptized under the impassive gaze of the shrine's famous statue of Mary.[151] The first inhabitants of the New World to emerge from baptismal waters on Spanish soil, Cristobal and Pedro, as these men would be known, were living trophies of their master's achievements—and testimony to Mary's presence at the dawn of a new era of military and spiritual conquest.

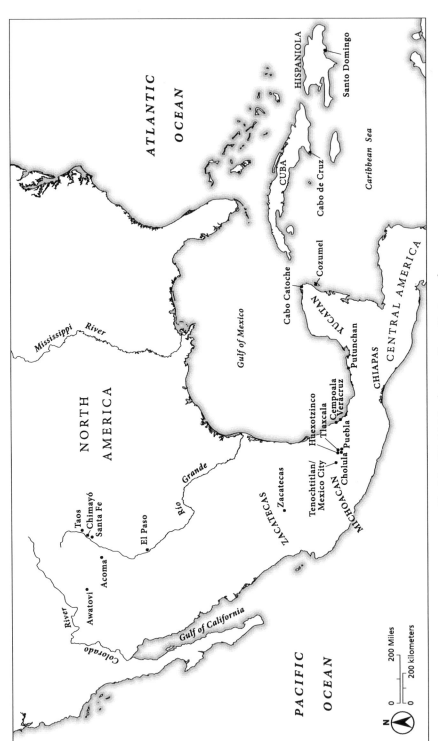

The New World. Map by Pease Press Cartography.

PART THREE

NEW WORLDS

Introduction

In 1528, just a few short years after captaining the conquest of an empire on the other side of the Atlantic, Hernán Cortés laid offerings from this distant land before the Virgin of Guadalupe at her shrine in Extremadura. These handsome gifts must have seemed strange and wondrous to the friars who watched over the renowned Marian statue. Cortés's donation consisted of Indian feather-work images of "exotic design and perfection" and a gold scorpion wrought with "the marvelous artifice in which the Indians excelled," to borrow the admiring description of Guadalupe's late sixteenth-century historian. These magnificent products of the high culture of Mesoamerica were just the sort of New World trophies the conquistador had sent to the Hapsburg ruler of Spain, Charles V, in 1520.[1]

A charismatic and unscrupulous man, Cortés was known for his ability to parlay difficult situations into advantageous ones. He could play people and win, as his astute maneuvers precipitating the violent collapse of the Triple Alliance (commonly known as the Aztec or Mexica Empire) in 1521 had taught his enemies and allies, Spanish and indigenous alike.[2] But by the time he came to Guadalupe, his game was off. Facing legal proceedings and serious accusations of misconduct by his compatriots in Mexico, Cortés returned to Spain in the hopes of setting the record straight with Charles V.[3] Perhaps an element of political calculation entered into his decision to stop at Guadalupe before making his appearance at court. Charles V did not cherish this Marian shrine with quite the fervor of his maternal grandparents, Isabel and Ferdinand, but he nonetheless continued the long tradition of royal patronage, visiting the monastery and enriching it with donations.[4] Surely Cortés expected that the monarch would listen favorably to reports of his own pious offering to this royal Virgin and interpret it as a sign of loyalty to the Crown.

Cortés's pilgrimage was more than political theater, however, for he gave every indication of at least some measure of personal devotion to Our Lady of Guadalupe.[5] In 1522, he sent his second shipment of booty from the defeated Mexica realm back to Spain, carefully apportioning the "royal fifth" for Charles V

209

but also designating certain "jewels" as offerings to her.[6] Because French corsairs intercepted the ship carrying these plundered New World treasures, Guadalupe would have to wait six years before receiving material evidence of the conquistador's devotion.

Cortés's wish to honor the Virgin of Guadalupe is one of the less surprising aspects of his personality. This Madonna belonged to his *tierra*, the word sixteenth-century Spaniards used to express allegiance to their community of origin.[7] Like so many of the Spaniards who shipped out to the Indies in the wake of Christopher Columbus's voyage of 1492, Cortés came from Extremadura, the rough and poor region where the shrine of Guadalupe was located.[8] He was born and raised in Medellín, a farming town situated some eighty kilometers southwest of the monastery along the main road to Seville.[9] In his youth he would have seen pilgrims pass through and perhaps had joined them once or twice as they traveled north into the forested hills surrounding the shrine. According to the monastery's late sixteenth-century historian, Gabriel de Talavera, Cortés knew the Virgin of Guadalupe as a wonder-worker on whom he could rely, even when thousands of miles away from Extremadura; poisoned by a scorpion's sting somewhere in the Indies, the conquistador "turned his eyes to Our Lady," begging her to save him from death. The gold scorpion Cortés brought to her shrine was thus an ex-voto offering, which, Talavera commented, contained the dried body of the guilty insect itself.[10]

Among the trove of gifts that other grateful pilgrims had left for the Virgin at Guadalupe, the scorpion must have stood out, its strong lines and use of color revealing its distinctly non-European manufacture.[11] Like many of the medieval offerings crowding the monastery's treasury, though, it was proof of Mary's willingness to aid men engaged in colonial projects of conquest. It thus connected the Old and New Worlds, a tangible sign of how the men who risked their lives to cross the Atlantic did not entirely leave behind the cultural universe from which they came. In many ways, they carried with them the attitudes, beliefs, and expectations of late fifteenth- and early sixteenth-century Spain.

Beginning with Columbus's voyage of 1492, Europeans landed on islands and then continents rich in sights strange to their eyes: scantily clad peoples dining on unfamiliar foods and speaking unknown languages, odd animals prowling jungles and forests dense with vegetation unlike any back home, soaring stone and earth pyramids, and much more. No wonder they called these lands a New World. Although during the early years of contact and colonization, Europeans collided with the unknown almost everywhere they looked, they did not always bring fresh eyes to their experiences. To understand, possess, and subdue this alien territory in all its teeming difference, the colonizers at first charted it with mental and cultural maps brought from home, trying to make the New World fit into Old World categories.[12]

Some of the reference points Europeans used during early years to orient themselves in the New World came from medieval traditions based on the texts of classical antiquity that detailed the monstrous and mythic beings an adventurer might expect to find beyond the known world.[13] Many of the Spaniards who colonized this new world, however, also tamed its novelty with more prosaic and familiar language. Faced with peoples so unlike themselves, the Spaniards could resort to a vocabulary grounded in generations of Aragonese and Castilian Christian experience of living with difference—that is, with Muslims and Jews.[14]

"Some Spaniards, considering certain rites, customs, and ceremonies of the indigenous peoples, judged them to be descendants of Moors. Others...said they were descendants of Jews."[15] The man who wrote these words was Toribio de Benavente, known as Motolinía, one of the first Franciscan missionaries to arrive in Mexico after the Spanish and their native allies toppled the Triple Alliance. The friar concluded that most Spaniards believed the indigenous to be neither Muslims nor Jews, but "gentiles." Yet by introducing this terminology, Motolinía and his compatriots implicitly placed the New World peoples into the category of long-familiar enemies and neighbors—and thus cast their trans-Atlantic enterprises in a rather medieval mode.

Although the conquistadors may well have exemplified the "Renaissance spirit" so prized by an earlier generation of modern historians, they were also under the sway of ideas inherited from the Middle Ages. The weight of this medieval legacy impressed itself on everything from the laws with which the Spanish ruled their Atlantic empire to the intricate geometries of the Mudejar ceilings gracing some New World churches.[16] It was equally palpable in the narratives of discovery and conquest. In the pages that the more literate of the conquistadors wrote about themselves, these men often displayed all the swagger and heroism of the knights of the chivalric romances whom Miguel de Cervantes mocked in *Don Quijote*.[17] After all, they had been raised on such medieval fare. Though conquistadors compared themselves flatteringly to the Romans of antiquity, only the most educated among them would have been exposed to the classical curriculum beloved of the humanists, and even then it did not always take.[18]

In their battles with the indigenous peoples of the New World, these men could resort to military tactics that did not resemble the chivalric combats of romance and epic, but nonetheless came from the late Middle Ages. Some of their strategies would have been recognizable to their fathers, especially to those who had participated in the campaigns against Granada, as Cortés's own parent had done.[19] As one contemporary observer wrote: "they conquered the land...following the example of the Catholic Monarchs when they conquered Granada."[20] Despite the conquistadors' much vaunted firearms, their most effective weapon was perhaps the one wielded by generations of medieval knights: the steel sword.[21] The men who crossed the Atlantic to lay bloody claim to the wealth and peoples of the New World also inherited the motivations that had driven soldiers and knights to wage war against Granada—that potent alloy of piety, ambition, and greed—along with a good dose of the reconquest ideology undergirding Ferdinand and Isabel's campaigns. Conquistadors could even write openly of their activities as an extension of the Granadan wars.[22]

The world from which these men set forth gave them every reason to believe that Mary would be a powerful patron of such violent Christian enterprise. In the years following the fall of Granada, legends commemorating the aid she had provided Christian knights, armies, and cities against their Muslim foes during the reconquest flourished. Reports of new Marian military glories over the infidel complemented the memories of older ones. After the Nasrid kingdom's demise, Isabel and Ferdinand were eager to take their wars against Muslims to the African shores of the Mediterranean. Motivated by a host of practical and political concerns, the monarchs also still burned with the spirit of holy war.[23] They intended their North African campaigns to continue the crusade they had begun years before against Granada. Not surprisingly, they, along with their contemporaries, drew explicit parallels between these expeditions and those being conducted thousands of miles away in the New World.[24] Some conquistadors even returned to Spain and fought in the Maghreb, as Cortés did.[25] Ferdinand and Isabel's successors, Charles V and Philip II, inherited these North African endeavors, although they would aim their military energies toward the Ottoman Turks, who reigned over an ever expanding empire from Constantine's old city on the Bosphorus.

Whether fighting against the Muslims of North Africa or against the Turks, sixteenth-century Spaniards could turn to Mary for aid. Any early sixteenth-century pilgrim to Guadalupe would have found there abundant evidence of her participation in the ongoing Spanish conquest of unbelievers. Perhaps the soft light cast by another grateful warrior's gift to the shrine's Madonna flickered over the golden scorpion offered by Cortés. It was an elaborate lamp engraved with the silhouettes of three Muslim cities, each bristling with towers, walls, and castles: Oran, Tripoli, and Bougie (Bejaïa).[26] The lamp was eloquent proof that the defenses of these North African cities had been of no avail against Spanish attacks of 1509 and 1510. The man who led these assaults, Count Pedro Navarro, had come to Guadalupe before setting off for the Maghreb. At the shrine, he apparently imitated many Christian knights before him, committing himself to Mary's care, giving the monastery "a great quantity of money, offer[ing] to Our Lady his expedition, and supplicat[ing] her for victory."[27]

Navarro must have felt that Mary had heard his prayers. A royal chronicler detailed how, after his victory at Tripoli, the count and his troops rendered thanks to God, the Virgin, and Saint James.[28] Some time later, Navarro offered the lamp to Guadalupe. As the monastery's late sixteenth-century historian wrote, the count recognized Mary as the author of his triumphs over the "barbarous Moors of Africa."[29] For good measure, he also sent her six Muslims taken captive during his North African campaigns, destined for perpetual servitude at the shrine.[30]

The men and women of Extremadura who packed the ships bound for the New World in the sixteenth century would surely have known the stories of the Virgin of Guadalupe's powers to bring about Christian victory. Some, such as Francisco Pizarro, had even been raised in towns that had their own conquering Madonnas. This man, who in 1532 sent news from the Andes of Spanish triumph over the Inca empire, came from Trujillo, a town west of Guadalupe. In Trujillo today, spiked cacti loom near flamboyant houses built by successful sixteenth-century emigrants returning from the New World, stone and living monuments to Spanish conquests on the other side of the Atlantic.[31] The young Pizarro, however, would have grown up hearing tales about a victory of the distant past: a battle of 1232 when Mary had appeared over the gates of Trujillo and helped Ferdinand III take the town from its Muslim lords. Of obscure origins, this legend was enshrined in the town's civic architecture and festive life by at least the early sixteenth century. In 1505, a statue of "Our Lady of Victory" was placed over the gateway known as the "Gate of Triumph." Sixteenth-century Trujillans dedicated a feast day to this Virgin's honor, and, as they walked by their town's public buildings and churches, they could glance up at their civic coat of arms, a bust of the Madonna floating above crenellated walls, a design supposedly confirmed by Ferdinand III himself.[32]

Trujillo's triumphant Virgin had many sisters in late medieval and early modern Iberia, as urban communities began to create for themselves histories glorifying their Christian identity and reducing the Muslim portions of their past to the moment of Christian conquest.[33] As they did so, Marian legends of the reconquest—some previously fostered by ecclesiastical communities, others plucked from the pages of old chronicles, and yet others apparently created ex nihilo—gained a certain vogue.[34] Perhaps nowhere was Mary's importance to the emerging civic traditions of early modern Spain more evident than in Seville, the city designated by the monarchs as the official gateway to the Indies, whose fourteenth-century residents made the preposterous claim that the Virgin had been born there.[35]

All emigrants to the New World were supposed to pass through Seville. Extremadurans determined to cross the Atlantic typically began the long journey by traveling south to this bustling city, where they lingered for weeks, even months, while making the complicated arrangements for passage.[36] Joining them in the endless wait for the necessary documents were men and women from all over Spain, including the region around Seville itself; Andalusia seems to have sent an even greater percentage of conquistadors to the Americas than did Extremadura.[37] Sevilleans too filled many berths aboard the ships that began the journey across the Atlantic from this port on the Guadalquivir.[38]

Wherever they came from, emigrants would have found much to wonder at in Seville. With a population of approximately 100,000, it was one of the largest cities in early modern Spain. In its urban magnificence, it boasted wide paved streets thronged with merchants and men of business from all over Europe, a floating bridge spanning the river that flowed through the city, public baths, elegant palaces—and a huge new cathedral dedicated to Mary.[39] Begun in the early fifteenth century and not completed until some hundred years later, this building replaced the Almohad mosque that had served as the city's main church since 1248.[40] The proud Gothic and Renaissance lines of the new cathedral, one of the largest ever built, helped erase the city's Muslim past. Like the old mosque-cathedral, obliterated all but for its minaret, the new structure bore Mary's name and housed important statues and paintings of her. Men and women heading to the New World would have stopped by, either to pray in the hope of securing the Virgin's aid for the dangerous voyage or to see a cathedral in the big city. Whether pious or merely curious, any visitor to Seville's cathedral found evidence there of the Madonna's powers to help Christians defeat their infidel enemies.

In the royal chapel, the crowned and imperious statue of Mary that had so impressed the German doctor Hieronymus Münzer in 1494 still watched over the tomb of Castile's saintly crusader king, Ferdinand III. At least some men and women departing for the New World from Seville would have heard the same story Münzer did: the tale of how this Madonna had helped her most famous royal devotee vanquish his unbelieving foes. By the time Seville became the headquarters for traffic to and from Spain's expanding possessions in the Indies, this legend belonged to the city's public self. Anyone present for the Corpus Christi procession in 1514 would have seen the pride Sevilleans took in the story of how together Mary and Ferdinand III had defeated the Almohads and recovered the city for Christendom. Enthroned in the middle of the float designed by the tailors' guild sat a depiction of Our Lady of the Kings, the statue Münzer had admired. Guild officials costumed to represent different eras of Seville's history posed in front of her. Reigning over this tableau of two Visigothic bishops, ten Muslim men, one Muslim woman, a Christian standard bearer, and Ferdinand III, the Madonna became the still point around which the tides of the city's Christian identity ebbed and flowed.[41]

In November 1532, an even more dramatic procession carrying the actual statue of Our Lady of the Kings and headed by the city's church and civic officials wound its way through Seville's broad streets.[42] Sevilleans turned out in great numbers to implore Mary to help Charles V defeat the Ottoman armies, then making their second attempt to storm Vienna. The Turkish retreat some months later proved to Seville's residents that their Madonna still had the powers to trounce Muslims. And so they joined together in a thanksgiving procession, and once again paraded the statue through their city.[43]

Other images of Mary that bore messages about Christian victory over unbelievers resided in Seville's cathedral in the sixteenth century. One particularly attracted the devotion of men who ventured to the New World: the delicate Italianate fourteenth-century painting known as the Virgen de la Antigua. Numerous conquistadors, Cortés among them, made offerings to her.[44] This youthful Mary cradled Jesus on her hip and gazed soft-eyed at the viewer, gold filigree ornamenting her robe and veil.[45] The many copies made of this celestial beauty in sixteenth-century Andalusia are testimony to the devotion she inspired at the start of Spain's imperial era.[46]

The Virgen de la Antigua is probably the enigmatic image of Mary that plays second fiddle to Our Lady of the Kings in the story Münzer heard when he visited Seville's cathedral in the 1490s. During the city's Islamic centuries, an "image of the blessed Virgin" had stayed in the Almohads' main mosque "from antiquity," wrote the doctor.[47] Alonso Morgado's history of Seville published in 1576 confirms that the Marian painting was exactly the kind of defiant icon of the city's enduring Christianity described by Münzer. "Nuestra Señora de la Antigua," wrote Morgado, "has been generally called thus from time immemorial because of her antiquity dating back to the time of the Goths. She remained always in Seville, as long as the Moors ruled it, against their perfidy. At various moments they tried to efface and destroy her, but she always remained, more beautiful and resplendent than ever."[48] Morgado admitted that he could not find written evidence to support this "pious tradition," but he assured his readers that the story was common knowledge in the city. Sevilleans, he said, would laugh at anyone suggesting the tale was not true.[49]

In the early sixteenth century, great ships bearing this Virgin's name set sail from Seville for the West Indies. So when Nicolás de Ovando left in 1502 to take up the governorship of the Spanish settlements in the Caribbean, he traveled on board the Santa María de la Antigua at the head of some thirty ships.[50] Perhaps Ovando and other men, such as Alonso de Hojeda and García de Ocampo, who sailed the Indies in carracks of the same name understood the part that the Virgen de la Antigua had played in the struggle between Christianity and Islam over Seville's soul.[51] Or perhaps they simply thought of their ships' namesake as the graceful, young mother of the painting enshrined in Seville's cathedral. In any case, they would have known that they journeyed under Mary's protection.

So too did all those men who set out for the New World in ships named after the many other Madonnas cherished in early modern Spain. So popular was Mary, the "star of the sea," as a patron of American-bound carracks and caravels that when the conquistador Pedrarias Dávila pulled away from Seville's docks in 1514, headed for the Caribbean coast of South America, ten of the sixteen ships in his fleet bore her name in one version or another.[52] His flagship itself was called Nuestra Señora de la Concepción ("Our Lady of the Conception"). Aloft on its mast flew a banner of white taffeta sporting an image of Santa María de la Antigua, one of only three flags given places of honor next to the royal pennant itself (the other two depicted Santiago and the Cross of Jerusalem).[53]

Two of the ships in Dávila's fleet were named for Our Lady of Victory, a Madonna in whom Sevillean-based sailors often placed their hopes for a safe voyage. In the sweltering heat of August 1519, Ferdinand Magellan and his crew made a solemn procession to the church bearing her name in Triana, the area of Seville that was home to the city's congested wharfs. There, they knelt in prayer. Magellan and his sailors then boarded the Santa María de la Victoria, the ship in which they would circle the globe. The Franciscan friars who tended this Madonna's church made it their mission to provide aid to sailors and navigators, a goal also cherished by the clergy of a nearby chapel built in 1526 and dedicated to Our Lady of Remedies. Watching over men bound for the New World was the task of both these popular Madonnas of the shipyards—and of Mary herself, whatever name she bore.[54]

By the 1530s, a painting of the Virgin housed in Seville announced that such in fact was the official ideology promoted by the royal representatives who oversaw Spain's imperial project in the Americas. Known as the "Virgin of the Seafarers" or the "Virgin of the Navigators," this portrait of Mary resided in the city's temple to commerce with the Americas, the Casa de Contratación.[55] Founded in 1503, the Casa was a royal institution, whose officials regulated the flow of goods and people across the Atlantic, dispensing the licenses necessary for emigration, imposing duties on goods arriving from the Indies, authorizing ships to sail and land, and dealing with the myriad details of administering this aspect of empire.[56]

In 1526, Charles V ordered the installation of a chapel in the Casa. Perhaps because the Casa's officials had to make do with limited space, they fulfilled the monarch's command rather creatively by having their Sala de Audiencias serve as both church and audience hall. The "Virgin of the Seafarers" would preside over the sacred and secular business conducted there, for the painting belonged to an altarpiece commissioned for the room from one of Seville's leading artists, Alejo Fernández (Figure 13.1). Presumably the Casa's officials determined the altarpiece's theme, though leaving the details to the painter. The resulting composition, completed by 1536, was as openly imperial in its message as it was Renaissance in its style, projecting what one recent commentator has called the "official vision of Spain's creation of a Christian empire across the ocean."[57]

In the altarpiece's central panel—its focal point—Mary balances on a cloud and spreads her cloak wide about her. Gazing up at her from its folds are the

Figure I.3.1 Alejo Fernández, *The Virgin of the Navigators.* Reales Alcazares, Seville, Spain. De Agostini Picture Library, A. Dagli Orti. The Bridgeman Art Library.

participants, willing and unwilling, in Spain's imperial project: figures representing the royal family, navigators, and conquistadors, with the dusky-skinned peoples of the New World crowded behind them. Ships gather on the sea below Mary's feet, enjoying her patronage and protection. This Virgin who watches over Spain's imperial drama is recognizably Our Lady of Mercy, the Madonna who lovingly extends her mantle over her devotees in so many medieval images. But it has been suggested that Fernández also painted into the "Virgin of the Seafarers" subtle references to Seville's Our Lady of the Kings. If so, this is only one of the ways that he cued his viewers to the ideological connection between Spain's New World ventures and its Old World crusades against Muslims.[58]

Mary's guiding role in the colonization of the Americas was no mere product of this artist's imagination or that of his patrons, the Casa officials. The stories that had circulated for centuries in Castile and Aragon about Mary's role in Christian victory shaped how the conquerors and colonizers saw their own ventures in the New World. Such is the picture painted by many of the early chronicles, letters, and other documents relating to the Spanish conquest of the Caribbean and Mesoamerica, the heart of the vast area designated in 1535 as the viceroyalty of New Spain. There is evidence suggesting that a similar Marian story could be told about the conquest and settlement of Spain's other massive viceroyalty in the Americas, Peru.[59] Yet New Spain and especially central Mexico left behind particularly rich sources.

Late fifteenth- and sixteenth-century texts presented the men who initiated the piecemeal process by which the lands of New Spain were gradually brought under the semblance of Spanish control as invoking Mary, much like both the Castilian knights and soldiers who had brought Granada to its knees and the Spaniards still campaigning against Muslims in the Mediterranean. But while drawing on traditional Marian language and imagery, conquistadors also relied on her in ways that their Old World counterparts would never have thought to, at least when faced with Muslims on the battlefield. They did so because of one of the key differences between the Old World crusades and the New World imperial project. In the Old World, Spaniards fought against Muslims to defeat them, but in the New World, Spaniards warred against indigenous peoples to defeat them *and* to bring Christianity to them.

Evangelization was not an overt goal of the medieval military campaigns against the Muslim polities of al-Andalus and North Africa. The treaties signed between Christian victors and conquered Muslim communities typically contained clauses assuring the vanquished of their right to continue practicing Islam.[60] In medieval Castile and Aragon, Muslims and Jews living under Christian rule were in fact guaranteed religious freedom. Late in 1491, when the citizens of the city of Granada, starving and suffering after living under siege, decided to surrender, the right to remain Muslim figured prominently on the long list of terms they requested from their new Christian lords. By agreeing that Granadans could indeed "live in their own religion," as the Capitulations of Granada say, Ferdinand and Isabel were only following tradition.[61]

A few years later, the natives of the New World would be granted a legal status that in most respects paralleled that of Jews and Muslims in medieval Castile and Aragon.[62] The degree to which the rights and privileges officially enjoyed by indigenous communities in the sixteenth century were modeled on the status of Jewish and Mudejar *aljamas* is yet another indication of the palpable presence of the Middle Ages in the New World—but the idea of religious coexistence itself did not cross the Atlantic. The protections that the Spanish Crown granted to the indigenous peoples of the New World pointedly did not extend to the religious beliefs and practices they had inherited from their ancestors.

Great changes in the Old World help explain why. Upheavals precipitated by the momentous events of 1492 shattered the religious equilibrium of medieval Iberia and made sixteenth-century Spain in some ways into a new world, one officially populated only by Christians, new and old. The story of how, within three decades of Ferdinand and Isabel's triumphant entry into Granada, the Jews and Mudejars of Castile and Aragon were transformed into Christians, and Judaism and Islam officially effaced from Spain, is not a pretty one. It is an anguished tale of book burnings, armed rebellion, mass deportations, mass baptisms, and the blatant breaking of promises. In it figure the Catholic Monarchs, their advisors, their grandson, a saintly archbishop and a fanatic one, and thousands of Muslims and Jews forced to choose between conversion or exile.

Few dates in Spanish history reverberate quite like 1492. On January 2, Isabel and Ferdinand formally took possession of Granada in a ceremony that sealed the death of the last Islamic polity on Spanish soil. Then, on March 31, they issued edicts giving their Jewish subjects three months within which to decide between baptism and exile. Thousands of Jews chose the latter option, the tortuous paths of diaspora leading to Portugal, Amsterdam, and Italy, as well as Muslim North Africa and the sophisticated cities of the Ottoman Empire. Thousands of others chose baptism, creating a host of converts of dubious Christianity who became fodder for the recently founded Spanish Inquisition. The reason Ferdinand and Isabel gave for their decrees was neither instinctive anti-Semitism nor fervent evangelism, but anxiety about the spiritual welfare of their converso subjects, Jewish men and women already converted to Christianity. In her edict, Isabel accused Jews of "try[ing] always and with all possible means to subvert and remove [conversos] from our holy Catholic faith" and return them to Judaism.[63] The solution, she and her husband believed, was for all Jews either to become Christian or to leave Spain.

The monarchs issued their notorious decree from newly conquered Granada. By then, the man they had appointed to be the city's first archbishop, Hernando de Talavera, was ready to take up his duties.[64] In his early years as Granada's pastor, Talavera made every effort to ensure that the religious terms under which the city had capitulated were observed scrupulously. By all accounts, this won him the respect and affection of the city's Muslim residents. But even while he protected their religious liberty, he worked assiduously to persuade them of Christianity's superiority to Islam. His methods were gentle, his touch light, and predictably, his harvest of souls disappointingly small.[65]

Observing the glacial pace of conversion in Granada with increasing impatience was one of Spain's most powerful prelates, Francisco Jiménez de Cisneros, archbishop of Toledo, and a strict Franciscan, a zealot even. In 1499, he came to Granada and initiated a series of increasingly violent measures aimed at bringing the city's Muslims to the baptismal font. Arresting and imprisoning some of the city's leading men in order to force them to renounce Islam, he impounded thousands of books in Arabic and had them publicly burned in a bonfire that consumed much of al-Andalus's rich textual legacy.[66] Enraged by Cisneros's blatant disregard of their right to religious liberty, Granada's Muslims took up arms against their Christian lords, joined by Muslims living outside the city in the terraced mountain valleys of the Alpujarras and elsewhere across southern Andalusia. The rebels were soon overcome by the superior military strength of Ferdinand and Isabel's forces.

In the aftermath of the uprisings of 1499–1501, the Catholic Monarchs abrogated the Capitulations of Granada and, in a replay of 1492, dealt with the problem of safeguarding the Christianity of the Moriscos—the Muslims whom Cisneros had forcibly converted—by compelling Granada's Muslims to choose between baptism and exile. By 1502, Isabel had imposed the same fate on all Mudejars in Castile. Though Ferdinand allowed the Muslims of his own kingdom to retain their religion, a decade after his death, his grandson Charles V ordered them to convert or leave the realm.[67] Thus thousands of Spain's Muslims fled to North Africa, at least while they were allowed to. Most of these royal decrees quickly shut off the option of exile, forcing baptism on the Muslims and turning them into Moriscos.

By the time Cortés came to Guadalupe to offer his golden scorpion to Mary, all of Spain was Christian, if in name only. To many of Ferdinand and Isabel's contemporaries, these mass conversions of Jews and Muslims following the fall of Granada seemed like the fulfillment of the apocalyptic prophecies predicting how in the world's last days, a universal ruler would appear, conquer Granada and Jerusalem, and then destroy Islam while the Jews and all the peoples of the world were baptized.[68] Charles V would inherit the mantle of apocalyptic universal monarch his grandfather had worn and pass it on to his own son, Philip II.[69]

This was the heady atmosphere in which the adventurers and mercenaries who became the conquistadors set forth from Spain. The volatile mixture of territorial ambitions and evangelical expectations underlying the prophecies was only intensified by the discovery of new peoples seemingly waiting to be converted—pagans, living in a spiritual darkness that Christians believed would readily yield to illumination by the faith, unlike the stubbornness of Jews and Muslims. Many of the conquistadors who fanned out across the Caribbean and then the Mesoamerican mainland would try to persuade New World peoples to renounce their gods in favor of Mary and her son. The Spanish Crown drew men of arms into this work of Christianization, for beginning early in the second decade of the sixteenth century, all were officially required to preface military action against indigenous peoples by reading aloud to them a text known as the "Requirement." Composed in 1512, it provided what the Crown believed was the legal sanction for conquest and thus for empire.[70]

The Requirement set forth a vision of the world shot through with imperial desire and evangelical fervor, demanding, in the monarch's name, that the indigenous acquiesce or suffer the consequences. The people to whom it was read were to recognize "the church as the lord and superior of the universe" and to acknowledge the pope's authority to "judge and govern all peoples, Christians, and Moors, and Jews, and gentiles, and of whatever other sect or belief they might be."[71] They were also to accept the monarchs of Spain as "the lords and superiors and kings" of the lands where they themselves lived, since the pope had given this territory to the Spanish Crown. Finally, they were to allow "religious fathers" to come and preach Christianity to them.

"If you will not do this," the conquistador was to admonish the indigenous, "I assure you that with God's help I will enter powerfully against you and I will make war against you everywhere and in every way that I can and I will subject you to the yoke and obedience of the Church and Our Highnesses."[72] In most cases, the recitation of the Requirement thus served as a declaration of war. How could native men and women possibly accept conditions announced in a language most of them could not comprehend? They could, however, understand the threatening stance of the Spanish, impatiently waiting for the ritual reading of the document to end, armed and ready for battle.[73]

Countless conquistadors muttered, hurried through, or shouted out the Requirement's ponderous legalese to indigenous men and women who were sometimes within earshot but just as often not, and who in most cases would not have understood the Spanish words anyway. This strange scene repeated itself on white sand Caribbean beaches, in the dense jungles of Central America, on the highlands of the Mexican plateau, and everywhere else the Spanish set foot in the Americas before 1573. Uncomfortably aware of how ludicrous the reading of the Requirement was, some conquistadors told sad jokes and bitter stories about the dubious situations it put them in, and one even consulted the document's author, the royal legist Juan López Palacios Rubios, about whether Christians could pronounce its words without fearing for their conscience.[74] Open criticism led to changes in the text by 1573.[75] But the new version expressed just as strongly how inextricably entangled conversion and conquest officially were in Spain's imperial project.

Anyone who entered the audience hall-cum-chapel of Seville's Casa de Contratación and took a good look at Alejo Fernández's painting of the Virgin would realize that the peoples of the New World were to be subjugated to both Spanish rule and Christian truth. Accompanying the Europeans who seek shelter under Mary's generous mantle are dark-skinned figures representing the natives of New Spain and Peru. Rather than being dressed in clothing signaling their various ethnicities, as was usual in Spanish art of the time, they sport the plain white cloths typically worn by adults about to be baptized.[76] Their faces as homogenous as their garb (unlike the crowd of Europeans whom Alejo paints as recognizable individuals), the indigenous melt into one indistinguishable mass of grateful converts. Their conversion, this portrait of Spain's imperial ideology implies, takes place under the Virgin's loving gaze.

In the conquistadors' own accounts of their evangelical efforts in the New World, Mary would watch over the Christianization of the indigenous. If her role in New World warfare owed much to Old World precedents, the part that the narratives of conquest assigned to her as mother of conversion was equally indebted to medieval traditions. But because in the New World, military and spiritual conquest went hand in hand from the beginning, some quite different patterns emerged. This convergence of conquest and conversion would shape not only the portrait of the Virgin drawn by the conquistadors, but also the legends commemorating her arrival in New Spain. These stories, which began to figure in the religious and civic traditions of many towns and cities in the late sixteenth century, had much in common with the tales about Mary nurtured by Old World urban communities such as Seville, yet they would bear the imprint of the New World. The coincidence between conquest and conversion would even affect how some of the native peoples of New Spain themselves understood the Virgin.

Much of the material in the following chapters suggests that those who have proposed that the sixteenth century tolled the death knell for the medieval Mary have foretold her demise too quickly.[77] True, from the confessional tumult of the Reformation and other radical changes of the sixteenth century, the early modern Virgin emerged as a figure in many ways quite different from her medieval sister. Late sixteenth-century Catholic preachers imbued with the ideals of the Counter-Reformation articulated at the Council of Trent increasingly instructed their audiences to see Jesus' mother as a passive figure, a model of feminine obedience to God, rather than the powerful wonder-worker of medieval tradition.[78] The brushes of some of Europe's greatest Baroque painters helped to strip away the power Mary had commanded in the Middle Ages. Seville's own Bartolomé Murillo rendered her as a meek young woman or a sorrowing mother helpless with grief over her son's death.[79] But the medieval Mary would linger in many corners of the new worlds of the early modern Spanish Empire, her active powers perhaps tempered by the changing religious climate, but certainly not effaced. Like the Spaniards who colonized the lands across the Atlantic, Mary took the medieval past with her into the New World. Otherwise, she would not have gained the title in sixteenth-century New Spain of La Conquistadora, the name that would cause such bitter controversy in New Mexico five hundred years after Columbus first made landfall on a Caribbean island.

Marian Conquistadors and
Lay Evangelists

The conquistador Alonso de Hojeda was Mary's man. Always eager to be "the first to draw blood wherever there was war," he was "very devoted to Our Lady and his motto was 'devotee of the Virgin Mary,'" wrote the Dominican friar Bartolomé de las Casas in the sixteenth century. Arriving in the New World in 1493, Hojeda voyaged widely in the Caribbean and Central America, often wielding his weapons against indigenous peoples as he went. Against all odds, his career culminated in a peaceful death, a good end that Las Casas believed he owed to Mary. Hojeda died in a Spanish settlement on the Caribbean island of Hispaniola, very poor and miserable, said Las Casas, but "in his bed, which was no small miracle, it seems because of the devotion he had for Our Lady."[1]

Mary had many devotees among the Spanish adventurers who crossed the Atlantic in the early years of the sixteenth century, men who prayed to her not just before setting out from home, but also after reaching their destination. Their prayers joined the ever larger chorus of voices invoking her in the land from which they came; in sixteenth-century Spain, Mary was increasingly edging local saints from Christians' affections.[2] Vasco Núñez de Balboa and Hernán Cortés were but two of the other conquistadors singled out by sixteenth-century chroniclers for their love of her.[3] Bernal Díaz del Castillo, a soldier who fought alongside Cortés in Mexico, even wrote that the man who would make offerings of New World feathers and gold at Guadalupe in 1528 "held the Virgin Mary Our Lady as his great advocate, she whom all of us faithful Christians should have as our intercessor and advocate."[4]

In his lengthy but lively book composed when he was in his seventies or eighties, the *Historia verdadera de la conquista de la Nueva España*, Díaz revealed his conviction that he himself had benefited from Mary's favor during his New World adventures. Surveying the landscape of his fallen companions at arms, he listed the names of the hundreds who had died during the conquest of New Spain and its aftermath. Contemplating this gloomy panorama, Díaz offered heartfelt thanks to Christ and "Our Lady the Virgin Saint Mary, his blessed mother, who saved me from being sacrificed" at the hands of the Indians.[5]

In his thanksgiving to the Madonna, Díaz flirted with the language of Marian miracle, a vocabulary that other conquistador authors openly embraced. Gonzalo Fernández de Oviedo y Valdés, a conquistador of impressive literary talent who lived for years in the Caribbean, celebrated the many times that Mary had cast her wondrous cloak of protection over the Spanish colonizers. In the section of his *Historia general y natural de las Indias* published in 1535, Oviedo gave numerous examples of her miraculous aid to the colonists and lauded "the pious mother of the Savior, the glorious Virgin without blemish, whose devotees are accustomed to receive such renowned help in their straits and necessities on land and sea."[6]

Stories showing Mary's renowned ability to tame the ocean's wrath particularly interested Oviedo, who had personal experience with nautical danger. In Seville and on Hispaniola, home to Spain's earliest New World colony, he interviewed the survivors of Caribbean shipwrecks and storms to discover what prayers had helped them escape alive. Their answers confirmed the truth of a somber proverb that he quoted—"If you want to learn to pray, learn to sail"—and proved that the Virgin's powers as the "star of the sea" extended over New World waters.[7] Oviedo collected seven stories of how Mary had saved Spanish men and women who had appealed to her when caught by the Caribbean's waves.[8] These people, he learned, had most often addressed their desperate pleas to either Our Lady of Guadalupe or Seville's Santa María de la Antigua, two Virgins with whom the many colonists from Andalusia and Extremadura would have been very familiar.

Some rather odd ex-voto offerings from the New World were even ferried across the Atlantic to arrive at the feet of these Madonnas. When Cortés showed up at Guadalupe in 1528 with his gold scorpion and Nahua featherwork, he would have seen a large rock among the shrine's more obviously precious treasures. According to Oviedo, this stone, doubtless an impressive chunk of Caribbean coral, had lodged itself in the hull of a ship that struck a reef in the Virgin Islands in 1523. The vessel had remained afloat due to a combination of the crew's ingenuity and their prayers to Mary.[9]

The ship traveling alongside this one ran aground in the shallows and sank. Its crew and passengers were saved, but the entire cargo was lost, with one exception: a "large image of Our Lady de la Antigua" which, Oviedo explained, was "a replica of the image…in the cathedral of Seville." Salvaged from the sea, this painting was later taken to Hispaniola and hung as a Marian ex-voto of sorts in the first cathedral ever to rise in the Americas, Santo Domingo's main church, whose sober façade carved from coral was itself a reminder of the Caribbean's relentless presence.[10] Enshrined over an altar next to the sacristy, this painting of the Madonna whose name was borne by so many ships sailing the Indies would serve as a comforting reminder of Mary's dominion over the waves and of her patronage of the conquest and colonization of the Americas.

Men like Hojeda, Cortés, and Díaz would call on Mary for help in their physical and spiritual battles with New World peoples. Yet the conquistadors would also present her to the indigenous as a powerful woman who granted loving protection to all willing to accept her dominion. The Spaniards, then, would both wield the Madonna against the natives of the New World and offer her to them. Exploring how this double-edged Marian strategy guided the conquistadors' actions during the early years of the conquest of the Caribbean and mainland Mesoamerica is not always easy, for these men's accounts of their exploits are full of self-aggrandizement and exaggeration.[11] Only by carefully comparing their narratives is it possible to recover some sense of how they actually invoked Mary during their early encounters with New World peoples—a challenging but important task. Over the centuries, many layers of wishful thinking have been built on the foundation of the conquistador era, and many tales that belong to the realm of legend have been taken as truths. In colonial Mexico, stories about Mary's role in the conquest figured prominently in the politics of identity, Spanish and indigenous. These tales in turn have become the cornerstone for modern stories summoning the colonial past as justification for the present. Hence it is well worth trying to reconstruct the nature of the encounters between Mary's conquistadors and the New World peoples whom they wished to dominate materially and spiritually.

Caribbean Conquests and Conversions

When Martín Fernández de Enciso reached Cuba's Cabo de Cruz, he must have been relieved by the warm welcome that he received in Mary's name from the Taino Indians who lived along this peninsula's shores, fishing and cultivating cassava and tobacco. The ship carrying this Sevillean-born conquistador dropped anchor off Cabo de Cruz's beaches in 1511 after having sailed from the coast of what the Spanish often called Tierra Firme, more or less modern-day Central America. In Tierra Firme, Enciso had clashed with natives whom he saw as the Madonna's enemies, but at Cabo de Cruz, he would be greeted by Indians who, he believed, were her friends. Both sides of his experience illuminate Mary's place in the earliest years of Spanish presence in the Caribbean.

A year or so before meeting Mary's Taino devotees on Cuba, Enciso had set off for Tierra Firme from Hispaniola, where most Spaniards then living in the New World resided. On Hispaniola the Spaniards had panned the island's streams in the hopes of finding gold, but soon realized that they could gain more by taking advantage of the tropical climate and cultivating sugar. The brutal work in the cane fields was forced on the indigenous, as was most of the heavy labor in the colony—at least until the native men and women began to die in such numbers from exhaustion and disease that the Spaniards had to replace them with enslaved Africans. By the second decade of the sixteenth century, a handful of settlers had made their way to Jamaica and Puerto Rico, but the Spanish had yet to turn the Caribbean into their preserve. Restless and ambitious men like Enciso nurtured hopes of doing so—and believed Mary would help them overcome any natives who resisted.

In 1510, Enciso co-captained an expedition of exploration and conquest aimed at Tierra Firme, a region thought so promising that the conquistadors would also dub it Castilla del Oro in honor of the precious metal they lusted after. He and his fellows would soon have to rely on Mary's support in staking their claim to this land. In dense jungles, Enciso's company encountered Caribs— Indians dressed in little more than the red dye with which they ornamented their bodies, and armed with poisoned arrows. Catching sight of these dreaded weapons in their opponents' quivers before one skirmish, the conquistadors fell to their knees, lifted their hands in desperate prayer to Mary and beseeched her to "give them victory," as one of their contemporaries wrote.[12] They placed their hope in Santa María de la Antigua, the elegant Madonna beloved in the Andalusian city from which Enciso came. If she would help them prevail over the Caribs, Enciso and his men promised, they would name the first church and town they founded in Castilla del Oro for her and send offerings of New World gold and silver to her chapel in Seville.[13] The conquistador kept this vow after surviving the confrontation with the Caribs, though the "town" he dubbed Santa María de la Antigua del Darién was no more than a scrappy village inhabited by a handful of Spaniards. An uncertain European presence in a sea of natives, it was one of the earliest Spanish settlements on the American mainland and the first of many New World towns that would bear Mary's name.[14]

When Enciso moored off Cuba's Cabo de Cruz en route back to Spain, disgraced and angry after a quarrel over command, he was greeted by Mary's allies, indigenous men and women who seemed so naturally inclined to Christianity that they already cherished her, or so he would claim. These Tainos, wrote the conquistador, lovingly venerated an image of the Madonna, clamored for baptism, and pressed the newly arrived Spaniards to recite the Ave Maria. During the three days that Enciso spent on Cabo de Cruz, he repeated this Marian prayer "many times" at the Tainos' insistence.[15]

In his manual of navigation and universal geography beautifully published at Seville in 1519, the *Suma de geographia*, Enciso explained how these indigenous men and women had become so enamored of the Ave Maria and its namesake. According to the conquistador, Cabo de Cruz's inhabitants had learned their devotion to Mary over a year before his own arrival on the peninsula, and thus sometime before the Spanish definitively established themselves on Cuba. Enciso described the Tainos' enthusiastic love for her as the result of the evangelical activity of a man not so dissimilar from himself—a layman seeking his fortune in the Indies.[16]

Early modern writers evidently thought the striking tale of Marian evangelism related by Enciso worth lingering over. This story, dating from the primordial decades of the Spanish colonization of the Americas, quickly became part of the lore surrounding the conquest of the New World. In the sixteenth and early seventeenth centuries, men who knew the Caribbean and Mexico firsthand would repeat this Marian tale as they chronicled how the Spanish had established themselves on the western side of the Atlantic. They would prune the narrative to fit their own agendas and to match their own perceptions of the right relationship between their compatriots and the natives of the Americas. Yet however they tailored their material, the Madonna almost always remained the medium for this relationship.

This story suggests that the adaptation of Old World Marian practices and mentalities to the New World would create patterns more complex than Enciso's invocation of the Virgin in his skirmish with the Caribs of Tierra Firme would lead one to suspect. In appealing to her to help him in combat, Enciso, along with his companions, echoed the prayers and battle calls uttered by generations of medieval Spanish knights—and by his contemporaries fighting Muslims in the Mediterranean. At almost exactly the same time that the conquistadors were dodging poisoned arrows in Tierra Firme's jungles, on the other side of the Atlantic, Count Pedro Navarro was piously making his way to the shrine of Guadalupe to petition the Virgin for aid in his North African campaigns. If Enciso's prayer to Mary would not have been out of place in an Old World clash with Muslims, the same cannot be said for the story he tells of how Cabo de Cruz's inhabitants came to their love of her. In this tale, a layman took on a missionary role quite foreign to the Christian men fighting against Muslims and opened a new field on which Mary could exercise her military talents.

Enciso claimed to have heard the story from the Tainos themselves during his stay at Cabo de Cruz, although it was perhaps a sailors' yarn. By the time the conquistador wrote it down, it was a rather fanciful narrative. Enciso presented it as the truth, however, as did a more famous author who published the story three years before the conquistador's *Suma de geographia* went to press: Peter Martyr d'Anghiera, the Italian-born humanist, priest, member of the Council of the Indies, and courtier who served Isabel and Ferdinand. His epistolary collection describing the Spanish exploration and conquest of the New World was widely read all across Europe.[17]

Peter Martyr never crossed the Atlantic, but he interviewed many men who had, including Enciso. In 1512, the conquistador came to the royal court to lodge a complaint against the man who had ousted him from Santa María de la Antigua del Darién, Vasco Núñez de Balboa. Among the influential people in Spain whom Enciso tried to win over to his cause was Peter Martyr. As the conquistador presented his versions of events to the Italian, he described his encounter with the Mary-loving Tainos of Cabo de Cruz. Impressed by the story, Peter Martyr incorporated it into his oeuvre about the New World. The courtier's rendering of this Marian tale became part of the more or less official chronicle of the Spanish Caribbean conquests when it appeared in the pages of his *De orbe novo* edicated to Pope Leo X and printed in 1516.[18] More artful than the account Enciso published three years later, the story that Peter Martyr recounted was nonetheless substantially the same as the conquistador's version.[19]

The narrative's Marian hero was an ailing Spanish sailor deposited on the beach by a ship anchored off Cabo de Cruz. Neither Enciso nor Peter Martyr recorded his name. Both described him as an ordinary man (Peter Martyr says he was illiterate), but a good one who was deeply devoted to Mary. Among the possessions he took ashore at Cabo de Cruz was an image of her. Though in the *Suma de geographia,* Enciso provided no details about its appearance, perhaps during his visit to court in 1512 he described it to Peter Martyr as a sewn piece of parchment worn on the chest, for that is how the Italian courtier characterized it in the *De orbe novo.* The sailor's Madonna could then have belonged to a scapular, that pious yoke of two pieces of cloth attached by strings and bearing representations of Mary and Jesus. The many Christians who donned this devotional garb believed that the portraits of the Madonna and her son offered some shelter from life's misfortunes.[20] The sailor, in any case, evidently considered his likeness of Mary a talisman that could protect him in this new and unpredictable world.

This man stayed at Cabo de Cruz for at least a year while convalescing from his illness, wrote Enciso. There he was taken in by the same group of Tainos whom the conquistador would encounter later, a community whose cacique (leader) called himself "Comendador," a Spanish title that Peter Martyr says the man had taken in imitation of a governor of Hispaniola.[21] Comendador's authority probably extended over the *caçicazago* of Macaca, a swath of southwestern Cuba closely hugging the Caribbean coastline.[22] As his name indicates, this cacique evidently had had some earlier contact with the Spanish. By the time the sailor arrived on Cabo de Cruz, Comendador had been baptized (by "Christians passing through," specifies Peter Martyr). But the other Tainos on the peninsula apparently had not been. According to Enciso, the sailor did his best to remedy this situation by undertaking an ambitious Christianizing project focused on his prized image of the Madonna.

First, the sailor created a church of sorts for Mary; Comendador allowed him to enshrine the image in a "small house" prominently situated in the Tainos' town. The Madonna's new home was next to the cacique's own, wrote Enciso. It probably faced out onto the central plaza around which the community's activities were oriented and would have been made with the thatch and wood construction characteristic of Taino architecture. Exactly how small it was is hard to know, but perhaps its rustling palm leaf roof covered a good-sized space, for the typical Taino house could hold several interrelated families.[23]

Next, the sailor instructed his indigenous hosts how to venerate the woman depicted in the image. Teaching the Ave Maria to Comendador and some other members of the community, he devised a simple form of Marian services: each afternoon, the cacique, urged on by the sailor, would lead his people to the building that Peter Martyr insisted on calling a "church." There, dressed in the brief loincloths and short skirts that so scandalized the Spanish, they would kneel before the image and listen while the sailor recited the Ave Maria. Then the Tainos would raise their voices in prayer: "Lady Saint Mary, save us and help us!" according to Enciso, and "Ave Maria, Ave Maria!" according to Peter Martyr.

This story is about conversion in the literal sense of the word, for it depicts the Tainos turning toward Christianity even in the absence of baptism. More precisely, it is about conversion to faith in the Madonna's image, an object serving as both the instrument and the focus of the sailor's evangelical efforts. This enterprise was not an entirely peaceful one, as it required the Virgin to deploy just those military skills in which Enciso had such confidence. In the rest of this tale of Marian evangelism, she wages war to defeat the earthly and supernatural forces seeking to reverse her spiritual conquest of Comendador's people.

According to Enciso, Mary had to join battle because the other Taino caciques in the area, angered that Comendador's community had abandoned the *zemis* for her, attacked her new devotees. As the conquistador knew, *zemis* were the potent sacred objects cherished by the Tainos (Figure 7.1). The Spanish would eventually describe *zemis* as demonic idols, although the earliest European observers realized that this label did not really fit objects taking such a variety of forms, only some of them figurative: stones, twisted roots, pieces of wood, carved coral, woven cotton figurines, or sculpted containers holding the bones of ancestors. Whatever their shape, *zemis* were worshipped for their great powers in the realms of politics, healing, weather—and war.[24]

As the Spaniards observed as early as 1498, Tainos consulted their "idols" to discover whether victory or defeat lay ahead in battle.[25] *Zemis* could even go to war themselves. Although these objects were usually too large to be easily carried, Tainos readying themselves for battle would decorate their foreheads with smaller versions of the *zemis*: carved amulets dangling from a cord or headpiece.[26] Thus arrayed, warriors must have been fearsome sights. The *idolillos*, as the Spanish called the amulets, would have stood out prominently against the flattened foreheads so admired as a sign of beauty by the Tainos that they bound infants' skulls into the desired shape.[27]

Figure 7.1 Zemi from Cuba. Museo de America, Madrid, Spain. Gianni Dagli Orti. The Art Archive at Art Resource, NY.

Perhaps those Tainos on Cabo de Cruz who objected to Comendador's affection for Mary ornamented themselves with such amulets before raising their spears and war clubs against him, if indeed the intra-Taino skirmishes over the Madonna described by Enciso and Peter Martyr actually took place. In any case, both the conquistador and the courtier portrayed the conflicts between Comendador and his enemies as a war between the Virgin and the *zemis*, hostilities at first prosecuted by indigenous proxies but eventually by Mary and her native counterparts in spectacular scenes of hand-to-hand combat.

Peter Martyr turned the clashes between Comendador's people and their adversaries into a veritable Marian crusade by describing how the cacique's followers, like generations of Castilian knights before them, loudly invoked the Madonna on the battlefield. The Italian even asserted that the image of the Virgin venerated by these Tainos was itself a warrior's talisman. The nameless sailor, Peter Martyr wrote, had introduced his Madonna to Comendador by telling the cacique that she had always "brought him victory" in battle. As for Enciso, he believed that "it was not Comendador or his followers who made war but instead a very beautiful woman dressed all in white who came to their aid with a stick, and who killed them all with blows and made them flee"—this, wrote the conquistador, was how the defeated Tainos explained their losses against Mary's indigenous champions.

Not only did the Madonna kill the *zemi*-worshipping Tainos who opposed her newly acquired indigenous devotees, but according to Enciso and Peter Martyr, she also defeated the *zemis* themselves. Both authors described how, humiliated and frustrated by Comendador's string of Marian victories, this cacique's adversaries persuaded him to pit Mary directly against their *zemis*. Each side chose a representative, a man whom the other side then tied up. These bound men were left overnight in a field with guards posted to keep watch. The Tainos on both sides agreed that if the *zemis* were more powerful than Mary, these beings would arrive during the night and free their man, whereas if she commanded superior force, she would be able to loosen hers first.

Midnight came. A *zemi* appeared and approached its champion. As the *zemi* began to unfasten the man, the Virgin arrived, dressed in her habitual heavenly white and armed with the same stick she had wielded to slaughter Tainos in battle. At the sight of her, the *zemi* fled. With her stick, Mary gently touched her man and released his restraints. Miraculously, his bonds were added to those already fettering the other man. The next morning, the guards reported the events to a set of incredulous caciques. The *zemis*' devotees insisted on repeating the test. Faced with the same outcome a second time, and then a third, they finally, in Enciso's words, admitted that Mary was indeed a "good cacique." They stopped harassing Comendador and his people and gave their own followers the choice between worshipping *zemis* or venerating her.

Despite Enciso's assertions that he learned of Mary's contest with the *zemis* and their devotees from his Taino hosts, it is hard to imagine that the tale owed much to the indigenous men and women living on Cabo de Cruz. Although Tainos believed that the cosmos was structured by opposing forces of order and disorder, the story's skirmishes read as enactments of the Christian European conception of the age-old conflict between good and evil.[28] In particular, Mary's midnight face-off with the *zemi* recalls the battles against the demons of Islam and Judaism that she often waged in miracle stories from the Iberian Peninsula.

Whatever Enciso had heard from the Tainos, he seems to have it recast according to the script of Mary's Old World conversion miracles, but with a

New World twist. In the wonders celebrated at Castilian shrines like Guadalupe, Mary herself was the evangelist, appearing to non-Christians and guiding them, whether gently or imperiously, to the path of truth. On Cabo de Cruz, a man who probably would have identified himself as a conquistador shared top billing with her. Serving as Mary's impresario, he becomes as much the agent of Christianization as she is.

The story Enciso told was unusual in granting so much place to Mary's missionizing miracles. Although the Madonna would be central to conquistadors' efforts to sow Christianity in the New World, they rarely told tales of how she exercised on Indians the wondrous talents of conversion that she had honed on Old World Jews and Muslims. Instead, conquistadors usually celebrated themselves as evangelical heroes who did not require her dramatic celestial back-up. Boasting words penned by Bernal Díaz in his old age underscored the pride some of these men took in themselves as evangelists. "With [Christ's] holy help, we, the true conquistadors, discovered and conquered this land and from the very beginning we took away [the Indians'] idols and we taught them to understand the holy faith, and so to us—after God and before anyone else, even religious men—is due the prize and reward for all this," wrote Díaz in his *Historia verdadera*. He willingly admitted that "good religious men," first Franciscans and then Dominicans, had accomplished missionary work that had born "much fruit." But these friars, he pointed out, only arrived in New Spain after "we true conquistadors...held all those lands in peace" and had already "instilled good and orderly habits of life [in the indigenous] and had taught them the holy faith." The men in robes had built on the spiritual foundation laid by the conquistadors, adventurers like Díaz who had braved "wars and battles and mortal danger."[29]

Díaz was perhaps exaggerating his more youthful accomplishments, embellishing the past here, as he did elsewhere, in service of his larger project. He wrote his history not just in order to relive his glory days, but also to correct an injustice. Previous chroniclers—most notably Francisco López de Gómara, a priest who had never been to the New World—had unduly lionized Cortés and unfairly ignored the men who had fought alongside him, or so Díaz thought. Claiming for himself and his former comrades a large share of the credit for the conversion of New Spain was just one of the strategies he used to gild the conquistadors as a company and justify their conquests.[30]

Guilty of hyperbole as Díaz could be, his proud words contain a certain truth. Some conquistadors did far more than merely mouth the formulaic phrases of the Requirement, actually taking it upon themselves to try to Christianize the peoples and places they encountered. Although noted long ago by historians, these lay evangelical efforts upon which Díaz congratulated himself and his companions have attracted much less attention than the richer set of sources and questions produced by the decades, even centuries, of missionary activity by the religious orders.[31] Yet there is much to be gained by closely examining the methods and self-image of the lay evangelists, since it was from men such as Díaz and the anonymous sailor that many New World peoples first heard of something called Christianity.

According to many stories told by the conquistadors, they presented their religion to indigenous men and women as exactly the Mary-centered faith of Enciso's story, a version of Christianity embodied by images of her. Perhaps they were imitating the preachers they had seen back in Spain, who relied heavily on visual props to convey spiritual messages.[32] In any case, with these Marian likenesses, conquistadors would often try to dislodge indigenous gods and rituals, or at least to leave a Christian mark on the New World's religious landscape, just as the anonymous sailor supposedly had at Cuba's Cabo de Cruz. On the same island, an image of Mary was key to a more documented case of conquistador evangelism involving Enciso's partner in the Tierra Firme venture, Alonso de Hojeda, the man whose Marian devotion had won Bartolomé de Las Casas's praise. Las Casas himself, who spent much time on Cuba, related this spiritually inspiring if harrowing story of lay Marian evangelism and conquistador experience in the island's deep forests, some time before its violent "pacification" by his compatriots.

Hojeda, wrote Las Casas, had braved the dangers of the New World protected by the likeness of the saint he so loved. This conquistador's image of Mary was much more elaborate than the one Enciso saw on Cabo de Cruz. Las Casas described it as a "marvelously" executed, if small, Flemish painting. With the rich colors, fine brushwork, and naturalism characteristic of northern European art, this portrait of the Virgin aroused Las Casas's admiration. He even admitted that he coveted it. But by the time the Dominican laid eyes on this Madonna, she must have been somewhat the worse for the wear. Hojeda had hauled the painting through jungle and swamp in his food bag, the logical place for a man often stalked by hunger to guard his most precious possessions.[33]

Las Casas did not record whether Hojeda prayed before this image in hopes of Mary's military aid when faced with the kind of threats that drove Enciso to invoke the Virgin de la Antigua in Tierra Firme's jungles; Hojeda had confronted the Caribs and their poison arrows some months before his partner would. In any case, when he fled Tierra Firme in 1510, exhausted and demoralized after months of waiting in vain to be resupplied by Enciso, he put his faith in the woman represented by his painting.

Hojeda and his men certainly needed a powerful celestial patron, for the ship carrying them toward Hispaniola's Spanish settlements foundered off the southern coast of Cuba. As the survivors wandered for over a month through the island's mangrove swamps, Hojeda took refuge in the little image of Mary tucked in his ever-thinning food bag. Propping the painting against a tree, he would kneel in prayer and exhort his companions to join him in beseeching the Virgin for rescue. He repeated this ritual as often as he could during their ordeal, each time vowing that if only she would guide his dwindling company to safety, he would leave the image in the first village he found. Ragged and famished, the men finally stumbled into a Taino town called Cueíba. Half of the party had perished among the mangroves. The sight of the village's houses gathered around the central plaza typical of Taino communities filled Hojeda with relief—and a rush of gratitude toward Mary. He entrusted his painting to Cueíba's cacique and instructed the Taino leader to create a suitable home for it—a small chapel with an altar, according to Las Casas.[34]

Enshrined in its own palm-roofed hut, the painting became Hojeda's votive offering to his saintly savior. He must also have hoped that after he and his men had departed, the Flemish Madonna would serve as a tangible trace of their passage, silently claiming this corner of Cuba for Christianity. His gift of the painting to Cueíba would even, Hojeda apparently believed, help shepherd the village's residents into the Christian fold. True, he and his men made no attempt to baptize anyone. They were hardly in a position to do so, given their abject condition. By this point in their odyssey, they might also have been lacking a priest. None of this stopped Hojeda from using the means at hand in order to give his hosts "some news of matters pertaining to God," to quote Las Casas. That means was the painting of Mary, according to Las Casas's succinct description of an impromptu sermon that Hojeda delivered to the villagers.

"This image signified the mother of God, God and Lord of the world who was in the sky. Her name was Saint Mary, the great intercessor for human beings," Hojeda told the Cueíbans. Perhaps he had picked up a smattering of Taino during his years in the Caribbean and communicated this Marian vision of Christianity to the villagers in their own language. Or maybe an interpreter—a Taino captured by the Spanish as a child, say—stood by Hojeda's side and translated as the conquistador preached about the woman in the painting. Perhaps Hojeda even pointed at the image of Mary while he spoke. However the conquistador overcame the linguistic barrier, according to Las Casas he offered the Tainos a version of Christianity largely reduced to one figure: Mary.

Las Casas may have exaggerated the cordiality of the welcome that the villagers gave this needy band of Spaniards. But there is no reason to doubt the essential truth of his account. Not only did Las Casas know some of Hojeda's men personally, but he passed through Cueíba shortly after the conquistador's stay and could have questioned the villagers about the image of Mary he saw in the humble "church." Perhaps he already had heard the Flemish Madonna's story from Hojeda's men. In any case, Las Casas exclaimed over the painting's beauty and praised the villagers' reverence for the woman it represented. He then brought to fruition the seed of Christianity that Hojeda had planted; he baptized the Cueíbans and left them to practice their Marian cult.[35]

The similarities between this episode of lay Marian evangelism on Cuba and the one described by Enciso make it tempting to identify Hojeda as the anonymous protagonist of the Cabo de Cruz tale. Yet by the time Enciso composed the *Suma de geographia*, he surely would have known if his partner in the Tierra Firme expedition and the nameless sailor who had visited Cabo de Cruz were one and the same. And Las Casas, who would relate his own version of the Cabo de Cruz story, clearly situated the two instances of Marian missionizing in different villages.[36] In two Taino villages on Cuba, then, lay evangelists bearing images of the Virgin preceded Christian priests and proposed to native peoples a Christianity largely consisting of God's mother.

From a perspective of some five hundred years later, these conquistadors' introduction of Mary into Taino communities can be seen as one more step in the destruction of the native cultures of the Caribbean. The triumphal tone of the tale told by Enciso and Peter Martyr about the Virgin routing *zemis* and slaughtering Tainos who did not believe in her eloquently evokes the violent stance that sixteenth-century Europeans could adopt when confronted with the religious cosmos of New World peoples. Yet it is also somewhat misleading. Neither the nameless sailor nor Hojeda undertook their Marian evangelism from positions of strength. Both men were dependent to a large extent on their Taino hosts' kindness and could not have forced Christianity on these Indian communities. Despite what must have been considerable preoccupation with their own worrisome situations, both Hojeda and the sailor took care to offer Christianity in the form of their own beloved Marian talismans to the villagers who gave them shelter. These Madonnas were not just instruments of lay evangelization and signs of Spanish presence. They were also the prized possessions of conquistadors, men who surely hoped that these images of Mary would soon displace the *zemis* in the villagers' affections but who intended them too as precious gifts to people who had provided help when it was so needed.

The conquistadors who ventured onto the Mesoamerican mainland just a few years later would often give images of the Virgin into the care of the peoples they encountered, usually first offering the same sort of Mary-focused, rudimentary explanations of Christianity as Hojeda and the anonymous sailor had. But neither the situations nor the results were exactly the same. When the Spaniards reached the Maya lands of the Yucatan Peninsula and then the Nahua areas further north, they were stepping into a new world for which the Taino culture of the Caribbean had not prepared them—a universe of towns and cities whose monumental architecture and complex social organization rivaled what they knew from home and whose wealth was guarded by disciplined, organized armies and elaborate political hierarchies, all paying homage to a pantheon of divinities housed in imposing buildings. It would prove far more difficult for the Spaniards to challenge Mesoamericans and their gods than it had been to prevail over Tainos and *zemis*. As the conquistadors sought to succeed in this very different human landscape, they would not hesitate to wage war, but they would just as often seek peace and even advantageous alliances. Mary would second them in all these enterprises.

The Marian Politics of War and Peace in Maya Lands

The thrill of excitement on board the first Spanish ships to sight a Maya town across the waves was palpable.[37] The rectangular masonry shrines standing sentinel along the coast and the outlines of the tall buildings clustered further inland promised something quite different from the Taino settlements, and must have stimulated expectant desire among the men who lined the decks and gazed at the shore during that expedition of 1517.[38] Bernal Díaz, who claimed to have been among this company but was probably borrowing memories from a fellow conquistador, wrote: "from the ships we saw a large town...and seeing that it was well populated and that we had not seen such a large town either on the island of Cuba or on Hispaniola, we named it 'Great Cairo.'"[39] Having dubbed the first Maya community they saw after a Muslim city, the conquistadors then named Yucatan for the saint who had so often helped Spaniards claim Islam's territory for Christianity: Mary. Baptizing it "Saint Mary of Remedies," they also honored the Madonna who was the patron of many Spanish ships sailing the Indies, including one of the earliest ever to set anchor off Mayan lands.[40]

In "Great Cairo" and other Mesoamerican towns, conquistadors would walk among buildings they would deem also worthy of appropriation in Mary's name. The sophistication of Maya architecture impressed the Spaniards, who, according to one of Cortés's contemporaries, were "astonished to see stone buildings, which up to this point they had not seen [in the New World]."[41] In Yucatan, as later in the Nahua lands of central Mexico, the conquistadors were particularly struck by the temples and shrines guarding sacred images of the indigenous gods. These buildings aroused in the Spaniards an uneasy mélange of admiration, fascination, and disgust—and provoked their passions as lay evangelists. They would often try to transform Mesoamerican sacred architecture into the stage for much more aggressive Marian evangelical theatrics than those enacted in Taino villages by men like Hojeda.

The conquistadors had seen nothing like these temples in the West Indies. Tainos mostly kept *zemis* in their homes, though in some towns the cacique's *zemis* occupied their own houses on the main plaza. A stranger might not have been able to tell the difference between the *zemi* houses and the surrounding structures, for all shared the same simple lines.[42] But as the Spanish immediately realized, the urban centers of both Mayan and Nahua lands were dominated by buildings whose style and materials announced their functions as places of sacrifice and as home to images that Christian eyes naturally interpreted as "idols." Some of these temples and shrines were tall "towers," as the Spanish described them, flanked with dizzyingly narrow stone treads leading to the shrine rooms perched at the top, while others were only a man's height (Figure 7.2). Their expertly crafted masonry walls were alive inside and out with the play of vividly colored friezes and frescoes, a dance of human and animal figures confirming the Spaniards' suspicion that these must be places of idolatry.[43]

Figure 7.2 Mexica temple. Post-classical period. Acatitlan, Mexico. Gianni Dagli Orti. The Art Archive at Art Resource, NY.

When searching for a word to capture the significance of these buildings, the conquistadors drew not just from the lexicon of paganism ("temples") but also from the vocabulary of Islam: they often called these Mayan and Nahua structures "mosques."[44] There was no compelling visual resemblance between the pyramidal structures of Mesoamerica and the rectangular prayer halls of Muslims. Yet both were monumental forms of religious architecture produced by sophisticated societies that the Spanish wished to dominate. If a Maya town glimpsed from afar conjured up visions of Muslim Cairo, Mesoamerican places of cult also could be fit, however awkwardly, into that familiar vocabulary evoking both civilization and difference. This language told the conquistadors not just how to see but also what to do: to purify these buildings of alien forces and then claim them for their own god—and his mother.

The ghost of the triumphant ceremonies with which Christian kings and knights had so often baptized the mosques of conquered Muslim towns in Mary's name would haunt the more makeshift rites with which conquistadors tried to place a Christian stamp on some Maya and Nahua cult sites by installing in them an image of the Virgin often accompanied by her son's symbol, the cross. New patterns also materialized during Mary's enthronement in native shrines. If during the long centuries of the reconquest, priests and bishops had performed the ritual gestures that transformed mosques into the Madonna's churches, the conquistadors would describe themselves as the heroes who actively introduced Mary into Mesoamerican temples. These men thus made themselves into her frontline soldiers in a "war of images," the often violent contest between Christian holy images and their indigenous rivals, idols.[45]

The Madonna herself could take up arms in these battles against New World idolatry. Yet in Mesoamerica, the conquistadors would also draft Mary and her images into the service of a calculated politics of friendship. Even when the "war of images" coincided with military campaigns against Maya and Nahua armies, the conquistadors would describe their introduction of the Madonna into Mesoamerican temples as the foundation for bonds of fraternity between victors and vanquished, a notion that never would have occurred to a medieval knight or king attending the conversion of a mosque into Mary's church.

Mary's prominence in these politics of war and peace is plain to see in the Spanish accounts of the third conquistador party to venture into Maya lands, captained by Hernán Cortés. Almost immediately, the members of this expedition would disregard the official charge laid upon them by the governor of Cuba, Diego de Velázquez—to explore, but not to conquer or colonize. To justify their actions, these men would have recourse to the language of friendship, and the images of the Madonna that they carried with them would be key terms in this vocabulary.

Cortés's little fleet weighed anchor from Spanish Cuba in February 1519.[46] Perhaps as their captain watched the coastline slip out of sight, he nervously

fingered his Marian pendant—Díaz would later write that this "jewel" hanging from a small golden chain was Cortés's preferred neckwear. On one side it
bore a portrait of the Madonna and Child, while the other sported an image of
John the Baptist.[47] Whether this talisman adorned with the likenesses of two of
his favorite saints was a mute witness to the beginning of a journey that would
eventually lead to the city of Tenochtitlan, Cortés pressed an image of Mary
into service at the very first place he and his men made landfall: the island of
Cozumel, home to a community of Chontal Maya.

In the early sixteenth century, Cozumel was a thriving port of trade, busy with
the great sea-going canoes of the Maya merchants who plied the waters of the
Gulf of Mexico.[48] The island also welcomed a flow of Maya pilgrims from the
mainland, who came to worship the goddess Ix Chel—"she of the rainbow"—at
an imposing shrine looming tall on the coast.[49] Although Cozumel's inhabitants
were accustomed to the constant arrival of strangers, they nonetheless chose the
prudent course of hiding when Spanish boats approached their shores in the
spring of 1519. Eventually, apparently encouraged by the messages Cortés sent
assuring them of his friendly intentions, the Maya slowly emerged from their
refuges. Waiting to greet them were men who not only read them the Requirement, but also wanted to acquaint them with Mary and her son.

In a letter to Charles V, Cortés boasted that he had left Cozumel "peaceful"
and its caciques "very happy and joyful" with what he had told them both about
their status in the Spanish empire and about the man and woman at the center
of this realm's religion.[50] Here, as elsewhere in his report to his monarch, Cortés
carefully depicted his actions on the island as a complete and bloodless "pacification" of its residents rather than as the sort of conquest he was not authorized
to make.[51] His companions would later confirm the essence and sometimes even
the spirit of his account. Their descriptions underscore even more dramatically
Mary's significance to a pattern of lay evangelism that would be repeated elsewhere during the conquistadors' progress across Mexico.

For his sovereign, Cortés sketched an uplifting scene of natives gladly
renouncing their religious practices and accepting Mary and Christ when he
commanded them to do so. He described how, when he admonished the island's
caciques to "live no longer in their pagan sect," they begged him "to give them
a religion" to follow. So, wrote Cortés, he "instructed them as well as he could
in the Catholic faith and left them a wooden cross placed on a tall building and
an image of Our Lady the Virgin Mary." This conquistador thus compressed
Christianity into Marian image and cross, objects that he declared Cozumel's
caciques had "accepted . . . with very good will."[52]

Cortés deliberately enshrined these emblems of Mary and her son in a building that lay at the core of Cozumel's religious life. Details given by other conquistadors indicate that the *casa alta* of his letter was the main temple of Ix Chel,

the rainbow goddess who drew so many pilgrims to the island.[53] In this towering structure visible from land and sea, Ix Chel, according to one member of Cortés's company, "talked" to her devotees; the temple housed a "hollow idol... of fired clay" through which a priest ventriloquized the goddess.[54] This temple's evident importance made it the logical place to claim for Mary and her son—and a very public stage on which to introduce them to Cozumel's residents. Although Cortés described his audience as the island's caciques, men from his company would remember a much larger crowd watching as the Christian images were installed.[55] Díaz, for example, recalled that the broad plaza stretching in front of the temple was "full" of Maya men and women who had come to burn incense for their gods and listen to their own priests but instead became witnesses to rites featuring Mary and her son's sign.[56]

Cortés chose his religious champions wisely. In Christian art, Mary and the instrument of Jesus' death were traditionally twinned, representing the faith's central truths of Incarnation and Passion. Other conquistador eyewitness reports suggest that the image of Mary perhaps overshadowed the cross in ceremonial importance and as an embodiment of the religion that these lay evangelists proposed to share with Cozumel's residents. The very different origins and manufacture of these two objects probably indicated as much to the Maya. Díaz related how, at Cortés's orders, Spanish carpenters pieced together a cross from wood found on the island.[57] As the Maya would have realized, however, the Marian image arrived on Cozumel with Cortés's company. It might have been the product of a workshop in the Spanish Caribbean but more likely had been imported directly from conquistadors' homeland. In this statue of the Madonna, then, resided an obvious Spanishness less easily summoned by a cross crafted from native wood.[58]

Another detail highlights the special role of the Madonna's image in these conquistador theatrics of Christianization: its location in Ix Chel's temple. The conquistador reports disagree over whether the cross was placed inside the temple or on top of it as a sign of Christian triumph "visible from far away on the sea."[59] There was no such disagreement about the statue of Mary. The Spanish clearly enthroned it in the temple, probably on an altar that Cortés ordered Maya masons to construct specifically for this purpose.[60] This stone surface where the conquistadors reverently set their Madonna was, wrote Díaz, "very clean," a distinct and deliberate contrast to the Mayas' own bloodstained altars holding "idols." It was the statue of Mary that the Spaniards particularly intended to displace the "idols" kept in Ix Chel's temple.

As different in shape and style as this Madonna had to have been from her Mayan counterparts, the conquistadors doubtless realized that the image bore more resemblance to these "idols" than did the cross; Mayan religious statuary usually possessed the contours of living beings, human or animal.[61] The statue of Mary perhaps offered a further advantage over her son's sign. The Maya, like other Mesoamericans, had long used cruciforms as religious symbols, if more sparingly than Christians.[62] Inspiring some Spaniards to believe that an apostle had reached the New World centuries ago, the visual coincidence between the indigenous sign and the Christian one could be useful, but it also could also be confusing, as the Europeans tried to explain the meaning they gave to this abstract form. But by pointing at images of Mary, the conquistadors clearly showed the Maya the woman whom they should worship.

Years later, the Franciscan missionary known as Motolinía would capture the prominence of Marian images in Cortés's battle against New World idolatry. In a letter of 1555 addressed to Emperor Charles V, Motolinía lauded Cortés, whom he knew personally, for having worked to bring Christianity to New Spain before the arrival of the friars. "Everywhere Cortés went," wrote the friar, "he raised the cross.... Having destroyed the idols, he put in their place the image of Our Lady."[63] Here Motolinía was probably exaggerating, as was the Franciscans' habit when describing Cortés, a man whom they believed fulfilled a divinely ordained role in opening the New World to conversion.[64] This conquistador and his company certainly did not replace "idols" with Marian images "everywhere," nor did they even raise crosses in all the places through which they passed. Yet in emphasizing how Cortés substituted the Madonna in particular for indigenous sacred images, Motolinía seems to have hit on the truth.

Although Díaz did not mention exactly where in Ix Chel's temple the Spaniards put the Madonna and her altar, given the layout of Mayan sacred architecture, Mary's new quarters must have occupied one of the shrine rooms at the top of the building, where "idols" were traditionally housed. All across Mesoamerica, these small dark spaces atop temple platforms reeked with the stench of encrusted human blood, the precious offering to the gods who sustained the cosmos, gods whose presence could be felt in the sacred images kept in the deep shadows of the shrine rooms. These statues, fashioned from clay, stone, wood, or even a paste of sacrificial blood mixed with seeds, had many layers of meanings for the indigenous peoples (Figure 7.3).[65] Such complexities usually did not interest conquistadors. If Maya and Nahua cult buildings were "temples" and "mosques," then their statues, too, were material signs of false belief and merited destruction.

At Cozumel, the Spanish made sure that their Madonna did not rub shoulders with images of the goddess whom the Maya revered. All accounts (except Cortés's own) declare that the conquistadors purged Ix Chel's temple from the stain of idolatry before entrusting Mary to this alien space. Díaz wrote of hurling the Maya images down the temple's steep stone stairs, while another Spaniard recalled burning them.[66] Other sources simply mention the statues' destruction.[67] As these writers might have known, this scene of pagan images lying broken before Mary literally re-enacted the famous Old World tale from the Gospel of Pseudo-Matthew about how hundreds of Egyptian idols spontane- ously shattered in her presence.

Spanish accounts asserted rather tendentiously that the violence with which the conquistadors demolished the Mayan images and cleared the way for Mary did not damage the good relations with Cozumel's residents that Cortés had underscored in his report to Charles V. Two members of the company even insisted that the Maya willingly acquiesced to the smashing of the "idols," while Díaz, who recalled the native priests staunchly resisting Cortés's exhortations to cast away their statues in favor of the Virgin and the cross, nonetheless framed his account with the terms of friendship.[68] Cortés, he wrote, announced to

Figure 7.3 Statue of Coatlicue, Mexica goddess. Late Post-classic period. Mexico. Gianni Dagli Orti. The Art Archive at Art Resource, NY.

Cozumel's leaders that in order to be "our brothers" they would have to give up idols and "put [in their place] an image of Our Lady which [Cortés] gave them, and a cross."[69] The vocabulary of Christian fraternity thus lay like a thick veneer over the Spaniards' memory of how they brought Mary and her son's symbol to Cozumel. For them, this rhetoric made the war against idols equally a Christian peace established through the Virgin and the cross.

Shortly thereafter, Cortés and his men sailed away, leaving the statue of the Madonna in the care of Cozumel's residents, and landed at another Chontal Maya merchant community, Putunchan.[70] There, practically in the shadow of the towering ceíba trees of the surrounding jungle, Cortés would again act as a lay evangelist, using as his visual aid yet another image of Mary that he hoped would unseat "idols" from their home high in a temple shrine room. This time, the war of images followed on the heels of actual battle. Cortés's presentation of the Virgin and the cross to the Maya of Putunchan as signs of Christian friendship provided the dramatic conclusion to several days of bloody hostilities during which the Spaniards hoped for—and received—Mary's military aid.

Maya warriors—thousands of them, as the Spanish remembered it—gathered in their canoes on the river that flowed by Putunchan, ready to drive away the strangers. A message was sent to the conquistadors, asking them to leave peacefully. When they refused, combat began. It was hard fought, long, and costly to both sides. Soon the action shifted to land, where for the first time natives of Mesoamerica heard the thunder of horses' hooves as Spanish riders bore down on them. They might have heard too for the first time the strange syllables of the newcomers' battle cries invoking Mary and her male saintly companions-at-arms. One Spaniard later insisted that Cortés rallied his men with words worthy of a medieval captain of war: "Forward, companions! Know that God and Saint Mary and the apostle Saint Peter are with us! Heaven's favor will not fail us if we do our duty!"[71]

Over the next few days, the conquistadors prevailed, despite being far outnumbered. Having routed the Maya on one of Mary's feast days—March 25, the feast of the Annunciation, or as Díaz wrote, "the day of Our Lady of March"—it was perhaps natural that the Spaniards named the defeated town for her. Yet rather than dubbing Putunchan Santa María de la Anunciación, the conquistadors called it Santa María de la Victoria and thus proclaimed the Madonna the author of their military success.[72]

Putunchan's Marian baptism was just one way in which the Madonna featured in the ceremonies of surrender, a crescendo of ritual orchestrated by the conquistadors to transpose the Maya gestures of submission into a Christian key. First, the Maya made the traditional offerings of the vanquished: food for the hungry Spaniards, gold that only whetted the strangers' appetite for more, and twenty slave women (one of whom would become famed as Malintzin,

Cortés's skillful translator).[73] Then the Maya leaders humbled themselves before Cortés.[74] Accepting their gifts, he sealed what he interpreted as their subjection to his power with a flourish of evangelical zeal. As he wrote to his sovereigns back in Spain, he "reprimanded [the Maya] for the evil they did in adoring their idols and gods and made them understand that they had to come into the knowledge of our holy faith." In the same letter he mentioned that he had left the Maya "a great wooden cross put on high," but provided no further information about his conversion efforts in Putunchan.[75]

Díaz, however, remembered Cortés giving the defeated Maya an image of Mary. In this account, the likeness of Christ's mother, rather than the cross, served as the conquistador's primary prop for his explanation of Christianity to the Maya. Cortés, wrote Díaz, had "shown them a very dear image of Our Lady with her precious son in her arms, and told them that we revered this holy image because she is in heaven and is the mother of our lord God." Then, according to Díaz, Cortés ordered the Maya to construct a "good altar" for Mary, as he had done at Cozumel. Only sometime later, said Díaz, did Cortés have two Spanish carpenters make a cross to keep her company.[76]

Cortés told his sovereigns that his evangelism in Putunchan rendered the Maya "our friends and the vassals of Your Royal Highnesses."[77] Yet the Madonna and her attendant cross were as much material reminders of the military defeat the Putunchans had suffered as they were symbols of friendship. The Christian rituals accompanying the installation of the Virgin and cross on the new altar had a similar double-edged meaning. When the altar was ready, wrote Díaz, the conquistadors called Putunchan's caciques and other notables together to watch as the Marian image from Spain and the newly carved cross were put in place, and Mass was celebrated. Then Fray Olmedo, the Mercedarian friar who accompanied Cortés, admonished the Maya about the dangers of idolatry and proceeded to baptize the twenty slave women.[78] By turning the Maya peace offering of women into an evangelical opportunity, the Spaniards had transformed the gift's meaning. The mass baptism made the Mayas' ritual admission of defeat into a proclamation of Christian religious triumph complementing the conquistadors' military victory. Mary watched over both.

Images of the Madonna would continue to preside over the baptism of indigenous women after Cortés's company left Putunchan to sail toward a realm of whose power and gold they had begun to hear rumors: the area controlled by the Triple Alliance, that Nahua confederation of Tetzcoco, Tlacopan, and Tenochtitlan dominated by the latter city and its ruler, or *tlatoani*, Moctezuma. In the lands of central Mexico, the Spaniards' presentation of Marian images to indigenous communities and the Christianization of native women given to the conquistadors would acquire added depth, becoming an exchange of women that signaled a new politics of coalition.

Toward Tenochtitlan: From Amity to Alliance

Landing on Mexico's mosquito-ridden Gulf Coast near a place they would soon christen as Veracruz, Cortés and his men almost immediately found themselves face to face with Moctezuma's emissaries, his loyal allies, and his bitterly unhappy tributaries. The conquistadors would slash their way through this challenging political landscape with words and weapons. When the moment was opportune, they would offer Christianity, in the shape of the Madonna and the cross, to the peoples they encountered.

In Mexico, the conquistadors would continue to use images of Mary and crosses to defeat the alien gods worshipped in temples and to establish what they termed "fraternal peace." They would also draw these two Christian symbols into a new type of negotiation with the indigenous. Enshrining the Madonna and cross in temples became as much the act of conquistadors seeking useful military alliances as it was the gesture of armed lay evangelists thirsting to claim territory for their own god. As the Spaniards joined forces with some indigenous groups, they would use the language of religious fraternity to intertwine images of Mary ever more tightly with their material ambitions. In the political theatrics of alliance that the conquistadors patched together in Mexico, they nonetheless would not hesitate to use force, for their Marian war on idolatry was hardly over.

The Totonacs of Cempoala, a large coastal town whose white-washed buildings shone so brightly in the tropical sun that some Spaniards at first thought they were made of silver, learned firsthand just how violent the Virgin's arrival could be, even when glossed with the language of friendship.[79] Cortés persuaded these disgruntled tributaries of the Mexica to throw their lot in with the Spanish. To seal the partnership, the Totonacs used the traditional Mesoamerican ritual form, bestowing eight high-ranking women on the conquistadors.[80] At Putunchan the Spaniards had been given women, but those were slaves. Whether or not Cortés and company realized it, the elevated status of the women now being presented to them indicated that this was a ritual of alliance between partners, not a ceremony of submission.[81] The Spaniards in turn offered a very special woman to the Totonacs. Her advent was heralded by a new campaign in the conquistadors' war on idolatry.

In order for true fraternity to prevail between these new partners, Cortés announced, the Totonacs would have to renounce "idols" and sacrificial offerings. Enraged, the caciques refused. In Díaz's dramatic retelling, the conquistadors took up their weapons and made their way to Cempoala's temple, climbing its high stairs to the shrine rooms, where they smashed idol after idol.[82] The native priests wept at the sight of the shards. Battle was avoided only when Cortés seized the caciques and threatened to kill them if the fully armed Totonac warriors did not back down. Having broken ties with Tenochtitlan, the Totonacs could not risk alienating their new allies.[83] "Now," Díaz remembers Cortés telling the Totonacs, the Spanish "would hold them as brothers" and defend them against Moctezuma.

After humiliating Cempoala's leaders, the conquistadors introduced Mary as the replacement for the shattered images. Díaz recalled how Cortés told the Totonacs that since they no longer had "idols" in their temples, "he wished to leave them a great lady, who is the mother of Jesus Christ, in whom we believe and whom we venerate, so that they could have her also as their lady and intercessor." The next day, according to Díaz, Cortés directed the Totonacs to wash the blood from their temples and had native masons build an altar. An image of Mary was enthroned on it, surrounded by beautifully woven cloths, and garlanded with leafy branches and "many roses" whose fragrance filled the air. Carpenters then made a cross and placed it atop a pillar nearby. As at Putunchan, the native leaders watched while Mass was celebrated before the Madonna and the cross, and Fray Olmedo baptized the women who had been given to the Spanish.

This tableau juxtaposing Mary and baptized native women would repeat itself elsewhere during Cortés's journey through Nahua lands. It was a dramatic visual statement of the crossed cultural codes and mutual misunderstandings that so profoundly marked this phase of the Spanish conquest of the New World.[84] Although each side proposed special women to the other as entryways into a new web of relationships, it is possible that neither party fully grasped the meaning of the other's gesture. The Nahuas offered human, if elite, women as a conduit for bonds of sex and marriage, while the conquistadors opened a door instead to religious brotherhood through material representations of a heavenly woman. This incongruent exchange of women could only create an uneasy peace between partners such as the conquistadors and the Totonac warriors who left Cempoala with Cortés's company some months later.

Heading inland, the conquistadors and their new allies began to pass through towns loyal to the Triple Alliance, where there was little chance of winning support. There, Cortés sometimes denounced idolatry during his exchanges with local caciques, but he knew that any attempt to destroy these people's images would have been suicidal, and he shared little of the friars' fervor for martyrdom.[85] Nor did the conquistadors apparently try to plant their own sacred symbols in these hostile towns.[86] At least once more before reaching Tenochtitlan, however, they would find the chance to repeat their Marian rituals of lay evangelism and political alliance. This time, the conquistadors' installation of an image of the Madonna in a temple belonged to the negotiations that gained them their most important ally: the great *altepetl* (or "ethnic state") of Tlaxcala, a wealthy, powerful, and militarily accomplished confederation of Nahuas who had resisted the Triple Alliance's imperialism.

This *altepetl* lay southeast of Tenochtitlan, its well-tended fields stretching out beneath a massive dormant volcano. Every day, in the thronged marketplace of what seemed to Cortés like a "city" larger and more impressive than Granada, residents of Tlaxcala's urban center shopped for luxuries and necessities—clothing, firewood, charcoal, pottery, feather work, gold, silver, jewelry—and used the services of barbers and bathing establishments. As the conquistadors approached Tlaxcalan territory, they found their way barred by a stone wall some nine feet high and twenty feet wide and topped with battlements. These fortifications snaked along the *altepetl*'s frontiers, guarding the Tlaxcalteca against their enemies, the Mexica.[87]

Cortés hoped that the Tlaxcalteca's hostility toward Moctezuma would naturally incline them toward peace and perhaps even alliance with his own company, but such was not the case initially. Over several weeks in September 1519, the conquistadors faced the well-trained and highly capable warriors of Tlaxcala in skirmishes and outright battles that left both sides deeply shaken. Having taken the strangers' measure, the Tlaxcalteca concluded that it would be better to have them as partners and eventually sought an alliance. The conquistadors, on the verge of collapse, accepted the Tlaxcalteca overtures.[88]

During the ensuing ceremonies to formalize the partnership, Tlaxcalteca caciques gave noble women to the Spaniards. Cortés responded with the conquistadors' harder-edged protocols of Christian fraternity. Denouncing the evils of idolatry, he proffered an image of Madonna and Child in place of the images he exhorted his new allies to abhor. As Díaz remembered it, Cortés "showed" the assembled Tlaxcalteca elite "an image of Our Lady with her son in her arms," presenting Christianity as the same kind of Marian creed he had preached at Putunchan and Cempoala. The image, Cortés explained through his interpreters, represented a powerful intercessor called "Our Lady, who is called Saint Mary, and who is high in the heavens and is the mother of Our Lord," and who had remained a virgin before, during, and after her son's birth.[89]

No riot of idol destruction accompanied Cortés's exposition of these finer points of Marian doctrine. In Tlaxcalteca territory, the Spaniards lacked the strategic advantages that had permitted them their iconoclastic frenzy at Cempoala. Despite Cortés's rhetorical claims that the Tlaxcalteca had accepted him as their lord, the conquistadors were very much the junior partners in this new alliance.[90] By persuading the *altepetl*'s rulers to grant them a temple (albeit only a small, recently built one) in which to make "a church," as one conquistador called it, they nonetheless managed to introduce an image of Mary into the Tlaxcalteca religious landscape. After ridding this shrine of idols and the blood of sacrifices, the Spaniards installed the Marian image that Cortés had used during his sermon. The conquistadors knelt on the temple's cleanly swept floor in front of the Madonna, while Fray Olmedo intoned the liturgy of the Mass, the rhythmic gestures of his hands further consecrating the space. Then the friar baptized the Tlaxcalteca noble women who had been given to the Spaniards.[91]

At Tlaxcala, as at Cempoala, the Spaniards summoned an image of Mary as champion in their war on idolatry and then drew the same object into the dialogues that established their military partnership with an indigenous group. This was a potent combination of roles for the Virgin. But it was not a very stable one, as became evident soon after the conquistadors arrived in the capital city of the Triple Alliance. There, during increasingly tense and angry exchanges between Cortés's company and Moctezuma's *altepetl*, the cloak of Christian fraternity slipped from Mary's shoulders, unveiling her image as an icon of conquest.

Tenochtitlan

When Cortés and his men left the region of Tlaxcalteca power, they were flanked by several thousand of the warriors against whom they had just fought so hard. This new military coalition would eventually prove disastrous for the Triple Alliance. But the battles that reduced Tenochtitlan to ruins did not seem inevitable in November 1519, when the conquistadors and their indigenous allies entered this sophisticated city built out over the waters of Lake Tetzcoco.[92] Over the previous six months, Cortés had had extensive dealings with Moctezuma's emissaries as the Mexica *tlatoani* had tried to assess these potentially dangerous strangers. Several times, in ceremonies that represented efforts to establish relations through ritual rather than through weapons, Moctezuma's ambassadors and the Spaniards had exchanged presents.[93] During some of the very earliest of these negotiations, the conquistadors' gifts had embodied their hopes of luring the Mexica into the world of Christianity through the power of Mary and her son.

Bernal Díaz remembered how the Mexica emissaries who had greeted the Spaniards almost as soon as they landed on the Gulf Coast had expressed wonder when the strangers knelt before a cross and repeated the Ave Maria. Seizing the moment, Cortés made a lengthy speech contrasting the evils of idolatry with the good of Christianity, and then bestowed on the Mexica an image of Mary and a cross. Cortés, wrote Díaz, made it plain that he wanted Moctezuma's ambassadors to take these Christian emblems back to Tenochtitlan and honor them instead of "idols."[94]

Months later, when the Spaniards and their Tlaxcalteca allies strode across the broad causeway leading into Moctezuma's city, neither the Madonna nor the cross had unseated the Mexicas' images. They had in fact never been brought to Tenochtitlan, according to Díaz. Moctezuma had refused to allow these symbols of alien forces and threatening newcomers to enter his city.[95] The *tlatoani* was no more inclined to accept images of Mary and other Christian symbols when Cortés proposed them soon after the conquistadors' arrival in Tenochtitlan. This time, Moctezuma's will would not prevail.

As all the Spanish sources agree, Cortés succeeded in ensconcing an image of the Virgin right at the heart of Tenochtitlan's political and religious life, that is, in the vast Templo Mayor complex dominating the city center. In twin shrines atop a beautifully built pyramidal temple so high that from its summit one could see out over the whole city and the surrounding lakes stretching toward the mountains, the Mexica kept images of some of their most important divinities (Figure 7.4). Blue paint marked the shrine on the temple's upper platform where Tlaloc, the god who brought life-giving rain to the highland plateaus, watched over the city, while red and black ornamented the shrine guarding Huitzilopotchli, the hummingbird war god who had led the Mexica from the wilds of the north to the marshy site where they had founded their empire.[96]

The cosmopolitan wealth on display in Tenochtitlan's marketplaces, the cleanliness of its streets, the exquisite art produced by its painters and sculptors, the sophisticated engineering behind the canals that drained the marshy site and allowed two-storied stone buildings to stand on this island in the middle of Lake

Figure 7.4 Mexica temples at Tenochtitlan, perhaps the Templo Mayor. Painting by indigenous artist in Diego Duran's *Historia de las Indias* (1597). Biblioteca Nacional, Madrid. Gianni Dagli Orti. The Art Archive at Art Resource, NY.

Tetzcoco—all of this dazzled the Spanish.[97] But they were not so entranced by Tenochtitlan's grandeur that they abandoned their political savvy. Treated as honored if unwelcome guests, the conquistadors spent their time observing Mexica ways, exploring the city, and gathering information.[98]

During the Spaniards' first few days in the city, Moctezuma allowed them to tour the great temple. He met them at the top of its more than one hundred stairs after a climb that left some of the men exhausted, although Cortés would not admit it. The conquistadors were impressed by the building's size and superb craftsmanship, though they probably did not realize that it was the symbolic axis of the Mexica universe and the stage for rituals proclaiming this people's expansionist ideology.[99] But its scale, location, and splendor indicated that it was terrifically important, more so than any temple they had seen in Mesoamerica. No wonder Cortés was inspired to try to mark this building with his own god's power. While his men admired the view from the temple's platform, he whispered to Fray Olmedo his plan to persuade Moctezuma to let them "make a church there," as Díaz later would remember.[100] As conquistadors pursued this project, an image of Mary would be their main instrument.

Díaz relates that Cortés's resolve hardened when the Spaniards received permission from Moctezuma to enter the Templo Mayor's shrine rooms. The conquistadors were repulsed by these chambers, where human hearts still fresh from the day's sacrifice smoldered over braziers of copal before massive sacred images. According to Bernal Díaz, the sight of the statues encrusted with precious stones, garlanded with carved snakes, and splashed with blood, unleashed Cortés's tongue. Denouncing them as nothing more than "devils" powerless to help human beings, he exhorted Moctezuma to renounce the vanity of idolatry and the hideous bloodshed of human sacrifice. If Moctezuma would only let him put an image of the Virgin in the shrine room and install a cross on the temple's summit, then the impotence of the "idols" would be laid bare. The Mexicas' statues, Cortés foretold, would "dread" the Marian image—or so Díaz recalled his captain's words. This account, even if much exaggerated, proves that at least one conquistador believed that Mary wielded exactly the awesome power over idols assigned her in the Gospel of Pseudo-Matthew.

Díaz enigmatically states that "Moctezuma had already seen this image [of the Virgin]."[101] Perhaps the Spaniards had shown it to the *tlatoani* a few days earlier when they came to his palace and had a rather spirited exchange about the respective merits of their religious beliefs.[102] Or Moctezuma might have noticed the Madonna among the Spaniards' possessions when he paid them a ceremonial visit in the quarters he had arranged for them.[103] Whatever the *tlatoani* knew of the Marian image was enough to make him angrily refuse to dishonor his own gods by making room for it in the great temple. To their chagrin, the Spaniards had to content themselves with making a "church" of sorts in their own lodgings.[104]

Within a few months, Cortés managed to overcome Moctezuma's resistance to his Marian project. By this time, the Mexica ruler probably had little choice but to accommodate the Spanish demand that an image of the Virgin be enshrined in the dark rooms where statues of his own gods resided. The conquistadors were now his handlers, his jailers even, for they had taken him hostage in circumstances that remain mysterious.[105] Equally murky are the details of the incidents leading to the installation of the image of Mary in Tenochtitlan's main temple. No two Spanish sources agree on exactly how it happened. Cortés and those writers who sought to lionize him paint an epic scene of idol destruction. They insist that he piously presided as the native statues were rolled off the edge of the temple's platform, or even that he himself smashed in their faces.[106] Other authors wrote less dramatic accounts of negotiations and pressures that led to the temple's idols being quietly removed from one of the shrine rooms by the Mexica priests, or just pushed aside to make room for Mary.[107]

However it happened, the Spaniards enthroned an image of the Virgin high above the city. This was perhaps an image particularly dear to Cortés. Francisco Cervantes de Salazar, a learned humanist who would join the faculty of the University of Mexico at its foundation in 1553 and knew Cortés personally, believed that this Marian image was one that the conquistador "always had with him on all his expeditions and journeys."[108] None of the Spaniards who had actually witnessed the events at the Templo Mayor confirmed this assertion. Yet even if this image of Mary originally was not in and of itself special, it became so once lodged in the temple. Some conquistadors remembered Cortés setting images of other saints at the Virgin's side, while some wrote of crosses as her companions. But when these men wrote of later events involving this temple, all but one of them named only the Madonna and omitted these other Christian symbols.[109] Mary distilled the essence of the Spaniards' claim to Tenochtitlan's ritual center.

This claim was not softened by the language of Christian fraternity that usually tempered the accounts of Cortés's Marian evangelism in other places. At Tenochtitlan, he attacked the same religious practices that had attracted his ire elsewhere, inveighing against idolatry and the rituals of human sacrifice. Díaz even remembered Cortés's installation of the Madonna in the Templo Mayor as participating in the kind of mutual if discordant exchange of important women that had occurred at Cempoala and Tlaxcala. Some days before the drama in the great shrine room, Moctezuma had offered his daughter to Cortés as a pledge of his "love" for the Spaniard. The conquistador had accepted her, stipulating that she be baptized. Such is the preface to Díaz's description of how Cortés prevailed in the struggle over whether or not a Madonna and a cross would grace Tenochtitlan's great temple.[110]

In this case, the ceremonial rhetoric of alliance established through women was not reciprocated by the Spaniards. In their accounts of Mary's arrival at the

Templo Mayor, neither Díaz nor Cortés used tropes of Christian friendship and fraternity. Instead, there was a tenacious insistence that the Mexica make space for the Madonna, an ambition that lays her bare as an instrument not of diplomacy but rather of the conquistadors' will to power. It is only partly camouflaged by Díaz's memory of how, late in the spring of 1520, Cortés admonished Moctezuma that the conquistadors would take it as a sign of the *tlatoani*'s "good friendship" if he protected the image of Mary from harm.[111] Largely lacking the vocabulary of amity and alliance, the Spaniards' accounts of the Madonna's installation in the Templo Mayor belonged instead to their stories of how they temporarily mastered Tenochtitlan.

Even when things started to unravel for the conquistadors, as was the case by the time of Cortés's exhortation to Moctezuma, they presented Mary as a figure of their power. In April or May of 1520, the Spaniards in Tenochtitlan received bad news. The governor of Cuba, Diego de Velázquez, had learned how blatantly Cortés had flouted his orders. Infuriated, Velázquez sent Pánfilo de Narváez to Mexico to squelch the upstart. When Cortés got wind of Narváez's arrival on the Gulf Coast, he left one of his lieutenants in charge of matters in Tenochtitlan and raced off to deal with this problem. According to Díaz, Cortés proudly told Moctezuma that Mary would help him crush this threat. Before the captain departed for the Gulf Coast, the *tlatoani* asked him how he could hope to win against Narváez's far larger company. Cortés, according to Díaz, responded: "Jesus Christ, in whom we believe, and Our Lady Saint Mary will give us force and strength greater than theirs."[112]

Soon Cortés would need the Madonna to help him fight against the Mexica themselves. After subduing Narváez in a battle at Cempoala, Cortés returned to Tenochtitlan. In his absence, the Spaniards had massacred hundreds, if not thousands, of Mexica men and women who had gathered to celebrate a religious festival, and Tenochtitlan's warriors had taken up arms to avenge the hideous slaughter. Cortés managed to re-enter the city, but almost immediately he and his men were forced to take refuge in their quarters. For some twenty days the Spaniards and their native allies attempted to hold out against the Mexica attacks, their situation growing more dire daily. The sorties they made did not much improve their lot, although during one, they gained some measure of success due to what Cortés described as the "help of God and his glorious mother."[113]

During what was literally the conquistadors' darkest hour—the night of June 30, 1520, later remembered as the Noche Triste (the Night of Sorrow)—some of Cortés's men turned to Mary. At midnight, the conquistador company made a desperate bid to escape the city. Closely pursued by Tenochtitlan's warriors, many of the fleeing conquistadors and even more of their indigenous allies lost their lives. Those Spaniards who had the misfortune to fall into the hands of the Mexica that night pierced the darkness with their screams, some shouting for God's help and others for Mary's mercy, according to one man's dramatic description.[114]

Neither Mary nor God saved those hapless conquistadors from the obsidian blade of sacrifice and the Mexica war club. Other Spaniards had more luck in obtaining such celestial protection. In his vivid recollection of the days of battle and skirmishes following this bloody night, Díaz described how "we commended ourselves sincerely to God and Saint Mary, and invok[ed] the name of Lord Santiago." In response to these prayers, wrote the conquistador, this trinity so familiar to Castilian military men had inspired in him and a handful of his fellows the strength to fight their way to safety.[115]

Days later, Cortés's forces limped into Tlaxcala. There they nursed their wounds and laid plans to return to Tenochtitlan. When they set out toward the Mexica capital, they marched as a well-organized army of conquerors in which the indigenous contingents dwarfed the Spanish ones. Some eighteenth-century Mexican writers would insist that fluttering over Cortés's head was a cloth standard bearing Mary's image, a visible sign of her patronage of his plan to attack Tenochtitlan. Whether or not the red damask banner portraying her and labeled *el estandarte de Cortés*, guarded today in Mexico City's Museo Nacional de Historia, ever flew in the winds of war gathering around Tenochtitlan in 1521, it appears that a Marian standard was carried by some of Cortés's men.[116]

The Spaniards, in any case, were confident in the Madonna's aid as they assaulted Tenochtitlan. Key to their strategy for taking the city protected by the waters of Lake Tetzcoco were thirteen fast, small ships called brigantines. Built at Tlaxcala according to the Spaniards' specifications, these boats apparently set sail armed with Mary's grace and that of two other powerful saints. A Christian priest, wrote one Spaniard, blessed the brigantines, intoning prayers to win for the warriors the "help and favor of the Virgin without blemish, and of all the saints, especially the advocates Saint Peter and Santiago."[117]

In August 1521, after months of siege and street fighting had made starving shadows of Tenochtitlan's once elegant people, the city fell to the conquistadors and their native allies. Many decades later, some Spaniards would insist that the Madonna of the Templo Mayor had survived the battles.[118] This was, however, rather improbable. Not only did the great temple suffer severe damage during the siege, but as Cortés himself would suggest, the image of Mary probably had fallen victim to the Mexicas' rage sometime before the Noche Triste.[119] Before her disappearance, this Madonna had borne witness to how rapidly the conquistadors could translate their Marian language of amity and alliance into the equally Marian rhetoric of dominance and discord.

The conquistadors and their chroniclers would write of Tenochtitlan's fall as the "conquest of New Spain." Their proud language, however, was deceptive. The Spaniards' military subjugation of Mesoamerica was a protracted process that continued for decades, even centuries after Cortés proclaimed himself master of Moctezuma's city.[120] Tenochtitlan's defeat did not signal the submission of all the peoples in the loose federation of allies and tributaries that had comprised the Triple Alliance's empire. In the wake of the city's fall, conquistadors undertook armed expeditions to "pacify" those peoples, as well as others who lived in regions on the fringes of the Mexica world.[121] During these conquests, the Spanish would continue to turn to Mary for help, as Pedro de Alvarado revealed in a letter he wrote Cortés in 1524.

Alvarado had fought in the campaigns that led to Cuba's colonization, and then in those leading to Tenochtitlan's demise. In 1523, he set off to conquer the region the Spaniards would call Guatemala. There he encountered stiff resistance from first the Quiches and then the Cakchiquels. In the midst of his struggles to subdue them—which he would eventually do through such savage means as burning captives alive—Alvarado sent a progress report to Cortés. After detailing his travails and triumphs, Alvarado confessed that he was "in the midst of the harshest land" ever seen and would be lost unless help came from the heavens. "So that God will give us victory," he wrote, "I ask that Your Grace command that a procession be held in [Mexico City] with all the friars and clerics, so that Our Lady will aid us, for we are so far from help if it does not come thence."[122] If a procession of clergy did wend its way through Mexico City's streets, imploring Mary to assist Alvarado in his battles in Central America, these men in robes probably carried images of her, perhaps even banners bearing her sacred portrait. A Marian war standard, in any case, flew over one conquistador company that set out in 1530 to conquer the "unpacified" region lying northwest of Mexico City.[123]

If conquest continued for decades, so did the kind of rough lay evangelism to which images of the Madonna were so important. In places like Michoacán, Chiapas, and the dense jungles of Central America, conquistadors would sometimes deliver impromptu sermons about the evils of human sacrifice and idolatry. There they would also on occasion destroy native images. Cortés boasted that he did so during his ill-advised and traumatic campaign of 1524–1526 into Las Hibueras, a region stretching into modern-day Honduras.[124] According to Díaz, Cortés even enjoined other conquistadors to follow in his evangelical footsteps.[125] Some of them did so, making good use of images of Mary. Díaz remembered watching Luis Marín, the captain of a 1523 expedition into Chiapas, as he exhorted the defeated Tzotzil Maya inhabitants of the town of Chamula to renounce idolatry and sacrifice, and then gave them "crosses and an image of Our Lady" to replace their idols.[126] When, in January 1524, Cristóbal de Olid set out for Las Hibueras at Cortés's command, his equipment for the campaign apparently included a supply of images of Mary intended for just such missionizing.

Olid was fresh from a campaign in Michoacán, an area to the west of Mexico City. There the Spaniards had urged the Tarascans to put away idols and had sent their coyote-shaped sacrificial stones crashing down temple stairs, while consigning ceremonial masks and feather work to the flames of bonfires.[127] Cortés intended Olid to undertake such evangelism in Las Hibueras. According to Díaz, Cortés sent his lieutenant off with not just two clerics and plenty of advice about how to combat idolatry and sacrifice, but also "many images of Our Lady for [Olid] to put in towns." Cortés also commanded Olid to "put crosses everywhere," but did not provide him with any, evidently assuming that they would be cobbled together on the spot, as they had been during the Spaniards' advance toward Tenochtitlan. The images of Mary, though, probably came from Europe, like those Cortés had used in service of his evangelical ambitions. Cortés even explicitly instructed Olid to model his missionary methods on those of the previous years of conquest: "Look, brother Cristóbal de Olid, take care to do all this in the manner in which you saw us to do it in New Spain."[128] In other words, at least as Díaz remembered it, Cortés told Olid to follow an established pattern— one in which lay evangelists scattered crosses cut from native wood across the landscape but placed Marian images of European manufacture on native altars.

The conquistadors, then, continued to use images of the Madonna to embody the faith they wanted the indigenous peoples of Mesoamerica to adopt. Yet they seem never to have forgotten Mary's more formidable martial side, any more than the anonymous sailor who brought the Madonna to the Tainos of Cuba's Cabo de Cruz apparently had. Nor did most of the chroniclers of the conquest, for they welcomed signs that the saints had been on the Spaniards' side. The conquistadors' double-edged vision of the Virgin did, however, have one fierce critic, a man who even went so far as to reshape the tale of Cabo de Cruz in order to deny that the Madonna was a military icon: Bartolomé de las Casas, the Spanish priest who had praised Alonso de Hojeda's Marian devotion.

Cabo de Cruz Redux

Over the long span of centuries considered by this book, Las Casas appears to have been the only author to condemn the idea that Mary could be involved in warfare. By the time he shed the sword of a conquistador for the robes of a Dominican, he had become convinced that the Spaniards' treatment of the inhabitants of the New World was a moral outrage and thus an unpardonable offense against God. Las Casas's conversion from conquistador to passionate defender of the Indians' human rights was a gradual process, though it was complete by 1514.[129] It was the bitter fruit of years of witnessing the atrocities committed by his fellow conquistadors against the native peoples of the

Caribbean—brutalities that Las Casas would describe in graphic detail in the books for which he became famous. The Spanish, Las Casas believed, had caused no less than "the destruction of the Indies."[130] He had witnessed much of the horror and even had had a hand in it.

Las Casas arrived as a young man in the New World just ten years after Columbus's first voyage.[131] When he disembarked on Hispaniola, he had probably already seen military action; he appears to have taken part in suppressing a Morisco uprising of 1497 in Granada. In the Caribbean, he participated in expeditions against the Tainos, serving as a priest ministering to the spiritual needs of his compatriots and perhaps wielding a weapon himself. He received a reward for his efforts in the form of *repartimientos* on both Hispaniola and Cuba—those grants of subject Indians and their labor so eagerly sought by conquistadors. In 1515, Las Casas renounced his *repartimientos*, declaring them an unjustifiable form of dominion over peoples he now believed were human beings deserving of liberty. It was this conviction that led him to excoriate the Spanish practice of invoking the Virgin in warfare against the Indians.

Las Casas's censure of the military Mary appears in his monumental *Historia de las Indias*, a chronicle on which he began work in the late 1520s. His belief in the dignity of the indigenous is etched into almost every page, including those passages decrying the conquistadors' misuse of Mary. The native peoples of the Caribbean, wrote Las Casas, were innocent and, for the most part, peace-loving individuals. The blameless victims of Spanish bloodlust, they were the targets of unjust warfare. The idea that conquistadors might call on God and Mary to help them triumph over these peoples in such patently immoral wars disgusted and incensed him. It was Las Casas who recorded how Enciso prayed to Seville's Santa María de la Antigua in battle against the Caribs of Tierra Firme—and his account is scathing, to say the least. Enciso's hope that "God and his mother Saint Mary" would provide him with victory was, Las Casas declared, tantamount to "making [them] accomplices in the robberies, murders, captures, infamies against the faith, and bloodbaths that [the conquistadors] perpetrated." Enciso and his men expected from God and Mary "services that belong to none other than the demons and their ministers." Santa María de la Antigua, Las Casas knew, would never find the "jewels" Enciso promised her in exchange for victory an "acceptable sacrifice."[132]

Not surprisingly, Las Casas dramatically recast this conquistador's account of the Marian image venerated by the Tainos of Cuba's Cabo de Cruz by purging it of all allusions to martial violence. Though citing both Enciso and Peter Martyr as his sources, in the *Historia de las Indias*, he shaped a story of completely peaceable Indians venerating a loving Virgin. Gone are the armed conflicts between Comendador and rival caciques in which Mary slaughtered Indians with her stick, along with the midnight struggles between the *zemi* and her. Only readers familiar with either Enciso's version of events or Peter Martyr's would have known exactly what spectacular marvels of Marian aggression lay behind Las Casas's off-hand reference to "miracles that Our Lady performed for [Comendador's people], such that devotion [to her] was engendered in those peoples with whom they had certain quarrels."[133]

Las Casas's sanitized version of this Marian story owes much to his own experiences with Cuba's Tainos. In 1513, he served as chaplain to Pánfilo de Narváez during this conquistador's campaign to "pacify" Cuba. The savagery that Las Casas saw his fellow Spaniards perpetrate there turned his mind for good. Since Narváez's bloody rampage began at Cuba's southeastern tip, perhaps even at Cabo de Cruz itself, Las Casas may have seen the Tainos who lived there.[134] In any case, he was sure that Cuba's natives were an especially nonbelligerent people, writing of them: "They lived peacefully. I do not remember that we ever heard of or observed war between these peoples or between their chiefs."[135] He may have been right, for Cuba's Tainos do seem to have had less occasion for warfare than their counterparts further east in the Antilles.[136] The notion of such peace-loving peoples invoking an aggressive Madonna in battle was as unconvincing to Las Casas as it was distasteful.

If Las Casas's newfound love for the indigenous peoples of the New World led him to roundly reject the military Mary beloved by generations of Castilian men of war, it also spurred him to approve of the conquistadors' use of the Virgin in the service of lay evangelism, a colonial project that often wrought violence on those very same peoples.[137] The conquistadors' introduction of the Madonna into the natives' religious cosmos was an effort that Las Casas, who himself burned to save souls, supported, even though it often went hand in hand with military conquest.

Las Casas in fact shared the conquistadors' confidence that native peoples were rational human beings who would accept Christianity once the fallacy of their own religious beliefs had been revealed to them. The willingness of Spanish men of war to deliver images of the Virgin into the keeping of Tainos, Maya, Totonacs, Tlaxcalteca, and Mexica cannot be ascribed solely to colonial desire and strategic concerns. Nor was it just evidence of pious zeal to win the "war of images" and render the New World and its temples an offering to Mary and her son. It also reveals faith in the capacity of the indigenous to perceive and receive the truths embodied in images of the Virgin at which the conquistadors so often pointed when explaining Christianity to their New World "brothers."[138]

The Spaniards had been raised to revere such images, yet repeatedly left them in the care of people who had not been ritually incorporated into the Christian community through the sacrament of baptism. The conquistadors would only have done so if they believed that they could trust the indigenous to take care of these important objects. At Cabo de Cruz, in Cueíba, on the island of Cozumel, and in Putunchan, Cempoala, Tlaxcala, and Tenochtitlan, conquistadors confidently instructed New World peoples how to revere the Madonna who had come to reside in their midst. Often these Spaniards addressed themselves to caciques and native priests, who they thought possessed some of the dignity of their own upper classes.[139] At Cempoala, as Díaz recalled, Cortés even deputed four Totonac priests to "serve the holy image of Our Lady," making them first don clean white garments and cut their long hair matted with sacrificial blood. The conquistadors ordered the native peoples to keep the Marian altars in their temples clean and adorned with garlands of flowers and fresh cut greenery, and the floors of the shrine room well swept. Candles were to burn in front of the Madonna, and the fragrant copal incense that Mesoamericans offered their own gods was to scent the air for her.[140]

Hope thus suffused the conquistadors' Marian evangelism. It was a hope perhaps as strong as that nurturing their faith in the Virgin's ability to aid them in their New World travails, whether of war or peace. Hope, along with less exalted qualities, inspired the impromptu sermons in which they told the indigenous peoples about God's mother. It allowed them to leave images of her in the hands of unbaptized men and women who they believed might thereby be brought to Christianity. Caution did occasionally tinge the conquistadors' belief that the native peoples would treat these images appropriately. Cortés left a Spanish soldier with a game leg behind in Cempoala, ordering him to make sure that the Totonacs tended to the Madonna and the cross.[141] At Tenochtitlan, an elderly conquistador was posted to keep watch over the Christian images newly installed in the Templo Mayor and to prevent Mexica priests from mishandling them.[142]

The conquistadors, then, were not complete religious idealists. Nor would their optimism about the indigenous peoples' innate inclination to Christianity survive for long after Tenochtitlan's conquest, as yet another retelling of Enciso's tale of Cabo de Cruz reveals. This time, it was conquistador author Gonzalo Fernández de Oviedo y Valdés who revived the story. In the section of his *Historia general de las Indias* published in 1535, he referred to the tale of Cabo de Cruz, only to dismiss it out of hand for two reasons. He had never heard the story himself when he was on Cuba, and his own experiences in the New World, the criterion by which he preferred to judge the truth, had led him to conclude that "few if any [natives] are Christian of their own will." It is "possible," wrote Oviedo, "that there are some faithful Indians, but I think they are very rare."[143]

Like Las Casas, Oviedo created from the Cabo de Cruz material a vehicle for his own opinion about the post-conquest spiritual state of the indigenous. He thought his fellow conquistadors deluded in believing that, as lay evangelists, they could bring the native peoples of the New World to Christianity. Las Casas for his part trimmed the tale to render the Tainos exemplars of a benevolent Christianity embodied by Mary's maternal love. To discover whether either of these authors were right, it is necessary to explore how the indigenous reacted to the conquistadors' introduction of Mary, the woman whose images had become as emblematic of the Spaniards' arrival as their guns, their horses, and their diseases.

8

Our Precious Mother

On the heels of the conquistadors came armies of friars determined to establish Christianity in the New World. Three years after the fall of Tenochtitlan, Hernán Cortés ceremoniously welcomed a deliberately apostolic number of Franciscans—twelve—to this city, where piles of rubble still marked the places where Mexica temples and houses had once stood. The "Twelve," as these friars were known, were the vanguard in a host of professional evangelists who attempted to win the indigenous peoples of Mesoamerica over to Christianity in the sixteenth and seventeenth centuries. First came more Franciscans, many hoping to hasten the second coming of Christ by converting the New World.[1] Soon they had competition from men belonging to religious orders less roiled by the currents of apocalyptic prophecy: Dominicans, Augustinians, and Jesuits. These men in robes would devote their lives to trying to instill love for their god, his son, and his mother in the hearts of the indigenous peoples.[2] Their efforts to instruct Nahuas, Mayas, Zapotecs, Tarascans, and myriad other inhabitants of New Spain in the practices and beliefs of Christianity dwarfed the sermonizing labor of the lay evangelists.

From the friars, the peoples of the Caribbean and Mexico would learn much about Mary. Yet the conquistadors' endeavors were not unimportant in shaping how the indigenous would see this woman so central to Christianity, as testimony given during Cortés's trial for malfeasance in 1529–1530 suggested. Witnesses in Cortés's favor recalled how in the decade following his 1519 sojourn on Cozumel, Spanish ships sailing into the turquoise waters fringing the island were offered a most Marian greeting from its Chontal Maya inhabitants. The Maya would set out to meet the Spanish in their majestic canoes. Usually they loaded these vessels with the trade goods from which they made their fortunes as sea-merchants—cacao, cotton cloth, metalwork, pottery—but when welcoming the Spaniards, they added special cargo: the image of Mary that Cortés had enshrined in Ix Chel's temple.[3] The Maya brought the Madonna out onto the water with them "so that [the Spanish] would know they were friends (*amigos*)," to borrow the words of witnesses at Cortés's trial. To further signal their peaceful intentions, the Maya would shout out "Cortés! Cortés!" across the waves. It is hard to imagine what effect this incantation had on conquistadors like Pánfilo de Narváez and Cristóbal de Olid, the first sailing westward in 1520 determined to overcome Cortés, while the other traveled south some years later in mutiny against him. But both men were among the Spaniards whom Cozumel's Maya apparently hailed with Cortés's name and the image of Mary he had left on their island.[4]

This scene that repeated itself off Cozumel's shores hints at the complexity of exploring how the conquistadors' introduction of Mary to the peoples of the Caribbean and Mexico influenced indigenous responses to her. The Maya's words and gestures suggest that the language of alliance and friendship with which Cortés had so often framed his presentation of the Virgin to the indigenous peoples of Mesoamerica was not lost on them. He had given these Maya every reason to see the image of her as a symbol of the Spaniards, and even as a medium through which to communicate with these strangers who came ever more frequently to their island. Perhaps they also naturally understood Mary as a link to Cortés himself. By pairing her image with the invocation of his powerful name, the Maya expressed their desired relationship to the Spanish.[5]

These Chontal Maya were not alone. Other Mesoamericans who had received images of Mary from the conquistadors would press her into the service of dialogue with the Spanish, even if the conversation was not always amiable. Indeed, as indigenous peoples evolved ways of asserting their place in a world irredeemably changed by the arrival of the Spaniards yet not completely dominated by the newcomers, they would often find Mary useful. But this is hardly the whole story, as a further detail relating to Cozumel's Madonna and mentioned by witnesses during Cortés's trial suggests; the Chontal Maya had dressed their image of Mary in "native clothes," probably diminutive garments cut from the same cotton fabric they themselves wore and perhaps even embroidered with the lustrous rainbow of feathers that hemmed the capes of their nobility.[6] This Madonna then must have been a statue. By adorning it with indigenous attire, Cozumel's residents fashioned new layers of meaning for the woman brought by the conquistadors and thus made the statue their own.

Mesoamericans understood their divinities not as fixed and stable personalities, but rather as embodiments of "clusters of possibilities" that "mov[ed] in constant complex interaction."[7] The fluid cascade of divinity manifested itself in the Mesoamerican practice of transforming physical objects and living people into temporary dwelling places for the gods and their power. These *ixiptla*, to use the Nahuatl term that the Europeans translated as "representation" or "image," were made and unmade through ritual, especially ceremonies of dressing and ornamentation. Men and women could don the raiment of the gods and thus become them, at least for a period of time. Images, too, whether carved from stone or shaped from seed-paste kneaded into dough, could be changed from mere matter into *ixiptla* by rituals of dressing.[8]

The Franciscan Bernardino de Sahagún learned this in the mid-sixteenth century from the Nahua noblemen who were his informants as he compiled his famed encyclopedic work about native culture, the *Historia general de las cosas de la Nueva España*. These men recalled pre-conquest ceremonies at Tenochtitlan during which the Mexica priests "ornamented and clothed all the images....On each of [the images] they placed precious feather, necklaces, and turquoise masks and they dressed them in gods' garments, quetzal-feathers garments, yellow parrot feather garments, eagle feather garments."[9] The clothing that Cozumel's Maya chose for their Madonna may not have been quite this sumptuous. Yet by dressing the image, they applied to Mary their traditional mode of behavior toward divinity and began to draw her into their religious universe.[10]

This is not how the Spaniards who described the statue's dress at Cortés's trial understood the significance of their evidence. To be sure, conquistadors aboard the Spanish ships that anchored at Cozumel in the 1520s would have been accustomed to seeing clothed statues of Mary. The Madonnas they had knelt before in Spain could wear dresses and capes of silk or of the scarlet cloth called *grana* that belonged to the wardrobe of one Aragonese Madonna in 1501; the practice of clothing Christian devotional images reached back to the Middle Ages.[11] Yet even if Europeans dressed saints' images as richly as Mesoamericans did *ixiptla*, the significance of the practice differed. By clothing a Marian statue, Spaniards honored the mother of their god, but did not seek to transform sculpted wood or stone or metal into the Virgin herself. At Cortés's trial, detail about the dress of Cozumel's Madonna appeared in testimony intended to whitewash this conquistador's deeds by proving that he had brought New World peoples into the fold of Spanish rule—and faith. Witnesses cited Cozumel's Madonna as a hopeful sign that the Maya had embraced the religion to which Mary was so important.

Such hopes were not exactly well founded. Just because the Chontal Maya dressed their Madonna, they had not therefore converted to Christianity. Yet the ways that the native inhabitants of New Spain interpreted Mary for themselves and came to find meaning in her did belong to the messy, ambiguous, and prolonged processes by which Christianity became part of the indigenous world. Religious change in the aftermath of Spanish conquest was far more gradual and complex than the simple term "conversion" suggests, just like the rhythm of change in other arenas of life.[12]

Some native peoples of central Mexico described the conquest as a cosmic war that had terminated one cycle of time and given birth to another—a new sun, a new world.[13] The arrival of the Europeans in Mesoamerica indeed caused demographic disruption and massive sociocultural transformation. If the former was immediate and cataclysmic, the latter was much less so. For many people, the fabric of existence remained largely intact, woven from the old warp and weft, although in some new hues. Mesoamericans were used to absorbing conquerors and their culture. And for much of the sixteenth century, the Spaniards were a tiny minority, hardly able to impose their ways completely on the native population, even if they had wanted to. In some parts of New Spain, indigenous peoples were forcibly assembled and moved to new sites where the Spaniards found it easier to supervise them. But many other Indian communities largely stayed in the same places their ancestors had lived and were often governed by the same families who had exercised power before 1521. Especially in the first decades after the conquest, the Spaniards were content to leave the native elite more or less in place in order to ensure the smooth governance of this vast realm.[14] As one of the greatest modern historians of the colonial Nahua world has commented, "by the late eighteenth century, almost nothing in the entire indigenous cultural ensemble was left untouched, yet at the same time almost everything went back in some form or other to a preconquest antecedent."[15]

Religion was no exception. The allegiance of the indigenous to their traditional forms of religious expression and even to the gods of their ancestors hardly evaporated with the holy water that the friars flung over the heads of crowds of thousands of Indians, an efficient if theologically suspect method of mass baptism. There was resistance, overt and covert, to the new religion.[16] But there was acceptance, too, if not always quite as the Spanish hoped; the indigenous peoples often tailored Christianity to fit the familiar patterns of their world.[17] As they reshaped the new religion, it changed perhaps as much as they themselves did.

The missionaries themselves participated in Christianity's transformation. As these men in robes translated teachings about God, his son, and his mother into native tongues that their audiences could understand, the conceptual structures of these languages colored the missionaries' message in unintended ways.[18] Sometimes, in their fervor to harvest as many souls as quickly as possible, friars even deliberately allowed indigenous elements to enter the religion they presented to their rapidly expanding flocks. Hence the façades of the mendicant churches that began to cover New Spain were ornamented not only with images of Christ and the saints, but also with shapes recalling glyphs of the pre-Columbian native writing system: the sun, water, the sacred hill among them.[19]

In the New World, Mary slowly emerged as a figure reinterpreted to make sense to indigenous peoples, although still recognizably herself to European eyes.[20] The colonized Nahuas of central Mexico eschewed many of the hierarchical titles that Spaniards bestowed on her. They focused instead on what the Europeans told them about her nature as a loving mother, always ready to offer compassionate intercession. In this sympathetic yet powerful role, Mary helped these Indians learn how to negotiate a world where they increasingly had to rely on less heavenly mediators—colonial officials—to defend their interests before a remote monarch.[21] Hence one of the terms Nahuatl speakers came to prefer for the woman whom Spaniards often addressed as "Our Lady" was the more intimate *Totlaçonantzin,* "Our Precious Mother."[22]

The friars instructed the Indians in Mary's loving nature, but so, too, had some of the conquistadors in their own impromptu sermons. Exploring what native responses to the Virgin owed to the conquistadors' lay evangelism requires beginning in the first decades of the sixteenth century and then listening to reverberations that echoed as late as the seventeenth century. The indigenous people did not forget that Mary had often first entered their world in the company of men who bore guns and steel swords. By the second half of the sixteenth century, this memory would begin to color how some Nahuas described the conversion of their people to Christianity and the dawning of the new world cycle. As they made Mary their own, some of these men and women would call her La Conquistadora.

Accepting Mary

The earliest evidence of what the native peoples of New Spain thought of Mary comes through the dense filter of Spanish texts. Only after the 1540s did indigenous voices directly describe the contours of existence in the aftermath of the Spaniards' arrival. None of these voices belonged to the peoples of the Caribbean. They simply did not survive the demographic apocalypse begotten by European germs and forced hard labor in Spanish mines and plantations long enough for their oral cultures to become written ones. But for generations before the conquest and decades afterward, Nahuas recorded their history and their world in the vivid colors and bold shapes of pictographic narratives painted on bark paper or deerskin.[23] Few of these painted books remain from the 1520s and 1530s, and those that do show signs of having been reworked later. The gradual Europeanization so perceptible in the artistic style of these books was not the only impact that the Spanish presence had on native systems of writing. After the friars devised ways of transposing the language of central Mexico into Latin letters, alphabetic writing in Nahuatl began to appear, if only in earnest in the 1540s.[24] To understand the period before the 1540s requires careful reading of Spanish texts as well as indigenous ones that were composed later but looked back to those chaotic decades immediately following the coming of the Europeans.

According to the conquistadors, both in the Caribbean and on the mainland, the images of Mary they bestowed upon the native peoples were often well received, even eagerly welcomed. Conveniently bolstering these men's self-portrayal as successful evangelists, these optimistic depictions of New World peoples enthusiastically entering the path of conversion involved some wishful thinking. Tensions fissure these stories, allowing glimpses of the truth. Indigenous peoples' tendency to accept the images of Mary offered by the conquistadors did not spring from innate affection for Christianity or necessarily mean that they were becoming Christians. Instead, it revealed their ability to assimilate the Virgin into their own religious world.

Martin Fernández de Enciso, Peter Martyr, and Las Casas all described Cuba's Tainos as enthusiastically adopting the Madonnas given to them by Alonso de Hojeda at Cueíba and the nameless sailor at Cabo de Cruz.[25] Enciso and Las Casas even witnessed the thriving indigenous cults that had burgeoned around these images of Mary. As Enciso observed at Cabo de Cruz, the cacique Comendador had continued the practice instituted by the sailor of collective afternoon Marian prayers at the house sheltering the Madonna. For his part, Las Casas marveled at the "devotion and reverence" that the inhabitants of Cueíba felt for their painting of Mary. When he came to the village sometime shortly after Hojeda's departure in 1510, he saw cotton cloths adorning the "church" where the image was housed and noticed how well kept the building was.

Something else Las Casas saw suggested that the villagers' reverence for the painting owed much more to their own ways of thinking about the sacred than to the natural inclination to Christianity he so eagerly imagined in New World peoples: the Cueíbans composed songs for Mary and danced to these rhythms in her honor. During his years in the Caribbean, Las Casas certainly would have watched the Tainos perform such choreographed devotions for their *zemis*.[26] Yet this keen observer of native culture chose not to remark on the decidedly indigenous quality to this aspect of the Cueíbans' veneration of their Madonna.

Enciso was more honest, noting that the Tainos of Cabo de Cruz provided their image of Mary with food and drink, just as they traditionally did their *zemis*.[27] Recognizing just how much these people expected Mary to be like their deities, the conquistador even recollected that they asked the Christian priest who came ashore with him why she did not consume their offerings, as *zemis* did. When the cleric explained that churchmen ate on her behalf and helped himself to the dishes arrayed in front of her, the Tainos threatened to kill him. They willingly lavished food, however, on those members of Enciso's crew who sang the Ave Maria over and over at their request.[28]

The Tainos' own assumptions about divinity might have inclined them to understand these images delivered to their communities by outsiders as new *zemis*, if rather strange ones given the contrast between the two-dimensional portraits of Mary and the rounded surfaces of their traditional objects of worship. Taino communities were used to incorporating new *zemis* into their devotional life, for they had a practice of stealing these objects from each other.[29]

Something that happened to Las Casas during his visit to Cueíba suggested that the villagers suspected the Spanish shared this tradition.

Las Casas had apparently heard reports of the painting's exquisite beauty before arriving in Cueíba. He came to the village determined to make the image his own, planning to replace it with a different Flemish portrait of Mary. But when he made this proposal to Cueíba's cacique, the man's face darkened. That night, the Taino leader disappeared into the surrounding hills with the coveted image. The next day, when Las Casas asked the villagers to summon the cacique for mass, he learned that the man had hidden himself away with the painting to keep it from the Spaniards. The Tainos were unhappy and restive as they delivered this news. Hoping to prevent violence, Las Casas sent messages to the cacique reassuring him of the Spaniards' honorable intentions. Unwilling to risk losing the painting, he stayed away until the Spaniards were gone. Las Casas tells this as a story demonstrating the villagers' ardent if naïve devotion to Mary, but the cacique's fear that Las Casas would abscond with the image was no mark of innocent simplicity. It was a perfectly rational expectation, given the Taino tradition of *zemi* theft. Like the dances and songs composed for the Virgin, and the food and drink offered to her at Cabo de Cruz, it suggests that this image of Mary was entering the world of the *zemis*.

In Maya lands too, images of Mary left by conquistadors were treated with respect. The inhabitants of Cozumel not only clothed the statue of the Virgin that Cortés had enshrined in Ix Chel's temple, but kept it as "clean and beautifully adorned" as the conquistador had apparently instructed them to do. So said witnesses at Cortés's trial of 1529, echoed some decades later by Bernal Díaz del Castillo in his *Historia verdadera*.[30] These men all recalled how, in the spring of 1519, Cortés's little fleet had set sail from Cozumel, only to return to shore almost immediately when one of the ships began to founder and required repair. Back on the island, the Spaniards were delighted to find the Maya taking good care of the Madonna. Díaz adds the telling detail that incense burned in front of the statue—doubtless *pom*, the aromatic resin whose smoke perfumed the air for Maya gods. Caressed by the fragrant scent and draped in Maya dress, the statue had already escaped the Spaniards, although they did not know it.

In adopting a sacred image brought by these strangers, Cozumel's residents followed the Maya custom of accepting gods who arrived with outsiders.[31] And so caciques further along the Yucatan coast seem to have readily welcomed the image of Mary that Cortés gave them. These were the leaders of Putunchan, men whom the conquistadors had just defeated after draining days of battle, men who listened during the surrender ceremonies as Cortes spoke of god's mother, and watched as he gestured toward an image of her. Díaz remembered them declaring that this "great *tececiguata*...seemed very good to them, and [asking] that she be given to them to have in their town."[32]

It is unlikely that these Maya would actually have used the word *tececiguata*, for it came not from their language, but from Nahuatl. Though misspelling it rather badly, Díaz glossed it accurately enough as a term of respect for "important ladies in those lands."[33] During his long years in New Spain, he would have heard Nahuatl speakers honor women of high rank with this title, properly written as *teuccihuatl*.[34] Yet it appears that Nahuas did not commonly use this word for Mary, although occasionally they applied it to Malintzin, Cortés's translator and sometime mistress, who was just as indelibly associated with the Spaniards' arrival in central Mexico—and often linked to the Virgin.[35] The "Malia *teuccihuatl*" of one mid-sixteenth-century Nahuatl text might in fact be Mary, or it might be Malintzin.[36]

Perhaps Díaz introduced this term from an indigenous language into his story to burnish the dialogue with the sheen of veracity. Or maybe the caciques at Putunchan actually had used some similar word in Mayan that the old conquistador misremembered. In any case, it certainly impresses on Díaz's readers the idea that Mary instantly commanded the respect of the Maya, as she might indeed have. The conquistadors' victory celebration would have communicated to the caciques that the woman of the image was the author of the strangers' triumph and thus a powerful force whom the Maya would do well to have on their side.[37] It is even possible that the caciques at Putunchan really asked Cortés to give them the image of Mary.

The chronicler Gonzalo Fernández de Oviedo y Valdés had heard a similar story about indigenous leaders in Nahua lands from Alonso de Zuazo, a conquistador and distinguished jurist who came to the New World in 1517. In 1524, while Cortés was slogging his way through Honduras, Zuazo was appointed to the unenviable task of governing Mexico City in conjunction with several other equally power-hungry men. During his brief time in office, he had to deal not only with his co-governors' machinations, but also with the fallout from the newly arrived Franciscans' campaign to extirpate "idolatry" from the city's indigenous population—a daunting religious project, which Zuazo supported, but one that sparked the fires of rebellion among the Nahuas. His punishment of the revolt's ringleaders was brutal. He ordered some of these men drawn and quartered, while others were tossed to mastiffs imported from Spain.[38] Such is the grim background for the story about Mary he related to Oviedo.

Zuazo remembered how in the wake of these executions, a group of Nahua nobles engaged him in a lengthy debate over sacred images. They pressed him hard to explain why Christian images were permissible if native ones had to be smashed and burned. According to Zuazo, the Nahuas gave in to his logic, his religion, and his images. They requested baptism, agreed to renounce their "idols," and spontaneously promised to "love the image of Our Lady, Virgin Saint Mary." And so Zuazo gave them an image of the Madonna, which, he told

Oviedo, they enshrined in "their biggest temple and destroyed all the idols they had in it."[39]

As it appears in Oviedo's *Historia*, this anecdote is intended to showcase Zuazo's pacification of the Nahuas and his talents as a lay evangelist. Stripped of his hyperbole and self-aggrandizing, the tale perhaps reveals Nahuas who harbored a Marian-tinged understanding of Christianity that strongly—and not coincidentally—echoed the version of the faith that men like Cortés had presented to them. If Zuazo can be believed on this point, these Nahuas even followed the conquistadors' lead by themselves installing an image of the Virgin in one of their most important temples (probably not the Templo Mayor, largely dismembered during the siege of Tenochtitlan). That they destroyed their idols to make way for Mary seems less likely.

Zuazo also remembered these Mexica noblemen declaring a distinct prefer- ence for Mary over the Christian god. He says they asked for an image of her because "they did not understand God and his image very well." The radical monotheism of Christianity indeed was at first incomprehensible to the Nahuas, not because they were unable to grasp the notion of one god (in the Nahua world- view, one divine principle was responsible for the universe), but because they could not imagine this god would demand exclusive worship and outlaw the sac- rifices upon which the continuance of the world depended.[40] Zuazo explained the Nahuas' predilection for Mary in another story he told Oviedo vaunting his own management of indigenous affairs and promulgation of Christianity dur- ing Cortés's absence. According to Zuazo, he had settled a vicious land dispute between two prominent Nahuas of Mexico City so effectively that they decided the religion professed by such an astute man must be better than theirs. They had themselves baptized and then destroyed "many idols in all their lands, keep- ing in veneration only the image of Our Lady, who they said was the god of the Christians and was good and better than their idols."[41]

"The god of the Christians"—the phrase is telling. If Spanish accounts of Taino and Maya reception of the conquistadors' images of Mary implied that indigenous peoples at first understood her as a deity, these words proclaimed it. They also suggested the importance that the Marian evangelical efforts of Zuazo's peers had in shaping these peoples' earliest impression of Christianity. By the time Zuazo governed Mexico City, Nahuas could only have gotten the idea that images of Mary were god from the conquistadors. The Franciscans had just arrived, and in their fervor to wrest Indians from idol-worship, they hesitated to use Christian images as anything but a didactic aid, lest native neo- phytes discover in the new religion camouflage under which to continue banned practices.[42] But Nahuas who had listened as interpreters translated Cortés's ser- mons and had watched him gesture toward images of Mary might naturally have understood this woman as the primary focus of the Spaniards' devotion.

One conquistador apparently had even declared to the Indians in so many words that Mary was a god. According to Enciso, the nameless sailor who convalesced on Cuba's Cabo de Cruz told his Taino hosts that the Virgin was the "the god of the Christians and the mother of god."[43] An Inquisition tribunal surely would have considered this formulation heretical, but it is easy to imagine that an unlettered man might have resorted to such misleading shorthand as he strove to explain Mary's exalted place in the celestial hierarchy to people whose language he spoke imperfectly, if at all. He might even have believed what he said, for the distinction between Mary's powers and the divine ones of her son was not always clear to the average Spaniard.

Not only did missionaries have to fight against native religious beliefs and practices, but sometimes they also had to undo these misunderstandings about Mary created by the conquistadors. Motolinía remembered how shocked he and his fellow Franciscans were to arrive in Mexico in 1524 and find that the native peoples "thought that by saying [Mary's] name, they were saying God, and that they called all the images they saw Saint Mary." "We had to explain to them who Saint Mary really was," he wrote.[44] Another missionary, probably also a Franciscan, ran into similar problems among the Tarascans of Michoacán. "They called crosses Saint Mary...and they believed crosses were god," he noted sometime between the late 1530s and 1550.[45]

This friar implied that the Tarascans stopped mixing up the Virgin, the cross, and God after they had received Christian teachings from the missionaries. To theologically sophisticated Spaniards, this confusion over Mary's nature was a potentially grave perversion of Christianity that could not be allowed to persist. Oviedo assured his readers that the Mexica noblemen mentioned by Zuazo only thought Mary was a god "because at that time they were not as well instructed in matters relating to our Catholic faith as they are now."[46] Decades later, however, Fray Sahagún still felt the need to spell out for his Nahua flock the difference between the Virgin and the Christian god. In a set of spiritual exercises that this Franciscan composed in Nahuatl during the 1570s, the *Exercicio quotidiano*, he directed his charges to pray to Mary as follows: "You who are God's mother...I acknowledge that although you are God's mother, you are not God, not a deity; you are only the beloved creation of the only Deity, God."[47]

Sahagún had reason to be so direct. Even Don Domingo de San Antón Muñon Chimalpahin Quauhtlehuanitzin, the learned Nahua historian who in the early seventeenth century made the surviving copy of the friar's *Exercicio*, slipped once and wrote about an "image of our lord God called Our Lady of Soledad."[48] In 1582, a Nahua nobleman named Alvaro Vázquez recalled how, decades ago, Cortés had brought "a god named Saint Mary" to Tlaxcala.[49] Vázquez spoke in Nahuatl, but as his words were recorded only in the Spanish translation provided by a mestizo contemporary, it is not clear what term he used for "god."

Was it *teotl*, a word that Nahuas tended to reserve for God and rarely applied to Mary?[50] Or did he interrupt the flow of his Nahuatl with the Spanish word *dios*, as Chimalpahin did when calling Our Lady of Soledad an image of God? In any case, one of the terms Nahuas often used for Mary—*Totlaçonantzin* (Our Precious Mother)—not only captured the intense emotional kinship they felt with her, but also echoed a title that often graced God in Nahuatl texts."[51]

None of this is to say that in the second half of the sixteenth century, Nahuas worshipped Mary as God, or even as a direct stand-in for the goddesses of their past, though they may have done so sometimes. Rather, their lingering susceptibility to speaking of her as god-like owed something to the way she had first come into their world: with the conquistadors and in the form of images. During the earliest years of contact, a Nahua gazing at a statue or painting of Mary would not have understood it as a mere representation of a sacred figure; such a concept was as foreign as the Spaniards themselves. Instead, he or she might well have believed the image to be an *ixiptla*, that living dwelling place for divinity that could take so many shapes. For decades after the conquest, Nahuas most often referred to saints' images by using the Spanish term (*imagen*) and the Nahuatl one (*ixiptla*) together.[52] People used to the dynamic play of divinity that swirled through the Mesoamerican cosmos—as one god blended into another or took on radically different forms and different names—would have found it perfectly logical to call *all* images brought by the conquistadors with the word so often on these strangers' lips: Mary.[53]

Nahuas would have had even more reason to believe at first in Mary's divinity, given how inseparable images of her must have seemed from the conquistadors. So the strangers' words and gestures would have suggested to the Nahuas, a people for whom worship of the gods coincided with and expressed social and political loyalties. Each *altepetl*—the ethnic corporate grouping constitutive of the Nahua sense of self—boasted its own particular deity. As Motolinía wrote, "they have in each town an idol or demon which they especially honor and invoke, and they adorn it with many gems and much clothing."[54] The *altepetl*'s protector and patron, this god also embodied the greatness of its people, their authority and prestige.[55] They honored this deity with a temple, usually the most magnificent and prominent one built with the *altepetl*'s labor. The bond fusing a people with its special god was eloquently captured by the glyph of flames bursting from the side of a toppling temple, which was used in the Nahuas' painted books to express an *altepetl*'s defeat in battle.[56] This glyph often came to life in the cities and towns of central Mexico, as members of a conquered *altepetl* watched victors signal triumph by setting fire to the local temple.[57]

Surely to the Nahuas, Mary must have seemed like a god of the strangers' *altepetl* and a guardian of their identity. The Nahuas therefore knew what to do with her. Like the Maya, they had a tradition of assimilating other peoples' divinities, often in precisely the circumstances surrounding the Spaniards' arrival: political rivalries and warfare. Sometimes Nahuas triumphantly carried home from military expeditions the images of a conquered *altepetl*'s gods, after having forced their own special deity on the defeated. Men and women who had just watched their god's temple go up in flames could even willing accept a divinity that had proved its strength by leading its warriors to triumph, especially as embracing the new god did not mean casting off the old one, at least not until the Christians showed up.[58]

For all these reasons, the Nahua would have been inclined to accept the images of Mary given to them by the conquistadors. They could put the images brought by these new, powerful men in the same places in their temples where they were accustomed to guard their own sacred statues, as Zuazo reported. Whether the Mexica nobles actually destroyed their idols in 1524–1525, as he insisted, is not so clear. Even Cortés's most important native allies, the Tlaxcalteca, did not do so. Franciscans preaching the gospel in Tlaxcala in 1524 were repelled to find images of Mary and her son mingled with idols, the familiar European figures suddenly strange in the shadow of native statues—feathered serpents, staring faces, bodies circled with carved snakes. "Christians had given them these images [of Mary and Christ]," wrote Motolinía, "thinking that they would worship them alone," but the Tlaxcalteca had simply added the Virgin and her son to their pantheon. "As they already had a hundred gods, they wanted to have a hundred and one," he concluded.[59]

It is tempting to wonder if one of these Marian images dwelling among Tlaxcala's idols was the Madonna that Cortés had installed during the autumn of 1519, but there is not enough evidence to decide. Rather more is known about the Madonna that Cortés bestowed on the Mexica sometime during his stay in Tenochtitlan in 1519–1520. Her fate suggests that the indigenous peoples did not always peacefully accept the images of Mary brought by the conquistadors.

Indigenous Marian Politics

Given how keenly aware Nahuas were of the political weight of introducing strangers' gods into their own shrines, their treatment of Marian images became a barometer to their changing relationship with the conquistadors. If in 1524, Mexica nobles living amidst the rubble remains of Tenochtitlan expressed their submission to Zuazo's power by placing a Madonna in one of their surviving temples, rather different political weather had been foretold by the sufferings of some of her sisters several years earlier when the city's stately buildings still stood.

A detail that Cortés let slip in a letter composed in 1520 for his sovereigns suggests that as the Mexica's relations with their European guests soured and eventually degenerated into open hostility, images of Mary became as unwelcome as the conquistadors themselves. Writing just after the retreat from Tenochtitlan on the Noche Triste, Cortés described a sortie the conquistadors and their native allies had made during their final fraught months in the city. The fighting, he said, surged up and down the steep stone stairs of a temple that he called Mary's "house"; he wrote that an image of her had been placed there sometime earlier. Yet when he and his men slashed their way to the temple's summit, forcing Mexica warriors to leap off its sides, they found that the image had vanished, presumably removed by the Mexica. To press his advantage, Cortés set the temple on fire.[60]

Cortés did not indicate when this Madonna had been expelled from the temple's shrine room, nor what happened to her afterward. Perhaps he did not know or did not wish to share this information with his sovereigns. He made remarkably little of the image's disappearance, for the Virgin's removal from the temple marred the portrait of willing indigenous proto-converts that he wanted to present to his monarch. It belied his detailed report in the same letter of how Moctezuma and the other leading men of Tenochtitlan earlier had docilely allowed the Spaniards to purge the Templo Mayor of its "idols" and to install images of Mary and other saints in its shrine rooms. Mexica who evicted images of the Virgin were engaged in a Marian politics of their own, countering that of the Spaniards—a politics of rejection that Cortés understandably was reluctant to highlight.

This shrine that so briefly housed the Marian image may have been Tenochtitlan's Templo Mayor.[61] Other evidence, in any case, strongly suggests that even before the outbreak of armed conflict with the Spaniards, the Mexica were intent on removing the Madonna from the home the conquistadors had tried to create for her in the city's most important and imposing temple. The Mexica's desire to eject the image of Mary from the Templo Mayor had in fact precipitated the hostilities, claimed Pedro de Alvarado, one of Cortés's lieutenants. Alvarado made this assertion in 1529 as he related his version of the tragedy that had unfolded in Tenochtitlan nine years earlier, when Cortés had left him in charge of matters in the city.

Alvarado described how he had observed the Mexica begin the preparations for the festival of Toxcatl, when the city's residents would assemble in throngs on the broad expanse of the Templo Mayor's patio and a young man who for a year had been feted as an *ixiptla* of the god Tezcatlipoca would end his reign under the obsidian blade of sacrifice in a shrine some fifteen miles away.[62] Alvarado's interest in the proceedings, which included the fashioning of a massive statue of Huitzilopochtli from seed paste and vegetables, soon turned to alarm. He saw stakes being erected in the Templo's patio and learned from native informants that their sharp points were intended for him and the other Spaniards—the Mexica customarily hung the skulls of sacrificial victims from such poles in the sacred precincts.[63] Warriors, Alavardo heard, were gathering with the express purpose of killing the conquistadors. According to his informants, the Mexica would celebrate the Spaniards' death with the overthrow of the Templo Mayor's Madonna and then would raise the statue of Huitzilopochtli in her place. Moctezuma personally urged Alvardo to come watch "how they would lift Huitzilopochtli up into the mosque and would hurl Our Lady from there." The conquistador mustered his men and went to the temple to defend Mary from the crowds who had gathered in anticipation of Huitzilopotchli's triumph over her.[64]

Alvarado made this declaration to a court of law in 1529. He was on trial, facing a long list of charges of misconduct, cruelty, and abuse of power. One of the accusations he worked hard to counter regarded his leading role in the infamous slaughter of the Mexica at the festival of Toxcatl—Alvarado and his men had massacred hundreds of unarmed men and women that day. To justify why he had taken such drastic action, Alvarado spun for his judges a story that cast him as a hero fighting to rescue the Virgin from idolaters and to save Spanish lives.

As tendentious as Alvarado's narrative is, it is probably true that the Mexica longed to restore Huitzilopochtli to the shrine room usurped by Mary. No fewer than six men were willing to swear under oath that the conquistador's version of events was correct, most of them claiming to have been eyewitnesses.[65] One remembered having seen sooty fingerprints smeared on the Madonna—evidence that the image had been handled by Mexica priests, who typically daubed themselves with ashes when officiating at rituals.[66] Even a witness hostile to Alvarado, Bernardino Vázquez de Tapia, gave evidence confirming that the Mexica wanted to reinstate Huitzilopochtli to his rightful place (he also said that they did not carry out their plan).[67]

The indigenous noblemen of Tenochtitlan-Tlatelolco, however, who shared their memories of the Spaniards' arrival with Sahagún in the mid-sixteenth century, did not mention any effort made during the Toxcatl festival or later to dislodge the European intruder from Huitzilopochtli's shrine.[68] Nor did the Nahuatl chronicle known as the *Anales de Tlatelolco*, produced in the same period by men from the Tlatelolco area of Mexico City.[69] Such silence could mean that there actually had been no struggle over sacred images, or it could mean that these people chose not to remember the episode. The indigenous shaped and managed the history of Tenochtitlan's fall as intensely as the Spaniards did.[70] In their post-conquest accounts of the Toxcatl massacre, the Mexica took pains to portray themselves as the noble victims of Alvarado's unjustified aggression, a picture of clear innocence that would have been marred by any suggestion of stubborn adherence to what Sahagún's informants called "devil-worship." By the mid-sixteenth century, the Christianized Mexica would have found it convenient to forget they had conspired to eliminate an image of Mary ensconced in their city by the conquistadors. Why deliberately remind anyone of how, decades ago, the faith that now held sway in Mexico had been so rudely scorned in Tenochtitlan? Doing so only would make the Mexica of the past seem as bad as the Jews, people who had willfully rejected the Christian truth. Better to remember themselves as having been pagans, people who simply had not yet found the path out of spiritual darkness provided by "Our Precious Mother" and her son. Hence the Mexica nobles who worked with Sahagún did not speak at all about the conquistadors' evangelism at Tenochtitlan or even hint that Cortés had put an image of Mary in the Templo Mayor.

The Tlaxcalteca, however, members of that powerful *altepetl* without whose military support the Spaniards never would have been able to bring down Tenochtitlan, would nurture a post-conquest memory of the Mexica as having destroyed an image of Mary during the violent aftermath of the Toxcatl massacre. Such is the message of a scene in the so-called *Lienzo de Tlaxcala*, a magnificent pictorial narrative painted by the Tlaxcalteca in the mid-sixteenth century to showcase the many times they had marched into battle at the conquistadors' side.[71] Though the *Lienzo* exists today only in the form of eighteenth- and nineteenth-century copies, something of the energetic movement that must have coursed through the original versions still vibrates in these schematic drawings. In one scene, the Tlaxcalteca and the Spaniards gather in their quarters at Tenochtitlan after the Toxcatl massacre (Figure 8.1).[72] Mexica warriors surround the building, their heavy war clubs drawn back, poised to strike. The attack has in fact already been launched, for flames leap from two Christian images. Both are framed paintings, one of Mary and the other of her son's passion.

These fiery images could represent a Tlaxcalteca memory of a real event witnessed during the struggle with the Mexica. Or perhaps the flaming images serve instead as a visual code reminiscent of the burning temple glyph, an improvised symbol for the defeat of the Spaniards and their *altepetl*. In either case, the Tlaxcalteca artists must have enjoyed sketching the fire that consumes these images of Mary and her son. Its flames branded the Mexica, the Tlaxcalteca's long hated enemies, as the foes too of Christianity and the conquistadors.[73] In contrast, the *Lienzo* depicted the Tlaxcalteca as having been willing converts, the Spaniards' faithful allies—and Mary's enthusiastic devotees—from the very first moment of contact. By the mid-sixteenth century, memories of the Virgin's arrival with the conquistadors could thus be tinted to express intense inter-*altepetl* rivalries and hostilities that endured deep into colonial period, as well as advantageous proximity to the Spaniards.[74] Another kind of indigenous Marian politics was emerging, in which the Virgin would gradually be acknowledged not just as "Our Precious Mother," but also as the powerful patron of battle who had watched over the Spaniards and their native allies during the long years of conquest. This too was part of the process by which the indigenous peoples made Mary their own.

Figure 8.1 An image of Mary and one of the Passion burn outside a building in
Tenochtitlan occupied by the Spaniards and Tlaxcalteca, while the Mexica attack.
Lienzo de Tlaxcala: Manuscrito pictórico mexicano de mediados del siglo XVI, ed. Próspero
Cahuantzi. Mexico City, 1939. Plate 10. Anne S. K. Brown Military Collection, Brown
University Library.

Native Marian Conquistadors

Sermons, catechisms, devotional manuals, and other texts of formal religious
instruction composed in Nahuatl in the sixteenth and early seventeenth centuries reveal no trace of the Virgin who watched over the conquistadors and led
them to bloody victories over native peoples.[75] Nor is the military Mary any
more apparent in those narratives of Tenochtitlan's fall related to Fray Sahagún
in elegant Nahuatl by elderly Mexica noblemen late in the sixteenth century.[76]
Yet this does not mean that the indigenous peoples of New Spain felt no affinity
for the Virgin in her more warlike manifestations. Latin and Spanish doctrinal
and devotional texts from the eleventh through the sixteenth centuries themselves rarely mention the Virgin of the battlefield who was so familiar to men
like Alfonso X and Enciso. On neither side of the Atlantic were these the literary
genres in which she tended to appear. As for Sahagún's informants, they were
men whose *altepetl* had been humiliated by the Spaniards. They would have had
little reason to want to associate "Our Precious Mother" with painful memories

of the war that had left their city in ruins.[77] The same was not true for those *alte-petl* that had provided the thousands of warriors who fought side by side with the conquistadors, assuring the victories that led to the expansion of the Spanish empire across Mesoamerica. The era of conquest meant something rather different for them.[78]

These *indios amigos*, as the Spaniards typically called them, came from *alte-petl* like Tlaxcala, Cempoala, Huexotzinco, and Chalco.[79] Sometimes they were pressed into service, accompanying the conquistadors into battle only reluctantly or even against their will. But just as often they were glad to join forces with the Spanish, whether to widen their own domains or simply to renew long-standing hostilities with other *altepetl*. Mesoamerica was no peaceful Eden when the Spaniards arrived. Rather, it was a warrior's paradise, where *altepetl* fought *altepetl* according to rituals different from European rules of engagement, but ones that left the landscape no less scarred.[80] No super-*altepetl* "Indian" identity existed that would have inspired the native peoples to make common cause against the strangers.[81] Instead, if the conquistadors exploited as best they could the rivalries and enmities with which the Mesoamerican political scene was riven, the native peoples often adroitly used the Spaniards as a new pawn on the chessboard. During the long decades of conquest, various *altepetl* willingly contributed men to military campaigns that they saw as furthering their own interests as much as those of the conquistadors.

Enthusiasm would eventually wane, especially when it became apparent that the Spaniards were reluctant to recompense indigenous war captains' services with the grants of land that victorious Mesoamerican leaders traditionally bestowed upon their warriors.[82] But often these native conquistadors prided themselves on the feats of arms that they accomplished during their expeditions with the Spaniards; after all, long before the Europeans' arrival, valor reigned among the virtues that defined the male elite in many Mesoamerican societies.[83] Individual warriors who fought alongside the Spanish could vaunt their own deeds, as did the Chalco lord Francisco de Sandoval Acazitli in his account of a campaign into western Mexico in 1541.[84] The relentlessly corporate nature of Nahua social identity also asserted itself in this realm. By the mid-sixteenth century, the elite members of *altepetl* like Huexotzinco and Tlaxaca elaborated expansive narratives casting their own people as the Spaniards' valiant allies who had provided the Europeans with warriors and supplies for campaign after campaign—and had even welcomed the newcomers' religion, immediately seeking baptism.

In the experiences and memories of these native conquistadors, one might logically expect to find the military Mary, albeit in indigenous translation. The warriors of these *altepetl* would have had ample opportunity to observe how their European companions at arms related to the Virgin. In the very early years of contact, for example, *indios amigos* must have thought that the divine forces invoked by their Spanish allies were as hungry for the blood of warriors as were their own gods and goddesses, although once they gained a more sophisticated understanding of Christianity (and of Spanish military strategy), they would have realized that the new god and his mother demanded the death of his enemies not on the stone of sacrifice, but on the battlefield. In the clamor of combat, they had heard the Spaniards shout out the names of figures whom first the conquistadors and then the friars urged them to venerate—"Dios!" or "Santa María!" or "Santiago!" They would also have noticed the war banners adorned with images of the conquistadors' holy protectors. When sixteenth-century Nahua artists drew scenes illustrating the wars that had led to Tenochtitlan's destruction, they made sure to include pennants flying over the Spaniards' heads.[85]

The Nahuas surely recognized the Spaniards' banners as battle standards, for many Mesoamerican peoples marched to war using something similar. Typically fashioned from feathers, Mesoamerican standards were attached to a harness and strapped to the body. In the *Lienzo de Tlaxcala*, they sway and dip with the movements of the native warriors who accompany the conquistadors into battle. Like the Spaniards' banners, the indigenous standards served both as highly visible signals during combat maneuvers and as colorful statements of corporate identities. Among the Mexica, each sub-group of warriors had its own standard, representing the section of the *altepetl* these men belonged to, while the army as a whole fought under the *tlatoani*'s sumptuous standard, its hammered gold ornaments competing with the blue-green iridescence of its quetzal feathers to catch the sunlight.[86] Men used to glancing up as they swung their war clubs to watch the feathered standard of their group would have well been able to understand the significance of the Spaniards' own banners. So they learned that the cross and the Virgin, as well as other saintly figures, were the signs of the Spanish warriors.

The leaders of the Huexotzinco *altepetl* who late in the 1520s had to sell twenty slaves in order to purchase the materials to make an extravagant war standard for the infamous conquistador Nuño Beltrán de Guzmán certainly grasped Mary's role as a battle patron. At Guzmán's command, Huexotzinca artists fashioned an image of her from the gold and feathers acquired by the sale of the slaves. Evidence given by members of the *altepetl* during a lawsuit against the conquistador in 1531 suggests that this banner must have been stunning.[87] According to the Huexotzinca testimony, it measured more than half an arm's length in both height and width. Nine plumed crests, each consisting of twenty "large and opulent feathers," formed a border around a field of gold.[88] Although the Huexotzinca witnesses did not describe how Mary herself was depicted, they drew the banner in a picture documenting the excessive tribute that Guzmán had squeezed from their community (Figure 8.2).

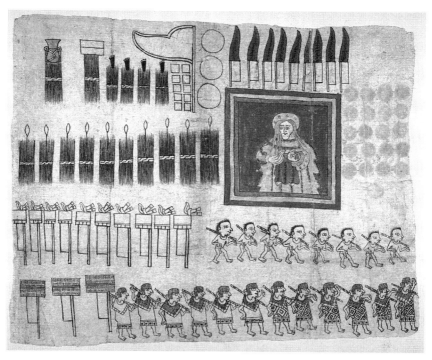

Figure 8.2 War banner decorated with an image of Mary made by members of the *altepetl* of Huexotzinco, painted next to other tribute demanded by Nuño de Guzmán. Huexotzinco Codex, 1531. Harkness Collection. Library of Congress, Washington, DC.

One of the earliest extant images of Mary created by any New World peoples, this small sketch of the war standard is recognizably European in its iconography, but follows a distinctly indigenous visual idiom, a combination that probably appeared on the banner itself.[89] Guzmán would have told the Huexotzinca artists what he wanted the mother and child to look like. Maybe they even already knew how to make images of Mary imitating ones imported from Spain; by 1525, indigenous artists were being trained in European painting styles.[90] But at Huexotzinco, they used native materials and their own techniques to produce a banner not so dissimilar from their own war standards.

The Huexotzinca knew Guzmán intended the banner for battle, for the witnesses of 1531 recalled how the conquistador had demanded this "image of Saint Mary made from gold in order to take it to war with him."[91] Guzmán had ordered the banner in 1530 as he prepared for an expedition into the area of western Mexico that would become New Galicia. When he set off, warriors from Huexotzinco whom he had forced into service marched alongside the Spanish contingents.[92] Perhaps these Huexotzinca eyed the feather and gold image of the Madonna with bitterness, for it was tangible evidence of Guzmán's abusive governance of their *altepetl*. Yet it depicted a woman whom they may have hoped would use her powers on their behalf. From the Franciscans who had established a large mission at Huexotzinco in 1525, the people of this *altepetl* had learned about Mary's boundless love for her devotees and the refuge she provided for her spiritual children beset by dangers like those threatening the men accompanying Guzmán; vicious armed conflict, violent storms, floods, and severe food shortages made the expedition so nightmarish that many *indios amigos* committed suicide when he refused to let them turn back. If the woman on the banner could watch over Spanish warriors, perhaps she could extend her protection over men from the *altepetl* that had spent so much to make this image.

During the campaign, the Huexotzinca may have bent their backs to a task that also would have impressed on them the connection between Mary and war: the building of a chapel for her on the hilltop site of a hard-won victory.[93] Or perhaps this heavy labor fell to men from Tlaxcala, another *altepetl* that contributed warriors to Guzmán's campaign. By the time the Tlaxcalteca war captains left for western Mexico with him, they were well aware of the association the Spanish saw between Mary and martial victory and may even have come to share this mind-set. A decade earlier, when Tlaxcalteca warriors had strode back into Tlaxcala, weary but triumphant after interminable months of fighting the Mexica, they had carried with them a Marian emblem of the resounding military success they had just achieved at Tenochtitlan with their Spanish allies. So three elderly Tlaxcalteca nobles remembered in 1582.[94]

These men recalled how, as young boys in 1521, they had watched with admiration as the Tlaxcalteca war captains returned laden with the spoils of battle including "great quantities of featherwork and painted mantles" plundered from Tenochtitlan's treasures. The boys' eyes had been especially drawn to Acxotecatl Cocomitzi, son-in-law to one of the *altepetl's tlatoque* (rulers) and a war captain who had been of invaluable aid to Cortés, as the special prize he brandished among his war trophies announced: a statue of the Virgin, or as one of the old men described it in 1582, "a god named Saint Mary" that Cortés had bestowed upon Tlaxcala.[95] Another witness recounted having heard Acxotecatl explain that "Cortés had given [the Tlaxcalteca war captains] this statue to take to this city and that they should keep it there as the most precious jewel he could give them because they had carried it with them during the whole conquest."

Acxotecatl had treated this Madonna with great care, or so the Tlaxcalteca elders would recount in 1582. They remembered how he kept the statue in his house and surrounded it with offerings of "painted mantles" and fragrant blossoms, thus drawing Mary into the world of the sacred that Nahuas believed bloomed from the petals of flowers.[96] When Axcotecatl went to festivals and dances, he brought the statue with him, carrying it in his hands "like a most precious object." This was exactly the sort of pride that Christianized Nahuas

later would typically take in saints' images, displaying them in public and tending them at home, as well as in churches, with attentive devotion.[97] It is perfectly possible that Acxotecatl made offerings to the image he probably believed
was an *ixiptla* of his Spanish allies' god—already in the 1530s, the Tlaxcalteca
brought to Christian feast days a profusion of flowering boughs and the richest *mantas* they could find.[98] Acxotecatl might also have considered this exotic
object an enhancement of his personal and political prestige, as Nahua nobility
would the Spanish insignia of rank—clothes and titles—that they were quick to
appropriate.[99]

There is, in any case, little reason to question the reliability of the Tlaxcaltecas'
boyhood recollections when it comes to the most important feature of their
story: that by 1521, their *altepetl* possessed a statue of Mary symbolizing the
defeat of Tenochtitlan and the military alliance with the Spanish. After all, these
old men told their stories in 1582 under oath, and Diego de Rangel, the friar
then in charge of the Franciscan convent in Tlaxcala, willingly confirmed the
substance of their testimony.[100] Cortés had indeed handed out Marian images to
his native allies in conjunction with his evangelical efforts. Had the old men's tale
emerged more from legend than history, it is also unlikely that Acxotecatl would
have figured as the attentive guardian of this Madonna. His posthumous reputation among Tlaxcalteca and Spaniards alike was just too dark.

Acxotecatl was a notorious idolater. So violently did he reject the Christian
god's demand for exclusive worship that he brutally murdered his own son
when the boy, under the sway of the Franciscans, tried to persuade him of the
evils of the old gods.[101] Acxotecatl was executed for his crimes in 1527, along
with three other prominent Tlaxcalteca leaders also accused of idolatry, while
his son, Cristóbal, was proclaimed a martyr. Repeated by Franciscan friars and
Tlaxcalteca chroniclers alike, the tale of Acxotecatl's heinous sin and Cristóbal's
holy death epitomized the bitter conflict over Christianity, which repeatedly
pitted Nahua boys educated by the friars against their elders.[102] In 1582, the
Tlaxcalteca men did not mention the shadow that lay over Acxotecatl's name,
though they surely knew of it. Members of the generation of Tlaxcalteca elite
youths co-opted by missionaries and raised as Christian zealots, these men
would have had little reason to try to rehabilitate his reputation. It is far more
probable that Acxotecatl features in their recollections simply because Cortés
really had given him the statue of Mary, as awkward a truth as that was.[103]

Acxotecatl did not enjoy possession of the Madonna for long, as the
Tlaxcalteca witnesses of 1582 remembered. When the Franciscans arrived in
1524 to spread the gospel in Tlaxcala, they were scandalized to find this image
in his home. Whether because they had caught the scent of idolatry, or simply
wanted to exercise control over such an important image, they confiscated the
Madonna and moved her to their improvised convent in the palace belonging

to Acxotecatl's father-in-law, the *tlatoani* Maxixcatzin. In her new location, this Virgin's importance to the Tlaxcalteca only increased. The old men remembered how, late in the 1520s, when rain clouds repeatedly failed to gather over the high volcanic sierra just beyond the city, endangering Tlaxcala's usually abundant harvest of beans, corn, and chili, the friars had processed through the streets with the statue, imploring Mary to end the drought.[104] Even before the ritual ended, fat rain drops began to fall. "From then on the [Tlaxcateca] had great faith in the image," declared one of the 1582 witnesses. When some years later, the Franciscan Juan de Rivas took this Madonna with him on a preaching mission only to return without her, the *altepetl*'s leaders were disturbed to learn that she had been left in far away Chocamán, a place feared among Spaniards for its "tigers and lions."[105]

The Tlaxcalteca had never seen this Madonna again, according to the testimony of 1582, but remembered exactly what she looked like. Little more than a foot high, the statue was gilded and brightly painted. Mary held her son in her arms and wore a removable crown. The aging Tlaxcalteca nobles also remembered the statue's name. This Madonna whose presence in Tlaxcala was the fruit of the *altepetl*'s military partnership with the Spaniards was called La Conquistadora. The testimony of 1582 seems to be the earliest written evidence of this distinctly martial title being used for Mary anywhere in the Spanish world. The Tlaxcalteca witnesses imply that they learned her name from the Franciscans, but even if the title originated in a Spanish milieu, it did not remain there. In 1582, the indigenous nobles called the statue "Santa María Conquistadora" and remembered other Tlaxcalteca as having done so decades ago. Their account suggests that she might have received her name shortly after the Franciscans removed her from Acxotecatl's possession.

A Virgin called Conquistadora was a fitting ornament for the proud self-image that the Tlaxcalteca elite forged during the years between Acxotecatl's death and the testimony of 1582. Through text and image, they articulated a portrait of themselves as an *altepetl* of native conquistadors—the loyal and Christian allies of the Spaniards, and their equals not their subordinates. With this expansive vision, the Tlaxcalteca created a history that was illustrious and eminently usable, as did other *altepetl* of *indios amigos* who shared the dispiriting experience of discovering that alliance with the Spaniards had not resulted in the expected rewards.[106]

In their increasingly desperate struggles to gain the recompense and respect they believed were their due, such *altepetl* invoked the power of the past. In a letter of 1560 to Phillip II, the *cabildo* (town council) of Huexotzinco begged the monarch to reconsider the crushing tribute payments he had levied on their *altepetl*. They reminded him that they were native conquistadors who had repeatedly seconded the Spanish in the conquests of other Indians and who (or so they said) had embraced Christianity the moment the Franciscans set foot in the *altepetl*'s territory. Given their long history as courageous Christian *indios amigos*, the new tribute requirement was an unjust imposition.[107]

For much of the sixteenth century, Tlaxcala, an *altepetl* that had contributed at least as many warriors as Huexotzinco to Spanish military efforts in Mesoamerica, would flood the court far across the ocean with such petitions and ambassadors.[108] Like the Huexotzinca, the Tlaxcalteca appealed to the king for privileges and exemptions, citing their early alliance with Cortés and carefully reworking history to create a narrative of prompt, wholehearted conversion to Christianity. By the mid-sixteenth century, the Tlaxcalteca and the Huexotzinca openly competed for Spanish favor, each *altepetl* striving to construct the more glorious conquest history for itself and to efface the role played by any other as *indios amigos*. As might be expected from a people who slurred their rivals, the Mexica, as having set fire to an image of Mary during the conquest, the Tlaxcalteca made much of their own love as *indios amigos* for this woman who they knew was so important to their Spanish allies and to the faith they now prided themselves on having adopted so quickly.

The *Lienzo de Tlaxcala* vividly demonstrates just how consciously Tlaxcala's elite integrated Mary into their revisionist history of their own career as native conquistadors. There were several versions of this chronicle-in-images of the Tlaxcalteca-Spanish alliance. One may have ornamented the walls of the *cabildo*'s spacious meeting hall in Tlaxcala, where it would have reminded the *altepetl*'s leading men of their community's distinguished history as they conducted their business.[109] Another was probably made to be sent across the Atlantic as part of a dossier intended to prove the Tlaxcaltecas' worth to the king.[110] By the time that Nahua artists, working under the close supervision of the *cabildo* sometime between 1550 and 1564, outlined the *Lienzo*'s eighty-eight scenes on a large cotton sheet, the Tlaxcalteca elite had figured out how best to remind the Spaniards of what loyal *indios amigos* were owed. In an earlier pictorial history of the conquest, they had depicted their partnership with the conquistadors in traditionally Mesoamerican terms as a relationship founded on the transfer of Tlaxcalteca noble women to the new allies. In the *Lienzo*, these women still are given away, but scene after scene proclaims the Tlaxcalteca as *indios amigos* by highlighting the qualities that the Spaniards valued in native allies: loyal military support and rapid conversion to Christianity.[111] Mary appears on both sides of this diptych of the Tlaxcalteca conquistadors.

Chronicling the destruction of the old cycle of time through the cosmic warfare unleashed by the Tlaxcalteca-Spanish partnership, the *Lienzo* explicitly announces the birth of a new sun, an era in which Mary symbolizes the *altepetl*'s central position and its privilege.[112] One of the earliest scenes depicts

a key moment in this process—the Tlaxcalteca's conversion to Christianity.
Flanked by frames depicting first the establishment of the military alliance
with the Spaniards and then Tlaxcalteca warriors' fierce slaughter of other
natives on behalf of their new allies, it shows the *altepetl's* four *tlatoque* receiving the eucharist while Cortés, another conquistador, and Malintzin look on
approvingly (Figure 8.3). Although this event doubtless occurred some time
later than the *Lienzo* claims, it is deliberately used to cast a Christian aura over
the Tlaxcalteca-Spanish alliance from its inception—and over all the battle
sequences in which the *altepetl's* warriors assist or, more often, lead the Spaniards
during a long string of military campaigns.[113] When in these subsequent frames
the Tlaxcalteca battle other Indians, they do so haloed by their leaders' conversion, even as Christian crusaders.[114]

Mary is the midwife for the spiritual birth of these native Christian conquistadors and the new Christian world cycle.[115] In the conversion scene, a large
image of the Madonna holding her son occupies center stage, demanding the
viewer's attention in a way that the smaller crucifix held up by Cortés does not.
The *Lienzo's* artists placed this image of Mary directly above the four *tlatoque*

Figure 8.3 Conversion of Tlaxcalteca tlatoque. *Lienzo de Tlaxcala: Manuscrito pictórico
mexicano de mediados del siglo XVI,* ed. Próspero Cahuantzi. Mexico City, 1939. Plate
3. Anne S. K. Brown Military Collection, Brown University Library.

who kneel before the Christian priest and the eucharistic wafer he holds over their heads. Diego Muñoz Camargo, a mestizo man who often wrote in the language of his Spanish father but could be fiercely loyal to his mother's Tlaxcalteca blood, gave voice to the Marian sentiment behind this scene in the version of Tlaxcala's history he composed in the 1580s.[116] The *tlatoque* decided to convert, Muñoz Camargo wrote, "because they were determined to believe in God and in Saint Mary, his most holy mother." The accompanying illustration is a less elegant version of the scene in the *Lienzo*. Muñoz Camargo continues: "When this general conversion to the honor and glory of Our Lord God and his most blessed virgin mother, Saint Mary, had been accomplished, [the Tlaxcalteca] began to hurl their idols down on the ground."[117]

Motolinía and the other Franciscans who worked to bring the Tlaxcalteca into the Christian fold would have been rather surprised by Muñoz Camargo's assurance that upon the conquistadors' arrival, his forebears had wholeheartedly renounced their idols in favor of Mary and the Christian god. During the friars' first years at Tlaxcala, they not only found images of Jesus and his mother among well-preserved idols, but also realized that native priests of the old religion were trying to rally the *altepetl* to reject these interloper gods. Motolinía tells a disturbing story of an indigenous priest who, adorned as the *ixiptla* of the Tlaxcalteca god of wine, proclaimed that any Tlaxcalteca who had angered this divinity by deserting his "house" for "Saint Mary's" would die. The priest was stoned to death by a band of young Tlaxcalteca boys being raised as Christians by the Franciscans. As the friars' protégés heaped rocks onto the bloody corpse, they shouted that now all the people would "see that [this priest] had been no god, and that God and Saint Mary are good"—another gruesome episode in the war between generations.[118]

The revisionist versions of Tlaxcala's conversion smoothed away such times when Mary and Christ's demands for exclusive worship had been pitted against loyalty to native gods. Muñoz Camargo was as aware as the *cabildo* members who had supervised the *Lienzo*'s creation that their cause would be well served by a version of history in which their people's conversion did not await the friars' arduous labor, but instead coincided with the coming of the Spanish conquistadors.[119] Perhaps these Tlaxcalteca's insistence that the Virgin had presided over their transformation into Christian conquistadors was a much reworked memory of the Marian gestures of Cortés and company at Tlaxcala in 1519: the sermon explaining the Virgin's importance followed by the installation of her image in the temple granted by the *tlatoque* to the conquistadors.[120] It was, in any case, logical for Tlaxcalteca to believe in the mid-sixteenth century that their community had converted in Mary's honor, for by then she was the *altepetl*'s patron saint and a symbol of its corporate identity—the era of conflict captured in Motolinía's macabre story was over.

Perhaps when the Franciscans moved out of their temporary quarters in 1527 and construction began on a purpose-built church, they exhorted Tlaxcala's leaders to elect Mary as the *altepetl*'s Christian celestial guardian; as the walls of a church rose in an indigenous town, friars often pushed the Indian community to take a patron saint.[121] For the Tlaxcalteca, Mary would have been the obvious choice, since the new church bore her name—"Our Lady of the Assumption," Motolinía calls it.[122] Yet the Tlaxcalteca told the story of how they acquired her patronage rather differently, ignoring the friars to privilege the *altepetl*'s military alliance with the Spanish conquistadors.

Mary occupies the center of the scene heading the *Lienzo*, a tableau depicting the *altepetl*'s identity and political structure as a cosmogram, a diagram of the world (Figure 8.4).[123] Each of Tlaxcala's four *tlatoque* stands below traditional glyphs indicating the number of lordly houses belonging to his territory. A retinue of richly attired nobles follows each *tlatoani*. Forming an inner circle are the Spanish authorities who wield power over the *altepetl*: viceroys, bishops, and members of the first and second Audiencias. Like the Tlaxcalteca, they face toward the middle, where a vertical row of emblems reveals the core of this *altepetl*'s colonial self-image and worldview. Among them is the military Mary.

Right in the middle of this central line sits an enlarged version of the glyph used in the Nahuas' painted books for an *altepetl*, a triangular-shaped hill, which gives shape to the word's literal meaning of "water mountain."[124] The glyph captured the coincidence between *altepetl* and guardian god, for Mexico's abundant rugged sierras and volcanic mountains were believed to be dwelling places of deities, a sacred geography deliberately echoed by the pyramidal forms of Mesoamerican temples.[125] But no indigenous deity lives in the *Lienzo*'s water mountain. Mary keeps watch over this *altepetl* of native conquistadors. Framing the diminutive portrait of her tucked into the stylized hill is a sketch of a church façade, a composition suggesting the new colonial version of the old indigenous trio of *altepetl*, temple, and deity.[126]

Mary's patronage of her *altepetl* is lent a distinctly martial hue by another sign of corporate identity adopted from the Spaniards and contained within the hill glyph: Tlaxcala's coat of arms, granted by Charles V in 1535 at the urging of a delegation that traveled to court to petition him for material recognition of the community's military services. By twinning this emblem with the Virgin, the *Lienzo*'s artists transformed the traditional *altepetl* glyph into a Marian monument to Tlaxcalteca Christian valor. The military dimension is further amplified by the sketch below, depicting a cross's miraculous appearance on the spot where the Tlaxcalteca and the conquistadors first met, and by the Habsburg coat of arms emblazoned above. In 1535, in recognition of the *altepetl*'s military support, Charles V had awarded Tlaxcala the coveted privilege of displaying the royal shield.[127]

Figure 8.4 Opening scene of the *Lienzo de Tlaxcala*. Mesolore.org.

Each of these elements offers the *Lienzo*'s viewers proof of Tlaxcala's much vaunted military alliance with the Spaniards. Time is collapsed, rendering the Tlaxcalteca's adoption of Mary as their patron simultaneous with their warm reception of Cortés and, by implication, the establishment of their partner-ship with him and the foundation of the new world order. "Mary presided over our alliance with the Spaniards," a learned Tlaxcalteca might have said as he explained the *Lienzo* to his indigenous audience; the reading of a *lienzo* was a public performance piece, complete with songs, poems, and dialogue.[128] This, in fact, is almost exactly how the seventeenth-century erudite Tlaxcalteca historian Don Juan Buenaventura Zapata y Mendoza and his somewhat younger associate and glossator, Don Manuel de los Santos y Salazar, told the tale of their ances-tors' decision to make her the *altepetl*'s patron.

"In the year 1521 news [of Tenochtitlan's fall] arrived [in Tlaxcala] which was celebrated. The four *tlatoque* asked those who arrived there: 'What do the Christians of Castile venerate?' They said, 'the ever Virgin Saint Mary of the Assumption,'" wrote Zapata y Mendoza.[129] This very Marian interpretation explains why, in 1526, as he goes on to say, "all the Tlaxcalteca lords and com-moners selected [Mary as] the intercessor"—that is, because she commanded the devotion of the Castilian conquistadors with whom they had achieved their great triumph over the Mexica. In a gloss on another of Zapata y Mendoza's entries for 1521, Santos y Salazar simply combines the Tlaxcalteca victory fes-tivities with Mary's formal election as the *altepetl*'s saint: "On Tuesday August 13, the feast day of Saint Hippolytus, Mexico was taken and the news arrived in Tlaxcala on Wednesday afternoon. On Thursday they celebrated the news and chose Our Lady of the Assumption as their patron."[130] The tradition preserved by these two learned Tlaxcalteca renders the *altepetl*'s designation of Mary as its saint a triumphant chapter in the history of the Tlaxcalteca-Spanish military partnership. It is a story vaguely reminiscent of the one that Tlaxcalteca elders told in 1582 about La Conquistadora. That statue of Mary had vanished from Tlaxcala, but the connection it embodied between warfare and the woman brought by the Spaniards belonged to the identity the *altepetl*'s elite manufac-tured for themselves in the colonial world.

Mirroring their European counterparts in making Mary an emblem of tri-umph, this altepetl of native Christian conquistadors also came to share the Spaniards' belief that she had actively helped her warrior devotees during the conquest. The elderly Tlaxclateca noblemen remembered having heard the war captains returning from Tenochtitlan declare that in the "travails of the con-quest," La Conquistadora had "aided them," a pronoun mustering all conquis-tadors, Spanish and Tlaxcalteca alike, under Mary's martial shield.[131] Just how La Conquistadora had supported her conquistadors the 1582 witnesses did not say. It is possible, however, that by the mid-sixteenth century, some Tlaxcalteca

believed that during the battle for Tenochtitlan, Mary had urged the native conquistadors on, commanding them to spill their enemies' blood.

Such is the interpretation recently suggested for some ambiguous lines in "The
Water Pouring Song," a poem-song composed in Nahuatl about a battle between
the Mexica and the Tlaxcalteca.[132] In this poem, which is roughly contemporaneous with the *Lienzo de Tlaxcala*, a woman called *Malia teuccihuatl* tells the
warriors where to put their "water jars." Modern readers have tended to understand this "great lady Mary" as Malintzin, who calls for water to relieve the thirst
of combat.[133] But despite her frequent association with Mary, Cortés's famous
female interpreter does not appear to usurp the Virgin's name anywhere else in
Nahuatl literature. This enigmatic *Malia* bearing the Nahuatl title of honor that
Díaz insisted the indigenous used for the Virgin could be Mary herself. As for
the water jars she mentions, a Nahua audience might have understood them as
a poetic allusion to the bloodshed of battle. Through the heart of Nahua culture
ran a river of symbols uniting water, rain, the blood of sacrifice, and the blood of
war—all those precious fluids necessary to nourish the earth and the gods, and
to maintain the cosmos in equilibrium.[134] Imagery linking these liquids saturates
the Water-Pouring Song. Perhaps it seeps into these lines about *Malia teuccihuatl*, making Mary into an indigenous version of the Spaniards' battle patron, a
woman as thirsty for blood in all its forms as some of the pre-Hispanic goddesses
had been.

A century or so later, the noblemen of San Juan de Cuauhtlantzinco, a small
village south of Tlaxcala, would have no hesitation in remembering a conquering Virgin actively fighting on their ancestors' behalf during the conquest. The
inhabitants of Cuauhtlantzinco were Cholulteca rather than Tlaxcalteca, but
they readily borrowed ideas and cultural traditions from their more powerful
neighbor. When sometime in the seventeenth century, the leaders of this community began to feel the pressures bearing down on indigenous people everywhere in central Mexico as the explosive growth in the number of Spanish
settlers threatened landholdings that Nahuas had long considered their own,
they commissioned the painting of a pictorial narrative reminiscent of the
Lienzo de Tlaxcala.[135] The twenty-odd frames of the *Mapa de Cuauhtlantzinco*
teach viewers a grandiose history lesson, reminding them that Cuauhtlantzinco's
privileges and land rights had been guaranteed by none other than Cortés himself, seconded by Charles V. Like the *Lienzo*, the *Mapa* is a proud tale of how the
forebears of the village's elite had eagerly become native Christian conquistadors, allying themselves immediately with Cortés, embracing his religion, and
then bravely fighting alongside the Spaniards against less enlightened native
peoples.[136] But as was perhaps natural in the later colonial period, the *Mapa's*
portrait of the Cuauhtlantzinca warriors as conquistadors is even more explicitly
Christian, and far more openly Marian.

Figure 8.5 Conversion of the Cuauhtlantzinca *tlatoque*. *Mapa de Cuauhtlantzinco*, scene 7. Codex Campos. The Latin American Library. Tulane University.

In one scene the Cuauhtlantzinca convert to Christianity under the Virgin's watchful eye (Figure 8.5). They kneel before a regal Marian statue while Cortés and another armored Spaniard render homage to her, grateful for "such a great favor," according to the Nahuatl caption.[137] In another frame, four Cuauhtlantzinca men reverently bear the Madonna on a litter while three other men carry branches heavy with blossoms signaling the presence of the sacred.[138] "This most pure Virgin whom you see here," explains the Nahuatl caption, "is the one brought by Lord Don Hernán Cortés." She shares a military title with another Madonna whom Cortés was reputed to have given to a contingent of native conquistadors. "This most beautiful Virgin [was] called the Virgin Conquistadora by Lord Don Hernán Cortés, the Marquis del Valle," declares the caption. It goes on to explain that this Conquistadora was herself actually a military champion: "she is the one who not infrequently appeared in the air, among the clouds, and helped us when we had to fight against and convert to the faith another people."[139] Hence in a scene in which "we triumphed over the inhabitants of Tecuanapan and brought them out of their errors and false beliefs," Mary hovers above her warriors as they achieve the victory of arms and faith over serpent-worshipping, skin-clad idolaters (Figure 8.6).[140]

The Cuauhtlantzinca—or at least the creators of the *Mapa*—knew Mary both as Conquistadora and, in the words of an ardent prayer quoted in one of the Nahuatl captions, as loving "mother of mercy."[141] Like the Spaniards, these

Figure 8.6 Mary hovers in the air, helping the Cuauhtlantzinca to conquer and convert the inhabitants of Tecuanapan. *Mapa de Cuauhtlantzinco,* scenes 19 and 20. Codex Campos. The Latin American Library. Tulane University.

indigenous people had come to believe that she had guided the work of military and spiritual conquest. To glorify their ancestors, the Cuauhtlantzinca commemorated them as brave Christian allies of the Spaniards—and as men who had both conquered and converted other indigenous peoples in Mary's service. With her help, the Cuauhtlantzinca warriors become missionaries, their Marian evangelizing efforts part and parcel of the military victories to which La Conquistadora leads them.[142] The *Mapa* reveals just how thoroughly some seventeenth-century indigenous communities had internalized the model of the Marian conquistador learned from the Spaniards.

An odd disjunction between word and image in the scene of Tecuanapan's military and spiritual defeat suggests that these Cuauhtlantzinca sometimes even conflated their forebears with the Spanish conquistadors. The pronoun "we" used in the caption proclaims that the men who fight under Mary's aegis here are the Cuauhtlantzinca, but in the scene itself, mail-clad Spaniards stand alone beneath the Virgin and the shield bearing the Castilian royal arms that appears in the sky next to her. Opposing them are the warriors of Tecuanapan ranged around the undulating rampart of their giant snake deity. The Cuauhtlantzinca themselves are nowhere to be seen. Yet when the seventeenth-century villagers looked at the armored men fighting with La Conquistadora's aid, they saw their own ancestors.

A similar scene appears in the *Mapa de Chalchihuapan*, a late seventeenth-century pictorial narrative that claims much the same illustrious past of alliance with the Spanish conquistadors, if in a cruder visual idiom, for this indigenous village some fifteen kilometers southwest of Cuauhtlantzinco.[143] No caption explains whether the late colonial inhabitants of this community followed the villagers of Cuauhtlantzinco by projecting their forebears onto the figures of the steel-plated Spaniards who slaughter semi-naked peoples while Mary looks on approvingly from her airy perch.[144] In any case, this scene, like its model in the *Mapa de Cuauhtlantzinco*, belongs to the cluster of indigenous texts, testimonies, and images produced in the Tlaxcalteca sphere of influence during the sixteenth and seventeenth centuries that limned a portrait of Mary as an icon of an *altepetl*'s conversion to Christianity and its subsequent military and even religious conquest of other native peoples.

This version of "Our Precious Mother" did not necessarily appeal to all residents of Tlaxcala, Cuauhtlantzinco, and Chalchihuapan. Commoners would not have been likely to nurture fond memories of the era of conquest, since the arrival of the Spaniards added more oppressive lords to their already difficult lives.[145] It was the elite, the *tlatoque* and war captains—the native conquistadors—who stood to profit from the coming of the Europeans. They sometimes tried to do so by asserting their right to rewards for their military services and attempting to persuade the Spaniards to confirm them in powers and privileges they in fact had not held before 1521.[146] Their efforts were less and less successful as the Spaniards' reliance on indigenous leaders diminished over the course of the sixteenth century. As members of the Nahua elite felt their power ebbing, they tried to tighten their grasp over commoners, igniting intra-*altepetl* conflicts that flared particularly fiercely in Tlaxcala and the surrounding region during the mid-sixteenth century and later seventeenth centuries.[147] Other changes introduced by the Europeans gradually eroded the status of the Nahua nobility, but not their pride, so manifest in the images of the *Lienzo de Tlaxcala* and the *Mapas*, and in the words of the histories composed by men like Muñoz Camargo and Zapata y Mendoza.[148] The elite sensibility palpable in these documents created during intense struggles over status extends to the Virgin Conquistadora herself. Like all of the ties to the Spaniards trumpeted in these texts, she becomes an emblem of rank, a badge of prestige flaunted by those people who hoped to make the past a basis for power in the present.[149]

Many Spaniards shared this attitude, as the fate of Tlaxcala's own Conquistadora shows. This Madonna had re-emerged from the wilds of Chocomán only to be appropriated by Puebla de los Angeles, a distinctly Spanish city that owed its prominence in part to the scorn the first bishop of Tlaxcala felt for the indigenous town where he was supposed to make his seat. Appointed to the see of Tlaxcala in 1527, Julián Garcés was dismayed at the thought of establishing his cathedral and residence in this community that the Crown had decided would not be open to Spanish settlers. After a spell of absentee governance conducted from Mexico City, Garcés eventually succeeded in having Puebla, a recently built Spanish town to the south of Tlaxcala, designated as the headquarters for the bishopric.[150] By the second half of the sixteenth century, enshrined in the new city's Franciscan convent was the Madonna that Cortés had bestowed on his loyal Tlaxcalteca allies in 1521 and that Juan de Rivas had whisked away to Chocomán some years later.

Rumors that La Conquistadora resided in Puebla had evidently reached Tlaxcala, for the elderly men said as much in their testimony of 1582. Some of the Tlaxcalteca who moved to Puebla for work could well have brought back home tales of the statue of Mary they had seen there in the church of San Francisco.[151] The seventy-one-year-old Tlaxcalteca *principal* Diego de Soto stated that although he "had never seen the said image or known where it was" after Juan de Rivas took it from Tlaxcala, he "had heard it was in" Puebla.[152] The emotional tone of this testimony is much attenuated, especially as these words were recorded not in Don Diego's Nahuatl but in the Spanish translation provided by the interpreter (who happened to be mestizo Diego Muñoz Camargo). Yet La Conquistadora's devotees in both Tlaxcala and Puebla may have understood how her new location underscored the transfer of ecclesiastical power from the indigenous city to the Spanish one.

The destiny of Tlaxcala's Conquistadora suggests that in colonial New Spain, people of Spanish descent also prized Madonnas linked to the gilded era of conquest. Otherwise, after her sojourn in Chocomán, La Conquistadora would simply have been returned to the indigenous community to which she originally belonged. So much did Puebla's residents care about this statue that they probably solicited the testimony given by Diego de Soto and the other Tlaxcalteca elders in 1582.[153] The Poblanos were evidently eager to firm up their Virgin's claim to the title of La Conquistadora and the illustrious past it represented. As they well knew, there were other Madonnas in the running for the honor. One was not at all far away from Puebla, as the *Mapa de Cuauhtlantzinco* revealed. Its captions sometimes called La Conquistadora by another name: Our Lady of Remedies.[154] The Cuauhtlantzinca were probably thinking of the Madonna who watched over the nearby community of Cholula from a chapel high atop the remains of one of the most massive temples ever built in Mesoamerica.[155] This church silhouetted against the snowy bulk of the volcano Popocatepetl was not, however, Our Lady of the Remedies' most celebrated shrine in sixteenth-century New Spain. That was in Mexico City, a place where Spaniards would celebrate this Virgin as a most worthy rival to Puebla's statue for the coveted title of Conquistadora. What did such Madonnas mean to Spaniards as they invoked the past in the service of the colonial present?

9

Relics of the Conquest

Some twenty years after the fall of Tenochtitlan, one of the leading men of Mexico City sat down to compose an eyewitness account of the conquest of the Mexica. Bernardino Vázquez de Tapia was a conquistador, the veteran of campaigns in Castilla del Oro, Cuba and Mexico, and a member of New Spain's elite. When, in the 1540s, he decided to write about the deeds of arms that had resulted in Spanish possession of the city the Mexica had once ruled, he had no thought of becoming a historian. Tapia addressed his text to Charles V and intended it to prove his own merits.[1] This piece of blatant self-promotion also happens to contain the earliest extant reference to a miracle that by the late sixteenth century would often enjoy center stage in stories told by New Spain's Spaniards about statues of Mary called La Conquistadora.

This miracle that would become such a celebrated part of Mary's colonial biography appears in Tapia's account of the conquistadors' plight after the Toxcatl massacre in 1520. Enraged at the murder of their people by Pedro de Alvarado's men, Mexica warriors had seized their weapons and driven the Spaniards and the allied *indios amigos* into a corner of the city. One day, remembered Tapia, the Mexica set fire to the door of the building where the conquistadors had holed up. "Tired and wounded," the Spaniards and their native allies were so demoralized that the Mexica could easily have made short work of them. Suddenly Moctezuma's warriors retreated, to the conquistadors' great relief and surprise. "Afterwards," wrote Tapia, "we asked the Indian noblemen who had been the war captains" why they had withdrawn that day. The Mexica, he said, explained that just as they had been about to seize the conquistadors, "a very beautiful Castilian woman who shone like the sun" had appeared and "thrown handfuls of dirt in their eyes."[2]

Though Tapia did not name this radiant woman warrior, he surely thought of her as the Virgin Mary. From sermons and paintings and perhaps even his own reading of the Bible, he would have known of the woman "robed with the sun" and crowned with the stars of Apocalypse 12:1, an incandescent figure long identified with Jesus' mother. This apocalyptic Mary haunting Tapia's text reveals that by the 1540s, the Virgin of the conquest already was moving into the enchanted realm of legend for Spaniards.

In subsequent decades, Mary would become ever more important in the commemorative traditions flourishing in Mexico's Spanish milieus. Legends about her sanctifying presence during the conquest were as much a mark of this colonial world as the cities and towns the Spaniards laid out, the neat grids of streets converging on central plazas lined with ornate churches, imposing government buildings, and the houses of the wealthy and powerful.[3] Like these Renaissance-inspired urban blueprints, New Spain's stories about Mary owed much to developments on the other side of the Atlantic. Tales about statues of her connected to the Old World reconquest crossed the ocean, providing the pattern for legends that would become attached to many images of her housed in colonial Mexican churches.

Although Spaniards on both sides of the Atlantic shared enthusiasm for Madonnas embodying a golden age of conquest, the New World Conquistadoras were hardly identical twins of the reconquest Virgins of Spain's civic legends. They came from the crucible of a colonial society where, by the late sixteenth century, not only did Spaniards born in Spain (*peninsulares*) vie with those born in the New World (*criollos*), but the alchemy of sex was transmuting the genes of Europeans, indigenous peoples, and Africans into a thick racial mélange.[4] In Mexico, the transformative powers of legend would endow the Virgin of the conquest with a genealogy just as distinctively colonial, marrying the native and the European.

If in the late sixteenth and seventeenth centuries, some indigenous people of central Mexico shaped their memories of Madonnas of the conquest in order to make statements about their place in the colonial order, so too did Spaniards. Important questions of Spanish colonial identity would play out through Marian interpretations of the past, especially by the late sixteenth century, when myth-making around the conquest and the attendant conversion of the indigenous peoples accelerated. As Spanish-identified men and women in New Spain fashioned a colonial culture, they articulated a history for the land where they now lived, a proud vision of the past in which the era of the conquistadors and of the first contingents of friars often occupied a special place as the heroic time of origins.[5] Hence images of Mary endowed with connections to the conquest became prized objects over which various sorts of largely Spanish communities could contend.

Competition and conflict were not all that lay behind the conquering Virgins of Spanish legends. These Madonnas belong to sweeping visions of colonial society, imaginative panoramas that have much to reveal about how Mexico's Spanish-identified residents—especially its *criollos*—conceived of their relationship to indigenous peoples and to the land they all shared. Indigenous actors were granted increasing space in these stories about the Virgin of the conquest, and not just as the targets of Mary's battlefield wrath. Gradually, they also were allotted the role of witness to her tender love for New Spain and all its inhabitants. In the first half of the seventeenth century, new legends about Mary would make this point even more effectively. Eventually, the Madonnas of these later stories would displace their elder sisters in the affections of the peoples of New Spain.

War Stories and Military Miracles

Some years after Bernardino Vázquez de Tapia wrote down the story of the nameless dirt-throwing miracle-worker, his fellow conquistadors began to repeat it in their chronicles of the conquest. Men like Gonzalo Fernández de Oviedo y Valdés and Bernal Díaz del Castillo announced this wondrous woman to their readers as Mary. Neither they nor other sixteenth-century authors such as Francisco López de Gómara and Francisco Cervantes de Salazar mentioned her unearthly radiance, but Mary's assault on the Mexica gained brilliance with each retelling, acquiring the reflected glory of two equally belligerent miracles that came to flank it. This trio of marvels sanitized the Toxcatl massacre, salving the conquistadors' conscience by proving that Mary had unflinchingly seconded them throughout the carnage.

In one of these wonders, the Marian battle miracle that blinded the Indians joined forces with a story about the Virgin's defiance of the Mexica during the Toxcatl debacle. Though many conquistadors asserted that before Alvarado and his men unleashed their weapons, the Mexica had tried to purge the Templo Mayor's shrine room of the Madonna enshrined there by Cortés, Spaniards liked to believe that this effort to banish Mary from Tenochtitlan's religious heart had failed. As early as 1529, a witness at Alvarado's trial declared that the Mexica had not been able budge the image.[6] His testimony suggests a miracle in the making, for only divine force could have stopped the Indians from simply carrying the image away.[7] As Christians, the conquistadors had been raised on stories of how saints' relics and statues of Mary could never be moved against their will or by unworthy people. By the mid-sixteenth century, the imaginative transformation of the Mexica's act of open resistance into Mary's miraculous triumph was complete. Gómara, Oviedo, Salazar, and Díaz all told the tale, relishing the details proving that it was God's will—and Mary's—that her image remain in the Templo Mayor.[8] Only Salazar admitted that this same image of Mary later disappeared from the temple, an awkward discrepancy that he never resolved.[9]

According to these sixteenth-century chroniclers, this intransigent Madonna was the one who rescued the conquistadors with handfuls of dirt in the aftermath of the Toxcatl murders. The Indians who retreated before her assault, wrote Díaz, recognized her as "another one like the one that was in their great temple." Gómara went so far as to declare that the Mexica believed she actually was "the woman of the [Templo Mayor's] altar," while Salazar insisted that Mary waged her warrior's campaign from the altar itself.[10] As the dirt-wielding Madonna acquired the features of the Templo Mayor's statue, one conquering Virgin emerged whose miracles declared that she and the Spaniards had come to Tenochtitlan to stay.

Her marvels were acts of war, as another attendant wonder unmistakably indicated. According to Oviedo, Díaz, Gómara, and Salazar, as Mary flung dirt into the Mexica's eyes, Santiago rode at her side, brandishing the sword he had acquired long ago on the other side of the Atlantic. His horse's hooves and mouth, according to Salazar and Gómara, inflicted as much damage on the Mexica as did the saint's steel blade, as late sixteenth-century visitors to Santiago's church at Tlatelolco in Mexico City could see in a painting of the holy pair coming to the conquistadors' aid.[11] Santiago's knightly presence in this miracle story honed its martial edge, forging Mary's fistfuls of earth into a weapon as devastating as his sword and his horse's hammering hooves. "Saint Mary and Santiago were fighting for the Spaniards," Gómara declared.[12]

For these "very great miracles," wrote Díaz in his *Historia verdadera*, "we should continuously give thanks to God and to the Virgin Mary Our Lady, his blessed mother, who helped us in all things, and to blessed Lord Santiago."[13] As this elderly conquistador thought back over the conquest, he remembered yet another Marian war marvel. It sweetened the bitter recollection of what he called the "first rout we ever suffered in New Spain," a clash near Veracruz late in 1519 between the Mexica and Juan de Escalante, the man whom Cortés left in charge of this hastily founded Spanish settlement while the rest of the conquistadors set off on the journey leading to the causeways of Tenochtitlan.[14]

As Díaz admitted, this fight had been disastrous for the Spanish and their Totonac allies. Though Juan de Escalante managed to retreat to Veracruz, he and six other Spaniards soon died of their battle wounds. The *Historia verdadera* softened the blow with a miracle story featuring Mary and Moctezuma. In Díaz's imaginative reconstruction of events, Moctezuma asks his war captains why their "thousands" of warriors had not "conquered" the handful of Spaniards who held Veracruz. Their arrows and war clubs, they tell the *tlatoani*, had suddenly fallen useless when a "great Castilian lady" had appeared and called out words of encouragement bolstering the conquistadors' courage. Moctezuma instantly recognizes the terrifying woman of his war captains' report as Mary, the "advocate of the Spaniards," whom he knows from Cortés's earlier gift of an image of her.[15] The moral of the story is plain. The Spaniards may have been defeated at Veracruz, but the Virgin was victorious.

Although Díaz knew this Marian tale only secondhand, having heard it from "certain conquistadors," he was inclined to believe it because "all of us soldiers who accompanied Cortés cherish the belief...that divine mercy and Our Lady the Virgin Mary were always with us."[16] In the decades after Tenochtitlan's fall, the Spaniards assiduously nurtured this conviction, feeding it on remembrance and imagination. Conquistadors would have swapped these anecdotes about the Veracruz battle and Tenochtitlan's dirt-throwing Virgin as they reminisced while drinking in Mexico City's crowded taverns or at the lavish parties that colonial aristocrats loved to throw. Perhaps each man added his own embellishments as the line separating memory and legend grew ever thinner and then vanished altogether. Both war stories helped the Spaniards retrospectively transform some traumatic moments of the conquest into a kind of glory. One of Mary's apparitions justified a particularly heinous atrocity, and the other reframed a serious Spanish military setback into a portrait of Mexica quailing before the conquistadors' saintly patron.

Why then did all the Spanish chroniclers—including Tapia—claim that these miracle tales actually originated as war stories told by Mexica witnesses to Mary's battlefield appearances? Tempting as it is to speculate that after the conquest, some Christianized Mexica elaborated such narratives to excuse their ultimate humiliating defeat, it is equally likely that Spanish colonial chroniclers were employing a literary device inherited from their medieval predecessors, who had cast Muslim men of arms in a similar role: if even the infidel enemy saw the Madonna fighting for Christians, her presence was undeniable.[17] Not until well into the seventeenth century would any indigenous text from central Mexico evoke Mary's combat apparitions—and these would be *indios amigos* celebrating military victories, not Mexica justifying losses. When the Nahua artists working on the *Mapa de Cuauhtlantzinco* picked up their brushes to paint the Virgin hovering above her native conquistadors, the stories of her two warrior appearances had already been popular for a century in Spanish colonial circles.

Even if these Marian tales began with the Spaniards, the conquistadors and chroniclers allowed the indigenous world to slip in around the edges.[18] Díaz, for example, introduces a Nahuatl word at the climax of his accounts of Mary's military apparitions. The Mexica, he writes, declared that they saw *una gran tecleciguata*—a "great lady"—the misspelled Nahuatl honorific he uses elsewhere to characterize indigenous people's understanding of the Madonna, and one that colonial Nahua singer-poets themselves may have bestowed on her.[19] Perhaps Díaz inserted this Nahuatl word in an effort to add authenticity to the apparitions—or perhaps he had heard both his fellow conquistadors and Nahuas tell these tales.

Another detail that gives pause belongs exclusively to the tale of the dirt-throwing Madonna, a story that became a fixture in conquest mythology.

The dirt is a peculiar choice of weapon. There seems to be only one other place where Mary would be remembered as having preferred this eccentric if effective arm. It happened also to be on the western side of the Atlantic—Peru, where, in the valleys and highlands of the Andes, the Spaniards subjugated yet another sophisticated imperial New World people. By the second half of the sixteenth century, a dirt-flinging Virgin, accompanied by the knightly Santiago, featured in legends commemorating a key moment of this conquest.[20] Circulating among Spaniards, mestizos, and pure-blood Andeans alike, these tales were doubtless offshoots of the well-known stories that had emerged much earlier in Mexico.[21]

The miracle was supposed to have occurred in 1536, the year in which Manco Inca, the puppet ruler whom the Spaniards had ushered to power, had been unable to stomach the conquistadors' brutality any longer and fought to regain control of Cuzco, the Incas' imposing imperial city. During this battle, Mary and Santiago rushed to the conquistadors' defense—she with her dirt and he with his sword—just as at Tenochtitlan. One of the famous drawings with which Incan nobleman and author Guaman Poma de Ayala illustrated his early seventeenth-century chronicle of his people's past energetically depicts the wonder (Figure 9.1).[22] Crowned and imperious, Mary stands on a cloud. Cringing Inca warriors sink to the ground or flee before the onslaught of earth that rains from her fingers.

Some beliefs and practices of the two New World peoples whom Mary blinds in these legends may illuminate her puzzling choice of weapon. In some versions of the tale, she tosses earth at her enemies, in others dust, and in yet others sand. None of these substances held special significance for the Spaniards, but they did for Mesoamericans and Andeans. The broad expanse of the sacred plaza at the center of Cuzco was covered with sand laboriously transported from the sea to this highland city; the grains polished by the waves helped sanctify the site.[23] The Mexica, a people whose ritual calendar included mysterious ceremonies called "Entering the Sand," may have consecrated sand and laid it out in patterns before their temples, as did their Mixtec neighbors in the Oaxaca Valley.[24] When Mary scooped up her ammunition at Tenochtitlan and Cuzco, she was perhaps turning the Incas' and Mexicas' own sacred stuff against them—a subtle prediction of the destruction of indigenous religions by Christianity. Whatever the origins of these stories, the Spaniards narrated them in terms that would have made sense to their indigenous neighbors. Mary's resulting miracles were the creations of the colonial New World, a place marked by cultural as well as biological *mestizaje*.

A Spaniard who crossed the Atlantic in 1599, intending to travel through both Peru and Mexico, recognized the New World quality to the dirt-throwing Virgin of the conquest. Diego de Ocaña was a Jeronymite friar, a member of the monastic community that tended the shrine of the Virgin of Guadalupe in

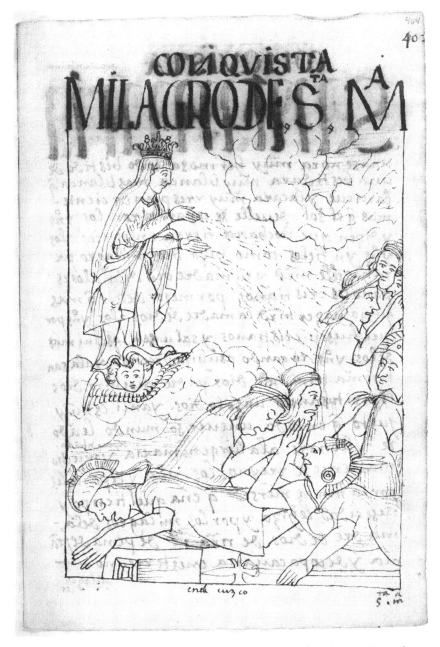

Figure 9.1 Mary casts sand in the eyes of the Incas at Cuzco. Felipe Guaman Poma de Ayala, *Nueva crónica y buen gobierno*. Danish Royal Library, Copenhagen MS GKS 2232 4°, folio 402 [404]. Image courtesy of the Danish Royal Library's Photographic Studio and reproduced with permission of the Danish Royal Library.

the hills of Extremadura.[25] He embarked for the New World to collect alms for this Madonna from her devotees in Peru and Mexico, who he knew tended to direct their generosity toward local images of her. Ocaña's journey took him first through the valleys and plateaus of Peru. There, using his considerable literary and artistic talents to publicize his cause, he orchestrated theatrical pieces starring the Virgin of Guadalupe that borrowed heavily from the *Moros y Cristianos* plays, an increasingly popular form of entertainment in the Spanish world on both sides of the Atlantic.[26]

In Ocaña's flamboyant dramas, Old World scenes mingled with ones set in the Andes. His large Peruvian audiences watched as Our Lady of Guadalupe defeated idolatry, converted Andeans to Christianity, and vanquished Muslims.[27] Ocaña drew much of his material from the history of his own monastery, where the pile of war trophies offered abundant proof of his beloved Virgin's ability to trounce her enemies. In a play performed first in Potosí in 1601 and then in Chuquisaca in 1602, he even decided to teach his New World audience about the iconic Old World victory achieved with Guadalupe's aid, Alfonso XI's triumph over the Muslims at Salado in 1340.[28] Ocaña spread this battle out over several scenes, building the tension to the moment when Mary miraculously arrives on stage to save the Christians from "Albohacem" and his men.

"Our Lady appears on high, with a dish of sand," specified Ocaña in his stage directions. Immediately a "Moor" cries out to his commander: "A woman, more beautiful than the moon…has blinded me! She threw dust in my eyes. I am not alone. All of your Moors are blind." In a fury, Albohacem shouts that he will kill "this woman," but "she throws a fistful of dirt and blinds this Moor." "What is this? I am dead!" he screams in agony, "help me Allah, for I am blind. Blind with sand! It is that woman for sure.… She has blinded me again. It has cost me dear to look at her." In the background, Christian knights chant "Victory! Victory!"[29]

This scene would have made sense to Ocaña's Peruvian public, but surprised his fellow friars back in Spain, for they told the tale of Salado differently.[30] His inspiration could not have been the stories circulating about the most recent Christian triumph over Muslims to bring an addition to Guadalupe's treasury: the battle of Lepanto, fought on October 7, 1571, in the eastern Mediterranean. The victory won that day by the combined forces of Spain, Venice, and the papacy over the seemingly unstoppable juggernaut of the Ottoman Turks was celebrated throughout western Christendom as a crusading triumph owed to the Virgin. At Lepanto, a banner bearing an image of Mary had flown high in the rigging of the Spanish flagship.[31] The Virgin "fought" for "us," remembered a Spanish lieutenant who had risked his life during the engagement.[32] From the brushes of artists such as Paolo Veronese came dramatic scenes of Lepanto with Mary presiding over a sea bristling with masts. Pope Pius V even decreed a new Marian feast to be held annually on the battle's anniversary. In thanksgiving, Philip II offered the lantern captured from the Turkish flagship to the Virgin of Guadalupe.[33]

Mary's role at Lepanto may have inspired Ocaña to write a scene for one of his dramas in which the Virgin of Guadalupe overcame Muhammad, represented by an actor dressed "in Turkish garb."[34] Yet in none of the tales about Lepanto does Mary cast sand into the Turks' eyes, nor does she reach for dirt during battle in any other text composed in medieval or early modern Spain.[35] Ocaña could only have appropriated this gesture for his Virgin from stories he had heard in the New World about Mary's martial methods. Maybe he was familiar with the Mexican version of the tale, or maybe he knew only about her assault on Manco Inca's troops at Cuzco. Whichever rendering of the legend he borrowed from, he did so in order to make his presentation of Salado ring true for New World spectators. To direct their devotion toward the Madonna of Guadalupe in her distant Castilian home, Ocaña somehow had to bring her into their world. He did so as much through his theatrical translation of Salado into a New World idiom as through the images of her that he painted and bestowed on churches in Peru. As his Virgin's hands blinded the Muslims, Ocaña invented a history for these New World legends about Mary that led across the Atlantic straight back to his monastery.

In 1605, Ocaña left the viceroyalty of Peru and made his way north to New Spain, where he would die in 1608. If sometime before his death he had a chance to stage his play about Guadalupe and Salado in Mexico City, his audience would not have been surprised to see Mary flinging sand at her enemies, for they knew she had done so during Tenochtitlan's conquest. But many would have wondered at Ocaña's claim that this aggressive Virgin was Guadalupe. By the time the friar arrived in Mexico City, many of its residents were certainly familiar with the Madonna from Extremadura. By the second half of the sixteenth century, increasing crowds of devotees made their way to a chapel dedicated to her on a hill just outside the city.[36] Some of them even believed that Guadalupe, accompanied by Saint Peter and Santiago, "had fought during the conquest for the Spanish," as a *criollo* author from Veracruz wrote in 1604.[37]

But the men and women of New Spain's capital identified the dirt-throwing Madonna who had rushed into battle with Santiago as instead Nuestra Señora de los Remedios (Our Lady of Remedies), who reigned over their city from another hilltop chapel. They often turned to Los Remedios as one of Mexico City's most important saintly patrons when their community was in need. Part of her rise to fame as a symbol of the city rested on the history she was acquiring as a relic of the conquest. By the end of the sixteenth century, this Madonna would even vie with the one who had belonged to the Tlaxcalteca war captain Acxotecatl for the title of La Conquistadora. The history of how Los Remedios earned this honorific and became the mythic dirt-throwing warrior Virgin is as emphatically a New World story as was the miracle that Ocaña tried to usurp for Guadalupe, though this time the accent would be on *criollo* pride.

Totoltepec

"Our Lady of Remedies" suggests a sweet-tempered Madonna, not one destined to become a Conquistadora. Men and women who departed for the New World from Seville in the sixteenth century knew her as the patron of a religious community whose mission matched her name: to provide aid and comfort to sailors.[38] As ships setting off to cross the Atlantic slipped down the Guadalquivir and left Seville behind, they could even salute this Virgin, whose church was perched on the river banks, practically in the busy boatyards of Triana. Emigrants headed to the New World might also kneel before the serene late fourteenth- or early fifteenth-century Italianate painting of her hanging in Seville's cathedral, or request her protection in any of the numerous churches scattered across Andalusia that bore her name.[39]

Knowledge of Los Remedios' tender powers traveled to New Spain with these men and women. In the nascent colony, the promise of succor held out by her name slowly but surely drew her into the commemorative traditions forming around the Noche Triste. That summer night of 1520, Cortés's company of Spaniards and indigenous allies had desperately needed solace from on high as they escaped from Tenochtitlan after the Toxcatl massacre. Fleeing across the causeways linking the city to the shore, they offered easy targets for Mexica archers. So many were killed and wounded that Díaz would remember Cortés declaring it a "miracle" that any of his men had survived at all. The battle remained fierce after the Spaniards and their native allies reached the shore. At Tacuba, on the northwestern side of Lake Tetzcoco, other contingents of warriors joined Tenochtitlan's forces and threatened to annihilate the conquistadors. Cortés and the remnants of his band managed to retreat to a temple on a nearby wooded hill, where they rested, assessed their losses, and tended to the wounded.[40]

Known to the Nahua as Totoltepec, this hill where the exhausted conquistadors found some respite would become indelibly associated with Los Remedios. Within a few years of Tenochtitlan's fall, a Christian chapel crowned this height and it bore Mary's name, according to the records of Mexico City's *cabildo* from 1528.[41] Some Spaniards already knew just which Madonna held sway there: Los Remedios, declared witnesses at a trial in 1529.[42] Some forty years later, Díaz explained in his *Historia verdadera* how "after the taking of the great city of Tenochtitlan, we made at that temple [on Totoltepec]...a...church which is called Our Lady of Remedies."[43]

It would take some time for the conquistadors' foundation to assume importance in the colonial landscape and for Los Remedios to establish exclusive claim
to this memorial site. In the 1550s, some residents of Mexico City who climbed
the hill at Totoltepec with offerings thought of her as the chapel's patron, while
others came to pay homage to "Saint Mary of Victory," the name that appears
in a lively map of New Spain's capital painted by a native artist sometime in the
mid-sixteenth century.[44] On this map, small figures clad in indigenous clothing
herd animals or shoulder burdens along the roads in and around Mexico City.
Several make their way toward the chapel on Totoltepec, which the artist drew
as a much simpler structure than most of the other churches scattered across
his cityscape. At the time, it was merely a building of "stone and mud" with a
"poor straw roof," as an early seventeenth-century *criollo* author remembered.[45]
He was much more impressed with the church that replaced the original chapel
in the mid-1570s. Los Remedios' new home sported a wooden roof sheltering a
tribune and an elevated choir. From its tall tower, four large bells pealed to summon her devotees to services.[46]

By the time this church's walls went up, Los Remedios' bit part in
Tenochtitlan's conquest had become a starring role. The remedy she had held
out to the Spaniards at Totoltepec was now commemorated as a dramatic military marvel, described in a text of April 1574 drawn up by the men from Mexico
City who funded the new building: after Cortés's retreat to Totoltepec, "in this
place where the said chapel is now, Our Lady appeared…and afterward the
[enemy] Indians admitted that because of their respect and fear of the vision
that they had seen, they were unable to continue with their pursuit. In gratitude
for this favor and boon, the [original] chapel of Our Lady of the Remedies was
built."[47] The men who signed this document may not have been the first individuals in New Spain to believe that on Totoltepec, Los Remedios had made a
battlefield apparition. Yet whether these patrons of Los Remedios' new chapel
were the authors of this Madonna's expanded role in conquest history or merely
its publicists, they were certainly eager to embrace it—and to plunge her into the
politics of colonial identity.

Prominent and powerful figures in the capital's political and social life, these
men all held seats on Mexico City's *cabildo*. Most were *criollos* and many were
proud descendants of conquistadors or of other early arrivals in New Spain.[48]
Like other *criollos* who claimed such ancestry, these men believed that their heritage set them apart from the masses and made them equal to any *peninsular*, no
matter how high born. They even thought their conquistador lineage entitled
them to the privileges enjoyed in Spain by the nobility, a point they relentlessly
asserted as they strove to establish themselves as a New World aristocracy.[49]

Criollos' efforts to enter the highest ranks of Spanish society were blocked on
many sides. *Peninsulares* often scorned the *criollos* for their arriviste pretensions

and unrefined ways, while Spanish monarchs were leery of creating a new nobility too far away from court to be controlled effectively. In 1542, Charles V sought to squelch this threat by enacting a set of laws that, among other things, prohibited the inheritance of *encomiendas*, those grants of indigenous labor and tribute that formed the basis of power in the early colonial New World. *Encomenderos* rightly interpreted this and other regulations as assaults on their stature. In Peru, some even greeted the announcement of the new laws with violent rebellion.[50] When Philip II renewed the legislative attack on *encomenderos* in the 1560s, New Spain's *criollo* elite were outraged. Some apparently plotted to crown their own monarch—Martín Cortés, son of Hernán and a Spanish noblewoman— who would embody *criollo* honor.[51] The scheme failed and leading *criollos* were arrested, some even executed. Nonetheless, in the later sixteenth century, *criollo* pride blossomed into what has been called "creole patriotism," a sentiment that was often backward looking and infused with nostalgia, even a bitter sense of "dispossession" at having not received just rewards.[52]

When Mexico City's *cabildo* members agreed in 1574 that Our Lady of the Remedies deserved a better church, they were spurred by the same *criollo* dignity that moved the conspirators of just a few years earlier.[53] This Madonna, the *cabildo* believed, had prevented the annihilation of their ancestors during the retreat from Tenochtitlan. The miracle with which she had illuminated the darkness of the Noche Triste and made the enemy cower at Totoltepec was, the *cabildo* declared in 1574, a "celebrated favor which Our Lady did for [Cortés] and the conquistadors and through them to all the other Spaniards who have come and will come to this land," a miracle joining past and present whose "memory," the council stipulated, should therefore be cultivated by their city.[54]

The *cabildo* envisioned Los Remedios herself, or rather the small statue of her housed in the chapel on the hill, as extending her protection over the whole city spreading out around her. Just when this image of the Madonna arrived on Totoltepec is not known, but it was in place by 1576, when it was carried in a solemn procession from the chapel into the heart of Mexico City (Figure 9.2). There it reigned on an altar in the cathedral for some time before being returned to Totoltepec. Over the next 120 years, the statue would repeat this journey some eighteen times. On each occasion, the citizens of the capital hoped to secure Los Remedios' loving intercession to help their city survive a disaster, whether the ravages of epidemic or the siege of drought. They respectfully received her with artillery salutes and the light of thousands of candles.[55]

People filled the streets to greet Los Remedios when she came down into the suffering city. As the Chalcan chronicler Don Domingo de San Antón Muñon Chimalpahin Quauhtlehuanitzin wrote of a 1597 procession: "everyone [went to see her], indigenous men and women, Spaniards and Spanish women. They went on foot, all carrying candles to light her way."[56] These processions may

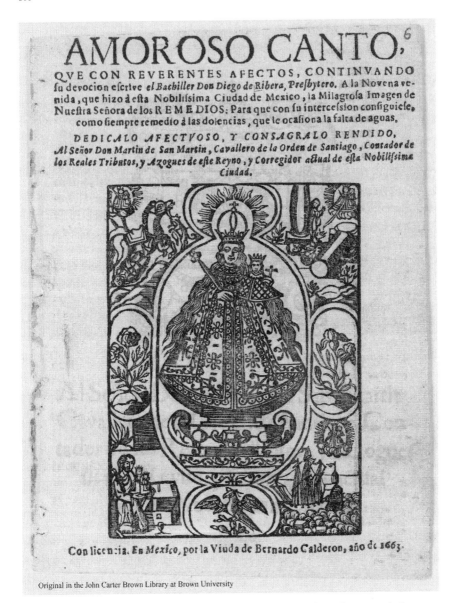

Figure 9.2 Frontispiece of a poem in honor of Los Remedios of Totoltepec, with the statue depicted below the title. Mexico City, 1663. Courtesy of the John Carter Library at Brown University.

have brought the city together, but they also showcased the *criollo* elite. As Los Remedios made her way through the crowds to the cathedral, officials representing Mexico City accompanied her, prominent among them members of the *cabildo*. The council tightly controlled the processions, deciding when to let the Madonna leave Totoltepec and selecting its own officials to serve as her honor guard and fulfill other ceremonial roles.[57]

Tending to the cult of this Virgin who had watched over their conquistador ancestors was one way *criollo* men and women sought to recover from the traumatic events of the 1560s. They might not have their own *criollo* king, but they could have their own Madonna and make her into a symbol of their city. That was not, however, the reason the *cabildo* members gave for their decision to rebuild the chapel in 1574; instead, they stated that they needed to "remedy" (the word play is theirs) the sad condition of Los Remedios' church. The chapel founded by the conquistadors, they said, was "ruined," prey to the wind, sun, and rain that swept in through gaping holes where doors had once hung. Masses were no longer sung there, nor was there anywhere in the dilapidated building where the faithful could attend novenas.[58] The *cabildo* may have been indulging in some self-interested hyperbole, for just six years earlier, Díaz had described Los Remedios' church as a still flourishing devotional center where "many residents and lords of Mexico City go . . . on pilgrimage and to attend novenas."[59] Whether he was right, *cabildo* members had every incentive to think of Los Remedios' chapel as in sore need of restoration. By rescuing this Virgin of the conquest from oblivion, they could style themselves her champions and prove themselves the worthy successors of their conquistador forefathers who had established the original church.

These self-proclaimed guardians of Los Remedios' cult created institutional structures designed to ensure that men like themselves would remain in charge of her newly resplendent shrine on Totlotepec. Though a priest was needed to say Mass at the chapel and perform other religious duties, he would be chosen by Mexico City's *cabildo*, not by the archbishop or any other religious official. In all matters, the chaplain had to obey the officers of the confraternity of Our Lady of the Remedies.[60] Founded in 1575, Los Remedios' confraternity had a governing board of five men, three of whom were always to be members of Mexico City's *cabildo*. The confraternity officers and their deputies spent perhaps as much time at the shrine as did the chaplain, and held the keys to the chapel doors. The most important key of all, which opened the small shrine protecting the statue of Los Remedios, belonged to the confraternity's highest official, always selected from among Mexico City's *regidores*.[61]

According to the confraternity's ordinances, drawn up in 1579, Los Remedios' chapel on Totoltepec offered a stage on which the pageantry of the liturgy would enact the continuity between the glories of the past and the high stature that *criollos* claimed in the present.[62] At the chapel, Mary's feast days were to be celebrated with all possible "sumptuosity," and special masses were to be performed weekly. On Mondays, stipulated the confraternity statutes, the ritual would benefit the souls of the "dead conquistadors who died on the day when the first miracle occurred during the conquest of this city on the hill where the holy chapel is, and for the rest who also died during the conquest." On Saturdays—Mary's day of the week—the chaplain would intone the mass of "Our Lady" on behalf of the confraternity's living members and its benefactors. Weaving together the dead and the living, these liturgical celebrations united conquistadors and *criollos* in a seamless spiritual community presided over by Los Remedios. The confraternity's founders even stipulated that if "any son or daughter, grandson or granddaughter of a conquistador should be so poor" that he or she could not afford the organization's entry fee, it would be waived. All descendants of the conquistadors deserved to participate in the confraternity's Marian cult of the conquest.

The confraternity's promotion of their Madonna as the special patron of the conquistadors soon met with success.[63] In his history of the Indies published in 1581, Diego Durán, a Dominican who lived most of his life in New Spain, wrote that the conquistadors had been especially devoted to Los Remedios. According to this friar, after the Toxcatl massacre, the Spaniards had implored her to ward off the grisly hallucinations—walking corpses and leaping disembodied heads—being visited upon them nightly by Mexica sorcerers. Durán's amplified version of Los Remedios' legend culminates with Cortés himself deciding to found a chapel in her honor on Totoltepec.[64]

By the late 1590s, pilgrims who climbed the hill to seek Los Remedios' aid would have realized that she was the Virgin of the conquest the moment that they stepped inside the church. Splashed across the chapel's interior walls were paintings and verses celebrating her virtues and miracles, among them all the major Marian marvels associated with the Spaniards' arrival in Tenochtitlan and their defeat of the Mexica.[65] These murals disappeared when a larger church was built for Los Remedios in the 1620s, but fortunately Luis de Cisneros, a Mercedarian friar from a prominent *criollo* family of Mexico City, included a detailed description of them in the history of the shrine he finished in 1616.[66] Ten large frescoes flanked by columns depicted Los Remedios' miracles, while clusters of smaller painted panels framed more scenes as well as poems in Latin and Spanish glossing the paintings and teaching Mariological lessons. This Marian festival in word and image owed its design to Joseph López, Totoltepec's chaplain in the 1590s and the son of a wealthy *criollo* benefactor of Mexico City, who in 1595 commissioned the artist Alonso de Villasana for the project.[67] The images and words decorating the church's walls were testimony to Mexico City's *criollo* elite's expanding vision of their Madonna's role in the conquest.

The first large painting on the chapel's right-hand wall boldly asserted that the image of Mary that Cortés had so famously enshrined in the Templo Mayor during his sojourn in Tenochtitlan was none other than the statue of Los Remedios guarded on Totoltepec. In the mural, Cortés installs the statue in the temple. One of the poetic octaves below explained the scene as one of religious struggle and eventual Christian victory, accomplished by Mary and the conquistadors' leader. It drew on imagery from classical antiquity to relate how the Madonna's presence in the Templo Mayor elicited the anger of the forces of darkness: "the Stygian lake sent forth its venom, the barbarian resistance. But against such a great Lady no one can resist nor is there any one who can counter the strength of the Marqués [sc. Cortés]."[68] In the next mural, the Mexica try to remove Los Remedios from the Templo Mayor, but fail.[69]

When visitors to the chapel turned to face the first mural on the left-hand wall, they were plunged into the chaos of the Noche Triste and reminded that the Spaniards and their native allies had found a savior in Los Remedios. In the fresco, she appears on Totoltepec and forces the conquistadors' enemies to fall back by blinding them with "sand and dust," as the accompanying poem relates. This painting and its verses are the earliest evidence that Los Remedios had become the famous sand-throwing Virgin of legend.[70] The poem trumpets her military prowess, proclaiming that she "gave to the people dear to her victory with a miracle worthy of memory" and protected "the invincible Christian army" from the "barbarian furor." The last line of the painted verse crowns Los Remedios with a title befitting her newfound status: "During that great campaign, this Lady won the name of Conquistadora."[71]

La Conquistadora—this is an honorific that the Mercedarian friar who so carefully copied down the verses adorning the chapel walls used for Los Remedios in his lengthy history of her shrine. To be more precise, Luis de Cisneros was wont to call her "the holy (*santa*) *conquistadora*."[72] To him, this title had its spiritual side; he wrote that Mary was the "most courageous captain that God had in all of his army in heaven and on earth" and that she led the fight against the devil.[73] Cisneros was well versed enough in biblical exegesis to cite the passages from the Song of Songs that generations of medieval clerics and monks before him had read as allusions to her powers in the pitched battle against Lucifer's minions: Mary was the Song's bride, "terrible as the array of a battle line," and David's tower bristling with weapons.[74]

From the Song of Song's tower, wrote Cisneros, Mary handed out to her devotees weapons intended "not only for spiritual wars, but for physical ones."[75] This friar, a proud *criollo* who, as he told his readers, had been born in Mexico City and lived there most of his life, emphasized how such Marian arms had been particularly efficacious during the foundation of European colonies like the one he loved as his homeland.[76] Some of his evidence came from distant realms. Who, Cisneros wrote, had "helped" Vasco da Gama during the "celebrated and famous" conquest of India in 1497 "if not holy Mary," offering "visible aid" in battle?[77] But this friar drew the bulk of his evidence for her ability to "attend...to her devotees not only in peace, but also in war" from Mexico and the Caribbean.[78] He retold, for example, the old tale about Mary and the Tainos of Cuba's Cabo de Cruz, restoring and amplifying the martial detail that Las Casas had pruned away.[79] In Cisneros's history, this story serves as a worthy prelude to Mary's much more glorious military miracles on Mexican soil, all of them executed by Los Remedios herself.

During the conquest of New Spain, Cisneros proclaimed, Los Remedios had "appeared" an "infinite number of times" to help the conquistadors.[80] This was hyperbole, since the friar actually described only one Marian battlefield apparition: the miracle of the dirt-throwing Madonna, which he appropriated for Los Remedios and the Noche Triste, just as the murals of the chapel on Totoltepec had.[81] For this wonder and the many others performed by Los Remedios during the conquest, declared Cisneros, the people of New Spain owed her an enormous debt of gratitude. They in fact owed "the whole conquest to her."[82] The friar described his fellow citizens as a sort of Marian elect, a people for whom the Virgin had done more than she had for any other—an implicit elevation of New Spain above Spain itself.[83]

According to the friar, Los Remedios had worked her Mexican miracles "by means of her most holy image," the civic icon venerated in the chapel on Totoltepec. He reiterated the claim made by the murals on the shrine's walls that this was the same statue of Mary that Cortés had placed in Tenochtitlan's Templo Mayor and the Mexica had been unable to remove.[84] Sure as Cisneros was of this image's importance to conquest history and of the veneration due it from his contemporaries in New Spain, he confessed that he knew very little about the statue's career before it so spectacularly dislodged the Mexica idols. Worried that uncertain origins would do little to enhance Los Remedios' appeal among the bevy of Madonnas vying for devotees' attention in early seventeenth-century Mexico City, he hastened to point out that many famous images of Mary had histories shrouded in mystery. [85]

Possessed by the spirit of research, Cisneros yearned to discover where the Marian statue that he and other prominent *criollos* of Mexico City so loved had come from. To unearth clues, he interviewed people and consulted old books and fragile manuscripts.[86] The results, he admitted to his readers, were frustratingly inconclusive—he had found conflicting accounts of the statue's deep past. From his sleuthing, he did learn that the image had entered New Spain with a member of Cortés's company. Some of Cisneros's sources identified this conquistador as Juan Rodríguez de Villafuerte, one of Cortés's close associates who had fought at Tenochtitlan and in later campaigns.[87] Other evidence suggested that the image had crossed the Atlantic with a man whose name Cisneros could not discover. According to the friar's sources, the statue originally belonged to this anonymous conquistador's brother, a soldier of the Spanish imperial army. He campaigned in Italy and Germany, where the image of the Madonna "saved him from the many dangers he faced during the wars." Hoping that Los Remedios' powers would extend to the wars of a new continent, he bestowed this Marian talisman on his conquistador brother.[88]

Cisneros prudently did not say which version of Los Remedios' provenance he judged to be closer to the truth. Both stories probably satisfied him, for each endowed the statue of Los Remedios with a military genealogy and reinforced the reputation that she was acquiring as La Conquistadora. Both also attest to this Madonna's growing stature in the vision of history evolving in Mexico City's *criollo* circles. Cisneros's contemporaries residing in and around New Spain's capital evidently gossiped about Los Remedios. Perhaps their curiosity was born from their increasing conviction that the statue was indeed what the friar proclaimed it to be: a precious "relic" of the conquest.[89]

Puebla

Not everyone in New Spain shared the belief that Los Remedios could take credit for all of Mary's military miracles during the colony's foundation. In particular, some residents of Puebla, the burgeoning town east of Mexico City that aspired to economic, social, and cultural prominence, rebelled against Los Remedios' reign as the queen of conquest history. These Poblanos worked to dethrone the capital's Madonna in favor of their own Virgin Conquistadora, the small statue of Mary that in 1521 Cortés had given to the Tlaxcalteca war captain, Acxotecatl. By 1582 this Madonna had made her way to the Franciscans' church in Puebla, where she can be seen today. She stands in a high wall niche, enclosed in a glass-fronted shrine from either side of which spring the talons, outstretched wings, and beaks of a silver double-headed Habsburg eagle. La Conquistadora has been ensconced in this imperial monument—or one like it—ever since the late seventeenth century, when Francisco de Florencia, a Jesuit who knew Puebla well, admired the artistry with which she was "inserted into the breast of a silver eagle. . . with its wings extended in a gesture of desiring to take flight." He marveled at the cost of this magnificent object, estimating the Madonna's silver casing at more than 2,000 pesos.[90]

Some citizens of colonial Puebla evidently believed that their Conquistadora deserved such a showy shrine and were willing to fund it. By at least the early seventeenth century, some of her devotees insisted that it was this Madonna who had played the starring role during the conquest. As they made their offerings to her, they believed they were in the presence of the statue that Cortés had installed in the Templo Mayor.[91] According to Florencia, "some" even "said that [Puebla's] image, and not the one of Los Remedios in Mexico City . . . performed the wonders of throwing dirt in the eyes of the pagans."[92]

Naturally, such claims infuriated Los Remedios' literary champion, Luis de Cisneros. He dismissed them on many grounds, including the impossiblity that Cortés would have deprived Mexico City of the Templo Mayor's image of Mary and bestowed it on another town. Cortés had known, declared Cisneros, that the only natural home for this Madonna who had served as "the royal standard" in the fight against idolatry was New Spain's capital. Puebla's pretensions also offended this friar's historical sensibilities. Puebla, he said, simply was not an old enough city for Cortés to have taken La Conquistadora there.[93] Cisneros had a point. Puebla was in fact a young city, created a decade after Tenochtitlan's fall—which was precisely why some of its residents were so eager to expand their Conquistadora's connections to conquest history.

Puebla had been founded in 1531 at the command of the Royal Audiencia, whose members saw the need for a town on the heavily traveled route between New Spain's capital and the ports of the Gulf Coast. The site they chose for the new city lay in a well-watered valley not far from the same volcano that loomed over Tlaxcala. Nearby Nahua altepetl, allied with the Spaniards, contributed the thousands of indigenous men and women with whose labor Puebla was built.[94] Though it would have its Indian barrios and mixed race residents, it was intended as a Spanish city—a conceit that may have been cherished later by its criollo elite.[95] Puebla's first bishop, the socially ambitious prelate who had scorned Tlaxcala as too indigenous a place for his see, was perhaps nonetheless disappointed by the Spaniards in his flock. Among the city's original settlers were none of the great names of the conquest. The men who moved into Puebla in the 1530s were much more humble figures, who had played only supporting roles—if any—in the conquest. Among the town's heads of household in 1534, only half had fought in New World battles, and even those who had borne arms were not granted their residences in Puebla as a reward for military service. The Audiencia had founded Puebla in part as a place to house Spaniards who would be content as farmers and artisans.[96]

Puebla soon grew rich from the profits of its agricultural enterprises and, above all, from the cloth woven on the clacking looms of its textile workshops.[97] This industry made the town a magnet for immigrants arriving from Spain.[98] New churches were built, their ornate façades and towers announcing the city's wealth. Grand houses began to jostle for space with the rude homes dating from Puebla's early years.[99] Yet none of this could hide the fact that the city did not possess a past worthy of its present dignity, a past, that is, anchored in the events that, by the late sixteenth century, Mexico's Spaniards increasingly invoked as the foundation for prestige in the present—the conquest.

Some canny Poblanos realized that enthroned within the thick walls of the city's oldest church sat a statue of Mary that could help solve the problem.[100] Through La Conquistadora—the Madonna who bore the illustrious title so many of their ancestors had lacked—they could forge a link between their community and the heroics of the conquest. Someone from Puebla likely motivated the formal inquiry of 1582 into the statue's history, which confirmed not just that this Virgin dated to at least 1521, but that she had won her name honestly in battle.[101] Whoever instigated the inquiry, the pages recording the Tlaxcaltecas' testimony soon ended up in the possession of Puebla's Franciscans.[102] In Puebla, La Conquistadora not only enjoyed the ministrations of the men and women belonging to her confraternity—an organization founded in the late sixteenth century—but, as the early seventeenth-century chronicler Juan de Torquemada wrote, was venerated as a wonder-worker and "a most precious relic."[103] Rumor had it, he continued, that "the first people to come from Spain had brought her and they had been favored by her on various occasions, or, to speak more truly, at all times."[104]

Records from a meeting of Puebla's *cabildo* in October 1631 confirm that it was fast becoming public opinion that La Conquistadora anchored the city in the right slice of the past. When town council members gathered that month, they reviewed documentary proof of this Madonna's distinguished history, the original copy of the 1582 testimony, presented to them by Fray Isidro Ordóñez, guardian of Puebla's Franciscan convent. The friar requested permission to donate the folios containing the Tlaxcalteca noblemen's memories of this Madonna to Puebla's archive. In his petition to the *cabildo*, he declared that it was only "right" that the "noble city" of Puebla celebrate La Conquistadora since she was a "relic" of the conquest—exactly the laurels Cisneros claimed for Mexico City's Los Remedios.[105]

The council members enthusiastically approved Fray Ordóñez's request and officially incorporated La Conquistadora into Puebla's civic memory. They directed the city's *escribano* to have the folios of the testimony bound between protective covers and then locked up securely. Then, proclaiming the statue "a great relic" with whose help "this kingdom had been won," the mayor urged the *cabildo* to commit civic monies to support the liturgical celebration of her cult that took place each January. One by one the council members voted in favor of his proposition.[106] With La Conquistadora's antiquity as a relic of the conquest established, their city had a stronger hand of cards to play in the game of colonial memory.

By 1653, the publicly funded pageantry on the opening day of La Conquistadora's novena visibly stated her place in Puebla's civic fabric and her status as one of the city's patron saints.[107] In a festive procession, this Madonna would leave her home in the Franciscans' church. After stopping briefly at the convent of the Poor Clares, women belonging to the religious order founded by one of Saint Francis's most ardent female devotees, La Conquistadora would go on directly to the cathedral, where *cabildo* members would welcome her and her fiesta would take place. She then would return to Santa Clara for the night before making her way back to San Francisco. This procession route proclaimed that La Conquistadora belonged to the friars, but her stay in the cathedral announced that she was the city's Madonna, too, as did other features of the celebration. Two of Puebla's high-ranking civic officers, *regidores*, oversaw the whole proceedings, as they usually did the city's religious ceremonies.[108] Less exalted residents had their own responsibilities, for the *cabildo* charged them with transforming Puebla into a palace worthy of receiving La Conquistadora. The night before the procession, *luminarias* would flicker from the window sills and balconies of the houses lining the streets through which the statue would pass. On the day of the procession, the citizens living along the route replaced the candles and lamps with a blaze of decorations more visible in the sunlight, hanging colorful cloths from their windows.

It is quite likely that as Puebla's *cabildo* and residents planned these festivities in honor of their Conquistadora, they cast an eye toward Mexico City. Other public demonstrations of Marian piety funded from the *cabildo's* coffers certainly betrayed signs of Puebla's competition with the capital. In the second decade of the seventeenth century, the city council members voted to pay for a lavish fiesta for the Virgin of the Immaculate Conception not only because she was their cathedral's saintly patron, but also because they knew that Mexico City's archbishop and *cabildo* had just instituted a spectacular celebration of this Madonna.[109] Yet it is important to notice also that as Puebla's council members embraced La Conquistadora as a civic symbol, they often acted with the prompting of the friars in whose church the statue resided.

The Franciscans hoped to use their Madonna to reassert the significance of their own order to Puebla at a time when the traditional bases of its power in New Spain were under assault. The late sixteenth century inaugurated a difficult period for Puebla's friars. The conflicts over ethnicity that roiled lay circles of Spanish society penetrated their convent's walls; wearing the humble robes prescribed by Saint Francis was no protection from the ravages of pride that spurred *peninsulares* and *criollos* to battle over prestige.[110] Fissured by such internal strife, the community was ill-equipped to withstand increasing external pressures. Beginning in the late sixteenth century, bishops and church councils commanded Franciscans all across New Spain to renounce the pastoral work among the indigenous that had led to the order's prominence in the New World. With the years of evangelization over, reasoned the bishops, the mendicant missionaries should hand over the care of souls to the secular clergy, to whom the job properly belonged.

This decree was announced at the Third Mexican Council of 1583, but the bishop of Puebla did not manage to strip the city's Franciscans of control over the churches frequented by the indigenous until 1640. Even before then, Puebla's friars must have felt threatened. They certainly knew about the new regulations and chafed under the increased constraints on their power as the secular clergy successfully drove home the idea that friars did not deserve to minister to the natives since their evangelical efforts had failed to stamp out idolatry. By the late sixteenth century, Puebla's Franciscans also had to field indigenous parishioners' increasing protests about heavy payments imposed by the Order. As epidemics winnowed the native population, the financial burden grew ever more onerous for each *altepetl*, and relations with the friars further soured.[111]

Surely it was no coincidence that just as the Franciscans felt their fortunes flagging, they eagerly shared La Conquistadora with the city of Puebla. These friars still possessed the dignity of history and apparently thought it could help shore up their reputation. After all, not only could they count among their predecessors men who had been the first to wage the wars of New Spain's spiritual conquest, but they also were the guardians of a Madonna with a glamorous past. By widening the space in Puebla's civic consciousness and memory for their Marian relic of the conquest, they subtly reminded the city's residents of the respect owed to their order.

Puebla's friars were not alone in understanding the considerable value of connections to a Madonna dating from the conquest. In the late 1580s, the Franciscan convent at Tacuba, just outside Mexico City, launched a vigorous effort to take over the nearby Marian shrine of Totoltepec, where Los Remedios was venerated. The politics surrounding this attempt are tangled, even by colonial standards. The official proposition apparently came not from the friars, but from Jerónimo López, the *regidor* of the institution that controlled Los Remedios' church, Mexico City's *cabildo*. His suggestion in 1586 that the city turn the management of the shrine's religious affairs over to the Franciscans caused an uproar among *cabildo* members. Many approved of the plan, but others were outraged at the thought of the friars getting their hands on this civic symbol. The heated debate lasted several years. The Franciscans began to press their claims to the chapel, pointing out that it originally had fallen under the jurisdiction of their convent at Tacuba. The viceroy intervened to support transferring the church to the friars, while the archbishop of Mexico was against it. The project was moving ahead when several of the plan's most staunch opponents occupied the shrine and refused to leave unless their demands were met. According to Cisneros, one of these men even kidnapped the statue of Los Remedios, hid it in Mexico City's cathedral, and would not reveal its whereabouts, even after being arrested and imprisoned. Calm was restored late in 1589, when the idea of giving the shrine to the friars was scrapped and Los Remedios returned to Totoltepec.[112]

Amidst this host of conflicting interests, the Franciscans were clearly determined to associate themselves with Los Remedios' increasingly successful cult. Painting these friars as religious opportunists, Cisneros alleged that their cupidity was stirred by the "greatness of [this] Virgin…the miracles Our Lord did through her intercession, and how she had enriched this kingdom," a perfectly plausible set of motivations for their claims.[113] But Jerónimo López, the *cabildo* member who first suggested the plan, emphasized what the friars could do for Los Remedios rather than what she could do for them. The rationale he outlined to his fellow *cabildo* members reveals another important dimension to *criollos'* understanding of their Virgins of the conquest.

López worried that dwindling numbers of indigenous men and women were attending the masses and religious festivities at Los Remedios' shrine, thereby diminishing the church's income from alms and offerings. In large part, he explained, the fault lay with the shrine's chaplains. They tended to celebrate services in Spanish, a language that the average native man or woman did not understand terribly well in this period.[114] Appointing Franciscans to oversee the chapel would solve this problem, as the friars were famed for their mastery of indigenous tongues. Beyond his interest in boosting the church's finances, López evidently believed Los Remedios' cult should include the indigenous, for that would prove her universal appeal. The initially warm hearing he was given by a majority of the *cabildo* members indicates that these *criollos* shared his view.

As the Spaniards in Mexico worked out a serviceable vision of the past through their Virgins of the conquest, these Madonnas acquired a distinctively colonial identity that embraced the indigenous world rather than rejecting it. This Marian history reflected the official conception of New Spain as composed of both a *república de los indios* and a *república de los españoles*, a powerful ideology despite its considerable distance from the rainbow-hued realities of race and ethnicity in colonial Mexico.[115] It also suggests another side to the image of conquest nurtured by New Spain's *criollos* in the late sixteenth and early seventeenth centuries.

The Other Side of Conquest History

Above one particularly elaborate fresco painted in the 1590s on the walls of Los Remedios' chapel on Totoltepec was an inscription in Latin proclaiming the gratitude of the "S.P.Q.M."—the "Mexican Senate and people"—to Mary, "their most faithful patron and helper." The allusion to ancient Rome evident in this reworking of the famous abbreviation "S.P.Q.R." was heightened by the classical touches in the depictions of Mexico City below the inscription, but more striking still in these frescoes was the emphasis on the indigenous as an embodiment of New Spain's capital, along with the painterly evocation of the conversion of the native world under Mary's tender tutelage.[116]

In one scene, entitled "Peace be to you," the Virgin held her son and at the same time reached out a caduceus—a Roman staff of office typically borne by peacemaking missions—to an "Indian." Unfurling from Mary's lips was a scroll quoting the welcoming words of Ephesians 2:19: "Now therefore ye are no more strangers and foreigners, but fellow citizens with the saints, and of the household of God." Nearby, a female figure representing the Church reclined on a vessel whose contents were pouring into Lake Tetzcoco, a scene glossed as one of baptismal purification with a quotation from Ezekiel 36:25: "Then will I sprinkle clean water upon you, and ye shall be clean." The biblically literate would have known how the verse ends, though these words apparently were not painted on the wall: "from all your filthiness and from all your idols, will I cleanse you." The theme continued with Isaiah 6:7—"thine iniquity is taken away"—emblazoned right above the Mexico City's coat of arms. This heraldic device, which sported an eagle devouring a serpent, was based on a colonial misreading of a famous Mexica legend about the foundation of Tenochtitlan.[117]

In this cascade of images and words, the native and autochthonous repeatedly represented the multiracial civic body of the "S.P.Q.M.," that colonial city enjoying Los Remedios' favor. Yet each could personify Mary's city only by being Christianized and purged of idolatry's taint, as the mural's evocations of exorcism and spiritual regeneration announced. This set of paintings created an optimistic narrative of New Spain's conversion and cast Mary—not conquistadors or friars—in the role of missionary. Proffering the staff of peace to a native person and, in her guise as the Church, cleansing the waters that lapped the shores of Tenochtitlan, she leads the city and its peoples into the embrace of the faith.

Cisneros reinforced the message in a chapter of his history devoted to the Virgin's labors to bring Christianity to the New World, declaring that "from its very beginnings, this conversion was the work of Our Lady."[118] Pondering the millions of souls to be saved, idolatry's tenacious hold on the indigenous, and the vastness of the land they inhabited, Cisneros concluded that the effort would have been impossible without "Mary's powerful directing hand."[119] Although citing no specific miracles from Mexico demonstrating her evangelical powers, Cisneros offered his audience the story of the Tainos from Cuba's Cabo de Cruz, as well as a yarn of how Mary converted a king of Mozambique by appearing to him in a dream, a technique she had perfected years before on the Muslims of al-Andalus and North Africa.[120]

Another painting in the Totoltepec chapel underlined Mary's prominence as evangelist in the evolving *criollo* vision of conquest history. This fresco, which depicted Los Remedios preventing the Mexica from taking her statue out of the Templo Mayor, proclaimed that conversion had been her aspiration even while she worked some of her most terrifying military miracles during the battles over Tenochtitlan. The accompanying verses framed this wonder that "honored our land" with language as suggestively evangelical as it was patriotic: although the Mexica's repeated efforts to "exile" Los Remedios from the Templo Mayor showed these Indians to be "blind" to spiritual truth as well as "ungrateful and scornful," "sweet and loving" Mary was waging this "war" for "their good" and would "conquer" them spiritually.[121] The Virgin Conquistadora fêted by Puebla also was believed to have her own connection to the spiritual dimension of the conquest, and not just because she had accompanied a Franciscan on an evangelizing mission to Chocomán. In 1582, Fray Diego Rangel, the Franciscan prior of Tlaxcala, testified that Cortés had chosen to give La Conquistadora to Tlaxcala "because it was the first part of this New Spain where the Holy Gospel was preached."[122]

This emphasis on the Madonna as the heroine of New Spain's conversion was new.[123] Although in deed and memory, conquistadors like Cortés and Díaz had often given a Marian cast to their own enterprises of Christianization, they carefully reserved the role of active missionizing for themselves. In the later sixteenth century, these men were still often commemorated as lay evangelists. The 1579 ordinances of Los Remedios' confraternity, for example, celebrated "the Spanish conquistadors who came to this New Spain to establish here the holy Catholic faith."[124] Yet these human actors were now dwarfed on the stage of conversion by the twinning of the military and spiritual conquests in the figure of the Virgin suggested by Cisneros and the frescoes on Totoltepec.

By the time these frescoes were painted, many residents of Mexico were increasingly inclined to believe that the missionary work of the early years had been much more than a divinely willed human project. Newly forged stories told how tangible support for the evangelization of the indigenous had come directly from heaven. Miracles attributed to holy crosses, saints, and sacred images became ever more common in narratives of New Spain's conversion and other forms of colonial religious literature. The Franciscan Bernardo de Lizana, who in the early seventeenth century worked among the Maya and wrote a devotional history of the image of Mary enshrined at Izamal in central Yucatan, explained that God had performed "many marvels and miracles" through this Madonna precisely in order to lure the indigenous away from their "false gods."[125] No wonder Cisneros dusted off the old story about the Tainos of Cuba's Cabo de Cruz and the sailor's wonder-working Virgin. This tale fit the temper of his time, an era when clerics imbued with Counter-Reformation ideals pointed to sacred images and miracles of holy men and women as evidence of Catholicism's triumph—and colonials (Spanish and native) sought to find the tangible imprint of God's hand in the history of conversion and on their land.[126] Perhaps this turn to miracle reflected pessimism among New Spain's churchmen about whether the indigenous could really be weaned from their love of "idolatry" by human effort alone.[127] In any case, it reveals how some criollos sought to create foundations for the Mexican church resting on higher and more morally secure ground than the bloodshed of the conquest or the efforts of the friars.[128] The new history of conversion proposed by Cisneros and the murals on Totoltepec—a history in which Mary played the starring role—could provide this alternative narrative of origins.

In underscoring the Virgin of the conquest's ability to be "sweet and loving" with the natives of the New World, the verses glossing one of the Totoltepec frescoes subtly suggested the ambivalence about the conquest that some *criollos* had come to feel by the turn of the sixteenth century. While still extolling the heroism of their forebears, they deplored the wanton violence of the Spanish entrance into the New World, the murder of countless indigenous men and women, and the destruction of monuments of Mesoamerican high culture. Linked with this "emotional distancing" from the horrors of the conquest was "a growing sympathy" for the indigenous.[129] Both of these shifting currents in the *criollo* perception of the past ran through the Marian conversion frescoes on Totoltepec, where they converged with another.

By the late sixteenth century, many *criollos* were enthusiastically incorporating the glories of indigenous culture into their patriotic histories of Mexico. They claimed the magnificence of the pre-Columbian past as part of their heritage, brandishing it as proof that New Spain was a worthy rival of the land across the Atlantic.[130] Some *criollos* went so far as to intimate that they counted among their own ancestors illustrious indigenous rulers and noblemen.[131] When it suited their political agenda, *criollos* could even masquerade as Indians. One night in 1566, two of the leading *criollos* who aspired to make Martín Cortés their king donned the rich dress of Mexica caciques. Followed by a retinue of other *criollos* clothed as native warriors, they made their way to Martín and offered him a crown of flowers, a scene intended to evoke Moctezuma's supposedly voluntary submission to Cortés the elder and his bestowal of Mexico on the conquistador.[132] In this piece of subversive political theater, the conflation of the *criollo* with the indigenous was crucial, as it was in the Marian conversion fresco in the chapel on Totoltepec, where the autochthonous stood for the grandeur of New Spain's colonial capital. Perhaps it was also quietly at work in the cult of another Virgin of the conquest, Puebla's Conquistadora.

During this Madonna's rise to prominence as a symbol of Puebla, there was never an effort to erase the years that she had spent in the care of the neighboring indigenous community of Tlaxcala. Instead, the elite Poblanos who devoted themselves to nurturing this Madonna's reputation carefully preserved that period of her history. In 1582, the formal inquiry into the statue's past even deliberately resurrected her time among the Tlaxcalteca. The detailed descriptions provided by several elderly noblemen from this *altepetl* created her official pedigree, guarded first at Puebla's Franciscan convent and then in the city's own archives.[133] Their testimony of course proved that this Conquistadora had the conquest background fashionable in Mexico's Spanish circles by the late sixteenth century. Yet as these native memories were marshaled in support of Spanish colonial identities, they also established a link between this Madonna and the Tlaxcalteca nobility of the conquest era that was almost as important to the story Puebla wished to tell of past and present as was her connection with Cortés. If this statue had been given to the city directly by the conquistador, rather than arriving there after a sojourn among this *altepetl* of native conquistadors, it might not have been so potent a civic symbol in the early seventeenth century, as developments in the cult of Mexico City's own Virgin of the conquest suggest.

By the 1590s, an important new chapter in Los Remedios' evolving biography as a relic of the conquest featured her prolonged stay in an indigenous man's house. Like La Conquistadora's native host in Tlaxcala, this man was a noble; in most of the texts to mention him, he merits the title "Don." Unlike Tlaxcala's Acxotecatl, however, he did not receive the image of Mary from a conquistador. Instead, he rescued the statue from obscurity some years after the Noche Triste, at least according to a miracle story promoted by the *criollo* caretakers of this Madonna's shrine at the end of the sixteenth century. The world of wonders evoked in this tale is far removed from the sober testimony given by the Tlaxcalteca noblemen in 1582 about Puebla's Conquistadora's years with their *altepetl*. Yet it too presents noble native testimony—whether fictive or not— as crucial to the genealogy of a Virgin of the conquest. In fact, the indigenous cultural world was fundamental to this new set of miracles attributed to Los Remedios—so fundamental that this tale must be read from two colonial perspectives, indigenous and *criollo*.

Even more explicitly than the conversion frescoes on Totoltepec, this new part of Los Remedios' story painted her as an icon of both sides of conquest history. The marvels it described balanced the miracle of the Noche Triste by presenting an indigenous man as witness to Mary's ability to inspire not just fear but also overwhelming love in those who beheld her. Terrifying and tender by turns, this Conquistadora is both the scourge of the conquistadors' enemies and the benevolent mother of Mexico's new Christians, indeed of all the colony's Christians, regardless of their race.

"Terrible and Bellicose ... Kind and Loving"

In the cycle of frescoes decorating the Totoltepec chapel, immediately following the large painting of Los Remedios blinding her enemies came one depicting her potential to deal more gently with the natives of New Spain. This mural offered the earliest known version of a story destined for fame: the legend of Los Remedios' intimate relationship with an indigenous nobleman named Don Juan. According to Cisneros, the painting showed "the miracle that the Virgin worked with her Indian devotee, Don Juan, when he found her and with his saintly simplicity put her in a box and she went back to the place where he found her, and how he gave her food and drink so she would not go away."[134] Fortunately, the friar provided a more detailed account elsewhere of the wonders that Los Remedios worked with Don Juan, starting with the Noche Triste. From this dark beginning, these miracles blossomed into a romance between Los Remedios and her native devotee.

On the Noche Triste, wrote Cisneros, a Spanish conquistador had the statue of Los Remedios in his keeping. When he took shelter with his fellows beneath the walls of the temple on Totoltepec, he set the image down in a safe place. There the statue stayed, forgotten and abandoned on the hill after the conquistadors' departure for Tlaxcala. Years passed, fifteen or twenty according to Cisneros' calculations. Then Los Remedios took matters into her own hands. She began appearing to Don Juan, an indigenous man from a village just west of Totoltepec. Not just once, but "many times" as he walked by the hill on his way to Mexico City, he saw a "resplendent and beautiful" statue of a woman urging him to come and find her.[135]

The native nobleman had no difficulty recognizing this apparition. "As [Don Juan] himself testified many times," wrote Cisneros, she was none other than Los Remedios, the Madonna "of the conquest." Don Juan remembered her from his battlefield experience of many years ago, for on the Noche Triste, he had been among the ranks of native warriors cowering before her terrifying wrath.[136] But the Franciscans in the convent at Tacuba refused to believe his tales of the lovely female figure haunting his trips from Tacuba to Mexico City—until proof came to confirm his insistence that she was indeed Los Remedios.

One day as Don Juan was out hunting with his dogs, he stumbled across the ruins of the temple where the conquistadors had holed up during the Noche Triste. There, beneath the spiky leaves of a large maguey, he found the statue of Mary that had appeared to him so many times. Filled with love for this *linda señora* (pretty lady) with her dainty beauty and "solemn blue eyes," he murmured endearments to her, took her home, and placed her in a box for safekeeping. But despite his affection for this Madonna, she would not stay with him—the statue kept vanishing from the box and returning to the spot on Totoltepec where he had found it. Don Juan tried to entice Mary into remaining at home by giving her food—tortillas, eggs, and chile—and drink. Eventually he slept on top of the box holding the Madonna and her meals. Even this did not stop the statue from escaping.

After twelve years, wrote Cisneros, Don Juan consulted Don Albaro Tremiño, the master of Mexico City's cathedral school, who ordered that an altar be constructed for her in the native nobleman's house. Soon word of the miraculous Madonna spread. Pilgrims—indigenous and Spanish, men and women—began to crowd into Don Juan's home, so many that he eventually asked Tremiño to move the image to a chapel in the nearby village of San Juan. There the statue

spent a year, performing miracles for pilgrims. Among them was Don Juan himself, who had fallen sick. Mary cured him, but not without a gentle scolding.
Why, she asked him, had he not yet understood that she wanted him to build
a shrine for her on Totoltepec? Joined by the other Indians in his village, Don
Juan finally constructed a humble chapel of straw and adobe atop the hill where
he had found the image years earlier. On this building's simple stone altar, he
enthroned the statue of Los Remedios.

This tale of the love between Don Juan and Los Remedios provided a new
story of origins for the chapel on Totoltepec, in which the indigenous displaced
the conquistadors. Asserting that native villagers had built the first Marian
church on the hill, this narrative granted a new prominence to indigenous people in this Virgin of the conquest's past, matching the realities of her cult in the
present. The records of life in New Spain's capital during the seventeenth and
eighteenth centuries present native people as active and full participants in the
civic veneration she enjoyed. Along with Mexico City's other residents, they
enthusiastically thronged the streets to greet Los Remedios on the days when
she traveled from her chapel to the cathedral. At other times of the year, crowds
of indigenous men and women gathered on Totoltepec to honor her with their
own festivities, sometimes wrangling with the *cabildo* over access to the statue or
even vying with each other to control the ceremonies.[137]

How much this indigenous affection for Los Remedios was engendered
by the legend of Don Juan is hard to know. It might, in any case, have made
sense to native men and women living in and around Mexico City to venerate
Mary—"Our Precious Mother"—on Totoltepec, since before the arrival of the
Spaniards, their ancestors had climbed this hill to worship at the shrine of the
goddess Toçi, "Our Grandmother."[138] But the story of Don Juan surely communicated to the indigenous that Los Remedios belonged to them as much as she
did to all the other people who prayed to her. Until the disappearance in the early
seventeenth century of the chapel's frescoes, native visitors to Totoltepec could
see their own traits reflected in the painted face of Don Juan as he received sign
after sign of the Virgin's miraculous favor just as they themselves hoped to.[139] In
Cisneros's day, displayed in a place of honor on the chapel's main altar was an
object whose contours communicated to the indigenous that this native man
stood at the center of Los Remedios's cult. It was a *tecomatl*, a deep round bowl
of the sort found in almost every Nahua house. Set in silver, it was reputed to be
the actual vessel in which Don Juan had given drink to Los Remedios' statue—a
sacred relic testifying to the image's many years in an indigenous home.[140]

It is possible that the Don Juan stories originated among the indigenous, as
Cisneros insisted. The friar worked hard to convince his readers that he had solid
evidence. He explained that he had talked to the sacristan of Los Remedios'
temporary chapel at San Juan, who provided him with eyewitness testimony to

the miracles she had performed there. Several times, Cisneros mentioned having also interviewed an elderly indigenous woman named Doña Ana, whom he
identifies as Don Juan's daughter.[141] His conversations with her could reveal that
the indigenous residents of the area around Tacuba told stories about how a loving Virgin had appeared to one of them on Totoltepec. By the later sixteenth
century, some indigenous men and women in central Mexico indeed believed
that Mary blessed them with her miraculous presence as generously as she did
Spaniards.[142] The Don Juan narrative exhibits the hallmarks of Nahua Christian
miracle tales, including the emphasis on sacred landscape and the prominence
of a nobleman in the experience of the miraculous.[143]

Perhaps in the story of Don Juan there even lingered a much reworked native
memory of how an indigenous nobleman really had acquired an image of Mary
abandoned or misplaced at some point by the Spaniards, maybe during the confusion of the Noche Triste. Nor is it farfetched to think that such a man would
have cherished the image, made a place for it at home, and plied it with offerings, for that is exactly how the Tlaxcalteca war captain Acxotecatl apparently
treated the Marian statue that Cortés bestowed on him. Nahuas indeed often
fostered domestic cults around saints' images. Sometimes they even transferred
especially prized images from their homes to local chapels so the saint could
enjoy more public attentions from the *altepetl*.[144]

Yet no indigenous writers living in central Mexico during the sixteenth century or the first few decades of the next so much as hinted that they knew the
tale of Don Juan and Los Remedios, nor suggested that the chapel on Totoltepec
was a native foundation. Doña Ana unfortunately did not provide Cisneros with
the sort of sworn testimony that officially documented the years that Puebla's
Conquistadora had spent among the indigenous. Whatever the origins of the
story of Los Remedios and her native rescuer, its emergence can only be tracked
in the *criollo* milieux so important in fostering her cult. The chronology of its
evolution neatly coincided with the crystallization of *criollo* patriotism and the
appearance of new versions of history that sought to eliminate the blemish of
conquest violence while preserving the conquistadors' heroic glow.

When the *criollo* men who sat on Mexico City's council announced their
intention in 1574 to replace Los Remedios' old church on Totoltepec with a
more magnificent building, they did not seem familiar with the story of Don
Juan. The document solemnizing their decision assumes that the original chapel owed its origins to their distinguished conquistador forebears and describes
no miraculous post-conquest apparitions by Los Remedios to a native nobleman, though it highlights her battlefield appearance on the Noche Triste. Had
these *criollos* known of the Don Juan wonders, they surely would have enlisted
these marvels in service of their project and thus bolstered their case that the
Totoltepec shrine was a special place worthy of a generous infusion of civic

monies. Their silence suggests that the story of Don Juan and Los Remedios became well known only sometime after the chapel's refoundation.[145]

By the 1590s, Don Juan's discovery of the statue and the playful evidence of Los Remedios' insistent affection for Totoltepec were painted on the chapel walls for all to see. According to Cisneros's description, these murals did not themselves announce the native nobleman as the chapel's first father.[146] The words of a *criollo* writing more than a decade before Cisneros in fact hint that the Don Juan wonders were at first grafted onto Totoltepec's illustrious history as a conquistador foundation. Baltasar Dorantes de Carranza, a civic official in Veracruz whose conquistador father had miraculously survived Pánfilo de Narváez's ill-fated expedition to Florida and the agonizing odyssey back to Mexico, included the story of Los Remedios in a treatise he composed in 1604 to promote the *criollo* cause. First he related how Cortés had ordered a chapel built on Totoltepec in gratitude for this Madonna's aid during the Noche Triste. Then he described the statue's apparition to "an Indian…named Don Alonso or Don Pedro" and its constant miraculous trips from this man's home to Totoltepec.[147]

Dorantes de Carranza confessed to his readers that despite his best efforts he had been unable to turn up more detail to flesh out this story. Perhaps he would have had better luck had he lived in Mexico City rather than Veracruz. But as his uncertainty about the native seer's name suggests, even in the capital the tale may have still been rather inchoate. Dorantes de Carranza also let slip that not everyone was as convinced as he was by the reports of Los Remedios' miracles involving the Indian noble.

Naturally enough, no such doubts clouded Cisneros's own fulsome version of the tale. By the time he wrote in 1616, Don Juan was both visionary and founder of Mary's chapel on Totoltepec. Over subsequent centuries, the church's conquistador origins would remain in more or less permanent eclipse and Don Juan would ascend in the firmament of Los Remedios' New World career as her devotees elaborated her biography. Colonial chroniclers and historians laying out the bright constellations of New Spain's past would often include the story of how a native nobleman's discovery of the statue on Totoltepec culminated in the chapel's establishment by indigenous men and women.[148]

To understand why Los Remedios' *criollo* promoters so enthusiastically incorporated this new chapter into the history of their Virgin of the conquest, it is important to remember their campaign to market her shrine to a civic public that included native men and women living in and around the capital. The Don Juan legend was the perfect imaginative complement to Jerónimo López's efforts to appoint bilingual chaplains for the chapel. It is equally important to remember that Mexican-born Spaniards seeking to construct new imaginative foundations for New Spain's church could project themselves onto ennobled indigenous figures not so very different from Don Juan. His story was a worthy addition to the history that proud *criollos* like Cisneros and Dorantes de Carranza labored to build for their land.

Rivaling miracles long familiar to Spanish Christians living on the other side of the Atlantic, the Don Juan wonders proved that Mary favored New Spain as much as she did Spain. Statues of the Madonna hidden in caves, perched in trees, or otherwise ensconced in nature and then miraculously revealed had peopled the peninsular devotional universe since the late Middle Ages.[149] To a modern observer, the pronounced similarities between Los Remedios' story and these Old World Marian legends—including repeated visions, religious authorities' reluctance to believe the seer, the image's insistent return to the site of its discovery, and the foundation of a chapel—suggest the latter as the blueprint for the former.[150] To a *criollo* writer of the 1620s like Juan de Grijalva, they suggested instead Los Remedios' stature as the equal of her Spanish sisters.

This Augustinian friar from Colima explicitly compared the Don Juan wonders to the miracles surrounding the finding of such famed peninsular Madonnas as Our Lady of Guadalupe. In doing so, Grijalva elevated Totoltepec's statue of Los Remedios to the illustrious category of revealed Marian images that "enjoy great veneration because of their antiquity and miracles."[151] If Los Remedios deserved the same honors as her Old World sisters, then surely *criollos* need not bow before *peninsulares'* pretensions. In this Madonna, "fortunate Mexico City" possessed "a sun" whose splendor illuminated the land, announced the painted verses accompanying the Totoltepec fresco of Don Juan's discovery of her statue.[152]

For *criollos*, the Don Juan legend also told a story about how New Spain had become as Christian a place as Spain itself. On the other side of the Atlantic, tales about Marian images that had patiently endured the centuries of Muslim domination, waiting in hiding for the arrival of Christian times, had long served as proof of the Iberian Peninsula's essential Christian identity. In early modern Spain, some civic boosters even bragged that their town's Madonna had spent her long years of concealment actually walled up in the masonry of a mosque.[153] The relationship between Spanish Christians and peoples who had held territory that Spain now considered its own also lay at the core of the story of Los Remedios and Don Juan. Yet this seer's identity suggests that New Spain's *criollos*, perhaps in conjunction with the indigenous, were articulating a vision of Christianization responding to their own needs.

In the Old World tales, it is Christians born and bred who find the concealed images of Mary.[154] Don Juan is instead a former military enemy and a convert; by the time he began to see the *linda señora* on Totoltepec, he had sincerely renounced his ancestors' religious ways in favor of Christianity, according to all versions of the story. Dorantes de Carranza even vaunted the Indian visionary as an exemplary convert, praising him as "an Indian who was among the first Christians [in New Spain] and a good Christian."[155] Cisneros for his part hinted

that Don Juan's privileged role in Los Remedios' history was the fruit of baptism. Contrasting the terrifying Marian apparition that had visited the native
nobleman during the Noche Triste "before his conversion" with the charming
visions years later "after his conversion," the friar implied that the Virgin would
never have chosen to reveal her tender side to an indigenous person still mired
in idolatry.[156] The peninsular Marian stories reassured early modern Spaniards
anxious about the threat of Ottoman expansion or worried about the orthodoxy
of the Moriscos, those converts of Muslim descent and markedly uneven adherence to Christianity, that Spain possessed an indelibly Christian core. But the
tale of Don Juan is a sort of Marian meditation on the conversion of New Spain's
people, figuring their peaceful incorporation into the church in the person of
this native nobleman.

   In the wake of the Los Remedios legend, stories about the miraculous discovery of images of Mary gained quite a vogue in New Spain—and very often the
seer was an indigenous convert to Christianity. Some of these Indian visionaries
would even share Don Juan's name, most famously Juan Diego, a humble native
resident of Mexico City, to whom the Virgin of Guadalupe repeatedly appeared
outside Mexico City, events which supposedly occurred in 1531, although no
writer mentioned them until the 1640s. The Guadalupe legend, whose origins
are much debated, took the imaginative world proposed by the Los Remedios
story several steps further to fashion a Madonna truly native to New Spain.[157]
The Virgin whom Juan Diego saw did not lead him to a statue of Mary that had
come to Mexico from Spain. Instead, this Madonna filled his *tilma* (cloak) with
Castilian roses and left her own likeness behind on the rough cloth, blessing
New Spain with an image sent directly from heaven. According to the earliest
written versions of the story, Juan Diego's *tilma* was woven from the fiber of the
maguey, a plant important to indigenous culture. And, these same texts note, the
"precious face" of the image was "dark," a skin tint this Virgin shared with native
men and women.[158]

   Almost anywhere people of Mexican descent settle today, they bring with
them reproductions of the Marian image that was miraculously revealed to Juan
Diego centuries ago. Standing serenely in a mandorla, her cloak scattered with
stars, Mexico's Guadalupe watches over the faithful from church altars and roadside shrines as well as taxi dashboards, appliquéd leather jackets, bottle cap earrings, even the hoods of low riders and tattoos inked onto her devotees' bodies
(Figure 9.3).[159] Every day in Guadalupe's basilica in Mexico City, hundreds of
pilgrims jostle for room on the moving walkways passing in front of the original
image—ingenious crowd control devices that let no devotee linger too long in
contemplation of the sacred *tilma*.

   Guadalupe's popularity far overshadows Los Remedios in modern Mexican
devotional life. But in the seventeenth century, these two Virgins shared the

Figure 9.3 Apparition of the Virgin of Guadalupe to Juan Diego. Roadside shrine, Texas. Author photo.

affections of Mexico City's residents. Both served as the saintly patrons of the colonial capital, exercising complementary powers to protect its residents.[160] Unlike her sister venerated on Totoltepec, however, Guadalupe was no relic of the conquest. The tale of Juan Diego precluded any connection between this miraculous Marian image and conquistadors.

Nor did the conquest figure in the stories told during the seventeenth century about other images of Mary unveiled in New Spain's natural landscape. Indigenous residents of Tlaxcala, for example, came to believe that an image of the Virgin venerated in the church of Ocotlán on the outskirts of their city had revealed itself miraculously to a native cacique in the 1540s. The tale, first put into writing by the learned Tlaxcalteca Don Manuel de los Santos y Salazar late in the seventeenth century, followed the familiar pattern.[161] As the story's nameless indigenous protagonist passes through the pine forests of Tlaxcala's sierra, he sees flames bursting from a tree. The vision repeats itself many times. Eventually the Tlaxcalteca nobleman brings his "spiritual fathers" (probably an allusion to the Franciscans) to observe the marvel. They cut down the pine and find at its heart the "sacred image" of the Virgin.

This legend presents a Tlaxcalteca leader as witness to the special qualities of a cherished image of Mary, a role that several elderly Tlaxcalteca noblemen had played in reality when they gave their testimony in 1582 about Puebla's Conquistadora. But in the late sixteenth century, these men had been summoned to verify the connections between a Madonna and conquest history, whereas the conquest was absent from the seventeenth-century legend of Ocotlán. Perhaps it is true that, as one historian has argued, the cult of the Virgin of Ocotlán consoled the Tlaxcalteca for the loss of La Conquistadora to Puebla.[162] The replacement Madonna, however, offered no link to the *altepetl*'s past as native Christian conquistadors, but instead was believed to have emerged from her fiery pine during the years when friars like Motolinía labored to cultivate Christianity in Tlaxcala.

In these legends about images of Mary springing from Mexico's natural fabric, the distancing from the conquest that already marked the story of Don Juan and Los Remedios had grown. The Virgin's miraculous conquest of the hearts of native men and women supplanted conquistador violence. In the early seventeenth century, when the residents of Puebla chose Mary as the official saintly patron of their city, they turned not to her incarnation as La Conquistadora, but instead to Our Lady of the Immaculate Conception.[163] The cult of Mexico City's Los Remedios responded to the changing spiritual fashions in which peaceful conversion upstaged savage conquest; as the story of Don Juan evolved in the seventeenth century, the chapel on Totoltepec shed its identity as a conquistador foundation and was remembered instead as having been established by indigenous converts acting under Mary's orders.

Yet the recent suggestion that "by the seventeenth century, Remedios lost all symbolic connection to the Conquest" might not be entirely correct.[164] After all, Cisneros, writing then, proclaimed Los Remedios "a holy *conquistadora*." Her heroic intervention on behalf of the conquistadors during the Noche Triste remained part of her legend. Many later authors would follow Cisneros's lead by invoking Don Juan as a witness both to Mary's awesome powers to overcome the Indians' armed resistance and to her abilities to inspire love in just those people.[165] Juan de Grijalva perhaps said it best in 1624. This friar believed that it was only because Don Juan had experienced the terrifying Virgin of the Noche Triste that he was able to identify the more benevolent figure who later appeared to him: "Don Juan... knew that this was the lady who had conquered them and put them to flight... on the day of the defeat he saw her as terrible and bellicose, but on this occasion as kind and loving." In fact, declared Grijalva, he himself was convinced of the truth of the Don Juan story precisely because of the "variety of [the Virgin's] appearances"—the friar knew that Mary was "terrible with the proud and gentle with the humble."[166] Los Remedios' legendary reputation as a Conquistadora would linger too in some indigenous circles; hence the Nahuatl captions for the seventeenth-century *Mapa de Cuauhtlantzinco*'s colorful drawings naming her as the Conquistadora who had fought for the Spaniards and their native allies.[167]

In the years when native artists were painting the *Mapa*, the association between Mary and the conquest remained potent enough that other Madonnas in New Spain acquired reputations as relics of the conquest. At the end of the seventeenth century, Francisco Antonio de Fuentes y Guzmán, the first *criollo* historian of Guatemala, proudly described a statue of Mary housed in the Mercedarian convent of Guatemala City as a "*conquistadora* who had been present in the battles... of the conquest of the Kingdom of Guatemala and Mexico... and had favored our brave and zealous soldiers." This Madonna, Fuentes y Guzmán insisted, was the statue that had hovered "in the air... above her army" and hurled down a blindingly "fine sand" on her Indian enemies— just the miracles described by his great-great grandfather Bernal Díaz del Castillo. Any visitor to the Mercedarian convent in the Guatemalan capital would find miraculous evidence that the image of Mary there was indeed the "powerful... valiant... brave and invincible... warrior (*guerrera*) and victorious veteran" who waged war on the Spaniards' behalf. An old arrow wound acquired during the conquest still pierced the base of the Madonna's neck. From the gash came a continuous flow of blood, oozing through the statue's varnish no matter how often it was wiped away.[168]

The stain of violence would prove just as hard to eradicate from the memory of the conquest, resurfacing again and again in the colonial consciousness. In fact, although Fuentes y Guzmán did not say so, the blood that trickled down the Guatemalan *conquistadora*'s neck seeped into his own world. In the seventeenth century, New Spain's conquering Madonnas were not confined to the realm of history. As a new round of conquistadors, Spanish and indigenous, set out to expand the frontiers of New Spain northward into the territory that would be baptized New Mexico, the legends forged in the sixteenth century about the Virgin *conquistadoras* would come to life.

10

The Return of the Virgin

In April 1598, the *criollo* Juan de Oñate and his company of 129 soldier-settlers, their families, a handful of Franciscans, and some Indian, mestizo, and black servants splashed across the Rio Grande near the place where today the twinned urban sprawl of El Paso and Ciudad Juárez defies the border between the United States and Mexico.[1] As they forded the river, they were leaving New Spain behind and entering the land they called New Mexico, a territory that Oñate had ceremoniously claimed for his monarch just days earlier. The Virgin Mary escorted them.

As the members of Oñate's party rode north among the mesas and buttes studding the desert landscape, their banners bobbed overhead. One was made of "figured white Castilian silk" trimmed with gold and crimson tassels. On one side, this banner sported Captain Luis Gasco de Velasco's familial coat of arms, and on the other, Oñate's own escutcheon. These emblems proclaiming the venture a joint enterprise of these two grandees lay small at the feet of much larger figures. The Virgin and John the Baptist stood serene over Oñate's arms, while Santiago and his horse pranced above the Velasco shield. Painted around the Madonna and her companion was a further Marian symbol, a rosary of large gold beads.[2] This standard placed Oñate's company under the patronage of that saintly pair so important to the colonial vision of conquest: Mary and Santiago. Two more banners showing the Virgin flanked by different celestial companions traveled with the party.[3]

Mary would soon demonstrate that her domain encompassed New Mexico itself. Oñate's soldier-settlers would rely on her to help sanction one of their most violent assaults on the indigenous men and women whom they would dub the Pueblo Indians, an ethnically and linguistically diverse set of peoples, as the colonists soon realized. In letters sent to the viceroy in Mexico City, Oñate compared the Pueblos' ways to the native cultures of Mexico. He observed that the Indians of New Mexico shared the skin color and general countenance of New Spain's indigenous population and that their "dress, grinding of meal, food, dances, and songs" were similar. He also described how, like the Nahuas and other peoples of Mexico, the Pueblos worshipped "idols," offering them "fire, painted reeds, feathers, and...little animals, birds, vegetables." In contrast to the centralized imperial order that the Spaniards had encountered in Moctezuma's Mexico, the Pueblos, Oñate believed, enjoyed a political existence "of complete freedom, for although they have some chieftains they obey them badly and in very few matters," a mischaracterization of the Pueblos' highly structured if localized political traditions.[4]

Oñate nonetheless found much to admire in these peoples. He believed that the corn and vegetables they cultivated ranked among the "best and the largest...anywhere in the world." He praised the buffalo robes the Pueblos wore ("these furs have a beautiful wool," he wrote), as well as the finely decorated black and white blankets they wove from cotton and agave fiber. The sophisticated architecture of Pueblo towns impressed him; to Spanish eyes, developed urban centers signaled a desirable degree of civilization. With graceful blocks of multistoried houses clustered around plazas, these towns inspired the Spaniards to name their inhabitants "Pueblos," a word meaning "town" or "municipality."[5]

Vastly exaggerated rumors of this urban civilization's magnificence already had reached New Spain in the late 1520s, inflaming the conquistadors' quixotic hopes that somewhere in the New World they might find the seven golden cities of ancient fable. Lured by this mirage, several expeditions had set out for New Mexico, including a company headed by Francisco Vázquez de Coronado in 1540.[6] This conquistador and his men had soon retreated when their expectations of finding streets paved with precious metal were proven wrong. The effort to colonize New Mexico would not be renewed until the later sixteenth century. Even then, the men and women who left the comforts of New Spain behind to venture northward would remain as much under the spell of potential riches as Coronado's company had been.

The colonization attempts of the late sixteenth century were impelled by the expansive energies of both miners and missionaries. The Franciscans, increasingly dispossessed of pastoral care over the indigenous in central New Spain, sought new fields in which to exercise their evangelical talents. In the northern reaches of Mexico, they struggled to convert the Chichimecs, indigenous peoples whom Spaniards and Nahuas alike saw as uncivilized barbarians, and who, in the friars' opinion, more than lived up to this reputation by fiercely resisting baptism.[7] Soon the Franciscans began to look beyond these *indios bárbaros* to the lands where Coronado's expedition had found a wealth of souls belonging to people seemingly more civilized than the Chichimecs and therefore perhaps more willing to embrace the Christian truth.[8] Other Spaniards living in Chichimec territory cast a greedy gaze in the same direction. Among them were men who had grown rich from the famous silver mines of Zacatecas, as well as prospectors still dreaming of a lucky strike. Like many of his companions on the expedition to claim New Mexico for Spain, Oñate hoped that the land north of the Rio Grande crossing would yield profitable lodes of precious metal.[9]

In Pueblo territory, Oñate's party mined little silver or gold. They encountered much the same difficulties that in the 1580s and early 1590s had plagued several Franciscan reconnaissance missions and two settlement attempts unauthorized by the Spanish Crown.[10] Unlike the men who led these latter, however, Oñate rode at the head of his company with the stamp of approval of the viceroy of New Spain, Luis de Velasco, who happened to be a personal friend. Oñate had won the much coveted official royal contract to settle and explore New Mexico and exploit its natural resources. In October 1595, Velasco named him the "governor, captain general, caudillo, discoverer and pacifier" of New Mexico.[11]

With these grand titles, Oñate entered into an elite conquistador fraternity that stretched back to the early years of Spanish colonization of the New World and included men such as Hernan Cortés. True, Velasco did not bestow the label of "conquistador" on his old friend. In 1573, Spanish officials had forbidden the men involved in vanquishing the indigenous and claiming new lands for the Crown from calling their endeavors conquests. The preferred term was now the softer-edged "pacification" that appears in Oñate's official instructions. According to the new doctrine, missionaries—not armed men—were to spearhead the enterprise of colonization, a policy that would profoundly mark the settlement of New Mexico.[12] The first century of the colony's existence would be dominated by the Franciscans and their evangelical drive, as they worked to claim New Mexico's land and people for Spanish Christendom by building imposing stone and adobe mission churches.

The proclamation of 1573 hardly ended Spanish violence against Indians, as New Mexico's Pueblos would learn firsthand.[13] Nor did it eliminate conquistadors, destroy conquistador sensibility, or even eradicate the word "conquest" from New Spain's colonial vocabulary.[14] Oñate envisioned himself as a conquistador equal to any who had gone before him. During his vexed progress toward the territory he was to govern, he was spurred on not only by his considerable material ambitions, but also by a desire to emulate and even outdo the heroes of the past. "With God's help," Oñate declared in a letter to the viceroy, " I am going to . . . give more pacified worlds, new and conquered to his majesty, greater than the good Marquis [sc. Cortés] gave him, despite his having done so much."[15] Cortés's exploits, much burnished by the tales so popular in colonial Mexico, haunted Oñate. In the "conquest dramas" he staged to try to persuade the Pueblos to submit to the powers he represented, he often tried to channel the ghost of Tenochtitlan's conqueror.[16] As Oñate and his companions strove to project their endeavors in New Mexico as a glorious continuation of the legendary conquest of old Mexico, their repertoire naturally included Mary, whose image adorned three of their banners.

Some modern historians believe that Oñate's "soldiers marched under a banner with an image of 'Our Lady of Remedies' identical to the one Hernán Cortés
had carried into Tenochtitlan in 1519."[17] This is probably wrong on all counts.
Not even in the late sixteenth- and seventeenth-century tales from Mexico that
fashioned Los Remedios into the conquistadors' special patron did Cortés bear
this Madonna's standard, never mind in 1519. As for Oñate, it would doubtless
dismay the organizers of a controversial commemoration at Santa Fe in 1998
of his expedition's quatercentenary to learn that the replica of his supposed
banner of Los Remedios presiding over the ceremonies might not have had a
1598 counterpart.[18] No contemporaneous evidence definitively identifies any of
those Madonnas emblazoned on the standards borne by Oñate's company as the
Virgin venerated in the chapel on Totoltepec.[19]

Whether or not a banner of Los Remedios fluttered overhead as Oñate and
the men and women in his party proceeded north in 1598, these people knew
that Mary belonged to conquistador mythos. In stories they would tell to justify
the bloodiest, ugliest, and most significant fight between their forces and the
Pueblos, she would in fact whitewash their violence and grace New Mexico with
a military miracle reminiscent of those attributed to the Madonna of Totoltepec.
Accompanied by Santiago, the Virgin would ride to these new conquistadors'
rescue, just as she had so often in Mexico's legends of the conquest.

According to a story first written down by one of Oñate's captains, Mary and
her male companion made their appearance during the terrible siege of Acoma
in 1599, which left some eight hundred Indians dead and delivered several hundred others into servitude to Oñate and his company. Crowning the summit of a
high mesa some sixty miles west of Albuquerque, the pueblo of Acoma deserves
its nickname of "Sky City." Its sixteenth-century residents climbed up and down
the sheer sandstone cliffs on trails consisting of hand- and foot-holds hewn into
the buff colored rock. A place spectacularly well fortified by nature, Acoma was
home to a large and powerful Pueblo community whom it was important for the
Spanish to establish good relations with and, ultimately, to control.

At first, things went relatively smoothly between the Acomas and the newcomers, despite the strategies of intimidation that the colonists used to strip
Pueblo communities of their resources. Soon, Oñate's oppressive demands for
tribute added tinder to the cultural misunderstandings that typically troubled
Spanish encounters with native peoples, igniting an explosion of violence. In
response to the colonists' offenses, Acoma warriors killed one of Oñate's captains and twelve of his men. Fearing that successful resistance by Acoma would
incite other pueblos to follow suit, the governor sent half his forces—some sev-
enty men—to lay siege to the mesa. A few days later, hundreds of Acomas lay
dead, and the remaining men, women, and children of the community had been
taken prisoner by Oñate's soldiers. These Indians were tried for murder, found

guilty, and sentenced with servitude and, for men over the age of 25, the amputa-
tion of one foot.[20] To complete the Acomas' humiliation, the Spaniards burned
down the town on the mesa top.[21]

The battle of Acoma was a just war won with "special aid from our God,"
wrote one of the victors, Alonso Sánchez, in a letter composed some weeks after
the bitter fight. With evident satisfaction, he related a miracle story that probably was already making the rounds among the colonists: after their defeat, the
Acomas looked in vain among Oñate's troops for a man who, astride "a white
horse, dressed in white, a red emblem on his breast, and a spear in his hand,"
had terrorized them "in the heat of battle."[22] Sánchez did not name this mysterious rider, nor did one of Oñate's captains also present at Acoma, Gaspar Pérez
de Villagrá, when he described the same episode in his monumental epic poem
about New Mexico published in 1610. But any reader familiar with conquistador legends from Mexico would have known to arm this knight with Santiago's
halo. There was, at any rate, no ambiguity about the "beautiful maiden…more
lovely than the sun and heaven" whom, according to Villagrá, the vanquished
Acomas described as the white rider's companion and thus also an author of
their defeat. Villagrá proclaimed her to be the Virgin Mary.[23]

Perhaps it was Villagrá who introduced the Madonna into the story of
Acoma's fall, but this captain with a gift for poetry was more likely repeating a
war story familiar by 1610 to his fellow participants in the battle. As the colonists talked about their triumph on the mesa, it would have been only natural
for Mary to feature in the tale eventually. After all, Villagrá claimed that "we won
this great victory" on one of her feast days.[24] More important, this captain and
the other colonists would have expected Mary to appear with a white knight
at her side and bestow her celestial benediction on conquistadors slaughtering
Indians. Many of the men and women accompanying Oñate came from Mexico;
from childhood, they would have heard the popular legends about her battle aid
to New Spain's conquerors.[25] As a *criollo* born in Puebla, the city that was home
to a Madonna named La Conquistadora, Villagrá would have known Mary as
Santiago's companion at arms.

Riding to war together at Acoma, the Virgin and the white knight endowed
this battle on the distant northern fringes of the Spanish empire with a distinguished lineage leading back to Cortés's day. Villagrá had every reason to so
heavily gild the events at Acoma, given the serious questions being raised by the
time he wrote about Oñate's treatment of the Pueblos. Disaffected members of
the expedition had accused the governor of excessive brutality in his suppres-
sion of the Acomas and of other atrocities against the Pueblos. After these allega-
tions made their way to the viceroy in Mexico City and then across the Atlantic
to Philip III, Oñate was recalled from New Mexico and subjected to official
investigations. Villagrá crafted his poem in the hopes of countering the charges

of misconduct that had begun to imperil not only Oñate's fortunes, but also his own; the inquiry into the expedition's misdeeds had broadened to include captains such as himself. Hence he shaped the battle of Acoma—the culmination of his epic, the point to which its 11,338 lines inexorably build—into a great, if tragic, victory that he hoped would vindicate the expedition and even ennoble the whole Spanish colonial project in the Americas.[26] Mary and Santiago lent their halos of history to this poetic apologia.

Thus the most important military engagement during the founding of New Mexico entered the Spanish-speaking public arena patterned in part on the Marian legends inherited from New Spain. Villagrá's poem was the first published history of New Mexico and would secure Mary's place in colonial commemorations of the events at Acoma. Although in the 1620s a Franciscan missionary questioned whether the white rider had been Santiago, he entirely agreed with Villagrá that the "beautiful maiden" was the Madonna.[27] Mary's ability to link events in New Mexico to the venerable conquistador past of old Mexico would shape the self-image of the Spanish colony that slowly established itself north of the Rio Grande in the seventeenth century. Yet heavy as the weight of history was, the colonists were on a new frontier, facing circumstances quite different from those that had prevailed in Mexico. In New Mexico, Mary would become part of new kinds of colonial encounters, including the most successful indigenous uprising against Spanish imperial power in the Americas.

La Conquistadora

In 1684, a leading New Mexican, Captain Alonso del Río, took up his duties as head of a confraternity dedicated to an image of Mary that apparently enjoyed considerable attention from the colony's settlers. He signed a formal document stating that he had received and reviewed the organization's valuables.[28] Among them must have been some of the finery listed in an inventory made two years later. Through her devotees' generosity, this Madonna had acquired an extensive wardrobe, including dresses of white lamé, green satin, and brightly flowered tapestry, as well as hoods of gold, silk, and, as befitted a frontier saint, snakeskin. She could also wear necklaces of pearl, brass and coral beads, earrings of gold and pearl, and other jewels such as a "gilded silver rose [set] with five stones." Over the Madonna's dresses and chemises might be draped mantles cut from blue or white satin, blue damask, or even dramatic black Sevillean silk.[29]

This inventory pays more attention to the Virgin's outfits than it does to the image that sported them, describing it only as a statue a little more than a *vara* in height—about a meter. But the title used for the image in these seventeenth-century documents identifies it as the one with which this book began: the twenty-eight-inch high willow- or olive-wood Madonna who today reigns over her devotees from a spacious side chapel in Santa Fe's cathedral—La Conquistadora.[30] That is the name by which Captain del Río knew his confraternity's patron saint, as did the thirty-odd men and women who in 1688 and 1689 paid their membership dues to the organization (a peso or even two, which most rendered in kind as wax candles, chickens, lengths of cloth, red ribbon, or even socks, shoes, and chocolate).[31]

Neither these documents nor any others explain how La Conquistadora's seventeenth-century New Mexican devotees understood her title. Yet surely the settlers did not happen upon this name for their Madonna by chance. Like Oñate, the men who colonized New Mexico saw themselves as conquistadors and tried to claim the martial prowess and military virtue associated with that word. When possible, they avoided farming or any kind of manual labor, leaving such work to enslaved Indians. Their own duty, they believed, was to protect, defend, and even avenge the colony's Franciscan friars against any offenses perpetrated by the Pueblos or Apaches. Hence, when the cruzada—a tax on non-combatants to provide support for crusading enterprises—was levied on New Mexico's settlers in 1633, they protested loudly. Since they themselves were engaged in a crusade against unbelievers, they argued, they should not have to pay.[32]

In reality, the colonists' daily lives in New Mexico bore little resemblance to European holy wars or even to the bloody exploits of men like Cortés. They more often took up arms to hunt than to fight, and knew the Pueblos better as neighbors, trading partners, household servants, and workers than as enemies on the battlefield.[33] But perhaps when they bowed their heads before their Virgin Conquistadora, they were reminded of their proud self-image and could reassure themselves that they indeed had a right to share this title with her.

Venerating a Madonna of this name in any case helped the colonists lend the sheen of a celebrated past and its attendant glories to their considerably less elevated present. The settlers' numbers were not large—by the second half of the sixteenth century, perhaps three thousand men and women. They were vastly outnumbered by the Pueblos, whose population had declined from perhaps some sixty thousand when the Spaniards arrived, but still counted seventeen thousand or so.[34] These colonists lived in what was very much a frontier society, with all its rough edges intact. Except for those few who could afford imported luxuries such as smoked oysters and fine china, the elegance of places like Mexico City and Puebla was a distant mirage.[35] Yet they had a Virgin whose title connected them to the renowned Madonnas embodying New Spain's legendary history.

There is every reason to believe that these men and women knew of Mexico's own Conquistadoras. Fully one-third of the 120 adult men in Oñate's company came from New Spain. Of these thirty-nine, fourteen were from Mexico City and three from Puebla, cities that were home to Virgins called Conquistadora. Though some of these men may have been among the flood of deserters who abandoned Oñate in 1601, those few colonists who straggled into New Mexico over the next decades largely came from New Spain. They too would have brought legends about Mexico's Conquistadoras with them.[36]

It is even possible that among the colonists were members of the *altepetl* of Tlaxcala, who themselves had a long history with a Madonna of this name. Today, some residents of New Mexico's capital city boast that the native conquistadors who had been so helpful to Cortés also lent their prestige to Santa Fe's early years. A white lettered sign in front of the chapel of San Miguel, one of the city's oldest churches, insists that it was "Tlaxcala Indians from Mexico" who in 1610 constructed this simple adobe building. Professional historians point out that the Tlaxcalteca were not part of New Mexico's settlement in any systematic way. But a contingent from the Nahua *altepetl* so famously allied with the Spaniards may have accompanied Coronado when he ventured into New Mexico in 1540, and in the 1590s, numerous Tlaxcalteca families participated in the colonization of areas of northern Mexico not so far from Pueblo territory.[37] One of the friars in Oñate's expedition in fact had a Tlaxcalteca "assistant." Any Tlaxcalteca who did make it to New Mexico probably thought of themselves as native conquistadors, for the members of this *altepetl* never forgot this prized identity, no matter how far from Tlaxcala they went.[38] If there were some Tlaxcalteca among the New Mexican Conquistadora's seventeenth-century devotees, they might have found in their veneration of her a way to distinguish themselves from the local indigenous population and instead align themselves with the Spanish settlers, as they did elsewhere.

Other of New Mexico's settlers may also have expressed ethnic pride through devotion to La Conquistadora. Most of the seventeenth-century colonists liked to think of themselves as Spaniards, even though few actually had pure Spanish blood flowing in their veins.[39] With the exception of the *peninsulares* who accompanied Oñate, the immigrants to New Mexico were already largely products of New Spain's own rich racial mélange. *Mestizaje* marked the succeeding generation of New Mexico's settler community even more profoundly. Since there were few women among the original settlers, male colonists often took Pueblo women as their bed partners. Despite the biological facts of miscegenation, the settlers' sense of Spanishness persisted. They eagerly sought cultural confirmation of their identity, trying to maintain what they saw as Spanish ways. Perhaps their devotion to La Conquistadora helped them in this quest, as well as in their efforts to distance themselves from the Christianized Pueblos with whom they so often shared the ties of kinship.

Given the reticence of the surviving documents, it is hard to go beyond these educated guesses about the meaning of La Conquistadora's title to her devotees

during the colony's early decades. The extant sources also provide no answers
to other important questions. We do not know how long La Conquistadora
had borne her title before Alonso del Río became the majordomo of her confraternity in 1684, for the document describing his acceptance of this office is
the earliest surviving reference to her name. Nor is it clear when the confraternity dedicated to her was founded, though the organization may have been in
existence as early as 1664 or even 1626.[40] By Captain del Río's day, however, La
Conquistadora evidently had been around for some time. In 1686, a Franciscan
who inspected her wardrobe rejected several garments as so "old" and thread-
bare that they were "unbecoming."[41]

Perhaps this Madonna was even old enough to have witnessed the early days
of Spanish New Mexico. The records for the colony's pre-1680 history are full of
gaps. Yet those documents that have survived reveal that within a few decades
of its founding, New Mexico was home to at least one important statue of Mary.
This Madonna arrived in the colony's capital of Santa Fe in 1626. Packed securely
in a crate, she had traveled from New Spain in the ample baggage train of Fray
Alonso de Benavides, a Franciscan eager to embark on the hard work of converting the Indians of New Mexico.[42]

This Madonna helped Benavides in his missionary labors, or so the friar
informed first the king in 1630 and then the pope in 1634 when he provided
them with deliberately optimistic and surely exaggerated reports about the friars' evangelical successes in the nascent colony. Benavides related how he had
enshrined the statue of Mary in a chapel, a building that was probably rather
humble and surely made from adobe like the rest of the colony's churches.[43]
Yet he made sure that even if the Madonna's accommodations were not grand,
she was well-tended and always appropriately "decorated." Soon, claimed the
friar, rumors of this Virgin's "great beauty" began to spread, reaching even some
Apaches living on the eastern side of the Rio Grande. Their leaders came to Santa
Fe to see her, arriving at night. In the Virgin's chapel, the darkness was dispelled
by candles, their soft light flickering on the statue's surfaces. Music was play-
ing. In this heightened atmosphere (doubtless orchestrated by Benavides), the
Apaches reverently kissed the Madonna's feet and promised her that they and all
their people would embrace Christianity. According to the friar, they remained
faithful to this vow. One Apache captain even supposedly died as Mary's martyr,
clutching a rosary a friar had given him and pleading in the name of this holy
object and of "the mother of God" for mercy from his murderer, who was an
Apache outraged by this renunciation of ancestral ways.[44]

The statue starring in Benavides's sanguine portrait of these Marian converts might very well be the Madonna who would be called La Conquistadora
some decades later. It has been pointed out that the dimensions of the box in
which Benavides transported his Virgin to Santa Fe would almost perfectly

accommodate the statue of Mary honored in the city's cathedral today.[45] La Conquistadora was, at any rate, present in Santa Fe by 1680 at the latest.[46] Perhaps she was even housed in a chapel dedicated to Mary that occupied a "fortified tower" in the governor's residence (*casas reales*), whose eighteen rooms stretched along one side of Santa Fe's main plaza.[47] Seventeenth-century Santa Fe residents called the tower chapel "Our Lady of the *Casas Reales*," evidence that they had inherited the old medieval association between Mary's protective powers and the bulwarks of military architecture.[48] Given its location, this chapel would have been a logical place to keep a Marian statue named La Conquistadora.

Wherever it was that Santa Fe's faithful went to venerate La Conquistadora, events of 1680 reveal that she evidently commanded the respect of the soldier-settlers in the colony's capital. In that year, the colonists, the missionaries, and some of their Pueblo converts abandoned Santa Fe, driven out by armed Indians. Fleeing south to safety, they abandoned some Madonnas to the rebels' fury—but not La Conquistadora. As these refugees accommodated themselves to their new home, a Spanish settlement near the site where El Paso would be founded a year later, they reaffirmed their devotion to the Madonna they had brought from Santa Fe. They paid hefty dues to belong to her confraternity and, by 1692, established a church in El Paso dedicated to her.[49] Perhaps these displaced men and women prized La Conquistadora even more than they had in Santa Fe, her name now a reminder of the lost fruits of conquest.

As the letters and reports of eyewitnesses to the Pueblo Revolt (or the Pueblo-Spanish War) reveal, the Virgin in fact belonged to both the Spanish and the Indian experiences of this uprising. All parties affected—the settlers, the friars, and the Pueblos—openly used Marian language, if very differently, to express their understanding of the events. Mary belonged to what many Pueblos saw as a war of the gods, the colonists as a war for their own survival against diabolically inspired rebels, and modern historians as the most successful instance of indigenous peoples in the Americas overthrowing a Spanish colonial regime. It would be years before La Conquistadora returned to Santa Fe.

Marian Prophecy and the Return of the Katsina

On August 10, 1680, the tribal leaders of New Mexico's Indians received the signal that they had awaited for months. Thousands of Pueblo and Apache warriors painted their bodies with the colors of war, took up their bows, arrows, and clubs, and executed a well-planned, coordinated series of attacks on the colonists' settlements and missions. For those Indians joining the revolt, August 10 was the joyous beginning of more than a decade of freedom from the heavy hand of Spanish rule, while for New Mexico's colonists and those Pueblos who sided with them, it was the start of a long nightmare. That day, 401 settlers and 21 friars lost their lives. Survivors of the first wave of attacks were practically hamstrung—the Pueblos had deliberately targeted the horses and mules they so relied on. Three days later, the rebels commanded almost all the territory the colonists had considered their own for nearly a century. Only Santa Fe remained in the settlers' hands. There, they holed up with their Pueblo allies, retreating to the governor's residence in the hopes that its thick walls and fortifications might help them withstand assault.[50]

The battle for Santa Fe lasted for over a week. The Virgin's chapel in the tower of the *casas reales* sustained damage when the attackers set fire to its doors.[51] As the men and women huddled inside the governor's residence smelled burning wood, they perhaps hoped that Mary would drape her cape of protection around them and prove as strong as the Song of Songs' tower, hung about with arms. With no sign of a miracle in sight, they grew desperate, especially after the Pueblos interrupted the town's access to water. Governor Don Antonio de Otermín soon realized that few options were left: surrender, death from thirst and starvation, or a final charge. He decided, as he put it, that it would be "a better and safer step to die fighting"—a conquistador's death—"than [to die] of hunger and thirst"—a coward's death. He and the men who fought beside him would call on Mary to help them break the siege.

At sunrise on August 20, Otermín rallied his handful of men and led them in a foray. As they plunged into the ranks of Pueblo and Apache warriors, they shouted out the name of the saint who had watched over the manly heroics of so many past conquistadors. The Indians would have heard the loud cries of "Santa María" as their attackers bore down on them. Mingling with the din of battle, these shouts accompanied the thrust of weapons as Otermín and his band killed some of their opponents and caused the rest to scatter long enough for the colonists to stage a hasty exit from Santa Fe.[52]

In a report composed just hours after the events, Otermín gave the Madonna much of the credit for the sally's success, declaring that "all [my men] seem to have been miraculously protected by the most serene Virgin Mary, who was invoked in the assaults and skirmishes."[53] A year later, during Otermín's failed effort to retake New Mexico, one of his lieutenants would express the same confidence in Mary's patronage. During this abortive expedition, eerily empty pueblos greeted Otermín and his men. When the Pueblos heard of the return of the Spanish, they simply abandoned their towns, leaving no one for the governor to subjugate—an effective strategy of resistance that they would use frequently.[54] The fruits of the 1681 *entrada* largely were limited to some important Christian sacred objects recovered from Pueblo houses. In the deserted pueblo of Alameda, Juan Domínguez de Mendoza found not only an intact set of vessels used for mass, but also "a precious figure of Our Lady." He sent the image of Mary to Otermín with a letter expressing his deep hope that the Madonna "will favor and protect us" against the Pueblos.[55]

Men like Domínguez de Mendoza and Otermín believed they were fighting to save the colony under Mary's aegis, but some Franciscans had a rather different theory about her role in the war. They believed that she had warned that this catastrophe would be visited upon the colony as a just punishment for its sinful disrespect toward the members of their order who had labored so long and hard there. In 1697, Fray Augustín de Vetancurt, a *criollo* Franciscan living in Mexico but well informed about New Mexican affairs, told the story. He related how, six years before the uprising, the ten-year old daughter of Santa Fe's *alguacil mayor* had been left partly paralyzed by a serious illness. When the girl prayed before an image of the Virgin for a cure, Mary not only miraculously restored her health, but also delivered a frightening message. "Child," she ordered, "get up and announce that this territory soon will see itself destroyed because of the little reverence that it shows my priests...if [the residents of New Mexico] do not wish to experience this punishment, then let them remedy their sins." Soon the terrible prediction became public knowledge, especially after a Mass during which the girl was present to offer her testimony to the Virgin's harsh words.[56]

The "priests" to whom Mary referred were certainly the Franciscans, a mendicant order characterized by passionate love for her. Whether or not this Marian prophecy actually was circulating in New Mexico in the 1570s, the Madonna's outrage at the treatment of her priests reflects the anger that so often stained the friars' reports from the pre-Revolt colony. Ever since New Mexico's foundation, the Franciscans had waged almost continuous war with the colony's governors for power. The Franciscans conceived of New Mexico as a theocracy of which they would naturally be the head, while the governors placed themselves at the top of the colony's ideal political ordering. The governors' efforts to wield what they saw as their right to supreme authority led to bitter wrangles with the friars.[57]

The Virgin's warning of imminent disaster ventriloquized the Franciscans' position: lack of respect for their rightful authority would have apocalyptic consequences. Mary's help in impressing this notion on New Mexico's inhabitants would have been particularly welcome to the friars in the 1570s. Not only had they just been embroiled in a vicious series of conflicts with a governor, but they were also facing increasing open resistance from the Pueblos. From the Franciscan perspective, the Indians were in fact now just as guilty as the governors of the "little reverence" condemned by Mary. The friars believed that a flood of Pueblos returning to the religious practices and beliefs of their ancestors threatened to sweep away the missionary work of decades.

Just how thoroughly the Franciscans had ever managed to wrest the Indians of New Mexico from their own religious customs is a matter of much debate. As their brethren had done in Mexico, the New Mexican missionaries adroitly accommodated Christianity to the indigenous world. They allowed Mary, for example, to take on some of the traits of powerful female spirits venerated by the Pueblos, and preached about her in mission churches that Indian artisans shaped as expressions of the old religious cosmos as well as the new. At times the friars also reached for the arms of spiritual and even physical coercion, especially in their bitter contests with native religious leaders.[58] Nevertheless, the Franciscans' evangelical achievements in New Mexico were not as impressive as champions of the order like Benavides liked to think.

Even in the pueblos that the Franciscans vaunted as success stories, Christianity was not always very deeply rooted. Take the great Hopi pueblo of Awatovi, which was located on Antelope Mesa. In the early seventeenth century, the Franciscans built a large convent there and, according to Benavides and other Spaniards, were pleased to see how rapidly their Indian charges adopted Christianity. Yet the designs that Hopi artists carved onto the sandstone cliffs stretching below the pueblo during the decades after the missionaries' arrival show little Christian influence. There are two crosses that might be Christian rather than Pueblo symbols, but they are overwhelmed by an abundance of masks, shields, and clan symbols entirely traditional to Hopi rock art.[59] Either the new religion had not made as much progress in Awatovi as the Spaniards believed, or those Awatovis who were not enthusiastic about Christianity prevented the more fervent converts from inscribing the cliffs with too many alien motifs.[60]

Elsewhere in New Mexico, fierce differences of opinion existed among Indians about the appropriate attitude toward the missionaries and the religion they sought to impose.[61] The darker side of Benavides's own rosy story of Apache Marian converts reveals just how violent these disagreements could be; this friar related how one of the Virgin's new devotees was murdered by a member of his own tribe precisely because of his baptism. Pueblo communities, too, were divided among those men and women who more or less embraced the new religion, those who tried to ignore it, and those who rejected it wholeheartedly. Encouraged by native religious leaders, some Pueblos fought to save their prayer sticks, fetishes, and ceremonial pipes from the friars' purges. Ridiculing, resisting, and sometimes even roughing up the Franciscans, these traditionalists maintained their own religious customs when they could. They venerated the Corn Mothers, who had ascended from the underworld to the earth's surface to bring life to all beings; they offered feathered prayer sticks to the katsina, the spirits of the Pueblo dead who could bring rain and other favors to the people; and they donned brightly colored masks while performing dances to invoke the favor of these spirits and of the deities who made New Mexico's landscape and animals alive with power.[62]

Other Pueblos, particularly the Christianized younger generation, renounced the communal and clan ceremonies performed in kivas—underground chambers where people gathered to fulfill the ritual requirements learned from their parents—in favor of masses at the mission church. Yet the courtyards of those same churches sometimes boasted fully functioning kivas constructed with the Franciscans' permission. This architectural oddity signaled not just the friars' efforts to adapt Christianity to the indigenous world, but also Pueblos' attempts to harness the spiritual powers of this new religion to their own ends.[63] Many Pueblos in fact incorporated Christian elements into their lives without giving up older beliefs and practices. Even those Indians who violently scorned the new religion might try to appropriate its spiritual prestige for themselves.

By the second half of the seventeenth century, Pueblo traditionalists were emboldened to adhere more openly to the time-honored beliefs and practices. It had become evident that the Franciscans' charismatic powers were not as great as they had claimed, nor was the religion they brought able to always protect against disease and drought. Those Indians who agitated for a return to the old ways found backing from some of New Mexico's governors, who during the 1660s allowed performances of the katsina dances—anything to goad the Franciscans and win Indian support in the perpetual feud with the friars. The traditionalists' voices grew louder in the 1660s and 1670s, when New Mexico was repeatedly scourged by the apocalyptic horsemen of drought, disease, and famine. The gods were angry, said some Pueblos. In the 1670s, they danced the katsina dances ever more frequently, imploring the cloud spirits to come back and help them. With waxing anger, the friars made draconian efforts to suppress native religious cults, but only succeeded in further tarnishing their own prestige and hardening the resolve of those Pueblos who had turned away from Christianity.

This was the turbulent backdrop against which the Virgin was supposed to have uttered the dire prediction reported by Vetancurt. To the Franciscans, it must have seemed as though the foundations of the New Mexican church were trembling. It was only natural that Mary—symbol of the Church, the saint beloved of their order, and a figure long associated with prophecy—would warn of imminent catastrophe. It was also natural for the friars to believe that her traditional enemy, the devil, was at work among the rebellious Pueblos.[64] "The demon had taken hold of the hearts of the infidel," thundered Vetancurt. He in fact deliberately preceded his description of Mary's apparition with a story of a diabolical one. Appearing to the Pueblos in the form of a "giant," the devil told them, "I am your old master," and announced his return among them. He instructed the Indians to kill the Spaniards, especially the missionaries. Once the settlers were dead, the churches burned, and the Christian images smashed, then all would be "as it formerly had been."[65] Mary's own warning of impending disaster eerily echoes this scene of devastation conjured up by Vetancurt's demon.

The friar intended his readers to see the two stories as a diptych portraying the epic struggle between the forces of good and evil that propelled Christian history. From this perspective, the revolt became one more battle in Mary's timeless war against the armies of hell. Many of the Pueblos who took up arms against the settlers and missionaries in August 1680 themselves believed that she was involved in the war they had just launched. They would cast her role, however, according to their own prophecies, not those of the colonists.

As the Pueblos laid their plans for the uprising, they learned that the katsina had visited one of their leaders. These spirits had promised to renew their intimate relationship with the Pueblos, if the settlers and Christianity could be eliminated.[66] Although it is not clear how many of the Indians who joined the revolt were inspired by prophecies that the ancestral spirits would soon again watch over them, the return of the katsina became the rebels' frequent rallying cry.[67] And if the old gods were alive and well, then the new ones—including Mary—were dead.

The Pueblos "were saying that...their own god whom they obeyed had never died" and that "now...[the Christian God] and Santa Maria were dead," wrote Otermín in a report composed just before he pulled out of Santa Fe in 1680.[68] This was not some Spanish fantasy. A Pueblo man captured a year later confessed to his Spanish interrogators that during the siege of Santa Fe, the Indian warriors had "shouted in loud voices: 'Now the god of the Spaniards, who was their father, is dead, and Santa Maria, who was their mother, and the saints, who were rotten pieces of wood,' saying that only their god lived."[69] A battle call countered by the settlers' yells of "Santa María" during the sortie on August 20, 1680, the Pueblo proclamation of Mary's death was a spectacular rejection of much of what the friars had struggled to teach the Indians. It rebutted the missionaries' preaching about Mary as the mother of humanity and God as the father of all Christians. Reduced to a genealogical symbol of the Spaniards alone, the Virgin was transformed into the hated oppressors' clan figure, a being who could claim no relation to the Pueblos themselves.

According to the Indian captive, as the Pueblo warriors shouted out these words delivering Mary to death, they set fire to a church in Santa Fe. There and in pueblos across New Mexico, they would ensure the demise of God, Mary, and the saints by destroying Christian buildings, holy objects, and images.[70] The devastation that greeted Otermín's soldiers when they entered the pueblo of Sandia in 1681 was typical. The burned-out hulk of the community's church sat shrouded in silence. While rummaging through one of the empty houses, the soldiers stumbled across the church's altarpiece, a panel painting of the Virgin of the Immaculate Conception. The Madonna's eyes and mouth "were ruined," and her body showed signs of having been stoned.[71]

Yet Mary was not so easily vanquished. The image of her found at Alameda in 1681 by Otermín's lieutenant Domínguez escaped the orgy of destruction. This Madonna's survival was not necessarily accidental, for sometimes the revolt's leaders deliberately preserved Christian objects and even donned the vestments of murdered Franciscans to perform their sacred dances.[72] Despite these Indians' desire to hasten Mary's death and to welcome the katsina back, there was no easy return to the old ways. During the thirteen years that the Pueblos would rule New Mexico in the revolt's wake, Christian crosses would disappear from pottery and Santa Fe would be rebuilt in the Indians' own urban style, but the old ways themselves were irrevocably changed.[73] After all, the world that most of these Pueblos had known from birth was colored by Christianity—by the friars, their sermons, their missions, their churches, their saints. Eighty years of missionary labor had subtly influenced the beliefs and practices of even those Pueblos who ostensibly rejected the new religion; many freely commandeered the charisma of Christian sacred paraphernalia and signs to enhance their own prestige.[74] As late as 1692, one leader of the revolt had in his possession a snippet of taffeta bearing a "printed image of Our Lady of Guadalupe" along with "a small silver image of Christ"—exactly the pair whose death he and his fellows had announced twelve years earlier.[75]

During the revolt period, Mary retained enough resonance for some Pueblos that they may have etched an image of her among the katsinas, snakes, and ritual clowns with which they decorated the rock walls of a remote area in Frijoles Canyon. This carving depicts a figure whose gender is unclear, but whose outline strongly recalls the iconography of well-known Madonnas such as the Virgin of Guadalupe. Encircling the figure's head is a jagged halo of the sort that typically crowned images of Mary made in New Spain and New Mexico but did not belong to the usual repertoire of rock art motifs. While this image stands out from its neighbors, it also shares with them some traits, including the rectangular box-like mouth traditionally used for katsinas. If this carving does represent Mary, she has been adapted to fit a world in which these spirits reign.[76]

Perhaps this image was intended to appeal to the more Christianized Pueblos among the participants in the Revolt. Or perhaps the Pueblos were celebrating their freedom from the friars by endowing a Christian figure with the features of the spirits the *padres* had so hated.[77] In either case, this carving suggests an equivocal attitude toward Mary and the religion she represented that occasionally surfaced in other ways during the years before the Spanish re-established control over New Mexico and even after they returned. Such ambivalence deeply marked what has been called the "final phase of the Pueblo-Spanish War," the tumultuous years from 1692 to 1696, when a new governor of New

Mexico would reconquer this territory.[78] As this man negotiated and fought with the Pueblos, he would play on their ambivalence toward Mary and counter the return of the katsina with the return of the Virgin. In the process, he would both re-enact and transform some famous legends about Mary that were inherited from Mexico. He would even usher La Conquistadora herself back to Santa Fe. During his campaigns, he would make every effort to prove that Mary was the mother not just of the Spaniards, but also of the Pueblos.

The Marian Reconquest of New Mexico

Late one day in June 1692, Don Diego José de Vargas Zapata Luján Ponce de León y Contreras attended novenas at the New Mexican refugees' church of La Conquistadora in El Paso.[79] As he recited the words of the rosary and listened to the other prayers of the service, perhaps he was dressed as richly as this church's statue of Mary. In the only extant contemporaneous portrait of him, Vargas stands sternly in Spanish aristocratic garb, holding a fur-trimmed hat of the sort that he surely did not wear in El Paso's summer heat (Figure 10.1). As his sumptuous dress and sonorous name suggest, Vargas belonged to one of Spain's distinguished noble families. He could trace his lineage back to knights who had helped Alfonso VI win Madrid from the Muslims late in the eleventh century.[80] To this man born and raised in Castile and accustomed to the vast expanses of its Gothic and Plateresque cathedrals, La Conquistadora's church in El Paso must have seemed humble indeed.

Yet by the time Vargas bowed his head in prayer before this Madonna, the simple contours of her home would not have surprised him. Almost twenty years earlier, he had left his wife and five children behind in Spain and crossed the Atlantic, driven by financial need. In New Spain, Vargas worked his way up the administrative ladder, frequenting the viceroy's court in Mexico City in an effort to win ever more prominent and lucrative posts. By 1688, he landed the office of governor of New Mexico and the accompanying task of re-imposing Spanish control there. The charge laid upon him was a heavy one, critical as it was to the maintenance of Spanish imperial power in the Americas. In the late seventeenth century, as the French threatened to push the frontiers of their Louisiana holdings ever westward, New Mexico suddenly assumed strategic importance in the calculus of empire.

Vargas made his way to El Paso in 1691 to oversee the organization of his first expedition into the territory he intended to govern. It took him almost a year and a half to pull his forces together. He and his soldiers—a mix of Spaniards and Pueblo allies—finally set out from El Paso on a date chosen for its symbolic importance: August 10, 1692, the thirteenth anniversary of the Pueblo

Figure 10.1 Portrait of Don Diego de Vargas, probably painted between 1640 and 1710. Courtesy of the Palace of the Governors Photo Archive (NMHM/DCA). Negative number 11409.

Revolt. As Vargas rode north, he believed that his mission was not only to re-impose royal authority on New Mexico but also to bring Christianity back to the Pueblos, and therefore to defeat the devil. In comparison to the lurid language used by Fray Vetancurt to characterize the black giant who had seduced the Indians into rebellion, Vargas's vocabulary of diabolism was mild. Yet the conquistador shared an understanding of the uprising as demonically inspired, describing Pueblos who smashed an image of Mary as being "overcome by the devil."[81] Vargas was confident of victory, for he had a powerful ally in the Virgin. "She protected this enterprise and guided my steps to conquer such a devil," he wrote of his New Mexico successes.[82] In 1693, he even boasted to some Pueblos whom he suspected of treachery that "the devil could not deceive me, because I brought with me the Virgin, Our Lady."[83]

Vargas's copious campaign journals, official reports, and letters display how profoundly he understood his reconquest of New Mexico to be willed by Mary. "My trust in Blessed Mary...who has been the pilgrim and patroness of this undertaking. I trust, as I repeat, in her Divine Majesty"; " with the protection and guidance of most holy Mary, I am going to make my *entrada*"; " the most holy Virgin in a nearly miraculous fashion permitted me to know the danger I was in"; "I gave thanks to Our Lady, for she had inspired my good judgment in the decisions I had made"—phrases like these form a powerful refrain in Vargas's narration of his New Mexican campaigns.[84] They echoed loudly in the ears of the writer Carlos de Sigüenza y Gongora, who in 1693 produced a popular account of Vargas's 1692 expedition. Working from Vargas's papers, Sigüenza y Gongora created for eager Mexico City readers a portrait of a conquistador always confident in "the patronage which he had so clearly received from the most holy Virgin, in whose name and with whose aid he had brought about this enterprise."[85]

At his death, Vargas had in his possession a small statue of a crowned Virgin named "Our Lady of Defense," perhaps an incarnation of the Madonna by the same name whom a mid-sixteenth century bishop of Puebla had bestowed on a California-bound conquistador.[86] But it was not this Madonna in whose "protection" Vargas declared his confidence and whom he said he "brought as [his] guide" to New Mexico.[87] Nor was it La Conquistadora, whose church he had visited in El Paso in 1692. Instead, the patron of Vargas's New Mexican campaigns was Our Lady of Remedies.

Vargas's devotion to Los Remedios ran deep. Her name appears repeatedly in his journals and letters chronicling his reconquest of New Mexico. In 1696, he would even pledge one of the silver mines he found there to her.[88] As he lay dying in April 1704, he mustered the strength to add a codicil to his will, stipulating that after his death, five hundred masses should be said, of which "two hundred will be for my soul and directed to the most holy Virgin of the Remedies, my advocate."[89] Unfortunately, in the thousands of pages Vargas wrote about his New Mexican experiences, he never once explained why he venerated this particular Madonna so fervently. He probably had not inherited this devotional preference from his family, which traditionally celebrated the farmer-saint who supposedly had tilled the lineage's Madrid lands in the thirteenth century, Saint Isidore.[90] It is more likely that Vargas's years in Mexico explain his passion for Los Remedios.

During the two decades Vargas spent in New Spain before he set out for New Mexico, he had ample opportunity to learn that this Virgin would be an appropriate saintly patron for a man with conquistador ambitions. In Mexico City, Los Remedios' cult was in full swing, with crowds of devotees fêting her as one of the city's most powerful protectors. By the late 1670s, Vargas had a house in the capital and preferred to reside there when he could.[91] He lived only a few blocks south of the Zócalo, the city's main plaza bordered on one side by the cathedral, where the statue from Totoltepec came to stay in 1678 and again in 1685, while throngs in the streets implored Los Remedios to end the terrible droughts of those years. Surely Vargas knew not only of this Madonna's status as Mexico City's benefactor, but also of her famous history and legendary association with Cortés and company. By taking her as his "advocate" and as the protector of his expeditions into New Mexico, he cast himself and these endeavors in the Cortesian mould.

Vargas even brought to life the venerable tales about Mexico's past by marching into New Mexico under a banner of Los Remedios. This Virgin was emblazoned on one side of his official standard, while the king's arms decorated the other.[92] It is unfortunate that neither Vargas nor his contemporaries recorded further details about the banner's appearance, because this piece of cloth served as much more than a public declaration of his affections for Mary and the royal sanction he enjoyed. During the fours years it took him to subdue the Pueblos, he repeatedly and intentionally used this standard to make Los Remedios' patronage of his enterprise startlingly real to all involved, including the Indians. After Vargas's death, it was preserved as a relic of the conquest and accorded due ceremonial honors when carried by the official standard bearer.[93]

Vargas first mentioned the banner of Los Remedios in his letters and reports of 1692, the year he entered New Mexico with his soldiers. As he doubtless knew from his Pueblo allies, interpreters, and informants, many Indian leaders were ready to parley.[94] The return of the katsina had not inaugurated an era of prosperity and peace as the participants in the Pueblo Revolt had hoped. The severe drought, famine, and disease that had ravaged New Mexico in the 1670s continued during the decade following the banishing of the Spanish and their gods, while Apache raids intensified. The fragile alliances that had held the tribes together during the uprising soon dissolved into wrangles over power,

internecine strife, and even civil war.[95] Just three years before Vargas would ride
into New Mexico, Governor Domingo Jironza Petrís de Cruzate led successful
attacks against the pueblos of Santa Ana and Zia, taking many Indian warriors
captive and leaving hundreds of others dead.[96] This bloody reminder of Spanish
military power was fresh in the Pueblos' minds in 1692 when they learned of
Vargas's approach.

Unlike Jironza, Vargas did not send armed men up the mesas to storm the
Pueblos' towns.[97] Though he hardly eschewed violence, he would manipulate
the language of diplomacy and political spectacle in an effort to impress upon
the Indians the necessity of returning to the fold of Spanish rule and Christian
belief. As Vargas spoke with the Pueblos through his interpreters and demanded
their renewed submission to Spanish authority, he deliberately made the banner
of Los Remedios central to the scene. He pointed at it to prove that he came in
the name of two monarchs: the king of Spain and the Virgin, "Queen of Heaven"
and "Divine Majesty," as he often called Mary. Vargas's description of his 1692
encounter with the Pueblos who held Santa Fe is typical: "I ordered the royal
alfarez to show them the image of the Virgin, as I myself took it into my hand,
showing it and saying to them that they had but to look at her and recognize her
to be Our Lady the Queen and the Blessed Virgin and that on the other side of
the royal standard were the arms of the king, our lord, so that they might know
he sent me."[98] Vargas repeated this piece of stagecraft several times at Santa Fe,
and then again near Taos.[99]

To induce the Pueblos to submit, Vargas promised pardon to those who had
participated in the rebellion. He granted this favor in the name of the king, but
the visual pledge of forgiveness that he held out to the Indians was the image
of the Queen of Heaven on his banner. As he explained in a letter to Charles
II: "I . . . assure[d] these rebels I had come in your name from where the sun rises
just to pardon them, bringing our divine Lady as a witness and symbol better
to combat their disbelief."[100] In fact, Vargas most often mentioned in his writings—and drew the Pueblos' attention to—Mary's side of the banner, allotting
the royal arms a rather bit part. This was not just because he believed that Mary,
with her renowned powers of intercession and her famously boundless maternal
love even for errant sinners, was the natural embodiment of pardon. He also
realized that none of the Pueblos had ever seen Charles II, a king located in a
faraway land. Instead of forcing the Pueblos to bow to this distant ruler, Vargas
demanded that they pay homage to the monarch whom they could actually see
on the banner and whom they had known for decades.

Although in 1680 these Indians had jubilantly proclaimed Mary's death and
rejected her along with the religion she stood for, Vargas was well aware that
they were familiar with her; after all, most adults among them had been baptized
years ago by the friars. He also believed that traces of respect for her lingered

among these people. After his negotiations at Santa Fe with Don Luis Picurí, one of the captains of the Revolt, Vargas must have been even more convinced that he was right. This Pueblo leader came out to meet the Spaniard bearing in his hands an image of Mary and another of her son.[101] Around Don Luis's neck hung another Marian sign, a rosary that Vargas had sent him earlier as "a sign of peace." Like those Pueblos who hastily put up crosses on their houses or at the entrances of their towns when they heard that Vargas was coming, Don Luis probably realized that it would be to his advantage to appear as Christian as possible in his dealings with the Spaniard.[102] But Vargas read this tactical choice as a devotional one presaging political capitulation and replied by pointing at the image of Los Remedios on his banner to indicate that he meant no harm.

Although this exchange of Marian pleasantries outside Santa Fe perhaps had very different meanings for the parties involved, Don Luis and Vargas each knew that the other would see significance in the Marian symbols they used. In his efforts to reclaim the Pueblos for Christianity, Vargas would relentlessly exploit this knowledge. Wielding Christian ritual and imagery, he sought to fan the embers of the Indians' appreciation for the power of the religion the friars had brought to them decades ago. He would give rosaries as signs of peace and pardon to other Pueblo leaders and try to tie these men to him through the bonds of spiritual kinship forged when he stood as godparent to their children.[103] Above all, Vargas would stage the first act of the Pueblos' return to Christianity as the triumphant return of the Virgin.

Events at the Hopi pueblo of Awatovi in the fall of 1692 demonstrated just how adroitly Vargas could play on the Indians' familiarity with Mary. The Hopis had heard rumors that the conquistador's offers of pardon were merely a show and that he actually intended to behead any Indian leaders he could get his hands on.[104] So when Vargas approached Awatovi, he was confronted outside the pueblo's entrance by a large group of armed warriors prepared to defend their community. Vargas halted his own forces and kept them at the ready "about a musket shot away," as he would later report. Rather than firing, he ordered the Spanish-speaking head of the pueblo to tell the Awatovis that he "came in peace"—and "show[ed] them as authority and proof Our Lady of the Remedies" on his banner.[105]

If Vargas's self-congratulatory accounts of events can be trusted, this was only the overture to the series of Marian maneuvers with which he managed to defuse the situation and to transform what started as a tense stand-off into the Madonna's triumph. He wrote that he had commanded the Awatovis to cast off their allegiance to the devil and to prove they remembered the deference good Christians owed the Virgin:

> I ordered them with imperious words to lay down their weapons if they were Christians and receive the divine Lady…on their knees…they

should do so and agree that they were Christians and not to let the
devil deceive them.... [S]howing them our divine Lady of Remedies,
I told them to be calm, as I had come so that they might adore her,
as the Christians they were...I ordered them...to immediately quit
their shouting, lay aside their weapons, and kneel in front of the divine
Lady...[D]id they not remember from when they were Christians that
in order to receive a saint and the Virgin, they should all be reverent,
silent and on their knees?

After prolonged debate among themselves, the Awatovis acceded to Vargas's
demand that they accord to the banner of Los Remedios the royal honors with
which the relics of saints were traditionally welcomed.[106] They dismounted from
their horses and knelt. Those who hesitated were "reprimanded" by Vargas "in
honor of the divine Queen." Then, in front of the crowd of humbled Hopi warriors, he "took the royal standard from the alfarez's hand," wheeled around on
his horse, and, "showing them the most holy Lady Mary," proclaimed Awatovi's
renewed entry into Spanish dominion. For good measure, Vargas repeated the
same scene shortly after entering the pueblo. Forcibly assembling the community's warriors on the main plaza, he commanded them to surrender their weapons
and "to kneel and receive the holy Virgin" while he again pronounced Awatovi a
royal possession.

The four fulsome accounts that Vargas penned of the confrontation on
Antelope Mesa are full of conceited boasting about his own prowess, but he ultimately credits the victory to Los Remedios herself. "I overcame, reduced, and
conquered" these hostile Indians, he wrote, through "a miracle from the most
holy Virgin, Our Lady of Remedies."[107] She "used miraculous means to make the
more than one thousand Indians, gathered...to tear me to pieces, kneel three
times and surrender their weapons."[108] Tellingly, he believed that Los Remedios
had worked this miracle not through fireworks of wonders, but through her
power over the Indians' souls. As he put it, "miraculously, the Virgin allowed the
efficacy of my faith to take hold of their hearts with such force and proper devotion that most of them knelt and fell silent."[109] This Marian miracle suggested the
rekindling, however faint, of the Christian spark of years ago.

The royal entry that Vargas forced the Awatovis to give Los Remedios would
not have had such weight if they had not already known who Mary was. In fact,
in the rhetoric Vargas used to try to recall these Indians to their Marian duties
as Christians, he made sure to remind them that she belonged as much to them
as she did to Spaniards like himself. Gathering Indians and Europeans alike
into Mary's maternal lap, he instructed the Hopis that the Virgin was not only
a "divine Lady" but also "our Mother."[110] Sigüenza y Gongora's literary rendering of the events at Awatovi put it more pointedly, portraying Vargas as angrily

upbraiding the Hopis for not immediately throwing themselves on the ground and adoring "the true mother of your god and mine."[111]

At Awatovi, Vargas thus endeavored to present himself to the Indians as bringing back to them the celestial and royal mother whose reign they had spurned years ago. But to the Spanish public he addressed in his letters and reports, Vargas revealed that Mary's maternal affections continued to favor his own side. When he rode south to El Paso some months after the events at Awatovi, he was convinced that he had, as he would write to the king in 1693, "left" New Mexico "humbled and conquered...by means of divine assistance and the protection of holy Mary, Our Lady of Remedies."[112] He had successfully persuaded most of the Pueblo leaders to play their part in the dramas of submission before her image on the royal banner. All that remained for him to do was to escort the group of settlers and their families who had gathered at El Paso northward and safely settle them in New Mexico, while he himself renovated the *casas reales* in Santa Fe, took up his duties as governor, and hunted for silver mines.

So thought Vargas in his arrogance when he set out in October 1693 for his second expedition into Pueblo territory. This time he was accompanied not just by soldiers, but also by families and slow-moving wagon trains laden with household goods. Vargas soon realized his rashness in bringing so many women, children, and unarmed men to New Mexico. Although some Pueblos would strike alliances with him to gain the advantage over their enemies in ongoing internecine conflicts, most were not as ready to accept the return of Spanish rule as they had seemed to him in 1692.[113] In his campaigns over the next four years to crush these Indians' armed resistance and gain control of New Mexico, Vargas would yet again rely on Mary's help.

The banner of Los Remedios was at Vargas's side when he rode back into New Mexico in 1693. During the following three years, he kept it there as he negotiated and skirmished with the Pueblos. He showed it to his Indian allies in order to demonstrate to them that they had the Virgin's power on their side.[114] When "rebels" came to Vargas and asked for pardon, as in 1692, he granted forgiveness in the name of the king while using as his "witness" Mary's side of the banner, which he made sure the Indians could see.[115] In his efforts to recall these men and women to the community of Christian rule, he again conjured Mary as universal mother, telling some Indian leaders in 1694 that the Pueblos were all children of "Our Mother, Lady and Advocate."[116] For a group of Pueblos fearful that his forgiveness of them was merely feigned, Vargas summoned Los Remedios as a powerful enforcer, who would not let him renege on his promise of pardon. Entering the kiva where these Pueblos had gathered, he pointed at the image of Mary adorning his banner and declared that the Indians' own leader "knew that her strength was so great that I could not break my word even if I thought to.

Before I would harm them in any way, the earth would open up, making a hole larger than this kiva. It would swallow me alive."[117]

If Mary's fiercer side belonged to Vargas's rhetoric of reassurance during these years, it also surfaced when he tried to impress and intimidate Pueblos of whose loyalty he was doubtful. During some tricky early morning negotiations with two Indians in November 1693, Vargas told them it was no use trying to outwit him "because I had brought with me Our Lady on the royal standard I kept with me in my tent." Gesturing at the banner of Los Remedios and some other powerful Christian objects in the tent, Vargas announced to the men that "with these, though the devil might deceive them into coming to see me and do evil, they could not harm me."[118]

A month later, Vargas had to convince his own men that Mary would exercise her formidable powers on their behalf. As winter brought snow and bitter cold to northern New Mexico, Vargas had not yet succeeded in persuading the Indians in possession of the colony's capital to render it to him. The settler families, who had barely survived the hard journey from El Paso, huddled in makeshift accommodations outside the walls of Santa Fe. Lacking adequate food and fuel, the weak among them began to sicken and die; according to one Franciscan's Christmas report to the governor, twenty-two children had already been buried.[119] Vargas stubbornly persisted in his attempts to negotiate with the Pueblos, but by December 29, his company's patience had come to an end.

A year earlier, Vargas had vaunted his negotiated "conquest" of Santa Fe as the Virgin's achievement.[120] Now he turned to her for support in violently overcoming the Indians holding the town. He gathered his soldiers, including several hundred Pueblo allies. All knelt while a Franciscan friar delivered a short sermon. Then Vargas and his captains mounted their horses. The governor turned to face his troops and exhorted them, as he wrote later, to remember that "God Our Lord and the most Holy Virgin [will] help us." Riding at his side was the "alfarez with the royal standard bearing an image of Our Lady of Remedies." Screaming "Santiago!" as their battle cry, but with Mary's banner streaming overhead, Vargas and his men stormed Santa Fe. It took them a day or two of fighting in the snowy streets to secure the town.[121]

Vargas was enraged to find among Santa Fe's ravaged buildings a maimed statue of the Madonna. Its wounds convinced him that the villa's Pueblo defenders had "relapsed into apostasy." Vargas had thought that during his earlier expedition, he—or rather Los Remedios—had brought these same Indians back into the Christian fold. In 1692, he had written: "I attribute the parting of the shadows of their blindness to the aurora and guiding light of my thoughts... the protectoress of our holy faith... the most holy Mary of the Remedies."[122] Either then or a year later, a settler in Vargas's company had been confident enough in these Indians' respect for Christianity to leave a statue of Mary in the house of a Pueblo acquaintance, a gift made perhaps in the spirit of the amicable trading that, until relations soured, occurred in 1693 between the colonists waiting outside Santa Fe and the Indians who held the town. This Marian pledge of Christian friendship did not survive to see Vargas's victory of December 1693. By the time the colonists took Santa Fe, wrote Vargas, the statue had been "beaten with a club and the head of the divine Lady had been broken." It was an act of desecration so shocking to the Spaniards that a century later, it would become the subject of a pious Marian legend circulating as far away as Mexico City.[123]

Vargas saw further damning evidence of these Indians' diabolically inspired apostasy in the shards of a cross lying shattered on the ground. In his eyes, the destruction of the Madonna and the cross were crimes warranting the sentences of execution he meted out. The statue's wreckage naturally looked rather different to the Pueblos involved. In attacking Mary, they had unleashed anew the iconoclastic frenzy that had exorcised the Spanish presence in 1680. Yet they were not just resorting to methods that had worked in the past, but were also making eloquent political statements targeting the man who sought to impose his authority on them. So too the "countless blasphemies" Vargas attributed to these same Indians—including "saying that the devil could do more than God and the Virgin"—signaled more than just a return to the battle cries of 1680.[124] These Pueblos doubtless knew just how effectively their assaults on Mary would communicate their rejection of Spanish authority to Vargas. Turning his own Marian rhetoric inside out, they announced that neither the Virgin nor the Christians who loved her would be allowed to come back to New Mexico.

Other Pueblos used their knowledge of the Madonna's importance to Vargas rather differently. In November 1693, as the long wagon train of colonists inched toward Santa Fe, four leaders of the Jemez pueblo came to Vargas's tent late one night. They belonged to a community that had responded to the news of the Spaniard's re-appearance in New Mexico by deciding to oppose him at all costs. By the time these four men showed up at Vargas's camp, the Jemez had abandoned their pueblo and relocated to a more easily defensible mesa top.[125] They had also urged other tribes to join them in a coordinated attack on Vargas's company. From his Pueblo informants and allies, the governor had learned of the Jemez's contribution to the "great storm ... [and] bloody war [that] was taking shape" among the "rebellious nations." Vargas was sure he could ride out the tempest with the help of Mary and her son. But the Jemez captains came to him as representatives of those members of their community who had begun to rethink their openly hostile stance. Their purpose was to show Vargas their good will, as the nine blankets they brought him as gifts indicated. If Vargas's memory can be trusted, during these negotiations the Jemez skillfully cribbed from the Marian script he himself had written.[126]

First, these men told Vargas how "happy" they were that he had come to their pueblo a year earlier and "pardoned them all in the most holy Virgin's name." Then, he reported, they "asked me to repeat before them that I pardoned them in the most holy Virgin's name, which I did." In his account, Vargas cast this request as a sign of the Jemez's willingness to submit to his authority. Far more likely, these men asked the governor to reiterate his lines in the Marian drama of redemption for their own benefit, not his. With this piece of political theater, the Jemez invoked the Virgin in order to ensure that Vargas would not take vengeance on them.

To further cement good relations, the Jemez captains even made Vargas a Marian offering of sorts. In Vargas's words, they told him that the pueblo's "women sent word that they would pray for the most holy Virgin to give me success in the *entrada* to the remaining pueblos."[127] Perhaps this startling message was the fruit of some earlier discussion among the Jemez about the best way to gain Vargas's favor, or perhaps it revealed that some respect for Mary actually had survived among the women of the pueblo. In either case, the captains' decision to convey these words to the governor belonged to a calculated strategy that took advantage of Vargas's own rhetoric of the Virgin's return.

Three years later, other Pueblos would just as astutely turn Mary into a bargaining chip in their dealings with the governor. During the final paroxysm of the Pueblo-Spanish War—the revolt of 1696 during which all but five tribes in New Mexico erupted into open warfare with the colonists—Indians seized images of the Madonna and held them hostage. Hence the message that El Zepe, a Cochiti man among the uprising's leaders, sent to one of Vargas's captains in June, just a few days after the Indians began attacking settlers and burning churches. El Zepe's envoy, an Indian woman from Zia, came down from one of the strongholds high up on the mesas to which the Pueblos had withdrawn. She informed Vargas's man that El Zepe had "sent her to ask for peace" and that he had in his possession livestock from Cochiti and "the most holy Virgin that belonged to [the pueblo of] Santo Domingo."[128] Whether this Madonna was a carved statue or a painting on wood, canvas, or even the elk skin New Mexican artists often used, no document reveals. But it seems that this image depicted none other than Los Remedios herself.[129]

According to information that Vargas extracted a few days later from a Keres captive, the rebels had singled this Madonna out as the most important item to take with them when they had rifled through the furnishings of Santo Domingo's church.[130] Even though these Indians set fire to Christian buildings, they perhaps wanted Mary's power on their side. It is equally possible that they had pragmatic purposes in absconding with the Virgin. If El Zepe's followers distinguished between Madonnas, it may have been no accident that they chose to carry off an image of just the Virgin whom Vargas had so often thrust into Indians' faces. In any case, El Zepe's message to the governor suggests that these Pueblos appreciated how useful the image could be in their dealings with the Marian-besotted Spaniard. Accordingly, as the Zia woman apparently emphasized to Vargas's lieutenant, they made sure that the Madonna suffered no harm.

Vargas was as disturbed by the news of this Madonna's captivity as El Zepe probably hoped he would be. Two days later, a reply was carried back up to the mesa. The governor offered full pardon to El Zepe and his followers, telling them that they were "guilty of no crime . . . since they have kept Our Lady safe, as they have said."[131] The conditions that Vargas dictated involved the Indians' return of all the plunder from Santo Domingo and Cochiti. At the top of the list was the Virgin kidnapped from Santo Domingo's church. In response to the Indians' unwelcome and unexpected move, Vargas was forced to adapt the Marian script he had used for years. Yet even under these new circumstances, he managed to preserve the Virgin's essential role as an icon of pardon. The Indians, however, were hardly inclined to speak the new lines Vargas had written for them. As the governor soon learned, El Zepe intended neither to yield his valuable hostage nor to surrender.

All through the summer of 1696, the rebels held the Madonna of Santo Domingo as they moved from mesa to mesa and fought the colonists. Despite Vargas's preoccupation with devising tactics to overcome the rebellion, his concern for her did not abate. He closely questioned captives about her condition and whereabouts, learning in August that she was hidden in a cave.[132] In that month, Vargas made a concerted effort to recover this Madonna and to induce El Zepe and the other leaders of the revolt to put down their arms. The governor charged an Indian captive with the mission of taking a message to El Zepe: as a pledge of good faith between Christians, Vargas proposed an exchange of female hostages. If the Indians would deliver the image of Mary, the governor would hand over El Zepe's daughter.[133] Vargas's willingness to trade such an important captive for the Madonna suggests the weight he attached to the Virgin's rescue.

The Pueblos were not interested in Vargas's offer then or a month later, when he tried again to bargain for the Madonna. By September 1696, the remaining rebels had gathered in a deep canyon in the wooded hills near Taos. On September 22, Vargas rode toward the canyon's mouth and spoke to some Indians who left the protection of its walls to meet him. Through an interpreter, he assured them of pardon if they would "hand over the most holy Virgin," along with some church furnishings in their possession and two Christian captives. In response, the Indians sent smoke signals to warn their forces of his arrival and then shot a shower of arrows at Vargas's Pueblo allies. As night was falling, Vargas withdrew. The next day, he returned to the canyon and proffered exactly the same terms, but received an even more defiant refusal.[134]

During the ensuing days of fighting, Vargas's men wore away at the Pueblos' position. Gradually, groups of Indians began to emerge from the canyon in surrender. Among them was a man bearing an image of the Virgin. Whether the Madonna that Felipe, "an Indian sacristan," turned over to Vargas on September 24 was the Madonna of Santo Domingo or another one in the rebels' possession is not clear. Vargas identified the recovered image of Mary as a painting on canvas, not of Los Remedios but of Our Lady of Aránzazu, a Virgin who was very popular among Basques both in their mountainous Iberian homeland and in New Spain.[135] Even if this was not the Madonna that the governor had bargained for all summer, he was willing to stage for her a most royal reception at Taos, the pueblo serving as his headquarters for the campaign.

Vargas first constituted the Virgin's honor guard: the lieutenant general of his cavalry, some *regidores*, and a squadron of soldiers. Then he sent this company to retrieve the Marian image from its hiding place. As they returned bearing the painting and approached Taos's main plaza, the rest of Vargas's officers and men came out to meet "the most holy effigy," as the governor called the image. They raised their guns into the air and fired what Vargas described as a "salvo of joy" in the Madonna's honor. With all eyes upon him, the governor fell to his knees as the painting was placed in his hands. He then reverently placed the Virgin in his own tent.[136]

Felipe would later deliver a host of other important Christian objects to Vargas, including vestments, missals, censers, and candlesticks.[137] Yet the governor staged no public ceremony to celebrate the return of these items, any more than he did when Pueblos elsewhere brought him objects salvaged from burned churches.[138] The performance at Taos in honor of the Virgin was special, an expression of heartfelt relief by this Marian devotee that he had rescued at least one Madonna from the rebels. More important, Vargas orchestrated it as a public spectacle designed to impress on everyone watching that Mary had returned to her rightful place—and that rightful political order therefore had been restored in New Mexico.

La Conquistadora Returns

What then of La Conquistadora, the Madonna in whose El Paso church Vargas had heard novenas that June afternoon in 1692? Despite her evocative name, Vargas never invoked her in battle against the Pueblos, instead relying on Los Remedios' aid. Yet he did not forget the refugees' Virgin. In 1692 or 1693, he became the majordomo of La Conquistadora's confraternity, an office that he must have realized befitted his status as governor.[139] He well understood this Madonna's importance to the handful of men and women who had hung on in

El Paso, waiting hopefully for a chance to return to New Mexico, even as they watched many of their fellows give up and head back to New Spain. He knew that years ago the settlers had "rescued her from the ferocity of those barbarians," as he put it in a letter of 1693 to the viceroy.[140] La Conquistadora was, Vargas informed the same dignitary in another letter, no less than "the patron saint and protectress" of New Mexico.[141] Therefore, as he contemplated the logistics of re-establishing the colony, he decided that she would have to accompany the thousand or so men, women, and children whom he planned to shepherd toward their new homes in Pueblo territory. It did not matter that most of these people—recently recruited to this frontier project—had not been acquainted for long with the Madonna who would travel beside them during the fall of 1693.[142] As the saintly patron of New Mexico and the icon of its settler community, La Conquistadora naturally had a role to play in Vargas's drama of the Virgin's return.

The governor believed that it was his duty to re-enthrone La Conquistadora in Santa Fe, the town from which she had escaped so ignominiously in 1680. "The glory and pride are mine," wrote Vargas to the viceroy in the fall of 1693, "in that I am the one who brings her back, not only to establish her again in her villa of Santa Fe, but also to set her up in her place on a new throne, which I am to rebuild for her sovereign and divine majesty." Vargas hoped thereby to render such service to this heavenly queen that she would "govern my actions so that they will foster not only the propagation of our holy faith, but also the royal service."[143] He intended "to personally build" a church in Santa Fe for La Conquistadora.[144]

A mere four days after the colonists arrived at Santa Fe in December 1693, Vargas was already trying to carry out this plan. His company certainly had more pressing practical needs, as they waited outside the town in the freezing cold while he pursued his fruitless negotiations with the Pueblos. Yet installing La Conquistadora in Santa Fe would serve as an unmistakable announcement to colonists and Indians alike that New Mexico's capital had returned to Spanish rule and to Christianity.

As Vargas wrote later, he reminded the Indians who held the town of their "obligation" to this Madonna: "if a lady came, they had a duty to give her a house." Invoking the idea of shared Christian responsibility, he warned these Pueblos that God "could punish us, seeing that we were Christians" if "we" did not "immediately buil[d] the church" for her. Whether or not the Indians were convinced by Vargas's rhetoric, some agreed to help him. They began to repair the damaged chapel of San Miguel, which the governor thought would make a suitable home for La Conquistadora. After only a day or two, the Indians halted work, telling Vargas that the snow and cold made it impossible for them to venture into the forests and cut down trees for roof beams. They proposed instead to transform one of their kivas into La Conquistadora's church.[145]

Vargas was open to the idea, especially given the military possibilities suggested to him by the kiva's location. This round chamber "jutted out from one corner of the fortress like a small tower" and the governor believed that in case of trouble, he could "order men-at-arms to break through the fortress and enter."[146] Under his supervision, the Indians whitewashed the kiva's walls, built a step before the place where the altar would stand, and added a fireplace. One Franciscan in Vargas's company inspected the refurbished space and approved of it. But a friar who outranked him disagreed vehemently, angrily declaring that the kiva could never be used for Christian rituals like Mass because "it had been the place of [the Indians'] idolatries and diabolical gatherings for their dances." Reluctantly, Vargas agreed to find another place for La Conquistadora.

Over the next decades, La Conquistadora would receive the generous attentions of her confraternity and other devotees. In 1770, as the colony's residents desperately sought celestial protection from attacks by Comanche Indians, they turned to La Conquistadora for aid—and officially elected her the patron saint of the kingdom of New Mexico. To cultivate her favor, New Mexico's *vecinos* decided to honor her every October with a feast and to keep "over three hundred candles of white wax" burning at her "altars." By then, La Conquistadora reigned over the faithful from a chapel attached to Santa Fe's main church, a place of honor that would surely have pleased the friar who had opposed Vargas's idea of setting her up in a kiva.[147]

Vargas himself doubtless would have appreciated La Conquistadora's chapel, had he lived to see it. But in late December 1693, as he argued to enthrone this Madonna in a kiva, he believed that history was on his side. After all, he was only proposing to do what generations of Spanish Christian men of arms had done before him. "The main cathedrals of Spain had been Moorish mosques," Vargas informed the recalcitrant Franciscan. Therefore, why couldn't a kiva serve as La Conquistadora's church? The friar riposted with his own interpretation of the reconquest, saying that the Spaniards "had driven off the Moors so that these mosques could be churches." Since Indians still lived in Santa Fe, kivas could not become churches.[148] Vargas found the flaw in this logic. "There was a big difference," he told the *padre*, between the conquered Muslims of Spain's past and the Pueblos of New Mexico's present. The former had remained unbelievers, while the latter were baptized Christians, even if the Franciscans had had to absolve them of apostasy.[149]

This heated discussion took place between two men on a frontier so distant from the land where mosques had once been common that Vargas thought of New Mexico as located "at the ends of the earth and remote beyond compare."[150] Yet as aware as he was of the thousands of miles separating him from Spain and New Spain, he believed that his identity as Mary's conquistador connected him both to the battles against the Muslims his forefathers had fought and to the legendary New World exploits of men like Cortés. Vargas knew his history well enough not to try to deny the differences between these earlier enterprises and his own. In his dispute with the friar, he pointed to what actually was one of the biggest contrasts between the reconquest and the Spanish imperial project in the Americas: the role of conversion. Vargas knew too that in New Mexico he faced challenges unlike those experienced by the men who had claimed Mexico for the Spanish crown. He shaped his Marian strategies accordingly. No captive to the past, Vargas was also no stranger to its spell, as his choice of Los Remedios for his special patron shows. In his argument with the friar, this conquistador even consciously conjured a Marian past that went all the way back to the Middle Ages. His willingness to house La Conquistadora in a kiva made him a worthy heir to the men in medieval Castile and Aragon who had transformed mosques into Mary's churches. Vargas thus eloquently integrated New Mexico into centuries of Marian history, just as surely as he had wielded the language of the Virgin's return to reincorporate its indigenous inhabitants into Christendom.

Epilogue

Medieval New Mexico and Mestizaje

In 1938, Bright Lynn, a worker for the WPA-sponsored Federal Writers Project (FWP), was collecting folktales in New Mexico. Among the people Lynn interviewed was Mrs. Guadalupe Gallegos. Mrs. Gallegos lived in Las Vegas, a small town on the edge of the Santa Fe National Forest that had often been used as a setting for Tom Mix films. One of the *cuentos* she shared with the FWP representative featured skirmishes between white hats and black hats worthy of a Western, but her characters were Moors and Christians, not Indians and cowboys.[1]

Mrs. Gallegos's story stars a virtuous married woman named Constancia, who more than lives up to her name. Her tribulations begin when a "wicked vagabond" tricks her husband into believing she has been unfaithful. Constancia's gullible spouse shuts her into a box and tosses it into the ocean. It soon washes up on the shore of a land where, Mrs. Gallegos said, "Moors were fighting against Catholics." After Constancia escapes from her box, she dresses in men's clothing. Then, she seeks guidance from the Virgin. Constancia's prayers are rewarded with an apparition of Mary worthy of those that graced Rodrigo Ponce de León, the marquis of Cádiz, during his campaigns against Granada at the end of the fifteenth century. In this fairytale place, in fact, the Madonna no more hesitates to send her devotees to war against the Moors than she had in medieval Iberia, though now her champion is a cross-dressing woman rather than a brawny knight.

"Fear not," Mary tells Constancia, "for you will triumph. You must go to the city and kill as many Moors as you can." Constantia obeys and fights hard "all day." Naturally, she is victorious. That night she invokes Mary, who comes to her a second time. "Fear not," the Madonna reassures her again, "for I am with you. Tomorrow the battle will start at eight o'clock." The next day, after Constancia kills "hundreds of Moors," the Christian army begins to wonder whether this new hero could be an angel or even a woman in disguise. When the Christian king tries to unmask this unexpected savior by tempting her with his crown, Mary helps Constancia preserve her male camouflage. Then "the Blessed Virgin appear[s] to Constancia and t[ells] her that she must conquer the Moorish King." In the ensuing fray, the Christian ruler is killed along with his Muslim counterpart. Constancia herself is crowned king of the Catholics. After ruling for six months, she returns to her homeland where she sheds her male clothing, proves her innocence to her husband, and is reunited with him. The tale ends with an even more resounding restoration of the proper hierarchy between men and women: Constancia places the crown on her husband's head and he reigns as king.

This story of a Marian-sanctioned, cross-dressing crusader unfolds in an eternal past that blends into twentieth-century New Mexico's present. Although Mrs. Gallegos never names the land where Constancia battles Moors at Mary's urging, this place—populated by martial Madonnas and warring Muslims and Christians—is surely reconquest Spain. This folktale makes medieval Iberia into modern New Mexico's next-door-neighbor, separated by a sea so narrow that Constancia does not even have to cross it when she comes home from her Marian wars.

Mrs. Gallegos has had much company in resurrecting the Iberian Marian past. Reconquest Spain haunts the politics of ethnicity in modern New Mexico, producing a charged vision of medieval New Mexico often articulated through the Madonna. In the twentieth century, civic rituals, erudite works of history, and folktales like the one told by Mrs. Gallegos imaginatively transformed the state's high desert landscape into a place where Moors and Christians still fought each other under Mary's watchful eye.

This geographical and chronological alchemy distilled the fierce pride in conquistador ancestry that emerged in the late nineteenth century among northern New Mexicans who earlier had identified as Mexican but increasingly eschewed that label after New Mexico's annexation by the United States in 1848. They did so partly to combat the conviction of many newly arrived Anglo-Americans that Mexicans belonged to a "mongrel race" in which the last vestiges of Spanish whiteness had long ago drowned in a sea of black and brown. Many northern New Mexicans responded to Anglo scorn by calling themselves Hispanos or Spanish-Americans, claiming to be culturally and biologically Spanish; their bloodlines, they boasted, led directly back to the conquistadors. In their quest for whiteness, these New Mexicans thus denied the centuries of *mestizaje*, that cultural and genealogical mixing of Europeans, native peoples of the Americas, and Africans imported to the New World as slaves. They also expanded the meaning of the word "conquistador," rendering it as much a marker of Spanish heritage as a reminder of how their putative ancestors had prevailed over the Pueblos.[2]

In their efforts to forge a racial and ethnic identity as white, pure, European, and ancient as that vaunted by Anglos, these new sons and daughters of Spain enlisted both Mary and the Middle Ages. Not only did they tell folktales like the one the FWP worker heard from Mrs. Gallegos, but they also turned to Santa Fe's Conquistadora, the statue bearing the title they believed had distinguished their colonial forefathers. In 1954, Spanish-identified New Mexicans revived this Madonna's confraternity, which had been defunct for many decades. In that same year, they watched with pleasure as Cardinal Francis Spellman laid a crown on her head. Then, in 1960, they engineered a second coronation for La Conquistadora by a papal emissary.[3] They also intertwined their genealogical claims to conquistador ancestry with her. A program from the 1960s for Santa Fe's fiesta—a annual civic celebration of Vargas's reconquest of New Mexico—promised that during the parades, La Conquistadora would be "carried by the caballeros de Vargas, a group of young men who are descendants of the Spanish conquistadors."[4] In 1970s, some of Santa Fe's Hispano families proudly showed an anthropologist their family trees stretching back to the conquistadors, in the front of which were glued images of La Conquistadora as if she were one of their conquistador foremothers.[5]

By integrating into their lineage the statue they called the "nation's oldest Madonna," these New Mexicans reinforced their claim to a European ancestry of even greater antiquity than that of Anglos: the colonial Spanish past. Fray Angélico Chávez, New Mexico's first native-born Franciscan friar, went much further than that.[6] A prolific author and a passionate Marian devotee, Chávez wrote the first authoritative historical studies of La Conquistadora, a Madonna with whom he was much in love (Figure E.1). He proved that, contrary to the scholarly consensus of his day, this statue had in fact been brought to Santa Fe by Diego de Vargas in 1693 and may even have come to New Mexico as early as 1625.[7] Chávez thus planted La Conquistadora firmly in the colonial past. But in a moving if odd little work about her that he wrote for a general audience in 1975—*La Conquistadora: The Autobiography of an Ancient Statue*—he suggested that through this Madonna, he and other proud New Mexican Hispanos could extend their family histories across the Atlantic all the way back to medieval Spain.

Chávez wrote this text in the first person as if he were the statue itself.[8] Further underscoring his merging with Mary, he opens the book with his own family tree. It is composed of men and women whom Chávez calls "Conquistadora progenitors," making them into the statue's kin as well as his. The text that follows often interweaves La Conquistadora's life story with the experiences of Chávez's conquistador ancestors who had tended her. But this time-traveling Virgin reaches even further into the past, helping Chávez transport his audience to a Marian medieval New Mexico.

Figure E.1 La Conquistadora and Fray Angelico Chávez, by Laura Gilpin (1891–1979). Gelatin silver print, 1953. Amon Carter Museum of American Art, Fort Worth, Texas. Bequest of the artist.

Chávez's Conquistadora intimates that her own venerable lineage began in reconquest Spain. To be sure, she counts among her ancestors the "first Conquistadora," that is, Puebla's colonial Mexican statue, but she also expresses her gratitude to the medieval Virgin of Guadalupe, whose story Chávez sets against a backdrop of epic struggle between Moors and Christians.[9] When Chávez describes La Conquistadora's original outfit, which was painted onto her wood body, he transforms this Madonna into a medieval princess—and a

Muslim one at that: she wore "the costume of Moorish princesses who once brightened the halls and courts of the Alhambra."[10] Here Chávez was more correct than he might have imagined. He evoked the Alhambra to embroider La Conquistadora with the exotic magic of Orientalist fantasy, not to reveal the Virgin's ability to straddle the lines between Muslims and Christians. Yet Mary actually belonged as much in the halls of the Alhambra as she did in the churches of northern New Mexico. The medieval Muslim princesses who had enjoyed the Granadan palace's comforts had even listened to poems reminding them that she was a woman beyond compare.

Like his medieval Christian predecessors, Chávez makes sure his readers understand that Mary nonetheless belongs to Christianity. His Conquistadora relates how she exchanged her Moorish garb for Christian wear after a clumsy woodworker altered the statue's shape and added new clothes over the original painted costume. "For more than two hundred years," she says, "from the day my carved gold arabesques had been spoiled by a cruel knife, I had worn the graceful regal tunics of a medieval Spanish queen."[11] As this resplendent Christian queen, Chávez's Conquistadora naturally deserved her own attendant knights. Chávez sometimes referred to the men who brought this Madonna to New Mexico and cared for her there as "knights."[12] And even when he called them conquistadors, he endowed them with a proudly medieval pedigree, insisting that they "knew that they descended from knights who vanquished the Moors."[13]

The medieval New Mexico that Chávez conjures through La Conquistadora resurrects the medieval Spain encountered in this book, although in a rather more romantic mode. Chávez did so for a purpose. If La Conquistadora, the spiritual progenitor of New Mexico's Hispanos, belonged to the Middle Ages—an unequivocally European slice of history—then Hispanos' genealogical connection to Spain was guaranteed. In gilding La Conquistadora with medieval language and speaking in her voice to create an imaginary medieval New Mexico populated by conquistadors of knightly descent serving a Marian princess clad in Moorish and Christian costumes, Chávez, much like Mrs. Gallegos, proclaimed that Hispanos' Spanish identity spanned the long centuries from the Middle Ages to the present. So at the end of her autobiography, Chávez's Conquistadora declares that she "bear[s] witness to" the "ancestry" of her modern devotees, while they "like their forefathers, bear uninterrupted witness to my glory."[14]

In the twentieth century, La Conquistadora was thus drawn into the myth of ethnic purity created by self-identified Hispanos in defiance of the centuries of *mestizaje*—intermarriage and sex across ethnic lines that render labels like "Spanish," "Pueblo," and "Anglo" so much fiction. But this Madonna also has had her partisans among the many modern New Mexicans who reject such terms and their heavy baggage in favor of identities that embrace *mestizaje*.[15] As these men and women celebrate their complex heritage, they too find meaning

Figure E.2 Cristina Acosta, *La Conquistadora/The Corn Maiden/Dine Spider Woman.*
Courtesy of Cristina Acosta.

in La Conquistadora. Among them is the artist Cristina Acosta, who in 2005
made her own image of this Madonna (Figure E.2). Mixing silver and copper
leaf, antique tiles, and gold glaze with vibrant swirls of oil paint, Acosta created a stunning Conquistadora with the body of a Corn Maiden and the face
of a Native American. At the fastening of this Madonna's beaded cloak is an
emblem evoking Spider Woman, a powerful figure who walks in many Pueblo
and Navajo tales. Acosta's Conquistadora emerges right from New Mexico's
soil, her roots sunk into its earth like the corn stalks that grow around her. She
stands tall against a backdrop of New Mexico's signature red rock landscape and
turquoise skies.

Acosta's meditations on the painting's creation reveal that Santa Fe's Conquistadora has added yet another role to the long repertoire she has starred in over the centuries. In the seventeenth century this Madonna was, for men like Diego de Vargas, a symbol of the justice of the Spaniards' return to New Mexico. Hundreds of years later, she became a link to the whitewashing prestige of the conquistador past for Hispanos like Angélico Chávez. By the summer of 1992, her title represented a bone of contention between Hispanos and Pueblos wrangling over the meaning of the colonial past. For a bold contemporary artist like Acosta, she offers a space for thinking about genealogical *mestizaje*.

Acosta explains that her own ancestors "were among the original Spanish colonists in the Southwest." She even grew up hearing her grandmother "continually claim to be pure Spanish." But Acosta confesses that she has come to regard her grandmother's words with skepticism. She describes something that she says her grandmother knew well: her grandmother's son—Acosta's own father –"made Indian regalia" and would dance the "old dances." It was in memory of her father, a man who danced in Indian dress yet was the son of a woman who boasted undiluted Spanish blood, that Acosta created her Conquistadora. She was inspired, she says, by a visit she made to Taos Pueblo shortly after her father's death from Alzheimer's disease. There, in this Native American community's church of San Geronimo, Acosta saw an image of Mary surrounded by corn stalks. Her Pueblo guide identified this Madonna as La Conquistadora.[16]

Though Acosta knows La Conquistadora's past is complicated, she chooses to see the statue of Mary in Santa Fe's cathedral as a "representation of the peaceful accord the Spanish settlers eventually reached with the Native American tribes... after decades of warfare." Those Hispanos who during the 1992 dispute over La Conquistadora's title insisted that its only proper translation was "Our Lady of Conquering Love" also tried to efface the divisiveness implicit in the name. Such optimistic interpretations of history are shadowed by the centuries of hard-edged interfaith and inter-ethnic Marian politics on both sides of the Atlantic that form this Madonna's true genealogy. Yet Acosta's Conquistadora and the Corn Maiden Conquistadora of Taos Pueblo hold out hope that Santa Fe's Madonna has the potential to become a bridge-builder. So, perhaps, does the resolution of the 1992 controversy.

In July of the Columbus quincentennial year, the Archbishop of Santa Fe succeeded in soothing his community's political passions when he announced that the cathedral's Madonna would bear a new title. Henceforth, he said, she would be called not just La Conquistadora, but also Our Lady of Peace. Despite its startling contradictions, this name is the one now in official use. Glossy tourist brochures in Santa Fe hotels advertise the cathedral and its historic statue of "Our Lady of Peace, La Conquistadora." Hand-painted tin devotional icons emblazoned "La Conquistadora" on one side announce on the other her identity

Figure E.3 Inscription on new shrine to La Conquistadora at Chimayó, New Mexico. Photo courtesy of Jeffrey Richardson.

as an icon of peace. At Chimayó, a new much larger shrine to her stands near the one with which this book began. Three figures, among them a cowboy and an Indian, gather reverently before a Madonna identified by an inscription as "Our Lady of Peace, formerly known as La Conquistadora" (Figure E.3). And in late August during Santa Fe's famed Indian Market, visitors to the cathedral sometimes find La Conquistadora wearing not her usual Spanish-inspired robes, but traditional Pueblo garb, her turquoise and silver jewelry rivaling the items for sale just outside on the Plaza. It remains an open question, however, whether after centuries at war, Santa Fe's Madonna finally is at peace.

ABBREVIATIONS

BAE   *Biblioteca de Autores Españoles.* Madrid, 1846–.
BRAH   *Boletín de la Real Academia de la Historia.*
CCCM   *Corpus Christianorum Continuatio Mediaevalis.* Turnhout, 1966–.
CSM   Alfonso X, *Cantigas de Santa María,* ed. Walter Mettmann, 3 vols. Madrid, 1986–1989.
MGH   *Monumenta Germaniae Historica.* Hanover (etc.), 1826–.
PL   *Patrologia Cursus Completus, Series Latina,* ed. Jacques Paul Migne, 221 vols. Paris, 1844–1864.

NOTES

Introduction

1. E.g., Flory, *Marian Representations*, pp. 22–23; Fulton, *From Passion to Judgment*; Elizabeth A. Johnson, "Marian Devotion in the Western Church," in *Christian Spirituality II: The High Middle Ages and Reformation*, ed. Jill Raitt (New York, 1987), pp. 392–414.
2. Robert Sullivan, "The Mystery of Mary," *Life*, December 1996, 56. Cf. "Hail Mary," *Newsweek*, August 25, 1997, 49–55.
3. In the Prado Museum, a security guard forcibly removed a woman who threw herself on the floor to pray before a painting of the Virgin by Murillo; *El Pais*, 4 January 1998.
4. Octavio Paz, *El laberinto de la soledad, postdada y vuelta a el laberinto de soledad*, 2nd ed. (Mexico City, 1996), p. 93. Feminist seekers: Beverly Donofrio, *Looking for Mary (or, the Blessed Mother and Me)* (New York, 2000); China Galland, *Longing for Darkness: Tara and the Black Madonna, a Ten Year Journey* (New York, 1990).
5. "Catechism of the Catholic Church," 1.2.3.9.6 (nos. 963–970) and 4.1.2.2 (nos. 2673–2679). Online. Available at: http://www.vatican.va/archive/ENG0015/_INDEX.HTM. [June 11, 2012].
6. Rosemary Radford Ruether, *Mary: The Feminine Face of the Church* (Philadelphia, 1977), esp. pp. 82–88.
7. Jeanette Rodriguez, *Our Lady of Guadalupe: Faith and Empowerment among Mexican-American Women* (Austin, 1994), pp. 107–110.
8. Sally Cunneen, *In Search of Mary: The Woman and the Symbol* (New York, 1996), p. xvi.
9. On the confraternity's history, see Chapter 10 in this volume. On La Conquistadora in Santa Fe's modern civic life, see Grimes, *Symbol and Conquest*, esp. pp. 213–264.
10. Personal conversation between the author and a woman she met at a hot spring resort in Santa Fe, 2001.
11. Cited in Chávez, "Nuestra Señora del Rosario," pp. 195–196. The custom of dressing Marian statues existed in the Spanish world since at least the thirteenth century; e.g., *CSM*, no. 295, 3:85–87. In general on this custom, see Trexler, "Dressing and Undressing Images."
12. Chávez, "Nuestra Señora del Rosario," p. 204.
13. Geoffrey Chaucer, *The Canterbury Tales*, Prologue, lines 160–162 in *The Works of Geoffrey Chaucer*, ed. F. N. Robinson (Boston, 1957), p. 18. The saying was perhaps coined by Virgil (*Eclogues*, 10.69 as edited in *The Eclogues and Georgics*, ed. R. D. Williams [New York, 1979], p. 24).
14. *La Conquistadora: Our Lady of Conquering Love, Nuestra Señora del Rosario* (Santa Fe, NM, no date), no pagination.
15. Tom Sharpe, "Historic Statue Renamed to Satisfy N.M. Indians," *Albuquerque Journal*, July 12, 1992.

16. "Hispano" is an identity category used by those New Mexicans who wish to emphasize their Spanish heritage; for discussion, see Gonzales, "Political Construction of Latino Nomenclatures"; idem, "History Hits the Heart," pp. 208–210; Nieto-Phillips, *Language of Blood*.

17. Letter of protest from the mayordomo of the *La Conquistadora* confraternity, Pedro Ribera-Ortega; "La Conquistadora Story Deceptive, False," *Albuquerque Journal*, July 15, 1992. See also the more vehement original version of the letter in the Fray Angélico Chávez History Library, Palace of the Governors, Santa Fe NM, vertical file: "La Conquistadora."

18. Although colonial Latin Americanists recognize the importance of the medieval era, typically they treat it as background. For a few exceptions, see Burkhart, *Before Guadalupe*; Lara, *Christian Texts*; Weckmann, *Medieval Heritage of Mexico*; the articles in *España medieval y el legado de occidente*; Daniel K. Richter, *Before the Revolution: America's Ancient Past* (Cambridge MA, 2011), pp. 37–63 (who largely focuses on North America). Medievalists generally do not venture into the New World, with some bold exceptions including: James Muldoon, *Popes, Lawyers, and Infidels: The Church and the Non-Christian World, 1250–1550* (Philadelphia, 1979); and his edited volumes including *The Spiritual Conversion of the Americas* and *Medieval Frontiers of Latin Christendom*, co-edited with Felipe Fernández-Armesto (Farnham, GB, 2008); Sabine MacCormack, *Religion in the Andes: Vision and Imagination in Early Colonial Peru* (Princeton, 1991); Valerie Flint, *The Imaginative Landscape of Christopher Columbus* (Princeton, 1992); David Abulafia, *The Discovery of Mankind: Atlantic Encounters in the Age of Columbus* (New Haven, 2008).

19. For the sake of convenience, this book often uses "Aragon" to refer to the areas comprised by the medieval Crown of Aragon.

20. See the many examples of Mary as a symbol of conquest in modern Spain and Latin America in Perry and Echeverría, *Under the Heel of Mary*.

21. This encyclopedic tendency appears for example in Pelikan, *Mary Through the Centuries*; Schreiner, *Maria*; Warner, *Alone of All Her Sex*.

22. "Advocaciones de la Virgen."

23. For excellent explorations of Mary's multiplicity, see *Mary: The Complete Resource*; Rubin, *Mother of God*; Signori, *Maria zwischen Kathedrale, Kloster und Welt*, esp. pp. 270–273; idem, "La bienheureuse polysémie: Miracles et pèlerinages à la Vierge: Pouvoir thaumaturgique et modèles pastoraux (Xe-XIIe siècles)," in *Marie: Le culte de la Vierge*, pp. 591–617.

24. Antonio Aradillas and José María Iñigo, *Vírgenes de Madrid: Devoción, historia, mito y leyendes* (Madrid, 1999). For a catalogue of Madonnas venerated in mid-twentieth century Spain, see Sánchez Pérez, *El culto mariano*.

25. On the iconography of different Madonnas, see among others Hans Belting, *Likeness and Presence: A History of the Image before the Era of Art*, trans. Edmund Jephcott (Chicago, 1994); Daniel Russo, "Les représentations mariales dans l'art de l'Occident: Essai sur la formation d'une tradition iconographique," in *Marie: Le culte de la Vierge*, pp. 173–291; Stratton, *Immaculate Conception in Spanish Art*; Manuel Trens, *María: Iconografía de la Virgen en el arte español* (Madrid, 1946).

26. Corral, "Santa María de Rocamadour," esp. pp. 589–610. On the multiplication of shrines to this Madonna, see Alphonse Dupront, "Les sacralités de Rocamadour," in *Saint-Louis pèlerin et le pèlerinage de Rocamadour au XIIIe siècle: Premier colloque de Rocamadour* (Rocamadour, 1975), p. 190.

27. The date of the shrine's establishment is much contested. See Poole, *Our Lady of Guadalupe*, pp. 49–68.

28. Zarebska, *Guadalupe*, pp. 106, 118–119.

29. Ocaña, *Un viaje fascinante*.

30. Ibid., chap. 28, pp. 210–212.

31. Mills, "La 'Memoria Viva.'"

32. Cf. Signori's brief remarks in her *Maria zwischen Kathedrale, Kloster und Welt*, p. 93.

33. See, for example, *Les miracles de Notre Dame de Rocamadour*, 2.6, 3.11, pp. 184–186, 260–262.

34. On Columbus's Marian devotion, see John V. Fleming, "The 'Mystical Signature' of Christopher Columbus," in *Iconography at the Crossroads*, ed. Brendan Cassidy (Princeton, 1993), pp. 197–214; Hall, *Mary*, pp. 47–57.

35. For this episode, see *Cristóbal Colón: Textos y documentos completos*, ed. Consuelo Varela and Juan Gil (Madrid, 2003), pp. 206, 210; Las Casas, *Historia de las Indias*, 1.69, 1.71, 3:676, 681–682.

36. On Columbus's 1486 pilgrimage, see Demetrio Ramos Pérez, "La primera estancia de Colón en Guadalupe," in *Extremadura en la evangelización del Nuevo Mundo*, pp. 211–228.

37. To be sure, Christians in the pre-modern world could evince skepticism about miracles; John Arnold, *Belief and Unbelief in Medieval Europe* (London, 2005), pp. 219-220; Susan Reynolds, "Social Mentalities and the Case of Medieval Skepticism," *Transactions of the Royal Historical Society*, 6th series, 1 (1991): 21–41.

38. See Introduction to Part Two in this volume.

39. Fernando de la Granja, "Milagros españoles en una obra polémica musulmana (el *kitab maqami' al sulban* del Jazrayi)," *Al-Andalus* 33 (1968): 311–365 (here 353–354).

Part I: Introduction

1. Ramón Llull, *Libre de Sancta Maria*, chaps. 16, 19, 29, pp. 1200, 1213, 1237.

2. Llull expresses these hopes in his *Llibre de l'orde de cavalleria*, ed. Marina Gustà (Barcelona, 1980). For discussion, see Martin Aurell, "Chevaliers et chevalerie chez Raymond Lulle," in *Raymond Lulle et le Pays d'Oc* (Toulouse, 1987; Cahiers de Fanjeaux, 22), pp. 141–168.

3. For modern examples, see Karlheinz Deschner, "Morden mit Maria," in his *Opus Diaboli: Fünfzehn unversöhnliche Essays über die Arbeit im Weinberg des Herrn* (Hamburg, 1987), pp. 231–224; Hall, *Mary*, pp. 198–204; Perry and Echeverría, *Under the Heel of Mary*. For non-Iberian medieval ones, see notes 9 and 11 below.

4. Powers, *Society Organized for War*, pp. 157–159; O'Callaghan, *Reconquest and Crusade*, pp. 124–151. In general on medieval European warfare, see Contamine, *La guerre au Moyen Age*; Helen Nicholson, *Medieval Warfare: Theory and Practice of War in Europe 300–1500* (New York, 2004).

5. E.g., *Los "miraculos romançados"*; and *Liber miraculorum sancte fidis*, ed. Luca Robertini (Spoleto, 1994).

6. E.g., *CSM*, no. 57, 1:195–198; *Les miracles de Notre Dame de Rocamadour*, 1.24, 1.47, 2.6, pp. 132–134, 158–160, 184–186.

7. Llull, *Libre de Sancta Maria*, chap. 16, p. 1200.

8. "Vita Barbati episcopi beneventani," *MGH: Scriptores rerum langobardicarum et italicarum saec. VI–IX* (Hannover, 1878), pp. 555–563 (here 560).

9. On the Latin translation, see Michel Huglo, "L'ancienne version latine de l'Hymnos Acathiste," *Muséon* 64 (1951): 27–61. On the Greek version, see Léena Mari Peltomaa, *The Image of the Virgin Mary in the Akathistos Hymn* (Leiden, 2001). On the well-developed Byzantine tradition associating Mary and warfare, see Norman H. Baynes, "The Supernatural Defenders of Constantinople," *Analecta Bollandiana* 67 (1949): 156–177; Averil Cameron, "The Theotokos in Sixth-Century Constantinople: A City Finds Its Symbol," *Journal of Theological Studies* n.s. 29 (1978): 79–108; Cutler, *Transformations*, pp. 111–141; Suzanne Lewis, "A Byzantine 'Virgo militans' at Charlemagne's Court," *Viator* 11 (1980): 71–93, esp. 82–84, 87–88; Bissera Pentcheva, *Icons and Power: The Mother of God in Byzantium* (University Park, PA, 2006), pp. 61–103.

10. For the development of European Marian devotion discussed in this paragraph, see: Barnay, *Le ciel sur la terre*; Fulton, *From Passion to Judgment*; Rubin, *Mother of God* (who uses the term "marianization"); Signori, *Maria zwischen Kathedrale, Kloster und Welt*. There has been no systematic study of the emergence of Marian devotion in medieval Iberia itself. Some hints can be found in Fernández-Ladreda, *Imaginería medieval mariana*; Antonio Viñayo González, "La devoción mariana en Asturias durante los primeros siglos de la Reconquista," *Archivos Leoneses* 17 (1963): 31–108.

11. Some examples from elsewhere in Europe include: Mazeika, "'Nowhere Was the Fragility of Their Sex Apparent,'" p. 247; Philippart, "Le récit miraculaire marial," pp. 569–570; Schreiner, *Maria*, pp. 262–263, 336–340, 368–409; Marian Dygo, "The Politics of the Cult of the Virgin Mary in Teutonic Prussia in the Fourteenth and Fifteenth Centuries," *Journal of Medieval History* 15 (1989): 63–80.

12. Most previous discussions of Mary on the battlefield in medieval Iberia have simply mentioned her as one among a number of saintly patrons of warfare; e.g., Goñi Gaztambide, *Historia de la Bula de cruzada*, pp. 33, 95; Lomax, *Reconquest*, p. 104; Herbers, "Politik und Heiligenverehrung," pp. 256–259; MacKay, "Religion, Culture, and Ideology," pp. 230–231; Muñoz Fernández, "Cultos, devociones y advociones religiosas," p. 138; O'Callaghan, *Reconquest and Crusade*, pp. 191, 193; Maricel E. Presilla, "The Image of Death and Political Ideology in the Cantigas de Santa María," in *Studies on the Cantigas de Santa María*, p. 429. More detailed discussion (which takes a different angle from this book) appears in Hall, *Mary*, pp. 17–44.

13. The expression originated with Lourie, "A Society Organized for War." For re-evaluation, see Rodríguez Molina, *La vida de moros*; Vann, "Reconstructing a 'Society Organized for War.' "

14. Rodríguez Molina, *La vida de moros*.

15. Helpful overviews of al-Andalus include: Fletcher, *Moorish Spain*; Pierre Guichard, *Al-Andalus 711–1492: une histoire de l'Espagne musulmane* (Paris, 2000); the essays in *The Legacy of Muslim Spain*.

16. Hrotsvit, "Passio sancti pelagii…" in her *Omnia opera*, ed. Walter Berschin (Munich and Leipzig, 2001), p. 63, lines 12–18.

17. Robert Hillenbrand, " 'Ornament of the World': Medieval Córdoba as a Cultural Center," in *The Legacy of Muslim Spain*, 1:112–135.

18. Pierre Bonnassie, "Le comté de Toulouse et le comté de Barcelone du début du IXe au début du XIIIe siècle (801–1213): Esquisse d'histoire comparée," in *Actes du vuitè col.loqui internacional de llengua y literatura catalanes / I: Tolosa de Llenguadoc, 12–17 de setembre de 1988* (Montserrat, 1989), p. 39; Peter Spufford, *Money and Its Use in Medieval Europe* (Cambridge, 1988), pp. 166–167.

19. Salvador de Moxó, *Repoblación y sociedad en la España cristiana medieval* (Madrid, 1979), pp. 17–125.

20. Peter C. Scales, *The Fall of the Caliphate of Córdoba: Berbers and Andalusis in Conflict* (Leiden, 1994); David Wasserstein, *The Rise and Fall of the Party-Kings: Politics and Society in Islamic Spain, 1002–1086* (Princeton, 1985).

21. *Cantar de mio Cid*; Richard Fletcher, *The Quest for El Cid* (Oxford, 1989).

22. For overviews of the Almoravid and Almohad periods, see Mahmoud Makki, "The Political History of al-Andalus, (92/711–897/1492)," in *The Legacy of Muslim Spain*, 1:60–77; the essays in *El retroceso territorial de al-Andalus*.

23. Reilly, *Contest of Christian and Muslim Spain*.

24. Ávila's walls: Lapunzina, *Architecture of Spain*, pp. 8–11. Civic militias: John L. Edwards, "A Society Organized for War? Córdoba in the Time of Ferdinand and Isabella," in *Jews, Muslims and Christians In and Around the Crown of Aragon*, pp. 75–96; Lourie, "A Society Organized for War"; Powers, *Society Organized for War*, esp. pp. 98–101.

25. For a representative range of opinions, see Barkaï, *Cristianos y musulmanes*; Alexander Pierre Bronisch, *Reconquista und Heiliger Krieg: Die Deutung des Krieges im christlichen Spanien von den Westgoten bis ins frühe 12. Jahrhundert* (Münster, 1998); Fletcher, "Reconquest and Crusade," esp. p. 34; García Fitz, *Las Navas de Tolosa*, pp. 391-441; Henriet, "L'idéologie de la guerre sainte"; Klaus Herbers, "Reconquista: Spaniens Christen gegen Spaniens Muslime?" in *Terror oder Toleranz? Spanien und der Islam*, ed. Raimund Allerband (Bad Honnef, 2004), pp. 35–59; Linehan, *History and the Historians*, pp. 95–127; Lomax, *Reconquest*, pp. 38–41; O'Callaghan, *Reconquest and Crusade*, esp. pp. 3–22.

26. On papal crusade bulls in Spain, see Goñi Gaztambide, *Historia de la Bula de cruzada*. Damian J. Smith attributes great weight to papal policy in the development of the reconquest; see his "Soli Hispani?".

27. María Judith Feliciano, "Muslim Shrouds for Christian Kings? A Reassessment of Andalusi Textiles in Thirteenth-Century Castilian Life and Ritual," In *Under the Influence: Questioning the Comparative in Medieval Castile*, ed. Cynthia Robinson and Leyla Rouhi (Leiden, 2004), pp. 101–131 (esp. 113–117, 119–124).

28. Jerrilynn D. Dodds, "Islam, Christianity, and the Problem of Religious Art," in *Late Antique and Medieval Art of the Mediterranean World*, ed. Eva R. Hoffman (Malden, MA, 2007), pp. 354–358.

29. On Christians fighting in the service of Muslim rulers, see Barton, "Traitors to the Faith?"; Hillgarth, *Spanish Kingdoms*, 1:157. For Muslims in the service of Christian rulers, see Brian A. Catlos, "'Mahomet Abenadallil': A Muslim Mercenary in the Service of the Kings of Aragon (1290–1291)," in *Jews, Muslims, and Christians In and Around the Crown of Aragon*, pp. 257–302; Ana Echevarría, "La guardia morisca: Un cuerpo desconocido del ejército medieval español," *Revista de Historia Militar* 90 (2000): 55–78; idem, "La conversion des chevaliers musulmans"; Hillgarth, *Spanish Kingdoms* 2:128, 234. For Muslim admiration of Christian knights, see Cristina Granda Gallego, "Otra imagen del guerrero cristiano (su valorización positiva en testimonios del Islam)," *En la España medieval: Estudios en memoria del profesor D. Claudio Sánchez Albornoz* 5.1 (1986): 471–480.

30. Erdmann, *Origin of the Idea of Crusade*, pp. 273–281; James B. MacGregor, "Negotiating Knightly Piety: The Cult of the Warrior Saints in the West, ca. 1070–ca. 1200," *Church History* 73 (2004): 317–345. Interestingly, Mary does not seem to have been an important battle patron of the crusades in the Levant (Bernard S. Bachrach, private conversation, April 1998). Indeed, it has been argued that "Mary is not a figure strongly associated with the Crusades": Annemarie Weyl Carr, "Thoughts on Mary East and West," in *Images of the Mother of God: Perceptions of the Theotokos in Byzantium*, ed. Maria Vassilaki (Aldershot, GB, 2005), p. 277. Chronology perhaps plays a role: the eastern crusades were largely over by the time Mary's role in knightly piety had expanded enough to make her into an important battle patron. It is telling that one significant example of her battlefield aid to Latins in the east comes from the end of that crusading era. It dates from the late thirteenth century and is recounted in an early fourteenth century text: Jean de Joinville, *Histoire de Saint Louis*, chap. 118, ed. Natalis de Wailly (Paris, 1868), p. 214. Further research into the question could prove fruitful.

31. Wolfgang Speyer, "Die Hilfe und Epipanie einer Gottheit, eines Heroen und eines Heiligen in der Schlacht," in *Pietas: Festschrift für Bernhard Kötting*, eds. Ernst Dassmann, K. Suso Frank (Jahrbuch für Antike und Christentum, Ergänzungsband 8; Munster, 1980), pp. 55–77; Frantisek Graus, "Die Heilige als Schlachtenhilfer: Zur Nationalisierung einer Wundererzählung in der mittelalterlichen Chronistik," in *Festschrift für Helmut Beumann zum 65. Geburtstag*, ed. Kurt-Ulrich Jäschke, Reinhard Wenskus (Sigmaringen, 1977), pp. 330–348; Christopher Holdsworth, "'An Airier Aristocracy': The Saints at War," *Transactions of the Royal Historical Society* 6th series 6 (1996): 103–122.

32. *Colección diplomatica de Irache*, ed. José María Lacarra, 2 vols. (Saragossa, 1965–1986), 1:12, no. 8 (see also 1: 9–10, no. 6). On the property dispute mentioned in the text, see Justo Pérez Urbel, *Sancho el Mayor de Navarra* (Madrid, 1950), p. 393.

33. Tolan, *Saracens*, esp. pp. 3–20.

34. *Crónica Najerense*, 2.40, 3.14, 3.16, pp. 62, 93.

35. Andrew of Fleury, "Miraculorum sancti Benedicti," 4.10, pp. 187–190 (here 187).

36. Erdmann, *Origin of the Idea of Crusade*, pp. 99–100; Goñi Gaztambide, *Historia de la Bula de cruzada*, p. 33; Fletcher, *Moorish Spain*, pp. 74–76; Bisson, *Medieval Crown of Aragon*, pp. 22–23.

37. On battle orations, see Bliese, "Rhetoric and morale."

38. On Andrew, see Thomas Head, *Hagiography and the Cult of the Saints: The Diocese of Orleans, 800–1200* (Cambridge, 1990), pp. 70–71.

39. Andrew of Fleury, "Miraculorum sancti Benedicti," 4.7–4.9, pp. 182–187.

40. Franco and his followers especially nurtured the memory of Covadonga, as is evident in Menéndez Pidal, *La Cueva de Covadonga*.

41. The accounts are interpolations in both redactions of the *Adefonsi tertia Chronica*; see *Crónicas Asturianas*, pp. 125, 128, 129. For discussion of the interpolations and their dating, see Henriet, "L'idéologie de la guerre sainte," pp. 203–208; Klaus Herbers, "Covadonga, Poitiers, Roncesvalles: Das Abendland und sein islamisches Feindbild?" in *Der europäische Gedanke: Hintergrund und Finalität*, ed. Reinhard Meier-Walser and Bernd Rill (Munich, 2000), pp. 97–113 (esp. 101–104); Luis A. García Moreno, "Covadonga, realidad y leyenda," *BRAH* 194 (1997): 353–380; Linehan, *History and the Historians*, pp. 101–106. On the representation of Christian-Muslim warfare in these chronicles, see Barkaï, *Cristianos y musulmanes*, pp. 30–53.

42. The *Ad Sebastianum* version of the Chronicle mentions a "cova sancta marie," while the *Rotense* describes a "domu[s] sancta virginis marie, qui intus est in coba"; *Crónicas Asturianas,* pp. 125, 128.
43. *Historia Silense,* p. 133. On the dating and authorship of this text, see *The World of El Cid: Chronicles of the Spanish Reconquest,* trans. Simon Barton and Richard Fletcher (Manchester, GB, 2001), pp. 9–23. Cf. Barkaï, *Cristianos y musulmanes,* pp. 113–114 (who does not mention the role attributed to Mary).
44. For example: *Primera crónica general,* chap. 568, 2:323; Lucas de Tuy, *Chronicon mundi,* 4.1–3, 1:323–326.
45. *Historia Silense,* p. 133. On the shrine's later development, see Menéndez Pidal, *La Cueva de Covadonga;* Muñiz López, "Pasado y mitos de origen," pp. 454–458.
46. On the developments discussed in this paragraph, see the references in note 10 above.
47. *Chronicon Adefonsi imperatoris,* 2.69, p. 227 (for other instances of these same militia men's battlefield invocations of God and Mary, see 2.22, 2.26, pp. 205, 207).
48. For comprehensive discussion of the development of James's cult, see Klaus Herbers, *Jakobsweg: Geschichte und Kultur einer Pilgerfahrt,* 2nd ed. (Munich, 2007), pp. 10–20; idem, "Politik und Heiligenverehrung"; Francisco Márquez Villanueva, *Santiago: trayectoria de un mito* (Barcelona, 2004).
49. *Liber sancti jacobi,* Bk. 2, pp. 155–177; *Santiago de Compostela: 1000 ans de pèlerinage européen* (Ghent, 1985).
50. *Historia Silense,* pp. 191–192; repeated in *Crónica Najerense,* 3.2, pp. 99–100; and Lucas de Tuy, *Chronicon mundi,* 4.51, 1:286–287.
51. Herbers, "Politik und Heiligenverehrung," pp. 203–209.
52. Claudio Sánchez Albornoz, "La auténtica batalla de Clavijo," *Cuadernos de historia de España* 9 (1948): 94–139; Fletcher, *Saint James's Catapult,* pp. 67, 293–294; Rodríguez Molina, *La vida de moros,* pp. 175–180. Some thirteenth-century renderings of the legend include: Lucas de Tuy, *Chronicon mundi,* 4.17, 1:238–239; *Primera crónica general,* chap. 568, 2:360–361; Rodrigo Jiménez de Rada, *Historia de rebus,* 4.13, p. 133.
53. Fletcher, *Saint James's Catapult.*
54. On Mary and James in this ecclesiastical rivalry, see the text edited by Fidel Fita, "Santiago de Galicia: Nuevas impugnaciones y nueva defensa," *Razón y Fe* 2 (1902): 190–194; and the discussions of Herbers, "Politik und Heiligenverehrung," pp. 256–262; Keller, "King Alfonso's Virgin of Villa-Sirga," and his "More on the Rivalry Between Santa Maria and Santiago de Compostela."
55. *Chronicon Adefonsi imperatoris,* 2.73–75, 2.77–78, pp. 229–231.
56. Gambra, *Alfonso VI,* no. 86, 2: 224–229; Mínguez, *Alfonso VI,* pp. 116–118; Francisco J. Hernández, "La cathédrale, instrument d'assimilation," in *Tolède, XIIe–XIII,* pp. 75–91.
57. For two contemporaneous accounts, see Rodrigo Jiménez de Rada, *Historia de rebus,* 9.13, p. 294; *Primera crónica general,* chap. 1037, 2:272. For discussion, see Barbé Coquelin de Lisle, "De la grande mosquée."
58. On mosques and sacred space, see Lucien Golvin, *La mosquée: Ses origines, sa morphologie, ses diverses functions, son rôle dans la vie musulmane…* Algiers, 1960), pp. 102–106; Hillenbrand, *Islamic Architecture,* pp. 31–32, 35, 61–64.
59. Rodrigo Jiménez de Rada, *Historia de rebus,* 6.24–25, 7.4, pp. 205–208, 225; for discussion, see Mínguez, *Alfonso VI,* pp. 116–118; Barbé Coquelin de Lisle, "De la grande mosquée," p. 150.
60. Edited in Gambra, *Alfonso VI,* no. 86, 2:224–229. As Gambra notes, questions have been raised about the authorship and dating of this text.
61. Valencia: *Historia Roderici vel gesta Roderici,* chap. 73 as edited by Emma Falque in *Chronica Hispana saeculi XII,* ed. Emma Falque, Juan Gil, Antonio Maya Sánchez, CCCM 71.1 (Turnhout, 1990), p. 97; and the text edited in Ramón Menéndez Pidal, *La España del Cid,* 7th ed., 2 vols. (Madrid, 1969), 2:868–871. Coria: *Chronicon Adefonsi imperatoris,* 2.66, p. 225.
62. Marie-Louise Thérel, *Le triomphe de la Vierge-Eglise: Sources historiques, littéraires et iconographiques* (Paris, 1984), esp. pp. 78–193. By the eleventh century, Mary was increasingly used to define the space of churches; Palazzo, "Marie et l'élaboration d'un espace ecclesial."

63. Remensnyder, "Colonization of Sacred Architecture."
64. *Colección diplomática de Pedro I de Aragón y Navarra*, ed. Antonio Ubieto Arteta (Saragossa, 1951), p. 251, no. 30.
65. Cf. the dedication of mosque of Toledo; Gambra, *Alfonso VI*, no. 86, 2:224–229. For some later examples, see Rodrigo Jiménez de Rada, *Historia de rebus*, 9. 27, p. 299; *Crónica latina*, pp. 72, 100. For discussion: Harris, "Mosque to Church Conversions," esp. pp. 162–163.
66. E.g., Gambra, *Alfonso VI*, no. 86, 2:224–229; Rodrigo Jiménez de Rada, *Historia de rebus*, 9. 27, p. 299; *Crónica latina*, pp. 72, 100; *Colección diplomática de Pedro I*, no. 30, pp. 251–252; Osbern, *De expugnatione Lyxbonensi*, p. clxxxi. On consecration as purification, see Amy G. Remensnyder, *Remembering Kings Past: Monastic Foundation Legends in Medieval Southern France* (Ithaca, NY, 1995), pp. 28–36.
67. Cf. the language used for the conversion of late medieval German synagogues into Marian churches; Hedwig Röckelein, "Marie, l'Eglise et la Synagogue: Culte de la Vierge et lutte contre les Juifs en Allemagne à la fin du Moyen Age," in *Marie: Le culte de la Vierge*, pp. 527–530.
68. "Advocaciones de la Virgen," pp. 11, 12, 26, 28.
69. Pascal Buresi, "Les conversions d'églises et de mosquées en Espagne aux XIe-XIIIe siècles" in *Villes et religion: Mélanges offerts à Jean-Louis Biget par ses élèves* (Paris, 2000), pp. 333–350; Harris, "Mosque to Church Conversions"; José Orlandis, "Un problema eclesiástico de la Reconquista española: la conversion de mezquitas en iglesias cristianas," *in Mélanges offerts à Jean Dauvillier* (Toulouse, 1979), pp. 595–604; Remensnyder, "Colonization of Sacred Architecture."
70. Barkaï, *Cristianos y musulmanes*, pp. 115–116, 145; Herbers, "Politik und Heiligenverehrung," pp. 177–275; Rodríguez Molina, *La vida de moros*, pp. 181–184.
71. Lucas de Tuy, *Chronicon mundi*, 4.98, 1: 337; *Primera crónica general*, c. 698, 1: 400–401. For discussion, see Fernández González, "Iconografía y leyenda del Pendón de Baeza," pp. 142–152; Muñoz Fernández, "Cultos, devociones y advociones religiosas," pp. 139–140; Lomax, *Reconquest*, pp. 103–104; O'Callaghan, *Reconquest and advocaciones*, pp. 193–199.
72. James I, *Llibre dels feits*, chap. 84, p. 178; Johannes Vincke, "Zur Geschichte des St. Georgskultes in den Ländern der Krone von Aragon," *Historisches Jahrbuch* 53 (1933): 458–465.

Chapter 1

1. On this crusading campaign and the battle itself, see among others Juan Batista González, *España estratégica: Guerra y diplomacia en la historia de España* (Madrid, 2007), pp. 137–141; García Fitz, *Las Navas de Tolosa*; López Payer and Rosada Llamas, *Las Navas de Tolosa*; O'Callaghan, *Reconquest and Crusade*, pp. 66–74; Pick, *Conflict and Coexistence*, pp. 34–46; Damian J. Smith, *Innocent III and the Crown of Aragon*, pp. 89–92, 95–99, 103–106, 111–115; idem, "*Soli Hispani*? Innocent III and Las Navas de Tolosa," *Hispania Sacra* 51 (1999): 487–512.
2. Garciá Fitz, *Las Navas de Tolosa*, pp. 489–491; López Payer and Rosada Llamas, *Las Navas de Tolosa*, pp. 52–54; Molenat, "L'organisation militaire des Almohades," p. 549.
3. Al-Nasir's tent and cape: López Payer and Rosada Llamas, *Las Navas de Tolosa*, p. 108.
4. Molenat, "L'organisation militaire des Almohades," pp. 561–562.
5. On Alfonso's centrality in the planning of the campaign and in the execution of the battle, see García Fitz, *Las Navas de Tolosa*, pp. 227–233.
6. The letter is edited in González, *El Reino de Castilla*, no. 897, 3:566–572 (here 570). On royal banners in Christian Iberia, see Percy E. Schramm, *Las insignias de la realeza en la Edad Media española* (Madrid, 1960), pp. 117–125 (none of those he considers features the Virgin Mary). Amador de los Ríos argues that the banner traditionally identified as the one Alfonso VIII used at Las Navas actually dates from the fourteenth century; see his *Trofeos militares de la Reconquista*, pp. 18–22. Some parts of this banner may have been belonged to the one Alfonso actually used; López Payer and Rosada Llamas, *Las Navas de Tolosa*, pp. 165–166.
7. The Isidore banner: Fernández González, "Iconografía y leyenda del Pendón de Baeza."
8. See Figure 5.1 below.
9. Rodrigo Jiménez de Rada, *Historia de rebus*, 8.10, p. 273.
10. Erdmann, *Origin of the Idea of Crusade*, pp. 35–56.

11. For this and the following details about the *alférez*, see Alfonso X, *Las Siete Partidas*, 2.9.16, 2.23.12–15, vol. 1, fols. 25v, 86r-v; Juan Manuel, *Libro de los estados*, 1.83–84, pp. 120–121; O'Callaghan, *Reconquest and Crusade*, p. 132–133; Powers, *Society Organized for War*, pp. 147–148.

12. E.g. Al-Himyari, *La péninsule ibérique*, pp. 18–19, 165.

13. E.g. *Crónica de Alfonso X*, chap. 63, p. 183; "Relacion circunstanciada," pp. 59–60. Some medieval Islamic war banners supposedly captured during the reconquest are still displayed in churches; Amador de los Ríos, *Trofeos militares de la Reconquista*; and *Al-Andalus: The Art of Islamic Spain*, no. 92, pp. 326–327.

14. The bishop's account appears in his *Historia de rebus*, 8.10, CCCM 72.1:273. The banner is also prominent in an account of the battle which purports to be a letter authored by Alfonso's daughter, Berenguela (d. 1246), edited in González, *El Reino de Castilla*, no. 898, 3:572–574. This letter was actually a forgery from late thirteenth-century France; Theresa M. Vann, "'Our Father Has Won a Great Victory': The Authorship of Berenguela's Account of the Battle Las Navas de Tolosa, 1212," *Journal of Medieval Iberian Studies* 3 (2011): 79–92.

15. Letter of Alfonso VIII in González, *El Reino de Castilla*, no. 897, 3:570–571.

16. Rodrigo Jiménez de Rada, *Historia de rebus*, 8.10, p. 273.

17. González, *El Reino de Castilla*, no. 899, 3:574–575.

18. García Fitz, *Las Navas de Tolosa*, pp. 76–78, 537–546 (and 40–58 for discussion of how pitched battles in general captured the imagaination of medieval writers).

19. *Primera crónica general*, chap. 1019, 2:702.

20. Gonzalo Argote de Molina, *Nobleza de Andalucía* (1588; reprint Jaén, 1957), 1.46, p. 97; and the early seventeenth-century text by the so-called Captive of Tunis: *Tratado e la defença de la santa fe Catolica Christiana, respondiendo à los argumentos que de nuestros sagrados escrituras nos opone el Mahometano*, Paris Bibliothèque Nationale ms. espagnol 49, fol. 76r.

21. On the cross in Rodrigo's descriptions of Las Navas, see Pick, *Conflict and Coexistence*, pp. 43–44.

22. Cross and reconquest: Alvarus Pelagius, *Speculum regum*, pp. 16–18; G. Menéndez Pidal, "El lábaro primitivo de la Reconquista," *BRAH* 156 (1955): 277–296. Cross and kings: Manuel Díaz y Díaz, "Apuntes sobre el rey en la liturgia visigótica," in *Religion, Text, and Society in Medieval Spain and Northern Europe: Essays in Honor of J. N. Hillgarth*, ed. Thomas E. Burman et al. (Toronto, 2002), pp. 20–24; A. Frolow, *Les reliques de la Vraie Croix: Recherches sur le développement d'un culte* (Paris, 1961), pp. 77–80, 238, 245–246, 263–264, 271, 287–290; Michael McCormick, *Eternal Victory: Triumphal Rulership in Late Antiquity, Byzantium and the Early Medieval West* (Cambridge, 1986), pp. 216, 247, 249, 297–326; Berent Schwinekörper, "Christus-Reliquien-Verehrung und Politik," *Blätter für deutsche Landesgeschichte* 117 (1981): 197–199.

23. Alberic of Trois-Fontaines, *Chronica*; MGH SS 23: 894–895.

24. Corral, "Santa María de Rocamadour," esp. pp. 589–610.

25. The donation to Rocamadour: González, *El Reino de Castilla*, no. 372, 2:642–643. For one of Alfonso's gifts to his two favorite Marian churches (Las Huelgas and Toledo), see his testament of 1204; ibid., no. 769, 3:347.

26. Signori, *Maria zwischen Kathedrale, Kloster und Welt*, pp. 202–228.

27. Jiménez de Rada, *Historia*, 8.10, CCCM 72.1: 273.

28. Linehan, *History and the Historians*, pp. 222–223, 313–349.

29. On Rodrigo, this crusade and the primacy dispute, see Damian J. Smith, *Innocent III and the Crown of Aragon*, p. 96.

30. *Die Ordines für die Weihe und Krönung des Kaisers und der Kaiserin*, ed. Reinhard Elze (MGH Fontes iuris Germanici…, 9; Hannover, 1960), pp. 52–55.

31. Linehan, *History and the Historians*, pp. 474–476.

32. Ibid., p. 289.

33. Lapunzina, *Architecture of Spain*, p. 20.

34. *Cantar de Mio Cid*, lines 215–225, pp. 116–117.

35. Ibid., lines 820–822, p. 150.

36. José Manuel Lizoain Garrido, *Documentación del monasterio de las Huelgas de Burgos (1116–1230)* (Burgos, 1985), no. 11, pp. 21–23; Rodrigo Jiménez de Rada, *Historia de rebus*, 7.33, p. 255; Lucas de Tuy, *Chronicon mundi*, 4.84, 1:324. The circumstances of the

abbey's foundation: Rose Walker, "Leonor of England, Plantagenet Queen of King Alfonso VIII of Castile, and Her Foundation of the Cistercian Abbey of Las Huelgas: In Imitation of Fontevraud?" *Journal of Medieval History* 31 (2005): 346–368.

37. Alfonso's patronage of Cistercians: V.A. Alvarez Palenzuela and M. Recuerdo Astray, "La fundación de monasterios cistercienses en Castilla: Cuestiones cronológicas y ideológicas," *Hispania Sacra* 36 (1984): 429–455 (esp. 434–439, 449–450, 453–454).

38. González, *El Reino de Castilla*, no. 769, 3:345.

39. Manuel Gómez Moreno, *El panteón real de Las Huelgas de Burgos* (Madrid, 1946); *The Art of Medieval Spain A.D. 500–1200* (New York, 1993), nos. 58–59, pp. 107–108.

40. On Alfonso and *Christianitas*: Linehan, *History and the Historians*, pp. 292–296.

41. Church architecture often connected Mary and the cross; Palazzo, "Marie et l'élaboration d'un espace ecclésial."

42. Juan Gil de Zamora, "Poesías inéditas," pp. 402–403.

43. For the points in this and the following paragraph, see: Linehan, *History and the Historians*, pp. 389–393, 426–428, 430–443, 507; Joseph O'Callaghan, *The Learned King: The Reign of Alfonso X of Castile* (Philadelphia, 1993), pp. 24–25; idem, *Alfonso X and the Cantigas*, pp. 72–76; Adeline Rucquoi, "De los reyes que no son taumaturgos: Los fundamentos de la realeza en España," *Temas Medievales* 5 (1995): 163–186; Teófilo F. Ruiz, "Une royauté sans sacre: La monarchie castillane du bas moyen âge," *Anales E.S.C.* 39 (1984): 429–453; idem, *From Heaven to Earth: The Reordering of Castilian Society, 1150–1350* (Princeton, 2004), pp. 133–150; Nikolas Jaspert, "El perfil transcendental de los reyes aragoneses, siglos XIII al XV: Santidad, franciscanismo y profecía," in *La Corona de Aragón en el centro de su historia 1208–1458* (Saragossa, 2010), pp. 183–218. For a contrary view, see José Manuel Nieto Soria, *Fundamentos ideológicos del poder real en Castilla (siglos XIII–XVI)* (Madrid, 1988), esp. pp. 49–109.

44. Alvarus Pelagius, *Speculum regum*, p. 22.

45. On the friars as shapers of high medieval Marian devotion, see Rubin, *Mother of God*, esp. pp. 197–216.

46. *CSM*, no. 38, 1:153.

47. E.g., Juan Manuel, *Libro de los estados* 2.9, p. 200; Schreiner, *Maria*, pp. 304–310.

48. Schreiner, "*Nobilitas Mariae*"; Marie-Louise Thérel, *A l'origine du décor du portail occidental de Notre-Dame de Senlis: Le triomphe de la Vierge-Eglise* (Paris, 1984), pp. 224–236.

49. Ilene H. Forsythe, *The Throne of Wisdom: Wood Sculptures of the Madonna in Romanesque France* (Princeton, 1972).

50. While Christ has fully commanded the attention of medieval historians of monarchy, his mother has yet to receive her due. Though historians have considered Mary's role as exemplar for queens (e.g., Patrick Corbet, "Les impératrices ottoniennes et le modèle marial: Autour de l'ivoire du château Sforza de Milan," and Dominique Iogna-Prat, "La vierge et les *ordines* de couronnement des reines au IXe siècle," both in *Marie: Le culte de la Vierge*, pp. 109–135, 101–107), much less sustained work has been done on Mary's importance to kings. For some exceptions, see Iogna-Prat, "Le culte de la Vierge"; Ernst Dieter Hehl, "Maria und das Ottonisch-Salische Königtum: Urkunden, Liturgie, Bilder," *Historisches Jahrbuch* 117 (1997): 271–310; Rubin, *Mother of God*, pp. 17–19, 32, 43–49, 67–69, 285–286, 292–295, 379–381.

51. On James's reign, see Bisson, *Medieval Crown of Aragon*, pp. 58–72; Stefano Maria Cingolani, *Jaume I: història i mite d'un rei* (Barcelona, 2007).

52. James I, *Llibre dels feits*, chap. 565, p. 527.

53. *Documentos de Jaime I*, no. 340, 2:116–117 (cf. James's reconfirmation of this wish in no. 748, 3:234–235.

54. Jaume Sobrequés i Callicó, *Els reis catalans enterrats a Poblet* (Poblet, 1983), pp. 10–11, 16–17.

55. James I, *Llibre dels feits*, chap. 564, p. 527.

56. Ibid., chap. 566, pp. 527–528.

57. Schreiner, *Maria*, pp. 465–490; Warner, *Alone of All her Sex*, pp. 315–331.

58. "Proleg," James I, *Llibre dels feits*, pp. 48–49. On James's models and intentions for the *Llibre*, see the translators' introduction to *The Book of Deeds of James I: A Translation of the Medieval Catalan Llibre dels fets*, trans. Damian Smith and Helena Buffery (Aldershot, GB, 2003), pp. 5–10; Márquez Villanueva, *El concepto cultural alfonsí*, pp. 229–235.

59. James I, *Llibre dels feits*, chaps. 563–564, pp. 524–526.
60. Robert I. Burns, "The Spiritual Life of James the Conqueror, King of Arago-Catalonia, 1208–1276," in his *Moors and Crusaders in Medieval Spain: Collected Studies* (London, 1978), p. 16.
61. James I, *Llibre dels feits*, chap. 57, pp. 143–44.
62. Ibid., chap. 62, p. 150.
63. Ibid., chap. 84, p. 178.
64. Ibid., chap. 85, pp. 180–181.
65. Cf. the editors' remarks in James I, *Llibre dels feits*, p. 179, note 701.
66. James I, *Llibre dels feits*, chap. 218, p. 291.
67. Matthew Strickland, *War and Chivalry: The Conduct and Perception of War in England and Normandy, 1066–1217* (Cambridge, 1996), p. 64.
68. James I, *Llibre dels feits*, chap. 84, p. 178.
69. Ibid., chap. 105, p. 198.
70. Ibid., chap. 450, p. 449.
71. Joaquín Bérchez Gómez and Arturo Zaragozá, "Iglesia Catedral Basílica de Santa María (Valencia)," in *Valencia: Arquitectura Religiosa*, ed. Joaquín Bérchez Gómez (Valencia, 1984), pp. 16–27; Robert I. Burns, *The Crusader Kingdom of Valencia: Reconstruction on a Thirteenth-Century Frontier*, 2 vols. (Cambridge, MA, 1967) 1:19–20.
72. The miniature is reproduced in Antoni Furió i Diego, *El rei conqueridor: Jaume I: entre la història i la llegenda* (Alzira, 2007), p. 49. For discussion, see Marta Serran Coll, *Jaime I el Conquistador: Imágenes medievales del reino* (Saragossa, 2008), pp. 133–136.
73. Although a bell tower was added soon after the Christian conquest, major alterations in the mosque's fabric were made only in the fourteenth century; Barral y Altet, "Palma: cathedral"; Durliat, *L'art dans le Royaume de Majorque*, pp. 150–167.
74. James I, *Llibre dels feits*, chap. 451, p. 450.
75. Juan Torres Fontes, *La reconquista de Murcia en 1266 por Jaime I de Aragón* (Murcia, 1967).
76. James I, *Llibre dels feits*, chap. 451, p. 450.
77. Ibid., chap. 443, p. 446.
78. Ibid., chap. 451, p. 450.
79. Ibid., chap. 450, p. 449.
80. Ibid., chap. 451, pp. 449–450.
81. Ibid., chap. 453, p. 451. The "la" to which James refers in this passage grammatically could be either *la ciutat* of Murcia itself or Mary. The ambiguity underlines how for James, Murcia had become Mary's city.
82. For an example of crusading fervor in a later Aragonese ruler, see Santiago Sobrequés Vidal, "Sobre el ideal de la cruzada de Alfonso V de Aragón," *Hispania* 12 (1952): 232–252. The patronage lavished by later Aragonese kings on the shrine of Montserrat showed their Marian devotion; Antoní M. Aragó I Cabañas, "El vot de Jaume III a Montserrat," *Analecta Montserratensia* 9 (1962): 33–38; J. Ernesto Martínez Ferrando, *Jaime II de Aragón: Su vida familiar*, 2 vols. (Barcelona, 1948), nos. 224, 232, 235–237, 2:159–160, 166, 169–171; Frederic Udina I Martorell, "Els privileges reials atorgats al monestir de Montserrat en una confirmació de Carles I (1519)," *Analecta Montserratensia* 9 (1962): 83–88; Münzer, "Itinerarium hispanicum," pp. 15–16.
83. James I, *Llibre dels feits*, chaps. 489–490, pp. 476–478.
84. *Primera crónica general*, chap. 1132, 2:772–773.
85. On Alfonso's efforts to live up to his father's model, see Salvador Martínez, *Alfonso X*, pp. 3–4, 42, 98, 213.
86. On the siege of Seville, see González, *Reinado y diplomas de Fernando III*, 1:363–391; González Jiménez, *Fernando III*, pp. 205–234.
87. Robert Irwin, *The Alhambra* (Cambridge, MA, 2004), pp. 70–71.
88. Ana Rodríguez López, "Fernando el Santo, 1217–1252: Evolución historiográfica, canonización y utilización política," in *Miscellània en homenatge al P. Agustí Altisent* (Tarragona, 1991), pp. 573–588; González Jiménez, *Fernando III*, pp. 284–290.
89. "Guillelmi Petri Calciata Rithmi de Iulia Romula seu ispalensi urbe," ed. Diego Catalán and Juan Gil, *Anuario de Estudios Medievales* 5 (1968): 549–558 (here 557, verse 47).

90. For non-Marian aspects of Alfonso's commemoration of his father, see González Jiménez, *Fernando III*, pp. 271–282.
91. González, *Reinado y diplomas de Fernando III*, 3:442, no. 852.
92. González, *Reinado y diplomas de Fernando III*, 3:409, no. 825.
93. *Diplomatario andaluz*, nos. 142, 186, 211–214, 233, 247; pp. 152–153, 205, 232, 236, 237, 239, 257–258, 275 (cf. similar language used for Ferdinand's conquest of Córdoba, no. 242, p. 269). On Alfonso's involvement in the siege of Seville, see Salvador Martínez, *Alfonso X*, pp. 93–94.
94. Alfonso's preference for Mary: Keller, "King Alfonso's Virgin of Villa-Sirga;" idem, "More on the Rivalry Between Santa Maria and Santiago de Compostela."
95. On reliquaries and ivory carvings: *Diplomatario andaluz*, no. 521, pp. 557–564. On Masses of the Virgin: Mariano Alcocer y Martínez and Hipólito Sancho de Sopranis, *Noticias y documentos referentes al Alcázar de Jérez de la Frontera en los siglos XII a XVI* (Larache, 1940), Appendix 1, p. 15.
96. Alfonso X, *Primera Partida según el manuscrito add. 20787 del British Museum*, ed. Juan Antonio Arias Bonet (Valladolid, 1975), Tit. 4, ley 18, pp. 58–59.
97. Lappin, "Thaumaturgy of Royal Piety"; Salvador Martínez, *Alfonso X*, pp. 234–235.
98. *Diplomatario andaluz*, no. 80, p. 81 (see also nos. 186, 211, 262, 451, 458, pp. 205, 232, 292, 475, 485).
99. Juan Gil de Zamora, "Biografías," p. 315. For discussion, see Márquez Villanueva, *El concepto cultural alfonsí*, pp. 119–126; Walter Mettmann, "Algunas observaciones sobre la génesis de la colección de las *Cantigas de Santa María* y sobre el problema del autor," in *Studies on the Cantigas de Santa María*, pp. 355–366; Salvador Martínez, *Alfonso X*, pp. 222–230; Snow, "Alfonso as Troubadour."
100. Alfonso el Sabio, *Cantigas de Santa María*, Escorial ms. T.I.1, fol. 5r.
101. Flory, *Marian Representations*, pp. 120–129; O'Callaghan, *Alfonso X and the Cantigas*; Snow, "A Chapter in Alfonso's Personal Narrative."
102. *CSM*, no. 122, 2:67.
103. Ibid., no. 221; 2:284–286.
104. Ibid., no. 292, 3:80.
105. *Crónica latina*, p. 60; *Primera crónica general*, chap. 1034, 2:718–719; González Jiménez, *Fernando III*, pp. 64–65. On dubbing and Castilian kings, see Linehan, *History and the Historians*, pp. 593–596.
106. *CSM*, no. 221, 2:284.
107. Ibid., no. 292, 3:78.
108. *Crónica latina*, p. 100; Rodrigo Jiménez de Rada, *Historia de rebus*, 9.27, p. 299; Lucas de Tuy, *Chronicon mundi*, 4.101, 1:341; *Primera crónica general*, chaps. 1071, 1125, 1129, 2:746–747, 767, 769.
109. Juan Manuel, *El conde Lucanor*, exemplo 41, ed. Guillermo Serés (Barcelona, 1994), p. 166.
110. Alfonso X, *Setenario*, ed. Kenneth H. Vanderford (Buenos Aires 1954, rpt. Barcelona, 1984), p. 21.
111. On the chapel's arrangement, see *CSM*, no. 292, 3:77–81; Juan Gil de Zamora, "Biografías," p. 321; and the early fourteenth-century text in Burriel, *Memorias*, pp. 215–216.
112. It is not known which of the many Marian statues belonging to the cathedral of Seville in the late thirteenth century enjoyed this honor. For conjectures, see O'Callaghan, *Alfonso X and the Cantigas*, p. 54. By the late fifteenth century, the chapel's Marian centerpiece was the "Virgin of the Kings" (see Chapter 2 of this volume). On Seville's Marian statues, see Enrique Pareja López and Matilde Megía Navarro, *El arte de la Reconquista* (vol. 3 of *Historia de la arte en Andalucía*, ed. Enrique Pareja López, 8 vols., Seville, 1988–1991), pp. 280–309; Hernández Díaz, *La Virgen de los Reyes*; idem, "Estudio de la iconografía mariana hispalense de la época Fernandina," *Archivo Hispalense: Revista histórico, literaria y artística*, 2d series, 9 (1948): 155–190; idem, *Iconografía medieval de la Madre de Dios*.
113. *CSM*, no. 292, 3:77–81.
114. Amy G. Remensnyder, "Marian Monarchy in Thirteenth-Century Castile," in *The Experience of Power in Medieval Europe, 950–1350*, ed. Robert Berkhofer, Alan Cooper and Adam Kosto (Aldershot, GB, 2005), pp. 247–264.

115. Lappin, "Thaumaturgy of Royal Piety," pp. 46–47. On these crises faced by Alfonso, see Salvador Martínez, *Alfonso X*, pp. 294–357, 368–383, 400–410, 437–503.
116. *CSM*, no. 200, 2:242–243.
117. Ibid., no. 409, 3:323.
118. Ibid., no. 345, 3:198.
119. Ibid., Prologue A, 1:53–54.
120. *Diplomatario andaluz*, no. 262, p. 292.
121. Ibid., no. 306, p. 330. This phrase probably refers not to Alfonso's initial conquest of Jerez in 1253, but to the military action of 1264 when he regained control of the city after the Mudejar rebellion.
122. *CSM* no. 200, 2:243.
123. Ibid., no. 348, 3:205–206.
124. Torres Fontes, "La orden de Santa María," pp. 99–100. On Mary and military orders in medieval Iberia, see Ditte Gurack, "Gottesmutter und Schlachtenhelferin: Die Marienverehrung bei den iberischen Ritterorden (12.–16. Jahrhundert)" (Ph.D. dissertation in progress at the Ruhr-Universität, Bochum).
125. Carlos de Ayala Martínez, "La monarquía y las Ordenes militares durante el reinado de Alfonso X," *Hispania* 51 (1991): 409–465 (esp. 452–456).
126. Salvador Martínez, *Alfonso X*, pp. 121–159, 174–184, 189–194, 199–208.
127. Manuel Alejandro Rodríguez de la Peña, "La Orden de Santa María de España y la Orden Teutónica: Apuntes en torno a un modelo de relación entre las Ordenes Militares y las monarquías europeas en el siglo XIII," *Mélanges de la Casa de Velázquez* 32 (1996): 237–246.
128. Torres Fontes, "La orden de Santa María," 99–100.
129. *CSM*, no. 200, 2:243.
130. Ariel Guiance, "To Die for Country, Land, or Faith in Castilian Medieval Thought," *Journal of Medieval History* 24 (1998): 313–332. Cf. Ron Barkaï, *Cristianos y musulmanes*, pp. 205–253; Ernst H. Kantorowicz, "*Pro patria mori* in Mediaeval Political Thought," *American Historical Review* 56 (1951): 472–494.
131. Alfonso X, *Siete Partidas* 4.24.4, vol. 2, fol. 60v (cf. 2.24.3, vol. 1, fol. 91v).
132. Cf. Rodrigo Jiménez de Rada's statement (*Historia de rebus* 8.10, CCCM 72.1: 273) that Mary was the "protector and patron" of "all of Spain" (*tocius Hispanie*). On the meaning of Spanish unity to the archbishop, see Pick, *Conflict and Coexistence*, pp. 44–45.
133. Victor Turner, "Hidalgo: History as Social Drama," in his *Dramas, Fields and Metaphors: Symbolic Action in Human Society* (Ithaca, NY, 1974), p. 152. Cf. the female allegories of the modern nation state; e.g., Margaret R. and Patrice L. Higonnet, "The Double Helix," in *Behind the Lines*, pp. 37–38; Maurice Agulhon, *Marianne into Battle: Republican Imagery and Symbolism in France, 1789-1880*, trans. Janet Lloyd (Cambridge, 1981).
134. Juan Gil de Zamora, "Poesías inéditas," p. 387.
135. Despres, "Immaculate Flesh and the Social Body," pp. 59–60.
136. Lucas de Tuy, *Chronicon mundi*, 4.84, 1:323. The story also appears in the "Biografía inédita de Alfonso IX, rey de León, por Gil de Zamora," ed. Fidel Fita *BRAH* 13 (1888): 291–295 (here 293).
137. *Diplomatario andaluz*, no. 487, p. 516. Cf. Alfonso X, *Las Siete Partidas*, 2.11.1, vol. 1, fol. 31v.
138. See the language of his donations to Seville and Niebla, cited above.
139. Alfonso's colonization of al-Qanatir: Manuel González Jiménez, "La ocupación de la zona de Cádiz," in *Repartimiento de El Puerto de Santa María*, ed. Manuel González Jiménez (Seville, 2002), pp. xiii–xxx (esp. xvii–xxi, xxiii, xxvi–xix); idem, "Repoblación de El Puerto de Santa María," in the same volume, pp. lxxxi–cxlii; and O'Callaghan, *Alfonso X and the Cantigas*, pp. 100–109; 172–180.
140. *Diplomatario andaluz*, no. 487, p. 517.
141. *CSM*, no. 328, 3:159–162. The poem adroitly papers over some rather complicated political circumstances; O'Callaghan, *Alfonso X and the Cantigas*, p. 105.
142. *CSM*, nos. 328, 356–359, 364, 366–368, 371, 372, 375–379, 381, 382, 385, 389, 391–393, 398, 3:159–162, 225–230, 237–239, 241–248, 256–259, 261–272, 274–278, 284–285, 289–290, 293–299. For differently oriented analysis, see Snow, "A Chapter in Alfonso's Personal Narrative;" O'Callaghan, *Alfonso and the Cantigas*, pp. 172–191.

143. *Diplomatario andaluz,* no. 487, p. 516.
144. Ibid., no. 487, p. 516.
145. Ibid., no. 487, p. 517.
146. *CSM,* no. 385, 3:284.
147. On this church, see Leopoldo Torres Balbás, "La mezquita de al-Qanatir y el santuario de Alfonso el Sabio en el Puerto Santa María," *Al-Andalus* 7 (1942): 417–437; Alfonso Jiménez, "Arquitectura gaditana de época alfonsí," in *Cádiz en el siglo XIII: Actas de las Jornadas Commemorativas del VII Centenario de la muerte de Alfonso X el Sabio* (Cádiz, 1983), pp. 143–144, 149.
148. Juan Gil de Zamora, "Poesías inéditas," p. 399. Cf. Vincent Ferrer, *Sermons,* ed. Josep Sanchis Sivera and Gret Schib, 5 vols. (Barcelona, 1932–1984), 3:74 (Sermon 64); "Advocaciones de la Virgen," pp. 32–33.
149. *CSM,* no. 185, 2:204–207.
150. Marian castle chapels: N. Huyghebaert, "Le comte Baudoin II de Flandre et le 'custos' de Steneland: A propos d'un faux précepte de Charles le Chauve pour Saint-Bertin," *Revue Bénédictine* 69 (1959): 64, note 2; Schreiner, "Nobilitas Mariae," pp. 227–29. Marian churches on Byzantine city walls and boundaries: Cutler, *Transformations,* pp. 113–115, 117–118, 136–141; Procopius of Caesarea, *Buildings,* 1.3, 6.7, ed. and trans. H. B. Dewing and Glanville Downey (Cambridge, MA, 1940), pp. 41, 393.
151. *Diplomatario andaluz,* no. 521, pp. 557–564. For discussion, Salvador Martínez, *Alfonso X,* pp. 511–518.
152. Salvador Martínez, *Alfonso X,* p. 512.
153. *Crónica de Alfonso X.*
154. Edited in Gómez-Menor Fuentes, "Preces por el rey en tiempo de guerra," pp. 71–77.
155. On the battle positions: Manuel López Fernández, "La batalla de Salado sobre la toponimia actual de Tarifa," *Aljaranda: Revista de studios tarifeños* 67 (2007): 2–10.
156. Nicolás Agrait, "The Reconquest During the Reign of Alfonso XI," in *On the Social Origins of Medieval Institutions: Essays in Honor of Joseph F. O'Callaghan,* ed. Donald J. Kagay and Therese M. Vann (Leiden, 1998), p. 165.
157. The text's dating and composition: Diego Catalan Menéndez Pidal, *Poema de Alfonso XI: Fuentes, dialecto, estilo* (Madrid, 1953).
158. *El Poema de Alfonso XI,* verse 290, p. 83.
159. Ibid., verses 1205–1207, pp. 335–337. The *Poema* identifies the church as Santa María del Pilar of Seville, but I have found no record of a church by this name in the city in the fourteenth century. There was, however, a chapel in Seville's cathedral associated with a military confraternity dedicated to Our Lady of the Pilar; cf. the contemporaneous references to this confraternity as being "de la catedral" in Manuel García Fernández, "Regesto documental andaluz de Alfonso XI (1312–1350)," *Historia, Instituciones, Documentos* 15 (1988): 1–125 (here nos. 295, 308, pp. 66, 68); Isabel Montes Romero Camacho, "La documentación de Alfonso XI conservada en el archivo de la catedral de Sevilla," *En la España medieval* 3 (1982): 135–156 (here 146, no. 38); Goñi Gaztambide, *Historia de la Bula de cruzada,* pp. 644–645.
160. *Poema de Alfonso XI,* verses 1519–1521, p. 425.
161. Ibid., verse 1551, p. 433.
162. Ibid., verse 1674, p. 467.
163. Ibid., verse 1686, p. 469.
164. Ibid., verse 1794, p. 501.
165. Burriel, *Memorias,* pp. 215–216.
166. *Poema de Alfonso XI,* verses 2457–2458, pp. 683, 685.

Chapter 2

1. *Colección documental de Alfonso XI,* no. 278, pp. 469–470. For discussion, see Crémoux, *Pèlerinages et miracles,* pp. 20–22; Peter Linehan, "The Beginnings of Santa María de Guadalupe and the Direction of Fourteenth-Century Castile," in his *Past and Present in Medieval Spain* (Aldershot, GB, and Brookfield, VT, 1992), pp. 284–304; María Isabel Pérez

de Tudela y Velasco, "Alfonso XI y el Santuario de Santa María de Guadalupe," in *En la España Medieval: Estudios en memoria del Profesor D. Salvador de Moxó* (Madrid, 1982), 2:271–285. The first mention of the shrine dates from 1326; García, "El Real Santuario," p. 374.

2. *Colección documental de Alfonso XI*, no. 278, p. 469.

3. Linehan, *History and the Historians*, pp. 619–620.

4. *Gran Crónica de Alfonso XI*, chaps. 331, 335, 2:438, 449.

5. Ibid., chap. 335, 2:449.

6. On the church's construction, see García, "El Real Santuario," pp. 386–388.

7. The statue's dating and manufacture: ibid., pp. 368–372.

8. The following paragraphs use the earliest extant version of the legend as it was told at Guadalupe (Archivo Histórico Nacional Clero Codice 48 B). I cite from the partial transcription in Christian, *Apparitions*, pp. 276–279; and the complete transcription (with modernized spelling) in Rubio, *Historia de Nuestra Señora de Guadalupe*, pp. 13–22. On this and the later fifteenth-century manuscripts that contain the legend, see Crémoux, *Pèlerinages et miracles*, pp. 7–10. The monastery's official website (http://www.monasterioguadalupe. com/) tells the legend as history.

9. For these changes in the legend, see Crémoux, *Pèlerinages et miracles*, pp. 13–17; idem, "Saint Jacques et Guadalupe: Un déplacement de sacralité vers le centre?" in *Relations entre identités culturelles dans l'espace ibérique et ibéro-américain*, ed. Augustin Redondo, 2 vols. (Paris, 1995–1998), 1:54–55.

10. Gretchen D. Starr-LeBeau, "'The Joyous History of Devotion and the Memory of the Grandeur of Spain': The Spanish Virgin of Guadalupe and Political Memory," *Archiv für Reformationsgeschichte / Archive for Reformation History* 93 (2002): 192–216 (esp. 193–198).

11. For a transcription and discussion of this text, see Christian, *Apparitions*, pp. 26–40, 245–250.

12. Mary and hawthorns: M. A. Hall, "An Ivory Knife Handle from the High Street, Perth, Scotland: Consuming Ritual in a Medieval Burgh," *Medieval Archaeology* (2001): 169–188 (here 185, note 82).

13. In the modern world, too, Marian apparitions bring messages; William A. Christian, *Visionaries: The Spanish Republic and the Reign of Christ* (Berkeley and Los Angeles, 1996); Élisabeth Claverie, *Les guerres de la Vierge: Une anthropologie des apparitions* (Paris, 2003); Sandra L. Zimdars-Swartz, *Encountering Mary: From La Salette to Medjugorje* (Princeton, 1991).

14. Christian, *Apparitions*.

15. J. N. Hillgarth, "Spanish Historiography and Iberian Reality," *History and Theory* 24 (1985): 23–43; Rafael González Fernández, "El mito gótico en la historiografía del siglo XV," in *Antigüedad y cristianismo: Monografías históricas sobre la Antigüedad Tardía* 3 (1986): 289–300; Isabel Beceiro Pita, "La conciencia de los antepasados y la gloria del linaje en la Castilla medieval," in *Relaciones de poder, de producción y parentesco en la Edad Media*, ed. Reyna Pastor (Madrid, 1990), p. 340; Muñiz López, "Pasado y mitos de origen," pp. 437–441; Patricia E. Grieve, *The Eve of Spain: Myths of Origins in the History of Christian, Muslim, and Jewish Conflict* (Baltimore, 2009), pp. 72–80.

16. Majorca: Barral y Altet, "Palma: cathedral"; Durliat, *L'art dans le Royaume de Majorque*, pp. 150–167. Seville: Rafael Cómez Ramos, "Sevilla: Catedral," in *La España Gótica, 11: Andalucía*, ed. José Fernández Lopez (Madrid, 1992), pp. 290–328 (esp. 290–293).

17. See the transcription of the legend in Christian, *Apparitions*, pp. 276–277.

18. Rubio, *Historia de Nuestra Señora de Guadalupe*, p. 22. Cf. the slightly later text (AHN Cod. 101B) transcribed in Crémoux, *Pèlerinages et miracles*, p. 20, note 40; as well as the early sixteenth-century account of Diego de Ecija, *Libro de la invención*, 2.7, p. 53.

19. Diego de Ecija, *Libro de la invención*, 2.7, p. 56. Cf. Rubio, *Historia de Nuestra Señora de Guadalupe*, p. 22; Talavera, *Historia de Nuestra Señora de Guadalupe*, 1.7, fol. 19r.

20. Domínguez Casas, *Arte y etiqueta*, pp. 349–354; Crémoux, *Pèlerinages et miracles*, pp. 26–30 (for the proverb, p. 26); Fernando Chueca, *Casas reales en monasteries y conventos españoles* (Madrid, 1966), pp. 165–172; Francisca de Paula Cañas Gálvez, *El itinerario de la corte de Juan II de Castilla (1418–1454)* (Madrid, 2007), pp. 135–140; Gretchen Starr-LeBeau, *In the Shadow of the Virgin: Inquisitors, Friars, and Conversos in Guadalupe, Spain* (Princeton, 2003), pp. 47, 162–163.

21. Linehan, *History and the Historians*, pp. 633–634.

22. Domínguez Casas, *Arte y etiqueta*, pp. 349–353.

23. Vicenç Beltran and Mercé López Casas, "Fernán Pérez de Guzmán," in *Diccionario filológico de literatura medieval española: Textos y transmisión*, ed. Carlos Alvar and José Manuel Lucía Megías (Madrid, 2002), pp. 498–502; Mercedes Vaquero, "Cultura nobiliaria y biblioteca de Fernán Pérez de Guzmán," *Revista Lemir* 7 (2003). [Online]. Available: http://parnaseo. uv.es/lemir/Revista/Revista7/Vaquero/MercedesVaquero.htm [January 2, 2012].

24. Fernán Pérez de Guzman, "Loores de claros varones de España," in *Cancionero castellano*, 1:735, 747.

25. MacKay, "Un Cid Ruy Díaz en el siglo XV," esp. p. 199.

26. Pérez de Guzman, "Loores de claros varones de España," in *Cancionero castellano*, 1:741.

27. Pérez de Guzmán's admiration for Ferdinand of Antequera: Regula Rohland de Langbehn, "Power and Justice in *Cancionero* Verse," in *Poetry at Court in Trastamaran Spain: From the Cancionero de Baena to the Cancionero General*, ed. E. Michael Gerli and Julian Weiss (Tempe, AZ, 1998), pp. 199–219 (here 200–201).

28. Valdeón Baruque, *Los Trastámaras*, pp. 77–120.

29. On this order's foundation, see Torres Fontes, "Don Fernando"; Boulton, *Knights of the Crown*, pp. 330–332.

30. Torres Fontes, "Don Fernando," p. 99.

31. Boulton, *Knights of the Crown*, pp. 330–331 (and xvii–xviii, 1–2, 46–95 for the relationship between chivalric orders and royal power). On chivalric orders, see also Maurice Keen, *Chivalry* (New Haven, 1984), pp. 179–199.

32. See the Catalan version of the Statutes, edited in Torres Fontes, "Don Fernando," pp. 112–117 (here 112–113).

33. The collar is described in the Statutes as edited in Torres Fontes, "Don Fernando," p. 113. For fifteenth-century and early sixteenth-century representations of it, see Boulton, *Knights of the Crown*, fig. 12.4, p. 334. On the griffin as a symbol of Christ, see Carola Hicks, *Animals in Early Medieval Art* (Edinburgh, 1993), p. 151; Paul Michel, *Tiere als Symbol und Ornament: Möglichkeiten und Grenzen der ikonographischen Deutung, gezeigt am Beispeil des zürcher Grossmünsterkreuzgangs* (Wiesbaden, 1979), p. 67.

34. Edited in Torres Fontes, "Don Fernando," p. 113.

35. Edited in ibid., p. 117.

36. *Cancionero de Juan Alfonso*, no. 4, 1:24–25 (cf. no. 65, 1:143). For further discussion, see MacKay, "Ferdinand of Antequera," p. 134.

37. Valdeón Baruque, *Los Trastámaras*, p. 122.

38. MacKay, "Religion, Culture, and Ideology."

39. The renewal of hostilities between Castile and Granada: Valdeón Baruque, *Los Trastámaras*, pp. 100, 122; Norman Housley, *The Later Crusades: From Lyons to Alcazar 1274–1580* (Oxford, 1992), pp. 282–284.

40. García de Santa María, *Crónica*, chap. 39, p. 118.

41. García de Santa María mentioned that the chapel where Ferdinand slept was built by "Pero de Tos" (*Crónica*, chap. 39, p. 118), whom the early modern legend of Our Lady of Iniesta would describe as the discoverer of the "Visigothic" Marian image; Morgado, *Historia de Sevilla*, pp. 348–349; and *Constituciones de la Hermandad de Nuestra Señora de la Yniesta* (Seville, 1671), pp. 3–4. On this Virgin's cult in Seville, see Marielena Mestas Pérez, *Nuestra Señora de la Iniestra de Capaya: Estudio etnohistórico* (Caracas, 2008), pp. 97–100.

42. The ceremony of 1407 recounted in this and the following paragraph is described by García de Santa María, *Crónica*, chap. 48, pp. 129–131.

43. García de Santa María, *Crónica*, chap. 137, p. 293.

44. See the fourteenth-century text in Burriel, *Memorias*, pp. 215–216.

45. García de Santa María, *Crónica*, chap. 48, p. 130.

46. Ibid., chaps. 82–83, pp. 189–191.

47. Ibid., chap. 54, p. 138.

48. Hilda Grassotti, *Las instituciones feudo-vassaláticas en León y Castilla*, 2 vols. (Spoleto, 1969), 1:141–162.

49. García de Santa María, *Crónica*, chap. 137, p. 293.

50. Ibid., chap. 143, 172, 178, pp. 305–306, 366–367, 384.
51. Edited in Hipólito Sancho de Sopranis, *Historia social de Jérez de la Frontera al fin de la edad media*, 3 vols. (Jérez, 1959), 2:105–106.
52. García de Santa María, *Crónica*, chap. 144, pp. 308–309.
53. Barrientos, *Refundición de la crónica*, chap. 7, p. 20.
54. Barrientos, *Refundición de la crónica*, chap. 7, p. 20.
55. *Cancionero de Juan Alfonso*, no. 4, 1:24–25. MacKay ("Religion, Culture, and Ideology," p. 231) argues that in the fifteenth century, Santiago "could still be invoked in battle, but his great age now lay well in the past."
56. *Los romances frontizeros*, 1:242; Roger Wright, *Spanish Ballads* (Warminster, England, 1987), p. 103. On the ballad's history, see Roger Wright, *Spanish Ballads* (London, 1991), pp. 45–47. General discussion of ballads about Antequera: Bautista Martínez Iniesta, "La toma de Antequera y la poética del heroísmo," in *Las tomas: Antropología histórica de la occupación territorial del reino de Granada*, ed. José Antonio González Alcantud and Manuel Barrios Aguilera (Granada, 2000), pp. 383–415.
57. MacKay, "Ferdinand of Antequera," 132–139. On the painting, see also Kristin Sorensen Zapalac, "Debate: Ritual and Propaganda in Fifteenth-Century Castile," *Past and Present* 113 (1986): 186–196 (here 191–192), and in the same issue, Angus MacKay, "A Rejoinder," pp. 197–208 (here 206–207).
58. *Le parti inedite della "Crónica de Juan II,"* p. 97.
59. Ibid., pp. 113–114.
60. Ibid., pp. 119–120.
61. Torres Fontes, "Don Fernando de Antequera," p. 111.
62. Ferdinand had its statutes copied sometime during his reign; Boulton, *Knights of the Crown*, p. 333.
63. On the painting's manufacture and iconography, see *Isabel la Católica en la Real Academia de la Historia* (Madrid, 2004), pp. 81–88.
64. Fournes, "*La Virgen,*" p. 4.
65. For these last two points, see Fournes, "*La Virgen,*" pp. 6–7.
66. For an excellent biography of Isabel, see Liss, *Isabel*.
67. Francisco Javier Sánchez Cantón, *Libros, tapices y cuadros que coleccionó Isabel la Católica* (Madrid, 1950), pp. 47 (the *Cantigas*); 101, 102, 111, 112, 114, 116, 120, 122–124, 126, 129, 133, 134, 140, 148 (Marian tapestries); 160, 166, 167, 170–184, 187–188 (Marian paintings).
68. On Isabel and the succession crisis, see Carrasco Manchado, *Isabel*.
69. Carrasco Manchado, *Isabel*, pp. 191, 272.
70. Ferdinand, "Carta á la ciudad de Baeza," p. 399.
71. Palma, *Divina retribucion*, chap. 14, p. 57.
72. Ferdinand, "Carta á la ciudad de Baeza," pp. 399–400; Palma, *Divina retribucion*, chap. 14, p. 58.
73. Ana Isabel Carrasco Manchado, "Isabel la Católica y las ceremonias de la monarquía: Las fuentes historiográficas," *e-Spania* 1 (2006). [Online]. Available: http://e-spania.revues.org/308 html [December 19, 2009].
74. Carrasco Manchado, *Isabel*, pp. 276–277.
75. Palma, *Divina retribucion*, chap. 15, pp. 63–64. On this antiphon, see Amnon Linder, *Raising Arms: Liturgy in the Struggle to Liberate Jerusalem in the Late Middle Ages* (Turnhout, 2003), pp. 2–3, 55–56.
76. Weissberger, *Isabel Rules*, p. 112. See also the references above, note 15.
77. On Ildefonsus and this legend, see Juan Francisco Rivera Recio, *San Ildefonso de Toledo: Biografía, época y posteridad* (Madrid, 1985), esp. pp. 8–16, 233–235, 281–290.
78. Palma, *Divina retribucion*, chap. 15, p. 61.
79. Ibid., chap. 15, pp. 61–62.
80. Barrientos, *Refundición de la crónica*, chap. 62, p. 114.
81. The incident at Toledo: Carrasco Manchado, *Isabel*, p. 272 (who ignores Mary's importance as a battle patron). Juan II's place in the Isabelline rhetoric of legitimacy: Liss, *Isabel*, p. 135.

82. Isabel's visits to Guadalupe during the succession crisis (including in 1477): Carrasco Manchado, *Isabel*, pp. 287–289, 357, 421–422, 477.
83. Isabel's Sevillean *entrada* and establishment of the Toro feast: Carrasco Manchado, *Isabel I*, pp. 296–309.
84. The image can be found at http://www.institucioncolombina.org/catedral/blanco.htm [December 13, 2009].
85. Carrasco Manchado, *Isabel*, pp. 307–308. If, as Machado suggests, the designers of the Sevillean miniature modeled their Madonna on the statue in the Seville's royal chapel, the illumination offers yet more evidence of how Isabel's supporters recruited Marian reconquest history for their cause: depicted kneeling before the Virgin who guarded Ferdinand III's memory and who had received the prayers of a previous prince claiming the saintly warrior king's legacy, Isabel becomes her predecessors' worthy heir.
86. For examples of Marian rhetoric in descriptions of Isabel, see *Crónica incompleta*, tit. 52; Diego de Valera, Letter 13, of his "Epistolas," in *Prosistas castellanos del siglo XV*, ed. Mario Penna (BAE, 116; Madrid, 1959), pp. 17–18; Pulgar, *Los claros varones*, tit. 25, p. 149; the text by Bartolomé de Zuloaga as edited in Vicente Rodríguez Valencia, *Isabela la Católica en la opinión de españoles y extranjeros*, 3 vols. (Valladolid, 1970), 1:249. For extensive discussion see Liss, *Isabel*, pp. 171–174, 157–160; and above all Weissberger, *Isabel Rules*, pp. 112–124 (whose trenchant analysis I follow in this paragraph).
87. Carrasco Manchado, *Isabel*, pp. 462–469.
88. José Luis del Pino García, "Las campañas militares castellanas contra el reino de Granada durante los reinados de Juan II y Enrique IV," in *Andalucía entre Oriente y Occidente*, pp. 673–684.
89. Among the many studies of Ferdinand and Isabel's Granadan campaigns, the following are particularly helpful: John Edwards, *The Spain of the Catholic Monarchs 1474–1520* (Oxford, 2000), pp. 101–140; Harvey, *Islamic Spain*, pp. 253–254, 275–323; Miguel Angel Ladero Quesada, *Castilla y la conquista del reino de Granada* (Valladolid, 1967).
90. García-Arenal and Bunes, *Los Españoles y el Norte de Africa*, p. 4; MacKay, "Andalucía y la guerra del fin del mundo," pp. 329–342; Milhou, "La chauve-souris," pp. 61–78; idem, "Propaganda mesiánica y opinión pública," pp. 51–62.
91. E.g., *Historia de los hechos*, chap. 31, pp. 244–247 (and the editor's discussion, pp. 89–121).
92. Marcuello, *Cancionero*, p. 311. For discussion see Peinado Santaella, "*Christo pelea por sus castellanos*," pp. 494–495.
93. *Historia de los hechos*, chap. 15, p. 200.
94. Diego de Ecija, *Libro de la invención*, 4.66, p. 338.
95. Ibid., 4.66, p. 337.
96. Münzer, "Itinerarium hispanicum," p. 112 (for both the quotation and the oratory)
97. On the dates of Ferdinand and Isabel's visits to Guadalupe and on the construction of the royal residence, see Domínguez Casas, *Arte y etiqueta*, pp. 350–354.
98. Carrasco Manchado, *Isabel*, pp. 317, 319.
99. See the text quoted in Carrasco Manchado, *Isabel*, p. 320, note 180 (where she also gives the years of Isabel and Ferdinand's attendance at these Sevillean civic rituals).
100. Nicolás de Popielovo, "Relación de viaje," trans. in *Viajes de extranjeros por España y Portugal...*, ed. J. García Mercadal, 6 vols. (Salamanca, 1999), 1:298.
101. The tombs would be installed there only in 1579; Alfredo J. Morales, *La capilla real de Sevilla* (Seville, 1979), pp. 73–83.
102. Münzer, "Itinerarium hispanicum," pp. 78–79.
103. On this statue, see: Introduction to Part Three; Carrero Rodríguez, *Nuestra Señora de los Reyes*; Hernández Díaz, *La Virgen de los Reyes*; Webster, *Art and Ritual in Golden-Age Spain*, pp. 75–83.
104. Münzer, "Itinerarium hispanicum," p. 78.
105. Ibid., p. 79. On the crown, see Percy Ernst Schramm, *Herrschaftszeichen und Staatsymbolik: Beiträge zu ihrer Geschichte vom dritten bis sechzehnten Jahrhundert*, 3 vols. (MGH Schriften, 13.1–3; Stuttgart, 1954–1956), 3:820–825.
106. *Historia de los hechos*, Prohemio and Chap. 2, pp. 142, 155.

107. Cintas del Bot, *Iconografía del Rey San Fernando*; Amanda J. Wunder, "Murillo and the Canonisation Case of San Fernando, 1649–52," *Burlington Magazine* (2001): 670–675.
108. Marcuello, *Cancionero*, p. 36.
109. Ibid., pp. 43, 70, 75, 77, 103–107, 115, 147, 178, 180–181, 187, 189, 195, 197, 213, 247, 256, 259, 263, 264, 269, 313.
110. Ibid., pp. 171–207 (fols. 77r–94v).
111. Ibid., pp. 247–267 (Salve Regina), 311–313 (prediction).
112. Ibid., pp. 76, 98, 102, 170, 212, 258, fols. 29v, 40v, 42v, 76v, 97v, 120v (Virgin Mary); pp. 78, 88, 126, 146, 148, 150, 152, 160, fols. 30v, 35v, 54v, 64v, 65v, 67v, 67v, 71v (Isabel and/or Ferdinand).
113. Ibid., p. 126, fol. 54v.
114. For discussion, see Ruiz-Gálvez Priego, " *Fállase*," p. 94.
115. Marcuello, *Cancionero*, pp. 132–133, 187, 261 (in one apostrophe to the Virgin, Marcuello even tells her that Isabel is "por ty guerrera"; p. 103). The Marian messianic motif: Ruiz-Gálvez Priego, " *Fállase*," pp. 93–94.
116. Olga Pérez Monzón, "La dimensión artística de las relaciones de conflicto," in *La monarquía como conflicto en la Corona castellano-leonesa (c. 1230–1504)*, ed. José Manuel Nieto Soria (Madrid, 2006), pp. 547–619 (here pp. 571–572).
117. Marcuello, *Cancionero*, pp. 31, 32, 68; for discussion, see Ruiz-Gálvez Priego, "*Fállase por profecía*," p. 87.
118. Pulgar, *Crónica*, chap. 176, 2:189.
119. Pulgar, *Crónica*, chaps. 47, 74, 2:70–71, 225; "Relacion circunstanciada," p. 54; Valera, *Crónica*, chap. 52, p. 167; Bernáldez, *Memorias*, chap. 56, p. 122.
120. *Historia de los hechos*, chap. 7, p. 183.
121. Valera, *Crónica*, chap. 76, pp. 232–233.
122. Ibid., chap. 69, p. 212.
123. Alhama: Pulgar, *Crónica*, chap. 132, 2:24 (cf. *Historia de los hechos*, chap. 15, p. 207). Álora: Pulgar, *Crónica*, chap. 160, 2:123. Ronda: Pulgar, *Crónica*, chap. 172, 2:173–174. Loja: Pulgar, *Crónica*, chap. 187, 2:227. Vélez-Málaga: Bernáldez, *Memorias*, chap. 82, p. 176; Pulgar, *Crónica*, chap. 202, 2:279; Valera, *Crónica*, chap. 78, p. 236. Málaga: Pulgar, *Crónica*, chap. 123, 2:334; D. Aguilar Garcia, "La Mezquita Mayor de Málaga y la Iglesia Vieja," *Boletín de Arte* 6 (1985): 55–70 (esp. 55–58); María Isabel Calero and Virgilio Martínez Enamorado, *Málaga, ciudad de Al-Andalus* (Málaga, 1995), pp. 174–177.
124. Pulgar, *Crónica*, chap. 123, 2:334.
125. Bernáldez, *Memorias*, chap. 85, p. 192. Cf. Valera, *Crónica*, chap. 87, p. 269.
126. Pulgar, *Crónica*, chap. 123, 2:334.
127. Bernáldez, *Memorias*, chap. 82, p. 176; Pulgar, *Crónica*, chap. 160, 2:123.
128. Pulgar, *Crónica*, chaps. 132, 172, 187, 202, 2:24, 173–174, 227, 279.
129. Ibid., chap. 132, 2:24.
130. José Cepeda Adán, "La ciudad de Santa Fe, símbolo de una época," *Cuadernos de Historia Modern* 13 (1992): 73–79.
131. The chronicler is quoted in Harvey, *Islamic Spain*, p. 310.
132. Text cited in Devid Paolini, "Los Reyes Católicos e Italia: los humanistas italianos y su relación con España," in *La literatura en la época de Los Reyes Católicos*, ed. Nicasio Salvador Miguel and Cristina Moya García (Madrid, 2008), pp. 189–206 (here 193). Cf. Carlo Verardi, *Historia baetica (Drama humánistico sobre la toma de Granada)*, ed. Maria Dolores Rincón González (Granada, 1992), pp. 308, 310.
133. Münzer, "Itinerarium," pp. 49, 66.
134. The mosque and its consecration as a Marian church: Leopoldo Torres Balbás, "La mezquita real de la Alhambra y el baño frontero," in his *Obra Dispersa I: Al Andalus, Crónica de la España musulmana*, 3 vols. (Madrid, 1981), 3:196–214 (esp. 198–201, 201–207). The lamps and mosaics: *Al-Andalus: the Art of Islamic Spain*, Catalogue no. 57, pp. 276–277; and in the same volume, Darío Cabanelas Rodríguez, "The Alhambra: An Introduction," p. 129. On the replacement of this cathedral-mosque by one in Granada itself, see Chapter 5 of this present book.

135. For the queen's letter, her offerings to Guadalupe, and the late sixteenth-century friar's comments, see Talavera, *Historia de Nuestra Señora de Guadalupe*, 2.33, 4.12, fols. 116r, 214r-v. On Granadan swords, see David Nicolle, *Granada 1492: The Twilight of Moorish Spain* (Oxford, 1998), pp. 30–31.
136. Diego de Ecija, *Libro de la invención*, 4.67, pp. 350–351; Domínguez Casas, *Arte y etiqueta*, p. 353.
137. Münzer, "Itinerarium," p. 113.

Chapter 3

1. Red hair: Bernáldez, *Memorias*, chap. 104, p. 239.
2. *Historia de los hechos*, chap. 51, p. 302.
3. Bernáldez, *Memorias*, chap. 104, pp. 239–240.
4. *Historia de los hechos* chap. 31, pp. 244–247.
5. Bernáldez, *Memorias*, chap. 54, p. 239.
6. In 1483 Ferdinand and Isabel granted him the right to the clothes they wore every year on Mary's September feast day; *Historia de los hechos*, p. 52.
7. *Historia de los hechos*, chaps. 22, 51, pp. 226, 302.
8. Ibid., "Prohemio," p. 142. On the author's use of this genealogy to rehabilitate Rodrigo, see the editor's comments in ibid., 30–37, 64–68.
9. Ibid., "Prohemio" and chap. 2, pp. 140–145, 146–159.
10. On Pelayo Correa's reputation, see Philippe Josserand, "Itineraires d'une rencontre: Les ordres militaires et l'idéal chevaleresque dans la Castille du Bas Moyen Âge (XIIIe–XVe siècle)," in *L'univers de la chevalerie en Castille*, pp. 92–98.
11. *Historia de los hechos*, "Prohemio," pp. 144–145. The earliest extant version of this story comes from a text composed in the 1480s: Pedro de Orozco and Juan de la Parra, *Primera historia de la Orden de Santiago, manuscrito del siglo XV*, chap. 14, ed. Marqués de Siete Iglesias (Badajoz, 1978), p. 368.
12. *La Chanson de Roland*, lines 2450–2459, ed. Pierre Jonin (Paris, 1979), p. 252.
13. *Historia de los hechos*, chap. 1, p. 152.
14. Ibid., chap. 3, pp. 159–160.
15. Christian, *Apparitions*, esp. p. 17. In general, see Barnay, *Le ciel sur la terre*.
16. *Historia de los hechos*, chaps. 3, 6, 7, 15, 17, 18, 22, 40, 41, 51; pp. 163–164, 181, 184, 199–200, 203, 207, 212–213, 215, 228, 264–266, 268, 291, 293, 298–299, 302.
17. Ibid., chaps. 8, 20, 36, 37, 51; pp. 186, 222, 258, 259, 302.
18. Ibid., chap. 15, pp. 199–200.
19. In the early fourteenth century, a group of "armed men" in Seville founded a confraternity in Mary's honor dedicated to fighting Muslims; see the text edited Goñi Gaztambide, *Historia de la Bula de cruzada*, pp. 644–645.
20. Augustine, "Sermo 190," *PL* 38:1008.
21. Díaz de Games, *El Victorial*, chap. 7, pp. 272–274. On this text, see among others Fernando Gómez Redondo, "*El Victorial* de Gutierre Díaz de Games," and Jesús D. Rodríguez Velasco, "El libro de Díaz de Games," both in *La chevalerie en Castille à la fin du Moyen Age*, pp. 191–210, 211–223.
22. On his position in this debate, see references in previous note as well as Carlos Heusch, "De la biografía al debate: Espejismos caballerescos en el *Victorial* de Gutierre Díaz de Games," *eHumanistica* 16 (2010): 308–327; Jesús D. Rodríguez Velasco, "El discurso de la caballería," in *L'univers de la chevalerie en Castille*, pp. 54–76.
23. Mexía, "Nobiliario vero," p. 163.
24. Ibid., p. 162. On the Cid as chivalric model, see MacKay, "Un Cid Ruy Díaz en el siglo XV."
25. On these churches, see Alberto Muntaner Frutos, "El Cid: Mito y símbolo," *Boletín del Museo e Instituto "Camon Aznar"* 27 (1987): 192 (and note 42).
26. E.g., *CSM*, nos. 16, 45, 63, 121, 137, 148, 152, 174, 195, 214, 233, 281, 312, 314, 336, 363, 1: 99–102, 168–171, 209–212, 2:65–67, 108–109, 133–134, 141–142, 181–182, 228–234, 270–272, 309–310, 3:54–57, 121–124, 127–129, 178–180, 236–237.

27. Richard Kaeuper, *Holy Warriors: The Religious Ideology of Chivalry* (Philadelphia, 2009), pp. 159–162.
28. Schreiner, "*Nobilitas Mariae*," pp. 235–236.
29. Louise Mirrer, "Representing 'Other' Men: Muslims, Jews, and Masculine Ideals in Medieval Castilian Epic and Ballad," in *Medieval Masculinities: Regarding Men in the Middle Ages*, ed. Clare A. Lees (Minneapolis, 1994), 171–172. For elsewhere in medieval Europe, see Dawn M. Hadley, "Introduction: Medieval Masculinities," and Matthew Bennett, "Military Masculinity in England and Northern France c. 1050–c. 1225," both in *Masculinity in Medieval Europe*, ed. Dawn M. Hadley (London, 1999), pp. 11, 71–88.
30. Marqués de Santillana, *Poesías completas*, Sonnet 17, no. 69, 1:278. On the marquis' life, see Luis Suárez Fernández, "El hombre y su tiempo," in *El Marqués de Santillana 1398–1458: Los albores de la España moderna*, 3 vols. (Hondarribia, 2001), 1:17–48.
31. On warfare and gender in general, I have found the following particularly helpful: *Behind the Lines*; Huston, "Matrix of War;" *The Women and War Reader*; Elshtain, *Women and War*.
32. *Poema de Fernán González*, ed. H. Salvador Martínez (Madrid, 1991), lines 240–241, p. 96.
33. Sarah Lambert, "Crusading or Spinning," and Michael R. Evans, "'Unfit to Bear Arms': The Gendering of Arms and Armour in Accounts of Women on Crusade," both in *Gendering the Crusades*, pp. 1–15, 45–58; MacLaughlin, "Woman Warrior."
34. Mazeika, "'Nowhere was the Fragility of Their Sex Apparent.'"
35. Dillard, *Daughters of the Reconquest*, pp. 14–16; Antonio Pérez Martín, "El estatuto jurídico de la caballería castellana," in *La chevalerie en Castille à la fin du Moyen Age*, pp. 16, 18.
36. For this and the preceding points, see Contamine, *La guerre au Moyen Age*, pp. 394–395; MacLaughlin, "Woman Warrior"; Helen Solterer, "Figures of Female Militancy in Medieval France," *Signs: Journal of Women in Culture and Society* 16 (1991): 522–549; Jean A. Truax, "Anglo-Norman Women at War: Valiant Soldiers, Prudent Strategists, or Charismatic Leaders," in *The Circle of War in the Middle Ages: Essays on Medieval Military and Naval History*, ed. Donald J. Kagay and L.J. Andrew Villalon (Woodbridge, GB, 1999), pp. 111–125.
37. *Crónica incompleta*, p. 238 (for further praise of Isabel as a manly war leader, pp. 239–242, 310, 318–320).
38. Barbara Weissberger, "'¡A tierra, puto!' Alfonso de Palencia's Discourse of Effeminacy," in *Queer Iberia*, pp. 291–324.
39. For citations from these Isabelline writers, see Chapter 2 of this volume and Peinado Santaella, "Christo pelea," pp. 509, 510–511.
40. *Chronicon Adefonsi imperatoris*, chap. 55, p. 220. For brief commentary, see Dillard, *Daughters*, p. 15; O'Callaghan, *Reconquest and Crusade*, p. 139.
41. Cf. Elena Lourie, "Black Women Warriors in the Muslim Army Besieging Valencia and the Cid's Victory: A Problem of Interpretation," *Traditio* 55 (2000): 182–209 (esp. 188, 191, 208).
42. Cf. the description in *The Chronicle of Ibn al-Athir for the Crusading Period from "al-Kamil fi' l-ta'rikh"*, trans. D.S. Richards, 2 vols. (Aldershot, GB, 2006–2007), 1:323.
43. Most descriptions of Christian women as warriors during the Crusades were written by Muslims to deride the enemy; Keren Caspi-Reisfeld, "Women Warriors During the Crusades, 1095–1254," in *Gendering the Crusades*, pp. 94–107.
44. Mirrer, *Women, Jews, and Muslims*, pp. 47–65.
45. Sahar Amer, *Crossing Borders: Love Between Women in Medieval French and Arabic Literatures* (Princeton, 2008), pp. 14–16; Daniel Eisenberg, "Juan Ruiz's Heterosexual 'Good Love,'" in *Queer Iberia*, pp. 257–259.
46. E.g.. *Los romances fronterizos*, 1:297, 301–302. For discussion, see Mirrer, *Women, Jews, and Muslims*, pp.17–30; Victorio Martínez, "La ciudad-mujer"; Carrasco Urgoiti, *El Moro de Granada*, p. 32.
47. Díaz de Games, *El Victorial*, chap. 19, p. 323.
48. *Primera crónica general*, chap. 568, 2:323. Cf. *Historia Silense*, p. 133.
49. Rubin argues that Mary's maternity was indeed her most important identity, *Mother of God* (esp. p. 424).
50. On Mary as maternal intercessor in general, see Ellington, *From Sacred Body to Angelic Soul*, pp. 102–141; Fulton, *From Passion to Judgment*, pp. 204–243; Rubin, *Mother of God*.

51. E.g. *Diplomatario andaluz*, no. 80, p. 81; James I, *Llibre dels feits*, chaps. 62, 84, 85, pp. 149–150, 178, 180; *Gran Crónica de Alfonso XI*, chap. 335, 2:449; Diego de Ecija, *Libro de la invención*, 2.7, p. 56.

52. *El Poema de Alfonso XI*, verse 1551, p. 433. For the version of the hymn quoted here, see Augustine Thompson, *Medieval Version of the Salve Regina*. [Online]. Available: http://www.newliturgicalmovement.org/2010/05/medieval-version-of-salve-regina.html [August 8, 2011].

53. Cited by Torres Fontes, "Don Fernando," p. 117.

54. Quoted in the editor's introduction to Díaz de Games, *El Victorial*, p. 11.

55. Gonzalo de Berceo, "Los loores de Nuestra Señora," stanza 218, in Gonzalo de Berceo, *El Duelo de la Virgen*, p. 108. Cf. "Advocaciones de la Virgen," p. 28; Atkinson, *Oldest Vocation*, pp. 103, 105–106, 118; Fulton, *From Passion to Judgment*, pp. 224–226; Iogna-Prat, "Le culte de la Vierge," pp. 86–87, 89, 98.

56. Díaz de Games, *El Victorial*, chap. 62, p. 488.

57. Ibid., chap. 44, p. 403.

58. Klaus Theweleit, *Male Fantasies*, trans. Stephen Conway, 2 vols. (Minneapolis, 1987–1989), 1:91–95, 99–108.

59. E.g., James I, *Llibre dels feits*, chap. 84, p. 178; *El Poema de Alfonso XI*, verse 1686, p. 469.

60. On captivity on both sides of the frontier in medieval Iberia, see Bensch, "From Prizes of War"; Brodman, *Ransoming Captives*, pp.1–14; Abdelghaffer Ben Driss, "Los cautivos entre Granada y Castilla en el siglo XV según las fuentes árabes," in *Actas del congreso "La frontera oriental nazarí"*, pp. 301–310; Lappin, *Medieval Cult of Saint Dominic*, pp. 337–341; Miller, *Guardians of Islam*, pp. 1521–175; Argente del Castillo Ocaña, "Cautiverio y martirio," p. 37; O'Callaghan, *Reconquest and Crusade*, pp. 148–149; Rodriguez, *Captives and Their Saviors*.

61. Signori, *Maria zwischen Kathedrale, Kloster und Welt*, pp. 46, 222–223, 234–240.

62. *CSM*, no. 359, 3:229.

63. Ibid., no. 227, 2:297–299.

64. Another of her miracles of liberation: *CSM*, no. 301, 3:99–100. Alfonso's affection for her: Keller, "King Alfonso's Virgin of Villa-Sirga"; idem, "More on the Rivalry between Santa Maria and Santiago de Compostela."

65. *CSM*, nos. 83, 158, 176, 183, 325, 359; 1:263–265, 2: 201–202, 152–154, 186–187, 3:152–155, 229–230 (see also miracles of liberation not attributed to a specific Virgin, nos. 95, 106, 245, 291, 363; 1:292–294, 2:25–27, 338–342, 3:75–77, 236–237); López de Ayala, *Rimado del Palacio*, stanzas 757, 762–770, 800–809, 870–886, pp. 264, 265–267, 272–274, 293–296.

66. See the miracles in Madrid Biblioteca Nacional MS 1176, fols. 9r–12v, 14r–15r, 19r–20r; Talavera, *Historia de Nuestra Señora de Guadalupe*, fols. 240v–242r, 246r–v, 260r–v, 262v–263r, 265v–266v, 269r–270v. For analysis, see Crémoux, *Pèlerinages et miracles*, pp. 133, 137, 149–151; Pilar González Modino, "La Virgen de Guadalupe como redentora de cautivos," in *La religiosidad popular: Vida y Muerte: La imaginación religiosa*, 3 vols., ed. Carlos Alvarez Santaló, María Jesús Buxó i Rey, and Salvador Rodríguez Becerra (Barcelona, 1989), 2:461–471.

67. Münzer, "Itinerarium hispanicum," p. 107.

68. Miguel de Cervantes Saavedra, *Persiles y Sigisimunda*, 3.5 in his *Obras completas*, pp. 769–770. On Cervantes's experience of captivity, see Garcés, *Cervantes in Algiers*.

69. Talavera, *Historia de Nuestra Señora de Guadalupe*, fol. 247v.

70. Cervantes, *El trato de Argel*, lines 2490–2521, in his *Obras completas*, p. 850. Cf. Garcés, *Cervantes in Algiers*, pp. 153–161.

71. *CSM*, no. 83, 1:265; cf. nos. 95, 227, 1:292, 2:297–299. Similar descriptions of Mary's mercy color the poems about the liberation of captives from other Christians: ibid., nos. 158, 291, 301, 363; 2:152–154, 3:75–77, 3:99–100, 3:236–237.

72. Ibid., no. 227, 2:299.

73. Remensnyder, "Christian Captives, Muslim Maidens," pp. 650–651.

74. Perdrizet, *La Vierge de Miséricorde*.

75. On the Mercedarians' institutional development, see Brodman, *Ransoming Captives*. On the introduction of Mary as the Order's patron, see Bruce Taylor, *Structures of Reform: The Mercedarian Order in the Spanish Golden Age* (Leiden, 2000), pp. 14–16.

76. Neumann, *Great Mother*, pp. 147–208; James J. Preston, "Conclusion: New Perspectives on Mother Worship," in *Mother Worship: Theme and Variations*, ed. James J. Preston (Chapel Hill, 1982), pp. 329, 337.

77. Subordinating women's power of giving birth to their roles as nurturers, representations of motherhood as benign love leave the gender hierarchy intact: Janine Chassaguet-Smirgel, "Being a Mother and Being a Psychoanalyst: Two Impossible Professions," in *Representations of Motherhood*, ed. Donna Bassin et al. (New Haven, 1994), pp. 114–128; John Carmi Parsons, "The Pregnant Queen as Counsellor and the Medieval Construction of Motherhood," in *Medieval Mothering*, ed. John Carmi Parsons and Bonnie Wheeler (New York, 1996), pp. 39–61.

78. On the language of maternity in the service of warfare, see Lorraine Bayard de Volo, "Drafting Motherhood: Maternal Imagery and Organizations in the United States and Nicaragua," in *The Women and War Reader*, pp. 240–253; Genevieve Lloyd, "Selfhood, War, and Masculinity," in *Feminist Challenges: Social and Political Theory*, ed. Carole Pateman and Elizabeth Gross (Boston, 1986), p. 76; Nancy Scheper-Hughes, "Maternal Thinking and the Politics of War," in *The Women and War Reader*, pp. 227–233.

79. *Cancionero de Juan Alfonso*, 3:1148, no. 572 (cf. 2:692, no. 317).

80. Perdrizet, *La Vierge de Miséricorde*, pp. 37–41. On the Las Huelgas painting, see Chapter 2 of the present volume.

81. *CSM*, no. 28, 1:128–132. On the siege, see George Ostrogorsky, *History of the Byzantine State*, rev. ed., (New Brunswick NJ, 1969), pp. 156–157.

82. Talavera, *Historia de Nuestra Señora de Guadalupe*, fol. 292r.

83. García de Santa María, *Crónica*, pp. 282–283.

84. Ibid., pp. 283–284.

85. López de Ayala, *Rimado del Palacio*, stanzas 757, 762–770, 800–809, 870–886, pp. 264, 265–267, 272–274, 293–296.

86. Ibid., stanza 897, p. 298.

87. Ibid., stanzas 762–770, pp. 265–267 (cf. stanzas 888–896, pp. 297–298). On this statue, see Willibald Sauerländer, *Le monde gothique: Le siècle des cathédrales* (Paris, 1989), p. 316 and fig. 296.

88. On male Marian devotion as sublimation of desire for the mother, see Atkinson, *Oldest Vocation*, pp. 129–131; Michael Carroll, *The Cult of the Virgin Mary: Psychological Origins* (Princeton, 1986), pp. 49–74; Philippart, "Le récit miraculaire marial," pp. 577–581.

89. Heusch, "L'amour et la femme," pp. 161, 173–175 (here 174).

90. Torres Fontes, "Don Fernando," Appendix, no. 1, p. 113.

91. *CSM*, no. 16, 1:99.

92. Ibid., no. 10, 1:84–85.

93. Llull, *Libre de Sancta Maria*, chap. 14, pp. 1194–1195. Cf. Diego García de Campos, *Planeta: Obra ascética del siglo XIII*, ed. Manuel Alonso (Madrid, 1943), Bk. 2, p. 270.

94. Llull, *Libre de Sancta Maria*, Prologue and chap. 14, pp. 1157–1158, 1194–1197. For discussion, Barnay, *Le ciel sur la terre*, pp. 184–198; Katherine Allen Smith, "Bodies of Unsurpassed Beauty."

95. *CSM*, no. 324, 3:150 (cf. nos. 295, 349; 3:85–87, 207–208).

96. Llull, *Libre de Sancta Maria*, Prologue, p. 1157–1158. Katherine Allen Smith, "Bodies of Unsurpassed Beauty," esp. pp. 174–176.

97. Warner, *Alone of All Her Sex*, pp. 149–159.

98. *CSM*, no. 10, 1:85.

99. Ibid., no. 16, 1:99–101.

100. Paull F. Baum, "The Young Man Betrothed to a Statue," *PMLA* 34 (1919): 523–579; Camille, *Gothic Idol*, pp. 237–241; Katherine Allen Smith, "Bodies of Unsurpassed Beauty," pp. 174–175, 176–178.

101. *CSM*, no. 42, 1:160–163; John E. Keller, "The Motif of the Statue Bride in the *Cantigas* of Alfonso the Learned," *Studies in Philology* 56 (1959): 453–458.

102. E.g., *CSM*, nos. 137, 152, 195, 312, 336; 2:108–109, 141–142, 228–234, 3:121–124, 178–180.

103. Ibid., no. 292, 3:77–81. See Lappin, "Thaumaturgy of Royal Piety," pp. 52–53.

104. Burriel, *Memorias*, pp. 215–216.

105. *CSM*, Prologue A, 1:54.

106. Ibid., Prologue B, 1:55. On Alfonso as Mary's troubadour, see Márquez Villanueva, *El concepto cultural alfonsí*, pp. 112–115; Connie L. Scarborough, *Women in Thirteenth-Century Spain as Portrayed in Alfonso X's Cantigas de Santa María* (Lampeter, Dyfed, Wales, 1993), pp. 20–38, 109–128; Snow, "Alfonso as Troubadour."

107. *CSM*, nos. 10, 130, 160; 1:84–85, 2:86–87, 2: 156.

108. Cf. the poem written to her by a Spanish soldier in 1574; *Memorias del cautivo*, p. 133.

109. Marqués de Santillana, *Poesías completas*, nos. 88, 105, 106; 1:295–296, 2:275–282.

110. Rafael Lapesa, *La obra literaria del marqués de Santillana* (Madrid, 1957), pp. 233–236.

111. E.g., Marqués de Santillana, *Poesías completas*, nos. 14–16, 20–26, 33–35, 39, 60–61, 66, 1:93–96, 101–107, 115–125, 136–138, 267–269, 274–275.

112. For Iñigo's appearance, see Pulgar, *Los claros varones*, p. 96.

113. Pero Díaz de Toledo, "Diálogo é razonamiento en la muerte del marqués de Santillana," *Opúsculos literarios de los siglos XIV à XVI* (Sociedad de Bibliófilos Españoles 29; Madrid, 1892), 280.

114. Elshtain, *Women and War*; Jennifer Turpin, "Many Faces: Women Confronting War," in *The Women and War Reader*, p. 16.

115. Bliese, "Rhetoric and Morale," pp. 211–212.

116. For examples from medieval romances, see Heusch, "L'amour et la femme," pp. 158–160; for general discussion see Elshtain, *Women and War*, pp. 160, 167–180; idem, "Women as Mirror and Other: Towards a Theory of Women, War, and Feminism," *Humanities in Society* 5 (1982): 29–44; as well as the editors' introduction to *Behind the Lines*, pp. 1–2.

117. Llull, *Romanç d'Evast e Blanquerna*, pp. 291–295, for the passage discussed here. On this text, see Lola Badier and Anthony Bonner, *Ramón Llull: Vida, pensamiento y obra literaria*, trans. J. M. Martos (Barcelona, 1993), pp. 170–175; Ramon Sugranyes de Franch, "Raymond Lull écrivain: Les romans," in *Raymond Lull et le Pays d'Oc* (Cahiers de Fanjeaux, 22, Toulouse, 1987), pp. 88–93.

118. Angus MacKay, "The Virgin's Vassals," in *God and Man in Medieval Spain: Essays in Honour of J. L. R. Highfield*, ed. Derek Lomax and David MacKenzie (Westminster, 1989), pp. 49–58.

119. *CSM*, no. 374, 3:260–261. On *almogávares*, see O'Callaghan, *Reconquest and Crusade*, p. 129; Rodríguez Molina, *La vida de moros*, pp. 50–53. On the chapel at Jérez, see Remensnyder, "Colonization of Sacred Architecture," pp. 215–216.

120. Here, as elsewhere in the *Cantigas*, Mary usurps her son's prerogatives. Cf. Salvador Martínez, *Alfonso X*, pp. 231–235.

121. See the foundation charter edited by Hipólito Sancho de Sopranis, *Rincones Portuenses* (Cádiz, 1925), p. 200.

122. *CSM*, no. 99, 1:302–303.

123. Alfonso el Sabio, *Cantigas de Santa María*, Escorial MS. T.I.1, fol. 144r.

124. *CSM*, no. 401, 3:303.

125. Ibid., 2:174. On the events described by the poem, see María José Funes Alenza, *Alfonso X el Sabio en Murcia: Sus Cantigas y la Virgen de la Arrixaca* (Murcia, 1992).

126. *Primera crónica general*, chap. 1019, 2:702.

127. Marqués de Santillana, *Poesías completas*, no. 106, 2:280, 282.

128. Münzer, "Itinerarium," p. 79.

129. Talavera, *Historia de Nuestra Señora de Guadalupe*, 1.7, fol. 19r.

130. Juan Méndez de Vasconcellos, *Liga deshecha por la expulsión de los moriscos de los Reynos de España* (Madrid, 1612), fols. 113r, 118v–119r. Mary also wields a sword against Muslims in a legend from Spanish Sicily, which, despite its modern editor's claims, probably does not predate the fifteenth century; Melchiorre Trigilia, *La Madonna dei Milici di Scicli* (Modica, 1990), esp. pp. 63–73.

131. Schreiner, *Maria*, pp. 371–373.

132. Pelikan, *Mary Through the Centuries*, pp. 27, 91.

133. Schreiner, *Maria*, pp. 371–373.

134. The text is in both the Roman liturgy ("Liber responsalis," *PL* 78:799) and the Mozarabic one (Gonzalo Gironés Guillem, "Notas sobre el texto de la fiesta mozárabe de la Asunción," in *Miscelánea en memoria de Dom Mario Férotin 1914–1965* [Madrid, 1966], p. 253).
135. Marqués de Santillana, *Poesías completas*, no. 105, 2:277.
136. Pelikan, *Mary Through the Centuries*, pp. 91–92; for examples drawn from high medieval Castilian and Valencian poetry, see Twomey, *Serpent and the Rose*.
137. Ewald M. Vetter, "Mulier Amicta Sole und Mater Salvatoris," *Münchner Jahrbuch der bildenden Kunst*, 3rd series, 9–10 (1958–1959): 32–71, esp. 34–36.
138. "Advocaciones de la Virgen," p. 15.
139. Ibid., p. 26.
140. Ibid., pp. 20–21, 26.
141. Bugge, *Virginitas*, pp. 47–58.
142. Ellington, *From Sacred Body to Angelic Soul*, p. 70.
143. As cited and translated in Twomey, *Serpent and the Rose*, pp. 86–87.
144. *CSM*, no. 28, 1:128. No wonder that, according to legend, King Arthur's shield bore an image of Mary; Geoffrey of Monmouth, *The History of the Kings of Britain*, ed. Michael D. Reeve (Woodbridge, GB, 2007), p. 199.
145. Edited in Gómez-Menor Fuentes, "Preces por el rey en tiempo de guerra" p. 76.
146. Claude Dagron, *Vie et miracles de sainte Thècle: Texte grec, traduction et commentaire* (Subsidia Hagiographica, 62; Brussels, 1978), no. 27, p. 361 (see also nos. 2, 5, 6, 13, 16, 26, pp. 293, 296–299, 332–335, 322–325, 356–359.
147. "Historia SS. Ursulae et sociarum ejus," *Analecta Bollandiana* 3 (1884): 13. On the cult of the 11,000 Virgins, see Scott B. Montgomery, *Saint Ursula and the Eleven Thousand Virgins of Cologne: Relics, Reliquaries and the Visual Culture of Sanctity in Late Medieval Europe* (Bern, Switzerland, 2010).
148. Weissberger, *Isabel Rules*, pp. 119–120.
149. E.g., Castelli, "Virginity," pp. 74–77; Kathleen Coyne Kelly, *Performing Virginity and Testing Chastity in the Middle Ages* (New York, 2000), pp. 98, 113, 169–170, note 28; Jane Tibbetts Schulenberg, *Forgetful of Their Sex: Female Sanctity and Society, ca. 500–1100* (Chicago, 1998), pp. 127–128.
150. Huston, "Matrix of War," p. 130. The Vestal Virgins of pagan Rome enjoyed such intermediary gender status: Mary Beard, "The Sexual Status of Vestal Virgins," *Journal of Roman Studies* 70 (1980): 17–18; Georges Dumézil, *La religion romaine archaïque avec un appendice sur la religion des Etrusques*, 2nd rev. ed. (Paris, 1974), pp. 577–578.
151. Bugge, *Virginitas*, pp. 52–54, 58; Castelli, "Virginity," p. 76–77. For some early modern examples, see Mary Elizabeth Perry, "From Convent to Battlefield: Cross-Dressing and Gendering the Self in the New World of Imperial Spain," in *Queer Iberia*, p. 407.
152. Gonzalo Gironés Guillem, "La Virgen María en la liturgia mozárabe," *Anales del Seminario de Valencia* 4 (1964): 72.
153. Caroline Walker Bynum, *Holy Feast and Holy Fast: The Religious Significance of Food to Medieval Women* (Berkeley, 1987), p. 278; Ellington, *From Sacred Body to Angelic Soul*, pp. 88–99; Rubin, *Mother of God*, pp. 130–137, 268–279, 307–308, 344–345. Mary's priesthood also served as a subversive model for some medieval women; Anne L. Clark, "The Priesthood of the Virgin Mary: Gender Trouble in the Twelfth Century," *Journal of Feminist Studies in Religion* 18 (2002): 5–24.
154. Some men of war found models in the feminine virtues of female saints; Helen J. Nicholson, "The Head of Saint Euphemia: Templar Devotion to Female Saints," in *Gendering the Crusades*, pp. 108–120.
155. *CSM*, no. 169, 2:172–174; Flory, *Marian Representations*, pp. 121–123.
156. *CSM*, no. 148, 2:133–134.
157. "Les miracles de Notre-Dame de Chartres: Texte Latin inédit," ed. Antoine Thomas, *Bibliothèque de l'Ecole des Chartes* 42 (1881): 526–527. For one example of Mary's virgin body as *integer*, see Juan Gil de Zamora, "Poesías inéditas," p. 387.
158. Miriam Cooke, *Women and the War Story* (Berkeley, 1996), p. 319, note 15; Huston, "Matrix of War," pp. 120–123.

159. Alvarus Pelagius, *Speculum regum*, p. 368. On Alvarus himself, see Linehan, *History and the Historians*, pp. 561–568.

160. For examples of the word *limpieza* in a Marian context, see *Cancionero de Juan Alfonso*, nos. 567–568, 3:1133, 1135; Juan Manuel, *Libro de los estados*, 1.40, p. 59.

161. Alfonso X, *Las Siete Partidas* 2.21.13, as cited in Carlos Heusch, *La caballería castellana en la baja edad media: Textos y contextos* (Montpellier, 2000), p. 61.

162. Díaz de Games, *El Victorial*, chap. 6, p. 269. For similar praise of Ferdinand, see García de Santa María, *Crónica*, pp. 283–284. The praise of knightly purity persisted in the sixteenth century: Hernan Pérez de Pulgar, *Breve parte de la hazañas del excelente nombrado Gran Capitán*, in *Crónicas del Gran Capitán*, ed. Antonio Rodriguez Villa (Nueva Biblioteca de Autores Españoles, 10; Madrid, 1908), p. 586.

163. Adeline Rucquoi, "Etre noble en Espagne aux XIVe—XVe siècles," in *Nobilitas: Funktion und Repräsentation des Adels in Alteuropa*, ed. Otto Gerhard Oexle and Werner Paravicini (Göttingen, 1997), pp. 288–294, 296–297; idem, "Noblesse des *conversos*?" in *"Qu'un sang impur": les conversos et le pouvoir en Espagne à la fin du Moyen Age*, ed. Jeanne Battesti Pelegrin (Aix-en-Provence, 1997), pp. 89–108.

164. *Cancionero de Juan Alfonso*, nos. 4, 65, 1:23, 141.

165. E.g., *Cancionero de Juan Alfonso*, nos. 324, 328, 568, 2:706–707, 720, 3:1135, and the many texts discussed in Twomey, *Serpent and the Rose*, 113–122.

166. MacKay, "Ferdinand of Antequera," pp. 133–134.

167. "Advocaciones de la Virgen," p. 32.

168. *Le parti inedite della "Crónica de Juan II,"* p. 119.

169. Ibid., p. 97. On white as Mary's color, see also Marcuello, *Cancionero*, p. 125.

170. *Historia de los hechos*, chap. 2, p. 149.

171. Ibid., chap. 7, p. 184 (cf. chap. 3, 22, pp. 159, 226).

172. Ibid., chap. 2, p. 158 (and the editor's remarks, pp. 18–19).

173. Feast in Castile: Twomey, *Serpent and the Rose*, pp. 13–15. For the doctrine in general, see Sarah Jane Boss, "The Development of the Doctrine of Mary's Immaculate Conception," in *Mary: The Complete Resource*, pp. 207–235.

174. Estella Ruiz Galvez Prigo, "Mácula y pureza: Maculistas, inmaculistas, y maculados (España s. XV a s. XVII)," in *Les conversos et la pouvoir en Espagne à la fin du Moyen Age*, ed. Jeanne Battesti Pellegrin (Aix-en-Provence, 1997), pp. 139–161.

175. Aristocratic and royal devotion to the Immaculate Conception: Stratton, *Immaculate Conception*, pp. 7–10.

176. *Historia de los hechos*, chap. 51, p. 302.

177. Ibid., chap. 36, p. 258.

178. Stratton, *Immaculate Conception*, pp. 46–66.

179. Juan Manuel, *Libro de los estados*, 1.40–41, pp. 59, 61.

180. Barkaï, *Cristianos y musulmanes*, pp. 137–140, 287–288; Echevarria, *Fortress of Faith*, pp. 154–155; Lappin, *Medieval Cult of Saint Dominic*, pp. 186–188; Tolan, *Saracens*, p. 152.

181. Alvarus Pelagius, *Speculum regum*, pp. 275–276.

182. Simon Barton, *Conquerors, Wives and Concubines: Power and Intimacy in Medieval Iberia* (University of Pennsylvania Press, forthcoming), chap. 4; Mirrer, *Women, Jews, and Muslims*, pp. 17–30.

183. Pérez de Guzman, "A la singular virginidat de Nuestra Señora," in *Cancionero castellano*, no. 306, 1:705.

Part II: Introduction

1. *CSM*, no. 165, 2:165.

2. Ibid., no. 185, 2:207.

3. See, for example, MacKay, "Religion, Culture, and Ideology"; idem, *Spain in the Middle Ages*, p. 199; Rodríguez Molina, "Relaciones," pp. 257–290; idem, *La vida de moros*.

4. Peter Linehan, "At the Spanish Frontier," in *The Medieval World*, ed. Peter Linehan and Janet L. Nelson (London, 2001), pp. 39–40; Rodríguez Molina, "Relaciones," pp. 264–265; idem, *La vida de moros*, pp. 90, 209, 235–250.

5. Hillgarth, *Spanish Kingdoms*, 1:274–275.

6. *Diplomatario andaluz*, no. 487. See also O'Callaghan, *Alfonso X and the Cantigas*, pp. 175–180. For an introduction to Iberian Jews in Mediterranean commerce, see Yom Tov Assis, "The Jews of Barcelona in Maritime Trade with the East," in *The Jew in Medieval Iberia*, pp. 180–226.

7. Hillgarth, *Spanish Kingdoms*, 1:275.

8. Yitzhak Baer, *Die Juden im christlichen Spanien*, 2 vols. (Berlin, 1929–1936), 2:13, 19, 74, 81, 87, 104–106, 225–226, 307, 321, 336–337, 341–344, 347, 381–382, 404, 423–425; Harvey, *Islamic Spain*, pp. 68–69; Ladero Quesada, *Los mudéjares de Castilla*, pp. 19–20, 66; Hillgarth, *Spanish Kingdoms*, 1: 181.

9. Ruiz, "Trading with the 'Other,'" pp. 68–69.

10. For the jurists' debates, see Khaled Abou El Fadl, "Islamic Law and Muslim Minorities: The Juristic Discourse on Muslim Minorities from the Second/Eighth to the Eleventh/Seventeenth Centuries," *Islamic Law and Society* 1 (1994): 141–187.

11. For the details in this paragraph, see Ferrer i Mallol, *El Sarraïns*; Harvey, *Islamic Spain*, pp. 41–150; Ladero Quesada, *Los mudéjares de Castilla*, pp. 11–89; Lourie, "Anatomy of Ambivalence: Muslims under the Crown of Aragon in the Late Thirteenth Century," in her *Crusade and Colonisation*, pp. 1–77; Meyerson, *Muslims of Valencia*. For a recent study of Mudejars with extensive bibliography, see Miller, *Guardians of Islam*.

12. The bibliography on the Jews of the Iberian Peninsula is vast. For overviews, see Baer, *History of the Jews*; Bango, *Remembering Sepharad*; Ray, *Sephardic Frontier*; the articles in *The Jew in Medieval Iberia*.

13. Burns, "Jews and Moors," p. 53.

14. On the illumination and archaeological finds, see Bango, *Remembering Sepharad*, pp. 65–73.

15. John V. Tolan, "Alphonse le Sage: Roi des trois religions," in *Toleranz und Intoleranz im Mittelalter / Tolerance et intolerance au Moyen Age* (Greifwald, 1997), pp. 123–136.

16. Bango, *Remembering Sepharad*, pp. 140–143.

17. Harvey, *Islamic Spain 1250 to 1500*, pp. 6–9; Hillgarth, *Spanish Kingdoms*, 1:29–32; Nirenberg, *Communities of Violence*, pp. 23–27.

18. Barcelona's call: Elena Lourie, "A Plot Which Failed? The Case of the Corpse Found in the Jewish *Call* of Barcelona (1301)," in her *Crusade and Colonization*, pp. 187–220.

19. Bensch, "From Prizes of War."

20. For the interfaith interactions mentioned in this paragraph, see Hillgarth, *Spanish Kingdoms*, 1:170–171, 176–181; Ladero Quesada, *Los mudéjares de Castilla*, pp. 68–75; Meyerson, *Muslims of Valencia*, pp. 99–142; Nirenberg, *Communities of Violence*.

21. Hillgarth, *Spanish Kingdoms*, 1:169–170; Rodríguez Molina, "Relaciones pacíficas," p. 279.

22. MacKay, *Spain in the Middle Ages*, p. 203.

23. Charles Burnett, "The Translating Activity in Medieval Spain," in *The Legacy of Muslim Spain*, 2:1047–1048; Norman Roth, "Jewish Collaborators in Alfonso's Scientific Work," in *Emperor of Culture*, pp. 59–71; Márquez Villanueva, *El concepto cultural alfonsí*, pp 73–81, 183–193.

24. Jerilynn D. Dodds, "Mudejar Tradition and the Synagogues of Medieval Spain: Cultural Identity and Cultural Hegemony," in *Convivencia*, pp. 113–131.

25. For an introduction to this subject, see Jerilynn D. Dodds, "The Mudejar Tradition in Architecture," in *Legacy of Muslim Spain*, 2:592–598.

26. *CSM*, no. 358, 3:227–229.

27. Ibid., no. 385, 3:284. For discussion, see Chapter 1 of the present volume.

28. Manuel Pedro Ferreira, " A Case of Cross-Fertilization: The Mediaeval Andalus, Islamic Music, and the *Cantigas de Santa Maria*," *Pol-e Firuzeh: Journal of the Dialogue Among Civilizations* 3 (2004): 91–117 (esp. 108–113).

29. The classic statement of *convivencia* is Américo Castro, *España en su historia: Cristianos, moros, y judíos* (1948; reprint Barcelona, 1983). For introductions to the value and historiographic evolution of this much debated concept, see Thomas F. Glick, "Convivencia: An Introductory Note," in *Convivencia*, pp. 1–9; Kenneth Baxter Wolf, "*Convivencia* in Medieval Spain: A Brief History of an Idea," *Religion Compass* 3 (2009): 72–85; Maya Soifer, "Beyond

Convivencia: Critical Reflections on the Historiography of Interfaith Relations in Christian Spain," *Journal of Medieval Iberian Studies* 1 (2009): 19–35.

30. Carpenter, "Minorities in Medieval Spain."

31. Meyerson, "Religious Change," p. 104; Nirenberg, *Communities of Violence*.

32. This paragraph draws on Nirenberg, *Communities of Violence*.

33. Ruiz, "Trading with the 'Other,' " p. 64.

34. On the administrative, financial, and juridical structure of Muslim *aljamas*, see Meyerson, *Muslims of Valencia*; on Jewish *aljamas*, see Bango, *Remembering Sepharad*, pp. 74–82.

35. Burns, "Jews and Moors in the *Siete Partidas*," p. 49; Benjamin R. Gampel, "Jews, Christians, and Muslims in Medieval Iberia: *Convivencia* in the Eyes of Sephardic Jews," in *Convivencia*, pp. 23–24.

36. Burns, "Jews and Moors in the *Siete Partidas*," p. 49.

37. Epalza, *Jésus otage*, pp. 13–14; Thomas F. Glick and Orial Pi-Sunyer, "Acculturation as a Concept in Spanish History," *Comparative Studies in Society and History* 11 (1969): 136–154; Mark Meyerson, "Introduction," in *Christians, Muslims and Jews in Medieval and Early Modern Spain: Interaction and Cultural Change*, ed. Mark D. Meyerson and Edward D. English (Notre Dame, 1999), pp. xiii–xiv; Nirenberg, *Communities of Violence*.

38. Jesus, too, was a figure through whom Jews, Muslims, and Christians expressed religious difference, as Epalza has shown in his *Jésus otage*. Cynthia Robinson's *Imagining the Passion in a Multi-Confessional Castile: The Virgin, Christ, Devotions and Images in the Fourteenth and Fifteenth Centuries* (University Park, PA, 2013) was published only when the present volume was already in press, so I have been unable to draw on its insights.

39. Devotion to the Immaculate Conception: Chapter 3 of this volume. Debates over Jewish converts: Nirenberg, "Mass Conversion."

40. The argument made by Albert A. Sicroff, *Los estatutos de limpieza de sangre: Controversios entre los siglos XV y XVII*, trans. Mauro Armiño, rev. ed. (Madrid, 1985) that these statutes reflected a widespread racial obsession and were successful has been much questioned; see, among others, Kamen, *The Spanish Inquisition*, pp. 231–247; Linda Martz, "Pure Blood Statutes in Sixteenth-Century Toledo: Implementation as Opposed to Adoption," *Sefarad* 54 (1994): 83–107.

41. Tabari, *Chronique traditionelle*, trans. Hermann Zotenberg, 5 vols. (Paris, 1980), 2:95–96, 2:116–117. For further discussion, see Chapter 4 of this present volume.

42. Epalza, *Fray Anselmo de Turmeda*, p. 320.

43. Diego Catalán, *Por campos del Romancero: Estudios sobre la tradicción oral moderna* (Madrid, 1970), pp. 270–280. For a different opinion about the ballad's development, see Manuel da Costa Fontes, "El Idólatra de María: An Anti-Christian Jewish Ballad," *Romance Philology* 48 (1995): 255–264.

44. Pelikan, *Mary Through the Centuries*, pp. 67–79, esp. pp. 67, 78.

45. *CSM*, no. 379, 3:270–272.

46. Ibid., no. 305, 3:107.

Chapter 4

1. On Almería's coastal guards, see José Enrique López de Coca Castañer, "Consideraciones sobre la frontera maritíma," in *Actas del congreso "La frontera oriental nazarí,"* pp. 401–404.

2. The story of the image's miraculous discovery is recounted in testimony given in 1502 and edited in Martínez San Pedro, "La Virgen en Almería," pp. 389–391. The legend of the image's discovery fits more or less into the common late medieval Castile pattern described by Christian, *Apparitions*, pp. 10–110.

3. Martínez San Pedro, "La Virgen en Almería," p. 385.

4. Ibid., p. 390.

5. See Chapter 2 of this volume.

6. *CSM*, nos. 99, 183, 345, 1:302–303, 2:201–202, 3:197–201.

7. Ibid., no. 215, 2:272–275. On this invasion, see Salvador Martínez, *Alfonso X*, pp. 395–399.

8. On the lack of evidence for Muslim destruction of Christian images, see Naef, *Bilder und Bilderstreit*, p. 26.

9. On medieval Islamic attitudes toward images, see Naef, *Bilder und Bilderstreit*, pp. 11–72; Marianne Barrucand, "Les fonctions de l'image dans la société islamique du moyen-âge," in *L'image dans le monde arabe*, ed. G. Beaugé and J.-F. Clement (Paris, 1995), pp. 59–67. On the prejudice against representing the human being in Islamic sacred spaces, see Hillenbrand, *Islamic Architecture*, p. 128; Thackston, "Role of Calligraphy," pp. 43–44.

10. E.g., Miguel Asín Palacios, *Abenházam de Córdoba y su historia crítica de las ideas religiosas*, 5 vols. (Madrid, 1927–1932), 1.19.11, 3:112.

11. Cardaillac, *Morisques et chrétiens*, pp. 330–331; Echevarria, *Fortress of Faith*, p. 163.

12. Marcuello, *Cancionero*, p. 40. On his attitude toward Muslims, see Peinado Santaella, "*Christo pelea por sus castellanos*," p. 459.

13. CSM no. 34, 1:143–144. Cf. Vincent of Beauvais, *Speculum historiale*, 7.119, 4:266. For discussion of the tale, see Blumenkranz, "Juden und Jüdische," pp. 431–432; Camille, *The Gothic Idol*, pp. 186–187; Schreiner, *Maria*, pp. 450–451; Joshua Starr, "An Iconodulic Legend and Its Historic Basis," *Speculum* 8 (1933): 500–503; E. M. Zafran, "An Alleged Case of Image Desecration by the Jews and Its Representation in Art: The Virgin of Cambron," *Journal of Jewish Art* 2 (1975): 62–71.

14. Tartakoff, *Between Christian and Jew*, p. 24; Vose, *Dominicans*, p. 179.

15. For an Aragonese example of the Christian rhetoric of Jewish blindness, see Francisca Vendrell Gallostra, "La obra polémica de Fray Bernardo Oliver," *Sefarad* 5 (1945): 303–336.

16. Gonzalo de Berceo, "El Duelo de la Virgen," stanzas 31–32, 56, in his *El Duelo de la Virgen*, pp. 21, 25.

17. Tolan, *Saracens*, pp. 127–128.

18. Patton, *Art of Estrangement*, pp. 111–119.

19. Hence the legends about how, in 711, treacherous Jews had delivered some Visigothic towns and cities into the Muslims' hands; e.g., *Primera crónica general*, chap. 561, 1:316. For further discussion of the increasing link between Muslims and Jews in Christian texts, see Jeremy Cohen, "The Muslim Connection or On the Changing Role of the Jew in High Medieval Theology," in *From Witness to Witchcraft: Jews and Judaism in Medieval Christian Thought*, ed. Jeremy Cohen (Wiesbaden, 1996), pp. 141–162.

20. CSM, no. 348, 3:205–206.

21. Ibid., no. 34, 1:143–44.

22. Ibid., no. 99, 1:302–303.

23. Ibid., no. 215, 2:274.

24. On the shifting tangle of alliances and enmities among Castilians, Granadans, and Marinids in the 1270s and 1280s, see Harvey, *Islamic Spain*, pp. 151–160.

25. CSM, no. 183, 2:201–202. The late twelfth-century versions of this story: Benedict of Peterborough, *Gesta*, 2:121–122; Roger of Hovedon, *Chronica*, 3:46–47. On the historical circumstances of the miracle, see Ferreiro Alemparte, "La ciudad mozárabe."

26. Text in Brou, "Marie 'Destructrice,'" pp. 321–322.

27. Brou, "Marie 'Destructrice,'" pp. 321–322.

28. Brou, "Marie 'Destructrice,'" describes two of these legends.

29. CSM, no. 6, 1:72–75. For another version of this popular legend, see Gautier de Coinci, *Les miracles*, 4:42–72.

30. CSM, Appendix 6, 1:322.

31. On the dangers that Jews posed to Christians through their proximity, see Ron Barkaï, "Les trois cultures entre dialogue et polémique," in *Chrétiens, musulmans et juifs: de la convergence à l'expulsion*, ed. Ron Barkaï (Paris, 1994), p. 251 (cf. Morrison, *Understanding Conversion*, pp. 128–129). On the Jewish perspective, see Abulafia, *Christians and Jews*, pp. 70–71; Epalza, *Jésus otage*, pp. 66–72. On the "proximate other" in general, see Jonathan Z. Smith, "What a Difference a Difference Makes," in his *Relating Religion: Essays in the Study of Religion* (Chicago, 2004), pp. 251–302.

32. On written polemic between Jews and Christians, and public disputations, see Abulafia, *Christians and Jews*; Chazan, *Fashioning Jewish Identity*; idem, *Barcelona and Beyond*; Cohen, *Friars and the Jews*, pp. 103–195; Lasker, *Jewish Philosophical Polemics*; Hanne Trautner-Kromann, *Shield and Sword: Jewish Polemics against Christianity and the Christians in France and Spain from 1100–1500* (Tübingen, 1993).

33. For examples from the Iberian Peninsula of these arguments in Christian-Jewish debate and polemic, see Abner of Burgos, *Mostrador de justicia* chap. 6, in Mettmann, *Die volksprachliche apologetische Literatur*, p. 5; Pacios López, *La disputa de Tortosa*, 2:217–219, 313, 316–317, 322–323; Millás, "Un tratado anónimo," p. 10; Martí, *Pugio fidei*, 2.7.5, 2.10.3, 2.11.15, 3.3.8, pp. 354–35, 396, 416, 755–764; Petrus Alfonsi, "Dialogi," *PL* 157:613–617; Yehuda Shamir, *Rabbi Moses Ha-Kohen of Tordesillas and His Book Ezer Ha-Emunah: A Chapter in the History of the Judeo-Christian Controversy* (Leiden, 1975), pp. 108–113. These Marian points were also debated by Jews and Muslims beyond the Iberian Peninsula; see, for example, *The Jewish-Christian Debate in the High Middle Ages: A Critical Edition of the Nizzahon Vetus*, ed. and trans. David Berger (Philadelphia, 1979), pp. 43–44, 179, 183–184, 214–215, 222–223. For discussion, see Abulafia, *Christians and Jews*, pp. 83–85; Lasker, *Jewish Philosophical Polemics*, pp. 153–159; Schreiner, *Maria*, pp. 429–437.

34. E.g., Alonso de Espina, *Fortalitium fidei* 3.5.3, as edited in McMichael,*Was Jesus of Nazareth the Messiah?* pp. 484–507 (for discussion, pp. 197–214); Millás "Un tratado anónimo," p. 20; Pacios Lopez, *La disputa de Tortosa*, 2:219–221, 319, 324; Martí, *Pugio fidei* 3.3.7, pp. 737–753; Petrus Alfonsi, "Dialogi" *PL* 157:613–617; Shem Tob ibn Shaprut, *La piedra de toque: Una obra de controversia judeo-cristiana...*, ed. José-Vicente Niclós (Madrid, 1997), p. 20. For discussion, see Abulafia, *Christians and Jews*, p. 101; Chazan, *Fashioning Jewish Identity*, pp. 39, 126, 131–133, 234; Epalza, *Jésus otage, pp.* 74–77; Schreiner, *Maria*, pp. 423–429; Naomi Seidman, "Immaculate Translation: Sexual Fidelity, Textual Transmission, and Jewish-Christian Difference in the Virgin Birth," in *Gendering the Jewish Past*, ed. Marc Lee Raphael (Williamsburg, VA, 2002), pp. 115–135.

35. Evelyn M. Cohen, "The Teacher, the Father, and the Virgin Mary in the Leipzig Mahzor," in *Proceedings of the Tenth World Congress of Jewish Studies, Jerusalem, August 16–24, 1989: Division D, Volume 2: Art, Folklore and Music* (Jerusalem, 1990), pp. 71–76; Ivan G. Marcus, *Rituals of Childhood: Jewish Acculturation in Medieval Europe* (New Haven, 1996), pp. 88–94, 102.

36. Arthur Green, "Shekinah, the Virgin Mary, and the Song of Songs: Reflections of a Kabbalistic Symbol in Its Historical Context," *Association for Jewish Studies Review* 26 (2002): 1–52; Peter Schäfer, *Mirror of His Beauty: Feminine Images of God from the Bible to the Early Kabbalah* (Princeton, 2002), pp. 118–134, 217–243.

37. For recensions of the *Toldedot Yeshu* (and dating of the first written versions), see Krauss, *Das Leben Jesu*; Jean-Pierre Osier, *L'évangile du ghetto: La légende juive de Jésus du IIe au Xe siècle* (Paris, 1984); *Ein jüdisches Leben Jesu: Die verschollene Toledot-Jeschu-Fassung Tam u-mu`ad...*, ed. and trans. Günter Schlichting (Tübingen, 1982). For further discussion, see Chazan, *Fashioning Jewish Identity*, pp. 72–76; Goldstein, *Jesus*, pp. 160–163; Rubin, *Mother of God*, pp. 56–59; and the articles in *Toledot Yeshu ("The Life Story of Jesus") Revisited*.

38. For different opinions about the Talmud passages, see Chazan, *Fashioning Jewish Identity*, pp. 68–72; Epalza, *Jésus otage*, pp. 93–96; Goldstein, *Jesus*, esp. 98, 105–183; Peter Schäfer, *Jesus in the Talmud* (Princeton, 2007); Schreiner, *Maria*, pp. 415–417. Many of the putative references are assembled in Gustaf Dalman, *Jesus Christ in the Talmud, Midrash, Zohar, and the Liturgy of the Synagogue with an Introductory Essay by Heinrich Laible*, trans. A. W. Streane (Cambridge, 1893) (this study's violently anti-Semitic commentary is to be used with extreme caution).

39. Petrus Alfonsi, "Dialogi" *PL* 157:573. For further evidence of the *Toledot Yeshu*'s presence in Iberia, see Krauss, *Das Leben Jesu*, pp. 146–149; *Records of the Trials of the Spanish Inquisition*, 1:323; Tartakoff, *Between Christian and Jew*, pp. 103, 121–123; idem, "The *Toledot Yeshu* and Jewish-Christian Conflict in the Medieval Crown of Aragon," in *Toledot Yeshu ("The Life Story of Jesus") Revisited*, pp. 297–309.

40. Jeremy Cohen, "The Mentality of the Medieval Jewish Apostate: Peter Alfonsi, Hermann of Cologne, and Pablo Christiani," in *Jewish Apostasy in the Modern World*, ed. Todd M. Endelman (New York, 1987), pp. 23–29.

41. Petrus Alfonsi, "Dialogi," *PL* 157:573.

42. On the Christian "discovery" of the Talmud, see Cohen, *Friars*, pp. 60–99.

43. William Chester Jordan, "Marian Devotion and the Talmud Trial of 1240," in *Religionsgespräche im Mittelalter*, ed. Bernard Lewis and Friedrich Niewöhner (Wiesbaden, 1992), pp. 61–76.

44. *Documentos de Jaime I*, 5: 65, 89. For discussion: Vose, *Dominicans*, pp. 170–173.
45. Llull, *Libre de Sancta Maria*, chap. 19, p. 1208.
46. Pacios López, *La disputa de Tortosa*, 2:573 (the Talmud's insults to Mary and Jesus), 2:600–601 (the pope's prohibitions).
47. *CSM*, nos. 4, 6, 286, 1:63–66, 72–75, 3:67–68. Cf. Hatton and MacKay, "Anti-Semitism in the *Cantigas.*" For an argument that the Cantiga artists portrayed Jews ambivalently, see Patton, *Art of Estrangment*, pp. 135–164.
48. Schreiner, *Maria*, p. 455. For abundant evidence of high medieval Marian devotion and rhetoric as a vehicle for anti-Semitism, see ibid., pp. 413–462; Denise L. Despres, "Mary of the Eucharist: Cultic Anti-Judaism in Some Fourteenth-Century English Devotional Manuscripts," in *From Witness to Witchcraft: Jews and Judaism in Medieval Christian Thought*, ed. Jeremy Cohen (Wiesbaden, 1996), pp. 375–401; idem, "Immaculate Flesh and the Social Body"; Rubin, *Gentile Tales*; idem, *Mother of God*, pp. 161–168, 228–236, 252–253, 300–301; Peter-Michael Spangenberg, "Judenfeindlichkeit in den altfranzösischen Marienmirakeln: Stereotypen oder Symptome der Veränderung der kollektiven Selbsterfahrung," in *Die Legende vom Ritualmord: Zur Geschichte der Blutbeschuldigung gegen Juden*, ed. Rainer Erb (Berlin, 1993), pp. 157–177; Carole Stone, "Anti-Semitism in the Miracle Tales of the Virgin," *Medieval Encounters: Jewish, Christian, and Muslim Cultures in Confluence and Dialogue* 5 (1999): 364–374. This association persisted at least into the sixteenth century; Allyson F. Creasman, "The Virgin Mary Against the Jews: Anti-Jewish Polemic in the Pilgrimage to the Schöne Maria of Regensburg, 1519–1525," *The Sixteenth Century Journal* 33 (2002): 963–980.
49. All quotations of the Qu'ran are from *Al-Qur'an: A Contemporary Translation*, trans. Ahmed Ali (Princeton, 2001).
50. Pelikan, *Mary Through the Centuries*, p. 69 (pp. 68–76 on the Qu'ran's description of Mary).
51. On Mary's solitude, see Valensi, *La fuite en Egypte*, p. 58.
52. "The Protoevangelium of James" in *New Testament Apocrypha*, rev. ed. by Wilhelm Scheemelcher, trans. R. McL. Wilson, 2 vols. (Louisville, 1991), 1:421–436; "Pseudo-Matthei evangelium."
53. ʿAbd el Jalil, "La vie de Marie selon le Coran et l'Islam," in *Maria: Etudes sur la sainte Vierge*, ed. H. du Manoir, 8 vols. (Paris, 1949–1971), 1:183–211; Epalza, *Jésus otage*, pp. 171–176; Pelikan, *Mary Through the Centuries*, pp. 69–76; Valensi, *La fuite en Egypte*, pp. 55–61, 82–85.
54. Peters, *Muhammad*, p. 141.
55. On Muhammad's wet nurse, the sermon of Quss, and the Arab and Ethiopian Christian communities in and around Mecca, see Shahid, "Islam and *Oriens Christianus*," pp. 15, 21, 24, 27–29. For other analysis of Muhammad's relations with the Christians of the Arabian Peninsula, see Fred M. Donner, *Muhammad and the Believers: At the Origins of Islam* (Cambridge, MA, 2010), pp. 69–72, 87, 212–214, 221–222; F. E. Peters, *Islam: A Guide for Jews and Christians* (Princeton, 2003), p. 50; idem, *Muhammad*, pp. 40–48, 66–67, 111; Jacques Waardenberg, *Muslims and Others: Relations in Context* (Berlin, 2003), pp. 94–99.
56. On these "oratories of Mary," see Shahid, "Islam and *Oriens Christianus*," p. 12–13.
57. On the Kaʾaba's rebuilding, see Ibn Ishaq, *Life of Muhammed*, pp. 84–87.
58. Peters, *Mecca*, p. 49.
59. Ibn Ishaq, *Life of Muhammed*, pp. 552, 774. See Peters's discussion in his *Mecca*, p. 49.
60. Ibn Ishaq, *Life of Muhammed*, p. 552, note 3.
61. Valensi, *La fuite en Egypte*, pp. 61–71.
62. Smith and Haddad, "The Virgin Mary in Islamic Tradition."
63. In this paragraph, I follow Fierro, "Women as Prophets," pp. 183–198. See also ʿAbd el Jalil, *Marie et l'Islam*, pp. 71–72; Hüseyin Ilker Çinar, *Maria und Jesus in Islam: Darstellung anhand des Korans und der islamischen kanonischen Tradition unter Berücksichtigung der islamischen Exegeten* (Wiesbaden, 2007), pp. 190–193; Smith and Haddad, "Virgin Mary in Islamic Tradition," pp. 177–178.
64. Epalza, *Jésus otage*, pp. 181–183.
65. ʿAbd el Jalil, *Marie et l'Islam*, pp. 74–76; McAuliffe, "Chosen of All Women"; Smith and Haddad, "Virgin Mary in Islamic Tradition," pp. 180–181; D. A. Spellberg, *Politics, Gender, and the Islamic Past: The Legacy of ʿAʾisha bint Abi Bakr* (New York, 1994), pp. 48–49,

79–80, 152–174. For a differently oriented analysis, see Mary F. Thurlkill, *Chosen Among Women: Mary and Fatima in Medieval Christianity and Shiʾite Islam* (Notre Dame IN, 2007).

66. McAuliffe, "Chosen of All Women"; Smith and Haddad, "Virgin Mary in Islamic Tradition." For a different opinion, see Louis Massignon, "La notion du voeu et la dévotion musulmane à Fatima," and his "L'oratoire de Marie à l'Aqca, vu sous le voile de deuil de Fatima," both in his *Opera Minora: Textes recueillis, classés, et présentés avec une bibliographie.* ed. Y Moubarac, 3 vols. (Paris, 1961), 1:573–591, 592–618.

67. Smith and Haddad, "Virgin Mary in Islamic Tradition," pp. 17, 22; Tim Winter, "Mary in Islam," in *Mary: The Complete Resource,* pp. 488–490.

68. Ron Barkaï, "Une invocation musulmane au nom de Jésus et de Marie," *Revue de l'Histoire des Religions* 200 (1983): 264–265; Alexandre Papadopoulo, "Introduction générale," in *Le mihrab dans l'architecture et la religion: Actes du colloque international tenu à Paris en mai 1980,* ed. Alexandre Papadopoulo (Leiden, 1988), pp. 18–19; and, in the same collection, S. E. Hamza Boubakeur, "Le mihrab," pp. 50–51; and Abdel Majid Wafi, "Les mihrab et leurs ornamentations décoratives," p. 73. On calligraphy, see Thackston, "Role of Calligraphy."

69. Burchard of Strasbourg's account in Arnold of Lübeck, "Chronica," p. 238 (I thank Benjamin Kedar for this reference); Valensi, *La fuite en Egypte,* pp. 104–111; Rudolf Kriss and Hubert Kriss-Heinrich, *Volksglaube im Bereich des Islam,* 2 vols. (Wiesbaden, 1960–1962), 1:84, 162, 172, 223, 227, 242.

70. Münzer, "Itinerarium hispanicum," pp. 61–62. On which palm tree was the pits' source, see Epalza, *Jésus otage,* pp. 184.

71. Münzer, "Itinerarium hispanicum," pp. 61–62.

72. Hence some modern Muslims give dates to new mothers; ʿAbd el Jalil, *Marie et l'Islam,* p. 83.

73. Johannes of Hildesheim, "Liber de gestis et translationibus trium regum," chap. 27, in *The Three Kings of Cologne: An Early English Translation of the Trium regum by John of Hildesheim,* ed. C. Horstmann (London, 1886), p. 246.

74. Gloria López de la Plaza, *Al-Andalus: Mujeres, sociedad, y religión* (Málaga, 1992), p. 140.

75. Lévi-Provençal, *Histoire de l'espagne musulmane,* 3:366; M. Ocaña Jiménez, "Algo más sobre la 'Bab al-Sura' de Córdoba," *Al-Qantara* 3 (1982): 447–455.

76. Lévi-Provençal, *Histoire de l'espagne musulmane,* 1:352; Al-Himyari, *La péninsule ibérique,* pp. 47–48.

77. Fierro, "Women as Prophets," pp. 184–185.

78. Epalza, *Jésus otage,* pp. 183–184.

79. On the poem's origins and transformations, see Menéndez Pidal, *Poesía árabe,* pp. 39–40; Rubiera Mata, "De nuevo sobre las tres morillas."

80. Rubiera Mata, "De nuevo sobre las tres morillas," p. 141 (my translation of her Spanish rendering of the poem). On Ibn al-Jayyab, see Irwin, *Alhambra,* pp. 58, 76, 82. For a less pious poem from al-Andalus invoking Mary, see *Andalus: Moorish Songs of Love and Wine,* trans. T. J. Gorton (London, 2007), p. 102.

81. Ladero Quesada, *Los mudéjares de Castilla,* pp. 144, 165, 166.

82. *Cancionero tradicional,* ed. José María Alín (Madrid, 1991), no. 66, p. 116; Menéndez Pidal, *Poesía árabe,* pp. 39–40; Rubiera Mata, "De nuevo sobre las tres morillas," pp. 134. On the eroticization of Muslim maidens in late-fifteenth and sixteenth-century Christian literature, see Carrasco Urgoiti, *El Moro de Granada.*

83. Ladero Quesada, *Los mudéjares de Castilla,* p. 165, nos. 71–72.

84. Münzer, "Itinerarium," p. 61.

85. Miller, *Guardians of Islam.*

86. Antonio Vespertino Rodríguez, "Las figuras de Jesús and María en la literatura aljamiado-morisca," in *Actas del coloquio internacional sobre literatura aljamiada y morisca* (Madrid, 1978), pp. 259–294, esp. 294.

87. *Records of the Trials of the Spanish Inquisition,* 1:560, 577.

88. Rubiera Mata, "De nuevo sobre las tres morillas," p. 141. A more literal translation would be "owner of the house of grief [or "of stress" or "of the idolaters"], as Jenny Oesterle has remarked (private conversation, May 2009). For further evidence of Muslim awareness in al-Andalus of Christians' strong identification with Mary, see Maribel Fierro, "Judíos, cristianos, y musulmanes," in *El retroceso territorial de al-Andalus,* p. 533.

89. According to an early fourteenth-century Christian chronicler, during the Templar trial on Majorca, elderly Muslims who had converted to Christianity testified that Mary had "taken" the island; the Christian battle cries of "Saint Mary" were apparently the origin of their belief. Pedro Marsili, *La cronica latina de Jaime I: Edición crítica, estudio preliminar e indices*, chap. 24, ed. María de los Desamparados Martínez San Pedro (Almeria, 1984), pp. 187–188.

Chapter 5

1. *CSM*, no. 165, 2:167.
2. Ibid., no. 329, 3:194–195.
3. Ibid., no. 169, 2:174. A later polemic against Islam mentions Mary's Arabic name as evidence of Islam's corruption of Christianity; Pseudo Pedro Pascual, *Sobre la se[c]ta*, tit. 1, p. 87.
4. Sancho IV, *Castigos*, chap. 21, p. 129; Juan Manuel, *Libro de los estados*, 2.3, pp. 182–183.
5. Llull, *Libre de Sancta Maria*, chap. 19 p. 1208. See also his "Libre d'Evast e d'Aloma e de Blanquerna," I.1.64 in *Obres Essencials*, 1:204–206. For other evidence, see Cuffel, "'Henceforth All Generations Will Call Me Blessed,'" pp. 47–48; Pseudo Pedro Pascual, *Sobre la se[c]ta*, tit. 3, p. 174.
6. Martí, *Pugio fidei*, 2.8.11, 3.3.7.14–15, pp. 365–366, 749–750.
7. Alonso de Espina, *Fortalitium Fidei*, 3.5.3, in McMichael,*Was Jesus of Nazareth the Messiah?* pp. 507–509.
8. This text may have been written by a Jewish convert to Christianity: "Alfonso de Valladolid" in *Medieval Iberia: An Encyclopedia* (London, 2003), p. 833; Carpenter, "Social Perception and Literary Portrayal," p. 73. For a different opinion, see Mettmann, *Die volkssprachliche apologetische Literatur*, pp. 35–36.
9. Carpenter's paraphrase of the original text (which I have not been able to consult) in his "Social Perception and Literary Portrayal," p. 73.
10. Van Koningsveldt and Wiegers, "Polemical Works," p. 182. For discussion of other ways the *Toledot Yeshu* functioned in polemic between Muslims and Jews, see Philip Alexander, "The *Toledot Yeshu* in the Context of Jewish-Muslim Debate," in *Toledot Yeshu ("The Life Story of Jesus") Revisited*, pp. 137–158.
11. On the city's name change, see Ferreiro Alemparte, "La ciudad mozárabe," pp. 406–411; Picard, "Sanctuaires et pèlerinages chrétiens," pp. 237–238.
12. On the pace of conversion to Islam in al-Andalus, see Thomas F. Glick, *From Muslim Fortress to Christian Castle: Social and Cultural Change in Medieval Spain* (Manchester, 1995), pp. 51–63.
13. Fierro, "Women as Prophets," p. 194.
14. *CSM*, no. 183, 2:201.
15. Picard, "Sanctuaires et pèlerinages chrétiens," pp. 245, 247.
16. On the pillars, see Ferreiro Alemparte, "La ciudad mozárabe," p. 410. It has been suggested that the eleventh-century Muslim author refers instead to a church in Santa María de Albarracín; Peñarroja Torrejón, *Cristianos bajo el islam*, p. 254. It is more likely that the eleventh-century author meant Faro, given its church's fame as a pilgrimage site.
17. Alemparte, "La ciudad mozárabe," pp. 407–409.
18. *CSM*, no. 183, 2:201–202; Benedict of Peterborough, *Gesta*, 2:121–122; Roger of Hovedon, *Chronica*, 3:46–47.
19. Biblioteca del Escorial MS T.I.1, fol. 242r.
20. Picard, "Sanctuaires et pèlerinages chrétiens," pp. 239–240.
21. See references above in note 18.
22. Al-Himyari, *La péninsule ibérique*, p. 140, note 4; Ferreiro Alemparte, "La ciudad mozárabe," p. 405; Peñarroja Torrejón, *Cristianos bajo el islam*, pp. 254–255.
23. Barton, "Traitors to the Faith?" pp. 28–30, 33, 36–37.
24. O'Callaghan, *Reconquest and Crusade*, p. 118.
25. *CSM*, no. 181, 2:196–197.
26. O'Callaghan, *Alfonso X and the Cantigas*, p. 136.
27. *CSM*, no. 167, 2:168–169.

28. On the confraternity at Teruel, see Nirenberg, *Communities of Violence*, p. 39. On Segovia's confraternity, see ibid., p. 39, note 72; the Marqués de Lozoya, *La morería de Segovia* (Madrid, 1967), p. 10; Wiegers, *Islamic Literature*, p. 81.

29. Jesús Montoya Martínez and Aurora Juárez Blanquer, *Historia y anécdotas de Andalucía en las Cantigas de Santa María de Alfonso X* (Granada, 1988), pp. 33–34.

30. *CSM*, no. 329, 3:162–165.

31. Ibid., no. 344, 3:196–197.

32. Alberto Bagby, "Alfonso and the Virgin Unite Christian and Moor in the *Cantigas de Santa María*," *Cantigueiros* 1 (1988): 112, 114; García Arenal, "Los moros en las *Cantigas*," p. 145.

33. François Clément, "Le pèlerinage à Lagrasse, d'après une source arabe du XIe siècle," *Annales du Midi* 100 (1988): 489–495.

34. Vincent of Beauvais, *Speculum morale*, 3.21.3, edited in *Speculum quadruplex sive Speculum maius*, 4 vols. (Douai, 1624; rpt. Graz, 1964–1965), 3:1087.

35. *CSM*, nos. 127, 172, 262, 271, 341, 2:80–82, 178–179, 3:12–14, 34–36, 189–192.

36. On modern Muslim devotion there, see William Dalrymple, *From the Holy Mountain: A Journey among the Christians of the East* (New York, 1997), pp. 186–191.

37. Bernard Hamilton, "Our Lady of Saidnaya: An Orthodox Shrine Revered by Muslims and Knights Templar at the Time of the Crusades," in *The Holy Land, Holy Lands, and Christian History*, ed. R. N. Swanson (Woodbridge, GB, 2000), pp. 207–215; Benjamin Z. Kedar, "Convergences of Oriental Christian, Muslim, and Frankish Worshippers: The Case of Saydnaya and the Knights Templar," in *The Crusades and Military Orders: Expanding the Frontiers of Medieval Latin Christianity*, ed. Zsolt Hunyadi and József Laszlovsky (Budapest, 2001), pp. 89–100.

38. Burchard of Strasbourg's report to Frederick I of Germany is quoted in Arnold of Lübeck, "Chronica," pp. 239–240. For discussion, see John V. Tolan, "*Veneratio Sarracenorum*: Shared Devotion among Muslims and Christians, According to Burchard of Strasbourg, Envoy from Frederic Barbarossa to Saladin (c. 1175)," in his *Sons of Ishmael: Muslims Through European Eyes in the Middle Ages* (Gainesville, 2008), pp. 101–112.

39. Burchard of Strasbourg in Arnold of Lübeck, "Chronica," p. 238.

40. For versions of this miracle story, see "Les premières versions occidentales de la légende de Saïdnaia," ed. Paul Devos, *Analecta Bollandiana* 65 (1947): 256; Gaston Raynaud, "Le miracle de Sardenai," *Romania* 11 (1882): 523, 536–537.

41. Baraz, "Incarnated Icon," pp. 188–189.

42. *CSM*, no. 9, 1:79–84; "Les premières versions occidentales"; Baraz, "Incarnated Icon"; Paul Peeters, "La légende de Saïdnaia," *Analecta Bollandiana* 25 (1906): 137–157; Raynaud, "Le miracle de Sardenai."

43. Burchard of Strasbourg in Arnold of Lübeck, "Chronica," p. 240.

44. Camille, *Gothic Idol*, p. 225; Fernández-Ladreda, *Imaginería medieval mariana*, pp. 9, 10; Jean-Marie Sansterre, "Sacralité et pouvoir thaumaturgique des statues mariales (Xe–première moitié du XIIIe siècle)," *Revue Mabillon* n.s. 22 (83) (2011): 53–57.

45. E.g., Jacques de Vitry, *Epistulae*, 2.359–364, 4.43–47, pp. 93–94, 102.

46. San Ginés's miracles for Muslims: Eulogio Varela Hervías, "Historia de San Ginés de la Jara (manuscrito del siglo XV)," *Revista Murgetana* 16 (1961): 114–117. Saint Ginés identified as Muslim: Juan Torres Fontes, "El monasterio de San Ginés de la Jara en la Edad Media," *Revista Murgetana* 25 (1965): 45–46.

47. MacKay, "Ballad and the Frontier," p. 19.

48. E.g., *El Tribunal de la Inquisición de Sigüenza, 1492–1505*, ed. Carlos Carrete Parrondo and Maria Fuencisla García Casar (Salamanca, 1997), nos. 368, 418–419, 425, pp. 131, 153, 157; Hillgarth, *Spanish Kingdoms*, 1:170.

49. Beguer Pinyol, *El Real Monasterio*.

50. Barcelona, Archivo de la Corona de Aragón, Cancilleria Reg. 3576, fols. 145r–146r. For discussion and partial translation (quoted here), see Meyerson, *Muslims of Valencia*, pp. 45–46.

51. Beguer Pinyol, *El Real Monasterio*, pp. 30–31. On the campaign for Tortosa in 1148, see Reilly, *Contest of Christian and Muslim Spain*, p. 214.

52. Beguer Pinyol, *El Real Monasterio*, pp. 56–57, 58.

53. González Jiménez, "Alfonso X y las minorías confesionales," p. 49; Harvey, *Islamic Spain*, pp. 65–67; Hillgarth, *Spanish Kingdoms*, 1:167–170.
54. Carpenter, "Alfonso el Sabio y los moros."
55. Meyerson, *Muslims of Valencia*, pp. 42–49 (here 46).
56. Beguer Pinyol, *El Real Monasterio*, pp. 45, note 1 (James II's decree), 45–46 (the site's architectural history).
57. *CSM*, nos. 192, 264, 2:221, 3:17. Alfonso's dislike of Islam: García Fitz, "El Islam visto por Alfonso X"; González Jiménez, "Alfonso X y las minorías confesionales," p. 87.
58. Burchard described Muslims making their own sorts of ritual offerings at Saidanya ("Sarraceni ceremonialia sua illuc offerunt"), but specified that they did so on Christian Marian feast days; Arnold of Lübeck, "Chronica," p. 239.
59. On Baybars, see Hillenbrand, *Crusades*, pp. 226–237.
60. *CSM*, no. 165, 2:164–167.
61. Jacques de Vitry, *Epistulae*, 2.359–364, pp. 93–94. The Marian chapel he mentions was in the cathedral; Folda, *Crusader Art*, p. 81.
62. Hillenbrand, *Crusades*, pp. 331, 373 (fig. 6.43).
63. Cf. the ways in which Christian authorities interpreted Mudejar practices and institutions in Christian terms; Robert I. Burns, "Spanish Islam in Transition: Acculturative Survival and Its Price in the Christian Kingdom of Valencia, 1240–1280," in his *Moors and Crusaders in Medieval Spain: Collected Studies* (London, 1978), pp. 87–105.
64. On changing attitudes toward Islam and Muslims in the fifteenth century, see Echevarria, *Fortress of Faith.*
65. Ferrer i Mallol, *El Sarraïns*, Appendix 6, p. 272.
66. Meyerson, *Muslims of Valencia*, pp. 44, 285.
67. "Liber denudationis," 9.9, p. 316 (on the translation of this passage, p. 317, note 3).
68. Ibid., 9.8, pp. 314–316. See also Pseudo Pedro Pascual, *Sobre la se[c]ta*, tit. 1, p. 105. On this enduring theme of Muslim-Christian polemic, see Cardaillac, *Morisques et chrétiens*, pp. 267–268; Echevarria, *Fortress of Faith*, p. 148; Pelikan, *Mary Through the Centuries*, pp. 73–75.
69. Echevarria, *Fortress of Faith*, p. 149.
70. Jerome, "De perpetua virginitate B. Mariae: Adversus Helvidium," *PL* 23:193–216; David G. Hunter, "Helvidius, Jovinian, and the Virginity of Mary in Fourth-Century Rome," *Journal of Early Christian Studies* 1 (1993): 47–71.
71. Burchard of Strasbourg in Arnold of Lübeck, "Chronica," p. 238; *CSM*, no. 329, 3:162–165; Juan Manuel, *Libro de los estados*, 2.3, p. 182.
72. Bernáldez, *Memorias*, chap. 47, p. 123.
73. Pedro de Rivadeneira, "Vida del padre Ignacio Loyola," chap. 3, *BAE* 60:17.
74. Bernáldez calls De Vera's opponent "un moro bencerraje," *Memorias*, chap. 47, p. 123. On the Banu Sarraj, see Harvey, *Islamic Spain*, pp. 244, 248–250, 253, 260–261, 264–265.
75. *CSM*, no. 165, 2:165.
76. Llull, *Libre de Sancta Maria*, chap. 19, p. 1208.
77. Ibid., p. 1235.
78. Epalza, *Fray Anselmo de Turmeda*, p. 376.
79. Ibid., p. 376. Cf. the polemic by a fourteenth-century Muslim described in Van Koningsveldt and Wiegers, "Polemical Works," p. 182.
80. The Captive of Tunis, *Tratado e la defença de la santa fe Catolica Christiana, respondiendo à los argumentos que de nuestros sagradas escrituras nos opone el Mahometano*, Paris Bibliothèque Nationale ms. espagnol 49, fols. 152v–153v.
81. "Tratado y Declaración y Guía para seguir y mantner el addin del alislam," ed. in Wiegers, *Islamic Literature*, p. 254.
82. Ibid., p. 243.
83. Wiegers, *Islamic Literature*, pp. 75–76, 153–161.
84. Miller, *Guardians of Islam.*
85. Wiegers, *Islamic Literature*, p. 80.
86. "Liber denudationis," 9.8, p. 314.
87. For the polemic described in this paragraph, see ibid., 10.4 and 10.14, pp. 342, 355.
88. See also ibid., 10.8–10.13, pp. 346–354.

89. Sancho IV, *Castigos*, chap. 21, p. 129.
90. Juan Manuel, *Libro de los estados*, 2.3, pp. 182–183.
91. Sancho IV, *Castigos*, chap. 21, p. 129.
92. Van Koningsveldt and Wiegers, "Polemical Works," pp. 195–196.
93. Echevarria, *Fortress of Faith*, esp. pp. 101–136; Van Koningsveldt and Wiegers, "Polemical Works," pp. 165, 167–168.
94. For the story, see Llull, *Romanç d'Evast e Blanquerna*, pp. 291–295.
95. Osbern, *"De expugnatione Lyxbonensi,"*, p. clxvi. On the author's identity, see C. W. David, "The Authorship of the *De expugnatione Lyxbonensi*," *Speculum* 7 (1932): 50–57.
96. Osbern, *"De expugnatione Lyxbonensi*," pp. clxxix, clxxxi.
97. Ibid., p. clxxxi.
98. *Historia de los hechos*, chap. 15, p. 207.
99. Pulgar, *Crónica*, chap. 132, 2:24.
100. Álora: Pulgar, *Crónica*, chap. 160, 2:123. Ronda: Pulgar, *Crónica*, chap. 172, 2:173–174. Loja: Pulgar, *Crónica*, chap. 187, 2:227. Vélez-Málaga: Bernáldez, *Memorias*, chap. 82, p. 176; Pulgar, *Crónica*, chap. 202, 2:279; Valera, *Crónica*, chap. 78, p. 236. Málaga: Pulgar, *Crónica*, chap. 123, 2:334, 55–58.
101. Münzer, "Itinerarium," p. 38. On this mosque's dedication to Our Lady of the Incarnation and use as a cathedral, see Christian Ewert, "El mihrab de la mezquita de Almería," *Al-Andalus* 36 (1971): 402; Martínez San Pedro, "La Virgen en Almería," pp. 375–376; María del Rosario Torres Fernández and María del Mar Nicolás Martínez, "Una aportación a la arqueología medieval almeriense: La mezquita mayor y la primitiva catedral de Almería," in *Andalucía entre Oriente y Occidente*, pp. 773–785.
102. On Granada's Christianization, see Coleman, *Creating Christian Granada*.
103. For these details about the cathedral, see Rosenthal, *Cathedral of Granada*, pp. 5 (note 1), 12, 107–108, 114–118.
104. For the details in this paragraph, see Rosenthal, *Cathedral of Granada*, pp. 7–9; Leopoldo Torres Balbás, "La mezquita mayor de Granada," in his *Obra Dispersa I: Al Andalus, Crónica de la España musulmana*, 3 vols. (Madrid, 1981), 3:94–96.
105. Rosenthal, *Cathedral of Granada*, pp. 7–8.
106. On Pulgar's tomb and epitaph, see Manuel Gomez-Moreno, *Guía de Granada*, 2 vols. (Granada, 1892; rpt. 1994), 1:287. For Charles V's 1526 *cedula*, see Francisco Martínez de la Rosa, *Hernan Perez del Pulgar, el del las hazañas: Bosquejo histórico* (Madrid, 1834), Appendix no. 1, pp. 227–228.
107. *Los romances frontizeros*, 1:407–414, 2:707–712, 719–720, 725–757.
108. Lope de Vega, "Los hechos de Garcilaso" and "Cerca de Santa Fe." For discussion, see María Soledad Carrasco Urgoiti, "*El cerco de Santa Fe* de Lope de Vega: Ejemplo de comedia épica," in *Homenaje a William L. Fichter: Estudios sobre el teatro antiguo hispánico y otros ensayos*, ed. A. David Kossoff and José Amor y Vázquez (Madrid, 1971), pp. 115–125; idem, *El moro de Granada*, pp. 39–40, 80–81; idem, "La escenificación," pp. 30–34.
109. "El triunfo del Ave María," in *Dramáticos posteriores a Lope de Vega*, ed. Ramón de Mesonero Romanos (*BAE* 49.2, Madrid, 1951), pp. 173–194; Carrasco Urgoiti, "La escenificación," pp. 36, 85–87; José Antonio Gonzáles Alcantud, "Para sobrevivir a los estereotipos culturales: Structuras paródicas de las fiestas de moros y cristianos: El caso andaluz oriental," in *Moros y Cristianos*, p. 49.
110. Joan Amades, *Las Danzas de Moros y Cristianos* (Valencia, 1966), pp. 61–66; Carrasco Urgoiti, "La escenificación," p. 36.
111. Lope de Vega, "Los hechos de Garcilaso," p. 44.
112. *Los Romances frontizeros*, 1:444–448.
113. Remensnyder, "Christian Captives."

Chapter 6

1. José Vives, "Las *Vitas sanctorum* del Cerratense," *Analecta sacra tarraconensia: Revista de ciencias histórico-eclesiásticas* 21 (1948): 157–176; Massimiliano Bassetti, "Per un' edizione delle 'Vitae sanctorum' di Rodrigo de Cerrato," *Hagiographica* 9 (2002): 73–159; Pascual

Martínez Sopena, "Sobre los cultos del camino de Santiago en los reinos de Castilla y León: Génesis y evolución," in *Viajeros, peregrinos, mercaderes en el Occidente medieval: Actas de la XVIII semana de estudios medievales*... (Pamplona, 1992), pp. 169–170.

2. For a recent assessment of thirteenth-century Dominican attitudes toward the evangelization of non-Christians, see Vose, *Dominicans*.

3. Edited in Fita, "El libro de Cerratense," p. 232.

4. *CSM*, no. 107, 2: 27–30.

5. Edited in Fita, "El libro de Cerratense," pp. 231–232.

6. Baer, *History of the Jews*, pp. 191–192.

7. Nirenberg, *Communities of Violence*, pp. 127–165; Lasry, "Marisaltos," pp. 301–302, 304.

8. *Los fueros de Sepúlveda*, tit. 68, 71, ed. Emilio Sáez et al. (Segovia, 1953), pp. 89, 90.

9. Lasry, "Marisaltos," pp. 301–303; Norman Roth, *Daily Life of the Jews in the Middle Ages* (Westport, CT, 2005), pp. 11–12; Ray, *Sephardic Frontier*, pp. 122–123, 139–140.

10. On the shift and Jewish law, see Lasry, "Marisaltos," pp. 302–306. For a different interpretation, see Mirrer, *Women, Jews, and Muslims*, pp. 39, 42–44.

11. "El libro del Cerratense," p. 232. On Segovia's Mudejars, see Harvey, *Islamic Spain*, pp. 68–69.

12. Fita, "El libro del Cerratense," pp. 231–232.

13. Catlos, *Victors and the Vanquished*, p. 252; Ferrer i Mallol, *El Sarraïns*, pp. 19–24; Meyerson, "Aragonese and Catalan Jewish Converts," p. 135; Tartakoff, *Between Christian and Jew*, pp. 70–75.

14. On the manipulation of the ideologies of the powerful by the less powerful, see James C. Scott, *Domination and the Arts of Resistance: Hidden Transcripts* (New Haven, 1990).

15. Benjamin Z. Kedar, "Multidirectional Conversion in the Frankish Levant," in *Varieties of Religious Conversion*, pp. 190–199.

16. Catlos, *Victors and the Vanquished*, p. 254; Nirenberg, *Communities of Violence*, pp. 185–190.

17. Christians converting to Islam: Epalza, *Fray Anselmo de Turmeda*; Nirenberg, *Communities of Violence*, p. 128, n. 4; O'Connor, *Forgotten Community*, pp. 132–133. The most well-known instances of Christians becoming Jews occurred outside the Iberian Peninsula; e.g., the cases discussed by Bernhard Blumenkranz in his "Du nouveau sur Bodo-Eléazar," *Revue des études juives* 112 (1953): 35–42; "Un pamphlet juif médio-latin de polémique antichrétienne," *Revue d'histoire et de philosophie religieuses* 34 (1954): 401–413; "La conversion au judaïsme d'André, Archevêque de Bari," *The Journal of Jewish Studies* 14 (1963): 33–36.

18. Catlos, *Victors and the Vanquished*, pp. 252, 254–255; Ferrer i Mallol, *El Sarraïns*, p. 72; Meyerson, *Muslims of Valencia*, pp. 230–232, 254; Tartakoff, *From Jew to Christian*.

19. Espina, *Fortalitium fidei*..., 3.10.8 (no pagination).

20. Espina, *Fortalitium fidei*, 3.10.8 (no pagination). See also the text of 1523 edited in Fita, "La judería," pp. 379–380. On conversion miraculously curing Jewish blindness, see Blumenkranz, "Juden und Jüdische," p. 422.

21. Fita, "La judería," p. 380.

22. Ibid., pp. 380–381.

23. John Esten Keller, "Daily Living as Presented in the *Canticles* of Alfonso the Learned," *Speculum* 33 (1958): 488.

24. F. X. Cabello de Castro, "El santuario de la Fuencisla," *Estudios Segovianos* 1 (1949): 390–401; F. J. Sánchez Cantón, "Textos viejos sobre el santuario de la Fuencisla," *Estudios Segovianos* 1 (1949): 240–246.

25. Jean-Lewis Flecniakoska, "Fêtes solennelles du transfert de la statue de la Vierge de Fuencisla (Ségovie, 12–22 septembre 1613)," in *Fêtes de la Renaissance*, ed. Jean-Jacquot, 3 vols. (Paris, 1956–1957), 3:485–504.

26. Edward Glaser, "Escenificación de una leyenda segoviana por Juan de Zabaleta," *Estudios Segovianos* 10 (1958): 153–178.

27. "Advocaciones de la Virgen," pp. 19, 21, 25, 26.

28. Neumann, *Great Mother*, pp. 158–159, 160–62, 170. Cf. Julia Kristeva, "Stabat Mater," in her *Histoires d'amour* (Paris, 1983), p. 297.

29. The Byzantine material: Cutler, *Transformations*, pp. 116–117.

30. Cf. the lyrical celebration of Mary as dawn in *CSM*, no. 340, 3:187–189.

31. "Advocaciones de la Virgen," p. 19.

32. Ibid., p. 17.
33. Ibid., p. 28.
34. Cuffel, " 'Henceforth All Generations Will Call Me Blessed,' " pp. 46–47.
35. "Pseudo-Matthei evangelium," chap. 23–24, pp. 475–481.
36. E.g., Vincent of Beauvais, *Speculum historiale, 6.*95, 4:206. Visual representations of this scene: Camille, *Gothic Idol,* pp. 1–9.
37. Peter Comestor, *Historia Scholastica, PL* 198: 1440.
38. Juan Gil de Zamora, *De preconiis civitatis Numantine,* ed. by Fitel Fita in "Dos libros (inéditos) de Gil de Zamora," *BRAH* 5 (1884): 179.
39. Juan Gil de Zamora, *Nocturno III,* in "Poesías inéditas," pp. 387, 388.
40. Madrid, Biblioteca Nacional, MS. 9503. On this text, see the editor's comments in Juan Gil de Zamora, "Poesías inéditas," pp. 405–408; Mussafia, "Studien zu den mittelalterlichen Marienlegenden (III)," pp. 26–35.
41. Kedar, *Crusade and Mission;* Tolan, *Saracens.*
42. David Berger, "Mission to the Jews and Jewish-Christian Contacts in the Polemical Literature of the High Middle Ages," *American Historical Review* 91 (1986): 576–591; Cohen, *Friars and the Jews,* pp. 19–32.
43. Robert I. Burns, "Christian-Islamic Confrontation in the West: The Thirteenth-Century Dream of Conversion," *American Historical Review* 76 (1971): 1386–1434.
44. John V. Tolan, *Saint François et le Sultan: Une rencontre vue à travers huit siècles de textes et images* (Paris, 2007).
45. For an argument that thirteenth-century Dominican involvement in such missionary activity has been overestimated, see Vose, *Dominicans.* For a critique of Vose's "minimalist" stance, see the review of his book by John V. Tolan in *Islam and Christian-Muslim Relations* 21 (2010): 99–100.
46. John V. Tolan, "Porter la bonne parole auprès de Babel: Les problèmes linguistiques chez les missionnaires mendiants, XIII⁰–XIV⁰ siècles," in *Zwischen Babel und Pfingsten : Sprachdifferenzen und Gesprächsverständingung in der Vormoderne (8.–16. Jahrhundert),* ed. Peter von Moos (Zurich/Berlin, 2008), pp. 533–547 (esp. 541–542, 545–546).
47. Muslim/Christian debates: Echevarria, *Fortress of Faith,* pp. 70–71; Tolan, *Saracens,* p. 235; Van Koningsveld and Wiegers, "Polemical Works," pp. 179–183. Barcelona: Chazan, *Barcelona and Beyond* (Vose, *Dominicans,* pp. 139–155, questions whether conversion was a goal of this debate). For the Latin text of the Tortosa debate, see Pacios López, *La disputa de Tortosa.*
48. Roth, *Conversos,* p. 16; Vose, *Dominicans,* pp. 135–139, 160–161.
49. On Llull's missionary activities, see among many others Pamela Drout Beattie, " 'Pro exaltatione sanctae fidei Catholicae': Mission and Crusade in the Writings of Ramon Llull," in *Iberia and the Mediterranean World,* 1:113–129; Johnston, "Ramon Llull"; Tolan, *Saracens,* pp. 256–274.
50. Ramón Llull, *Libre de contemplació,* chap. 287.7–12, in his *Obres Essencials,* 2 vols. (Barcelona, 1957), 2:887–888. For discussion, Cohen, *Friars and the Jews,* pp. 224–225.
51. Jacques de Vitry, *Epistulae,* 2.224–227 in *Lettres,* p. 88. For discussion, Tolan, *Saracens,* pp. 199–200.
52. *Liber sancti jacobi,* Bk. 2, pp. 155–177.
53. *Los "miraculos romançados".* For discussion, Lappin, *Medieval Cult of Saint Dominic,* pp. 171–195, 275–390.
54. *Los milagros de san Isidoro (s. XIII) (facsímil del códice)* (Madrid, 1993), p. 83.
55. *CSM,* nos. 28, 46, 167, 205, 192, 397 (repeat of no. 192), 1: 128–132, 171–173, 2:168–169, 2:218–223, 2:251–253, 3:297 (conversions of Muslims); nos. 4, 25, 85, 89, 107, 1:63–66, 1:117–122, 1:268–270, 1:278–281, 2: 27–30 (conversions of Jews); nos. 196, 335, 2:234–236, 3:175–178 (conversion of pagans).
56. Hatton and MacKay, "Anti-Semitism in the *Cantigas,*" esp. p. 195; García Arenal, "Los moros en las *Cantigas,*" esp. pp. 145–147.
57. *CSM,* nos. 4, 25, 28, 46, 85, 89, 1:63–66, 117–122, 128–132, 171–173, 268–270, 278–281 (possibly also nos. 196, 335, 2:234–236, 3:175–178). On the history of the Marian *miracula,* see among others: Mussafia, "Studien zu den mittelalterlichen Marienlegenden"; James W.

Marchand, "Vincent de Beauvais, Gil de Zamora, et le *Mariale Magnum*," in *Encyclopédies médiévales: Discours et savoirs*, ed. B. Baillaud, J. de Gramont, D. Hüe (Rennes, 2004), pp. 101–115; Jesús Martínez Montoya, *Las colecciones de milagros de la Virgen en la Edad Media (el milagro literario)* (Granada, 1981); R. W. Southern, "The English Origins of the 'Miracles of the Virgin,'" *Mediaeval and Renaissance Studies* 4 (1958): 176–216.

58. Philippart, "Le récit miraculaire marial," pp. 568–570.

59. One of the best discussions of this quality of the Marian *miracula* remains R. W. Southern's *The Making of the Middle Ages* (New Haven, 1953), pp. 246–254.

60. Cervantes, *El ingenioso hidalgo Don Quijote*, 1.4.39–41, 1:464–502; and his *Los baños de Argel*. Lope de Vega, *La tragedia del rey Don Sebastián y bautismo del príncipe de Marruecos*, Acts 2 and 3, in Lope de Vega, *Comedias*, ed. Manual Arroyo Stephens, 15 vols. (Madrid, 1993–1998), 8:452–517. For discussion, see Remensnyder, "Christian Captives, Muslim Maidens."

61. On the ambivalence provoked by the crossings of religious borders, see Nirenberg, *Communities of Violence*.

62. García-Arenal, "Dreams and Reason," p. 89.

63. Elukin, "From Jew to Christian?" pp. 127–128; García-Arenal, "Dreams and Reason," p. 89; Nirenberg, *Communities of Violence*, pp. 127–128; Tartakoff, *Between Christian and Jew*.

64. Alfonso X, *Las Siete Partidas*, 7.24.6–7, 7.25.2, 7.25.4, vol. 3, fols. 75v, 76v, 77r; Robert Burns, "Journey from Islam"; Carpenter, "Alfonso el Sabio y los moros," pp. 231–232; Catlos, *Victors and the Vanquished*, pp. 253, 257; Nirenberg, *Communities of Violence*, pp. 127–128, 185–190; O'Connor, *Forgotten Community*, pp. 132–133; Tartakoff, *Between Christian and Jew*, pp. 106–116.

65. García-Arenal, "Dreams and Reason"; Jean-Claude Schmitt, *La conversion d'Hermann le juif: Autobiographie, histoire et fiction* (Paris, 2003), pp. 89–142.

66. García-Arenal, "Dreams and Reason," pp. 89–91.

67. Tartakoff, *Between Christian and Jew*, pp. 78–80.

68. E.g., Alfonso X, *Las Siete Partidas*, 7.24.6, 7.25.2, vol. 3, fols. 75v, 76v.

69. Alfonso X, *Las Siete Partidas*, 7.25. 2, vol. 3, fol. 76v. On the Christian suspicion of converts, see Catlos, *Victors and the Vanquished*, p. 258; Ferrer i Mallol, *El Sarraïns*, pp. 67–68; O'Connor, *Forgotten Community*, p. 132.

70. Morrison, *Understanding Conversion*, pp. 73–74, 81; Tartakoff, *Between Christian and Jew*, pp. 93–94.

71. Elukin, "From Jew to Christian?" pp. 177–182; Tartakoff, *Between Christian and Jew*, pp. 67–69.

72. Catlos, *Victors and the Vanquished*, p. 258; Nirenberg, "Mass Conversion."

73. Elukin, "From Jew to Christian?" pp. 180–182.

74. Espina, *Fortalitium fidei*, 3.10.8 (no pagination).

75. Hence seventeenth-century Spaniards staged the baptism of Muslims as jubilant public ceremonies. Bernard Vincent, "Musulmans et conversion en Espagne au XVIIe siècle," in *Conversions islamiques*, pp. 193–205.

76. Converts' own narratives of conversion are usually judged against a "conversion script" created by the group they are joining; Brock Kilbourne and James T. Richardson, "Paradigm Conflict, Types of Conversion, and Conversion Theories," *Sociological Analysis* 50 (1989): 15–16.

77. On medieval sermons, see Carolyn Muessig, "Audience and Preacher: Ad Status Sermons and Social Classification," in *Preacher, Sermon and Audience in the Middle Ages*, ed. Carolyn Muessig (Leiden, 2002), pp. 255–276.

78. *CSM*, no. 46, 1:171–173. For another example, see the legend discussed in Brou, "Marie 'Destructrice de toutes les hérésies.' "

79. Cf. José Filgueira Valverde's commentary in Alfonso X, el Sabio, *Cantigas de Santa María* (Madrid, 1985), p. 90.

80. Gautier de Coinci, *Les miracles*, 3:23–25; Vincent de Beauvais, *Speculum historiale*, 7.119, 4:266; John of Garland, *Stella Maris*, no. 7, p. 106.

81. Alfonso's knowledge of Islam: García Fitz, "El Islam visto por Alfonso X," p. 408.

82. Talavera, *Historia de Nuestra Señora de Guadalupe*, fols. 234v–235r.

83. Ibid., fols. 247v–248v, 315v–316v; and the miracle story edited in Crémoux, *Pèlerinages et miracles*, pp. 206–208.

84. Talavera, *Historia de Nuestra Señora de Guadalupe,* fols. 234v–235r, 315v (cf. fols. 301v–301r for similar language in another story of a Muslim man's conversion).

85. Barcelona, Archivo de la Corona de Aragón, C Jaume II Cartas extra series, caixa 136, no. 517. The text has been edited with some errors of transcription in *Acta Aragonensia,* 2:757–8.

86. Biblioteca del Escorial MS T.I.1, fol. 252v.

87. *CSM,* no. 192, 2:218–223.

88. Ferrer i Mallol, *El Sarraïns,* pp. 74–77.

89. Bensch, "From Prizes of War"; Burns, "Journey from Islam"; Catlos, *Victors and the Vanquished,* p. 255; Ferrer i Mallol, *El Sarraïns,* pp. 74–77; Kedar, *Crusade and Mission,* pp. 149–150; Meyerson, *Muslims of Valencia,* pp. 230–232.

90. *CSM,* no. 85, 2:268–270; cf. Vincent of Beauvais, *Speculum historiale* 7.111, 4:262.

91. *CSM,* no. 28, 1:128–132. Cf. Gautier de Coinci, *Miracles,* 4:31–4.

92. *CSM,* no. 25, 1:117–122. Cf. Vincent of Beauvais, *Speculum historiale,* 7.82, 4:251; Gautier de Coinci, *Miracles,* 4:110–133; Fidel Fita, "Cincuenta leyendas por Gil de Zamora, combinadas con las 'Cantigas' de Alfonso el Sabio," *BRAH* 7 (1885): 85–87; John of Garland, *Stella maris,* no. 19, pp. 115–166 (173–175 on the legend's origins).

93. Burns, "Journey from Islam"; Catlos, *Victors and the Vanquished,* pp. 258–259; Johnston, "Ramon Llull," pp. 35–36; Meyerson, *Muslims of Valencia,* pp. 230–232; O'Connor, *Forgotten Community,* pp. 121–134.

94. O'Connor, *Forgotten Community,* p. 128; Vose, *Dominicans,* pp. 155, 160.

95. This and the preceding quotations are from Alfonso X, *Las Siete Partidas,* 7.24.6, 7.25.2, vol. 3, fols. 75v, 76v. In general on Jews and Muslims in the *Siete Partidas,* see Burns, "Jews and Moors"; Carpenter, "Alfonso el Sabio y los moros"; idem, "Minorities in Medieval Spain"; González Jiménez, "Alfonso X y las minorías confesionales."

96. Cohen, *Friars and the Jews,* p. 106.

97. Cohen, *Friars and the Jews,* p. 82; Ferrer i Mallol, *El Sarraïns,* pp. 63–66; O'Connor, *Forgotten Community,* p. 127; Roth, *Conversos,* pp. 15–17; Vose, *Dominicans,* pp. 153–154, 160 (who points out that James "rescinded the most important clause of his edict after only one day"). Further evidence of Aragonese rulers' ambivalent about conversion efforts is discussed in Paola Tartakoff, "Christian Kings and Jewish Conversion in the Medieval Crown of Aragon," *Journal of Medieval Iberian Studies* 3 (2011): 27–39.

98. Burns, "Journey from Islam"; Cohen, *Friars and the Jews,* p. 84.

99. Johnston, "Ramon Llull"; Kedar, *Mission and Crusade,* pp. 189–199; Tolan, *Saracens,* pp. 256–274.

100. Kedar, *Mission and Crusade.*

101. Some preachers even capitalized on outbreaks of popular violence against Jews, delivering evangelizing sermons to them "in the presence of threatening Christian mobs"; Vose, *Dominicans,* p. 158.

102. Burns, "Social Riots"; Catlos, *Victors and the Vanquished,* p. 256; Nirenberg, *Communities of Violence,* p. 78.

103. For vivid accounts of the events of 1391, see Baer, *History of the Jews,* 2:95–117; Philippe Wolff, "The 1391 Pogrom in Spain: Social Crisis or Not?" *Past and Present* 50 (1971): 1–18.

104. Fifteenth-century Aragonese lords adamantly opposed conversion efforts directed toward their Mudejar tenants; Meyerson, *Muslims of Valencia,* pp. 230–232. Some late medieval Christians declared that all people could be saved in their own faith—Christians in Christianity, Muslims in Islam, and Jews in Judaism; Pedro M. Cátedra, *Sermón, sociedad y literatura en la Edad media: San Vicente Ferrer en Castilla (1411–1412)* (Salamanca, 1994), pp. 245–246; John Edwards, "Religious Faith and Doubt in Late Medieval Soria c. 1450–1500," *Past and Present* 120 (1988): 16–17; Kamen, *The Spanish Inquisition,* p. 6.

105. Rubin, *Gentile Tales,* pp. 37, 71.

106. For yet another example, see Talavera, *Historia de Nuestra Señora de Guadalupe,* fol. 289r–v.

107. Talavera, *Historia de Nuestra Señora de Guadalupe,* fols. 273v–274r, fols. 301v–301r.

108. Ibid., fol. 249v. Cf. the similar statement about the conversion of a Mudejar woman; *CSM,* no. 167, 2:168.

109. Here I am influenced by Mirrer's interpretation (*Women, Jews, and Muslims*, pp. 17–80) of a different set of literary representations of Muslims and Jews.

110. For discussion, see Blumenkranz, "Juden und Jüdische," pp. 441–442; Rubin, *Gentile Tales*, pp. 7–29; Schreiner, *Maria*, pp. 440–442.

111. *CSM*, no. 4, 1:63–66.

112. On the medieval idea of children as malleable, see Shulamith Shahar, *Childhood in the Middle Ages* (London, 1990), pp. 88–89, 100–101.

113. Cf. Rubin's comments on Gautier de Coinci's version, *Gentile Tales*, p. 14.

114. Talavera, *Historia de Nuestra Señora de Guadalupe*, fols. 249v–250r.

115. Cf. a similar miracle in Jacques de Vitry, *Epistulae* 2.380–385, pp. 94–95.

116. On such motivations in the conversion of adolescent Jews, see Jordan, "Adolescence and Conversion," p. 82.

117. Muslim examples: Echevarria, "La conversion des chevaliers musulmans"; Robert I. Burns, "Almohad Prince and Mudejar Convert: New Documentation on Abu Zayd," in *Medieval Iberia: Essays on the History and Literature of Medieval Spain*, ed. Donald J. Kagay and Joseph I. Snow (New York, 1997), pp. 171–188; Catlos, *Victors and the Vanquished*, pp. 251–252; Evariste Lévi-Provençal, "La 'mora Zaida,' femme d'Alphonse VI de Castille et leur fils l'Infant Sancho," *Hespéris* 18 (1934): 1–8; Reilly, *Contest of Christian and Muslim Spain*, pp. 92, 96; M. J. Rubiera de Mata, "Un insolito caso de conversas musulmanas al cristianismo: Las princesas toledanas del siglo XI," in *Las mujeres en el cristianismo medieval: Imágenes teóricas y cauces de actuación religiosa*, ed. Angela Muñoz Fernández (Madrid, 1989), pp. 343–345.

118. Baer, *History of the Jews*, 2:139–150.

119. On Jews and the military profession, see Elena Lourie, "A Jewish Mercenary in the Service of the King of Aragon," *Revue des Études Juives* 137 (1978): 367–373. The most famous adolescent male medieval Jewish convert dreamed of acquiring the accoutrements of Christian knighthood; Jordan, "Adolescence and Conversion," pp. 84–85.

120. Echevarria, *Fortress of Faith*, pp. 126–127; Katherine Ludwig Jansen, *The Making of the Magdalene: Preaching and Popular Devotion in the Later Middle Ages* (Princeton, 2000), pp. 210–211; Rubin, *Gentile Tales*, pp. 37, 71.

121. E.g., Meyerson, "Aragonese and Catalan Converts," pp. 138–139.

122. *CSM*, nos. 89, 167, 1:280, 2:169.

123. Ibid., no. 89, 1:278–281. For two other versions, see Vincent of Beauvais, *Speculum historiale*, 7.99, 4:258; John of Garland, *Stella maris*, no. 37, p. 127. On the tale's possible origins in the Iberian Peninsula, see Faye's comments in *Stella maris*, pp. 189–190.

124. Elisheva Baumgarten, *Mothers and Children: Jewish Family Life in Medieval Europe* (Princeton, 2004), pp. 114–115. On Christian women appealing to Mary during childbirth, see "Advocaciones de la Virgen," p. 11; *Cancionero de Juan Alfonso*, 2:413 (no. 226).

125. *CSM*, no. 167, 2:168–169. On Salas, see Pedro Aguado Bleye, *Santa María de Salas el siglo XIII: Estudio sobre las Cantigas de Alfonso X el Sabio* (Bilbao, 1916); Ricardo del Arco, "El santuario de Nuestra Señora de Salas," *Archivo Español de Arte* 19 (1946): 110–130; Balaguer, "Santa María de Salas."

126. *CSM*, no. 122, 2:67–68. For further details, see Amy G. Remensnyder, "Cantiga 122" in "Cantigas de Santa María," *Teaching Medieval Lyric with Modern Technology* (CD Rom Application; Project Directors: Margaret Switten and Robert Eisenstein).

127. On Mudejar speakers of Romance, see Harvey, *Islamic Spain*, p. 99. On the importance of cross-faith conversations among women, see *Conversing with the Minority: Relations among Christian, Jewish and Muslim Women in the High Middle Ages*, ed. Monica Green (special issue of *Journal of Medieval History* 34 [2008]).

128. Talavera, *Historia de Nuestra Señora de Guadalupe*, fols. 231r–233r.

129. The French story is edited in *"Comment lhymage n[ost]re Dame de Liesse autrement ditte de Lience fut trouvee, avec les miracles": Notre Dame de Liesse, sa légende d'après le plus ancien texte connu*, ed. Conte Hennezel d'Ormois (n.p., 1934). For discussion, see Remensnyder, "Christian Captives."

130. *CSM*, no. 205, 2:251–253. For the historical circumstances, see O'Callaghan, *Alfonso X and the Cantigas*, pp. 89–90.

131. On Téllez de Meneses' service to Ferdinand III, see González Jiménez, *Fernando III*, pp. 62, 78, 89, 97, 105, 154; *Primera crónica general*, chaps. 1031, 1037, 1079, 1086, 1082, 1110, 1113, 2: 716, 722, 750, 751, 753, 762, 764.

132. Jacques de Vitry, *Epistulae*, 2. 224–227, p. 88.

133. *CSM*, no. 46, 1:171–173; Gautier de Coinci, *Les Miracles*, 3:23–25; Vincent de Beauvais, *Speculum historiale*, 7.119, 4:266. For yet another version, see John of Garland, *Stella Maris*, no. 7, p. 106.

134. Talavera, *Historia de Nuestra Señora de Guadalupe*, fols. 247v–248v; 315v–316v; Crémoux, *Pèlerinages et miracles*, pp. 206–208.

135. Cervantes, *El ingenioso hidalgo Don Quijote*, 1.4.39–41, 1:464–502.

136. Cervantes, *Los baños de Argel*.

137. Remensnyder, "Christian Captives."

138. On captivity as trauma, see Garcés, *Cervantes in Algiers*.

139. Ferrer i Mallol, *El Sarraïns*, pp. 74–81; Lappin, *Medieval Cult of Saint Dominic*, pp. 293–296; *Los "miraculos romançados,"* pp. 65–67, 95–96, 109; Francisco de Asís Veas Arteseros and Juan Francisco Jiménez Alcázar, "Notas sobre el rescate de cautivos en la frontera de Granada," in *Actas del congreso "La frontera oriental nazarí"*, pp. 233–234; Rodríguez, *Captives and Their Saviors*, pp. 67–93. For the early modern period: Bartolomé Bennassar and Lucile Bennassar, *Les Chrétiens d'Allah: L'histoire extraordinaire des renégats XVIe et XVIIe siècles* (Paris, 1989), esp. pp. 202–340; Friedman, *Spanish Captives*, pp. 58, 77, 88–89, 90; García-Arenal and Bunes, *Los Españoles y el Norte de África*, pp. 212–239.

140. Hence the Christian ransoming efforts. Ferrer i Mallol, *El Sarraïns*, pp. 71–81; Argente del Castillo Ocaña, "Cautiverio y martirio," p. 47; Friedman, *Spanish Captives*, pp. 81, 146; Rodríguez, *Captives and Their Saviors*, pp. 67–93.

141. E.g.. *CSM*, no. 325, 3:152–155; García de Santa María, *Crónica*, p. 282; Madrid BN MS. 1176, fols. 9r–12v; Talavera, *Historia de Nuestra Señora de Guadalupe*, fols. 240v–242v.

142. Barcelona, Archivo de la Corona de Aragón, C Jaume II Cartas extra series, caixa 136, nos. 515–517. No. 517 is edited *Acta Aragonensia…*, 2:757–758. For other examples of the political weight of Christian stories about the conversion of high-ranking Muslims, see Adam Knobler, "Pseudo-Conversions and Patchwork Pedigrees: The Christianization of Muslim Princes and the Diplomacy of Holy War," *Journal of World History* 7 (1996): 181–197.

143. Dufourcq, *L'Espagne catalane*, pp. 493–494.

144. Barcelona, Archivo de la Corona de Aragón, C Jaume II Cartas extra series, caixa 136, no. 517; ed. in *Acta Aragonensia…*, 2:758.

145. Baptism as political bait: Dufourcq, *L'Espagne catalane*, pp. 488–494; Remensnyder, "Christian Captives," pp. 663–665; Vose, *Dominicans*, pp. 240–242.

146. On *alcayts*: Dufourcq, *L'Espagne catalane*, pp. 101–104, 412–413, 436–437.

147. Aragonese ambitions in North Africa: Ibid.

148. Transcribed by Crémoux, *Pèlerinages et miracles*, pp. 206–208.

149. García-Arenal and Bunes, *Los Españoles y el Norte de África*, pp. 120–121.

150. Crémoux, *Pèlerinages et miracles*, p. 67.

151. Sebastián García and Elisa Rovira López, "Guadalupe en Indias: Documentación del archivo del monasterio," in *Extremadura en el evangelización del Nuevo Mundo*, p. 703; Crémoux, *Pèlerinages et miracles*, pp. 29, 67.

Part III: Introduction

1. Talavera, *Historia de Nuestra Señora de Guadalupe*, fols. 168r, 178r. For an earlier description of Cortés's pilgrimage to Guadalupe, see Díaz, *Historia*, chap. 195, pp. 523–524. On Cortés's 1520 gift to Charles V, see Peter Hess, "Marvelous Encounters: Albrecht Dürer and Early Sixteenth-Century German Perceptions of Aztec Culture," *Daphnis: Zeitschrift für Mittlere Deutsche Literatur und Kultur der Frühen Neuzeit* 33 (2004): 161–182.

2. Other conquistadors also used such maneuvers; Restall, *Seven Myths*, pp. 19–26.

3. Thomas, *Conquest*, pp. 596–598. On Cortés's itinerary in Spain, see Amada López Meneses, "El primero regreso de Hernán Cortés a España," *Revista de las Indias*, 14 (1954): 69–91.

4. Crémoux, *Pèlerinages et miracles*, p. 30.

5. Antonio Ramiro Chico, "Bibliografía de Hernán Cortés en Guadalupe," in *Hernán Cortés y su tiempo: Actas del congreso "Hernán Cortés y su tiempo: V centenario (1485–1985)"* (Merida, 1987), pp. 820–826.

6. Johnson, "Negotiating the Exotic," pp. 102–103.

7. On this term, see Altman, *Emigrants and Society*, p. 23.

8. Altman, *Emigrants and Society*, esp. pp. 165–209.

9. Thomas, *Conquest*, p. 118.

10. Talavera, *Historia de Nuestra Señora de Guadalupe*, fol. 178r.

11. For conjectures about its appearance, see Federico Gómez de Orozco, "¿El exvoto de Hernando Cortés?" *Anales del Instituto de Investigaciones Estéticas* 8 (1942): 51–54.

12. Pagden, *European Encounters*, esp. p. 36.

13. Salvador Rueda Smithers and Guillermo Turner Rodríguez, "Nuevas formas y viejos ritos y costumbres: Imaginario medieval en Nueva España," in *España medieval y el legado*, pp. 259–268; Weckmann, *Medieval Heritage of Mexico*, pp. 46–71.

14. Mercedes García-Arenal, "Moriscos e indios: Para un estudio comparado de métodos de conquista y evangelización," *Chronica Nova* 20 (1992): 153–175, esp. 162, 171.

15. Motolinía, *Memoriales*, 1.29, p. 131; idem, *Historia de los Indios*, p. 8. For other examples of Spaniards comparing the indigenous peoples to Muslims, see Weckmann, *Medieval Heritage of Mexico*, pp. 180–181.

16. Monica Martí Cotalero, "El medioevo en Nueva España: Una permanencia velada," in *España medieval y el legado*, pp. 273–280; Weckmann, *Medieval Heritage of Mexico*.

17. Jennifer R. Goodman, *Chivalry and Exploration, 1298–1630* (Woodbridge, GB, 1998), esp. pp. 149–167; Stuart B. Schwartz, "New World Nobility: Social Aspirations and Mobility in the Conquest and Civilization of Spanish America," in *Social Groups and Religious Ideas in the Sixteenth Century*, ed. Miriam Usher Chrisman and Otto Gründler (Kalamazoo, MI, 1978), pp. 34–35; Weckmann, *Medieval Heritage of Mexico*, pp. 135–154.

18. Elliott, "Mental World of Hernán Cortés," pp. 30–32; Lupher, *Romans in a New World*, pp. 8–42.

19. Elliott, *Empires of the Atlantic World*, p. 20; Weckmann, *Medieval Heritage of Mexico*, pp. 85–115. On Cortés's father, see Thomas, *Conquest*, p. 118.

20. Motolinía, *Memoriales*, 3.5.3, p. 139.

21. Restall, *Seven Myths*, p. 143.

22. Oviedo, *Historia*, 2.4, 1:22.

23. García-Arenal and Bunes, *Los Españoles y el Norte de Africa*, pp. 19–61; Hillgarth, *Spanish Kingdoms*, 2:570–575.

24. Miguel Angel de Bunes Ibarra, "El descubrimiento de América y la conquista del Norte de Africa: Dos empresas paralelas en la Edad Moderna," *Revista de Indias* 45 (1985): 225–233; idem, "Lo americano y lo africano," pp. 159–173.

25. Bunes Ibarra, "Lo americano y lo africano," pp. 160–161.

26. Talavera, *Historia de Nuestra Señora de Guadalupe*, fols. 155r–v.

27. Ibid., fol. 155v.

28. Bernáldez, *Memorias*, chap. 224, p. 565.

29. Talavera, *Historia de Nuestra Señora de Guadalupe*, fol. 155r.

30. Ibid., fol. 155v. By 1510, one of these slaves had converted to Christianity. The friars of Guadalupe helped him ransom his wife and daughter from captivity in Valencia. Crémoux, *Pèlerinages et miracles*, p. 165.

31. On Trujillan emigration to the New World and the houses at Trujillo, see Altman, *Emigrants and Society*, pp. 165–205, 259, 270–271.

32. For the details in this paragraph about Our Lady of Victory, see José Antonio Ramos Rubio, *Historia del culto a Nuestra Señora de la Victoria y su coronación canónica* (Trujillo, 1994), pp. 14, 65, 67, 72.

33. On the creation of urban histories and the effacing of the Muslim past, see Richard L. Kagan, "Clio and the Crown: The Writing of History in Hapsburg Spain," in *Spain, Europe, and the Atlantic World*, ed. Richard L. Kagan and Geoffrey Parker (Cambridge, 1995), pp. 84–99; idem, "*Urbs* and *Civitas* in Sixteenth-Century Spain," in *Envisioning the City: Six Studies in*

Urban Cartography, ed. Davis Buisseret (Chicago, 1998), pp. 75–108, esp. 95–96; idem, *Urban Images.*

34. Rodríguez Molina, "Santos guerreros," pp. 456–461; idem, *La vida de moros,* pp. 190–194. These legends have exercised such a tenacious hold on Spanish imagination that some modern historians take them as fact; e.g., Muñoz Fernández, "Cultos, devociones y advociones religiosas;" and esp. Sánchez Pérez, *El culto mariano.*

35. Seville and shipping to the New World: Pike, "Seville in the Sixteenth Century," in *Globe Encircled,* pp. 154–191. The claim about Mary's birth in Seville appears in the text edited in F. A. Ugolini, "Avvenimenti, figure e costumi di Spagna in una cronaca italiana del Trecento," in *Italia e Spagna: Saggi sui rapporti storici, filosofici ed artistici tra le due civiltà* (Florence, 1941), p. 104. For discussion, Linehan, *History,* pp. 657–658.

36. On Extremaduran emigrants' experience in Seville, see Altman, *Emigrants and Society,* pp. 205–208.

37. Mena García, *Sevilla y las flotas,* pp. 139–142, 145; Restall, *Seven Myths,* p. 37.

38. Perry, *Gender and Disorder,* p. 14.

39. Thomas, *Conquest,* p. 126. For further detail, see Pike, "Seville."

40. Teodor Falcón Márquez, *La catedral de Sevilla (estudio arquitectónico)* (Seville, 1980), esp. pp. 13–30.

41. Cintas del Bot, *Iconografía del Rey San Fernando,* pp. 49–50.

42. Carrero Rodríguez, *Nuestra Señora de los Reyes,* p. 83; Webster, *Art and Ritual in Golden-Age Spain,* p. 78.

43. Carrero Rodríguez, *Nuestra Señora de los Reyes,* pp. 83–84.

44. Cortés's offering: Johnson, "Negotiating the Exotic," pp. 102–103. Conquistador devotion in general to this Madonna: Chapter 7 of this volume; Medianero Hernández, "La gran Tecleciguata."

45. The image and its dating: Valdivieso, *Historia de la pintura sevillana,* pp. 21 (fig. 2), 22–23; Alfredo J. Morales, "'Quien no vio a Sevilla, no vio maravilla': Notas sobre la ciudad del Trescientos," in *Sevilla, siglo XIV,* ed. Rafael Valencia (Seville, 2006), p. 74.

46. Valdivieso, *Historia de la pintura sevillana,* p. 23; Medianero Hernández, "La gran Tecleciguata," pp. 367–368. Already in 1403, Ferdinand of Antequera had chosen her as the patron for his Order of the Jar and Griffin; Torres Fontes, "Don Fernando," p. 98.

47. Münzer, "Itinerarium," p. 78.

48. Morgado, *Historia de Sevilla,* p. 350.

49. Ibid., p. 350.

50. Mena García, *Sevilla y las flotas,* p. 25 (note 1); Thomas, *Conquest,* p. 127.

51. Hojeda and Ocampo's ships of this name: E. Roukema, "Some Remarks on the La Cosa Map," *Imago Mundi* 14 (1959), p. 40, note 4.

52. Mena García, *Sevilla y las flotas,* pp. 158–159.

53. Ibid., pp. 25 (note 1), 59.

54. For these details about the two Marian churches in Triana, see *Andalucía Americana,* pp. 190–192; Mena García, *Sevilla y las flotas,* p. 25 (note 1).

55. The Casa's quarters: *Andalucía Americana,* pp. 224–227.

56. Elliott, *Empires of the Atlantic World,* pp. 9–50, 108–109; Phillips, "Visualizing *Imperium,*" pp. 815–816.

57. Phillips, "Visualizing *Imperium,*" p. 653 (*passim* for the information in this paragraph).

58. In this paragraph I follow Rahn's analysis in "Visualizing *Imperium.*"

59. Hall, *Mary,* pp. 73–76.

60. Robert I. Burns, *Islam under the Crusaders: Colonial Survival in the Thirteenth-Century Kingdom of Valencia* (Princeton, 1973), pp. 117–138; Meyerson, *Muslims of Valencia,* pp. 13–14.

61. From Harvey's translation of the Capitulations of Granada in his *Islamic Spain,* p. 316 (309–314 on the negotiations themselves).

62. Seed, *Ceremonies of Possession,* pp. 80–87.

63. Text of the decree in Bango, *Remembering Sepharad,* pp. 207–208. Here I follow the interpretation in Meyerson, "Religious Change," pp. 96–112.

64. Coleman, *Creating Christian Granada,* pp. 82–88.

65. Ibid., p. 84; Harvey, *Islamic Spain,* p. 329.

66. On Cisneros in Granada, see Coleman, *Creating Christian Granada*, pp. 38–39; Harvey, *Islamic Spain*, pp. 329–334.
67. Historians debate the reasons for Ferdinand's decision; e.g., L. P. Harvey, *Muslims in Spain 1500 to 1614* (Chicago, 2005), pp. 80–101; Meyerson, "Religious Change."
68. Prophecies of the world ruler: Milhou, "La chauve-souris," pp. 61–78; idem, "Propaganda mesiánica y opinion pública," pp. 51–62; Carriazo Rubio's introduction to his edition of the *Historia de los hechos*, pp. 89–121. Fifteenth-century Spanish associations of the apocalypse with the Jews' conversion: Steven McMichael, "The End of the World, Antichrist, and the Final Conversion of the Jews in the *Fortalitium fidei* of Friar Alonso de Espina (d. 1464)," *Medieval Encounters: Jewish, Christian and Muslim Culture in Confluence and Dialogue* 12 (2006): 224–273. Cf. MacKay, "Andalucía y la guerra del fin del mundo," pp. 329–342.
69. Brading, *Mexican Phoenix*, pp. 33–36.
70. In this paragraph, I follow Seed, *Ceremonies of Possession*, pp. 69–99.
71. This paragraph and the next quote the version of the *Requirimiento* in Oviedo, *Historia*, 10.7, 3:227–228.
72. Oviedo, *Historia*, 10.7, 3:228.
73. Restall, *Seven Myths*, pp. 94–95.
74. Oviedo, *Historia*, 10.7, 3:227, 230–231; 10.9, 3:237. For discussion: Restall, *Seven Myths*, p. 94; Seed, *Ceremonies of Possession*, pp. 71, 95.
75. Seed, *Ceremonies of Possession*, pp. 95–96.
76. Phillips, "Visualizing *Imperium*," pp. 833–835.
77. For an argument that Mary underwent such changes in the sixteenth century, see Ellington, *From Sacred Body to Angelic Soul*. For a powerful counter-argument, see Rubin, *Mother of God*, esp. pp. 356, 385–399.
78. Perry, *Gender and Disorder*, pp. 37–43; Ellington, *From Sacred Body to Angelic Soul*, especially pp. 188–207.
79. Perry, *Gender and Disorder*, p. 41 and figures 5 and 6.

Chapter 7

1. Las Casas, *Historia de las Indias*, 1.82, 2:849. For biographical details on Hojeda, see Paredes Ferrer, *Alonso de Ojeda*, a book to be used with caution. On Las Casas's portrait of Hojeda, see María Christen Florencia, *El caballero de la Virgen: La narración de Alonso de Ojeda en la "Historia de la Indias" de Fray Bartolomé de las Caas* (Mexico City, 1988), which, despite its title, says little about his Marian devotion.
2. Christian, *Apparitions*, pp. 93–94; idem, *Local Religion in Sixteenth-Century Spain* (Princeton, 1981), pp. 73–75. Rubin (*Mother of God*) argues that by the sixteenth century, European Christianity had been "marianized."
3. Peter Martyr, *De orbe novo*, 3.3, fol. 41r; Díaz, *Historia*, chap. 166, p. 418.
4. Díaz, *Historia*, chap. 204, p. 557.
5. Ibid., chap. 205, p. 573.
6. Oviedo, *Historia*, prologue to Book 50, 5:308. On the dating of this section of Oviedo's text, see O'Gorman, *Cuatro historiadores*, p. 81. On Oviedo's life, see Myers, *Fernández de Oviedo's Chronicle*, pp. 12–25.
7. Oviedo, *Historia*, prologue to Book 50, 5:308.
8. Ibid., 50.1, 50.3–4, 50.6–9, 5:308–309, 310–314, 316–322.
9. Ibid., 50.6, 5:317.
10. Ibid., 50.6, 5:317. Of the two early modern paintings of this Madonna still in the cathedral, legend identifies one as the image saved from the shipwreck of 1523, but it actually dates from the eighteenth century; the other dates from the early sixteenth century and is a more likely candidate. Medianero Hernández, "La gran *Tecleciguata*," pp. 370–373, and figs. 1–2. On coral in Santo Domingo's cathedral and the building's early construction history see Palm, *Los monumentos arquitectónicos*, 1:90, 184, 2:25–51.
11. Adorno, *Polemics of Possession*.
12. Las Casas, *Historia de las Indias*, 2.63, 4:1554.
13. Ibid, 2.64, 4:159.

14. By 1514, Santa María de la Antigua del Darién had only two hundred houses; Palm, *Monumentos arquitectónicos*, 1:71.
15. Enciso, *Suma de geographia*, fol. h ii recto.
16. Ibid., fols. h verso–h ii recto.
17. On Peter Martyr, see O'Gorman, *Cuatro historiadores*, pp. 11–44; Geoffrey Eatough, "Peter Martyr's Account of the First Contacts with Mexico," *Viator* 30 (1999): 397–421.
18. On the chronology of the composition and publication of this section of Peter Martyr's *De orbe novo*, see O'Gorman, *Cuatro historiadores*, pp. 14, 43.
19. Peter Martyr, *De orbe novo*, 2.6, fols. 30r–31r.
20. Warner, *Alone of All Her Sex*, pp. 328–329.
21. Peter Martyr, *De orbe novo*, 2.6, fol. 30r. Peter Martyr must have meant Francisco de Bobadilla, governor of Hispaniola from 1499 to 1502, who was often referred to in Spanish sources as "comendador Bobadilla" (e.g., Oviedo, *Historia*, 3.6–3.7, 1: 65–70).
22. Las Casas, *Historia de las Indias*, 3.24, 5:1858. On this *caçicazgo's* location, see Dacal Moure and Rivero de la Calle, *Art and Archaeology*, p. 26.
23. Taino architecture: Rouse, *Tainos*, pp. 9, 13.
24. This discussion of *zemis* is based on Gruzinski, *La guerre des images*, pp. 25–27, 30–37; Rouse, *Tainos*, pp. 13–16, 118–119. For illustrations of *zemis* from Cuba, see Dacal Moure and Rivero de la Calle, *Art and Archaeology*, color plates 5–7 (pp. 59–61), and figs. 12–47 (pp. 76–95). *Zemis* from Hispaniola and elsewhere in the Antilles appear in Onorio Montás, Pedro José Borrell, and Frank Moya Pons, *Arte Taíno*, 2nd ed. (Santo Domingo, 1985), pp. 35–37.
25. Fray Ramón Pané, *Relación acerca de las antiguedades de los Indios*, chaps. 19, 25, ed. José Juan Arrom, 8th ed. (Mexico City, 1998), pp. 33, 40; Oviedo, *Historia*, 5.3, 1:123.
26. Dacal Moure and Rivero de la Calle, *Art and Archaeology*, pp. 39–40, and color plates 5–7 (pp. 59–61) and figs. 12–47 (pp. 76–95); Rouse, *Tainos*, p. 17. Peter Martyr writes simply that Tainos took *zemis* into battle; *De orbe novo*, 2.6, fol. 30v.
27. Infant head binding: Rouse, *Tainos*, p. 11.
28. Taino conceptions of the cosmos: José R. Oliver, "The Taino Cosmos," in *The Indigenous Peoples of the Caribbean*, ed. Samuel M. Wilson (Gainesville, FL, 1997), pp. 140–153.
29. Díaz, *Historia*, chap. 208, p. 579.
30. Adorno, *Polemics of Possession*, pp. 149–153, 184.
31. For recent studies focusing on the religious orders' evangelical work, see Chapter 8 of this volume. Ricard's classic book mentions the conquistadors' missionizing: *Spiritual Conquest of Mexico*, pp. 15–21; for more recent if generally brief discussion, see Adorno, *Polemics of Possession*, pp. 135–136; Cervantes, *Devil in the New World*, pp. 11–13; Gruzinski, *Guerre des images*, pp. 56–62; Trexler, "Aztec Priests."
32. On this aspect of late medieval preaching, see Lara, *Christian Texts*, pp. 43–48.
33. For the details in this paragraph, see Las Casas, *Historia de las Indias*, 2.60, 3.29, 2:1543, 3:1876–1877.
34. Las Casas, *Historia de las Indias*, 2.60, 2:1543–1544. For some discussion of Hojeda's stay at Cueíba, see Paredes Ferrer, *Alonso de Ojeda*, pp. 219–232.
35. Las Casas, *Historia de las Indias*, 2.60, 3.29, 2:1544, 3:1876–1877.
36. For further confirmation that these were two episodes occurring in different villages, see Olga Portuondo Zúñiga, *La Virgen de la Caridad del Cobre: Símbolo de cubanía* (Santiago de Cuba, 2001), pp. 58–66. For Las Casas's version of Cabo de Cruz, see below.
37. For evocative analysis of the early Maya-Spanish encounters, see Clendinnen, *Ambivalent Conquests*.
38. For eyewitness description, see Díaz, "Itinerario de la armada," pp. 37–38. On Mayan coastal shrines, see Freidel and Sabloff, *Cozumel*, p. 45.
39. Díaz, *Historia*, chap. 2, p. 5.
40. Oviedo, *Historia*, 17.8, 2:119–120; *America pontifica*, no. 24, 1:142.
41. Gómara, *Historia general*, chap. 52, p. 75.
42. Rouse, *Tainos*, pp. 13, 18.
43. For an introduction to Mayan temples, see Morley and Brainerd, *Ancient Maya*, esp. pp. 261–361. On Nahua temples, see Broda, Carrasco, and Matos Moctezuma, *Great Temple*; and

Moctezuma's Mexico: Visions of the Aztec World, ed. Davíd Carrasco and Eduardo Matos Moctezuma (Niwot, CO, 1992), esp. pp. 99–148; *Aztecs* (London, 2002), figs. 287–291, pp. 320–321.

44. E.g. Cortés, "Segunda relación" and "Quinta relación," in Cortés, *Cartas,* pp. 191, 195, 237, 238, 269, 59; "Conquistador anónimo," *Relación de la Nueva España,* ed. Jesús Bustamante (Madrid, 1986), pp. 84, 120, 132, 148; Oviedo, *Historia,* 17.3, 2:114; Peter Martyr, *De orbe novo,* 4.8, fol. 61v. See also Elliott, *Empires of the Atlantic World,* p. 20; Weckmann, *Medieval Heritage of Mexico,* pp. 181–182. Conquistadors also called Incan temples "mosques"; e.g., *Las relaciones primitivas de la conquista del Perú,* ed. Raúl Porras Barrenchea (Paris, 1937), pp. 60–61.

45. "War of images": Gruzinski, *La guerre des images.*

46. Recent discussions of Cortés and his company's experiences in Yucatan and central Mexico include: Hassig, *Mexico and the Spanish Conquest;* Martínez, *Hernán Cortés;* Townsend, *Malintzin's Choices.* Other discussion of Mary's importance to Cortés appears in Hall, *Mary,* pp. 58–72.

47. Díaz, *Historia,* chap. 204, p. 557.

48. Morley and Brainerd, *Ancient Maya,* pp. 147, 157, 257.

49. Ibid., p. 476; Clendinnen, *Ambivalent Conquests,* p. 17; Díaz, *Historia,* chap. 27, p. 44.

50. Cortés, "Primera relación," in *Cartas,* pp. 124–125.

51. On the conquistadors' language of "complete" conquest, see Restall, *Seven Myths,* pp. 64–76.

52. Cortés, "Primera relación," in *Cartas,* p. 125.

53. "Interrogatorio presentado," pp. 318–319; Tapia, "Relación," pp. 72–73; Díaz, *Historia,* chap. 27, pp. 44–45. Perhaps Ix Chel's temple was the "white tower" where the first Spaniards to set foot on Cozumel—Juan de Grijalva's expedition of 1518—celebrated Mass; Díaz, "Itinerario de la armada," p. 39.

54. Tapia, "Relacion," p. 69. See also Gómara, *La conquista de México,* p. 62. For the identification of this shrine with Ix Chel, see Freidel and Sabloff, *Cozumel,* p. 44; David A. Freidel, "Preface," in *Ancient Maya Political Economies,* ed. Marilyn A. Masson and David A. Freidel (Walnut Creek, CA, 2002), pp. viii–ix.

55. Tapia, "Relacion," p. 72; "Interrogatorio presentado," p. 318.

56. Díaz, *Historia,* chap. 27, p. 44. On incense in Maya religious practice, see Morley and Brainerd, *Ancient Maya,* pp. 481–482. On Mayan temple plazas as ritual space, see Freidel and Sabloff, *Cozumel,* pp. 46–47.

57. Díaz, *Historia,* chap. 27, p. 45.

58. Trexler, "Aztec Priests," p. 483. For evidence that it was a statue, see Chapter 8 of this volume. Gruzinski (*La guerre des images,* p. 61) conjectures that all the Marian images used by Cortés were statues.

59. In the temple: Díaz, *Historia,* chap. 27, p. 44; Tapia, "Relacion," p. 73. On top of the temple: "Interrogatorio presentado," p. 319 (quoted here); Peter Martyr, *De orbe novo,* 4.6, fol. 59v. Interestingly, the most distinguished translator of Cortés's letters into English chooses to render "una cruz de palo puesta en un casa alta" as "a wooden cross fixed on top of a high building;" Hernan Cortés, *Letters from Mexico,* trans. Anthony Pagden (New Haven, 1986), p.18.

60. "Interrogatorio presentado," p. 319; Peter Martyr, *De orbe novo,* 4.6, fol. 59v; Díaz, *Historia,* chap. 27, p. 45.

61. Morley and Brainerd, *Ancient Maya,* pp. 461, 493–494.

62. Fariss, *Maya Society,* pp. 303, 315; Lara, *Christian Texts,* pp. 128–130.

63. "Carta de Fray Toribio de Motolinia al Emperador Carlos V," in Motolinía, *Historia de los Indios,* pp. 219, 220.

64. On the Franciscans' view of Cortés, see Elliott, "Mental World of Hernán Cortés," pp. 594–598; Phelan, *Millennial Kingdom,* pp. 29–38.

65. See Chapter 8 of this volume.

66. Díaz, *Historia,* chap. 27, p. 45; "Interrogatorio presentado," p. 318. Cf. Salazar, *Crónica,* 2.30, p. 122.

67. Tapia, "Relación," p. 73; Peter Martyr, *De orbe novo,* 4.6, fol. 59v.

68. Tapia, "Relación," p. 73; "Interrogatorio presentado," p. 318.

69. Díaz, *Historia*, chap. 27, p. 45.

70. On Mayan Putunchan, see Townsend, *Malintzin's Choices*, pp. 25–26. On the location of this town and its colonial Spanish successor (neither extant), see Ulises Chávez Jiménez, "Potonchan y Santa María de la Victoria: Una propuesta geomorfológico/arqueológica a un problema histórico," [Online]. Available: http://www.granadacollection.org/Publicaciones.htm [February 16, 2008].

71. Salazar, *Crónica*, 2.33, p. 128. For vivid reconstructions of these conflicts at Putunchan and nearby Cintla, see Hassig, *Mexico and the Spanish Conquest*, pp. 59–63; Townsend, *Malintzin's Choices*, pp. 33–36.

72. Díaz, *Historia*, chaps. 33, 36, pp. 54, 59. Cf. Motolinía's use of this name for the town in his *Historia de los Indios*, 3.5, p. 138.

73. For a moving biography of this woman, see Townsend, *Malintzin's Choices*.

74. Tapia, "Relación," p. 77.

75. Cortés, "Primera relación," in *Cartas*, p. 132.

76. Díaz, *Historia*, chap. 36, pp. 59–60.

77. Cortés, "Primera relación," in *Cartas*, p. 132.

78. Díaz, *Historia*, chap. 36, pp. 59–60.

79. Ibid., chaps. 45, p. 76.

80. Hassig, *Mexico and the Spanish Conquest*, pp. 28–29, 39–40, 74.

81. Townsend, *Malintzin's Choices*, p. 45. On the Nahua use of marriage politics to secure alliances, see Pedro Pizana Carrasco, "Royal Marriages in Ancient Mexico," in *Explorations in Ethnohistory: Indians of Central Mexico in the Sixteenth Century*, ed. H. R. Harvey and Hanns J. Prem (Albuquerque, 1984), pp. 41–81.

82. For the events described in this and the next paragraph, see Díaz, *Historia*, chaps. 51–52, pp. 87–89. Salazar mentions only that Cortés installed crosses in Cempoala's temples, but in his description of events several months later at Cempoala twice refers to "un *cu* que dicen de Nuestra Señora;" Salazar, *Crónica*, 3.24, 4.82, 4.86, pp. 186, 435, 441.

83. Hassig, *Mexico and the Spanish Conquest*, p. 76.

84. For superb discussion of cultural misunderstandings between the Mexica and Cortés and his men, see Clendinnen, "'Fierce and Unnatural Cruelty.'"

85. Hassig, *Mexico and the Spanish Conquest*, p. 78.

86. In one town, Cortés apparently wanted to plant a cross, but was dissuaded by cooler heads in his company; Díaz, *Historia*, chap. 61, p. 104.

87. Pre-conquest Tlaxcala and Tlaxcalteca relations with Cortés: Gibson, *Tlaxcala*, pp. 1–27. Structure and definition of pre-conquest Nahua *altepetl* and the layout of their urban cores: Lockhart, *Nahuas*, pp. 14–28. The details about Tlaxcala's size, its market, houses, and walls come from Cortés, "Segunda relación," in *Cartas*, pp. 173–174, 184–185.

88. For the events described in this paragraph, see Hassig, *Mexico and the Spanish Conquest*, pp. 79–90.

89. Díaz, *Historia*, chap. 77, pp. 132–133.

90. Hassig, *Mexico and the Spanish Conquest*, p. 90.

91. For the events described in this paragraph, see Díaz, *Historia*, chap. 77, p. 133; Tapia, "Relación," p. 94.

92. A point emphasized by Restall, *Seven Myths*.

93. On the different meanings such rituals held for the Spaniards and the Mesoamericans, see Clendinnen, "'Fierce and Unnatural Cruelty,'" p. 70; Hassig, *Mexico and the Spanish Conquest*, p. 92.

94. Díaz, *Historia*, chap. 40, pp. 68–69.

95. Ibid., chap. 41, p. 70.

96. On the Templo Mayor, see Broda, Carrasco, and Matos Moctezuma, *Great Temple*; Eduardo Matos Moctezuma, "The Templo Mayor: The Great Temple of the Aztecs," in *Aztecs*, pp. 48–55 (and the images, pp. 277–321); Eduardo Matos Moctezuma, "Excavations at the Templo Mayor," and Juan Alberto Román Berrelleza, "The Templo Mayor at Tenochtitlan," both in *Aztec Empire*, pp. 132–145, 146–148.

97. On Tenochtitlan's grandeur, see Inga Clendinnen, "City in America—Tenochtitlan: The Public Image," in *Globe Encircled*, pp. 193–240.

98. Townsend, *Malintzin's Choices*, pp. 85–96. For somewhat different reconstructions of the Spaniards' time in Tenochtitlan, see Hassig, *Mexico and the Spanish Conquest*, pp. 103–107; Martínez, *Hernán Cortés*, pp. 241–258.

99. On the temple's symbolic and political significance, see Broda, Carrasco, and Moctezuma, *Great Temple*.

100. For the details in this and the following paragraph, see Díaz, *Historia*, chap. 92, pp. 172–177.

101. Ibid., chap. 92, p. 175.

102. Ibid., chap. 90, pp. 164–165.

103. Ibid., chap.89, pp. 162–163.

104. Ibid., chap. 93, pp. 177.

105. Townsend, *Malintzin's Choices*, pp. 92–95.

106. Cortés, "Segunda relación," in *Cartas*, pp. 238–239; Tapia, "Relación," p. 110–112; Gómara, *La conquista de México*, pp. 197–200.

107. "Interrogatorio presentado," pp. 343–344; Díaz, *Historia*, chap. 107, pp. 207–208; Salazar, *Crónica*, 4.3031, pp. 342–345. Modern scholars tend to find these accounts more credible; see, for example, Clendinnen, "'Fierce and Unnatural Cruelty,'" p. 74; Gruzinski, *La guerre des images*, pp. 64–66; Henry R. Wagner, *The Rise of Fernando Cortés* (Berkeley, 1944), pp. 258–263.

108. Salazar, *Crónica*, 4.31, p. 345.

109. Cortés, "Segunda relación," in *Cartas*, p. 275; Peter Martyr, *De orbe novo*, 5.6, fol. 75r; Salazar, *Crónica*, 4.109, 4.118, pp. 473, 487–488; *Procesos de residencia*, p. 67. Díaz does mention the cross once more but focuses on the Marian image; *Historia*, chap. 125, p. 246.

110. Díaz, *Historia*, chap. 107, pp. 207–208.

111. Ibid., chap. 115, p. 222.

112. Ibid., chap. 115, p. 221.

113. Cortés, "Segunda relación," in Cortés, *Cartas*, p. 275. On the Spaniards' worsening situation and the Noche Triste, see among others: Townsend, *Malintzin's Choices*, pp. 96–108; Hassig, *Mexico and the Spanish Conquest*, pp. 107–120; Martínez, *Hernán Cortés*, pp. 258–274.

114. Oviedo, *Historia*, 33.47, 4:230.

115. Díaz, *Historia*, chap. 128, p. 259. Cf. Salazar, *Crónica*, 4.129, p. 503.

116. Elisa Vargaslugo argues for this banner's identification with Cortés, but in support cites only late eighteenth-century texts and a passage from Díaz that does not appear in modern editions; see her otherwise useful "Imágenes de la Inmaculada Concepción en la Nueva España," *Anuario de Historia de la Iglesia* 13 (2004): 67–71.

117. Salazar, *Crónica*, 5.72, p. 609.

118. See Chapter 8 of this volume.

119. See Chapter 8 of this volume.

120. Restall, *Seven Myths*, pp. 64–76.

121. On some of these expeditions, see Martínez, *Hernán Cortés*, pp. 347–358, 365–371.

122. Pedro de Alvarado, *An Account of the Conquest of Guatemala*, ed. Sedley J. Mackie (New York, 1924).

123. See Chapter 8 of this volume.

124. Cortés, "Quinta relación," in *Cartas*, pp. 545–546, 559–560, 574, 576; Díaz, *Historia*, chap. 183, p. 485. On this expedition, see Martínez, *Hernán Cortés*, pp. 417–445.

125. Díaz, *Historia*, chaps. 164, 165, pp. 410, 416.

126. Ibid., chap. 166, p. 425.

127. *Relación de Michoacán*, p. 274. On Tarascan coyote sacrificial stones, see Roberto Velasco Alonso, "Tarascan Art," in *Aztec Empire*, pp. 322–331 (here 325).

128. Díaz, *Historia*, chap. 165, p. 416.

129. Adorno, *Polemics of Possession*, pp. 61–98; Castro, *Another Face of Empire*.

130. Bartolomé de Las Casas, *Brevísima relación de le destruición de la Indias*, ed. André Saint-Lu, 10th ed. (Madrid, 1996).

131. For biographical details about Las Casas, see Manuel Giménez Fernández, "Fray Bartolomé de Las Casas: A Biographical Sketch," in *Bartolomé de las Casas in History: Toward an Understanding of the Man and His Work*, ed. Juan Friede and Benjamin Keen (DeKalb IL, 1971), pp. 67–125; O'Gorman, *Cuatro historiadores*, pp. 124–138.

132. Las Casas, *Historia de las Indias,* 2.63, 4:1556–1557.
133. Ibid., 3.24, 5:1858–1860.
134. Narváez's route: Rouse, *Tainos,* p. 156.
135. Las Casas, *Historia de las Indias,* 3.23, 5:1852.
136. Rouse, *Tainos,* p. 18.
137. Las Casas's attitude toward the Indians was shot through with such complexities; Castro, *Another Face of Empire.*
138. Cervantes, *Devil in the New World,* p. 11.
139. Trexler, "Aztec Priests," pp. 469–492.
140. For Spaniards' instructions about the care of Marian images and crosses, see Díaz, *Historia,* chaps. 28, 36, 52, 107, pp. 45, 60, 89, 208; Enciso, *Suma de geographia,* fol. h verso; Las Casas, *Historia de las Indias,* 2.60, 2:1544; Peter Martyr, *De orbe novo,* 2.6, fol. 30v.
141. Díaz, *Historia,* chap. 52, p. 89.
142. Ibid., chap. 107, p. 208.
143. Oviedo, *Historia,* 17.4, 2:115. Oviedo's emphasis on experience: Myers, *Fernández de Oviedo's Chronicle,* esp. pp. 33–40, 63–81; idem, "The Representation of New World Phenomena: Visual Epistemology and Gonzalo Fernández de Oviedo's Illustrations," in *Early Images of the Americas: Transfer and Invention,* ed. Jerry M. Williams and Robert E. Lewis (Tucson, 1993), pp. 183–213; Pagden, *European Encounters,* pp. 56–70.

Chapter 8

1. Phelan, *Millennial Kingdom.*
2. For introductions to the vast bibliography on the evangelization of New Spain, see Burkhart, *Slippery Earth*; Nicholas Griffiths, "Introduction," in *Spiritual Encounters,* pp. 1–42; Lara, *Christian Texts*; Osvaldo F. Pardo, *The Origins of Mexican Catholicism: Nahua Rituals and Christian Sacraments in Sixteenth-Century Mexico* (Ann Arbor, MI, 2004); Reff, *Plagues, Priests, and Demons*; and the essays in *The Spiritual Conversion of the Americas.* Mark Christensen's *Nahua and Maya Catholicisms: Texts and Religion in Colonial Central Mexico and Yucatan* (Stanford, 2013) appeared too late for me to incorporate its insights here.
3. Maya trade goods: Morley and Brainerd, *Ancient Maya,* p. 257.
4. "Interrogatorio presentado," p. 319. See also Cisneros, *Historia,* fol. 11v; Gómara, *La conquista de México,* pp. 60–61.
5. There is no indication that the cross Cortés had installed at Cozumel was used similarly.
6. "Interrogatorio presentado," p. 319. Maya clothing: Morley and Brainerd, *Ancient Maya,* pp. 235–240.
7. Clendinnen, *Aztecs,* p. 248.
8. On *ixipitla,* see Clendinnen, *Aztecs,* pp. 248–253; Gruzinski, *La guerre des images,* pp. 86–87; Hvidfeldt, *Teotl and *Ixiptlatli,* pp. 70–169 (esp. 98 on dress and ornament).
9. "Book Twelve of the Florentine Codex," chap. 28, p. 187 (and fig. 112, p. 181).
10. Clendinnen suggests this in general for the dressing of Marian statues by post-conquest Nahuas and Maya; "Ways to the Sacred," pp. 126–128.
11. For medieval examples, see *CSM,* no. 295, 3:85–87; Camille, *Gothic Idol,* p. 227; Hernández Díaz, *Iconografía medieval de la Madre de Dios,* p. 13. For analysis, see Trexler, "Dressing and Undressing Images." The Aragonese Madonna's wardrobe: Balaguer, "Santa María de Salas," pp. 218–219.
12. On the limitations of the term "conversion," see Griffiths, "Introduction," in *Spiritual Encounters,* p. 24; Lockhart, *Nahuas,* p. 203.
13. Bakewell and Hamman, "Painting History," p. 187; Kerpel, "Imágenes de la conquista."
14. For recent discussion, see Karen B. Graubart, "Learning from the Qadi: The Jurisdiction of Local Rule in the Early Colonial Cacicazgo" (unpublished article in progress).
15. Lockhart, *Nahuas,* p. 5. In this paragraph I largely follow the arguments of his luminous study. Cf. Lara, *Christian Texts,* p. 13.
16. For example, J. Jorge Klor de Alva, "Spiritual Conflict and Accommodation in New Spain: Toward a Typology of Aztec Responses to Christianity," in *The Inca and the Aztec States 1400–1800,* ed. George A. Collier, Renato I. Rosaldo, John D. Wirth (New York, 1982), pp. 345–366.

17. E.g., Cervantes, *Devil in the New World*, esp. pp. 40–73; Clendinnen, "Ways to the Sacred"; Farriss, *Maya Society under Colonial Rule*, pp. 286–351; Lara, *Christian Texts*; Lockhart, *Nahuas*, pp. 202–260; Taylor, *Magistrates*, pp. 47–62; Cynthia Radding, "Cultural Boundaries between Adaptation and Defiance: The Mission Communities of Northwestern New Spain," in *Spiritual Encounters*, pp. 116–135.

18. See the brilliant discussion in Burkhart, *Slippery Earth*.

19. Christian Duverger, *Pierres métisses: L'art sacré des indiens du Mexique au XVIe siècle* (Paris, 2003). On other ways that New Spain's colonial ecclesiastical architecture reflected indigenous religious beliefs, see Edgerton, *Theaters of Conversion*, pp. 1–105, 154–245.

20. Burkhart, *Before Guadalupe*. Cf. Hall, *Mary*, p. 105.

21. Burkhart, *Before Guadalupe*, pp. 4–5, 116, 131–148; Taylor, "Virgin of Guadalupe in New Spain," pp. 20–21; idem, *Magistrates*, pp. 292–293.

22. Burkhart, *Before Guadalupe*, p. 11; Lockhart, *Nahuas*, pp. 252–253.

23. Boone, *Stories in Red and Black*.

24. For chronologies of post-conquest writing, see Lockhart, *Nahuas*, p. 330–331; Serge Gruzinski, *La colonization de l'imaginaire: Sociétés indigènes et occidentalisation dans le Mexique espagnol XVIe–XVIIIe siècle* (Paris, 1988), pp. 15–100.

25. This pargraph and the next four draw on Enciso, *Suma de geographia*, fols. h verso–h ii recto; Las Casas, *Historia de las Indias*, 2.60, 3.29, 2:1544, 3:1876–1877; Peter Martyr, *De orbe novo*, 2.6, fols. 30r–31r.

26. Rouse, *Tainos*, p. 14.

27. On the feeding of *zemis*, see Rouse, *Tainos*, p. 14.

28. For another miracle story about the Tainos' love for the Ave Maria, see Enciso, *Suma de geographia*, fol. h ii recto.

29. Rouse, *Tainos*, p. 26.

30. "Interrogatorio presentado," p. 319; Díaz, *Historia*, chap. 28, p. 46.

31. This tradition: Farriss, *Maya Society under Colonial Rule*, p. 287.

32. Díaz, *Historia*, chap. 36, p. 59.

33. Medianero Hernández, "La gran *Tecleciguata*," pp. 379–380.

34. E.g., Lockhart, *Nahuas*, p. 120 (table 2.4); John Bierhorst, *A Nahuatl-English Dictionary and Concordance to the Cantares Mexicanos with an Analytic Transcription and Grammatical Notes* (Stanford, 1985), pp. 317, 594.

35. The term is not used for Mary in the numerous Nahuatl texts examined by Burkhart, *Before Guadalupe*; and Lockhart, *Nahuas*, pp. 252–253. For an example of the term applied to Malintzin, see the Nahuatl *Libro de los guardianes y gobernadores de Cuauhtinchan (1519–1640)*, ed. Constantino Medina Lima (Mexico City, 1995), p. 30. On the Malintzin/Mary association, see Navarrete, "La Malinche"; Townsend, *Malintzin's Choices*, pp. 78–79.

36. See below.

37. Cf. Farriss's argument that the Maya saw advantages in adopting the Christian god because of the military victories he gave the Spaniards; *Maya Society under Colonial Rule*, p. 287.

38. Oviedo, *Historia*, 50.10.29, 5:346–347. On the Spaniards' use of dogs, see John Grier Varner and Jeannette Johnson Varner, *Dogs of the Conquest* (Norman, OK, 1983) (p. 73 on Zuazo in particular).

39. Oviedo, *Historia*, 50.10.30, 5:347–349. For discussion, see Rodrigo Martínez, "La Virgen del licenciado Zuazo," in *Manifestaciones religiosas*, 2:131–149.

40. Burkhart, *Slippery Earth*, pp. 37 ff; Cervantes, *Devil in the New World*, p. 43.

41. Oviedo, *Historia*, 50.10.31, 5:349–350.

42. Gruzinski, *La guerre des images*, pp. 105–110; Lara, *Christian Texts*, pp. 49–57. Interestingly, despite the Franciscans' devotion to Mary, there is no mention of her in the extant version of their earliest sermons in Mexico; "El libro perdido de las Pláticas o Coloquios de los doce primeros misioneros de México," ed. José María Martín in *Miscellanea Francesco Ehrle*, 5 vols. (Rome, 1924), 3:281–333. This odd omission may be due to a later reworking of the texts; Martínez Baracs, *La secuencia tlaxcalteca*, p. 169, note 12.

43. Enciso, *Suma de geographia*, fol. h verso.

44. Motolinía, *Historia de los Indios*, 1.4, p. 24. For brief discussion, see Gruzinski, *Guerre des images*, pp. 69, 107.

45. *Relación de Michoacán*, chap. 27, p. 285. On this text's authorship and composition, see James Krippner-Martínez, "The Politics of Conquest: An Interpretation of the *Relación de Michoacán*," *The Americas* 47 (1990): 177-197.

46. Oviedo, *Historia*, 50.10.31, 5:350.

47. Sahagún, "Exercicio quotidiano," in Don Domingo de San Antón Muñon Chimalpahin Quauhtlehuanitzin, *Codex Chimalpahin: Society and Politics in Mexico Tenochtitlan, Tlatelolco, Texcoco, Culhuacan, and Other Nahua Altepetl in Central Mexico*, ed. and trans. Arthur J. O. Anderson and Susan Schroeder, 2 vols. (Norman, OK, 1997), 2:141.

48. Chimalpahin Quauhtlehuanitzin, *Annals*, p. 63.

49. López de Mendoza, *Información juridica*, pp. 8-9.

50. Burkhart, *Before Guadalupe*, p. 11.

51. Lockhart, *Nahuas*, pp. 252-253; cf. Burkhart, *Before Guadalupe*, p. 11.

52. Lockhart, *Nahuas*, pp. 237-238.

53. Gruzinski, *La guerre des images*, p. 107.

54. Motolinía, *Memoriales*, 26.3, p. 227.

55. Lockhart, *Nahuas*, pp. 16, 55.

56. Boone, *Stories in Red and Black*, p. 33 (fig. 3e), p. 207 (fig. 135).

57. Clendinnen, "'Fierce and Unnatural Cruelty,'" p. 78.

58. On the Nahua propensity to assimilate new gods, see Cervantes, *Devil in the New World*, pp. 42-43; Clendinnen, "'Fierce and Unnatural Cruelty,'" p. 78; Gruzinski, *La guerre des images*, p. 265; Lockhart, *Nahuas*, p. 203. (Cervantes, Gruzinski, and Lockhart argue that this attitude allowed Mesoamericans to accept Christian sacred figures, though not monotheism itself.)

59. Motolinía, *Historia de los Indios*, 1.3, p. 22.

60. Hernán Cortés, "Segunda relación," in *Cartas*, p. 275; Peter Martyr *De orbe novo*, 5.6, fol. 75r; Salazar, *Crónica*, 4.118, pp. 487-488.

61. On the vexed question of this temple's identity, see Thomas, *Conquest*, p. 731, note 52.

62. On the festival, see Carrasco, *City of Sacrifice*, pp. 118-139; Clendinnen, *Aztecs*, pp. 104-110; Doris Heyden, "Dryness Before the Rains: Toxcatl and Tezcatlipoca," in *To Change Place: Aztec Ceremonial Landscapes*, pp. 196-200; Hvidfeldt, *Teotl and *Ixiptlatli*, pp. 123-125.

63. Motolinía, *Memoriales*, 20.2, p. 207.

64. For Alvarado's account summarized in this paragraph, see *Procesos de residencia*, p. 67. Sahagún's native informants provided both a detailed description of the Toxcatl ceremonies and an entirely different account of the events precipitating the massacre; "Book Twelve of the Florentine Codex," chaps. 19-20, pp. 127-136, and figs. 57-58.

65. *Procesos de residencia*, pp. 113, 119, 127, 130, 134, 150 (cf. 93).

66. Ibid., p. 130. On Mexica priests' use of ashes, see Boone, *Stories in Red and Black*, p. 46.

67. *Procesos de residencia*, pp. 36-37.

68. "Book Twelve of the Florentine Codex."

69. *Anales de Tlatelolco: Unos anales históricos de la nación mexicana y Códice de Tlatelolco*, trans. and ed. Heinrich Berlin and Robert H. Barlow (Mexico City, 1948), pp. 62-63.

70. As well as the specific cases discussed below, see Kerpel, "Imágenes de la conquista"; and the classic studies of Miguel León Portilla, *The Broken Spears: The Aztec Account of the Conquest of Mexico*, rev. ed. (Boston, 1992); Nathan Wachtel, *La vision des vaincus: Les indiens de Pérou devant la Conquête espangnole, 1530-1570* (Paris, 1971), pp. 37-64.

71. On the Lienzo's complex history, see among others Asselbergs, "Conquest in Images"; Bakewell and Hamman, "Painting History," pp. 172-174; Gordon Brotherston and Ana Gallegos, "El Lienzo de Tlaxcala y el manuscrito de Glasgow (Hunter 242)," *Estudios de cultura Nahuatl* 20 (1990): 117-140; Kranz, "Sixteenth-Century Tlaxcalan Pictorial Documents."

72. For some discussion, see Martínez Baracs, *Secuencia tlaxcalteca*, pp. 121-129.

73. Gillespie, *Saints and Warriors*, p. 71.

74. For discussion of a similar situation in the Andes, see MacCormack, "From the Sun of the Incas," (esp. 48-50).

75. See the texts edited in Burkhart, *Before Guadalupe*.

76. "Book Twelve of the Florentine Codex."

77. Burkhart, *Before Guadalupe*, p. 3.
78. Wood, *Transcending Conquest*.
79. For extensive discussion of native conquistadors, see the essays in *Indian Conquistadors*.
80. Hassig, *War and Society in Ancient Mesoamerica*.
81. Wood, *Transcending Conquest*, p. 8.
82. Michel R. Ouijk and Matthew Restall, "Mesoamerican Conquistadors in the Sixteenth Century," in *Indian Conquistadors*, pp. 54–56. For an example, see the change of attitude by the Tlaxcalteca as recorded in *Tlaxcalan Actas*, pp. 106–108.
83. Adorno, *Polemics*, pp. 138–139, 144.
84. Francisco de Sandoval Acazitli, "Relación de la jornada," in *Colección de documentos para la historia de México*, 2:307–332.
85. E.g., "Book Twelve of the Florentine Codex," p. 185, figs. 114–116.
86. Hassig, *War and Society in Ancient Mesoamerica*, pp. 50, 97, 140, 143, 152, 153. On the Mexica *tlatoani's* standard, see Manuel Aguilar Moreno, *Handbook to Life in the Aztec World* (New York, 2006), p. 118, fig. 5.12a.
87. On the circumstances of the lawsuit, see Martínez, *Hernán Cortés*, pp. 613, 629–632.
88. Transcription of the testimony in "Harkness 1531 Huejotzingo Codex," p. 108.
89. Tom Cummins, "The Madonna and the Horse: Becoming Colonial in New Spain and Peru," in *Native Artists and Patrons in Colonial Latin America*, eds. Emily Umberger and Tom Cummins (Tempe, AZ, 1995), pp. 58–68.
90. Edgerton, *Theaters of Conversion*, pp. 111–127, 133–153; Gruzinski, *La guerre des images*, pp. 114–119.
91. "Harkness 1531 Huejotzingo Codex," p. 108 (cf. p. 116).
92. Altman, "Conquest, Coercion, and Collaboration," pp. 147–159.
93. On the chapel, see Juan de Sámano, "Relación de la conquista de los teules chichimecas," in *Colección de documentos para la historia de México*, 2:270. For Guzmán's exploitation of *indios amigos* for heavy labor, see Altman, "Conquest, Coercion, and Collaboration," pp. 152–153.
94. For their statements quoted over the next paragraphs, see López de Mendoza, *Información jurídica*, pp. 3–19.
95. On Acxotecatl, see Gibson, *Tlaxcala*, pp. 10–11, 23–24; Martínez Baracs, *La secuencia tlax-calteca*, pp. 139–142 (and 143–160 for discussion of the Marian statue).
96. Nahua association of flowers with the sacred: Louise M. Burkhart, "Flowery Heaven: The Aesthetic of Paradise in Nahuatl Devotional Literature," *Res: Anthropology and Aesthetics* 21 (1992): 88–109.
97. Lockhart, *Nahuas*, pp. 235–244; Serge Gruzinski, "Indian Confraternities, Brotherhoods and Mayordomías in Central New Spain," in *The Indian Community of Central Mexico*, ed. Arij Ouweneel and Simon Miller (Amsterdam, 1990), pp. 208–210, 215–218. For an Augustinian friar's remarks on the intense indigenous devotion to saints' images, see Gríjalva, *Crónica*, 2.6, p. 162.
98. Motolinia, *Memoriales*, chaps. 28–9, pp. 235–241.
99. On the Nahua use of Spanish insignia to enhance their prestige, see Lockhart, *Nahuas*, pp. 123–125; Wood, *Transcending Conquest*, pp. 49–59.
100. López de Mendoza, *Información jurídica*, pp. 1–2.
101. Gibson, *Tlaxcala*, pp. 34–37.
102. Muñoz Camargo, *Descripción de la* ciudad, pp. 265–267 (see also figs. 12, 14); Zapata y Mendoza, *Historia cronológica*, nos. 68, 135, pp. 105, 137; Mendieta, *Historia eclesiástica*, 3.25–26, 1:388–393. On generational warfare over Christianity, see Lara, *Christian Texts*, pp. 60–61; Richard C. Trexler, "From the Mouths of Babes: Christianization by Children in 16th Century New Spain," in *Religious Organization and Religious Experience*, ed. J. Davis (New York, 1982), p. 115–135.
103. Martínez Baracs, *La secuencia tlaxcalteca*, pp. 165–166.
104. On Tlaxcala's rain pattern and agricultural fertility, see Motolinía, *Memoriales*, 55.5–6, pp. 352–353.
105. For some biographical details about Juan de Rivas, see Ricard, *Spiritual Conquest*, pp. 58, 65. Chocomán's "lions and tigers:" Motolinía, *Memoriales*, 51.11, p. 329.
106. Wood, *Transcending Conquest*.

107. "Letter of the Cabildo of Huejotzingo to the King, 1560," in *We People Here*, pp. 288–297 (and pp. 45–46 for analysis).

108. Gibson, *Tlaxcala*, pp. 158–181.

109. *Tlaxcalan Actas*, no. 158, p. 58. On the *cabildo* building itself, see Gibson, *Tlaxcala*, pp. 125–126.

110. *Tlaxcalan Actas*, no. 122, p. 51. For extensive discussion, see Kranz, "Sixteenth-Century Tlaxcalan Pictorial Documents," pp. 11–13.

111. Kranz, "Sixteenth-Century Tlaxcalan Pictorial Documents," pp. 16, 18–19. For other discussion of indigenous consciously adopting "the values of Christian militancy," see Adorno, *Polemics*, pp. 139–146.

112. New sun and Tlaxcalteca privilege: Bakewell and Hamman, "Painting History," p. 187. Mary as embodiment of Tlaxcalteca centrality: Navarrete, "La Malinche," pp. 304–305. Neither article notes Mary's militarization.

113. The dating of the actual conversion event: Gibson, *Tlaxcala*, p. 30.

114. On the *Lienzo's* militarized depiction of the Tlaxcalteca's conversion and Christianity itself, see Gillespie, *Saints and Warriors*, esp. pp. 57–60, 83–110. The suggestion that the Lienzo's imagery shows a Tlaxcalteca crusading mentality was made by Alfred J. Andrea, "The Crusades in the Context of World History" (lecture, St. Louis University, November 3, 2006) [Online]. Available: http://www.crusades-encyclopedia.com/andrealecture.html [July 1, 2008].

115. A huge cross does loom over the *Lienzo's* depiction of the very first encounter between the Spaniards and the Tlaxcalteca. According to colonial legends, this cross appeared miraculously; Martínez Baracs, *Secuencia tlaxcalteca*, pp. 83–119.

116. Muñoz Camargo's complicated ethnic loyalties: Marilyn Miller, "Covert Mestizaje and the Strategy of 'Passing' in Diego Muñoz Camargo's *Historia de Tlaxcala*," *Colonial Latin American Review* 6 (1997): 41–58.

117. Muñoz Camargo, *Descripción de la ciudad*, 4:246 and fig. 33.

118. Motolinía, *Historia*, 3.14, pp. 174–176 (cf. Mendieta, *Historia eclesiástica*, 3.24, 1:385–386). The "casa...de Santa María" of Motolinía's story was probably the Franciscan convent in Tlaxcala, given that the Tlaxcalteca often called the friars the "padres de Santa María"; Martínez Baracs, *La secuencia tlaxcalteca*, p. 177.

119. In the 1580s, Muñoz Camargo went to Spain in order to present the Tlaxcalteca case to the king; Gibson, *Tlaxcala*, pp. 167–169.

120. See Chapter 7 of this volume. For a suggestion that the Marian painting depicted in the *Lienzo's* conversion scene refers to the image Cortés installed in the temple in 1519, see Martínez Baracs, *Secuencia tlaxcalteca*, pp. 76–82.

121. Lockhart, *Nahuas*, p. 244.

122. Motolinía, *Memoriales*, 5.9, p. 354; Gibson, *Tlaxcala*, pp. 44–45.

123. The scene as cosmogram: Bakewell and Hamman, pp. 174–175; Navarrete, "La Malinche," pp. 304–305. For other analysis of this scene, see Gillespie, *Saints and Warriors*, pp. 37–44.

124. Kranz, "Sixteenth-Century Tlaxcalan Pictorial Documents," p. 9.

125. Carrasco, *City of Sacrifice*, pp. 223–224, note 5. In the colonial era, hills and caves remained important to Nahua self-representation; Osowski, "Passion Miracles," p. 608.

126. On the transfer of loyalty owed the *altepetl's* god and temple to Christian saints and their churches, see Lockhart, *Nahuas*, pp. 235–237.

127. Asselbergs, "Conquest in Images," pp. 74–76.

128. Ibid., p. 91.

129. Zapata y Mendoza, *Historia cronológica*, no. 60, p. 103.

130. Gloss in Zapata y Mendoza, *Historia cronológica*, no. 129, p.133.

131. López de Mendoza, *Información jurídica*, p. 4.

132. "Water-Pouring Song," in *Cantares Mexicanos*, pp. 328–329. In this paragraph, I largely follow the provocative argument in Gillespie, *Saints and Warriors*, pp. 1–25, 123–133. Though Bierhorst's translation of the *Cantares* has been criticized (James Lockhart, "Care, Ingenuity, and Irresponsibility: The Bierhorst Edition of the *Cantares Mexicanos*," in his *Nahuas and Spaniards: Postconquest Central Mexican History and Philology* [Stanford, 1991], pp. 141–158), Louise Burkhart confirmed the accuracy of his rendering of the lines discussed here (private conversation, June 2013).

133. E.g., Townsend, *Malintzin's Choices*, p. 123 (though she notes that Malintzin here "bears a name reminiscent of the Virgin").
134. Gillespie, *Saints and Warriors*; Lawrence E. Sullivan, "Reflections on the Miraculous Waters of Tenochtitlan," in *To Change Place: Aztec Ceremonial Landscapes*, pp. 205–218.
135. On the land conflicts, see Lockhart, *Nahuas*, pp. 163–165.
136. For extensive analysis of the *Mapa*, see Wood, *Transcending Conquest*, pp. 77–106; and her "Nahua Christian Warriors," pp. 254–287.
137. For the text (in Spanish translation), see Starr, *Mapa de Cuauhtlantzinco*, nos. 19a–20a, p. 32 (cf. pp. 36–37).
138. Wood, "Nahua Christian Warriors," p. 267, fig. 8.17.
139. For the text (in Spanish translation), see Starr, *Mapa de Cuauhtlantzinco*, no. 18a, pp. 31–32 (cf. p. 36).
140. For the text (in Spanish translation), see Starr, *Mapa de Cuauhtlantzinco*, no. 7a, p. 31. Cf. the scene entitled the "conversion" of the inhabitants of Malacatepec, in which the Cuauhtlantzinca wield the steel swords of Castile to beat their club-bearing enemies into submission; Wood, "Nahua Christian Warriors," p. 261, fig. 8.5; Starr, *Mapa de Cuauhtlantzinco*, no. 5a, p. 30.
141. Starr, *Mapa de Cuauhtlantzinco*, no. 20a, p. 32.
142. There is evidence of indigenous peoples actually taking on missionizing roles; Jason Dyck, "Multiethnic Missionaries: The Myths of the 'Spiritual Conquest,' " unpublished paper presented at the John Carter Brown Library, 2013.
143. Castro Morales, "El Mapa de Chalchihuapan." On the relationship of this pictorial, the *Mapa de Cuahtlantzinco*, and the *Lienzo de Tlaxcala*, see Wood, *Transcending Conquest*, pp. 85, 88–90.
144. Castro Morales, "El Mapa de Chalchihuapan," figure 7.
145. Wood, *Transcending Conquest*, p. 95.
146. Lockhart, *Nahuas*, p. 132.
147. Hoekstra, *Two Worlds Emerging*, pp. 195–226.
148. The *Lienzo* as an expression of elite interests: Kranz, "Sixteenth-Century Tlaxcalan Pictorial Documents," p. 11. The *Mapas* as celebrations of local leaders' ancestors: Wood, *Transcending Conquest*, pp. 82–83, 95, 104. Lockhart (*Nahuas*, p. 391) notes Zapata y Mendoza's tendency to denigrate "political enemies" by making "snide remarks" about "their low social origins."
149. The Nahua elite claimed special connection to other miraculous Christian objects in an effort to shore up their own status in the colonial world; Osowski, "Passion Miracles."
150. Gibson, *Tlaxcala*, pp. 54–56, 59.
151. By 1575, some Tlaxcalteca lived and worked in Puebla; Gibson, *Tlaxcala*, p. 181.
152. López de Mendoza, *Información juridica*, pp. 6–7.
153. See Chapter 9 of this volume.
154. Starr, *Mapa de Cuauhtlantzinco*, no. 18a, p. 32 (cf. p. 36).
155. For a contemporaneous description of the chapel, see Vetancurt, *Chronica*, 4.2.3, pp. 55. See also Gauvin Alexander Bailey, *Art of Colonial Latin America* (London, 2005), p. 218 and fig. 117.

Chapter 9

1. Tapia, "Relación," pp. 127–129.
2. Ibid., p. 144.
3. Kagan, *Urban Images*, pp. 32–36; Alfonso Ortiz Crespo, "The Spanish American Colonial City: Its Origins, Development, and Functions," in *The Arts in Latin America 1492–1820*, ed. Joseph J. Rishel and Suzanne Stratton-Pruitt (New Haven, 2006), pp. 23–37 (esp. 25–26, 32).
4. For an introduction to colonial New Spain's racial politics, see Cope, *Limits of Racial Domination*.
5. Brading, *First America*, p. 3 and *passim*.
6. *Procesos de residencia*, p. 130.
7. Thomas (*Conquest*, p. 385) suggests that the image was fixed to a surface by nails, and that the Mexica could not figure out how to unfasten these unfamiliar devices. This assumes a

rather unbelievable naïveté in the Mexica, a people whose technical expertise consistently impressed the Spaniards.

8. Díaz, *Historia*, chap. 125, p. 246; Oviedo, *Historia*, 33.47, 4:277; Salazar, *Crónica*, 4.109, p. 473; Gómara, *La conquista de México*, p. 231.

9. Salazar, *Crónica*, 4.118, pp. 487–488.

10. Díaz, *Historia*, chap. 125, p. 246; Gómara, *La conquista de México*, p. 231; Salazar, *Crónica*, 4.110, p. 474.

11. Durán, *Historia de las Indias*, 1.78, 1:645; Robert H. Barlow, "Una pintura de la conquista en el templo de Santiago," in *Tlatelolco: Fuentes y historia* (vol. 2 of *Obras de Robert H. Barlow*, ed. Jesús Monjarás-Ruiz, Elena Limón, and María de la Cruz Paillés H., 7 vols. [Mexico City, 1987–1999]), pp. 211–216.

12. Gómara, *La Conquista de México*, pp. 231–232. Here he also states that "la mujer que peleaba era madre de Cristo."

13. Díaz, *Historia*, chap. 125, p. 246.

14. Ibid., chaps. 93–94, pp. 179–181.

15. Ibid., chap. 94, p. 181.

16. Ibid., chap. 94, p. 181. This sentiment was echoed in 1604 by Dorantes de Carranza, *Sumaria relación*, p. 17.

17. For a medieval parallel, see Chapter 1 of this volume at note 65.

18. On other colonial miracles stories in which the Spanish drew on "native rhetoric," see Osowski, "Passion Miracles," p. 637.

19. See Chapter 8 of this volume.

20. Brading, *First America*, p. 140; MacCormack, "From the Sun of the Incas," p. 58, note 37.

21. In the earliest Andean versions of the story, an unidentified Castilian woman on the roof of a burning church smothers the flames (Juan de Betanzos, *Narrative of the Incas*, 2.32, trans. Roland Hamilton and Dana Buchanan [Austin, 1996], p. 290)—and only Santiago fights beside the Spaniards (Juan de Matienzo, *Gobierno del Peru (1567)*, chap. 2 [Paris/Lima, 1967], pp. 13–14). The later introduction of the dirt-throwing Madonna suggests Mexican influence.

22. Felipe Guaman Poma de Ayala, *Nueva crónica y buen gobierno*, ed. John V. Murra, Rolena Adorno, and Jorge L. Urioste, 3 vols. (Madrid, 1987), 2:408–410, 2:686–289 for the story and 2:411 for the image. For an introduction to this author, see Rolena Adorno, "Felipe Guaman Poma de Ayala: Native Writer and Litigant in Early Colonial Peru," in *Human Tradition in Colonial Latin America*, pp. 140–163.

23. Johanna Broda, "The Provenience of the Offerings: Tribute to *Cosmovisión*," in *The Aztec Templo Mayor: A Symposium at Dumbarton Oaks October 8th and 9th, 1983*, ed. Elizabeth Hill Boone (Washington, DC, 1986), p. 217, note 6.

24. Sand patterns: Gordon Brotherstone, "Sacred Sand in Mexican Picture-Writing and Later Literature," *Estudios de cultura náhuatl* 11 (1974): 303–309. The enigmatic ritual of "Entering the Sand": María Elena Bernal-García, "The Dance of Time, the Procession of Space at Mexico-Tenochtitlan's Desert," in *Sacred Gardens and Landscapes: Ritual and Agency*, ed. Michel Conan (Cambridge, MA, 2007), pp. 84, 101 (note 204); Clendinnen, *Aztecs*, p. 218; Charles E. Dibble, "The *Xalaquia* Ceremony," *Estudios de cultura náhuatl* 14 (1980): 197–202.

25. Ocaña recounts his journey in his remarkable *Un viaje fascinante*. For discussion, see the forthcoming study by Kenneth Mills, as well as his "Diego de Ocaña: Holy Wanderer," in *Human Tradition in Colonial Latin America*, pp. 121–139; and his "La 'Memoria Viva.'"

26. On *Moros y Cristianos* plays, see Max Harris, *Aztecs, Moor and Christians: Festivals of Reconquest in Mexico and Spain* (Austin, TX, 2000); the articles in *Moros y Cristianos*.

27. For one example, see Ocaña, *Un viaje fascinante*, Appendix 5, pp. 332–347.

28. The two performances: Ocaña, *Un viaje fascinante*, Appendix 5, p. 330; the play's text, Appendix 6, pp. 367–433.

29. Ibid., Appendix 6, pp. 428–429.

30. E.g., Talavera, *Historia de Nuestra Señora de Guadalupe*, 1.7, fol. 19r.

31. *Memorias del cautivo*, p. 129.

32. Ibid., p. 127.

33. Talavera, *Historia de Nuestra Señora de Guadalupe*, fol. 156v.
34. Ocaña, *Un viaje fascinante*, Appendix 5, pp. 339–340.
35. At least not to my knowledge.
36. The date of the chapel's foundation is much debated; Poole, *Our Lady of Guadalupe*, pp. 34–68.
37. Dorantes de Carranza, *Sumaria relación*, p. 35.
38. *Andalucía Americana*, pp. 190–192; Mena García, *Sevilla y las flotas*, p. 25, note 1.
39. Valdivieso, *Historia de la pintura sevillana*, pp. 23–24 and figure 5.
40. Here I follow the account in Díaz, *Historia*, chap. 128, pp. 25–257.
41. Cited in Miranda Godínez, *Dos cultos*, pp. 41–42.
42. "Interrogatorio presentado," p. 364.
43. Díaz, *Historia*, chap. 128, p. 257. Cf. Salazar, *Crónica*, 4.126, p. 499.
44. S. Linné, *El valle y la ciudad de Mexico en 1550: Relación histórica fundada sobre un mapa geográfico, que se conserva en la biblioteca de la Universidad de Uppsala, Suecia* (Stockholm, 1948), esp. the plate entitled "Mapa III." Perhaps the chapel was sometimes called "Saint Mary of Victory" because the Spaniards had named the indigenous shrine on Totoltepec "the Temple of Victory"; Salazar, *Crónica de la Nueva España*, 4.126, p. 499.
45. Cisneros, *Historia*, 1.9, fol. 40r.
46. Ibid., 1.10, fols. 44v–44r.
47. The text is edited from the *Actas* of Mexico City's *cabildo* by Miranda Godínez, *Dos cultos*, pp. 49–50 (here 49).
48. Miranda Godínez, *Dos cultos*, pp. 73–77.
49. On *criollo* pride in this period, see among others: Brading, *First America*, esp. pp. 2–5, 293–313; Cañizares Esguerra, "Racial, Religious, and Civic Creole Identity."
50. Alan Knight, *Mexico: The Colonial Era* (Cambridge, 2002), pp. 18–19.
51. On the plot and *criollo* pride, see Pagden, "Identity Formation," pp. 54–56.
52. Brading, *First America*, pp. 2, 293.
53. Miranda Godínez, *Dos cultos*, pp. 23, 27, 111.
54. Text edited in Miranda Godínez, *Dos cultos*, p. 49.
55. On these processions, see Cisneros, *Historia*, 2, fols. 80r–132v; Curcio-Nagy, "Native Icon," pp. 378–380; Miranda Godínez, *Dos cultos*, pp. 147–163.
56. Chimalpahin Quauhtlehuanitzin, *Annals*, p. 61.
57. Cisneros, *Historia*, 2.3, fols. 91v–95r; Miranda Godínez, *Dos cultos*, pp. 151–153.
58. Text edited in Miranda Godínez, *Dos cultos*, p. 49.
59. Díaz, *Historia*, chap. 128, p. 257. The two most important modern historians of Los Remedios' cult believe that it was in decline by the 1570s, but neither mentions Díaz's remark; Curcio-Nagy, "Native Icon," pp. 370, 374; Miranda Godínez, *Dos cultos*, p. 112.
60. Miranda Godínez, *Dos cultos*, p. 91.
61. On the confraternity, see Miranda Godínez, *Dos cultos*, pp. 62–64, 155–156.
62. All quotations in this paragraph are from the confraternity's ordinances edited in Miranda Godínez, *Dos cultos*, pp. 65–69.
63. E.g.. the language of Pope Gregory XIII's 1576 privilege for Los Remedios' chapel and confraternity; *America Pontifica*, no. 340, 2:1059. An official in the papal chancery drafted these phrases, but the sentiment animating them originated in Mexico.
64. Durán, *Historia de las Indias*, 1.75–76, 1:623–624, 627–629, 631.
65. Federico Gómez de Orozco, "Las pinturas de Alonso de Villasana en el Santuario de Los Remedios," *Anales del Instituto de Investigaciones Estéticas* 15 (1946): 65–80.
66. Cisneros's *Historia* was published posthumously in 1621. On the construction of the new church beginning in the 1620s, see Miranda Godínez, *Dos cultos*, pp. 184–191.
67. Cisneros, *Historia*, fols. 49v–50r, 57v.
68. Ibid., fols. 57v–58r. On the use of classical imagery in colonial Spanish America, see Lupher, *Romans in a New World*.
69. Cisneros, *Historia*, fol. 58v.
70. At least to my knowledge.
71. Cisneros, *Historia*, fols. 50v–51v.
72. Ibid., 1.10, fols. 41v, 42v.

73. Ibid., 1.1, fols. 3r–v, 4r.
74. Ibid., 1.6, fols. 26r–v.
75. Ibid., 1.6, fol. 26v.
76. Cisneros's statement of his *criollo* identity is in the unpaginated prologue to the *Historia*.
77. Cisneros, *Historia*, 1.2, fols. 6v–7r.
78. Ibid., 1.6, fol. 26r.
79. Ibid., 1.2, fol. 7r–v.
80. Ibid., 1.2, fol. 7v.
81. Ibid., 1.2, fol. 8r–v.
82. Ibid., 1.2, fols. 7v, 8v.
83. Ibid., 1.2, fol. 7v.
84. Ibid., 1.6, fols. 27r–28r.
85. Ibid., 1.4, fols. 15v–19r. For the many Madonnas in Mexico City, see the ones he lists (*Historia*, 1.6, fols. 20r–23v) and those mentioned by Chimalpahin, *Annals*, pp. 33, 47, 75, 77.
86. On the research methods of colonial "sacred historians" like Cisneros, see Dyck, "The Sacred Historian's Craft," pp. 91–199.
87. On Villafuerte's activities in New Spain, see Martínez, *Hernán Cortés*, pp. 136, 319, 320, 35, 356, 671; Thomas, *Conquest*, pp. 423, 454, 476, 495–496, 533, 541, 549, 558.
88. For both versions of Los Remedios' past, see Cisneros, *Historia*, 1.6. fols. 25v–26r.
89. Ibid., 1.6, foli. 28r.
90. Florencia, *Zodiaco Mariano*, p. 201. Cf. Vetancurt, *Chronica*, 4.2.3, 4.5.4, pp. 49–50, 132. On Florencia, see Dyck, "The Sacred Historian's Craft."
91. Cisneros reports these claims in his *Historia*, 1.6, fols. 27r–28r.
92. Florencia, *Zodiaco Mariano*, p. 202.
93. Cisneros, *Historia*, 1.6, fols. 27v–28r.
94. Puebla's site and foundation: Motolinía, *Memoriales*, 57.1–12, pp. 363–368.
95. Ramos, *Identity, Ritual and Power*, pp. xxii, 13, 182.
96. For the material in this paragraph, see Gamboa Ojeda, "Los españoles," pp. 23–24, 26.
97. Porras y López and Porras de Hidalgo, *Puebla*, pp. 69–79.
98. Gamboa Ojeda, "Los españoles," p. 25; Altman, *Transatlantic Ties*.
99. Porras y López and Porras de Hidalgo, *Puebla*, pp. 133–136.
100. On the church, see Porras y López and Porras de Hidalgo, *Puebla*, pp. 124–125.
101. True, the aging Nahua noblemen gave their testimony at Tlaxcala and not Puebla. But by the later sixteenth century, Puebla "dominated the religious affairs of Tlaxcala"; Gibson, *Tlaxcala*, pp. 60–61 (here 61).
102. See below.
103. This confraternity lasted until at least the late seventeenth century; Florencia, *Zodiaco Mariano*, p. 202; Vetancurt, *Chronica*, 4.2.3, 4.5.4, pp. 49–50, 132. On some of its sixteenth-century members, see Altman, *Transatlantic Ties*, p. 123.
104. Juan de Torquemada, *Monarquía Indiana*, 3.30, ed. Miguel León Portilla, 3 vols. (Mexico City, 1969), 1:315. On Torquemada, see Brading, *First America*, pp. 275–292.
105. The text is edited in López de Villaseñor, *Cartilla vieja*, p. 239.
106. Ibid., pp. 239–241.
107. For the details in this paragraph, see the document of 1653 in ibid., pp. 241–242. On the city's many patron saints, see Ramos, *Identity, Ritual, and Power*, pp. 82–83.
108. On Puebla's cabildo as leaders of religious ritual, see Ramos, *Identity, Ritual, and Power*, pp. 67–68, 70–74, 103.
109. López de Villaseñor, *Cartilla vieja*, pp. 222–228, 244–246. Through this fiesta, Puebla's civic government was also expressing loyalty to the Spanish monarchs, fervent promoters of this Virgin; Loreto López, "La fiesta de la Concepción." Other aspects of Puebla's Marian cult also expressed the city's relation to the ruler; Montserrat Galí Boadella, "El regio patronato indiano y el retablo principal de la catedral de Puebla," in *Presencia española*, pp. 91–105. For extensive discussion of ritual as shaping force in Puebla's civic and political life somewhat later in the colonial period, see Ramos, *Identity, Ritual, and Power*. On Mexico City's festive

life, see Linda A. Curcio-Nagy, *The Great Festivals of Colonial Mexico City: Performing Power and Identity* (Albuquerque, 2004).

110. López de Villaseñor, *Cartilla vieja*, p. 448. Such strife was widespread among New Spain's Franciscans; Brading, *First America*, p. 298.

111. Hoekstra, *Two Worlds Emerging*, pp.161–171, 192. On the Franciscans' declining control over the indigenous in general, see Brading, *First America*, pp. 235–236.

112. For the details in this paragraph, see Cisneros, *Historia*, fols. 79r–v; Miranda Godínez, *Dos cultos*, pp. 80–83, 132–137.

113. Cisneros, *Historia*, fols. 79r–v.

114. For López's argument, see Miranda Godínez, *Dos cultos*, p. 80. On the slow progression of Spanish among the Nahuas, see Lockhart, *Nahuas*, pp. 319–320.

115. On this ideology and its lack of congruity with racial realities, see Cope, *Limits of Racial Domination*, esp. pp. 3, 50.

116. On the trope of Mexico City as a New Rome, see Kagan, *Urban Images*, p. 151. In general on the use of Roman imagery in New Spain, see Lupher, *Romans in a New World*.

117. The paintings were described by Cisneros, *Historia*, 1.12, fol. 62v.

118. Ibid., 1.3, fols. 9v–14r (here 10v); cf. 1.2, fol. 7r.

119. Ibid., 1.3, fol. 11v.

120. Ibid., 1.2, fol. 7r–v. I thank Jorge Flores for his generous help in identifying *Benopotama* as Mozambique.

121. Cisneros, *Historia*, 1.12, fol. 58v.

122. López de Mendoza (scribe), *Información jurídica*, p. 2.

123. True, after watching indigenous nobles from "forty provinces and pueblos" solemnly gather to celebrate Easter and Marian prayer in 1544, Motolinía wrote that indeed it seemed to him that "all generations called" Mary "blessed" as she had predicted in the Gospel of Luke. Yet he did not did not proclaim her the actual agent of their conversion; Motolinía, *Memoriales*, 31.4, pp. 246–247.

124. Text edited in Miranda Godínez, *Dos cultos*, p. 65.

125. Bernardo de Lizana, *Devocionario de Nuestra Señora de Izamal y conquista espiritual de Yucatán*, 1.1.13, ed. René Acuña (Mexico City, 1995), p. 89.

126. For the preceding points about miracle, see Gruzinski, *La guerre des images*, esp. pp. 165–167, 202; Osowski, "Passion Miracles"; Rubial García, "Tierra de prodigios," pp. 357–364. In this period, Jesuits on New Spain's northern frontier even expressed their missionary achievements in the language of miracle, a rhetorical technique earlier evangelists had avoided; Reff, *Plagues, Priests, and Demons*, pp. 216–217.

127. Here I draw on Rubial García's ideas about the miraculous as a weapon against idolatry ("Tierra de prodigios," esp. p. 358) and on Fernando Cervantes's analysis of the growing pessimism about whether it was possible to extirpate native idolatry (*Devil in the New World*, pp. 34–35).

128. Brading, *Mexican Phoenix*, pp. 46–47.

129. Brading, *First America*, p. 297.

130. Ibid., esp. pp. 2–3, 295–297, 306–310; Cañizares Esguerra, "Racial, Religious, and Civic Creole Identity."

131. Cañizares Esguerra, "Racial, Religious, and Civic Creole Identity," pp. 425–428.

132. Pagden, "Identity Formation," pp. 54–55.

133. Native testimony was often crucial to the *criollo* men who wrote New Spain's "sacred history"; Dyck, "The Sacred Historian's Craft," pp. 193-198.

134. Cisneros, *Historia*, 1.12, fol. 52r.

135. For Cisneros's tale described in this and the following paragraphs, see his *Historia*, 1.6–1.10, fols. 28v–30r, 31r–41v.

136. The indigenous peoples around Tacuba—largely Otomís—in fact had fought against the Spaniards.

137. Curcio-Nagy, "Native Icon," pp. 380–381, 383–388.

138. Durán, *Historia de las Indias*, 2.15, 2:148–149.

139. The cycle of murals also contained numerous paintings of the sun, intended to evoke the dawning of a new era as Mary and her son brought Christianity to Mexico, but also

reminiscent of pre-Columbian solar disks signaling divinity in Mesomerica; Curcio-Nagy, "Native Icon," pp. 375–376.

140. Cisneros, *Historia*, 1.8, fol. 35r. On *tecomatl*, see Lockhart, *Nahuas*, pp. 70, 193.
141. Cisneros, *Historia*, 1.7 and 1.9, fols. 32v, 34r, 38v.
142. Burkhart, " 'Here Is Another Marvel,' " pp. 131–132; idem, *Before Guadalupe*, p. 131.
143. On these traits of Nahua miracle stories, see Osowski, "Passion Miracles."
144. Lockhart, *Nahuas*, pp. 240–242.
145. Miranda Godínez, *Dos cultos*, p. 167.
146. Cisneros, *Historia*, 1.12, fols. 52r–53r.
147. Dorantes de Carranza, *Sumaria relación*, pp. 30–31. On this author's *criollo* patriotism, see Brading, *First America*, pp. 295–297; Merrim, *Spectacular City*, pp. 135–140.
148. For example, Grijalva, *Crónica*, pp. 182–185; Florencia, *Zodiaco Mariano*, pp. 116–120; Vetancurt, *Cronica*, 4.54, pp. 128–130.
149. Christian, *Apparitions*, pp. 16–149.
150. Curcio-Nagy, "Native Icon," pp. 371–372; Alberro, "Remedios y Guadalupe," pp. 161–162.
151. Grijalva, *Crónica*, 2.14, pp. 188–189.
152. Cisneros, *Historia*, 1.12, fol. 53r.
153. For one example, see Bravo Navarro and Sancho Roda, *La Almudena*, p. 32.
154. A rare exception is the Muslim in the legend of Nuestra Señora de la Yedra; Martín de Ximena Jurado, *Catalogo de los obispos de las iglesias cathedrales de la diocesis de Jaén...* (Madrid, 1654), p. 381.
155. Dorantes de Carranza, *Sumaria relación*, pp. 30–31.
156. Cisneros, *Historia*, 1.7, fol. 31r.
157. On legend's origins and meaning, see among many others: Brading, *Mexican Phoenix*; Jeanette Favrot Person, "Creating the Virgin of Guadalupe: The Cloth, Artist, and Sources in Sixteenth-Century New Spain," *The Americas* 61 (2005): 571–610; idem, "Canonizing a Cult: A Wonder-Working Guadalupe in the Seventeenth Century," in *Religion in New Spain*, ed. Susan Schroeder and Stafford Poole (Albuquerque, 2007), pp. 125–156; Poole, *Our Lady of Guadalupe*; William B. Taylor, "Mexico's Virgin of Guadalupe in the Seventeenth Century," in *Colonial Saints: Discovering the Holy in the Americas, 1500 to 1800*, ed. Allan Greer and Jodi Bilinkoff (New York, 2003), pp. 277–298; idem, "Virgin of Guadalupe in New Spain."
158. *Story of Guadalupe*, pp. 89, 139.
159. Dunnington and Mann, *Viva Guadalupe!*; Zarebska, *Guadalupe*.
160. Alberro, "Remedios y Guadalupe," pp. 151–164; Brading, *Mexican Phoenix*, pp. 68–69, 71–72, 153–154.
161. The story appears in his preface to Zapata y Mendoza, *Historia cronológica*, p. 81. On the legend's development, see Martínez Baracs, *La secuencia tlaxcalteca*, esp. pp. 13–43.
162. Martínez Baracs, *La secuencia tlaxcalteca*. For different interpretations, see Serge Gruzinski, *Man-Gods in the Mexican Highlands: Indian Power and Colonial Society, 1520–1800* (Stanford, 1989), pp. 89–104; Hall, *Mary*, pp. 134–136.
163. Loreto López, "La fiesta de la Concepción."
164. Curcio-Nagy, "Native Icon," p. 377.
165. Florencia, *Zodiaco mariano*, p. 117.
166. Grijalva, *Crónica*, 2.14, p. 183.
167. See Chapter 8 of this volume.
168. Francisco Antonio de Fuentes y Guzmán, *Recordación florida: Discurso historial y demonstración natural, material, military y politica del Reyno de Guatemala*, 6.2, 3 vols. (Guatemala, 1932–1933), 1:164–165. On Fuentes y Guzmán's *criollo* patriotism and his relation to Díaz, see Brading, *First America*, pp. 306–310.

Chapter 10

1. The account of the Oñate expedition in the following pages draws on Kessell, *Pueblos, Spaniards*, pp. 25–43; Riley, *Kachina and Cross*, pp. 37–49; Simmons, *Last Conquistador*; Wilcox, *Pueblo Revolt*, pp. 129–134.

2. See the description of 1597 cited by Ralph Emerson Twitchell, *Old Santa Fe: The Story of New Mexico's Ancient Capital* (Santa Fe, 1925), p. 27. Simmons (*Last Conquistador*, p. 59) mistakes the Velasco banner as a gift to Oñate from the viceroy Luis de Velasco. On Captain Luis Gasco de Velasco, see Knaut, *Pueblo Revolt*, pp. 137–138.

3. Inventory in *Don Juan de Oñate*, 1:251.

4. Oñate's description of New Mexico's natural and human wealth is edited in *Don Juan de Oñate*, 1:483–485.

5. On this meaning of "pueblo," and Spaniards' association of urban life and civilization, see Kagan, *Urban Images*, pp. 26–28.

6. On these earlier expeditions, see Weber, *Spanish Frontier*, pp. 45–49; Wilcox, *Pueblo Revolt*, pp. 105–113.

7. On the Chichimecs' reputation, see Charlotte M. Gradie, "Discovering the Chichimecs," *The Americas* 51 (1994): 67–88.

8. Kessell, *Kiva, Cross, and Crown*, pp. 31–37; idem, "Restoring Seventeenth-Century New Mexico," pp. 46–48.

9. Weber, *Spanish Frontier*, pp. 78–81.

10. On these earlier expeditions, see Kessell, *Kiva, Cross, and Crown*, pp. 37–62; Wilcox, *Pueblo Revolt*, pp. 113–129.

11. Kessell, *Kiva, Cross, and Crown*, p. 70–71.

12. On the 1573 proclamation and the foregrounding of mission over conquest, see: Seed, *Ceremonies of Possession*, p. 95; Weber, *Spanish Frontier*, p. 78.

13. On the violence of the Spanish colonization of New Mexico, see Wilcox, *Pueblo Revolt*, esp. pp. 75–79, 105–148.

14. Weber, *Spanish Frontier*, p. 78.

15. *Don Juan de Oñate*, 1:485.

16. "Conquest dramas": Gutiérrez, *When Jesus Came*, pp. 48–49.

17. Gutiérrez, *When Jesus Came*, p. 48, who cites Manuel Espinosa, *First Expedition of Vargas into New Mexico, 1692* (Albuquerque, 1940), p. 59, note 2. Yet Espinosa provides no supporting documentation. As early as 1948, Angélico Chávez pointed to the dearth of evidence for any such banner in Oñate's company: see his *Our Lady of the Conquest*, p. 27, note 41. But the legend of Oñate's banner continues to cast its spell, as is evident not only from Gutiérrez's statement but also the assertion by some leading contemporary historians of colonial New Mexico that the banner of Los Remedios used by Diego de Vargas in the 1690s was "Oñate's original royal standard"; *To the Royal Crown Restored*, p. 373. On Vargas's banner, see below.

18. Monica Soto, "Banner Greets Spanish Dignitaries," *Santa Fe New Mexican*, April 28, 1998, pp. A1, A3.

19. The same is true of a banner flaunting Mary and Santiago brought to New Mexico in 1600 by the official standard bearer for one of Oñate's captains' companies: G. P. Hammond, "The Founding of New Mexico: Chapter XI," *New Mexico Historical Review* 2 (1927): 168 (Appendix B); see also Chávez, *Our Lady of the Conquest*, p. 27, note 41.

20. On the battle as well as divergent accounts of its precipitating events, see: Kessell, *Kiva, Cross, and Crown*, pp. 84–86; Knaut, *Pueblo Revolt*, pp. 36–46; Riley, *Kachina and Cross*, pp. 79–81; Wilcox, *Pueblo Revolt*, pp. 130–133. Kessell (*Pueblos, Spaniards*, pp. 41–42) believes that the maimings were probably never carried out. In any case, the savagery of this punishment still sears Pueblo memory; Gonzales, "'History Hits the Heart.'"

21. Ward Alan Mingus, *Acoma: Pueblo in the Sky*, rev. ed. (Albuquerque, 1991), pp. 20–21.

22. Both passages from Sánchez's letter: *Don Juan de Oñate*, 1:427.

23. Villagrá, *Historia*, Canto 34, lines 183–194, 223–227, pp. 298–299. On this poem, see Luis Leal, "Gaspar Pérez de Villagrá," in *A Luis Leal Reader*, ed. Ilan Stavans (Evanston, IL, 2007), pp. 90–114.

24. There is some confusion over the exact date. The editors of Villagrá's poem say it was January 22 or 24 (Villagrá, *Historia*, p. 299, notes 5 and 19), but I can find no major Marian feast day on either of those dates that would have been celebrated in this period. On January 23, however, sixteenth-century Christians celebrated Mary's espousal to Joseph. By the 1620s, a Franciscan would assert that the victory occurred on January 25; see below.

25. On the geographic origins of Oñate's company, see references below in note 36.

26. Miguel R. López, "Disputed History and Poetry: Gaspar Pérez de Villagrá's *Historia de la Nueva México*," *Bilingual Review* 26 (2001): 43–55.

27. Benavides, *Revised Memorial*, pp. 166, 196–197.

28. Text edited in Chávez, *Our Lady of the Conquest*, p. 79. Chávez's archivally based study is much more reliable than J. Manuel Espinosa's "The Virgin of the Reconquest of New Mexico," *Mid-America: An Historical Review* 18 (1936): 79–87.

29. This wardrobe is listed in the inventory of 1686 edited in Chávez, *Our Lady of the Conquest*, pp. 79–81.

30. On the statue's measurements and appearance, see Chávez, *Our Lady of the Conquest*, pp. 29–32. On the type of wood from which it is made, see Chevalier, *La Conquistadora*, pp. 29–31, 34.

31. Text edited in Chávez, *Our Lady of the Conquest*, pp. 88–89.

32. On the colonists' self-image, see Gutiérrez, *When Jesus Came*, pp. 98, 101–108, 130.

33. Kessell, *Pueblos, Spaniards*; idem, "Restoring Seventeenth-Century New Mexico," p. 52.

34. For these population figures, see Gutiérrez, *When Jesus Came*, p. 92; David J. Weber, "Introduction," in *What Caused the Pueblo Revolt?* p. 16, note 3. These estimates have been questioned by Wilcox, *Pueblo Revolt*, pp. 122–123, 207–208.

35. Kessell, "Restoring Seventeenth-Century New Mexico," p. 52; Knaut, *Pueblo Revolt*, pp. 136–151; Riley, *Kachina and Cross*, pp. 127–139, 143–155.

36. On the colonists' geographical origins, see Jones, *Los Paisanos*, p. 130; Kraemer, "Dynamic Ethnicity," pp. 80–81, 84.

37. The Chalcan chronicler Chimalpahin Quauhtlehuanitzin remembered their ceremonious departure in 1591 for what he called "New Mexico"; see his *Annals*, p. 37.

38. On the Tlaxcalteca in the Spanish colonization of northern Mexico and their persistent identity as native conquistadors, see Andrea Martínez Baracs, "Colonizaciones tlaxcaltecas," *Historia Mexicana* 43 (1993–1994): 195–250. On the vexed question of their presence in New Mexico, see Jones, *Los Paisanos*, p. 131; Kraemer, "Dynamic Ethnicity," p. 87; and especially Marc Simmons, "Tlascalans in the Spanish Borderlands," *New Mexico Historical Review* 39 (1964): 101–110.

39. For the details about race and ethnic identity in this paragraph, see: Jones, *Los Paisanos*, p. 130; Kessell, "Restoring Seventeenth-Century New Mexico," pp. 48, 50–51; idem, "Ways and Words," pp. 30–32; Kraemer, "Dynamic Ethnicity," 80–81, 84.

40. Chávez, *Our Lady of the Conquest*, pp. 15–16.

41. Ibid., pp. 6, 15–16, 79.

42. The supply train's inventory: Benavides, *Revised Memorial*, p. 121.

43. On pre-1680 Santa Fe and the early colony's ecclesiastical architecture, see Riley, *Kachina and Cross*, pp. 131–133; Wilson, *Myth of Santa Fe*, pp. 24–26.

44. *A Harvest of Reluctant Souls: The Memorial of Fray Alonso de Benavides, 1630*, chap. 30, trans. Baker H. Morrow (Niwot, CO, 1996), pp. 76–78; Benavides, *Revised Memorial*, chap. 49, pp. 91–92.

45. Chávez, *Our Lady of the Conquest*, pp. 34–35. For the crate's dimensions, see Benavides, *Revised Memorial*, p. 121.

46. Diego de Vargas's declaration in 1693 that he had brought the statue" back" to Santa Fe to "establish her again in her place … and to set her up in her place in a new throne" surely indicates that La Conquistadora had been in Santa Fe before the Spanish fled the town in 1680; *To the Royal Crown Restored*, p. 384.

47. On the governor's palace in this era, see José Antonio Esquibel, "The Palace of the Governors in the Seventeenth Century," *El Palacio* 11(2006): 24–29.

48. Governor Don Antonio de Otermín mentioned the chapel in two texts dated September 1680; *Revolt of the Pueblo Indians*, 1:101, 113.

49. Chávez, *Our Lady of the Conquest*, p. 8, note 10.

50. Recent discussion of the Pueblo Revolt includes Galgano, *Feast of Souls*, pp. 132–143; Gutiérrez, *When Jesus Came*, pp. 130–135; Kessell, *Pueblos, Spaniards*, pp. 118–148; Knaut, *Pueblo Revolt*; Wilcox, *Pueblo Revolt* (esp. pp. 153–159); and the essays in *Archaeologies of the Pueblo Revolt*.

51. Letter and *auto* of Otermín of September 1680; *Revolt of the Pueblo Indians*, 1:101, 113.

52. This paragraph quotes and follows the account in Otermín's *auto*, August 1680, in *Revolt of the Pueblo Indians*, 1:15.
53. Otermín's *auto*, August 1680 in *Revolt of the Pueblo Indians*, 1:16.
54. Wilcox, *Pueblo Revolt*, pp. 95–138, 146–148.
55. Letter of December 1681 in *Revolt of the Pueblo Indians*, 2:220.
56. Vetancurt, *Chronica*, 4.3.6, pp. 103–104. For brief analysis, see Katzew, "Virgin of the Macana," p. 172.
57. On these conflicts, see Galgano, *Feast of Souls*, pp. 89–91, 105–116; Gutiérrez, *When Jesus Came*, pp. 95–101, 108–127; Riley, *Kachina and Cross*, pp. 80–103, 156–192.
58. On the friars' missionary strategies, see Edgerton, *Theaters of Conversion*, pp. 271–297; Galgano, *Feast of Souls*, pp. 47–60; Gutiérrez, *When Jesus Came*, pp. 71–94; Riley, *Kachina and Cross*, pp. 104–125.
59. Crosses had belonged to the Pueblos' pre-Christian symbol world.
60. For the details in this paragraph, see Kurt E. Dungoske and Cindy K. Dungoske, "History in Stone: Evaluating Spanish Conversion Efforts through Hopi Rock Art," in *Archaeologies of the Pueblo Revolt*, pp. 114–131.
61. On the reactions discussed in this and the following paragraph, see Galgano, *Feast of Souls*, pp. 64–79; Gutiérrez, *When Jesus Came*, pp. 64–65, 117–130.
62. For introductions to Pueblo religion, see among others Frank G. Anderson, "The Pueblo Kachina Cult: A Historical Reconstruction," *Southwestern Journal of Anthropology* 11 (1955): 404–419; Riley, *Kachina and Cross*, pp. 21, 63–70; Hamilton A. Tyler, *Pueblo Gods and Myths* (Norman, OK, 1984).
63. Edgerton, *Theaters of Conversion*, pp. 276–279; Galgano, *Feast of Souls*, pp. 73–75.
64. On the Spanish association between Indians and the devil, see Cervantes, *Devil in the New World*.
65. Vetancurt, *Chronica*, 4.3.6, p. 103.
66. *Revolt of the Pueblo Indians*, 2:246–248. Discussion in Galgano, *Feast of Souls*, pp. 135–136; Gutiérrez, *When Jesus Came*, p. 132.
67. On the question of how widespread religious motivation was among the rebels, see Van Hastings Garner, "Seventeenth-Century New Mexico, the Pueblo Revolt, and Its Interpreters," in *What Caused the Pueblo Revolt?* pp. 57–80.
68. *Revolt of the Pueblo Indians*, 1:13.
69. *Revolt of the Pueblo Indians*, 2:239–240.
70. Testimony in *Revolt of the Pueblo Indians*, 2:213, 247.
71. See the text edited in Jerry R. Cradock and Barbara de Marco, "La profanación de lo sagrado: Modalidades medieval y novomexicana," *Anuario de Letras* 35 (1997): 193–213 (here 198) (English translation in *Revolt of the Pueblo Indians*, 2:231).
72. Dances: *Revolt of the Pueblo Indians*, 1:195. Preservation of Christian objects: Galgano, *Feast of Souls*, p. 142; Wilcox, *Pueblo Revolt*, p. 230.
73. Crosses: Jeannette L. Mobley-Tanaka, "Crossed Cultures, Crossed Meanings: The Manipulation of Ritual Imagery in Early Historic Pueblo Resistance," in *Archaeologies of the Pueblo Revolt*, pp. 77–84 (esp. 80–81). Rebuilding of Santa Fe: Wilson, *Myth of Santa Fe*, p. 27.
74. Galgano, *Feast of Souls*, p. 65; Gutiérrez, *When Jesus Came*, pp. 161–163.
75. *By Force of Arms*, p. 407.
76. On this carving, see Liebmann, "Signs of Power," pp. 136–138 and Figures 9.4–9.5.
77. Liebmann, "Signs of Power," pp. 136–138.
78. I borrow this terminology for this period of Pueblo-Spanish relations from Kessell, "Ways and Words," p. 30.
79. See his letter of June 17, 1692, cited by Chávez, *Our Lady of the Conquest*, p. 8, note 10.
80. For biographical detail about Vargas in this and the following paragraph, see John L. Kessell, "Introduction" in *Remote beyond Compare*, pp. 3–93.
81. *To the Royal Crown Restored*, p. 532–533; cf. *Blood on the Boulders*, 1:51.
82. *By Force of Arms*, p. 416.
83. *To the Royal Crown Restored*, p. 417.
84. *By Force of Arms*, p. 410, 417; *Blood on the Boulders* 1:60, 64.

85. Sigüenza y Gongora, *Mercurio Volante*, p. 119.
86. Puebla's Our Lady of Defense: Florencia, *Zodiaco Mariano*, pp. 210–222 (esp. 217–219); Ramos, *Identity, Ritual, and Power*, pp. 160–161.
87. *To the Royal Crown Restored*, p. 186.
88. *Blood on the Boulders*, 2:701.
89. *A Settling of Accounts: The Journals of Don Diego de Vargas, New Mexico, 1700–1704*, trans. John L. Kessell, Rick Hendricks, Meredith D. Dodge, Larry D. Miller (Albuquerque, 2002), p. 234.
90. Kessell, "Introduction," in *Remote beyond Compare*, pp. 3, 5. Among Vargas's possessions at his death was a statue of this saint (ibid., p. 91).
91. Kessell, "Introduction," in *Remote beyond Compare*, p. 37.
92. For one among many of Vargas's descriptions of this banner, see *By Force of Arms*, p. 390.
93. Chávez, *Our Lady of the Conquest*, p. 26, note 41.
94. On the role of Pueblo go-betweens in Vargas's expeditions, see Kessell, "Ways and Words."
95. Gutiérrez, *When Jesus Came*, p. 139.
96. Kessell, *Spain in the Southwest*, pp. 154–156.
97. The Indians had relocated many of their pueblos to mesa tops for defensive purposes; Rick Hendricks, "Pueblo-Spanish Warfare in Seventeenth-Century New Mexico: The Battles of Black Mesa, Kotyiti, and Astialakwa," in *Archaeologies of the Pueblo Revolt*, p. 184.
98. *By Force of Arms*, p. 390.
99. Ibid., pp. 395, 397, 450.
100. *To the Royal Crown Restored*, p. 186. For other examples of Vargas using the Marian image as pledge of peace and pardon, see *To the Royal Crown Restored*, pp. 425, 451.
101. *By Force of Arms*, p. 407.
102. Liebmann, "Signs of Resistance," pp. 134–135. Crosses: *To the Royal Crown Restored*, p. 405, 434.
103. Rosaries: *To the Royal Crown Restored*, pp. 188, 190, 195, 404; *Blood on the Boulders* 1:403. Godparentship: Kessell, "Ways and Words," p. 37.
104. *Blood on the Boulders*, 1:63–64.
105. In this and the following two paragraphs, all quotes are from Vargas's multiple accounts of the stand-off at Awatovi: *By Force of Arms*, pp. 59–560, 602, 612; *To the Royal Crown Restored*, 209–210.
106. Royal honors for relics' arrival: Nikolaus Gussone, "Adventus-Zeremoniell und Translation von Reliquien: Victricius von Rouen, *De laude sanctorum*," *Frühmittelalterliche Studien* 10 (1976): 125–133.
107. *By Force of Arms*, p. 602.
108. *Blood on the Boulders*, 1:64.
109. *To the Royal Crown Restored*, p. 209.
110. *By Force of Arms*, p. 612.
111. Sigüenza y Gongora, *Mercurio Volante*, p. 123.
112. *To the Royal Crown Restored*, pp. 374–375.
113. On Pueblos allying with Vargas, see Kessell, "Ways and Words," pp. 30, 34–36, 39–41.
114. *To the Royal Crown Restored*, p. 451.
115. *Blood on the Boulders*, 1:64, 386–387, 403.
116. Ibid., 1:386. Vargas would also use the language of paternity, presenting himself to the Pueblos as their father: e.g., *To the Royal Crown Restored*, pp. 432, 471; *Blood on the Boulders*, 1:60, 65, 386, 2:1026. Thus he appropriated the patriarchal role the Franciscans formerly claimed vis-à-vis the Indians. On the friars' use of this language, see Gutiérrez, *When Jesus Came*, pp. 74–80.
117. *Blood on the Boulders*, 1:64.
118. *To the Royal Crown Restored*, p. 417.
119. Ibid., p. 506.
120. *By Force of Arms*, p. 416.
121. *To the Royal Crown Restored*, p. 530. The colonists' situation and the taking of Santa Fe: Kessell, *Spain in the Southwest*, pp. 171–173.
122. *By Force of Arms*, p. 416.

123. Vargas's reports of late 1693 and early 1694 in *To the Royal Crown Restored*, pp. 552–553; *Blood on the Boulders*, 1:51. On the eighteenth-century legend, see Katzew, "Virgin of the Macana" (who seems not to be aware of the Vargas evidence).

124. *To the Royal Crown Restored*, p. 533.

125. On this and the other strategies of resistance used by the Jemez, see Wilcox, *Pueblo Revolt*, pp. 147–148, 159–207.

126. *To the Royal Crown Restored*, pp. 401, 404, 405, 416 (Jemez's initial reactions to Vargas's return); pp. 415, 439 (war they were preparing and Vargas's confidence in Mary's aid); pp. 438, 443 (Jemez captains' visit to Vargas).

127. *To the Royal Crown Restored*, p. 443.

128. *Blood on the Boulders*, 2:765.

129. Ibid., 2:998.

130. Ibid., 2:769.

131. Ibid., 2:767.

132. Ibid., 2:767, 982.

133. Ibid., 2:998.

134. Ibid., 2:1017–1018.

135. Our Lady of Aránzazu in colonial Mexico: Vetancurt, *Cronica*, 4.2.3, pp. 39–40; Clara García Ayluardo, "El milagro de la Virgin de Aránzazu: Los vascos como grupo de poder en la ciudad de México," in *Manifestaciones religiosas*, pp. 331–347.

136. *Blood on the Boulders*, 2:1022–1023, 1025.

137. Ibid., 2:1023.

138. Ibid., 2:1037, 1038.

139. Chávez, *Our Lady of the Conquest*, pp. 8–9, 85.

140. *To the Royal Crown Restored*, p. 112.

141. Ibid., p. 384 (cf. 112).

142. La Conquistadora in wagon accompanying colonists: *To the Royal Crown Restored*, p. 477. Composition of the 1693 colonists: "Introduction" in *To the Royal Crown Restored*, pp. 18–19; "Introduction," in *Remote Beyond Compare*, p. 93.

143. *To the Royal Crown Restored*, p. 477.

144. Ibid., p. 112.

145. For the material in this and the following paragraph, see Vargas's accounts in *To the Royal Crown Restored*, pp. 477, 483; *Blood on the Boulders*, 1:68–69.

146. If the "fortress" Vargas referred to was the former governor's palace, it is possible that this tower-like kiva occupied the space that in pre-Revolt Santa Fe housed the *casas reales'* Marian chapel.

147. A text of 1777 describes La Conquistadora's election as New Mexico's patron and the establishment of her annual feast; "Noticias of Juan Candelaria," *New Mexico Historical Review* 4 (1929): 274–297 (here 293, 295, 297).

148. There is in fact little evidence of kivas being transformed into churches in New Mexico, in part because these underground chambers were not consonant with the sort of monumental ecclesiastical architecture with which the friars proclaimed Christianity's power; Edgerton, *Theaters of Conversion*, pp. 274–276.

149. *Blood on the Boulders*, 1:68–69 (cf. *To the Royal Crown Restored*, p. 485).

150. *Remote Beyond Compare*, p. xiv.

Epilogue

1. Santa Fe, Fray Angélico Chávez Historical Library, WPA 5-5-6, #6.

2. For the developments discussed in this paragraph, see among others Gonzales, "'History Hits the Heart,'" pp. 208–210; idem, "Political Construction of Latino Nomenclatures," esp. pp. 160–171; Nieto-Phillips, *Language of Blood*, pp. ix–17, 47–92, 138–143, 171–212.

3. On the coronations, see Grimes, *Symbol and Conquest*, pp. 51–52.

4. "In Old Santa Fe: 248th Fiesta, September 2-3-4-5, 1960," Fray Angélico Chávez Historical Library, Santa Fe NM, vertical file: "Fiesta, 1960–1969."

5. Grimes, *Symbol and Conquest*, pp. 233–235.

6. On his life and work, see the essays in *Fray Angélico Chávez.*

7. Marc Simmons, "Fray Angélico Chávez: The Making of a Maverick Historian," in *Fray Angélico Chávez*, pp. 13–15.

8. On his literary technique, see Luis Leal, "*La Conquistadora* as History and Fictitious Autobiography," in *Fray Angélico Chávez*, pp. 37–44.

9. Chávez, *La Conquistadora: The Autobiography*, pp. 33–36, 39–40.

10. Ibid., p. 10.

11. Ibid., p. 84.

12. Ibid., pp. 48, 58, 61, 64, 79, 90.

13. Ibid., p. 36.

14. Ibid., p. 91.

15. On these other identity categories, see the discussion and bibliography in Gonzales, " 'History Hits the Heart,' " pp. 210–213; idem, "Political Construction of Latino Nomenclatures;" Wilson, *Myth of Santa* Fe, pp. 156–163.

16. Quotations in this and the following paragraph from the author's personal correspondence with Acosta and from Acosta's website: http://www.cristinaacosta.com/.docs/pg/10089 [June 13, 2012].

SELECT BIBLIOGRAPHY

(contains only those works cited more than once; volumes of collected essays are cited by title)

Manuscript and Archival Sources

Paris Bibliothèque Nationale
 MS espagnol 49. "Captive of Tunis," *Tratado e la defença de la santa fe Catolica Christiana, respondiendo à los argumentos que de nuestros sagradas escrituras nos opone el Mahometano.*
Barcelona, Archivo de la Corona de Aragón
 Cancilleria Reg. 3576.
 C Jaume II Cartas extra series, caixa 136, nos. 515–517.
Madrid, Biblioteca Nacional.
 MS 1176.
Fray Angélico Chávez History Library, Palace of the Governors, Santa Fe, NM
 vertical file: "Fiesta, 1960–1969."
 vertical file: "La Conquistadora."
 WPA 5-5-6, #6

Primary Sources

Acta Aragonensia..., ed. Heinrich Finke. 3 vols. Berlin, 1908–1922.
"Advocaciones de la Virgen en un códice del siglo XII." Ed. Atanasio Sinués Ruíz. *Analecta Sacra Tarraconensia: Revista de ciencias histórico-eclesiásticas* 21 (1948): 1–34.
Al-Himyari, Ibn ʿAbd al-Munʾim. *La péninsule ibérique au Moyen Age d'après le Kitab ar-rawd al-miʾtar.* Ed. and trans. Evariste Lévi-Provençal. Leiden, 1938.
Alfonso X. *Cantigas de Santa María.* Ed. Walter Mettmann. 3 vols. Madrid, 1986–1989.
———. *Cantigas de Santa María: Edición facsímil del Codice Rico T.I.1 de la Biblioteca de San Lorenzo el Real de El Escorial (siglo XIII).* Madrid, 1979.
———. *Las Siete Partidas...glosadas por el licenciado Gregorio Lopez.* 1555. 3 vol. Reprint, Madrid, 1985.
Alvarus Pelagius. *Speculum regum.* Ed. Miguel Pinto de Meneses as *Espelho dos reis.* Lisbon, 1955.
America pontifica primi saeculi evangelizationis 1493–1592. 3 vols. The Vatican, 1991–1995.
Andrew of Fleury. "Miraculorum sancti Benedicti liber quartus." In *Les Miracles de saint Benoît écrits par Adrevald, Aimoin, André, Raoul Tortaire et Hugues de Sainte-Marie, moines de Fleury.* Ed. Eugène de Certain. Paris, 1858.
Arnold of Lübeck. "Chronica." *MGH Scriptores* 21:100–250.
Barrientos, Lope. *Refundición de la crónica del halconero.* Ed. Juan de Mata Carriazo. Madrid, 1946.

Benavides, Alonso de. *Revised Memorial of 1634*. Trans. Frederick Webb Hodge, George P. Hammond, Agapito Rey. Albuquerque, 1945.

Benedict of Peterborough. *Gesta regis henrici secondi*. In *The Chronicle of the Reigns of Henry II and Richard I, A.D. 1169–1192*. Ed. William Stubbs. 2 vols. Rerum Britanicarum medii aevi scriptores, 49.1–2; London, 1867.

Bernáldez, Andrés. *Memorias del reinado de los reyes católicos*. Ed. Manuel Gómez-Moreno and Juan de Mata Carriazo. Madrid, 1962.

Blood on the Boulders: The Journals of Don Diego de Vargas, 1694–97. Trans John L. Kessell, Rick Hendricks, Meredith D. Dodge. 2 vols. Albuquerque, 1998.

"Book Twelve of the Florentine Codex." In *We People Here*, pp. 48–255.

Burriel, Andrés Marcos. *Memorias para la vida del santo Rey Don Fernando III*, ed. Miguel de Manuel Rodríguez. 1800. Reprint, Barcelona, 1974.

Cancionero castellano del siglo XV. Ed. R. Foulché Delbosc. Nueva Biblioteca de Autores Españoles, 19; Madrid, 1912.

Cantares Mexicanos: Songs of the Aztecs. Ed. and trans. John Bierhorst. Stanford, 1985.

By Force of Arms: The Journals of Don Diego de Vargas, New Mexico, 1691–1693. Trans. John L. Kessell and Rick Hendricks. Albuquerque, 1992.

Cancionero de Juan Alfonso de Baena. Ed. José María Azáreta. 3 vols. Madrid, 1966.

Cantar de mio Cid. Ed. Alberto Montaner. Barcelona, 1993.

Cervantes, Miguel de. *Los baños de Argel*. Ed. Jean Canavaggio. Madrid, 1983.

———. *El ingenioso hidalgo Don Quijote de la Mancha*. Ed. John Jay Allen. 19th ed. 2 vols. Madrid, 1998.

———. *Obras completes*. Ed. Florencio Sevilla Arroyo. Madrid, 1999.

Chimalpahin Quauhtlehuanitzin, Don Domingo de San Antón Muñon. *Annals of His Time*. Ed. and trans. James Lockhart, Susan Schroeder, and Doris Namala. Stanford, 2006.

Chronicon Adefonsi imperatoris. Ed. Antonio Maya Sánchez in *Chronica Hispana saeculi XII*. CCCM, 71.1; Turnhout, 1990.

Cisneros, Luis de. *Historia de el principio y origen, progressos y venidas à Mexico, y milagros de la santa ymagen de Nuestra Señora de los Remedios, extramuros de Mexico*. Mexico City, 1621.

Colección de documentos para la historia de México. Ed. Joaquín García Icazbalceta. 2 vols. Mexico City, 1858–1866.

Colección diplomática de Pedro I de Aragón y Navarra. Ed. Antonio Ubieto Arteta. Saragossa, 1951.

Colección documental de Alfonso XI: Diplomas reales conservadaos en el Archivo Histórico Nacional Sección de cleros pergaminos. Ed. Esther González Crespo. Madrid, 1985.

Cortés, Hernán. *Cartas de relación*. Ed. Ángel Delgado Gómez. Madrid, 1993.

Crónica incompleta de los Reyes Católicos (1469–1476). Ed. Julio Puyol. Madrid, 1934.

Crónica Najerense. Ed. Antonio Ubieto Arteta. Valencia, 1966.

Crónica latina de los reyes de Castilla. Ed. Luis Charlo Brea. Cádiz, 1984.

Crónicas Asturianas: Crónica de Alfonso III (Rotense y "A Sebastian"), Crónica Albedense (y "Profética"). Ed. Juan Gil Fernández, Jose L. Moralejo, and Juan I. Ruiz de la Peña. Oviedo, 1985.

Crónica de Alfonso X según el ms. II 12777 de la Biblioteca del Palacio Real (Madrid). Ed. Manuel González Jiménez. Murcia, 1998.

Díaz de Games, Gutierre. *El Victorial*. Ed. Rafael Beltrán Llavador. Salamanca, 1997.

Díaz del Castillo, Bernal. *Historia verdadera de la conquista de la Nueva España*. Ed. Joaquín Ramírez Cabañas. 21st ed. Mexico City, 2004.

Díaz, Juan. "Itinerario de la armada del Rey Católico a la isla de Yucatán en la India, el año de 1518." In J. Díaz, A. Tapia, B. Vázquez and F. Aguilar. *La conquista de Tenochtitlan*. Ed. Germán Vázquez. Madrid, 1988.

Diego de Ecija, *Libro de la invención de esta santa Imagen de Guadalupe y de la erreción y fundación de este Monasterio . . . .* Ed. Angel Barrado Manzano. Cáceres, 1953.

Don Juan de Oñate: Colonizer of New Mexico 1595–1628. Ed. George P. Hammond and Agapito Rey. 2 vols. Albuquerque, 1953.

Documentos de Jaime I de Aragón. Ed. Ambrosio Huici Miranda and María Desamparados Cabanes Pecourt. Textos Medievales, 49–51, 55, 77; Valencia, 1976–1988.

Diplomatario andaluz de Alfonso X. Ed. Manuel González Jiménez. Seville, 1991.

Dorantes de Carranza, Baltasar. *Sumaria relación de las cosas de la Nueva España*...Ed. José María de Agreda y Sánchez. 1902. Reprint, Mexico City, 1970.

Durán, Diego. *Historia de las Indias de Nueva España e isles de tierra firme*. Ed. Rosa Camelo and José Rubén Romero. 2 vols. Mexico City, 1995.

Enciso, Martin Fernández de. *Suma de geographia que trata de todas las partidas y provincias del mundo, en especial de las Indias*...Seville, 1519.

Espina, Alonso de. *Fortalitium fidei*...Strasbourg, 1470/1471.

Ferdinand II of Aragon. "Carta á la ciudad de Baeza, haciéndole saber la victoria conseguida en la batalla de Toro." In *Colección de documentos inéditos para la Historia de España* 13:396–400.

Florencia, Francisco de (with Juan Antonio de Oviedo). *Zodiaco Mariano*. Ed. Antonio Rubial García. Mexico City, 1995.

García de Santa María, Alvar. *Crónica de Juan II de Castilla*. Ed. Juan de Mata Carriazo. Madrid, 1982.

Gautier de Coinci. *Les miracles de Nostre Dame*. Ed. V. Frederic Koenig. 4 vols. Geneva, 1955–1970.

Gómara, Francisco López de. *La conquista de México*. Ed. José Luis de Rojas. Madrid, 1987.

———. *Historia general de las Indias y vida de Hernán Cortés*. Ed. Jorge Gurria Lacroix. Caracas, 1979.

Gonzalo de Berceo. *El Duelo de la Virgen; Los himnos; Los loores de Nuestra Señora; Los signos del juicio final*. Ed. Brian Dutton. London, 1975.

Gran Crónica de Alfonso XI. Ed. Diego Catalán. 2 vols. Madrid, 1977.

Grijalva, Juan de. *Crónica de la Orden de N.S.P. Agustín en las provincias de la Nueva España*. Mexico City, 1985.

"The Harkness 1531 Huejotzingo Codex." In *The Harkness Collection in the Library of Congress: Manuscripts Concerning Mexico, a Guide*, ed. J. Benedict Warren, pp. 49–209. Washington, DC, 1974.

Historia de los hechos del marqués de Cádiz. Ed. Juan Luis Carriazo Rubio. Granada, 2003.

Historia Silense. Ed. J. Pérez de Urbel, A. González Ruiz-Zorrilla. Madrid, 1959.

Ibn Ishaq. *The Life of Muhammed ("Sirat Rasul Allah")*. Trans. A. Guillaume. Oxford, 1955.

"Interrogatorio presentado por el dicho Don Hernando Cortés, al exámen de los testigos que presentaré..." In *Colección de documentos inéditos relativos al descubrimiento, conquista, y organización de América y Oceanía*, 27:301–445. Ed. J. Pacheco and J. de Cárdinas. 42 vols. Madrid, 1864–1884.

Jacques de Vitry. *Epistulae*. In *Lettres de Jacques de Vitry (1160/1170–1240) évêque de Saint-Jean-d'Acre*. Ed. R. B. C. Huygens. Leiden, 1960.

James I of Aragon. *Llibre dels feits*. In *Les Quatre grans Cròniques*, vol. 1 (of a number of volumes as yet to be determined). Ed. Ferrán Soldevila, rev. Jordi Bruguera and Maria Teresa Ferrrer i Mallol. Barcelona, 2007.

John of Garland. *Stella Maris*. Ed. Evelyn Faye Wilson as *The "Stella Maris" of John of Garland*. Cambridge, MA, 1946.

Juan Gil de Zamora. "Biografías de San Fernando y de Alfonso el Sabio." Ed. Fidel Fita. *BRAH* 5 (1884): 308–328.

———. "Poesías inéditas." Ed. Fidel Fita. *BRAH* 6 (1885): 379–409.

Juan Manuel. *Libro de los estados: Edición según el manuscrito de la Biblioteca Nacional*. Ed. José María Castro Calvo. Barcelona, 1968.

Las Casas, Bartolomé de. *Historia de las Indias*. In his *Obras completas*, vols. 3–5. Ed. Miguel Angel Medina, Jesús Angel Barrada, Isacio Pérez Fernández. 14 vols. Madrid, 1988–1998.

"Liber denudationis sive ostensionis aut patefaciens." In Thomas E. Burman, *Religious Polemic and the Intellectual History of the Mozarabs, c. 1050–1200*, pp. 240–385. Leiden, 1994.

Liber sancti jacobi: Codex calixtinus. Ed. Klaus Herbers and Manuel Santos Noia. Santiago de Compostela, 1998.

Lienzo de Tlaxcala: Manuscrito pictórico mexicano de mediados del siglo XVI. Ed. Próspero Cahuantzi. Mexico City, 1939.

Llull, Ramón. *Libre de Sancta Maria*. In *Obres Essencials*, 1:1145–1242. 2 vols. Barcelona, 1957.

———. *Romanç d'Evast e Blanquerna*. Ed. Albert Soler Llopert and Joan Santach. Barcelona, 2009.

Lope de Vega, "Cerca de Santa Fe." In Lope de Vega, *Comedias*, 5:103–170. Ed. Manuel Arroyo Stephens. 15 vols. Madrid, 1993–1998.

———."Los hechos de Garcilaso y moro Tarfe." In Lope de Vega, *Comedias*, 1:1–58. Ed. Manuel Arroyo Stephens. 15 vols. Madrid, 1993–1998.

López de Ayala, Pero. *Rimado del Palacio*. Ed. Germán Orduna. Madrid, 1987.

López de Mendoza, Bernardino (scribe). *Información juridica, recibida en el año de mil quinientos ochenta y dos, con la que se acredita, que la Imágen de María Santisima, baxo la advocación de Conquistadora, que se venera en su capilla del convento de Religiosos Observantes de San Francisco de la Ciudad de la Puebla de los Angeles, es la misma que el Conquistador Hernando Cortés endonó al gran capitan Alxotecatlcocomitzi*… Puebla de los Angeles, 1804.

López de Villaseñor, Pedro. *Cartilla vieja de la nobilísima ciudad de Puebla (1781)*. Ed. Arturo Córdova Durana. Puebla, 2001.

Lucas de Tuy. *Chronicon mundi*. In *Lucae Tudensis: Omnia opera*. Ed. Emma Falque. 2 vols. CCCM 74.1–2; Turnhout, 2003–2009.

Marcuello, Pedro. *Cancionero*. Ed. José M. Blecua. Saragossa, 1987.

Marqués de Santillana. *Poesías completas*. Ed. Miguel Angel Pérez Priego. 2 vols. Madrid, 1983.

Martí, Ramón. *Pugio fidei adversus Mauros et Judaeos*. Ed. J. B. Carpzov. 1687. Reprint, Farnborough, GB, 1967.

Memorias del cautivo en La Goleta de Túnez (el Alférez Pedro de Aguilar). Ed. Pascal de Gayangos. Madrid, 1875.

Mendieta, Gerónimo de. *Historia eclesiástica indiana*. Ed. Antonio Rubial García. 2 vols. Mexico City, 1997.

Mexía, Ferrán. "Nobiliario vero." In *La caballería castellana en la baja edad media: textos y contextos*. Ed. Carlos Heusch and Jesús D. Rodríguez Velasco. Montpellier, 2000.

Les miracles de Notre Dame de Rocamadour au XII siècle. Ed. Edmond Albe with Jean Rocacher. Toulouse, 1996.

Los "miraculos romançados" de Pero Marin: Edición crítica. Ed. Karl-Heinz Anton. Silos, 1988.

Morgado, Alonso. *Historia de Sevilla*… Seville, 1587.

Motolinía (Benavente), Toribio de. *Historia de los Indios de la Nueva España*. Ed. Edmundo O'Gorman. 3rd ed. Mexico City, 1979.

———. *Memoriales (Libro de oro, MS JGI 31)*. Ed. Nancy Joe Dwyer. Mexico City, 1996.

Muñoz Camargo, Diego. *Descripción de la ciudad y provincia de Tlaxcala*. In *Relaciones geográficas del siglo XVI*, vol 4. Ed. René Acuña. 10 vols. Mexico City, 1982–1988.

Münzer, Hieronymus. "Itinerarium hispanicum." Ed. Ludwig Pfandl. *Revue Hispanique* 48 (1920): 1–179.

Ocaña, Diego de. *Un viaje fascinante por la América Hispana del siglo XVI*. Ed. Arturo Alvarez. Madrid, 1969.

Osbern. "De expugnatione Lyxbonensi." In *Itinerarium peregrinorum et gesta Regis Ricardi*. Ed. William Stubbs, Rerum Britanicarum Medii Aevi Scriptores, 38.1:cxliv–clxxxii. London, 1864.

Oviedo, Gonzalo Fernández de. *Historia general y natural de las Indias*. Ed. Juan Pérez de Tudela. 5 vols. *BAE*, 117–121.

Palma, El Bachiller (Alonso). *Divina retribucion sobre la caida de España en tiempo del noble rey Don Juan el primero*. Ed. José María Escudero de la Peña. Madrid, 1879.

Le parti inedite della "Crónica de Juan II" di Alvar García de Santa María. Ed. Donatella Ferro. Venice, 1972.

Peter Martyr d'Anghiera, *De orbe novo decades*. Acalá de Henares, 1530.

Petrus Alfonsi. "Dialogi." *PL* 157:527–672.

El Poema de Alfonso XI. Ed. Yo Ten Cate. Madrid, 1956.

"Les premières versions occidentales de la légende de Saïdnaia." Ed. Paul Devos. *Analecta Bollandiana* 65 (1947): 245–278.

Primera crónica general de España que mandó componer Alfonso el Sabio y se continuaba bajo Sancho IV en 1289. Ed. Ramón Menéndez Pidal. 2nd ed. 2 vols. Madrid, 1955.

Procesos de residencia, instruidos contra Pedro de Alvarado y Nuño de Guzman. Ed. José Fernando Ramírez. Mexico City, 1847.

"Pseudo-Matthei evangelium." In *Libri de nativitate Mariae*. Ed. Jan Gijsel and Rita Beyers. Corpus Christianorum Series Apocrypha 9; Turnhout, 1997.

Pseudo Pedro Pascual. *Sobre la se[c]ta mahometana*. Ed. Fernando González Muñoz. Valencia, 2011.

Pulgar, Fernando del. *Los claros varones de Castilla*. Ed. Robert B. Tate. Madrid, 1985.

————. *Crónica de los reyes católicos.* Ed. Juan de Mata Carriazo. 2 vols. Madrid, 1943.

Records of the Trials of the Spanish Inquisition in Ciudad Real. Ed. Haim Beinart. 4 vols. Jerusalem, 1974–1985.

"Relacion circunstanciada de lo acaecido en la prision del rey chico de Granada." In *Relaciones de algunos sucesos de los últimos tiempos del Reino de Granada,* pp. 47–67. Madrid, 1868.

Relación de Michoacán. Ed. Leoncio Cabrero. Madrid, 1989.

Remote beyond Compare: Letters of Don Diego de Vargas to His Family from New Spain and New Mexico, 1675–1706. Trans. John L. Kessell. Albuquerque, 1989.

Revolt of the Pueblo Indians of New Mexico and Otermín's Attempted Reconquest, 1680–1682. Trans. Charles W. Hackett. 2 vols. Albuquerque, 1942.

Rodrigo Jiménez de Rada. *Historia de rebus sive historia gothica.* Ed. Juan Fernández Valverde. CCCM 72.1; Turnhout, 1987.

Roger of Hovedon. *Chronica.* In *Chronica magistri Rogerii de Hovedene.* Ed. William Stubbs. Rerum Britanicarum medii aevi scriptores, 51.1–4; London, 1868–1871.

Los romances frontizeros. Ed. Pedro Correa Rodríguez. 2 vols. Granada, 1999.

Salazar, Francisco Cervantes de. *Crónica de la Nueva España.* Ed. Juan Miralles Ostos. Mexico City, 1985.

Sancho IV. *Castigos e documentos para bien vivir.* Ed. Agapito Rey. Bloomington, IN, 1952.

Sigüenza y Gongora, Carlos de. *Mercurio Volante*... In *The Mercurio Volante of Don Carlos Sigüenza y Gongora: An Account of the First Expedition of Don Diego de Vargas into New Mexico in 1692.* Ed. and trans. Irving A. Leonard. Los Angeles, 1932.

The Story of Guadalupe: Luis Laso de la Vega's "Huei tlamahuiçoltica" of 1649. Ed. and trans. Lisa Sousa, Stafford Poole (C.M.), and James Lockhart. Stanford, 1998.

Talavera, Gabriel de. *Historia de Nuestra Señora de Guadalupe consagrada a la sobrana magestad de la Reyna de los Angeles, milagrosa patrona de este santuario.* Toledo, 1597.

Tapia, Bernardino Vázquez de. "Relación de meritos y servicios." In J. Díaz, A.Tapia, B. Vázquez, and F. Aguilar. *La conquista de Tenochtitlan.* Ed. Germán Vázquez. Madrid, 1988.

The Tlaxcalan Actas: A Compendium of the Records of the Cabildo of Tlaxcala (1545–1627). Ed. and trans. James Lockhart, Frances Berdan, Arthur J. O. Dibble. Salt Lake City, 1986.

To the Royal Crown Restored: The Journals of Don Diego de Vargas, New Mexico, 1692–1694. Trans. John L. Kessell, Rick Hendricks, Meredith Dodge. Albuquerque, 1995.

Valera, Mosén Diego de. *Crónica de los reyes católicos.* Ed. Juan de Mata Carriazo Madrid, 1927.

Vetancurt, Augustín de. *Chronica de la Provincia del Santo Evangelio.* In *Teatro mexicano: Descripcion breve de los sucessos Exemplares, Historicos, Politicos, Militares, y Religiosos del Nuevo mundo Occidental de las Indias,* vol. 1. 1697–1698. One volume reprint, Mexico City, 1971.

Villagrá, Gaspar Pérez de. *Historia de la Nueva México, 1610.* Ed. Miguel Encinas, Alfred Rodríguez, Joseph P. Sánchez. Albuquerque, 1992.

Vincent of Beauvais. *Speculum historiale.* In his *Speculum quadruplex sive Speculum maius,* 4 vols. 1624. Reprint Graz, 1964–1965. Vol. 4.

We People Here: Nahuatl Accounts of the Conquest of Mexico. Ed. and trans. James Lockhart. Berkeley, 1993.

Zapata y Mendoza, Juan Buenaventura. *Historia cronológica de la Noble Ciudad de Tlaxcala.* Ed. and trans. Luis Reyes García and Andrea Martínez Baracs. Tlaxcala, 1995.

Secondary Sources

ʿAbd el Jalil, J. M. *Marie et l'Islam.* Paris, 1950.

Abulafia, Anna Sapir. *Christians and Jews in the Twelfth-Century Renaissance.* London, 1995.

Actas del congreso "La frontera oriental nazarí como sujeto histórico": Lorca-Vera, 22 a 24 de noviembre de 1994. Ed. Pedro Segura Artero. Alicante, 1997.

Adorno, Rolena. *The Polemics of Possession in Spanish American Narrative.* New Haven, 2007.

Al-Andalus: the Art of Islamic Spain. Ed. Jerilynn D. Dodds. New York, 1992.

Alberro, Solange. "Remedios y Guadalupe: de la unión a la discordia." In *Manifestaciones religiosas,* 2:151–164.

Altman, Ida. "Conquest, Coercion, and Collaboration: Indian Allies and the Campaigns in Nueva Galicia." In *Indian Conquistadors,* pp. 145–174.

———. *Emigrants and Society: Extremadura and Spanish America in the Sixteenth Century.* Berkeley, 1989.

———. *Transatlantic Ties: Brihuega, Sapin, and Puebla, Mexico, 1560–1620.* Stanford, 2000.

Amador de los Ríos, Rodrigo. *Trofeos militares de la Reconquista: Estudios acerca de las enseñas musulmanes del real monasterio de Las Huelgas (Burgos) y la catedral de Toledo.* Madrid, 1893.

Andalucía Americana: Edificios vinculados con el descubrimiento de las Indias y la carrera de las Indias. Seville, 1989.

Andalucía entre Oriente y Occidente (1236–1492): Actas del V Coloquio internacional de historia medieval de Andalucía. Ed. Emilio Cabrera. Cordoba, 1988.

Archaeologies of the Pueblo Revolt: Identities, Meaning, and Renewal in the Pueblo World. Ed. Robert W. Preucel. Albuquerque, 2007.

Argente del Castillo Ocaña, Carmen. "Cautiverio y martirio de doncellas en la Frontera." In *IV Estudios de Frontera: Historia, tradiciones y leyendas en la Frontera,* ed. Francisco Toro Ceballos and José Rodríguez Molina, pp. 31–72. Jaén, 2002.

Asselbergs, Florine G. L. "The Conquest in Images: Stories of Tlaxcalteca and Quauhquecholteca Conquistadors." In *Indian Conquistadors,* pp. 65–101.

Atkinson, Clarissa. *The Oldest Vocation: Christian Motherhood in the Middle Ages.* Ithaca, NY, 1991.

The Aztec Empire. New York, 2004.

Baer, Yitzhak. *A History of the Jews in Christian Spain.* Trans. Louis Schoffman, 2 vols. Philadelphia, 1961.

Bakewell, Eliza, and Byron Ellsworth Hamman. "Painting History, Reading Painted Histories: Ethnoliteracy in Prehispanic Oaxaca and Colonial Central Mexico." In *A Companion to Mexican History and Culture,* ed. William H. Beezely, pp. 163–192. Chichester, 2011.

Balaguer, Federico. "Santa María de Salas: Sus problemas históricos." *Argensola: Revista del Instituto de Estudios Oscenses* 8 (1957): 203–231.

Bango, Isidro G. *Remembering Sepharad: Jewish Culture in Medieval Spain.* Madrid, 2003.

Baraz, Daniel. "The Incarnated Icon of Saidnaya Goes West: A Re-examination in Light of New Manuscript Evidence." *Le Muséon* 108 (1995): 181–191.

Barbé Coquelin de Lisle, Geneviève. "De la grande mosquée à la cathédrale gothique." In *Tolède, XIIe–XIIIe,* pp. 147–157.

Barkaï, Ron. *Cristianos y musulmanes en la España medieval (el enemigo en el espejo).* Trans. M. Bar-Kochba and A. Komay. Madrid, 1984.

Barnay, Sylvie. *Le ciel sur la terre: Les apparitions de la Vierge Marie au Moyen Age.* Paris, 1999.

Barral y Altet, Xavier. "Palma: cathedral." In *La España Gótica 5: Baleares,* ed. Joan de Sureda Pons, pp. 82–116. Madrid, 1994.

Barton, Simon. "Traitors to the Faith? Christian Mercenaries in al-Andalus and the Maghreb, c. 1100–1300." In *Medieval Spain: Culture, Conflict, and Coexistence,* ed. Roger Collins and Anthony Goodman, pp. 23–45. New York, 2002.

Beguer Pinyol, Manuel. *El Real Monasterio de Santa María de la Rápita de la sagrada y soberana milicia hospitalaria de San Juan de Jerusalén (Orden de Malta).* Tortosa, 1948.

Behind the Lines: Gender and the Two World Wars. Ed. Margaret Randolph Higonnet et al. New Haven, 1987.

Bensch, Stephen P. "From Prizes of War to Domestic Merchandise: The Changing Face of Slavery in Catalonia and Aragon, 1000–1300." *Viator* 25 (1994): 63–93.

Bisson, Thomas N. *The Medieval Crown of Aragon: A Short History.* Oxford, 1986.

Bliese, John R.E. "Rhetoric and Morale: A Study of Battle from the Central Middle Ages." *Journal of Medieval History* 15 (1989): 201–226.

Blumenkranz, Bernhard. "Juden und Jüdische in christlichen Wundererzählungen: Ein unbekanntes Gebiet religiöser Polemik." *Theologische Zeitschrift* 10 (1954): 417–446.

Boone, Elizabeth. *Stories in Red and Black: Pictorial Histories of the Aztecs and Mixtecs.* Austin, TX, 2000.

Boulton, D'Arcy Jonathan Dacre. *The Knights of the Crown: The Monarchical Orders of Knighthood in Later Medieval Europe 1325–1520.* Woodbridge, GB, 1987.

Brading, David A. *The First America: The Spanish Monarchy, Creole Patriots, and the Liberal State, 1492–1867.* Cambridge, 1991.

———. *Mexican Phoenix: Our Lady of Guadalupe: Image and Tradition across Five Centuries.* Cambridge, 2001.

Bravo Navarro, Martín and José Sancho Roda. *La Almudena: Historia de la Iglesia de Santa María la Real y de sus imágenes.* Madrid, 1993.

Broda, Johanna, Davíd Carrasco, and Eduardo Matos Moctezuma. *The Great Temple of Tenochtitlan.* Berkeley, 1987.

Brodman, James William. *Ransoming Captives in Crusader Spain: The Order of Merced on the Christian-Islamic Frontier.* Philadelphia, 1986.

Brou, Louis. "Marie 'Destructrice de toutes les heresies' et la belle légende du répons *Gaude Maria Virgo.*" *Ephemerides liturgicae* 62 (1948): 321–353.

Bugge, John. *Virginitas: An Essay in the History of a Medieval Ideal.* The Hague, 1975.

Bunes Ibarra, Miguel Angel de. "Lo americano y lo africano en las crónicas de Indias: Algunos ejemplos." In *Lecturas y ediciones de crónicas de Indias: Una propuesta interdisciplinary,* pp. 159–173. Madrid, 2004.

Burkhart, Louise M. *Before Guadalupe: The Virgin Mary in Early Colonial Nahuatl Literature* (Albany NY, 2001).

———. "'Here Is Another Marvel': Marian Miracle Narratives in a Nahuatl Manuscript." In *Spiritual Encounters: Interactions between Christianity and Native Religions in Colonial America,* ed. Nicolas Griffiths and Fernando Cervantes, pp. 91–115. Lincoln, NB, 1999.

———. *The Slippery Earth: Nahua-Christian Moral Dialogue in Sixteenth Century Mexico.* Tucson, 1989.

Burns, Robert I. "Jews and Moors in the *Siete Partidas* of Alfonso X the Learned: A Background Perspective." In *Medieval Spain: Culture, Conflict and Coexistence: Studies in Honor of Angus MacKay,* ed. Roger Collins and Anthony Goodman, pp. 46–62. Basingstoke, 2002.

———. "Journey from Islam: Incipient Cultural Transformation in the Conquered Kingdom of Valencia (1240–1280)." *Speculum* 35 (1960): 337–356.

———. "Social Riots on the Christian-Moslem Frontier (Thirteenth-Century Valencia)." *American Historical Review* 66 (1961): 378–400.

Camille, Michael. *The Gothic Idol: Ideology and Image-Making in Medieval Art.* Cambridge, 1989.

Cañizares Esguerra, Jorge. "Racial, Religious, and Civic Creole Identity in Colonial Spanish America." *American Literary History* 17 (2005): 420–437.

Cardaillac, Louis. *Morisques et chrétiens: Un affrontement polémique (1492–1640).* Paris, 1977.

Carpenter, Dwayne E. "Alfonso el Sabio y los moros: Algunas precisiones legales, históricas, y textuales con respecto a *Siete Partidas* 7.25." *Al-Qantara* 7 (1986): 229–252.

———. "Minorities in Medieval Spain: The Legal Status of Jews and Muslims in the *Siete Partidas.*" *Romance Quarterly* 33 (1986): 275–287.

———. "Social Perception and Literary Portrayal: Jews and Muslims in Medieval Spanish Literature." In *Convivencia,* pp. 61–81.

Carrasco Manchado, Ana Isabel. *Isabel I de Castilla y la sombra de la ilegitimidad: Propaganda y representación en el conflicto successorio (1474–1482).* Madrid, 2006.

Carrasco Urgoiti, María Soledad. "La escenificación del triunfo del cristiano en la comedia." In *Moros y Cristianos,* pp. 25–44.

———. *El Moro de Granada en la literatura (del siglo XV al XX).* 1956. Reprint Madrid, 1989.

Carrasco, Davíd. *City of Sacrifice: The Aztec Empire and the Role of Violence in Civilization.* Boston, 1999.

Carrero Rodríguez, Juan. *Nuestra Señora de los Reyes y su historia.* Seville, 1989.

Castelli, Elizabeth. "Virginity and Its Meaning for Women's Sexuality in Early Christianity." *Journal of Feminist Studies in Religion* 2 (1986): 61–88.

Castro Morales, Efraín. "El Mapa de Chalchihuapan." *Estudios y documentos de la región de Puebla-Tlaxcala* 1 (1969): 5–22.

Castro, Daniel. *Another Face of Empire: Bartolomé de Las Casas, Indigenous Rights, and Ecclesiastical Imperialism.* Durham, 2007.

Catlos, Brian. *The Victors and the Vanquished: Christians and Muslims of Catalonia and Aragon, 1050–1300.* Cambridge, 2004.

Cervantes, Fernando. *The Devil in the New World: The Impact of Diabolism in New Spain.* New Haven, 1994.

Chávez, Fray Angélico. *La Conquistadora: The Autobiography of an Ancient Statue*. Rev. ed. Santa Fe, 1983.

———. "Nuestra Señora del Rosario la Conquistadora." *New Mexico Historical Review* 23 (1948): 94–128, 177–216.

———. *Our Lady of the Conquest*. Santa Fe, 1948.

Chazan, Robert. *Barcelona and Beyond: The Disputation of 1263 and Its Aftermath*. Berkeley, 1992.

———. *Fashioning Jewish Identity in Medieval Western Christendom*. Cambridge, 2004.

La chevalerie en Castille à la fin du Moyen Age: Aspects sociaux, idéologiques et imaginaires. Ed. George Martin. Paris, 2001.

Chevalier, Jaima. *La Conquistadora: Unveiling the History of Santa Fe's Six Hundred Year Old Religious Icon*. Santa Fe, 2010.

Christian, William A. *Apparitions in Late Medieval and Renaissance Spain*. Princeton, 1981.

Cintas del Bot, Adelaida. *Iconografía del Rey San Fernando en la pintura de Sevilla*. Seville, 1991.

Clendinnen, Inga. *Ambivalent Conquests: Maya and Spaniard in Yucatan, 1517–1570*, 2nd ed. Cambridge, 2003.

———. *Aztecs*. Cambridge, 1991.

———. "'Fierce and Unnatural Cruelty': Cortés and the Conquest of Mexico." *Representations* 33 (1991): 65–100.

———. "Ways to the Sacred: Reconstructing 'Religion' in Sixteenth-Century Mexico." *History and Anthropology* 5 (1990): 105–141.

Cohen, Jeremy. *The Friars and the Jews: The Evolution of Medieval Anti-Judaism*. Ithaca, NY, 1982.

Coleman, David. *Creating Christian Granada: Society and Culture in an Old-World Frontier City, 1492–1600*. Ithaca, NY, 2003.

Contamine, Philippe. *La guerre au Moyen Age*. Paris, 1980.

Conversions islamiques: Identités religieuses en Islam méditerranéen. Ed. Mercedes García Arenal. Paris, 2001.

Convivencia: Jews, Muslims, and Christians in Medieval Spain. Ed. Vivian B. Mann, Thomas F. Glick, and Jerilynn D. Dodds. New York, 1992.

Cope, R. Douglas. *The Limits of Racial Domination: Plebeian Society in Colonial Mexico City, 1660–1720*. Madison WI, 1994.

Corral, José María de. "Santa María de Rocamadour y la milagrosa salvación de una Infanta de Navarra en el siglo XII." *Hispania: Revista Española de Historia* 7 (1947): 554–610.

Crémoux, Françoise. *Pèlerinages et miracles à Guadalupe au XVIe siècle*. Madrid, 2001.

Cuffel, Alexandra. "'Henceforth All Generations Will Call Me Blessed': Medieval Christian Tales of Non-Christian Marian Veneration." *Mediterranean Studies* 12 (2003): 37–60.

Curcio-Nagy, Linda. "Native Icon to City Protectoress to Royal Patroness: Ritual, Political Symbolism and the Virgin of Remedies." *The Americas* 52 (1996): 367–391.

Cutler, Anthony. *Transformations: Studies in the Dynamics of Byzantine Iconography*. University Park, PA, 1975.

Dacal Moure, Ramón, and Manual Rivero de la Calle. *Art and Archaeology of Pre-Colombian Cuba*. Trans. Daniel H. Sandweiss. Ed. Daniel H. Sandweiss and David R. Watters. Pittsburgh, 1996.

Despres, Denise L. "Immaculate Flesh and the Social Body: Mary and the Jews." *Jewish History* 12 (1998): 47–69.

Dillard, Heath. *Daughters of the Reconquest: Women in Castilian Town Society, 1100–1300*. Cambridge, 1984.

Domínguez Casas, Rafael. *Arte y etiqueta de los Reyes Católicos: Artistas, residencias, jardines y bosques*. Madrid, 1993.

Dufourcq, Charles Emmanuel. *L'Espagne catalane et le Maghrib aux XIIe et XIVe siècles: De la bataille de Las Navas de Tolosa (1212) à l'avènement du sultan mérinide Abou-l-Hasan (1331)*. Paris, 1966.

Dunnington, Jacqueline Orsini, and Charles Mann. *Viva Guadalupe! The Virgin in New Mexican Popular Art*. Santa Fe, 1997.

Durliat, Marcel. *L'art dans le Royaume de Majorque: Les débuts de l'art gothique en Roussillon, en Cerdagne et aux Baleares*. Toulouse, 1962.

Dyck, Jason C. "The Sacred Historian's Craft: Francisco de Florencia and Creole Identity in Seventeenth-Century New Spain." Ph.D. dissertation, University of Toronto, 2012.

Echevarria, Ana. "La conversion des chevaliers musulmans dans la Castille du XVe siècle," in *Conversions islamiques*, pp. 119–138.

————. *The Fortress of Faith: The Attitude toward the Muslims in Fifteenth Century Spain.* Leiden, 1999.

Edgerton, Samuel Y. *Theaters of Conversion: Religious Architecture and Indigenous Artisans in Colonial Mexico.* Albuquerque, 2001.

Ellington, Donna Spivey. *From Sacred Body to Angelic Soul: Understanding Mary in Late Medieval and Early Modern Europe.* Washington DC, 2001.

Elliott, J. H. *Empires of the Atlantic World: Britain and Spain in America 1492–1830.* New Haven, 2006.

————. "The Mental World of Hernán Cortés." In his *Spain and Its World 1500–1700*, pp. 27–41. New Haven, 1989.

Elshtain, Jean Bethke. *Women and War.* New York, 1987.

Elukin, Jonathan M. "From Jew to Christian? Conversion and Immutability in Medieval Europe." In *Varieties of Religious Conversion*, pp. 171–189.

Emperor of Culture: Alfonso X the Learned and His Thirteenth-Century Renaissance, ed. Robert I. Burns. Philadelphia, 1990.

Epalza, Mikel de. *Fray Anselmo de Turmeda ('Abdallah al-Taryuman) y su polémica islamo-cristiana: Edición, traducción y estudio de la Tuhfa.* 2nd ed. Madrid, 1994.

————. *Jésus otage: Juifs, chrétiens et musulmans en Espagne (VIe–XVIIe s.).* Paris, 1987.

Erdmann, Carl. *The Origin of the Idea of Crusade.* Trans. Marshall W. Baldwin and Walter Goffart. Princeton, 1977.

España medieval y el legado de occidente. Mexico City, 2005.

Extremadura en el evangelización del Nuevo Mundo: Actas y estudios: Congreso celebrado en Guadalupe durante los días 24 al 29 de octubre de 1988. Ed. Sebastián García. Madrid, 1990.

Farriss, Nancy M. *Maya Society under Colonial Rule: The Collective Enterprise of Survival.* Princeton, 1984.

Fernández González, Etelvina. "Iconografía y leyenda del Pendón de Baeza." In *Medievo Hispano: Estudios in Memoriam del Prof. Derek W. Lomax*, pp. 141–157. Madrid, 1995.

Fernández Ladreda, Clara. *Imaginería medieval mariana.* Pamplona, 1988.

Ferreiro Alemparte, Jaime. "La ciudad mozárabe de Santa María del Faro y el milagro de la Cantiga CLXXXIII en fuentes anteriores al Rey Sabio." *Grial* 38 (1972): 405–430.

Ferrer i Mallol, Maria Teresa. *El Sarraïns de la Corona Catalono-Aragonesa en el segle XIV: Segregació i discriminació.* Barcelona, 1987.

Fierro, Maribel "Women as Prophets in Islam." In *Writing the Feminine: Women in Arab Sources*, ed. Manuela Marín and Randi Deguilhem, pp. 183–198. London, 2002.

Fita, Fidel. "La judería de Segovia: Documentos inéditos." *BRAH* 9 (1886): 270–293.

————. "El libro de Cerratense." *BRAH* 13 (1888): 226–237.

Fletcher, Richard A. *Moorish Spain.* Berkeley, 1992.

————. "Reconquest and Crusade in Spain c. 1050–1150." *Transactions of the Royal Historical Society* 5th series 37 (1987): 31–47.

————. *Saint James's Catapult: The Life and Times of Diego Gelmírez of Santiago de Compostela.* Oxford, 1984.

Flory, David A. *Marian Representations in the Miracle Tales of Thirteenth-Century France and Spain.* Washington, DC, 2000.

Folda, Jaroslav. *Crusader Art in the Holy Land, from the Third Crusade to the Fall of Acre, 1187–1291.* Cambridge, 2005.

Fournes, Ghislaine. *"La Virgen de los Reyes Católicos*, masque et miroir de la royauté." *e-Spania* 3 (2007). Online. Available: http://e-spania.revues.org/index87.html. December 12, 2009.

Fray Angélico Chávez: Poet, Priest, and Artist. Ed Ellen McCracken. Albuquerque, 2000.

Freidel, David A., and Jeremy A. Sabloff. *Cozumel: Late Maya Settlement Patterns.* Orlando, FL, 1984.

Friedman, Ellen G. *Spanish Captives in North Africa in the Early Modern Age.* Madison, 1983.

Fulton, Rachel. *From Passion to Judgment: Devotion to Christ and the Virgin Mary, 800–1200.* New York, 2002.

Galgano, Robert C. *Feast of Souls: Indians and Spaniards in the Seventeenth-Century Missions of Florida and New Mexico.* Albuquerque, 2005.

Gamboa Ojeda, Leticia. "Los españoles en la historia de la ciudad de Puebla." In *Presencia española*, pp. 23–30.

Gambra, Andrés. *Alfonso VI: Cancillería, curia e imperio.* 2 vols. León, 1997–1998.

Garcés, María Antonia. *Cervantes in Algiers: A Captive's Tale.* Nashville, TN, 2002.

García, Sebastían. "El Real Santuario de Santa María de Guadalupe en el primer siglo de su historia." *Revista de estudios extremeños* 57 (2001): 359–410.

García Arenal, Mercedes. "Dreams and Reason: Autobiographies of Converts in Religious Polemics." In *Conversions islamiques*, pp. 89–118.

———. "Los moros en las *Cantigas* de Alfonso X el Sabio." *Al-Qantara* 6 (1985): 133–151.

García Arenal, Mercedes, and Miguel Angel de Bunes. *Los Españoles y el Norte de Africa: Siglos XV–XVIII.* Madrid, 1992.

García Fitz, Francicso. "El Islam visto por Alfonso X." In *Cristianos y musulmanes en la Península Ibérica: La guerra, la frontera y la convivencia*, pp. 394–432. Avila, 2009.

———. *Las Navas de Tolosa.* Barcelona, 2005.

Gendering the Crusades. Ed. Susan B. Edgington and Sarah Lambert. New York, 2002.

Gibson, Charles. *Tlaxcala in the Sixteenth Century.* Stanford, 1952.

Gillespie, Jeanne. *Saints and Warriors: Tlaxcalan Perspectives on the Conquest of Tenochtitlan.* New Orleans, 2004.

Glick, Thomas F. *Islamic and Christian Spain in the Early Middle Ages.* 2nd ed. Leiden, 2005.

The Globe Encircled and the World Revealed. Ed. Ursula Lamb. Aldershot, GB, 1995.

Goldstein, Morris. *Jesus in the Jewish Tradition.* New York, 1950.

Gómez-Menor Fuentes, José-Carlos. "Preces por el rey en tiempo de guerra, según un documento abulense medieval." In *Estudios sobre Alfonso VI y la reconquista de Toldeo*, 4:71–77. 4 vols. Toledo, 1987–1989.

Goñi Gaztambide, José. *Historia de la bula de cruzada en España.* Vitoria, 1958.

Gonzales, Phillip B. "'History Hits the Heart': Albuquerque's Great Cuartocentenario Controversy, 1997–2005." In *Expressing New Mexico: Nuevomexicano Creativity, Ritual, and Memory*, ed. Phillip B. Gonzales, pp. 207–232. Tucson, 2007.

———. "The Political Construction of Latino Nomenclatures in Twentieth-Century New Mexico." *Journal of the Southwest* 35 (1993): 158–185.

González Jiménez, Manuel. "Alfonso X y las minorías confesionales de mudéjares y judíos." In *Alfonso X: Aportaciones de un rey castellano a la construcción de Europa*, ed. Miguel Rodríguez Llopis, pp. 71–90. Murcia, 1997.

———. *Fernando III el Santo.* Seville, 2006.

González, Julio. *Reinado y diplomas de Fernando III.* 3 vols. Cordoba, 1980–1986.

———. *El Reino de Castilla en la época de Alfonso VIII.* 3 vols. Madrid, 1960.

Grimes, Ronald L. *Symbol and Conquest: Public Ritual and Drama in Santa Fe, New Mexico.* Ithaca, NY, 1976.

Gruzinski, Serge. *La guerre des images: De Christophe Colomb à "Blade Runner" (1492–2019).* Paris, 1990.

Gutiérrez, Ramón A. *When Jesus Came, the Corn Mothers Went Away: Marriage, Sexuality, and Power in New Mexico, 1500–1846.* Stanford, 1991.

Hall, Linda B. *Mary, Mother and Warrior: The Virgin in Spain and the Americas.* Austin, 2004.

Harris, Julie. "Mosque to Church Conversions in the Reconquest." *Medieval Encounters* 3 (1997): 158–172.

Harvey, L. P. *Islamic Spain 1250 to 1500.* Chicago, 1990.

Hassig, Ross. *Mexico and the Spanish Conquest.* 2nd ed. Norman, OK, 2006.

———. *War and Society in Ancient Mesoamerica.* Berkeley, 1992.

Hatton, Vikki and Angus MacKay. "Anti-Semitism in the *Cantigas de Santa María*." *Bulletin of Hispanic Studies* 60 (1983): 189–199.

Henriet, Patrick. "L'idéologie de la guerre sainte dans la haut moyen âge." *Francia* 29 (2002): 171–220.

Herbers, Klaus. "Politik und Heiligenverehrung auf der Iberischen Halbinsel: Die Entwicklung des politischen Jakobus." In *Politik und Heiligenverehrung im Hochmittelalter*, ed. Jürgen Petersohn, pp. 177–275. Vorträge und Vorschungen, 42; Sigmaringen, 1994.

Hernández Díaz, José. *Icongrafía medieval de la Madre de Dios en el antiguo reino de Sevilla: Discurso académico*...Madrid, 1971.

―――. *La Virgen de los Reyes: Patrona de Sevilla y de la archidiocesis*....Seville, 1947.

Heusch, Carlos. "L'amour et la femme dans la fiction chevaleresque castillane du moyen âge." In *La chevalerie en Castille à la fin du Moyen Age*, pp. 145–189.

Hillenbrand, Carole. *The Crusades: Islamic Perspectives*. New York, 2000.

Hillenbrand, Robert. *Islamic Architecture: Form, Function and Meaning*. New York, 1994.

Hillgarth, J. N. *The Spanish Kingdoms 1250–1516*. 2 vols. Oxford, 1976.

Hoekstra, Rik. *Two Worlds Emerging: The Transformation of Society in the Valley of Puebla, 1570–1640*. Amsterdam, 1993.

The Human Tradition in Colonial Latin America. Ed. Kenneth J. Andrien. Wilmington, DE, 2002.

Huston, Nancy. "The Matrix of War: Mothers and Heroes." In *The Female Body in Western Culture: Contemporary Perspectives*, ed. Susan Rubin Suleiman, pp. 119–136. Cambridge, MA, 1986.

Hvidfeldt, Arild. *Teotl and *Ixiptlatli: Some Central Conceptions in Ancient Mexican Religion*. Copenhagen, 1958.

Iberia and the Mediterranean World of the Middle Ages: Studies in Honor of Robert I. Burns. Ed. Larry J. Simon, P. E. Chedevven, et al. 2 vols. Leiden, 1995–1996.

Indian Conquistadors: Indigenous Allies in the Conquest of Mesoamerica. Ed. Laura E. Matthew and Michel R. Oudijk. Norman OK, 2007.

Iogna-Prat, Dominique. "Le culte de la Vierge sous le règne de Charles le Chauve." In *Marie: Le culte de la Vierge*, pp. 65–98.

Isabel la Católica y su época: Actas del congreso internacional. Ed. Luis Ribot, Julio Valdeón, and Elena Maza. 2 vols. Valladolid, 2007.

IV Estudios de Frontera: Historia, tradiciones y leyendas en la Frontera. Ed. Francisco Toro Ceballos and José Rodríguez Molina. Jaén, 2000.

The Jew in Medieval Iberia. Ed. Jonathan Ray. Boston, 2012.

Jews, Muslims and Christians In and Around the Crown of Aragon: Essays in Honour of Professor Elena Lourie. Ed. Harvey J. Hames. Leiden, 2004.

Johnson, Carina Lee. "Negotiating the Exotic: Aztec and Ottoman Culture in Habsburg Europe, 1500–1590." Ph.D. dissertation, University of California, Berkeley, 2000.

Johnston, Mark D. "Ramon Llull and the Compulsory Evangelization of Jews and Muslims." In *Iberia and the Mediterranean World*, 1:3–37.

Jones, Oakah L. *Los Paisanos: Spanish Settlers on the Northern Frontier of New Spain*. Norman, OK, 1996.

Jordan, William C. "Adolescence and Conversion in the Middle Ages: A Research Agenda." In *Jews and Christians in Twelfth-Century Europe*, ed. Michael A. Singer and John Van Engen, pp. 77–93. Notre Dame, 2001.

Kagan, Richard L. *Urban Images of the Hispanic World 1493–1793*. New Haven, 2000.

Kamen, Henry. *The Spanish Inquisition: A Historical Revision*. New Haven, 1998.

Katzew, Ilona. "The Virgin of the Macana: Emblem of a Franciscan Predicament in New Spain." *Colonial Latin American Review* 12 (2003): 169–198.

Kedar, Benjamin Z. *Crusade and Mission: European Approaches toward the Muslims*. Princeton, 1984.

Keller, John Esten. "King Alfonso's Virgin of Villa-Sirga: Rival of Saint James of Compostela," and "More on the Rivalry Between Santa Maria and Santiago de Compostela." Both in his *Collectanea Hispanica: Folklore and Brief Narrative Studies*, ed. Dennis P. Seniff and María Isabel Montoya Ramírez, pp. 61–76. Newark, DE, 1987.

Kerpel, Diana Magaloni. "Imágenes de la conquista de México en los codices del siglo XVI: Una lectura de su contenido simbólico." *Anales del Instituto de Investigaciones Estéticas* 82 (2003): 5–45.

Kessell, John L. *Kiva, Cross, and Crown: The Pecos Indians and New Mexico, 1540–1840*. 2nd ed. Albuquerque, 1989.

―――. *Pueblos, Spaniards, and the Kingdom of New Mexico*. Norman, OK, 2008.

————. "Restoring Seventeenth-Century New Mexico, Then and Now." *Historical Archaeology* 31 (1997): 46–54.

————. *Spain in the Southwest: A Narrative History of Colonial New Mexico, Arizona, Texas, and California*. Norman, OK, 2002.

————. "The Ways and Words of the Other: Diego de Vargas and Cultural Brokers in Late Seventeenth-Century New Mexico." In *Between Indian and White Worlds: The Cultural Broker*, ed. Margaret Connell Szasz, pp. 25–43. Norman OK, 1994.

Knaut, Andrew L. *The Pueblo Revolt of 1680: Conquest and Resistance in Seventeenth-Century New Mexico*. Norman, OK, 1995.

Kraemer, Paul. "The Dynamic Ethnicity of the People of Spanish Colonial Mexico in the Eighteenth Century." In *Transforming Images: New Mexican Santos in between Worlds*, ed. Claire Farago and Donna Pierce, pp. 80–98. Albuquerque, 2006.

Kranz, Travis Barton. "Sixteenth-Century Tlaxcalan Pictorial Documents on the Conquest of Mexico." In *Sources and Methods for the Study of Postconquest Mesoamerican Ethnohistory*, ed. James Lockhart, Lisa Sousa, and Stephanie Wood, pp. 1–21. Online. Available: http://whp. uoregon.edu/Lockhart/index.html. September 29, 2007.

Krauss, Samuel. *Das Leben Jesu nach jüdischen Quellen*. Berlin, 1902.

Ladero Quesada, Miguel Angel. *Los mudéjares de Castilla y otros estudios de historia medieval andaluza*. Granada, 1989.

Lappin, Anthony J. *The Medieval Cult of Saint Dominic of Silos*. Leeds, 2002.

————. "The Thaumaturgy of Royal Piety: Alfonso X and the *Cantigas de Santa Maria*." *Journal of Hispanic Research* 4 (1995–1996): 39–59.

Lapunzina, Alejandro. *Architecture of Spain*. Westport, CT, 2005.

Lara, Jaime. *Christian Texts for Aztecs: Art and Liturgy in Colonial Mexico*. Notre Dame, IN, 2008.

Lasker, Daniel J. *Jewish Philosophical Polemics Against Christianity in the Middle Ages*. New York, 1977.

Lasry, Anita Benaim de. "Marisaltos: Artificial Purification in Alfonso el Sabio's Cantiga 107." In *Studies on the Cantigas de Santa María*, pp. 299–311.

The Legacy of Muslim Spain. Ed. Salma Khadra Jayyusi, 2 vols. Leiden, 1994.

Lévi-Provençal, Evariste. *Histoire de l'espagne musulmane*. Rev. ed. 3 vols. Paris, 1950–1953.

Liebmann, Matthew J. "Signs of Power and Resistance: The (Re)Creation of Christian Imagery and Identities in the Pueblo Revolt Era." In *Archaeologies of the Pueblo Revolt*, pp. 132–144.

Linehan, Peter. *History and the Historians of Medieval Spain*. Oxford, 1993.

Liss, Peggy K. *Isabel the Queen: Life and Times*. Rev. ed. Philadelphia, 2004.

Lockhart, James. *The Nahuas after the Conquest: A Social and Cultural History of the Indians of Central Mexico, Sixteenth through Eighteenth Centuries*. Stanford, 1992.

Lomax, Derek. *The Reconquest*. London, 1978.

López Payer, Manuel Gabriel and María Dolores Rosada Llamas. *Las Navas de Tolosa: La batalla*. Madrid, 2002.

Loreto López, Rosalva. "La fiesta de la Concepción y las identidades colectivas, Puebla (1619–1636)." In *Manifestaciones religiosas*, 2: 87–104.

Lourie, Elena. *Crusade and Colonisation: Muslims, Christians, and Jews in Medieval Aragon*. Aldershot, GB, 1990.

————. "A Society Organized for War: Medieval Spain." In her *Crusade and Colonisation*, pp. 54–76.

Lupher, David A. *Romans in a New World: Classical Models in Sixteenth-Century America*. Ann Arbor, MI, 2003.

MacCormack, Sabine. "From the Sun of the Incas to the Virgin of Copacabana." *Representations* 8 (1984): 30–60.

MacKay, Angus. "Andalucía y la guerra del fin del mundo." In *Andalucía entre Oriente y Occidente (1236–1492): Actas del V coloquio internacional de historia medieval de Andalucía*, ed. Emilio Cabrera, pp. 329–342. Cordoba, 1988.

————. "The Ballad and the Frontier in Late Medieval Spain." In MacPherson and MacKay, *Love, Religion and Politics*, pp. 1–27.

————. "Un Cid Ruy Díaz en el siglo XV: Rodrigo Ponce de León, marques de Cádiz." In *El Cid en el Valle de Jalón: Simposio internacional*, pp. 197–207. Calatayud, 1991.

————. "Ferdinand of Antequera and the Virgin Mary." In MacPherson and MacKay, *Love, Religion and Politics*, pp. 132–139.

————. "Religion, Culture, and Ideology on the Late Medieval Castilian–Granadan Frontier." In *Medieval Frontier Societies*, ed. Robert Bartlett and Angus MacKay, pp. 217–243. Oxford, 1989.

————. *Spain in the Middle Ages: From Frontier to Empire, 1000–1500*. Basingstoke, 1977.

MacLaughlin, Megan. "The Woman Warrior: Gender, Warfare and Society in Medieval Europe." *Women's Studies* 17 (1990): 193–209.

MacPherson, Ian, and Angus MacKay. *Love, Religion and Politics in Fifteenth Century Spain*. Leiden, 1998.

Manifestaciones religiosas en el mundo colonial Americano. Ed. Clara García Ayluardo and Manuel Ramos Medina. 2nd ed. 2 vols. Mexico City, 1993–1994.

Marie: Le culte de la Vierge dans la société medieval. Ed. Dominique Iogna-Prat, Eric Palazzo, and Daniel Russo. Paris, 1996.

Márquez Villanueva, Francisco. *El concepto cultural alfonsí*. Madrid, 1994.

Martínez, José Luis. *Hernán Cortés*. Mexico City, 1990.

Martínez Baracs, Rodrigo. *La secuencia tlaxcalteca: Orígenes del culto a Nuestra Señora de Ocotlán*. Mexico City, 2000.

Martínez San Pedro, María Desamparados. "La Virgen en Almería tras la conquista." In *IV Estudios de Frontera*, pp. 373–393.

Mary: The Complete Resource. Ed. Sarah Jane Boss. New York, 2007.

Mazeika, Rasa. "'Nowhere Was the Fragility of Their Sex Apparent': Women Warriors in the Baltic Crusade Chronicles." In *From Clermont to Jerusalem: The Crusades and Crusader Societies*, ed. Alan V. Murray, pp. 229–248. Turnhout, 1998.

McAuliffe, Jane Dammen. "Chosen of All Women: Mary and Fatima in Qur'anic Exegesis." *Islamochristiana* 7 (1981): 19–28.

McMichael, Stephen J. *Was Jesus of Nazareth the Messiah? Alphonso de Espina's Argument Against the Jews in the Fortalitium Fidei*. Atlanta, 1994.

Medianero Hernández, José María. "La gran *Tecleciguata*: Notas sobre la devoción de la Virgen de la Antigua en Hispanoamérica." In *Andalucía en el siglo XVI: Actas de las II jornadas de Andalucía y América*, 2:365–380. 2 vols. Seville, 1983.

Mena García, María del Carmen. *Sevilla y las flotas de Indias: La gran armada de Castilla del Oro (1513–1514)*. Seville, 1998.

Menéndez Pidal, Luis. *La Cueva de Covadonga: Santuario de Nuestra Señora de la Virgen María*. Madrid, 1956.

Menéndez Pidal, Ramón. *Poesía árabe y poesía europea*. Buenos Aires, 1941.

Merrim, Stephanie. *The Spectacular City, Mexico, and Colonial Hispanic Literary Culture*. Austin, 2010.

Mettmann, Walter. *Die volksprachliche apologetische Literatur auf der Iberischen Halbinsel im Mittelalter*. Opladen, 1987.

Meyerson, Mark D. "Aragonese and Catalan Jewish Converts at the Time of the Expulsion." *Jewish History* 6 (1992): 131–149.

————. *The Muslims of Valencia in the Age of Fernando and Isabel: Between Coexistence and Crusade*. Berkeley, 1991.

————. "Religious Change, Regionalism, and Royal Power in the Spain of Fernando and Isabel." In *Iberia and the Mediterranean World*, pp. 96–112.

Milhou, Alain. "La chauve-souris, le nouveau David et le Roi caché: Trois images de l'empereur des derniers temps dans le monde ibérique (XIIIe–XVIIe siècles)." *Mélanges de la Casa de Velazquez* 18 (1982): 61–78.

————. "Propaganda mesiánica y opinion pública: Las reacciones de las cuidades del reino de Castille frente al proyecto Fernandino de cruzada (1510–1511)." In *Homenaje a José Antonio Maravall*, 3:51–62. 3 vols. Madrid, 1985.

Millás, José María. "Un tratado anónimo de pólemica contra los judíos." *Sefarad* 13 (1953): 3–34.

Miller, Kathryn. *Guardians of Islam: Religious Authority and Muslim Communities in Late Medieval Spain*. New York, 2008.

Mills, Kenneth. "La 'Memoria Viva' de Diego de Ocaña en Potosí." *Archivo y Biblioteca Nacionales de Bolivia: Anuario* (1999): 197–241.

Mínguez, José María. *Alfonso VI: Poder, expansion y reorganizacíon interior.* Hondarribia, 2000.

Miranda Godínez, Francisco. *Dos cultos fundantes: Los Remedios y Guadalupe (1521–1649), historia documental.* Zamora, Michoacan, 2001.

Mirrer, Louise. *Women, Jews, and Muslims in the Texts of Reconquest Castile.* Ann Arbor, MI, 1996.

Molenat, Jean-Pierre. "L'organisation militaire des Almohades." In *Los Almohades: problemas y perspectivas,* ed. Patrick Cressier, Maribela Fierro and Luis Molina, 2:547–565. 2 vols. Madrid, 2005.

Morley, Sylvanus G., and George W. Brainerd, *The Ancient Maya.* 4th ed. Rev. by Robert J. Sharer. Stanford, 1983.

Moros y Cristianos: Representaciones del otro en las fiestas del Mediterráneo occidental. Ed. Marlène Albert-Llorca and José Antonio González Alcantud. Granada, 2003.

Morrison, Karl. *Understanding Conversion.* Charlottesville, VA, 1992.

Muñiz López, Iván. "Pasado y mitos de origen al servicio del poder: La imagen de la monarquía asturiana en la España de los Reyes Católicos." In *Isabel la Católica y su época,* 1:435–462.

Muñoz Fernández, Angela. "Cultos, devociones y advociones religiosas en los orígenes de la organización eclesiástica cordobesa (siglos XIII–XIV)." In *Andalucía entre Oriente y Occidente,* pp. 135–144.

Mussafia, Adolpho. "Studien zu den mittelalterlichen Marienlegenden." *Sitzungsberichte der philosophisch-historischen Classe der kaiserlichen Akademie der Wissenschaften* 113 (1886): 917–994, 115 (1888): 5–92, 119 (1889): 1–66, 123 (1890): 1–85, 139 (1898): 1–74.

Myers, Kathleen Ann. *Fernández de Oviedo's Chronicle of America: A New History for a New World.* Austin, 2007.

Naef, Silvia. *Bilder und Bilderstreit im Islam: Vom Koran bis zum Karikaturenstreit.* Trans. Christiane Seiler. Munich, 2007.

Navarrete, Federico. "La Malinche, la Virgen y la montaña: El juego de identidad en los codices tlaxcaltecas." *História, São Paulo* 26 (2007): 288–310.

Neumann, Eric. *The Great Mother: An Analysis of the Archetype.* Princeton, 1955.

Nieto-Phillips, John. *The Language of Blood: The Making of Spanish-American Identity in New Mexico, 1880s–1930s.* Albuquerque, 2004.

Nirenberg, David. *Communities of Violence: Persecution of Minorities in the Middle Ages.* Princeton, 1996.

———. "Mass Conversion and Genealogical Mentalities: Jews and Christians in Fifteenth-Century Spain." *Past and Present* 174 (2002): 3–41.

O'Callaghan, Joseph F. *Alfonso X and the Cantigas de Santa Maria: A Poetic Biography* Leiden, 1998.

———. *Reconquest and Crusade in Medieval Spain.* Philadelphia, 2003.

O'Connor, Isabel A. *A Forgotten Community: The Mudejar Aljama of Xàtiva 1240–1327.* Leiden, 2003.

O'Gorman, Edmundo. *Cuatro historiadores de Indias, siglo XVI: Pedro Mártir de Anglería, Gonzalo Fernández de Oviedo y Valdés, Fray Bartolomé de las Casas, Joseph de Acosta.* Mexico City, 1979.

Osowski, Edward W. "Passion Miracles and Indigenous Historical Memory in New Spain." *Hispanic American Historical Review* 88 (2008): 607–638.

Pacios López, Antonio. *La disputa de Tortosa.* 2 vols. Madrid, 1957.

Pagden, Anthony. *European Encounters with the New World: From Renaissance to Romanticism.* New Haven, 1993.

———. "Identity Formation in Spanish America." In *Colonial Identity in the Atlantic World, 1500–1800,* ed. Nicholas Canny and Anthony Pagden, pp. 51–93. Cambridge, 1987.

Palazzo, Eric. "Marie et l'élaboration d'un espace ecclésial au haut Moyen Age." In *Marie: Le culte de la Vierge,* pp. 313–325.

Palm, Walter. *Los monumentos arquitectónicos de la Española con una introducción a América.* 2 vols. Santo Domingo, 1955.

Paredes Ferrer, Alvaro. *Alonso de Ojeda: El descubridor de Colombia.* Bogota, 2006.

Patton, Pamela A. *Art of Estrangement: Redefining Jews in Reconquest Spain.* University Park, PA, 2012.

Peinado Santaella, Rafael G. "*Christo pelea por sus castellanos*: El imaginario cristiano de la guerra de Granada." In *Las tomas: Antropología historórica de la ocupación territorial del reino de Granda*, ed. José Antonio González Alcantud and Manuel Barrios Aguilera, pp. 453–524. Granada, 2000.

Pelikan, Jaroslav. *Mary Through the Centuries: Her Place in the History of Culture*. New Haven, 1996.

Peñarroja Torrejón, Leopoldo. *Cristianos bajo el islam: Los mozárabes hasta la conquista de Valencia*. Madrid, 1993.

Perdrizet, Paul. *La Vierge de Miséricorde: Étude d'un thème iconographique*. Paris, 1908.

Perry, Mary Elizabeth. *Gender and Disorder in Early Modern Seville*. Princeton, 1990.

Perry, Nicholas, and Loreto Echeverría. *Under the Heel of Mary*. London, 1988.

Peters, F. E. *Mecca: A Literary History of the Muslim Holy Land*. Princeton, 1994.

———. *Muhammad and the Origins of Islam*. Albany, 1994.

Phelan, John Leddy. *The Millennial Kingdom of the Franciscans in the New World*. 2nd ed. Berkeley, 1970.

Philippart, Guy. "Le récit miraculaire marial dans l'Occident medieval." In *Marie: Le culte de la Vierge*, pp. 563–590.

Phillips, Carla Rahn. "Visualizing *Imperium*: The Virgin of the Seafarers and Spain's Self-Image in the Early Sixteenth Century." *Renaissance Quarterly* 48 (2005): 815–856.

Picard, Christophe. "Sanctuaires et pèlerinages chrétiens en terre musulmane: L'Occident de l'Andalus (Xe–XII siècles)." In *Pèlerinages et croisades: Actes du 1118e congrès national annuel des sociétés historiques et scientifiques, Pau, octobre 1993*, pp. 235–247. Paris, 1995.

Pick, Lucy K. *Conflict and Coexistence: Archbishop Rodrigo and the Muslims and Jews in Medieval Spain*. Ann Arbor, 2004.

Pike, Ruth. "Seville in the Sixteenth Century." In *The Globe Encircled*, pp. 154–191.

Poole, Stafford. *Our Lady of Guadalupe: The Origins and Sources of a Mexican National Symbol, 1531–1797*. Tucson, 1995.

Porras y López, Armando, and Martha Porras de Hidalgo. *Puebla: Biografía de una ciudad*. Puebla, 2002.

Powers, James F. *A Society Organized for War: The Iberian Municipal Militias in the Central Middle Ages, 1000–1284*. Berkeley, 1988.

Presencia española en Puebla, siglos XVI–XX. Ed. Agustín Grajales and Lilián Illades Puebla, 2002.

Queer Iberia: Sexualities, Cultures, and Crossings from the Middle Ages to the Renaissance. Ed. Josiah Blackmore and Gregory S. Hutcheson. Durham, NC, 1999.

Ramos, Frances L. *Identity, Ritual, and Power in Colonial Puebla*. Tucson, 2012.

Ray, Jonathan. *The Sephardic Frontier: The Reconquista and the Jewish Community in Medieval Iberia*. Ithaca, NY, 2006.

Raynaud, Gaston. "Le miracle de Sardenai." *Romania* 11 (1882): 519–537.

El retroceso territorial de al-Andalus: Almorávides y almohades siglos XI al XII. Ed. María Jesús Viguera Molíns. Historia de España Menéndez Pidal, 8.2; Madrid, 1997.

Reff, Daniel T. *Plagues, Priests, and Demons: Sacred Narratives and the Rise of Christianity in the Old World and the New*. Cambridge, 2005.

Reilly, Bernard F. *The Contest of Christian and Muslim Spain 1031–1157*. Oxford, 1992.

Remensnyder, Amy G. "Christian Captives, Muslim Maidens and Mary." *Speculum* 82 (2007): 642–677.

———. "The Colonization of Sacred Architecture: The Virgin Mary, Mosques, and Temples in Medieval Spain and Early Sixteenth-Century Mexico." In *Monks and Nuns, Saints and Outcasts: Religious Expression and Social Meaning in the Middle Ages*, ed. Sharon Farmer and Barbara Rosenwein, pp. 189–219. Ithaca, NY, 2000.

Restall, Matthew. *Seven Myths of the Spanish Conquest*. New York, 2003.

Ricard, Robert. *The Spiritual Conquest of Mexico: An Essay on the Apostolate and the Evangelizing Methods of the Mendicant Orders in New Spain 1523–1572*. Trans. Lesley Byrd Simpson. Berkeley, 1966.

Riley, Carroll L. *The Kachina and the Cross: Indians and Spaniards in the Early Southwest*. Salt Lake City, 1999.

Rodríguez, Jarbel. *Captives and Their Saviors in the Medieval Crown of Aragon*. Washington, DC, 2007.

Rodríguez Molina, José. "Relaciones pacíficas en la frontera con el reino de Granada." In *Actas del congreso "La frontera oriental nazarí"*, pp. 257–290.

———. "Santos guerreros en la frontera." In *IV Estudios de Frontera*, pp. 447–470.

———. *La vida de moros y cristianos en la Frontera*. Alcalá la Real, 2007.

Rosenthal, Earl E. *The Cathedral of Granada: A Study in the Spanish Renaissance*. Princeton, 1961.

Roth, Norman. *Conversos, Inquisition, and the Expulsion of the Jews from Spain*. Madison, 1995.

Rouse, Irving. *The Tainos: The Rise and Decline of the People Who Greeted Columbus*. New Haven, 1992.

Rubial García, Antonio. "Tierra de prodigios: Lo maravilloso cristiano en la Nueva España de los siglos XVI y XVII." In *La iglesia católica en México*, ed. Nelly Siguat, pp. 357–364. Michoacán, 1997.

Rubiera Mata, María J. "De nuevo sobre las tres morillas." *Al-Andalus* 37 (1972): 133–143.

Rubin, Miri. *Gentile Tales: The Narrative Assault on Late Medieval Jews*. Philadelphia, 1999.

———. *Mother of God: A History of the Virgin Mary*. New Haven, 2009.

Rubio, Germán. *Historia de Nuestra Señora de Guadalupe...* Barcelona, 1926.

Ruiz-Gálvez Priego, Estrella. "*Fállase por profecía*: Les prophètes, les prophéties et la projection sociale: Le *Rimado o Cancionero* de Pedro Marcuello et le prophétisme de la fin du XVe siècle." In *La prophétie comme arme de guerre des pouvoirs (XVe–XVIIe siècles)*, ed. Augustín Redondo, pp. 75–95. Paris, 2000.

Ruiz, Teofilo. "Trading with the 'Other': Economic Exchanges between Muslims, Jews, and Christians in Late Medieval Northern Castile." In *Medieval Spain: Culture, Conflict, and Coexistence: Studies in Honour of Angus MacKay*, ed. Roger Collins and Anthony Goodman, pp. 63–78. Basingstoke, 2002.

Salvador Martínez, H. *Alfonso X, the Learned: A Biography*. Trans. Odile Cisneros. Leiden, 2010.

Sánchez Pérez, José Augusto. *El culto mariano en España*. Madrid, 1943.

Schreiner, Klaus. *Maria: Jungfrau, Mutter, Herrscherin*. Munich, 1994.

———. "*Nobilitas Mariae*: Die edelgeborene Gottesmutter und ihre adeligen Verehrer: Soziale Prägungen und politische Funktion mittelalterlicher Adelsfrommigkeit." In *Maria in der Welt: Marienverehrung im Kontext der Sozialgeschichte 10.–18. Jahrhundert*, ed. Claudia Opitz et al., pp. 213–242. Zurich, 1993.

Seed, Patricia. *Ceremonies of Possession in Europe's Conquest of the New World, 1492–1640*. Cambridge, 1995.

Shahid, Irfan. "Islam and *Oriens Christianus*: Makka 610–622 AD." In *The Encounter of Eastern Christianity with Early Islam*, ed. Emmanouela Grypeou, Mark N. Swanson, and David Thomas, pp. 9–31. Leiden, 2006.

Signori, Gabriela. *Maria zwischen Kathedrale, Kloster und Welt: Hagiographische und historiographische Annäherungen an eine hochmittelalterliche Wunderpredigt*. Sigmaringen, 1995.

Simmons, Marc. *The Last Conquistador: Juan de Oñate and the Settling of the Far Southwest*. Norman, OK, 1991.

Smith, Damian J. *Innocent III and the Crown of Aragon: The Limits of Papal Authority*. Aldershot, GB, 2004.

———. "*Soli Hispani*? Innocent III and Las Navas de Tolosa." *Hispania Sacra* 51 (1999): 487–512.

Smith, Jane I., and Yvonne Haddad. "The Virgin Mary in Islamic Tradition and Commentary." *The Muslim World* 79 (1989): 16–187.

Smith, Katherine Allen. "Bodies of Unsurpassed Beauty: 'Living' Images of the Virgin in the High Middle Ages," *Viator* 37 (2006): 167–187.

Snow, Joseph T. "Alfonso as Troubadour: The Fact and the Fiction." In *Emperor of Culture*, pp. 124–140.

———. "A Chapter in Alfonso's Personal Narrative: The Puerto de Santa Maria Poems in the Cantigas de Santa Maria." *La Corónica: Spanish Medieval Language and Literature Newsletter* 8 (1979): 10–21.

The Spiritual Conversion of the Americas. Ed. James Muldoon. Gainesville, 2004.

Spiritual Encounters: Interactions between Christianity and Native Religions in Colonial America. Ed. Nicholas Griffiths and Fernando Cervantes. Birmingham, UK, and Lincoln, NB, 1999.

Starr, Frederick. *The Mapa de Cuauhtlantzinco or Códice Campos*. Chicago, 1898.

Stratton, Suzanne L. *The Immaculate Conception in Spanish Art*. Cambridge, 1994.

Studies on the Cantigas de Santa María: Art, Music, and Poetry.... Ed. Israel J. Katz and John E. Keller. Madison, 1987.

Tartakoff, Paola. *Between Christian and Jew: Conversion and Inquisition in the Crown of Aragon, 1250–1391.* Philadelphia, 2012.

Taylor, William B. *Magistrates of the Sacred: Priests and Parishioners in Eighteenth-Century Mexico.* Stanford, 1996.

———. "The Virgin of Guadalupe in New Spain: An Inquiry into the Social History of Marian Devotion." *American Ethnologist* 14 (1987): 9–33.

Thackston, Wheeler M. "The Role of Calligraphy." In *The Mosque: History, Architectural Development and Regional Diversity,* ed. Martin Frishman and Hasan-Uddin Khan, pp. 43–52. London, 1994.

Thomas, Hugh. *Conquest: Montezuma, Cortés, and the Fall of Old Mexico.* New York, 1993.

To Change Place: Aztec Ceremonial Landscapes. Ed. Davíd Carrasco. Boulder, 1991.

Tolan, John V. *Saracens: Islam in the Medieval European Imagination.* New York, 2002.

Tolède, XIIe–XIIIe: Musulmans, chrétiens et juifs: Le savoir et la tolerance. Ed. Louis Cardaillac. Paris, 1991.

Toledot Yeshu ("The Life Story of Jesus") Revisited: A Princeton Conference. Ed. Peter Schäfer, Michael Meerson, and Jaacov Deutsch. Tübingen, 2011.

Torres Fontes, Juan. "Don Fernando de Antequera y la romántica caballeresca." *Miscellanea Medieval Murciana* 5 (1980): 85–120.

———. "La orden de Santa María de España." *Miscellanea Medieval Murciana* 3 (1977): 73–118.

Townsend, Camilla. *Malintzin's Choices: An Indian Woman in the Conquest of Mexico.* Albuquerque, 2006.

Trexler, Richard C. "Aztec Priests for Christian Altars: The Theory and Practice of Reverence in the New Spain." In his *Church and Community 1200 to 1600: Studies in the History of Florence and New Spain,* pp. 469–492. Rome, 1987.

———. "Dressing and Undressing Images: An Analytic Sketch." In his *Religion in Social Context in Europe and America, 1200–1700,* pp. 374–408. Tempe, AZ, 2002.

Twomey, Lesley K. *The Serpent and the Rose: The Immaculate Conception and Hispanic Poetry in the Late Medieval Period.* Leiden, 2008.

L'univers de la chevalerie en Castille: Fin du Moyen Age—début des temps modernes. Ed. Jean-Pierre Sánchez. Paris, 2000.

Valdeón Baruque, Juan. *Los Trastámaras: El triunfo de una dinastía bastarda.* Madrid, 2001.

Valdivieso, Enrique. *Historia de la pintura sevillana: Siglos XII al XX.* Seville, 1986.

Valensi, Lucette. *La fuite en Egypte: Histoires d'Orient et d'Occident.* Paris, 2002.

Van Koningsveld, P. S., and G. A. Wiegers. "The Polemical Works of Muhammad al-Qaysi (fl. 1309) and Their Circulation in Arabic and Aljamiado among the Mudejars in the Fourteenth Century." *Al-Qantara: Revista de Estudios Arabes* 15 (1994): 163–199.

Vann, Theresa M. "Reconstructing a 'Society Organized for War.'" In *Crusaders, Condottieri and Cannon: Medieval Warfare in the Societies around the Mediterranean,* ed. Donald J. Kagay and L. J. Andrew Villalon, pp. 388–416. Leiden, 2003.

Varieties of Religious Conversion in the Middle Ages. Ed. James Muldoon. Gainesville, 1997.

Victorio Martínez, Juan. "La ciudad-mujer en los romances fronterizos." *Anuario de estudios medievales* 15 (1985): 553–560.

Vose, Robin. *Dominicans, Muslims and Jews in the Medieval Crown of Aragon.* Cambridge, 2009.

Warner, Marina. *Alone of All Her Sex: The Myth and Cult of the Virgin Mary.* New York, 1976.

Weber, David J. *The Spanish Frontier in North America.* New Haven, 1992.

Webster, Susan Verdi. *Art and Ritual in Golden-Age Spain: Sevillan Confraternities and the Processional Sculpture of Holy Week.* Princeton, 1998.

Weckmann, Luis. *The Medieval Heritage of Mexico.* Trans. Frances López-Morillas. New York, 1992.

Weissberger, Barbara F. *Isabel Rules: Constructing Queenship, Wielding Power.* Minneapolis, MN, 2004.

What Caused the Pueblo Revolt? Ed. David J. Weber. Boston, 1999.

Wiegers, Gerard. *Islamic Literature in Spanish and Aljamiado: Yça of Segovia, His Antecedents and Successors.* Leiden, 1994.

Wilcox, Michael V. *The Pueblo Revolt and the Mythology of Conquest: An Indigenous Archaeology of Contact*. Berkeley, 2009.

Wilson, Chris. *The Myth of Santa Fe: Creating a Modern Regional Tradition*. Albuquerque, 1997.

The Women and War Reader. Ed. Lois Ann-Lorentz and Jennifer Turpin. New York, 1998.

Wood, Stephanie. "Nahua Christian Warriors in the Mapa de Cuauhtlantzinco, Cholula Parish." In *Indian Conquistadors*, pp. 254–287.

———. *Transcending Conquest: Nahua Views of Colonial Mexico*. Norman OK, 2003.

Zarebska, Carla. *Guadalupe*. Mexico City, 2005.

INDEX

Page numbers in italics refer to illustrations.

29081078R00265

Made in the USA
Lexington, KY
25 January 2019